NUCL

NUCLEAR ARMS RACE
Technology and Society

Second Edition

Paul P. Craig
Department of Engineering
University of California—Davis

John A. Jungerman
Department of Physics
University of California—Davis

McGraw-Hill Publishing Company

New York St. Louis San Francisco Auckland Bogotá Caracas
Hamburg Lisbon London Madrid Mexico Milan Montreal New Delhi
Oklahoma City Paris San Juan São Paulo Singapore Sydney Tokyo Toronto

This book was set in Times Roman by Waldman Graphics, Inc.
The editors were Denise T. Schanck and Bernadette Boylan;
the production supervisor was Denise L. Puryear.
The cover was designed by Fern Logan.
New drawings were done by Caliber Design Planning, Inc.
Arcata Graphics/Halliday was printer and binder.

NUCLEAR ARMS RACE
Technology and Society

1 2 3 4 5 6 7 8 9 0   HAL   HAL   8 9 4 3 2 1 0 9

ISBN 0-07-013347-6

Library of Congress Cataloging-in-Publication Data

Craig, Paul P.
    Nuclear arms race: technology and society / Paul P. Craig,
John A. Jungerman.—2nd ed.
       p.   cm.
    Bibliography: p.
    Includes index.
    ISBN 0-07-013347-6
    1. Nuclear weapons.   2. Nuclear warfare.   3. Arms race—
History—20th century.   I. Jungerman, John A.   II. Title.
U264.C73   1990
355.8′25119—dc20
                                         89-8361

ABOUT THE AUTHORS

Paul P. Craig is fascinated by the ways in which societies use and misuse technology. His courses and research focus on social decision making on issues with major technical components, especially the arms race and energy. His current fascinations are the international implications of man induced climate change, and toxic waste. The latter involves practical politics. He is a member of the review and negotiations committee on a super-incinerator proposed in his back yard which would process over 100 kilotons of carcinogens a year. His frequent habitat is the High Sierra.

John A. Jungerman is professor of physics at the University of California, Davis. There he has served as founding director of the Crocker Nuclear Laboratory and chair of the Physics Department. He began his professional career as a physicist on the Manhattan Project during World War II at Oak Ridge, Tennessee, and Los Alamos, New Mexico. He studied for the doctorate in nuclear physics at the University of California, Berkeley with Emilio Segrè and did a year's postdoctoral study with Hans Bethe at Cornell University. He has served as a consultant to the International Atomic Energy Agency and has pursued research at a number of institutes abroad, including the Atlantic Institute of International Affairs, Paris.

CONTENTS

Part 3   Consequences

Appendixes

PREFACE

Get your facts first, and then you can distort them as much as you please.

MARK TWAIN

GENERAL COMMENTS

Measured in terms of its implications for human survival, the nuclear arms race is the single most important activity on the face of the earth. For over 40 years, since the Trinity nuclear test shot was detonated in Alamogordo, New Mexico, on July 16, 1945, nuclear weapons have been the dominant feature of international geopolitics. Today there are an estimated 50,000 warheads in the arsenals of the world, the bulk of them under the control of the United States and the Soviet Union. These weapons affect all of our lives. There is no way to avoid this.

Since 1945 no nuclear weapons have been used in warfare. It may or may not be true that the fact that the United States and the Soviet Union are holding each other hostage in a strategy termed Mutually Assured Destruction, or MAD, is responsible for the absence of nuclear war over most of these four decades. One could, for instance, note that there has been no earthquake in San Francisco since 1906. Does this fact give one comfort? Of course, the analogy is weak because mankind has no control over earthquakes.

Should nuclear war occur, it will be the result of human decisions. What human decision one can't say. Decisions to undertake the physics research that made the weapons possible? Decisions to build nuclear weapons? Deliberate decisions to fight a war? Mechanical accident? Institutional accident? A misinterpretation of an act of God? (The Strategic Air Command was once alerted because radar interpreted the rising of the moon as a Soviet attack.)

The situation is complex and controversial. Does a nuclear freeze proposal contribute to or detract from the prospects for nuclear weapons stability? How many weapons and of what type are "enough"? Do the Soviets cheat on arms agreements? Is an MX missile needed? Will our strategic submarine fleet be vulnerable in the 1990s? What can and cannot be verified by "national means"? Is space defense or other defense viable? These and many, many more questions are being raised, and will be extensively debated in the coming years. For the nation—if not for the individual—there is no avoiding the questions.

THEMES

We believe, with Jefferson, that the strength of a democracy lies in the wisdom of its citizens. Nuclear issues are complex, to be sure, but they are not outside the scope of understanding of any American who wishes to inform himself or herself about them.

This text was written with two audiences in mind. One is the student interested in obtaining background on the arms race. Another larger audience is the citizen intent on gaining technical understanding of the scientific basis of the arms race. The book is arranged so that it can readily be used as a reference. Many technical questions of the form ''What is it?'' and ''How does it work?'' are addressed in an understandable way that should be of use to citizens of all orientations. We particularly hope that high school students will use the book to help find answers to some of their questions about the implications of the arms race for their lives.

The text grew out of a course we offered for the first time in the winter of 1983 at the University of California at Davis. It is intended for students from all backgrounds, and all political persuasions. We created in the course a microcosm of C. P. Snow's ''two cultures.'' The humanities-oriented person (a member of one of the cultures) may often be intimidated by equations and numbers. The scientifically oriented student (a member of the other culture) may be bored at times with the technical level of the course but disturbed by having to deal with issues which are impossible to quantify. Both perspectives are important. We can learn from each other how to wrestle with the almost overwhelming problem of nuclear arms. This question is a survival issue, and it is truly interdisciplinary.

Applied to the question of nuclear arms, ''two cultures'' attitudes can lead on the one hand to leaving the technical matters to the ''experts,'' and on the other to a situation in which technically trained persons are so ignorant of the way in which people think that they commit themselves to solutions which are made risky by human factors. We can afford neither attitude.

We believe that every informed citizen should be familiar with the technical facts of life in a nuclear age. An informed citizen should be able to discuss, for example: how an atomic weapon works; what is the difference between an A-bomb and an H-bomb; what is the trade-off between accuracy and warhead size; what are the effects of blast, heat, and radiation; what is fallout and what will it do; what are MAD, the strategic triad, MIRV, LOW, Cruise, SS-18, MX. What are the capabilities to absorb the effects of nuclear war of people, cities, the ecosphere? What does it mean for the fabric of the nation if 50 percent of the populace is killed? If the industrial infrastructure is decimated? If oil refineries and electricity generating plants are destroyed? What would such losses mean for the Soviet Union? How much could a vigorous civil defense program protect? What might a nuclear terrorist hope to accomplish? What are the consequences of a global exchange of nuclear arsenals of the superpowers to humankind and the ecosystem?

The text does not attempt to answer all of these questions. But it does provide a foundation that makes possible the understanding of the issues, and it will ease the interpretation of information appearing in the press and elsewhere.

Our goal is to provide you with the tools to make your own judgments about political and technical issues surrounding the nuclear arms race. As informed citizens you will be better able to be meaningfully involved in the political process on the critical issue of nuclear arms.

Development of common ground required that we include some material that will be elementary to everyone. Remember this, and pass quickly over topics you know well.

STRUCTURE OF THE TEXT

The text is divided into three main sections. Part 1 (Chapters 1–6) considers the nuclear status quo, and the history of how we arrived where we are. Section II (Chapters 7–18), the most technical part of the book, examines the technical background of the nuclear arms race. A summary (Chapter 7) introducing Part 2 makes it possible to draw on this material without going into it in detail. Part 3 (Chapters 19–26) explores present and potential consequences of the nuclear arms race, prospects for defense against nuclear attack (e.g., a "star wars" defense against ICBMs), proliferation of nuclear weapons, and psychological and economic factors.

The chapters that involve technical discussion (chiefly found in Part 2) present ideas and results in nonquantitative fashion at the beginning of the chapters, with more detail and quantification at the end of each chapter. These technical sections begin with a prefix "P", and are keyed to the descriptive sections.

WAYS TO USE THE TEXT

The text can be used in several ways:

1. If interest is principally in the nontechnical areas of the nuclear arms race, Part 2 could be eliminated entirely and only the first part of other chapters containing technical material utilized.
2. If a quick résumé of technical background is desired, Choice 1 may be supplemented with the summary of Part 2, found in Chapter 7.
3. If some understanding of the science and technology of nuclear weapons and their effects is desired, section II may be included, using only the first, nonquantitative, part of the chapters.
4. Finally, if the technical material is to be fully utilized, all of the material in these chapters can be used as well as the "Additional Physics" sections of other chapters.

In our course at the University of California, Davis we interweave technical and descriptive chapters so as to introduce the technical material gradually. The following chapter sequence is one way to accomplish this: 1, 8, 9, 2, 3, 10, 11, 4, 5, 12–18,

7, 22, 19–21, 6, 23–26. Because of our backgrounds (physics), we place relatively greater emphasis on technical considerations.

An instructor's manual to the text is available. It includes lists of films and general references (with sources), discussion of subtle points in each chapter, and solutions to all problems.

SYNOPSIS

Part 1 Present Status and History and Policies of the Nuclear Arms Race

Chapter 1 overviews the nuclear predicament. It includes a brief discussion of the nuclear arsenals and delivery systems, our vulnerability to nuclear attack, and the consequences of a nuclear exchange.

Chapter 2 provides a historical overview of the development of the arms race. The material is descriptive and anecdotal. It is intended to provide some feeling for the tenor of the times when the atomic bomb was developed, and the institutional dynamic that led to its use even after the fall of Nazi Germany. There is no escaping from the shaping forces of history; the arms race today has many roots going back 40 years or more.

Weapons are useless without delivery systems. Trade-offs between weapon megatonnage and accuracy of the delivery systems are examined in Chapter 3.

Chapter 4 introduces key elements of nuclear weapons policy. There are many specialized terms and phrases, such as MAD (mutually assured destruction), LOW (launch on warning), and ICBM (intercontinental ballistic missile), which must become a part of one's vocabulary in order to discuss arms race issues.

Chapter 5 is concerned with the processes by which nuclear weapons are kept under control. How might decisions to launch nuclear weapons be made, and how might these decisions be communicated to the personnel in physical possession of the weapons? What kind of safeguards exist against unauthorized launch?

Discussions of the arms race tend to focus on nuclear weapons, and this is the primary focus of the text. Conventional weapons have advanced enormously in recent decades. Many conventional weapons are capable of the same amount of destruction as even fairly large nuclear weapons. In Chapter 6 we review the characteristics of modern nonnuclear weaponry. The point is made that the elimination of nuclear arsenals, even if it could be accomplished, would by no means eliminate the enormous destructiveness of war in the late twentieth century. It would also not end the risk of nuclear war since the knowledge of how to make nuclear weapons would remain.

Part 2 Technical and Scientific Background, Bomb Building, and Nuclear Weapon Effects

These chapters (7–18) contain the most technical material in the book. They are introduced with a summary of key concepts (Chapter 7), which may be drawn upon by the nontechnical reader, or for reference.

The chapters of the section assume little conversance with the language of science. Chapter 8 introduces notation, particularly exponential notation and units. The question of "orders-of-magnitude" is explored. We have found that even among students with substantial backgrounds in science there is a poor appreciation of the importance of "back of the envelope" calculations. In arms race issues especially there is so much uncertainty that calculations valid to within an order of magnitude, i.e., a factor of ten, are frequently quite adequate for understanding the major effects.

An example is the difference in destructive power associated with a one-kiloton weapon, as contrasted to that of a one-megaton weapon, and the fact that while the destructive energy is increased by a factor of 1000, the destroyed area increases by only a factor of 100.

Chapter 9 develops the concept of energy and the important idea that mass can be converted to energy. Elementary nuclear structure is described including the concepts of isotopes, atomic number, and atomic weight.

Chapter 10 introduces key ideas of radioactivity and fission. It discusses the absorption of alpha, beta, and gamma rays in matter permitting the student to estimate shielding needed for protection from these radiations. The special characteristics of the isotopes critical to weaponry are examined, particularly ^{235}U, ^{238}U, ^{239}Pu, deuterium, and tritium.

Chapter 11 describes how nuclear weapons work. The basic ideas are relatively simple, but they are far from obvious. This chapter provides understanding of the differences between "A-bombs" and "H-bombs", and why we can build H-bombs of any desired destructive capability. The "secret of the H-bomb" is revealed—at least in so far as this information is to be found in the public domain.

Chapter 12 introduces concepts from electromagnetism and quantum theory that are needed to understand thermal radiation, the Compton effect, and the generation and effects of the electromagnetic pulse.

Chapters 13–17 examine physical effects of individual nuclear weapons. Included are blast effect, thermal radiation, initial nuclear radiation, fallout, and the electromagnetic pulse. Chapter 18 is concerned with the biological effects of nuclear weapons including those that are short-term as well as long-term carcinogenic and genetic effects. These chapters also introduce new concepts of physics and radiation biology including attenuation of neutrons, the photoelectric effect, the roentgen, rad, and rem.

Part 3 Consequences of the Nuclear Arms Race and other Considerations

Chapter 19 explores estimates of the short-term and long-term casualties from several nuclear exchange scenarios. The impact of a global nuclear war on humankind and the ecosystem—including the hypothesis "nuclear winter"—is discussed, including fallout exposure, ozone depletion, sunlight obscuration, and pyrotoxin generation.

Chapter 20 focuses on possibilities from a technical point of view of defense against a nuclear attack. It includes a discussion of terminal defense and examines extensions of present technology into a possible "space wars" or "high frontier" era that has the goal to provide defense in the ''boost'' and ''mid-course'' phases of a missile trajectory.

Chapter 21 examines concepts of civil defense—what can we do to protect ourselves from nuclear attack. The discussion explores not only physical defense mechanisms, but also the implications of civil defense for national attitudes of aggression or fear, and the implications for the United States of Soviet civil defense practices.

The prospect of nuclear war leads to psychological impact on everyone. These effects are difficult to quantify, yet painfully real. Many—perhaps most—students studying the nuclear arms race experience dreams, and occasionally nightmares. In Chapter 22 we explore the psychological impact of nuclear war on survivors, and the effect of of the prospect of nuclear war on all of us.

The uranium and plutonium used in nuclear weapons is similar to material in nuclear reactors. This is the ''weapons connection'' of civilian nuclear power, which is examined in Chapter 23.

Chapter 24 examines issues associated with verifying compliance with treaties.

Chapter 25 discusses the economic implications of the arms race. Dollars spent on the machinery of war are dollars not spent on developing civilian technology, or on feeding the hungry of the world. Arming ourselves in an unfriendly world may be a price of survival, but the issues of ''how much is enough'' demand that we understand the kind of trade-offs we are making.

In the final chapter we offer our views on the nuclear dilemma.

Appendixes provide useful references, a glossary of the nuclear arms race, and a compendium of useful numerical data.

Practical units are used throughout. While the SI (Système Internationale) units offer the advantage of consistency, we found these advantages outweighed by the confusion that results when students read other material. Thus, pressures (which appear primarily in the discussion of blast effects) are given in pounds per square inch. An appendix provides conversion factors.

CONCLUSION

One of us, JAJ, was an observer of the Trinity test. The other, PPC, served in Washington as a part of the federal government. Both of us have worked at Los Alamos, New Mexico, the government laboratory where the world's first nuclear bombs were designed and built. These experiences, supplemented by many years of observation of the nuclear arms race, have convinced us that the nuclear arms escalation practiced in both the United States and the Soviet Union—with each side responding to actions of the other—is leading to a decrease in the security of both Americans and Russians.

It is our hope that this text will contribute to citizen understanding of the arms race, and thereby to a reduction of tensions and a much needed increase in the security of our children, their children, and the citizens of all nations.

ACKNOWLEDGMENTS

We are grateful to the many individuals who gave generously of their time and knowledge to comment on the ideas in and the drafts of this book, especially to: Robert Ehrlich, George Mason University; Gary R. Goldstein, Tufts University; Gerald W. Meisner, University of North Carolina at Greensboro; G. M. Temmer, Rutgers University; and Valery Thomas, Princeton University. We are grateful for the cogent comments of Glenn T. Seaborg and Freeman Dyson, who reviewed the first edition in some detail. We particularly wish to thank Robert Nard, John Beldock, Avrom Blumberg, Annette Bodzin, Bernadette Boylan, Ray Coppock, Catharine Craig, Chris Craig, Maria Craig, Paul C. Craig, Sara Craig, Robert Ehrlich, Bruce Glassburner, David Hafemeister, Michael Harrington, Garth Isaak, Phillip C. Jessup, Sanford Lakoff, John Lamperti, Guy Letteer, Julius Margolis, Gerald Meissner, David C. Morrison, James Neel, Lester G. Paldy, Horst Porembski, William Potter, Timothy Prout, Joseph Romm, Dietrich Schroeer, Randolph Siverson, Robert Socolow, G. J. Temmer, Sylvia Warren, Claudio Zanelli, and our editors at McGraw-Hill, Denise Schanck and John Zumerchik. Students in our arms race course at Davis and summer institutes contributed extensively to the text through their comments and constructive criticisms. Nancy Jungerman and Kathleen Cox displayed enormous patience during the long periods when we were chained to our computers. We are most grateful to them for their encouragement and support. Although this book was prepared on computers, we still needed a great deal of secretarial support, which was ably supplied by Christine Baldocchi, Sue Chan, Silvia Hillyer, Trisha Risley, and Barbara Woolf.

Paul P. Craig
John A. Jungerman

NUCLEAR ARMS RACE
Technology and Society

PART I

THE CONTEXT

CHAPTER

1

OUR
NUCLEAR
PREDICAMENT

I know of no way of judging the future but by the past.

Joseph Henry 1775

We live in the birth era of the nuclear fire. That fire was first ignited in a squash court at the University of Chicago in December 1942, where Enrico Fermi and his group started the world's first nuclear reactor. The overwhelming fact of the nuclear fire is that it is more powerful by a factor of 10 million to 100 million than chemical fires. This major advance in the ability of human beings to influence the environment has arrived into a world afflicted with deadly rivalry among nation-states. The challenge we all face is to somehow change our modes of international behavior soon enough to avoid mutual annihilation.

The world's first atomic bomb was exploded near Alamogordo, New Mexico, on July 16, 1945. Two weeks later, on August 6, a uranium-fueled atomic weapon nicknamed "Little Boy" killed about 100,000 Japanese in Hiroshima. Three days after Hiroshima, on August 9, 1945, a plutonium bomb, "Fat Man," killed an estimated 70,000 Japanese in Nagasaki. Within a week Japan surrendered to the United States, and World War II was over.

The primitive Hiroshima and Nagasaki bombs created a blast equivalent to 15,000 and 21,000 tons of chemical explosive, respectively. The largest individual bombs carried by British Lancaster bombers in World War II, called "blockbusters," contained 4000 pounds (or about 2 tons) of TNT each. The atomic bombs were roughly 10,000 times more powerful. In an instant, the character of warfare had changed for all time.

Since 1945 the United States and the Soviet Union have developed vast arsenals based on the fission of uranium and plutonium (*A-bombs*), and on the fusion of

3

deuterium and tritium (*H-bombs*). Britain and France each have nuclear arsenals which, though much smaller than those of the superpowers, are quite sufficient to destroy a large number of cities. India and China have exploded nuclear weapons. China, in particular, has had an extensive nuclear weapons program and has an arsenal of nuclear weapons; Israel has not exploded nuclear weapons but is generally believed to have at least a dozen, and perhaps hundreds, of reliable bombs.

A 1-megaton bomb, the size of a strategic warhead in the 1980s, is equivalent to 67 Hiroshimas. The effects of even one such bomb exploded over a large city defy the imagination. But in 1988 there were in the combined strategic arsenals of the Soviet Union and the United States over 20,000 strategic warheads containing about 12,000 megatons that could be delivered to each other's societies by intercontinental ballistic missiles (ICBMs), submarine-launched ballistic missiles (SLBMs), or by aircraft. All the bombs used by all combatants in World War II amounted to about 3 megatons or 200 Hiroshimas. The combined strategic arsenals of the superpowers contain approximately 1 million Hiroshimas.

There are about 200 cities in the United States with a population of 100,000 or more. Sacramento, California, has a population of about 600,000. A 1-megaton bomb hitting Sacramento on a normal working day would kill about 400,000 people outright and seriously injure the remainder. The same megatonnage, but divided into three bombs of about one-third megaton, or 22 Hiroshimas, each, would be more "efficient" and leave hardly any survivors.

There are an additional 400 cities in the United States with a population of 25,000 or more. The combined population of all 600 cities is about 132 million people. If 1000 megatons exploded over these 600 cities, about 84 percent of the population of these cities, or 111 million people, would be killed directly. This does not take into account indirect casualties due to fallout, epidemics, and starvation. All of this could be accomplished with about 14 percent of the Soviet arsenal and all within 30 minutes time, any time. The United States can produce a similar catastrophe in the Soviet Union, and on the same scale. Such is the balance of terror.

The tremendous power of nuclear weapons has turned the advantage overwhelmingly to the offense. There is simply no technical way to provide assurance that no missiles will reach their targets. Vulnerability of both sides is a fact of the nuclear age.

The strategy of *mutually assured destruction* (MAD), which has been the de facto situation between the Soviet Union and the United States for over two decades, states that any nuclear attack on the United States would result in an overwhelming attack on its adversary. Hence the adversary is *deterred*. In order for deterrence to be successful one's retaliatory forces must be largely invulnerable to nuclear attack and the adversary must believe in your intent to actually carry out the second strike. This the United States has accomplished by means of the *strategic triad*, which places forces in land-based missiles, on aircraft, and on submarines. The submarines are difficult to locate and hence are an important part of our second-strike retaliatory capability. The Soviets, with less access to the sea, have chosen to concentrate their nuclear forces in land-based missiles.

One can argue that deterrence has been a success, because, after all, there has not been a nuclear war, or a war of any kind, between the superpowers since the beginning of the nuclear era in 1945, even though there have been many provocations that in other times might have led to war. The United States fought a conventional war in Vietnam, and the Soviet Union fought a conventional war in Afghanistan. The superpowers, despite frequent rhetoric of confrontation, have actually been circumspect in avoiding provocation of each other by actions.

The most dangerous superpower confrontation in the nuclear era probably was the Cuban missile crisis in 1962. That October the world peered into the nuclear abyss. The confrontation was over the emplacement of nuclear weapons. The United States felt threatened by the prospect of Soviet nuclear-tipped missiles able to hit points in the United States from Cuba. Fortunately, prudence on both sides was used. Chastened governments soon signed a treaty banning atmospheric testing of nuclear weapons (1963). Even though the Soviet Union at that time was outnumbered in nuclear weaponry (Figures 1-1 and 1-2), the threat of nuclear destruction of cities in the United States was very real, since only a few nuclear weapons can wreak incredible havoc.

The Soviet Union vowed never to be caught in such an inferior position again. Currently the United States retains its lead in numbers of strategic warheads (Figure 1-1), while the Soviet Union is ahead in numbers of strategic launchers (Figure 1-2). The arsenals are diverse, and it is possible to develop indicators which show each side to be ahead. These matters are explored in depth in Chapter 3. Suffice it to say, however, that both the United States and the Soviet Union have overwhelming de-

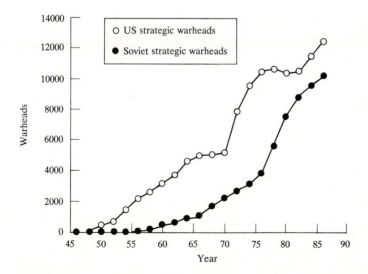

FIGURE 1-1

The total number of U.S. and Soviet strategic warheads are shown. The United States has always had a lead in the number of strategic warheads. *Source:* Robert Norris, William Arkin, and Thomas Cochran. Nuclear Weapons Databook Working Paper NWD 87-1, NRDC, Washington, D.C.

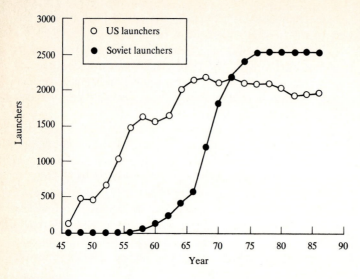

FIGURE 1-2

The total number of launchers for the United States and the Soviet Union since the inception of the nuclear arms race. The total includes bombers, intercontinental ballistic missiles, and submarine-launched ballistic missiles. The curves show the achievement of nuclear parity by the Soviet Union in the late sixties after an earlier period of dominance by the United States. *Source:* Robert Norris, William Arkin, and Thomas Cochran. Nuclear Weapons Databook Working Paper NWD 87-1, NRDC, Washington, D.C.

structive capability, as measured by their capabilities to destroy each other's societies many times over.

The United States and the Soviet Union also have a combined total of about 30,000 nuclear warheads of generally smaller size called *tactical nuclear weapons.* These weapons are fully integrated into military planning. If these so-called "battle-field weapons" are ever used, there is a risk that control will be lost and escalation to strategic nuclear weapons will occur.

The sheer amount of megatonnage now in the superpowers' arsenals represents a wholly new threat. Nuclear weapons are no longer just a threat to the cities and societies of nations, but to citizens of all nations, to the ecosystem of the earth, and to humankind itself. In the 40 years since Hiroshima the world has been slowly but surely crafting a "doomsday machine."

A simple estimate of radiation exposure will illustrate the danger. In a nuclear war between the superpowers with thousands of nuclear explosions, wind will quickly distribute fallout over the entire northern hemisphere. If 10,000 megatons are exploded, it is estimated that the *average* external radiation exposure in the mid-latitudes of the northern hemisphere for a person shielded during the first 48 hours will be 100 rad (radiation absorbed dose), with a further internal exposure of 100 rad to some body organs as a result of ingesting radioactive materials (Turco et al., 1983).* The

---

*The Reference section following the text gives complete citations for all sources cited in the text.

HERMAN

"Thank you, Burrows, for that
descriptive insight into
the nuclear arms race."

mid-latitudes contain most of the United States, the Soviet Union, and Western Europe. Those individuals in combatant nations who were in the downwind plume of the nuclear explosions would be exposed to a large additional radiation dose from local fallout.

A radiation dose of 200 rad is an extremely serious radiation exposure. A dose of 400 rad would produce death in 50 percent of a normal adult human population within 30 days. For the infirm or young the lethal dose is lower. Thus many of the people in the northern hemisphere might die from radiation exposure alone within a few months of the explosions. Among survivors there would be many cases of permanent sterility; an approximate doubling of the genetic mutation rate, giving rise to genetic deaths in future generations; and a shortened life span as a result of cancer or other radiogenic diseases.

Radiation exposure would not be the only disastrous and long-term consequence of a large-scale nuclear war. After a 10,000-megaton exchange, the sunlight could be reduced appreciably in northern latitudes for a period of several months and mid-continental temperatures could drop as much as 10 degrees Celsius for several weeks. Such reductions in the intensity of sunlight and the temperature would have serious consequences for the ecosphere and for agriculture, especially in a summer war. This effect has been called ''nuclear winter'' because initial calculations indicated more severe effects. More recently it has been termed ''nuclear fall'' by some authors (see Chapter 19, Strategic Nuclear Exchange by the Superpowers).

It is estimated that in a 10,000-megaton nuclear war from 15 to 30 percent of the human population of the earth might be killed directly (from 800 million to 1.5 billion people), principally by blast, thermal radiation, and nuclear radiation (Ambio, 1983). See Chapter 19. A similar number would probably die of indirect, long-term effects of radioactive fallout, famine, excessive ultraviolet radiation, and epidemics of disease.

In the 1960s Secretary of Defense Robert McNamara estimated that 400 megatons would be sufficient to destroy the Soviet Union as a functioning society. With the expansion of nuclear arsenals to more than 10,000 megatons, much more is involved if deterrence fails than the destruction of the societies of the adversaries. The stakes are now much higher. Nuclear war threatens the entire human race.

The existence of nuclear weapons has changed the nature of international conflict. Some would say it has made warfare obsolete as a method for resolving tensions between nations possessing nuclear weapons. The central fact of life in the nuclear age is the unquestioned and unambiguous ability of nations possessing nuclear weapons to destroy each other. We may mourn this fact, but there is no realistic chance of changing it.

The very existence of the United States depends on decisions made in the Soviet Union not to use nuclear weapons against us, and vice versa. Whether or not we trust the government and people of the Soviet Union is an important issue, but one which cannot be allowed to distract us from the technical reality of their ability to destroy us. We and the Soviets must learn to live together, or we shall certainly die together.

CHAPTER 2

HISTORY
OF THE
NUCLEAR
ARMS
RACE

Not everything that is more difficult is more meritorious.

St. Thomas Aquinas

2-1 THEMES

In the twentieth century advances in physics led to the discovery of the interconvertibility of mass and energy and to the understanding of the internal properties of atomic nuclei. By the mid-1930s physicists recognized the possibility of using this knowledge in constructing powerful weapons. As the threat to freedom from Nazi Germany grew more apparent, the United States began what was to become the Manhattan Project to develop an atomic weapon. Germany surrendered before the project was successful, but in 1945 two atomic bombs were used against Japan. The "atomic genie" has dominated international politics ever since. Technologists have developed increasingly powerful weapons and delivery systems, while diplomats have made only marginal progress in restraining a nuclear arms race.

2-2 BEGINNINGS

From the scientific point of view the nuclear arms race began in 1905 when Einstein derived his famous equation, $E = mc^2$ (Chapter 9). The knowledge that mass is equivalent to energy meant that in principle a very small amount of mass might be converted to an enormous amount of energy. The large energy release from a small mass is due to the very large value of c, the speed of light (see Chapter 9). The question was how to produce the energy release in significant amounts. Individual nuclear reactions were known to release energy, but no mechanism was known to produce a sustained release. In the 1930s a series of discoveries occurred in nuclear physics that made such a **mass-energy conversion** possible.

Advances in Nuclear Physics

The discovery of the neutron by James Chadwick in England in 1932 was followed shortly thereafter by the creation of artificial radioactivity by Frédéric Joliot-Curie in France. Enrico Fermi's group in Rome reasoned that since neutrons are not charged, hence there is no coulomb repulsion (Chapter 12), they can be captured by nuclei to form new and often radioactive nuclei (**isotopes**) of the same element. Fermi succeeded in producing many radioactive isotopes in this way. However, he failed to observe that when uranium is bombarded with neutrons, the uranium nucleus sometimes **fissions**, releasing a large amount of energy as well as radioactive fragments of lighter elements such as barium and strontium (see Chapter 9).

In 1939, just before World War II, Otto Hahn and Fritz Strassman in Germany discovered fission. One of their colleagues, Lise Meitner, was Jewish and had to leave Nazi Germany. Hahn wrote a letter to Meitner soliciting her confirmation of their discovery. She and her nephew, Otto Frisch, were able to explain Hahn's results, which were quite revolutionary at the time, using a liquid-drop model of the uranium nucleus (see Figure 2-1). She communicated their interpretation to Hahn and Strassman, who then published their fission discovery. Meitner and Frisch had been working in Niels Bohr's laboratory in Copenhagen. Bohr in turn quickly communicated the fission discovery to scientists of Great Britain and the United States. Enrico Fermi and Leo Szilard, now both at Columbia University, and others (e.g., Joliot-Curie in France) quickly discovered a truly spectacular aspect of fission: when fission occurs, two or three neutrons are released from the atom's nucleus. See Figure 2-2. Here at

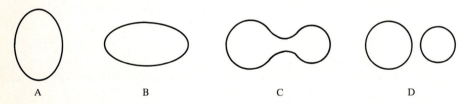

A   B   C   D

FIGURE 2-1
The liquid-drop model of fission. In this model the nucleus of the atom is conceived as a liquid drop which begins to oscillate violently when, for example, it absorbs a neutron. As a result of the oscillation the drop may become unstable to the repulsive coulomb forces of its electric charge with respect to the normal "surface tension" produced by the attractive nuclear forces. In A a uranium nucleus is shown in its normal state as a prolate spheroid (rather like a lemon in shape). Under the excitation produced by neutron capture it begins to oscillate in B, becoming more elongated. In C a neck appears and the positive charge of the nuclear protons pulls the nucleus apart into two fragments. The fragments are generally unequal in size. Finally in D the fragments are completely separate and fly apart violently with large kinetic energies. For more detail of the fission process see Chapters 9, 10, and 12.

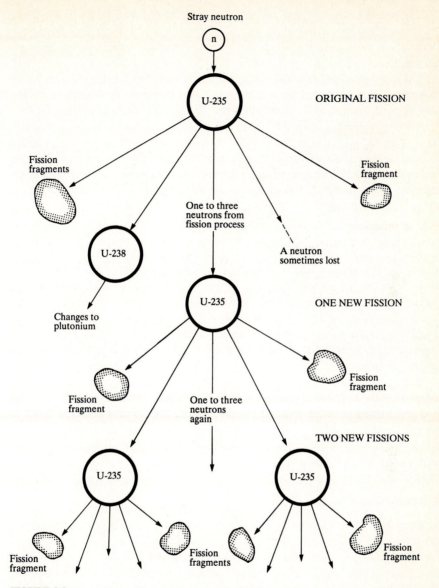

FIGURE 2-2

A neutron strikes a uranium 235 nucleus which then undergoes fission, releasing from one to three neutrons. On the average 2.46 neutrons are released per fission. Since more than one neutron is released per fission on the average, the possibility of a chain reaction exists. Occasionally, a neutron may be absorbed in a uranium 238 nucleus. The latter often subsequently undergoes spontaneous nuclear transformations to become plutonium. However, this neutron is lost in terms of producing more fissions and more neutrons to continue the chain reaction. Sometimes a neutron escapes from the assembly and is also lost to the chain reaction as is shown to the right in the figure.

last was a key to a possible huge release of energy: the neutrons from a given fission could perhaps find new uranium nuclei and produce fission in them, and this in turn could produce more neutrons which in turn could produce more fissions—giving a **chain reaction**.

The network of international communication that led to the discovery of fission is characteristic of unfettered science. At this point, however, the history of nuclear science became dominated by political events. Szilard and others proposed that there be a voluntary moratorium on publication of information on any aspect of fission in order to minimize information given to Nazi Germany. The moratorium was generally successful, although Joliot-Curie did publish the critical fact that two to three neutrons are released during fission of uranium. Soon official government censorship was imposed: documents were classified, and there were restrictions on communications outside of classified areas.

The Atom Bomb Project Begins

Most of the important research in nuclear physics during the 1930s was done in Europe. When the war started, physicists worried that the Nazis would develop atomic weapons. Leo Szilard implored Albert Einstein (by far the most prestigious scientist in the world at that time) to write a letter to President Franklin Delano Roosevelt advising him of the possible peril. Although Einstein was very much a pacifist, he did indeed write the letter. It was dated August 2, 1939, just a month before the war began in Europe.

Roosevelt appointed a study committee which reported in the summer of 1941 that they thought a "pile" (what we now call a **nuclear reactor**) producing a controlled chain reaction could be made in $1\frac{1}{2}$ years and that a bomb could probably be developed in about 4 years. As it turned out, this report was uncannily accurate— "uncannily" because many critical principles of nuclear physics and bomb design were not known at that time.

The Manhattan Project

After Pearl Harbor (December 7, 1941) a crash program was begun on the atomic bomb project under President Roosevelt's authorization. In the end several billion dollars (1943 dollars) were spent on the program, which was given the code name Manhattan Project. For reasons of security only key members of Congress were informed. In June 1942, J. Robert Oppenheimer, a physics professor at the University of California, Berkeley, was appointed head of the project. General Leslie Groves

FIGURE 2-3
(a) The Los Alamos staff worked a 6-day week; Sundays there was time for recreation. Shown here on a Sunday hike in the mountains above Los Alamos, left to right, standing Emilio Segrè, Enrico Fermi, Hans Bethe, Hans Staub, Victor Weisskopf; seated, Erika Staub, Elfriede Segrè. The photograph is reproduced here by courtesy of Professor Segrè. (b) Theoretician Robert Oppenheimer (left) and experimentalist Ernest O. Lawrence on an excursion from the physics department of the University of California, Berkeley in the 1930s. *Source:* Lawrence Berkeley Laboratory.

A.

B.

was put in charge of managing the military's unprecedented coordination with civilian industry. By the project's completion there were several hundred thousand employees working at three sites: site X was at Oak Ridge, Tennessee; Site Y, at Los Alamos, New Mexico; and Site W, at Hanford, Washington.

The Manhattan Project was aided immensely by the large number of outstanding European scientists who had fled the Nazis. Among them were Leo Szilard, Enrico Fermi, Hans Bethe, Victor Weisskopf, Neils Bohr (known at Los Alamos for security purposes as "Mr. Baker"), and George Kistiakowsky (see Figure 2-3). Many of the best American physicists simply packed up and headed for New Mexico to work on the project, taking their best students with them.

Scientific Knowledge in 1942

In 1942, what was known scientifically about the possibilities of nuclear fission? It was known that the most common fissionable isotope, uranium 238 (^{238}U—the U is the symbol for the element uranium and 238 is the atomic weight of a particular isotope of uranium on a scale where the atomic weight of hydrogen is one), was not suitable for a nuclear weapon because:

1. There is a high probability that a neutron upon entering a ^{238}U nucleus will be inelastically scattered (scattered with a loss of kinetic energy). Its kinetic energy would thus become less than the threshold energy required for fission in ^{238}U [about 1 mega-electronvolt (MeV)]. (For a discussion of energy concepts, see Chapter 9).
2. There is fairly high probability that the entering neutron would be captured to form ^{239}U.

Either process would remove the nucleus as a candidate for fission. Thus, although uranium 238 fission can take place when such nuclei are struck by neutrons, it does not occur often enough to make a self-sustaining chain reaction possible, and hence it cannot be used to make a bomb.

However, another uranium isotope, uranium 235, has a high fission probability. Of natural uranium only 0.7 percent is uranium 235; the remainder is other isotopes. Since uranium 235 is an isotope, it cannot be separated chemically from uranium 238. That is, uranium 235 behaves chemically in an identical manner to uranium 238, although they are two distinct forms of the element uranium. The Manhattan Project site at Oak Ridge was designed specifically to perform the isotopic separation of uranium 235 using physical means. The location was chosen because of the ready availability of electricity from the Tennessee Valley Authority (TVA), the isolation of the area, and the fact that there was an ample supply of labor to operate the separation plants.

Isotopic Separation at Oak Ridge

The separation process was pursued in two different ways. One was **electromagnetic separation**, which had been developed at the University of California Radiation Laboratory in Berkeley. Full-scale production facilities were immediately constructed at Oak Ridge. One of us (J.A.J.) was involved with this effort. It used a huge ring-shaped magnet which was energized by TVA power and which utilized conductors made of silver, on loan from the nation's depository at Fort Knox. The uranium was in the form of uranium tetrachloride, a thick liquid. It was ionized in an electric arc, and then accelerated into the magnetic field. The heavier ^{238}U isotope described a semicircle of slightly larger radius in the magnetic field than the ^{235}U. (See Chapter 12, Electromagnetism, Section 12-7, for a more detailed discussion.) Collectors for the ^{235}U at the smaller radius and ^{238}U at a slightly larger radius then permitted partial separation of the two isotopes. Uranium enriched in ^{235}U was obtained from the ^{235}U collector. The whole process had to be repeated several times because weapons-grade ^{235}U (better than 90 percent ^{235}U) could not be produced in a single separation.

A story is told that when some British scientists arrived in Berkeley to assist in the project they were confused because they had calculated that the electromagnetic separation method was impractical. It is a tribute to the capacity of American industry and to the imagination and tenacity of American physicist Ernest Orlando Lawrence that the project was successful—but it was also expensive, costing an estimated half-billion 1944 dollars.

The second separation process was **gaseous diffusion**. In this process uranium in a gaseous compound is diffused through a series of about 4000 cells. Because of its lower mass the ^{235}U diffuses slightly faster than the ^{238}U. This approach eventually superseded electromagnetic separation.

The uranium in the Hiroshima bomb came from the Oak Ridge project.

Fermi's Atomic Pile

Researchers in Berkeley found that when ^{238}U captures a neutron to form ^{239}U this isotope decays with a 23-minute half-life (half of the isotope decays spontaneously in 23 minutes) to form a new element, neptunium 239. This in turn decays again in a few day's time by spontaneously emitting an electron to produce plutonium 239. The latter has a long half-life, about 24,000 years. It decays by emission of a helium nucleus (alpha particle) to ^{235}U (see Chapter 10). Plutonium 239 was thus a candidate for a nuclear bomb, providing its nuclear properties, such as having a low probability for inelastic scattering or capture of neutrons, were satisfactory.

In order to pursue the plutonium avenue for the production of fissionable material for a bomb, Enrico Fermi worked with a group at the University of Chicago to construct a pile capable of a self-sustaining chain reaction. To be self-sustaining, at least one neutron must be available after each fission to begin a new generation. The idea was that if one took chunks of natural uranium and distributed them in a lattice in a very pure graphite the neutrons would scatter (bounce) from the graphite and slow down. Slower neutrons have a much better probability of being captured to form uranium 239. One might imagine the uranium chunks occupying the corners of a three-dimensional array of small cubes that were fitted together to form a large cube. With proper design the capture of neutrons by the ^{238}U could be minimized, and the probability of fission produced by the neutrons maximized, so the process would be self-sustaining. The graphite had to be very pure to avoid capture of neutrons by impurities. The neutrons that did get captured in ^{238}U would produce plutonium 239, which was the desired product.

About 2.5 neutrons are emitted per fission, on the average. Thus the pile would barely chain-react if 1.5 neutrons were lost before the next fission cycle began. To reduce loss of neutrons to the outside the pile was made larger and larger (carefully) until finally it reached a size at which it "went critical." This first controlled nuclear reaction occurred in December 1942 in a squash court underneath the University of Chicago football stadium.

Nuclear Reactors at Hanford

Since **plutonium** is a different element from uranium, it can be separated from uranium chemically. However, at the beginning of the Manhattan Project, no one knew enough about the chemistry of plutonium to produce it on a large scale. The problem was undertaken at the University of Chicago in what was termed the "metallurgical laboratory" under the direction of Dr. Glenn Seaborg, a chemistry professor from the University of California, Berkeley. The full-scale production of plutonium would require design and construction of special remote handling equipment because the radioactivity levels were vastly larger than any that had been previously encountered.

In order to develop this "hot chemistry," i.e., the chemistry necessary for separation of plutonium from the highly radioactive reactor fuel rods, it was necessary to produce a very small amount of this new radioactive element. Since the reactors had not yet even been designed, the plutonium needed was made by heroic efforts at the cyclotron at Washington University, St. Louis by irradiating 300-pound batches of uranium nitrate hexahydrate for months at a time. Ultramicrochemistry techniques were then developed to work with tiny quantities of plutonium—tenths of a microgram (10^{-6} gram). These almost invisible specks of plutonium were extracted from the irradiated uranium and were used to ascertain the chemical, physical, and nuclear properties of plutonium so that full-scale reactors could be built and the plutonium extracted. Three reactors were constructed at Hanford, Washington (site W). It required a tremendous extrapolative effort to go from the Chicago reactor, with its 0.6-watt power output, to the multimegawatt reactors at Hanford.

In the Hanford reactors several hundred grams of plutonium were eventually produced each day. The heat released was not recovered but was removed by using water from the nearby Columbia River.

After the plutonium was extracted by hot chemistry, it was cast into the shape needed for a bomb. The operations involved were very delicate and dangerous; they required strict precautions, since plutonium is extremely toxic if ingested (see Chapter 10). The atomic bomb that was dropped on Nagasaki was made from the plutonium created at Hanford.

Bomb Design at Los Alamos

One of us (J.A.J.) arrived at Los Alamos in 1945, just before the first atomic bomb test. At Los Alamos Emilio Segrè's group had discovered that the **spontaneous fission** rate of plutonium 239 is about 300 times larger than that of uranium 235, and that plutonium 240 is 40,000 times as large. The spontaneous fission rates were so large that the neutrons released would probably cause a nuclear weapon of the "gun" type to explode prematurely. The gun-type weapon (an example of which was the uranium 235 bomb that would eventually be dropped on Hiroshima) consisted of two pieces of fissionable material that were literally shot toward each other to form a supercritical assembly or bomb (see Chapter 11). If a stray neutron should initiate a chain reaction before the two pieces were entirely assembled, there was a risk of a "fizzle" rather than a high-yield explosion. This, as Segrè's group showed, is much more likely to happen with plutonium than with uranium 235.

The Implosion Technique—The Trinity Test

Seth Neddermeyer, a physicist from the University of Minnesota, developed the idea of using explosive charges to compress a sphere of plutonium very rapidly (in a millionth of a second) to a density sufficient to make it go supercritical and produce a nuclear explosion. Neddermeyer and James Tuck, a British scientist who had brought the latest technology on shaped explosive charges to Los Alamos, worked together under the direction of George Kistiakowsky, a chemist from Harvard University, in developing this compression scheme, or **implosion** technique, as it was called. (More detail on the construction of nuclear bombs is given in Chapter 11.)

The idea of an implosion was so novel and untested that it was decided that a test explosion would be needed. It was called *Trinity,* and took place in the Alamogordo Desert about 100 miles south of Albuquerque, New Mexico, on July 16, 1945.

One of us (J.A.J.) witnessed the test informally at a distance of about 20 miles. The group he was with was lucky because 20 miles is just beyond the distance at which a nuclear bomb blast begins to cause retinal burn or permanent eye damage to unprotected eyes. There was an awesome flash of radiation—much brighter than the sun in the dawn light of July 16—and the now-familiar mushroom cloud began to form. The group hastened from the scene, knowing that the cloud was filled with fission products and unfissioned plutonium, both of which are serious health hazards.

J.A.J. had the intuitive feeling that the world had changed in some ill-defined but fundamental way. There was a collective feeling of sympathy for the Japanese, who, it was assumed, would feel the effects of this new weapon in the near future.

For more detailed information on the Manhattan Project and the development of the atomic bomb the reader is referred to the *Smyth Report* (Smyth, 1945) and *The Making of the Atomic Bomb* (Rhodes, 1987).

2-3   THE ATOMIC BOMBING OF JAPAN

Bomb Data and Casualties

The first use in war of a nuclear weapon occurred on August 6, 1945, at Hiroshima, Japan. Hiroshima had been spared from conventional bombing in order to provide a more impressive demonstration of the power of the new bomb. As a result of this first nuclear bombing 80,000 to 140,000 people were killed and 100,000 more were seriously injured. Hiroshima ceased to exist as a functioning society. Although a similar number of casualties had occurred previously in conventional bombing of Japanese cities (e.g., the Tokyo firebombing), it required thousands of bombs delivered over a period of many hours to accomplish. The explosive yield of Little Boy, the ^{235}U gun-type bomb dropped on Hiroshima, was about 15 kilotons of TNT, only about one-twentieth of the megatonnage of warheads carried on today's strategic missiles (see Figure 2-4). [An eyewitness account by a 16-year-old Japanese Kamikaze fighter pilot is given in Kuwahara (1957). The psychological effects on the victims are examined in Chapter 22.]

On August 9 a plutonium-implosion bomb—Fat Man—was dropped on Nagasaki (see Figure 2-5). The yield was 21 kilotons. The casualties in Nagasaki were somewhat less than in Hiroshima because of the hilly terrain, which provided a partial shield from the blast pressure and radiation. Nevertheless 40,000 to 70,000 people were killed immediately and a like number injured (Committee for the Compilation of Materials, 1981, p. 478). Because of the utter chaos at the time and the loss of population records the casualty figures are approximate.

Should Japanese Cities Have Been A-Bombed?

On August 14 Japan surrendered unconditionally. It is often argued that without use of the atomic bombs the war would have continued for several more months, with a terrible loss of both United States and Japanese lives as Japan itself was invaded.

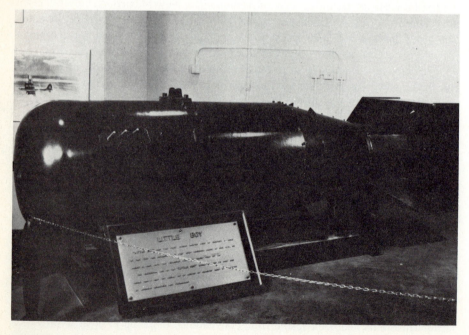

FIGURE 2-4
Little Boy—a replica of the uranium 235 bomb that was dropped on Hiroshima on August 6, 1945.

Estimates made on the basis of experience gained in the invasion of Okinawa suggest that several hundred thousand Allied casualties, and at least a comparable number of Japanese casualties, would have resulted if the planned invasion of the main islands of Japan had taken place.

The Committee for the Compilation of Materials on Damage Caused by the Atomic Bombs in Hiroshima and Nagasaki (Committee for the Compilation of Materials, 1981, p. 335) has a different view. It states: "This historically unprecedented devastation of human society stemmed from essentially experimental and political aims. . . . The A-bomb attacks were needed not so much against Japan—already on the brink of surrender and no longer capable of mounting an effective counteroffensive—as to establish clearly America's supremacy in the anticipated cold war setting."

The question of whether or not the atomic bombs should have been used as they were will be long debated. It is important to try to consider this decision in the context of that time. According to Bernstein (1983), "There was not really a decision as such to use the atomic bomb. The use of the weapon had already been decided early in the Manhattan Project and reaffirmed almost every year. Truman was a new president and too weak to change this policy and was basically in favor of it anyway."

A government committee had studied questions of targetry and other technical matters, but had never considered the possibility of not using the bomb. Several scientists from the Manhattan Project, including Lawrence, Oppenheimer, and A. H. Compton, proposed in late spring 1945 that a noncombat demonstration be made. This proposal was disposed of in a 10-minute discussion over lunch with government officials because the scientists could not guarantee that the bomb would not be a dud or that the Japanese would not place prisoners of war in possible target areas. [About a dozen American prisoners of war lost their lives in the atomic bombing of Hiroshima (Committee for the Compilation of Materials, 1981, p. 478).] (See Figure 2-6).

FIGURE 2-5
Fat Man—a replica of the implosion-type plutonium bomb dropped on Nagasaki on August 9, 1945.

FIGURE 2-6
The devastation caused by the atomic bomb dropped on Hiroshima.

Although the Hiroshima bombing might have been avoided by modifying the Allies' unconditional surrender formula, this was unacceptable domestically since "unconditional surrender" had long been a war goal. The Japanese peace feelers to Switzerland and the Soviet Union were ambiguous. We now know that the Japanese cabinet was split 3 to 3 and unable to decide whether or not to continue the war. Only the historically unprecedented intervention of Emperor Hirohito broke this stalemate and made it possible to surrender, and even then a group of young officers attempted a coup at the last moment and tried to suppress the emperor's address of surrender to the Japanese nation. They were narrowly defeated. Hirohito's decision to surrender unconditionally was made just before the Nagasaki attack so, with hindsight, we can surmise that that attack, at least, may not have been necessary.

However, although the Nagasaki bombing occurred on August 9, the official Japanese acceptance of surrender terms did not finally occur until August 15, 1945.

In the climate of August 1945 the use of the atomic bombs against Japanese cities was quite acceptable to most Americans. The United States had come to accept the idea of using saturation bombing to devastate entire cities with conventional bombs. This was a routine practice during the final months of both the European and the Japanese war. Retribution against the Japanese was also a popular idea. There was also the attractive political objective of possibly making the Russians more tractable. It would have been very difficult politically *not* to have used such a special weapon.

Retrospection

Although the original objective of the Manhattan Project was to develop the atomic bomb before the Nazis did, we now know that the Nazi bomb was never a real threat. Just after hostilities ended, the U.S. physicist Samuel Goudsmit made a special study of the German atomic bomb effort for the U.S. Army. In his book *Also* he shows that the German atomic bomb effort was never given high priority by Hitler, nor did it use the best German scientists (Goudsmit, 1947).

An interesting vignette regarding the Nazi effort is that German scientists ruled out a graphite-moderated reactor because of erroneous measurements made by a prominent German professor. Apparently no one dared to remeasure or confirm his results. Fermi knew of the situation, but published nothing so as not to alert the Nazis. As a result the German effort concentrated on a heavy water (deuterium water) moderator. While it is possible to construct a reactor in this way, it is difficult and expensive. The heavy water was made in a special plant in Norway which the Royal Air Force bombed dutifully and regularly to reassure the Germans of its importance (Irving, 1967).

As Herbert York (1970, p. 3) points out: "The Manhattan Project, then, was based on the first of a long series of mistaken beliefs in our being 'raced.' Because this was the first such case, our mistake in this regard was, in my view, entirely justified, but our subsequent failure to learn anything from repeatedly making the same mistaken judgment about the existence of a 'race' is less so." In the 1960s Presidential politics focused on missile and bomber gaps which later turned out to be nonexistent. A cautious approach to "windows of vulnerability" (see Section 2-6) is warranted.

After the defeat of Germany the original motivation for the atomic bomb development, namely, to obtain an atomic bomb before the Germans did, had vanished, yet the work at Los Alamos went forward with undiminished intensity. In fact there was overtime activity to bring the bomb to fruition for use in the war against Japan. This is the recollection of one of us (J.A.J.) and also of R. R. Wilson of Cornell University, as he comments in the film *The Day After Trinity*.

2-4 THE IMMEDIATE POSTWAR PERIOD

Atomic Diplomacy

For a short time the United States enjoyed a monopoly in nuclear weapons. During this period there were several contradictory political developments. For a brief period (until December 1945) Secretary of State James Byrnes tried unabashed "atomic diplomacy." He stated that he would not recognize Soviet spheres of influence and, for example, insisted that the Soviets change the method of the Bulgarian elections. This antagonized the Soviet Union and helped to lose what Secretary of War Henry Stimson had recognized as a unique postwar opportunity to avoid a nuclear arms race. Atomic diplomacy was soon recognized as an impractical policy and was abandoned.

Smyth Report

Just after the war a detailed volume on the Manhattan Project was released—the *Smyth Report* (Smyth, 1945) prepared by Henry D. Smyth of Princeton University. It described the main lines of the American effort and pointed out some of the technical difficulties that had been encountered. The details undoubtedly were helpful to any country developing atomic projects. On the other hand the general data revealed would have been difficult to keep secret for long in peacetime, and the Soviet Union already had access to many of the U.S. secrets through their espionage activities.

Weapons Tests

The military quickly began tests to explore the capabilities of the new weapons. One example was the Navy's Operation Crossroads tests at Bikini Atoll in the Pacific in July 1946. These explored the effects of airborne and underwater nuclear explosions on naval vessels of various types—mostly ships waiting to be scrapped. The most spectacular event was the shallow underwater explosion code-named Crossroads. This bomb had roughly the same yield (about 20 kilotons) as those used against Japan. The underwater explosion formed an immense hollow column of water about $\frac{1}{2}$ mile in diameter which rose initially at the rate of $\frac{1}{2}$ mile per second to a height of $1\frac{1}{2}$ miles. Several million tons of water were in this column, and a base surge was formed that initially had a wave 100 yards high. A battleship was lifted out of the water and smashed, and several other ships were sunk or swamped. Figure 2-7 shows the column of water.

In January 1946 the first General Assembly of the United Nations met in London. It created the U.N. Atomic Energy Commission as a dependent body of the U.N. Security Council. Part of the Commisson's charge was to eliminate all major weapons of mass destruction, including the atomic bomb. Undersecretary of State Dean Acheson was appointed to chair a committee to formulate the U.S. position. This report, largely the work of Oppenheimer, became known as the Acheson-Lilienthal report. It recommended what appeared to be rather revolutionary steps to control nuclear weapons. It defined as "dangerous activities" installations for production of uranium 235, plutonium reprocessing plants in connection with nuclear power, and even uranium mines. Thus, almost the entire nuclear fuel cycle was classified as dangerous. The report recommended that it be illegal for any nation to indulge in these dangerous activities, all of which should be placed under international management.

Only the proposed international authority was to have the right to conduct research on nuclear explosives. The transition from national to international control of nuclear weapons was to be effected in stages. One of the first steps was to make an international inventory of uranium mines, which would have required on-site inspection of these facilities.

President Truman assigned Bernard Baruch, a veteran statesman, to pursue the delicate negotiations with the Soviet Union concerning this proposal. Baruch persuaded the president to add to the U.S. proposal the restriction that the veto in the United Nations Security Council would not apply to atomic energy control. This right

FIGURE 2-7
Column formed as a result of a shallow underwater explosion (about 20 kilotons, at a water depth of 200 feet). *Source:* Glasstone and Dolan, 19, Fig. 2.67b.

of veto had been one of the conditions for the Soviet Union's participation in the formation of the United Nations. Without the veto any country deemed in breach of its formal promise not to develop atomic weapons would have been condemned by majority vote. Thus it was unlikely that the Soviet Union would accept the idea.

Andrei Gromyko of the Soviet Union soon made a counterproposal calling for an absolute prohibition of nuclear weapons and destruction of present stockpiles, all of which belonged at the time to the United States. Signatory states were to enact legislation which would severely punish any breach of the treaty. The signatory states themselves would ensure observation of the treaty—so there was to be self-control rather than international inspection, a condition that was deemed unrealistic and unacceptable by the United States.

The Soviet Union used the Baruch veto proposal as an excuse for rejecting the U.S. plan. The basic Soviet objections were to international inspection (an excuse for espionage, in their view) and to the fact that the proposed plan prohibited Soviet development of nuclear weapons while allowing the United States to preserve some nuclear weapons for an indefinite transition period. This would have effectively maintained the American monopoly. The Americans, stung by the Soviet rejection of the Oppenheimer-Baruch plan, rejected the Soviet proposal without much serious consideration.

The Cold War Begins

The late 1940s were a time of increasing hostility. The Truman doctrine was designed to prevent communist takeovers in Greece, Turkey, and elsewhere. The Soviets managed a coup d'état in Czechoslovakia. By 1948 the Cold War was in full swing.

In June 1947 the Soviet Union proposed to the United Nations that international control and inspection of all civil nuclear activities—from mining to the production of fissile materials and energy—be subject to Security Council veto. The United States considered this proposal inadequate. The effect of the treaty would have been similar to the nonproliferation treaty agreed to in the late sixties, but with the important difference that all countries would have been bound by its provisions. (Under the present treaty members of the ''nuclear club''—those nations that already had nuclear weapons at the time the treaty was signed—are excluded from having their facilities inspected by the International Atomic Energy Agency.)

The Soviet A-Bomb

The Soviet Union exploded its first atomic bomb in August 1949. Many American scientists had pointed out that there were no real secrets of the atomic bomb and that given sufficient time any industrial nation could build one. However, the consensus was that it would take from 5 to 10 years (General Groves thought it would be 20 years). According to York (1970, p. 34), ''At that time it seemed to many of us that espionage must have been far and away the main reason they were able to accomplish the job so quickly, especially after the devastation that had been wreaked on them by World War II. Having since seen some excellent Russian technological progress in other fields, we are no longer quite so sure that this was the case.''

Espionage

Soviet knowledge of the Manhattan Project was extensive. Klaus Fuchs, a British scientist in the theoretical division at Los Alamos during the war, had access to a wealth of classified material, much of which he passed to the Russians. Fuchs was tried and convicted in Britain in the 1950s. He served 10 years of a 14-year sentence, the maximum permitted under British law for giving classified information to an ally, as the Soviet Union was during World War II. He then emigrated to East Germany.

The most celebrated American espionage at Los Alamos involved David Greenglass, a skilled mechanic who gave to a Soviet agent (the same one who received Fuchs's information) details of how to calculate the critical mass of a plutonium bomb.

While this information was not nearly so useful or extensive as that provided by Fuchs, Greenglass's testimony against his sister, Ethel Rosenberg, and her husband, Julius Rosenberg, both of whom were also involved, led to their execution in June 1953. The sentence was believed by many to be unusually severe—the result of an almost hysterical fear of alleged and often unfounded internal communist threats. This attitude, sometimes called McCarthyism after a senator of the period who achieved notoriety by making political capital from such threats, increased fears of espionage.

The Rosenberg affair stimulated worldwide protest and much anti-American propaganda. The case remains controversial to this day.

2-5 THE H-BOMB

After the Russian A-bomb success, the idea of the hydrogen bomb (often called the "super") received fresh impetus in the United States. In this bomb deuterium or tritium (heavy isotopes of hydrogen) are fused into helium, releasing nuclear energy. There is no limit to the size of a hydrogen weapon, whereas fission bombs are limited in yield due to the restriction of the critical mass (see Chapter 11).

The H-Bomb Decision

In October 1949 the General Advisory Committee (GAC) of the United States Atomic Energy Commission (AEC), chaired by Robert Oppenheimer, met to consider the technical and political aspects of pursuing the hydrogen bomb.

The committee decision to reject the bomb was unanimous. (Glenn Seaborg, who probably would have opposed that decision, was abroad and hence missed the meeting.) They recommended instead that the development of atomic weapons, including tactical nuclear weapons for battlefield use, be accelerated. There were three major considerations. First, the H-bomb was considered to be technically difficult. Second, the production of tritium—then thought essential to an H-bomb—would interfere with the production of fissionable material for A-bombs. Finally—and this was a point that assumed great importance—the GAC agreed that the production of such a weapon should be avoided for broader reasons, reasons having to do with acceleration of the arms race and morality.

In a separate report, some members of the committee, including Oppenheimer, declared that the H-bomb was a weapon of genocide and that the psychological effect of possessing it would not be in the best interests of the nation. Two other members, the Nobel prize winners Enrico Fermi and Isadore Rabi, wrote their own addendum stating that "since no limit exists to the destructiveness of this weapon, its very existence and knowledge of its construction is a danger to humanity as a whole." They called on the President to declare before the American public and the world that "it was contrary to basic ethical principles to initiate the development of such a weapon," and asked that the President invite all nations to make a solemn pledge to join the United States in renouncing research leading to production of the hydrogen bomb.

This discussion must be considered in the context of an escalating Cold War with the Soviet Union. A group of scientists supporting development of the H-bomb, led by Edward Teller, made direct approaches to the military and to the Joint Committee on Atomic Energy (JCAE), to which the GAC reported. The JCAE was convinced by the arguments of Teller's group that the H-bomb was the appropriate reply to the Russian A-bomb. The Korean war, which erupted in June 1950, buttressed this approach. However, although the Air Force favored H-bomb development, the Navy did not. Truman appointed a special three-man committee—consisting of Dean Acheson, secretary of state, Louis Johnson, secretary of defense, and the chairman of the AEC, David Lilienthal—to study the question. Many believe that Truman selected the membership so that the outcome would be predictable.

Lilienthal was the only committee member opposed to H-bomb development. He focused on the probability that an H-bomb would lead to an even fiercer arms race, which would further reduce the chance of acceptance of the Acheson-Lilienthal-Baruch plan for international control of nuclear weapons. During the committee's last meeting it learned of Klaus Fuch's arrest and the importance of the information he had passed on to the Soviets—which included some preliminary calculations on the H-bomb. This lent force to Acheson's and Johnson's arguments, which were strongly in favor of continued development of the "super". Truman announced his decision the same day: The AEC was to pursue its work on all possible atomic weapons, including the hydrogen bomb.

The United States and the Soviet Union: The H-Bomb Race

By 1951 a test at Eniwetok Atoll demonstrated release of energy from **nuclear fusion**. The apparatus was an experimental device, not a weapon, that had been constructed on the basis of principles developed by Edward Teller and Stanislaw Ulam.

The rate of progress, though, was too slow for Teller and his group. They proposed setting up a new nuclear weapons laboratory to compete with Los Alamos. This facility, formed using staff of the Berkeley Radiation Laboratory (now the Lawrence Berkeley Laboratory), was established in September 1952 on an old Air Force base near Livermore, California. It is now known as the Lawrence Livermore National Laboratory (LLNL).

In late 1952 a 10-megaton thermonuclear explosion (the "Mike" shot) ushered in the thermonuclear age in earnest. The island in the Eniwetok Atoll upon which the test occurred disappeared. This bomb was a thousand times more powerful than the one that had been used on Hiroshima just 7 years before. A photograph of the Mike explosion is shown in Figure 2-8.

In August 1953 the Soviet Union exploded a device which had a fusion component. Analysis of atmospheric samples showed that the energy came in part from lithium deuteride. Lithium deuteride is much more practical to use for this purpose than deuterium or tritium, which had been used in the Mike shot, because the deuterium and tritium had to be maintained as liquids at extremely low temperatures. This demonstrated that the Soviets had an impressive capability and that, in this case at least, espionage had not played a significant role.

Sixteen months after Mike, on March 1, 1954, a deliverable H-bomb using solid lithium deuteride was tested by the United States on Bikini Atoll in the United States protectorate in the Marshall Islands. Operation Bravo yielded 15 megatons, far more than had been planned. It left a crater more than $\frac{1}{2}$ mile wide and several hundred feet deep and ejected several million tons of radioactive debris into the atmosphere.

Bravo produced extensive radioactivity in local fallout. An unanticipated change in meteorological patterns shifted the wind so that Rongelap Atoll, about 100 miles

FIGURE 2-8
This fusion test explosion—the ''Mike'' shot—took place on October 31, 1952, on Eniwetok Atoll, in the Marshall Islands, at the Atomic Energy Commission's Pacific Proving Ground. The test demonstrated the feasibility of the H-bomb. The explosion left a crater about 1 mile in diameter and 200 feet deep. The mushroom cloud went up 25 miles and spread out visibly for over 100 miles.

from Bikini, received high doses (see Chapter 16). On the northwesterly part of Rongelap Atoll radiation levels were over 3000 rad, which would have been fatal for several hundred residents. Fortunately all the islanders were in the extreme southerly part of the atoll attending a religious ceremony. However, by the time the inhabitants were evacuated, 44 hours after the explosion, the accumulated doses were of the order of 175 rad. (Ironically, evacuation was delayed so long in part because U.S. personnel suspected their radiation instruments were not functioning because they indicated off-scale—i.e., very high—levels of radioactivity). Long-lasting effects of this exposure, such as thyroid abnormalities and cancer, have been observed in Rongelap islanders.

The **fallout** pattern of lethal radioactivity extended about 160 miles downwind from the explosion. About 7000 square miles were contaminated to such an extent that evacuation or protective measures were necessary. Within a few weeks ocean currents and fish migration brought radioactive fish into the waters around Japan. This necessitated radiation monitoring of fish consumed in Japan (Hibakusha, 1977, p. 183), where fish are a staple of the diet. There were 682 contaminated fishing boats in the eastern Pacific by the end of November 1954. More detail of the fallout pattern and ocean contamination is given in Chapter 16.

The Bravo test covered the Japanese fishing boat the *Fifth Lucky Dragon* with radioactive ash. The crew was unaware of the danger and ingested the radioactivity. Two deaths, and severe health problems for the other sailors, particularly skin burns and loss of hair, caused a strong emotional reaction to these events in Japan. Public opinion throughout the world was outraged by the effects of Bravo on innocent victims. This contributed to a process that ultimately led, in 1963, to a ban on testing of nuclear weapons in the atmosphere (the Partial Test Ban Treaty).

In November 1955 the Soviet Union tested an H-bomb with an energy release of several megatons. This began a series of Soviet H-bomb tests culminating in 1962 in an explosion of about 60 megatons. Premier Nikita Khrushchev boasted that "it could have been bigger, but then it might have broken all the windows in Moscow, 4000 miles away." The sizes of current weapons are determined by the size of projected targets and by the military mission, not by technical limits.

Hindsight: Should the United States Have Waited?

Herbert York (1975) wrote that the American decision to build the H-bomb could have awaited an actual Russian H-bomb test without in any way jeopardizing the nation's security. His argument is summarized in Figure 2-9. The worst-case scenario is that the United States decided not to initiate H-bomb development until after a Soviet test and meanwhile the Russians proceeded at their actual rate. A more plausible scenario is one in which the Soviets would not have proceeded at their actual rate, but more slowly, because there would have been less urgency. As the figure shows, even in the worst case both nations would probably have tested a practical, deliverable H-bomb at about the same time, the end of 1955. Certainly the moral position of the United States would have been enhanced. And, because at that time the United States had several thousand deliverable fission weapons, national security would not have been threatened.

The Oppenheimer Security Hearings

In late 1953 the chairman of the AEC, Lewis Strauss, moved to deny Robert Oppenheimer's security clearance. Strauss, long an opponent of Oppenheimer in matters of nuclear policy, had been appointed 6 months before by President Dwight D. Eisenhower as chairman of the AEC. The Oppenheimer affair was ostensibly based on an incident 10 years earlier in which Oppenheimer had failed to inform security officials promptly of a purported attempt by a university colleague to contact him for espionage purposes. When he did so, he gave security officials two different versions of the incident.

The AEC deprived Oppenheimer of his position as a government adviser despite his prominence and his dedicated leadership during World War II. The decision,

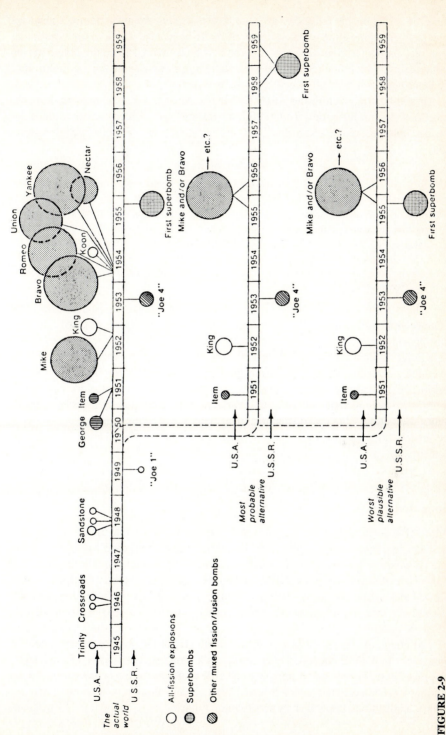

FIGURE 2-9

Scenarios for H-bomb development suggest that the United States could have waited for a Soviet H-device test before starting its own H-bomb program.

ostensibly based on his reliability as a security risk, was almost certainly a result of Oppenheimer's opposition to construction of the H-bomb. He was a victim of political infighting, particularly between the Air Force, which favored H-bomb development, and the Army, which favored emphasis on tactical fission weapons for use in Europe. The latter approach was advocated by Oppenheimer.

In the hearings before the AEC, Edward Teller was a key witness against Oppenheimer. In his testimony Teller said, in response to a query as to whether he considered Oppenheimer a security risk ("In the Matter of J. Robert Oppenheimer," 1954):

> In a great number of cases I have seen Dr. Oppenheimer act—I understood that Dr. Oppenheimer acted—in a way which for me was exceedingly difficult to understand. I thoroughly disagreed with him on numerous issues and his actions frankly appeared to me confused and complicated. To this extent I feel that I would like to see the vital interests of this country in hands which I understand better, and therefore trust more.
>
> In this very limited sense I would like to express a feeling that I would feel personally more secure if public matters would rest in other hands.

The hearing was a sad episode in American history. It was personally devastating to Oppenheimer and divided the American scientific community, most of whom sided with Oppenheimer. It was also unnecessary politically since the Strauss–Teller–Air Force point of view on H-bomb development had by then been accepted by the U.S. government. Oppenheimer retired from public life and spent the rest of his life (he died in 1967) as director of the Institute for Advanced Study at Princeton. Eventually the injustice was recognized. In 1963 President John F. Kennedy awarded Oppenheimer the nation's highest distinction in nuclear science, the Enrico Fermi award. The medal was presented by President Lyndon B. Johnson after the assassination of Kennedy.

Atoms for Peace

In 1954 President Eisenhower proposed withdrawing fissile material from military stockpiles to use for peaceful purposes. Under his "atoms for peace" proposal, fissile material would be provided by an international agency if the nation requesting it agreed to on-site inspection, verifying that it was not being used for military purposes. This proposal was subscribed to by the Soviet Union. In the fall of 1955 the U.N. General Assembly created the International Atomic Energy Agency (IAEA) to administer the safeguard system.

Although the IAEA was successful as a vehicle for the development of peaceful applications of nuclear energy, it was powerless to prevent continuation of the nuclear arms race. Initially only small amounts of fissile material were supplied to the IAEA by either the United States or the Soviet Union. Meanwhile the amount available for military applications grew ever larger in both countries.

2-6 NUCLEAR TEST BAN TREATIES

The Comprehensive Test Ban Negotiations

With public pressure growing because of radioactivity in the environment due to the testing of nuclear weapons, a conference of experts from the Soviet Union, the United States, and the United Kingdom was convened in Geneva in 1958 to study methods of detection of nuclear explosions at long distances. They concluded that such detection would be possible, even with underground testing, down to a level of only a few kilotons. In the autumn of 1958 during the negotiations on a comprehensive test ban the Soviet Union announced that it would unilaterally cease testing. The United Kingdom and the United States also ceased testing, and the moratorium continued for 3 years. It was ended in September 1961 by an extensive series of Soviet tests at Novaya Zemlya in the Soviet arctic. The Geneva negotiations on a comprehensive test ban treaty (CTBT) were terminated in 1961, after 350 sessions.

Cuban Missile Crisis

On October 15, 1962, the Soviet Union was detected attempting to install intermediate-range missiles in Cuba that would have been capable of reaching the United States and for two weeks the world looked into the nuclear abyss. Soviet Premier Nikita Khrushchev was gambling that he could intimidate the newly elected President John F. Kennedy and could at a stroke greatly improve the Soviet strategic nuclear capacity. Kennedy responded with a naval blockade of incoming Soviet ships to Cuba. There was also a proviso that an air strike at the missiles in Cuba would be made if the blockade failed. Men and materiel were assembled in Florida for the air strike and possible invasion to follow.

On October 26 a Soviet freighter was boarded, was found not to have missiles or nuclear warheads aboard, and was allowed to proceed. Since work on the Cuba missile sites had proceeded almost to the point of their becoming operational, word was passed to the Soviets that an air strike would be delayed only two days longer. At this time a secret letter arrived from Khrushchev hinting at a deal in which the missiles would be removed if the United States would promise not to invade Cuba (as had already been abortively attempted in the Bay of Pigs fiasco). The next day, October 27, a second letter arrived demanding removal of U.S. missiles from Turkey as the price of withdrawal of Soviet missiles from Cuba. This seemed to be the product of a committee, was more "hard line," and was viewed as politically unacceptable. On the advice of Robert Kennedy, then Attorney General of the United States, President Kennedy ignored the second letter and accepted the first.

As this diplomatic progress was taking place in very limited time, a U-2 reconnaissance plane was shot down over Cuba and the pilot lost. Tension increased greatly. The air strike was scheduled for Monday morning, October 29. Any Soviet missiles that survived might have been fired. It was expected that the Soviets would at least retaliate by moving on Berlin and perhaps elsewhere. In this course of events nuclear weapons would probably have been used on a wide scale. Western civilization hung by a slender thread.

On Sunday, October 28, a message came that the Soviets had agreed to remove the missiles with no mention of the missiles of the United States in Turkey. The Cuban missile crisis was over. The U.S. missiles in Turkey were quietly removed the following spring. Secretary of State Dean Rusk characterized this superpower confrontation as ''the gravest crisis the world has known.''

Limited Test Ban Treaty (LTBT)

Soon after the Cuban missile crisis it became politically possible to renew discussions of a nuclear test ban treaty. Such discussions were at least partially in response to a worldwide concern about pollution of the earth's atmosphere as a result of continued testing.

Negotiations were rather quickly concluded for a limited test ban. (The assumption was that the LTBT would be followed later by a CTBT—which never materialized.) The arrangement permits underground testing, and in practice it has not slowed the arms race. Because the treaty was limited to atmospheric testing, it avoided Soviet objections to any agreement involving on-site verification and U.S. objections to a treaty that would supposedly make it difficult to develop or maintain the quality of nuclear weapons.

France and China did not sign the LTBT. The United Kingdom, having exploded its first A-bomb in 1952 and an H-bomb in 1957, signed the treaty. So did over 100 other nations. Before the treaty went into effect there had been about 500 atmospheric tests: about 345 by the United States, 166 by the Soviet Union, 23 by the United Kingdom, and 9 by France. It is estimated that about 10 tons of plutonium were dispersed into the atmosphere by these tests. Since the residence time is about 1 to 2 years in the stratosphere and only a month or two in the troposphere, this plutonium is now part of the ecosystem.

Table 2-1 gives the number of tests by each nation that had publicly conducted nuclear tests at the time of the signing of the LTBT and the total conducted by 1988. See also Table 2-3, which shows the known nuclear tests by year and nation.

TABLE 2-1

U.S.	U.S.S.R.	U.K.	France	China	India
Tests conducted before signing of LTBT					
345	166	23	9	0	0
Tests conducted from 1945 to December 31, 1988					
910	635	41	172	34	1

Source: Countdown on the Comprehensive Test Ban, Neil Joeck and Herbert F. York, University of California Institute on Global Conflict and Cooperation and the Ploughshares Fund and Table 2-3.

Tests conducted by the United States, U.S.S.R., and United Kingdom since the signing of the LTBT in 1963 have been underground. French tests since the middle 1970s have also been underground.

Between the time the LTBT went into effect and 1986 there were about 450 underground explosions by each of the two superpowers. Ironically, the LTBT, while safeguarding the atmospheric environment, indirectly contributed to the nuclear arms race because it kept the magnitude of the U.S. and Soviet stockpile buildups from public awareness for over 20 years.

For further reading on the Cuban missile crisis and the limited test ban the reader is referred to *Kennedy, Krushchev, Test Ban* by Glenn T. Seaborg (1981), who was chairman of the Atomic Energy Commission during that period.

Will There Be a CTBT?

Jerome Wiesner, presidential science adviser, and Herbert York, the first director of the Livermore Laboratory, have stated that a CTBT would not be detrimental to having an adequate stockpile of nuclear weapons (Wiesner, 1964). However, officials of the weapons laboratories continue to stress the need for continued testing to ensure reliability of nuclear weapons (DeWitt and March, 1984, and *Effects of a Comprehensive Test Ban Treaty,* 1978).

In 1980, agreement on a CTBT seemed close. The Soviet Union had agreed to on-site seismic inspection stations, which had long been a point of contention in negotiations. In 1983, negotiations were abandoned by the Reagan administration in the United States and the Thatcher administration in Britain.

The British Nuclear Force

Early in World War II British scientists had taken the lead in assessing the feasibility of constructing an atomic bomb. The British decided that developing the bomb in Britain under wartime conditions was not promising, but they did share their knowledge with United States authorities. It was this fundamental work that made it possible for the United States government under President Roosevelt to proceed with some confidence in the initial research that eventually developed into the Manhattan Project. It was therefore natural to include British scientists in that project, and they made many noteworthy contributions to it. For more detailed information on the British contribution to the development of the atomic bomb during World War II the reader is referred to *The Making of the Atomic Bomb* by Richard Rhodes (1987).

However, in 1946 with the passage of the McMahon Act by the Congress, which established the Atomic Energy Commission of the United States, international cooperation in nuclear weapon research was terminated. The British felt betrayed by the Americans, who they considered were in their debt for having been alerted to the scientific possibility of an atomic bomb in the first place.

Although the British could have abandoned their own nuclear weapon development, leaving it to the Americans and to the Soviets, this was never seriously considered. Having their own nuclear weapons program was seen as a natural consequence of Britain's long scientific and technical leadership, and its recent status as a great power. As the Cold War developed, the idea that Britain should have an independent nuclear force also gained favor. Winston Churchill also argued that if the British would demonstrate their capacity to design and build a bomb, eventually the United States could be persuaded to restore atomic collaboration. In this respect he was correct, but it took 10 years and a dozen nuclear tests in the atmosphere to accomplish it.

All of Britain's tests of atomic bombs occurred in or near Australia. Their legacy in terms of radiation exposure and environmental contamination and the accompanying financial costs is destined to be a continuing source of friction between current Australian governments and Britain for some time in the future.

The first British test took place in 1952 and was of 25-kiloton yield. This fission bomb was exploded in the Monte Bello islands off the northwest coast of Australia. Two more tests were conducted in the Great Victoria Desert in 1953, and here seven more nuclear tests took place in 1956 and 1957.

Quite separately the British conducted nine thermonuclear atmospheric tests at Malden and Christmas Islands in the Pacific Ocean from May 1957 to September 1958. Two nuclear tests had previously taken place in the Monte Bello islands in 1956 as precursors for the hydrogen bomb development.

Throughout the British nuclear program, they were behind the Soviets (and the Americans). When the British cabinet made their secret decision to develop an atomic bomb in January 1947, they were confident they would beat the Soviets at becoming a nuclear power by several years. In fact the Soviets exploded their first fission bomb in 1949, 3 years before the first British test.

Again in the case of the hydrogen bomb the Soviets and Americans had already conducted H-bomb tests before the British even decided to build their own thermonuclear bomb, a decision taken in July 1954. The reason for doing so was a matter of international politics and national prestige. The cabinet record states: "No country could claim to be a leading military power unless it possessed the most up-to-date weapons, and the fact must be faced that, unless we possessed thermonuclear weapons, we should lose our influence and standing in world affairs."

Since 1962 Anglo-American collaboration has been resumed, and tests of British nuclear weapons are conducted at the Nevada Test Site in the United States. Since the United Kingdom is also a signatory to the Limited Test Ban Treaty, all of its tests since 1963 have been conducted underground.

The French Nuclear Force

During and after World War II, the French were systematically excluded from the Anglo-American nuclear program and were vexed by the policy of two-nation control needed to fire NATO nuclear weapons. General Charles de Gaulle moved to develop an independent nuclear capability, the *force de frappe*.

The first French A-bomb test occurred in 1960 in the Sahara, then under French control. Later tests, including the first French H-bomb in 1968, were made in the South Pacific. The French argued that they had every right to pursue the development

TABLE 2-2
Total beta activity in the air near the ground at several sites in Chile after French tests in the South Pacific on June 25, July 1, and July 29, 1972

Month	Beta activity, picocuries per cubic meter		
	Santiago	Antofagasta	Easter Island
January	0.10		
February	—		
March	0.11		
April	0.09		
May	0.09		
June	0.03	0.06	0.06
July	3.61	5.15	1.33
August	0.55	1.66	0.13
September	0.07	0.06	
October	0.04	0.04	
November	0.03		
December	0.03		

of nuclear weapons for their own security, as other states had done, including tests in the atmosphere if necessary. This is still their official policy.

Radioactivity from the French tests on the South Pacific island site had commonly fallen about 3 or 4 days later on the Andean watershed. This elicited strong protests from Peru and Chile, culminating in Peru's severing diplomatic relations with France.

Table 2-2 shows the dramatic increase in radioactivity in various parts of Chile as measured by the Chilean Atomic Energy Commission. It was about 30 to 100 times the normal level in Santiago and Antofagasta, respectively, during the peak period. This was the result of three French atmospheric tests totaling about 60 kilotons that took place in June and July 1972 on islands in the Tuamotu Archipelago, over 4000 miles west of Chile. As a result of meteorological conditions, Easter Island, which is only about 2000 miles from the test site, received less fallout. (See Chapter 10 for a discussion of radioactivity and Chapter 16 for further discussion of fallout.)

Australia and New Zealand carried protests against the French tests to the International Court of Justice at the Hague in 1973. The French atmospheric tests, which had taken place annually since 1968, were discontinued in 1974. As of this writing (1988) the French continue to conduct nuclear explosions beneath coral atolls in French Polynesia even though there is considerable opposition to them by inhabitants of the area. Through these tests, the French have been able to develop a hydrogen warhead for the submarine missile component of the *force de frappe*. [Much of the history of the French effort and the French view of the arms race is given by Goldschmidt (1982).]

The Chinese Nuclear Force

The Chinese also refused to sign the LTBT. Their nuclear program began during a period of cooperation with the Soviet Union in the 1950s. Demands by the Soviets

TABLE 2-3
Known nuclear tests by year, 1945 to December 31, 1988

Year	U.S.	U.S.S.R.	U.K.	France	China	Total
1945	3	—	—	—	—	3
1946	2	—	—	—	—	2
1947	0	—	—	—	—	0
1948	3	—	—	—	—	3
1949	0	1	—	—	—	1
1950	0	0	—	—	—	0
1951	16	2	—	—	—	18
1952	10	0	1	—	—	11
1953	11	4	2	—	—	17
1954	6	7	0	—	—	13
1955	18	5	0	—	—	23
1956	18	9	6	—	—	33
1957	32	15	7	—	—	54
1958	77	29	5	—	—	111
1959	0	0	0	—	—	0
1960	0	0	0	3	—	3
1961	10	50	0	2	—	62
1962	96	44	2	1	—	143
1963	44	0	0	3	—	47
1964	38	6	1	3	1	49
1965	36	9	1	4	1	51
1966	42	15	0	7	3	67
1967	34	17	0	3	2	56
1968	45	13	0	5	1	64
1969	38	16	0	0	2	56
1970	35	17	0	8	1	61
1971	17	19	0	6	1	43
1972	19	22	0	3	2	46
1973	16	14	0	5	1	36
1974	14	18	1	8	1	42
1975	20	15	0	2	1	38
1976	18	17	1	4	4	44
1977	19	18	0	6	1	44
1978	17	27	2	8	3	57
1979	15	29	1	9	0	54
1980	14	21	3	13	1	52
1981	16	22	1	12	0	51
1982	18	31	1	6	0	56
1983	17	27	1	9	2	56
1984	17	29	2	8	2	58
1985	17	9	1	8	0	35
1986	14	0	1	8	0	23
1987	14	23	1	8	1	47
1988	14	17	0	8	1	40
TOTAL	910	635	41	172	34	1,793

In more than four decades the five nations that currently possess nuclear arsenals have conducted almost 1,800 known nuclear test explosions. The United States and Soviet Union share approximately 87 percent of the total. For the entire period the average has been one test every nine days. As a result of the Soviet moratorium there were fewer tests in 1986 than in any year since 1960. In 1987, testing resumed normal levels.

The United States does not announce all of its tests. The U.S. total includes 114 unannounced tests, 68 of which have recently been added to the list of known test explosions by an examination of past seismic data; see Robert S. Norris, Thomas B. Cochran, and William M. Arkin, "Known U.S. Nuclear Tests, July 1945 to 31 December 1988," Nuclear Weapons Databook Working Paper 86-2 [Rev. 2C], January 1989. It is likely that several dozen more remain to be discovered. Twenty-seven of the total were "peaceful" nuclear explosions conducted between 1961 and 1973. Recent annual budgets for testing are approximately $650 million. Vertical shaft tests cost around $30 million apiece and the more complicated horizontal tunnel tests, to test the effects of explosions, $50-$60 million each.

The total number of Soviet tests is unknown. According to the Swedish National Defense Research Institute, an additional 18 tests took place between 1949 and 1958 for which a breakdown by year is not available; these are included in the total. The French ministry of defense has revealed additional Soviet tests for the time period 1963–77, but since dates are not specified they have not been included. It is likely that a significant number of Soviet tests have either been undetected or unreported. More than 100 of the Soviet tests are peaceful nuclear explosions.

Beginning in 1962 the United Kingdom conducted 20 of its 41 tests jointly with the United States at the Nevada Test Site.

A French ministry of defense document revealed five additional French tests between 1975 and 1984, not included in any other listing (two in 1980, one in 1981, and two between 1975–1977, which have been included in the total).

In 1986 several official Chinese publications stated that China had conducted 32 nuclear tests since 1964, three more than the available data suggested. The three are included in the total. The French ministry of defense shows two Chinese tests in 1983, where other sources show only one.

The overall total includes one Indian test in May 1974.

Source: Bulletin of the Atomic Scientists, "Nuclear Notebook," April 1989, p. 48. Reprinted by permission of the Bulletin of the Atomic Scientists. Copyright © 1989 by the Educational Foundation for Nuclear Science, 6042 S. Kimbark Ave., Chicago, IL 60637, USA.

---

for control over Chinese nuclear weapons led to severing of Chinese-Soviet nuclear cooperation.

As a result, the Chinese denounced their agreement with the Soviets in 1959, and in August 1960 all Soviet nuclear experts were suddenly withdrawn. This action is described by the Chinese in bitter terms as "treachery by the socialist imperialists who overnight tore up their contracts and recalled their technicians." However, the Soviet Union was only following a policy it has also used in Eastern Europe, which is to retain Soviet control of nuclear weapons.

In October 1964 the Chinese exploded an A-bomb at Lop Nor in the Sinkiang Desert of northwestern China. This bomb was made with uranium 235, which probably came from a uranium enrichment plant the Russians had built in Manchuria. In 1967, a year before the French exploded their first hydrogen bomb, the Chinese exploded a 3-megaton H-bomb. As early as 1973 the Chinese had developed a missile with a 5600-kilometer range. By 1976 they had exploded over 20 nuclear bombs and had a nuclear strike capability that could cover a large part of the Soviet Union (Wang, 1983).

Intercontinental Ballistic Missiles (ICBMs)

In the early 1950s intelligence reports indicated that the Soviet Union had an advanced program for producing **ICBM**s. These devices were correctly viewed as revolutionary.

FIGURE 2-10
Craters formed at the Nevada test site by decades of nuclear testing. *Source:* Lawrence Livermore National Laboratory.

They can deliver a nuclear warhead from the Soviet Union to the United States within $\frac{1}{2}$ hour. They enter the target area at around 15,000 miles per hour, which makes defense against them very difficult.

Although the United States had at this time a vastly superior bomber force, it started six crash programs to match the Soviet missile threat. In 1957 the Soviets tested an ICBM. Two months later they launched their first satellite, Sputnik. This event had been expected, but the public display of a Soviet satellite orbiting overhead produced a strong reaction in the United States. There were calls to close the "missile gap." We now know that there was in fact no missile gap at the time; it existed only in the nation's apprehensions. According to York (1970): "By the time the numbers of deployed ICBMs became a significant factor in the strategic balance between the two superpowers, the United States was well ahead of the U.S.S.R. . . . The Soviet leaders made things more confusing by deliberately using their genuine early space lead to imply an ICBM threat (nonexistent) against the U.S. even as early as 1958."

By the time of the Cuban missile crisis in 1962, the United States had a superiority in delivery systems and nuclear warheads of about 5 or 6 to 1. Although, even with this advantage, the United States could not have prevented a devastating nuclear assault, the Soviets perceived the lopsided strategic balance as placing them at a disadvantage. They began a long-range build-up of nuclear warheads and delivery systems, principally land-based ICBMs but also a fleet of nuclear-powered submarines equipped with nuclear missiles.

The Non-Proliferation Treaty

The non-proliferation treaty of 1968 was the result of an interest shared by the United States and the Soviet Union in limiting the spread of nuclear weapons to other nations. The treaty is not as useful as it would have been had the more comprehensive Soviet proposal of 1947 been successfully negotiated (see Section 2-4). Nevertheless, in exchange for assistance in developing peacetime uses of nuclear energy, most nations have agreed to renounce the acquisition of nuclear weapons. The treaty prohibits signatory nations from transferring nuclear weapons technology to other states and therefore attempts to limit the members of the nuclear club to the 1968 number.

The nuclear powers, particularly the superpowers, were enjoined by the treaty to negotiate in good faith to end the arms race as soon as possible and to formulate a general and complete disarmament treaty with strict and effective controls. By 1988, over 130 countries had signed the treaty. The non-nuclear signatory states contend— with justification—that the nuclear powers have done little to limit their nuclear arms as the treaty requires. Nonsigners of the treaty include a number of nations with potential interest in obtaining nuclear weapons. Among them are Pakistan, Brazil, Argentina, South Africa, Israel, Spain, India, Algeria, and Saudi Arabia. India has conducted an atmospheric nuclear test, and some of the other nations are thought to have acquired nuclear weapons (Israel, possibly South Africa).

The ''Peaceful'' Indian Explosion

In 1974 India exploded a plutonium bomb in a desert bordering on Pakistan. The Indians claimed the explosion was in pursuit of peaceful objectives. However, the Canadians, who had furnished a research reactor from which the plutonium was extracted in India, reacted strongly and prohibited any future collaboration on atomic matters with India. The United States also restricted such collaboration and successfully persuaded India not to carry out a second test. When Indira Gandhi was defeated in the 1977 elections, her successor, Morarji R. Desai, officially abandoned further tests.

SALT I

In the early 1970s President Nixon recognized the reality of the strategic balance and undertook discussions with the Soviet Union. This led to a period of detente during which the SALT I (strategic arms limitation talks) treaty was successfully negotiated. Part of the SALT agreement put a strict limitation on ABM (*a*nti *b*allistic *m*issile) systems. Only two sites per country were permitted to be defended in its protocol, one of which must be located so as to defend the capital city. The United States agreed to this, since its ABM system (Safeguard) was having severe technical problems and also because it was believed that the single Soviet ABM system defending Moscow could be easily penetrated by missiles equipped with *m*ultiple *i*ndependently targetable *r*eentry *v*ehicles (MIRV missiles). An amended protocol dated July 3, 1974 limited each nation to only one ABM site.

More recently, the Strategic Defense Initiative (SDI) (see Chapter 20, Strategic Nuclear Missile Defense) was initiated by the Reagan administration as a possible defense against strategic nuclear attack. The SDI, if deployed, would certainly require renegotiation or abrogation of the SALT I ABM provisions. As the SDI program progresses, increasing pressure to test components in realistic environments such as outer space has developed. Such testing is forbidden by the SALT I treaty according to its U.S. negotiators and many legal experts. However, the Reagan administration proposed a "broad interpretation" of the treaty that would indeed permit such testing. This interpretation has met with considerable opposition in Congress and the Soviet Union. In fact six former secretaries of defense have supported the traditional interpretation of the ABM treaty (Brown, 1987). Pursuit of the "broad interpretation" could have deleterious effects on arms control negotiations.

The Standing Consultative Commission

SALT I established a commission—the Standing Consultative Commission (SCC)—that meets at least every 6 months to monitor compliance with the treaty and to clarify ambiguous information. The SCC operates as a bilateral silent service; that is, it operates quietly and efficiently out of public view. There is one Soviet commissioner and one United States commissioner and their associated staffs. There are no public meetings unless both commissioners agree. Since the treaty's inception, there have been four United States commissioners. The third in this succession, Ambassador Robert Bucheim, had the following comments about the work of the SCC (Bucheim, 1983):

> The commission sticks to business, there is no rhetoric. A good, productive, working arrangement is formed by the commissioners through their months of contact which promotes mutual respect and efficiency. Questions are brought to the SCC early and defused. There never has been any evidence of Soviet cheating on any of the provisions of SALT I. When the Reagan administration came into office, two zealous staff members, convinced that the Soviets cheated on SALT I, brought no less than 70 complaints in this regard. They were patiently dealt with one by one and found to be groundless. The two staff members were subsequently removed from service in the administration.
>
> The monitoring is done like bird watching: not too early, which would reveal sources, and not too late or the situation may get out of hand (perhaps politicized). As an example the Soviets complained that we were illegally covering one of four missiles in Montana, which they noted by satellite observation. It turned out to be true. Repairs were being made in the inclement winter weather and a temporary structure had been erected to assist. It was removed. This example shows how communication is important to resolve questions concerning non-intentional interference with national technical means of treaty verification.

The SCC is one of the best examples of continuing cooperation between the United States and the Soviet Union. Article 17 of the proposed SALT II agreement provides for a similar commission.

SALT II

Except for the ABM provision, SALT I was really an interim agreement to be superseded by SALT II. It did limit the number of ICBMs to 1400 on the Soviet side and 1054 on the U.S. side. Although negotiations for SALT II were completed during the Carter administration, the treaty was never ratified by the U.S. Senate. This was the result of a shift in the domestic political climate, at least partly in response to Soviet incursions into Angola, Ethiopia, and Afghanistan. Adherents of the philosophy of "negotiating from strength" pointed to the continuing Soviet buildup of nuclear forces and insisted that there was now a "window of vulnerability" that needed to be redressed before any serious negotiations would be possible. Until November 1986 both the Soviet Union and the United States voluntarily observed the terms of SALT II. At that time President Reagan authorized exceeding the SALT II limits in connection with an increase in U.S. bomber forces. This action led to continuing rebuffs from Congress, and at this writing the SALT II treaty does not appear seriously compromised.

On the Soviet side the Krasnoyarsk radar has been considered a serious violation of the ABM treaty, since it is not on the periphery of the U.S.S.R. as the treaty requires and could be used, if operational, for ballistic missile defense. In response to these criticisms in 1988 President Gorbachev offered to place the radar under U.N. supervision for space research.

Although the SALT II treaty has not been ratified by the U.S. Senate and will probably be superseded by the START treaty presently under negotiation, it has nevertheless been a useful step in arms control for the superpowers.

SALT II took a long time to negotiate because it is ambitious in scope and sets limits on almost every category of strategic nuclear weapons, including those that are not yet built. It establishes numerical limits for land and sea-based missiles, heavy bombers, MIRVs, aircraft equipped with cruise missiles, and several other types of strategic weapons.

The treaty sets an overall ceiling of 2400 on ICBMs, submarine-launched ballistic missiles (**SLBMs**), and heavy bombers. It provides for the reduction of this number to 2250 by 1981. To be in conformance, the Soviets would have to dismantle about 250 strategic weapons systems. If the U.S. Senate were to ratify the SALT II treaty (the only act necessary for it to be put formally in force), the United States could obtain this reduction in Soviet strategic force.

The treaty also provides sublimits on all major strategic categories. The total number of MIRVed missiles may not exceed 1200, and neither side can have more than 820 ICBMs equipped with MIRVs. There may be no more than 10 warheads on existing ICBMs. This puts a limit on the total number of warheads either side could build. Thus the immense Soviet SS-18, which can easily carry 20 or 30 warheads, is limited to 10. Further, each side is allowed to build and deploy one new type of

ICBM, but it may not carry more than 10 MIRVs. Missile reloading is banned as is missile storage near silos. Mobile ICBMs that could be moved around on trucks or trains were a source of concern. The Soviets are not to produce, test, or deploy their SS-16 mobile ICBMs or to build mobile launchers for heavy ICBMs. Since the SS-20 is just the first two stages of the three-stage SS-16, the United States was concerned that the Soviets might try to convert their SS-20s into longer-range SS-16s, or launch SS-16s from SS-20 launchers. Both options are banned. Chapter 3 gives more detail on these weapons systems.

The last part of the treaty has a section on principles and guidelines for subsequent negotiations. The treaty is complex and involves comprehensive verification requirements that two decades ago would have been completely unthinkable.

The Intermediate Nuclear Force (INF) Treaty

At the Reykjavik summit meeting of President Reagan and General Secretary Gorbachev in October 1986 the Soviet Union linked progress on an INF treaty to resolution of the dispute over the broad interpretation of the ABM treaty and the Strategic Defense Initiative (SDI). On February 28, 1987, however, Gorbachev announced that the Soviet Union was willing to conclude a separate treaty on land-based intermediate-range nuclear forces. The Reagan administration quickly welcomed this decision. Negotiations proceeded rapidly and the treaty was signed in a ceremony in Washington, D.C., in December 1987. It was ratified by the U.S. Senate in May 1988 just before the Moscow summit meeting of the two superpower leaders in June.

This treaty is noteworthy in that for the first time a whole class of nuclear weapons and their delivery systems will be destroyed. These weapons, deployed by the Soviets in both Europe and Asia and by NATO in Europe, have ranges from 300 to 3400 miles. Although they represent only about 4 percent of the nuclear arsenals, the fact that an agreement has been reached which has nuclear arms reductions is most important. The treaty also broke new ground in agreements for innovative and quite intrusive on-site inspection. For example, Americans will be stationed at an intermediate missile factory in the Soviet Union and Soviets will monitor a U.S. factory similarly to verify compliance with the treaty. These inspections will continue for 13 years to assure both sides that no new missiles of this type are being fabricated. In addition destruction of existing missiles will be verified (see Chapter 24, Verification).

Because the Pershing II and SS-20 missiles can destroy the other side's command and control facilities in as little time as 10 minutes, they could be used as part of a sudden first strike. Their removal will reduce pressure on Soviet or NATO officials to strike first in a military crisis.

The INF treaty also shows that the present Soviet regime is willing to accept asymmetrical cuts in its forces. As Table 2-4 demonstrates, the Soviets will be destroying missiles that are capable of carrying four times as many warheads as the missiles that will be destroyed by the United States.

The successful negotiation and ratification of the INF treaty establishes momentum for future arms control agreements. It demonstrates that, given the political will, the United States and U.S.S.R. can negotiate mutually beneficial agreements to reduce

TABLE 2-4

A summary of deployed missiles to be destroyed and warheads eliminated under the provisions of the INF treaty

U.S.	No.	U.S.S.R.	No.
Ground-launched cruise missiles	309	SS-20 missile	405
		SS-4 missile	65
Pershing II missiles	120	SS-12 missile	220
		SS-23 missile	167
Number of warheads eliminated	429		

Source: Center for Defense Information, Vol. XVII, No. 2, 1988.

the number of nuclear arms. At the same time the treaty helps to ease tensions and improve relations between the United States and the Soviet Union.

Those who support the "peace through strength" concept argue that the Soviets are responding to the fact that NATO proceeded with the Pershing/cruise missile deployments in spite of massive public protests in Europe. This strength in turn permitted Gorbachev to argue the case internally for the INF treaty, which will remove the Pershing/land-based cruise missile threat not only to the Eastern bloc nations but to the Soviet Union itself.

Table 2-4 gives a summary of the missile types and numbers that will be destroyed under provisions of the INF treaty.

It is to be noted that the INF treaty does *not* require destruction of warheads. This provision is at the behest of the United States. It was the position of the Reagan administration that there was a shortage of nuclear materials, such as plutonium or uranium 235. Further it was argued that if the Soviets were allowed to inspect the destruction of U.S. nuclear warheads, they would learn too much about their secret designs. Robert Barker, Assistant Secretary of Defense for Atomic Energy, told Congress in March 1988, "It is . . . the desire of the Defense Department that the Department of Energy retain those warheads in their entirety without tearing them down."

Since the nuclear warheads can be fitted into missiles not covered by the treaty, this omission is not in the spirit of true arms reduction and is a poor precedent for future arms control agreements. It is to be hoped in the START negotiations that not only missiles will be destroyed but the warheads as well.

2-7 TRENDS IN THE NUCLEAR ARMS RACE

Concerns over the destabilizing effects of the MIRV have unfortunately proved only too true. In the decade of the 1970s the number of U.S. warheads tripled and the number of Soviet warheads more than quadrupled, even though the number of ICBMs had been frozen by SALT I. The MX missile and the Soviet SS-18 are evidence of this escalation. Increased missile accuracy is also contributing to instability because of mutual fear of first-strike capability. The theory here is that a single highly accurate attacking warhead can destroy many MIRVed enemy warheads if it hits them on the ground. This provides an incentive for first strike.

United States attitudes toward nuclear war fighting are changing dramatically. In the immediate post-World War II period the United States had nuclear dominance, and it explored "atomic diplomacy," although without much success (see Section 2-4). Later the doctrine of massive retaliation was adopted, which evolved, as Soviet nuclear capability increased, into a policy known as *mutual assured destruction,* or MAD. President Nixon led a search for more flexible targeting which would provide him with more extensive options. Under President Jimmy Carter the search for flexibility led to a key policy document, Presidential Directive No. 59 (PD-59). This document has never been made public, but the general contents have been reported in the press. Targeting emphasis was shifted from economic targets to military targets (*counterforce* instead of *countervalue* targeting). The policy required that U.S. forces be able to endure a protracted nuclear war. PD-59 represents a profound policy shift— from a dependence on deterrence to prevent nuclear war to the development of nuclear war-fighting capability.

Wieseltier (1985) comments that the United States had a pure MAD policy for only a very short time: "Indeed the United States probably never had a pure version of MAD as an actual plan. Recent studies of American targeting policy deduced from the declassified information reveal that, with the exception of a short-lived and bureaucratically inspired adoption of the doctrine of mutual assured destruction by the McNamara Pentagon, it has never been the American intention to strike first against cities . . . the notions of 'flexible response' and 'nuclear options' made their appearance shortly after missiles became the means (of delivery)."

The Reagan administration adapted the philosophy of PD-59, and introduced the idea that the goal of U.S. policy in any nuclear war is to "prevail." Whether it is possible to prevail in a nuclear war, or whether it is possible to fight a limited nuclear war, is unknown—but both are doubtful. The current national planning for nuclear war fighting is embodied in the single integrated operational plan (SIOP), which attempts to coordinate all nuclear capabilities. Under this plan some 40,000 targets are identified in the Soviet Union and its allies. There are, however, only about 900 Soviet cities with populations greater than 25,000, and less than 3500 key military installations, including the 1400 or so land-based missiles, 500 airfields, and smaller numbers of submarine bases, military headquarters facilities, etc. (Pringle and Arkin, 1983).

START (Strategic Arms Reduction Talks)

Shortly after the Reagan administration began in 1982 a proposal was made to the Soviets to reduce the number of warheads on land-based intercontinental ballistic missiles (ICBMs) to 1100 for those systems with the range and accuracy necessary to attack hardened targets (i.e., the land-based missile silos themselves). This proposal referred to the USSR's SS-18 "heavy" missile and to the U.S. counterpart, the MX missile. It also called for an overall sublimit of 2,500 on all ICBM warheads. This proposal was intended to address the vulnerability of ICBM silos to increasing effectiveness of the "heavy" missiles, but even if it were adopted the threat would still remain. In the usual scenario only 2000 accurate warheads are needed to destroy 1000 missile silos, the current land-based strategic arsenal of the United States. At present there are intense negotiations for a modified START treaty which would reduce the *strategic* nuclear arsenals of both sides. There is now an agreed overall limit of 3300 ICBM warheads, with a sublimit of 1540 warheads on "heavy" missiles.

One might ask why arms control negotiations had not flourished sooner. The advocates of "peace through strength" argue that the buildup of the U.S. armed forces during the Reagan administration made meaningful negotiations possible. Others assert that the new Soviet regime under Gorbachev with its emphasis on far-reaching changes in that society—glasnost (openness), perestroika (restructuring), and an attempt to reduce defense spending in order to provide more funds for domestic use—also have contributed substantially. Quite possibly there is some truth to both positions. President Reagan's own attitude about Soviet society also had changed dramatically in his second term in office. In any event the period 1978 to 1986 offered little progress in arms control, whereas the period from 1986 to date has produced significant and valuable achievements.

Other Current Nuclear Policy Questions

A nuclear war-fighting capability requires survivability not only of weapons, but also of weapons control. Current military budgets contain many billions of dollars designed specifically to improve command, control, communications, and intelligence (C-cube-I) functions (see Chapter 5). Whether or not control is possible in the aftermath of an initial nuclear exchange is at best dubious.

A related current policy theme is the ability of the nation to defend itself against attacking nuclear weapons. President Reagan called for development of defense systems against guided missiles—the "strategic defense initiative" (see Chapter 20). Even if such a defense can be developed (and this is extremely doubtful for present missile levels), defenses will still be needed against short-range SLBMs, cruise missiles, and other delivery systems.

Negotiation of arms control agreements offers an alternative to expanded armaments and continual expansion of military expenditure. At this time the United States is faced with serious problems of deficits in the federal budget, and the U.S.S.R. desperately needs more funds domestically to bolster its sagging economy. Therefore, there is a common need to decelerate the arms race from the economic perspective alone. This situation coupled with an energetic and imaginative new leadership in the Soviet Union will present President Bush with a historic opportunity to reassess the U.S. force structure, including nuclear arms. The fact that the INF treaty is in force underlines the new directions that may be possible. The conclusion of a START treaty, however, will be much more difficult because it involves the strategic missiles that can strike at the heartland and armed forces of each superpower.

2-8 SOME ROOTS OF THE
NUCLEAR ARMS RACE

Lord Solly Zuckerman, for many years chief scientific adviser for the minister of defense of the United Kingdom, sums up the current status of the nuclear arms race in his book *Nuclear Illusion and Reality* (1982) as follows:

> In 1971, during the course of the SALT I talks, Henry Kissinger admitted—presumably with the authority of the President he represented—that there was no longer any such thing as 'nuclear superiority'. He may not have been consistent over the years in his pronouncements on nuclear matters, but he could not have been more to the point on that occasion.
>
> Ten years later, after both sides have added substantially to their nuclear arsenals, neither enjoys any superiority. Both armories have long since passed the level that would be necessary to assure overwhelming mutual destruction. Only political determination based upon an understanding of what are the immutable facts of destruction can break the deadlock of the nuclear arms race.

Zuckerman suggests some reasons why the race persists:

> The world's leaders have declared that they want to see an end to the nuclear arms race. That this has not happened is due to the fact that the leadership in the USA and the USSR is fearful of taking action because the defense scientists and ''intelligence'' experts who are at the heart of the race are always able to generate alarm about what the other side is doing, or may be doing.
>
> But this need not go on forever. The success of SALT I and the more limited success of SALT II became possible because space surveillance and other techniques of intelligence allowed both sides to learn a great deal about each other's progress in the ABM race, and about the development of land-based missiles. On the other hand, while new technologies can help inform the two sides of certain facts, I doubt if they could ever give each side the assurance it would want that it knew enough not only of the opponent's capabilities, but, more important, his intentions.

York (1970) wrote that the arms race is fueled in part by ''overreactions and technical excesses,'' which are the result of ''patriotic zeal, exaggerated prudence, and a sort of religious faith in technology.'' In answering the question why the United States has been responsible for the majority of the actions that have set the rate and scale of the arms race, York says, ''We are richer and more powerful, our science and technology are more dynamic, we generate more ideas of all kinds. For these very reasons, we can and must take the lead in cooling the arms race, in putting the genie back in the bottle, in inducing the rest of the world to move in the direction of arms control, disarmament and sanity.''

Figure 2-11 illustrates some important historical points in the nuclear arms race. It shows that very often, though the first satellite in orbit and ABMs are exceptions, the United States has taken the lead in introducing new weapons, but the Soviets have always followed its lead within a few years' time.

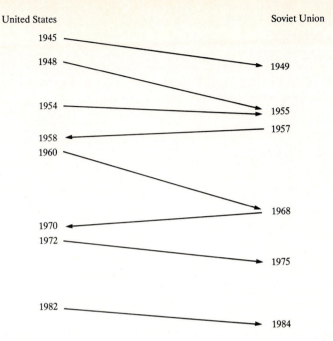

United States   Soviet Union

1945

1948   1949

1954   1955
                                                   1957
1958
1960

                                                   1968
1970
1972

                                                   1975

1982

                                                   1984

FIGURE 2-11
Chronological development of weapons systems by the United States and the Soviet Union.

QUESTIONS

1. What was the size of the explosion produced by the atomic bomb on Hiroshima and what were the casualties?
2. How did the decision to use the atomic bomb on Hiroshima come about?
3. Discuss Albert Einstein's role in the development of the atomic bomb.
4. When did the Soviet Union explode its first atomic bomb? Its first deliverable H-bomb?
5. Discuss H. York's reasoning that the United States could have delayed H-bomb development until the Soviet Union had exploded an H-device without endangering our national security.
6. Discuss the Bravo test of 1954 with particular reference to the radioactive fallout and its consequences.
7. What were the political pressures that resulted in the LTBT?
8. What nations conducted atmospheric tests after the LTBT went into effect?
9. Give a brief summary of the Manhattan Project.
10. What is the charge to the Standing Consultative Commission under the provisions of the SALT I treaty? How effectively has this commission performed?
11. Give some of the major provisions of the SALT II treaty.
12. Discuss the official current nuclear war policy of the United States.
13. According to H. York and S. Zuckerman, what are some of the factors that drive the nuclear arms race?

14. What were the chief provisions of the Oppenheimer-Baruch proposal to the United Nations for control of nuclear weapons?

15. Discuss the motivation for development of the atomic bomb in the United States during World War II. How was the Manhattan Project affected by the surrender of Germany?

16. Summarize the history of the United States decision to proceed with development of the H-bomb. Who were the proponents and who opposed the development?

17. Trace the history of negotiations concerning a comprehensive test ban treaty. What are the arguments pro and con for such a treaty?

18. Discuss some ways in which the United States might have demonstrated that it had an atomic bomb other than exploding one over a populated area. Would any of these alternatives have been preferable?

19. What are novel features of the INF treaty?

KEY WORDS

chain reaction   a process taking place in an atomic bomb or nuclear reactor in which a given fission releases neutrons and energy. The neutrons in turn produce more fissions, releasing more energy, and form a *chain* of nuclear fissions.

cruise missile   an air-breathing subsonic missile that is powered by a jet engine and travels very close to the earth in order to avoid radar detection.

electromagnetic separation   separation of uranium isotopes by electromagnetic means (to produce uranium 235 for an atomic bomb).

fallout   radioactive debris from a nuclear explosion that drifts to the earth.

gaseous diffusion   separation of isotopes by the process of diffusion through a barrier.

ICBM   intercontinental ballistic missile, a missile with a range of about 6000 miles or 10,000 kilometers that can attack the heartland of either superpower from launching sites in the other.

implosion   a technique for compressing plutonium with chemical high explosives in order to make its mass "critical" and produce a nuclear explosion.

isotope   forms of the same element having identical properties, but differing in their atomic masses due to different numbers of neutrons in their respective nuclei.

mass-energy conversion   a result of Einstein's famous equation that $E = mc^2$ or that a given mass m is equivalent to energy if multiplied by the square of the velocity of light.

nuclear fission   the process whereby the nucleus of a heavy element splits into two nuclei of lighter elements. Fission can occur spontaneously or by the absorption of neutrons.

nuclear fusion   release of nuclear energy by combining light nuclei to form heavier ones.

nuclear reactor   a device for producing a controlled chain reaction in order to produce plutonium or electric power.

plutonium   an artificial element produced in a nuclear reactor and suitable as fissionable material for an atomic bomb.

SLBM   submarine launched ballistic missile, a missile that can be launched from a submerged submarine.

spontaneous fission   a form of radioactivity in which a nucleus fissions without stimulation by another particle (such as a neutron).

CHAPTER 3

STRATEGIC ARSENALS AND DELIVERY SYSTEMS

That is the biggest fool thing we have ever done. The atomic bomb will never go off, and I speak as an expert in explosives.

Admiral William Leahy, 1945

3-1 THEMES

A 1-**megaton** nuclear weapon detonated about 2 miles above a major city on a clear day would create a blast overpressure of 5 pounds per square inch and deliver about 20 calories per square centimeter of thermal energy at a radius of 5 miles from ground zero (an area of almost 80 square miles). The blast would ignite virtually all inflammable material and knock down most buildings out to 5 miles distance. The immediate death toll would approach 1 million persons, with many serious injuries and many deaths occurring later. The same weapon, if delivered with the precision now achieved by ICBMs and bombers, would destroy virtually any hardened target in the world.

The nuclear arsenals of the United States and of the Soviet Union each contain many thousands of nuclear weapons. In addition, France and Great Britain each have enough strategic weapons to destroy much of any nation that either might choose to attack. These weapons are integrated into delivery systems, which are controlled through a chain of command extending to the commander-in-chief of the nation. There are in addition elaborate intelligence gathering and control systems that are designed to compromise between two conflicting requirements: to prevent unauthorized or accidental release (''negative control'') while assuring that the weapons can be used expeditiously if this is deemed in the national interest (''positive control'').

In this chapter we review the characteristics of the weapons and the delivery systems. We then discuss some of the technical characteristics of these systems that determine their effectiveness for various military functions.

Public-domain data on the arsenals are compiled by examining national documents, from reports in newspapers, and from interviews. It is likely that publicly available data for the United States are more accurate than data for the Soviet Union. Despite the uncertainties, there is little disagreement over the general characteristics of the arsenals. The best sources of information are the annual reports of the Stockholm International Peace Research Institute (SIPRI), the International Institute for Strategic Studies (London) (IISS), the Nuclear Weapons Databook Project (NWDP), administration reports to the Congress (particularly the reports of the Secretary of Defense), the Center for Defense Information (CDI), and congressional hearings. SIPRI and CDI tend to be a bit on the dovish side, while IISS is a bit more ''hawkish.''

3-2   THE ARSENALS

There are an estimated 50,000 nuclear warheads in the arsenals of the United States and the U.S.S.R. In recent years, the total has been growing exponentially, with a doubling time of about a decade. The weapons systems are generally classified in three categories: *strategic weapons systems, theater nuclear weapons,* and *tactical weapons systems.*

Strategic weapons are those used by the United States to threaten the Soviet heartland and by the Soviets to threaten the United States directly. Strategic weapons are delivered by **ICBMs,** by long-range manned aircraft, or by pilotless cruise aircraft. ICBM delivery systems are generally divided into two subcategories: land-based ICBMs and submarine-based ICBMs. The latter are often referred to as submarine-launched ballistic missiles (**SLBMs**). Tactical weapons systems are designed for use on foreign territory or for local defense at sea (e.g., nuclear depth charges). Tactical warheads are generally smaller than those on strategic systems. These weapons can be delivered by an enormous variety of systems, including field artillery, aircraft, short- and intermediate-range ballistic missiles, unmanned cruise aircraft, and ships. Nuclear delivery systems with ranges from 500 to 5000 kilometers are generally designated as theater nuclear weapons. It is the land-based weapons in this class of delivery system (which included conventional as well as nuclear weapons) which was eliminated by the Intermediate Nuclear Force (INF) treaty of 1988 (see Chapter 2).

Despite the precise language of the INF treaty, the boundaries between categories is hazy. Weapons which have been tested at long ranges can be targeted at nearby targets. Systems designated ''theater'' by the United States may have the capability of reaching the Soviet heartland, and hence may be considered strategic by them. This was the case with the Pershing II missile, eliminated under the INF Treaty. Cruise missiles are particularly difficult to categorize, since the same device can be used with either nuclear or conventional munitions and can be targeted at a variety of ranges. **Cruise missiles** can be launched from submarines (submarine-launched cruise

ROTHCO
ORIGINAL

"DID I HAVE A NIGHTMARE LAST NIGHT! I DREAMED THEY
HAD A BILLION MISSILES AND WE HAD ONLY A MILLION!"

missiles, or **SLCM**s), launched from the ground (ground-launched cruise missiles, or **GLCM**s), or launched from aircraft (air-launched cruise missiles, or **ALCM**s). Cruise missiles are also extremely difficult to detect and hence to deal with in arms control agreements.*

United States strategic doctrine focuses on the *strategic triad*: land-based ICBMs, SLBMs, and air-delivered weapons. (The historical development of the triad will be discussed in Chapter 4). It is unlikely now and will remain unlikely into the foreseeable future that any single technical development could negate all three legs of the triad simultaneously.

The three legs act synergistically. The locations of the ICBMs and the bomber bases are known, and so these systems are subject to preemptive attack. Submarines at sea cannot be located with presently known technology, and they can wait for long periods (months) before firing their missiles. While with present accuracy, SLBMs are incapable of destroying **hardened** missile sites, the Trident D-5 warhead soon to be deployed will have accuracy comparable with that of land-based missiles. (These weapons use satellites for fixing their precise location after launch.) SLBMs have traditionally been regarded as retaliatory weapons which could be used to destroy the Soviet Union even after a successful attack on the other two legs of the strategic triad.

---

*Thus one finds jargon-laden discussions about the difficulty of dealing with SLCMs, GLCMs, and ALCMs (pronounced "sliccoms, gliccoms, and alcoms").

However, as the accuracy of SLBMs increases, they must be considered not only survivable second-strike weapons but also as potential counterforce or first-strike weapons as well. With improvement in accuracy, a weapons system that at one time looked defensive can increasingly appear to the other side as offensive—a generic problem.

One-third of U.S. strategic bombers are on 15-minute alert. The transit time for ICBMs fired from the Soviet Union toward the United States is about half an hour, which would permit the bombers to become airborne and thus safe. In order to destroy United States bombers on the ground, the Soviet Union would have to use missiles fired from offshore submarines. However, at the first indication of nuclear weapons hitting United States bomber fields, the United States could fire its ICBMs. The bombers and the ICBMs thus offer a security against preemptive attack which exceeds that of either system separately. This situation will probably change in the near future, as the aiming accuracy of Soviet submarine-based missiles improves to the point at which these missiles can attack ICBM silos. The situation will also change if the Soviet Union deploys accurate submarine-based missiles close in to the United States shoreline. The warning time for these missiles is only seven or eight minutes, so both hardened land-based missiles and aircraft could be at risk. The geography of the United States makes this nation far more vulnerable to this threat than is the Soviet Union.

The Soviet Union has placed the bulk of its strategic firepower in ICBMs. They have only a very limited manned bomber capability and normally keep relatively few of their submarines at sea at any given time. Figures 3-1 and 3-2 show the percentage distribution of United States and Soviet launchers as of 1986. The pie-chart representation shows clearly the emphasis by the United States on SLBMs and by the Soviet Union on ICBMs. Each SLBM-based launcher is highly MIRVed and carries a number of warheads. Further, a number of these launchers are carried on each submarine. The submarines are extremely vulnerable if they can be found, but at present they are not detectable when on station. MIRVed ICBMs are vulnerable to

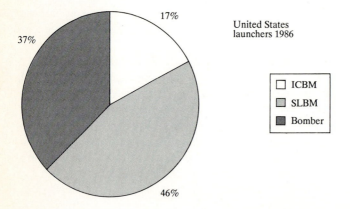

FIGURE 3-1
The percentage distribution of United States launchers as of 1986. The United States has elected to mount most of its warheads on submarines. *Source:* Nuclear Databook Project.

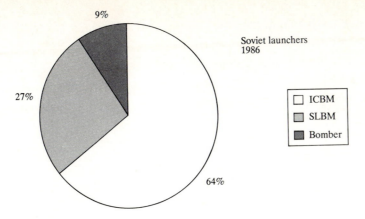

9%

Soviet launchers
1986

27%

☐ ICBM
▨ SLBM
■ Bomber

64%

FIGURE 3-2
The percentage distribution of Soviet launchers as of 1986. The Soviet Union has elected to mount most of its warheads on land-based ICBMs. *Source:* Nuclear Databook Project.

accurate missiles, which is the reason why the Soviet Union is moving toward mobile land-based missiles (SS-24s and SS-25s).

The United States strategic arsenal as of 1986 included over 4000 EMT, divided among some 12,000 warheads. As of 1984 the Soviet Union had a strategic arsenal of over 7000 EMT in about 10,000 warheads. Soviet warheads tend to be somewhat larger on average than United States warheads, while the targeting precision of United States delivery systems is better than that of the Soviet Union. The aiming accuracy for ICBMs and bombers on both sides is within a few hundred yards (see Section 3-3).

In evaluating the destructive power of a weapons system it is usual to use the concept of *equivalent megatons* (**EMT**). Equivalent megatonnage is defined as the actual megatonnage raised to the two-thirds power:

$$\text{EMT} = Y^{2/3} \qquad \text{where } Y \text{ is the yield in megatons*} \qquad (3\text{-}1)$$

This relation stems from the fact that the destructive power of a bomb does not vary linearly with the yield. As we shall see in Chapter 13, a given blast pressure occurs at a distance from ground zero which varies as the cube root of the weapon yield. The area destroyed by blast is proportional to the square of the distance d, and hence the two-thirds root of the yield Y.

Because the destructive power of a given megatonnage depends nonlinearly on the yield, division of megatonnage among a number of warheads increases the total amount of destruction possible. Table 3-1 illustrates this. A total yield of 1 megaton is assumed. It is also assumed that the individual warheads will not overlap (the so-

*The units involved in the nuclear arms race are complex. We use units which are common to the field. For a fuller discussion of units, see Chapter 8. For discussion of units related to particular aspects of the arms race, see the appropriate chapter in Part 2.

TABLE 3-1
**Destructive power of 1 megaton distributed
in several ways**

No. of bombs and yield per bomb	EMT	Destroyed area, square miles
1 × 1 Mt	1	80
8 × 125 kt	2	160
20 × 50 kt	2.7	216
100 × 10 kt	4.6	368

called "cookie cutter" assumption). The destroyed area is calculated assuming 80 square miles per effective megaton, which corresponds to an overpressure of about 4 pounds per square inch (psi). (This assumes the weapon is exploded at a height which maximizes what is known as the *mach stem overpressure*. See Chapter 13.)

The evolution of the superpower arsenals is shown in Tables 3-2 for the United States and 3-3 for the Soviet Union. The tables give a considerable amount of data. They show the number of launchers and warheads for each of the three major delivery systems: ICBMs, SLBMs, and Bombers. The last two columns show the totals. Figure 1-1 is a graph of the totals. Close examination of these basic data is useful. The Soviet Union started behind the United States, and moved vigorously to achieve parity. The relative emphasis of the Soviet Union on land-based ICBMs and the United States on SLBMs is apparent. Until the early 1960s the United States relied heavily on bombers carrying enormous warheads of up to 8 Mt. As other legs of the triad developed and accuracy improved, the number of bombers decreased, and so did the total megatonnage in the United States arsenal (Table 3-1). The Soviets strove vigorously and effectively to catch up, and today the strategic arsenals of the two nations are generally comparable, especially when it is considered that a small fraction of the firepower now in place in both countries would be enough to destroy the civilizations of either.

Some of the strategic delivery systems carry a single warhead; others (**MIRVs**) carry multiple warheads capable of being independently targeted. A short history of MIRV development was given in Chapter 2. In a MIRV missile a single rocket launcher carries aloft a platform (called the **bus**) containing a number of subunits. Shortly after boost phase the individual warheads are released, each to follow its own trajectory. The trajectories of the individual warheads are determined immediately after they are released, hence the notion of *independent* targeting. The individual warheads must all be targeted within a restricted region. The region (the "**footprint**") is elliptical in shape, with the long axis of the ellipse lying along the line of flight of the bus. The ellipse can be of the order of 200 miles long and tens of miles wide. The footprint of the MX may be as much as 1000 miles long and 50 miles wide. Thus a MIRV bus may be able to attack 10 or more targets, but there are restrictions on how far apart they can be.

The Pershing II missiles removed from Europe under the INF treaty had radar terminal guidance systems and were substantially more accurate than MIRVs. Future missiles will undoubtedly be **MaRVs**—maneuverable reentry vehicles. All cruise mis-

TABLE 3-2
The evolution over time of the three legs of the United States strategic triad

Year	ICBMs Launchers	ICBMs Warheads	SLBMs Launchers	SLBMs Warheads	Bombers Launchers	Bombers Warheads	Total launchers	Total warheads
1946					125	9	125	9
1948					473	50	473	50
1950					462	400	462	400
1952					660	660	660	660
1954					1035	1418	1035	1418
1956					1470	2123	1470	2123
1958					1620	2610	1620	2610
1960	12	12	32	32	1515	3126	1559	3170
1962	203	203	144	144	1306	3358	1653	3705
1964	907	907	320	320	785	3405	2012	4632
1966	1004	1004	560	560	575	3481	2139	5045
1968	1054	1044	656	656	481	3389	2191	5089
1970	1054	1244	656	656	390	3336	2100	5236
1972	1054	1644	656	2384	457	3843	2167	7871
1974	1054	1944	656	3824	396	3818	2106	9586
1976	1054	1944	656	4688	382	3834	2092	10466
1978	1054	1944	656	5120	376	3568	2086	10632
1980	1054	1944	592	4896	376	3568	2022	10408
1982	1049	2139	544	4992	328	3384	1921	10515
1984	1030	2120	616	5536	297	3844	1943	11500
1986	1005	2165	640	5632	312	4589	1957	12386

The kind of data presented here tends to vary considerably from one source to another. The Nuclear Databook Project has developed the best available synthesis. Their data are used in the annual SIPRI reports.

Source: Nuclear Databook Project.

55

TABLE 3-3
The evolution over time of the Soviet Union's nuclear arsenal

Year	ICBMs		SLBMs		Bombers		Total launchers	Total warheads
	Launchers	Warheads	Launchers	Warhead	Launchers	Warheads		
1956					20	80	20	80
1958					50	200	56	206
1960	4	4	6	6	104	416	138	450
1962	30	30	30	30	134	536	236	638
1964	180	180	72	72	163	652	415	904
1966	333	333	72	72	159	636	570	1047
1968	909	909	78	78	159	636	1203	1680
1970	1361	1361	135	135	145	580	1817	2252
1972	1547	1647	311	311	145	580	2189	2724
1974	1587	1909	497	497	145	580	2405	3162
1976	1539	2419	673	673	145	580	2527	3842
1978	1398	3438	843	843	145	580	2536	5657
1980	1398	5122	993	1639	145	580	2530	7495
1982	1398	5982	987	1793	145	580	2530	8805
1984	1398	6540	987	2243	145	580	2534	9542
1986	1398	6540	976	2362	160	640	2523	10174
			952	2742	173	892		

Source: Nuclear Databook Project.

siles include terrain contour matching systems (TERCOM) which gives them accuracies to within a few tens of meters under favorable conditions.

Table 3-4 summarizes estimates of the accuracy of the strategic arsenals of the United States and the U.S.S.R. The *circular error probable* (CEP) is a measure of the accuracy of the delivery system.* It is the radius of the circle within which one-half of the warheads will hit. The importance of CEP is discussed in Section 3-3.

More extensive data on the strategic and tactical nuclear weapons of the United States, the Soviet Union, the United Kingdom, and France are given in Section 3-8.

The mix of weapons delivery systems changes constantly. There are a large number of different existing systems and frequent revisions of these systems are made. Keeping track of this diversity is a difficult and time-consuming task.† Some general observations on the changing characteristics of the arsenals can be made. A rapid improvement in accuracy of delivery has led both the United States and the Soviet Union to shift from large warheads on low-precision missiles to smaller warheads on high-accuracy missiles. This trend is particularly apparent in the changes in the Minuteman ICBMs. Minuteman I was replaced by the more accurate Minuteman II, which has been partially replaced by the MIRVed Minuteman III. There is also a trend toward smaller delivery systems, particularly cruise missiles, which will be very difficult to monitor as a part of treaty enforcement. At the tactical level there is growing realization that small weapons close to an enemy border are at risk of capture, leading to very difficult problems of control. Small tactical weapons are therefore being partially phased out.

Figure 3-3 shows a Minuteman II in its silo. The silos are manned 24 hours a day by duty crews composed of two officers each. There are 1000 Minutemen in the land-based leg of the triad. The highly reinforced concrete silos protect the missile from all but very accurate nuclear weapons. Figure 3-4 shows a Minuteman III with exposed warheads. Fourth-generation Soviet ICBMs are shown in Figure 3-5.

The bomber element of the strategic triad consists of over 300 active B-52s and FB-111s. B-52s have been a part of the Air Force for more than three decades. They are continually being modified and improved. The letters (e.g., the "H" in B-52H) indicate the revision. The FB-111 has a range of 4700 kilometers, which means that

---

*There is a story, possibly apocryphal but still instructive, attributed to former Secretary of State Henry Kissinger. On examining a report on missile accuracy he observed that the error estimate for the Soviet weapons was substantially less than that for United States weapons. He properly pointed out that it must be true that accuracy estimates for our own weapons must be superior to those for Soviet weapons. The story points up the obvious facts that accuracy estimates are based on relatively few trials and that United States estimates of Soviet missile accuracy must include large uncertainty.

†For example, the British International Institute of Strategic Studies (IISS) and the U.S. Congressional Research Service (CRS) agree that there is a Soviet SS-18 land-based ICBM that carries ten 500-kT MIRVs. Both organizations designate this as the mod 4. The IISS claims it was deployed in 1982, while the CRS claims it was deployed in 1979. The IISS claims that the CEP is 300 meters, while the CRS claims that the CEP is 0.14 nautical miles, which is 259 meters. IISS says the range is 11,000 km, while CRS says the range is 5500 miles (or about 8800 kilometers). In other cases there are even larger discrepancies between the figures given by different sources.

TABLE 3-4
Technical characteristics of the strategic arsenals of the United States and the Soviet Union

Delivery vehicle	Number of vehicles	Warheads per vehicle	Yield per warhead, Mt	Total warheads N	Equivalent megatons $NY^{2/3}$	Range, km	
United States							
ICBMs							
Titan II	29	1	9.0	29	125	15,000	1300-m CEP
Minuteman II	450	1	1.2	450	508	11,300	370-m CEP
Minuteman III	250	3	0.17	750	230	13,000	280-m CEP
Minuteman III (Improved)	300	3	0.335	900	440	n.a.	220-m CEP
SLBMs							
Poseidon C-3	304	10	0.05	3040	413	4,600	450-m CEP
Trident C-4	288	8	0.1	2304	497	7,400	450-m CEP
Aircraft							
B52G	151			1208		12,000	0.95 Mach
Gravity bombs		4	~1				
SRAMs[a]		4	0.2				
B-52H	90			720		16,000	0.95 Mach
Gravity bombs		4	~1				
SRAMs[a]		4	0.2				
FB-111A	60	2	~1	120	120	4,700	2.5 Mach
Soviet Union							
ICBMs							
SS-11 Mod 1	580[b]	1	1.00	580	580	10,500	1400-m CEP
2		3	0.1 to 0.3			8,800	1100-m CEP
SS-13 Mod 1	60	1	0.75	60	50	10,000	2000-m CEP
SS-17 Mod 1	150[b]	4	0.75	~600[c]	~495[c]	10,000	450-m CEP
2		1	6.00			11,000	450-m CEP

SS-18 Mod 1		1	20.00	~2500[d]	~2300[d]	12,000	450-m CEP
2		8	0.90			11,000	450-m CEP
3	308[d]	1	20.00			10,500	350-m CEP
4		10	0.50			9,000	300-m CEP
5		10	0.75			9,000	250-m CEP
SS-19 Mod 2	360[d]	1	5.00			10,000	300-m CEP
3		6	0.55	~1500[e]	~1200[e]	10,000	300-m CEP
SLBMs							
SS-N-5	45	1	1.00	45	45	1,400	2800-m CEP
SS-N-6 Mod 1		1	1.00			2,400	900-m CEP
2	368[d]	1	1.00	~400	~400	3,000	900-m CEP
3		2	0.2			3,000	1400-m CEP
SS-N-8 Mod 1		1	1.0			7,800	1300-m CEP
2	292[d]	1	0.8	~300[f]	~250[f]	9,100	900-m CEP
3		3	0.2			n.a.	450-m CEP
SS-NX-17	12	1	1.0	12	12	3,900	1500-m CEP
SS-N-18 Mod 1		3	0.45			7,400	1400-m CEP
2	224[d]	1	0.45	~1040[g]	~430[g]	8,300	600-m CEP
3		7	0.2			6,500	600-m CEP
Aircraft							
TU-95 (Bear)	100	2[h]	1	210	210	12,800	0.78 Mach
Mya-4 (Bison)	43	2[h]	1	90	90	11,200	0.87 Mach

[a] Short-range air missile.
[b] Allocation among types is unknown.
[c] Assuming all SS-17s are Mod 1.
[d] Allocation among types is unknown.
[e] Assuming 300 SS-19s are Mod 3 and 60 are Mod 2.
[f] Assuming all SS-N-8 ICBMs are Mod 2.
[g] Assuming half the SS-N-18 ICBMs are Mod 2 and Half are Mod 3.
[h] Either gravity bombs or air-to-surface missiles.

Source: Updated from B. Levi, *Physics Today*, March 1983. Data from the International Institute for Strategic Studies, *The Military Balance: 1984–85*, London, 1984 and Congressional Research Service Report 84-163S (1984).

FIGURE 3-3
A Minuteman II in its silo.

FIGURE 3-4
A Minuteman III with exposed warheads. The three warheads are MIRVs, and each one has a nuclear yield of 170 kilotons, an accuracy of slightly more than 0.1 mile, and a range of about 8000 miles. Each warhead would be virtually certain to destroy any target hardened less than 80 psi. The probability of such a warhead destroying a concrete silo hardened to 2000 psi is about 60 percent. (See Section 3-3 for a discussion of kill probability.)

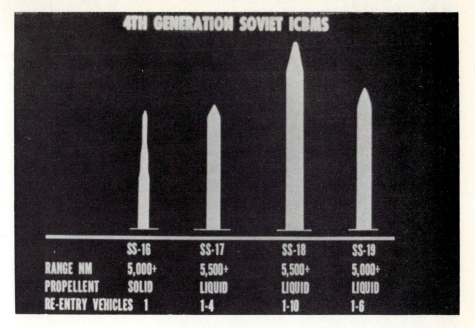

FIGURE 3-5

Fourth-generation Soviet ICBMs: SS-16s, SS-17s, SS-18s, and SS-19s. As of July 1981 the Soviet Union had deployed 150 SS-17 missiles, 308 SS-18 missiles, and 300 SS-19 missiles. The SS-17 Mod 1 carries four 900-kiloton MIRVs, and the Mod 2 has had one 5-megaton warhead. The SS-17 has a range of 6100 miles and a throw weight of 6000 pounds. It was first deployed in 1975. The SS-19 Mod 1, which was also first deployed in 1975, has six 550-kiloton MIRVs and a throw weight of 7500 pounds. The SS-19 Mod 2 has been tested with a 5-megaton warhead and has a range of 6300 miles. About 310 SS-18 missiles are deployed by the Soviets, most of which are Mod 2 with eight 2-megaton MIRVs and a range of about 5500 miles. The new SS-18 Mod 4 has a single 10- to 50-megaton warhead.

without in-flight refueling or forward basing it is incapable of strategic attacks on the U.S.S.R.

Submarine-based missiles are carried on nuclear submarines. The Poseidon C-3 SLBMs are carried on the 19 Lafayette class nuclear submarines, each of which has 16 launch tubes. Twelve of these have been modified to carry the longer-range Trident I missiles. Figure 3-6 shows a Poseidon submarine with its missile tubes. Trident I missiles are also carried on Ohio class submarines, each of which is 560 feet long and 10 or more stories in height, has a displacement of 18,700 tons, and costs almost $2 billion. There are elaborate and comfortable quarters for the crews, who must stay submerged for months at a time. Each submarine has two complete crews to permit shore leave and training.

Cruise missiles can be fitted with either nuclear or nonnuclear warheads. The nuclear warheads are typically 200 kilotons or less. Since there is no way to tell whether a particular cruise missile is nuclear or nonnuclear, an enemy must assume they are all nuclear. This problem, together with the very small size of the cruise missiles (20 feet long, weighing about 3100 pounds, with wings that fold for storage)

FIGURE 3-6
Each Poseidon submarine carries 16 missiles and each missile has 10 to 14 MIRVs. Thus each submarine can carry up to 224 warheads.

makes the cruise a particularly severe problem for arms control. Cruise missiles fly at speeds of about 500 miles per hour for distances of up to 1500 miles. They are equipped with terrain-following navigation radar and computer target matching, and can stay within a few hundred feet of the surface of the earth, making them difficult to detect. A U.S. ALCM is shown in Figure 3-7.

Soviet weaponry is similar to U.S. weaponry. The Yankee class nuclear submarine has 16 launch tubes holding MIRVed SS-N-6 missiles.* The Delta III nuclear submarine carries 16 MIRVed SS-N-18 missiles. Typically 30 percent of Soviet submarines are at sea at any time, in contrast to U.S. nuclear submarines, of which about two-thirds are at sea. The Soviet Backfire bomber is considered by the United States to be an intercontinental bomber, although the range (8000 kilometers) would not permit it to return from an attack without refueling.

---

*Names of Soviet weapons are generally assigned by the United States. The Soviet Union does not release the designations used internally. At arms control negotiations the United States nomenclature is routinely used by both sides.

FIGURE 3-7
The air-launched cruise missile (ALCM) is one of the new weapons for the 1980s. It is a pilotless jet plane powered by a turbofan engine and is carried by B-52-G bombers and any follow-on aircraft, such as the B-1. The ALCM weighs about 3000 pounds and has an overall length of about 20 feet. This extremely high accuracy missile is designed to fly at very low altitudes, with a very small radar signature, so that it can penetrate existing defenses.

How Much Is Enough? — The McNamara Limit

If nuclear weapons are used against cities, a small portion of the installed arsenals of either the United States or the Soviet Union could destroy either nation as a functioning society. The reason for this is the highly concentrated nature of the populations and the industrial capacities of both. When Robert McNamara was Secretary of Defense he answered the question "How much is enough?" by stating that "enough" is the assured capability to destroy $\frac{1}{3}$ the Soviet population and 75 percent of Soviet industry. He estimated this as 100 EMT, then doubled this to account for reliability problems, and finally doubled it again to be sure. The result, 400 EMT, is an important number because it provides a technical answer to the question (see Enthoven and Smith, 1974). The actual number could be very much less because no sane leader would accept the loss of even a single major city.

The McNamara figure is important in designing a pure *mutual assured destruction* (**MAD**) strategy. A major problem with such a strategy, and one reason why the

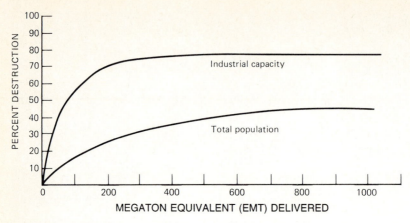

FIGURE 3-8
Concentration of population and industrial capacity in the Soviet Union. A 200-EMT attack would destroy 70 percent of Soviet industry and kill at least 25 percent of the population. The effects of long-term radiation and climate changes have been neglected. The curve for the United States is similar. (*Adapted from Enthoven and Smith, 1973.*)

United States arsenal has so much more megatonnage than 400 EMT, is that MAD does not permit graduated response to limited threats. The perceived need to respond to smaller Soviet threats led to the development of our current strategy of **flexible response**. A flexible-response doctrine attempts to provide means to respond to a threat of any conceivable scale. Since there is no limit to the number and type of threats that can be imagined, there is no limit to the number and type of weapons that can be justified.

Figure 3-8 shows the concentration of population and of industry in the Soviet Union. According to this figure 200 EMT would kill about 25 percent of the population and destroy about 70 percent of the Soviet Union's industrial capacity. The figure for the United States is almost identical, although U.S. industrial capacity is slightly less concentrated than that of the Soviet Union.

3-3 ACCURACY-YIELD TRADE-OFF— KILL PROBABILITY

An attack against a city requires aiming accuracy that is easy to obtain with current technology. The destructive power of nuclear weapons is so great and cities are so vulnerable that aiming errors are of little consequence. The situation is very different when attacks are contemplated against hardened targets. The difference between the two types of targets is best described in terms of the ability to resist blast damage. A pressure of 10 psi will devastate most urban buildings (see Chapter 13), but structures can be designed that will withstand very much greater pressures. Missile silos are typically hardened to withstand blast pressures of thousands of psi. The idea is to build the silos that are sufficiently strong to withstand a direct enemy attack so that they can then be used to launch a counterattack. This section explores the major

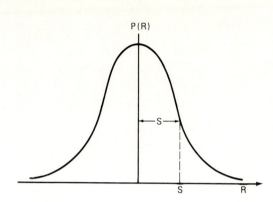

P(R)

FIGURE 3-9
The **normal distribution** or bell-shaped, curve. The frequency distributions of many situations or events in nature (such as the scores on an IQ test or the landing spots of darts thrown at a target) are like that shown in the figure. The area under the curve is unity—that is, for example, it is certain that a given dart will hit somewhere within that area. The distributions of hits on both sides of the origin ($R = 0$) is relatively even, but the farther away we move from the point of the curve's maximum height, the less likely it is that a hit will occur. There is a negligible chance that a hit will occur at a very great distance from the origin (see Section 3-7).

factors that must be considered in analyzing how to attack and how to defend a hardened target. (For more detail see Tsipis, 1983.)

Consider the problem of throwing darts at a dartboard. The darts tend to scatter. Often no dart will hit the intended target, yet most will hit somewhere near it. Suppose we throw a large number of darts, and make a graph of the number that fall outside a circle of radius R. The graph will look something like the curve in Figure 3-9. The most likely place to hit is the center, and the chance of hitting very, very far away is zero. The chance of hitting *somewhere* is exactly unity (100 percent), so the area under the curve is unity. Curves having this sort of shape are very typical of random processes. The accuracy of a missile, or **CEP**, is the radius of a circle such that on the average half the missiles will fall inside, and half outside. Typical modern missiles have CEPs of a few hundred meters, which means that they are able, for example, to place a warhead within Candlestick Park from a starting point a continent away.

With modern accuracy there is no question that a city can be hit and destroyed by an intercontinental missile. The problem is more complex for hardened targets. There are three critical parameters, two of them under control of the attacker and one under control of the defender. The attacker has control over the size of the warhead and the accuracy of the missile. The defender has control over the hardness of the silo. A technical analysis of how these quantities interact is given in Section 3-7 below.

The trade-off between missile yield and targeting accuracy is expressed by what is known as the **kill ratio**. This is defined as the EMT of the weapon (the yield to the two-thirds power) divided by the CEP squared. The kill ratio is far more sensitive to accuracy than to yield. An improvement in CEP by a factor of 2 permits a reduction in warhead size by a factor of $2^3 = 8$ without altering the probability of destroying the target. Improvements in accuracy have been the primary reason why the average size of warheads in both United States and Soviet stockpiles has decreased in recent years.

The probability of destroying a target depends upon the kill ratio divided by the target hardness to the two-thirds power [see Eq. (3-9)]. Target hardness, however, is

TABLE 3-5
Accuracy (CEP) of U.S. and Soviet missiles

Soviet weapons (selected)	CEP (meters)	Entered service (year)
ICBMs:		
SS-6	3700	1968
SS-7 mod 3	2800	1979
SS-8	1900	1964
SS-9	900	1966
SS-11 mod 1	1400	1966
SS-13 mod 1	1900	1969
SS-13 mod 2	1500	1973
SS-17 mod 1	440	1975
SS-17 mod 2	430	1978
SS-17 mod 3	370	1981
SS-18 mod 1	430	1974
SS-18 mod 2	430	1977
SS-18 mod 3	350	1977
SS-18 mod 4	260	1979
SS-19 mod 1	350	1975
SS-19 mod 2	300	1978
SS-19 mod 3	250	1981
SS-24	250	1986
SLBMs:		
SS-N-4	4000	1958
SS-N-5	2800	1963
SS-N-6 mod 3	1900	1974
SS-N-8 mod 2	1600	1977
SS-N-18	1400	1978
SS-N-20	1000	1983
SS-NX-23	1000	1987
U.S. weapons (selected):		
ICBMs		
Titan II	900	1963
Minuteman II	500	1966
Minuteman III	220	1970
MX	120	1986
SLBMs:		
Poseidon C3	460	1963
Trident I C4	460	1977
Trident II D5	120	1988

Accuracy has improved considerably over time. Traditionally SLBMs have been less accurate than ICBMs, though this situation has now changed for the United States with the introduction of the Trident II D5 SLBM.

Sources: World Weapons Data Book (Soviet data) and Nuclear Weapons Data Book (U.S. data).

not likely to be known exactly by the attacker because details of silo construction are highly classified. Should a silo an attacker believes to be hardened to 2000 psi actually be hardened to 2500 psi, for example, the calculations of kill ratio will be far off.

The probability curve in Figure 3-9 changes gradually when the distances involved are small but very rapidly when the distances are great. This variation leads to the conclusion that there comes a point at which further improvements in accuracy do not significantly increase the kill probability.

In a hypothetical first strike the attacker must be totally confident that the kill probability for every one of the attacked silos is high. This assurance is hard to attain, especially since there is no experience with firing large numbers of missiles in a short time, and first strike would be a very risky business for the attacker as well as the attacked. However, the accuracy of missiles has increased spectacularly. The United States has always been ahead in accuracy. Schroeer (1984) observes that the Soviet Union has tended to lag behind the United States by about 7 years. Table 3-5 and Fig. 3-10 present illustrative CEP data for the Soviet Union and the United States. Over the past quarter century Soviet ICBM accuracy improved from a CEP of 3700 meters to 250 meters. U.S. accuracy improved from 900 meters for the Titan II to 80 meters for the MX ICBM and also for the new Trident II D5 SLBM.

With the introduction of the Trident II, the accuracy of submarine-launched missiles has for the first time approached that of land-based missiles. This improvement is a result of the use of satellite navigation systems for corrections following launch.

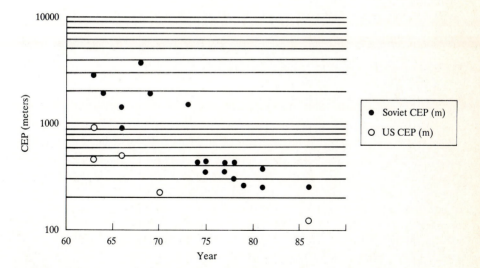

FIGURE 3-10
A semilogarithmic graph showing the improvement over time of aiming accuracy of ICBMs. The United States has always been ahead of the Soviet Union by about seven years. Accuracy may now be approaching a limit where fundamental uncertainties (e.g., in local winds during warhead reentry) limit accuracy. However, the accuracy is so good that it may no longer be possible to build shelters which can provide reliable protection. Data from Table 3-5.

Current accuracy is so great that hardening of missile silos is probably no longer possible, since the CEPs are becoming less than the crater size.

Extremely high targeting accuracy may eventually mean that nonnuclear weapons will become feasible for attacking even hardened targets, although this is controversial. This means that it would no longer be necessary to use nuclear weapons to attack nuclear weapons, and an entirely new perspective would be brought to the design of strategic arsenals and to deterrence strategy.

Bias Error and Fratricide

A major problem for any nation contemplating a preemptive attack is *bias error*. Even when the CEP is small, bias error can result in the center of the target circle being in the wrong place.

The trajectories of ICBMs are controlled by inertial navigation systems. These systems integrate the newtonian equations of motion, and thereby compute the location of a missile at each point in its trajectory relative to the known initial point. Inertial navigation systems are subject to drift, which could lead to errors of 100 meters or more with present systems. Errors in the detailed gravitational field of the earth could also lead to trajectories different from those intended. Actual missile testing by the United States is in the Pacific Ocean—from Vandenberg Air Force Base to Kwajalein Atoll in the South Pacific. This trajectory is quite different from any that would be used in time of war. The Soviet Union tests over Siberia. An attack on the United States would have to pass near the North Pole, a region over which no ICBM has ever flown. The earth's gravitational field can be accurately mapped by satellites, but uncertainties remain.

It might not be too serious for an attacker if a single missile had a bias error. However, gravitational bias would affect not just a single missile but *every* missile. An error of only a few hundred meters would allow all U.S. Minuteman silos (hardened to about 2000 psi) to escape unharmed. For a review of the sources of bias error, see Bunn and Tsipis (1983).

The final approach of a missile to its target is through the atmosphere. An attacker will inevitably be uncertain about local wind conditions, and strong "wind shear" can introduce significant errors. The situation will be very much worse if a missile follows another, for in that case the atmosphere will be highly turbulent with the strong winds that follow any substantial nuclear explosion. In addition, particles of dirt thrown up by an earlier explosion can ablate a missile, introducing more error or even destroying the missile. The effects of the interaction between one incoming missile and another are called **fratricide.** There is no real-world experience whatsoever, and such effects are extraordinarily hard to predict theoretically.

Launch on Warning (LOW)

An attacker must consider the possibility that the enemy's silos will be empty, the missiles having been fired before the attacking warheads arrive. Such a consideration might give rise to a shift by either the United States or the Soviet Union to a *launch-*

on-warning (**LOW**) system, in which warheads are launched when radar detects incoming missiles. LOW is extremely risky, for warning systems have been known to be wrong, and the price any nation would pay for an incorrect launch decision would be very high indeed. Should the Soviet Union move to launch-on-warning, the security of Europe (and of the United States as well) will depend on the reliability of Soviet computers. The destruction over the Sea of Japan of Korean Airlines flight 007 in the fall of 1983 provides perhaps a hint of the risk involved.

3-4 STRATEGIC CONSIDERATIONS

If calculated kill probabilities could really be trusted, an attacker could design a first-strike attack capable of destroying an arbitrarily large fraction of the other side's missiles. The prospect of such an attack has led to many proposals for new weapons systems. The increasing accuracy of Soviet missiles led the United States to believe that Minuteman silos were becoming vulnerable. The response was a proposed new missile system, the MX (Figure 3-11). The years between the time when the Soviet Union might conceivably launch a preemptive attack on the Minuteman silos and the time when the MX would be deployed has been called a "window of vulnerability." (Note that the arguments for the existence of such a window fail to take full account of the other two legs of the U.S. strategic triad—the bombers and the submarines.

FIGURE 3-11
The MX missile. This new ICBM is large—71 feet long with a weight of 96 tons—almost $2\frac{1}{2}$ times the weight of the Minuteman III. Each MX missile carries ten 350-kiloton MIRVs. With a reported accuracy of 300 feet, the MX could be perceived by the Soviets as being a first-strike threat to their hardened missile silos.

Missiles in the MX system are equipped with as many as 10 warheads. One problem with such a highly MIRVed system relates to *exchange ratios*. A single Soviet missile could destroy ten U.S. warheads. A highly MIRVed system thus provides incentive to an enemy to launch a preemptive strike. This destabilizing aspect of the MX was one of the key points in the congressional debates on the advisability of the system. The committee charged by the administration with examining these issues (the Scowcroft Commission) noted the advantages of a system of missiles equipped with single warheads. The proposed system, called "midgetman," would consist of a large number of small ICBMs without MIRVs. Since at least two warheads would be required to assure the destruction of a single midgetman, an attack would disarm the attacker faster than it would the nation attacked. Midgetman is therefore a stabilizing system relative to MIRVed systems. The midgetman proposal is a return to the single warhead missiles of the 1960s which implicitly recognizes the destabilizing results of the decision to equip U.S. warheads with MIRVs.

3-5   TACTICAL NUCLEAR WEAPONS SYSTEMS

United States tactical nuclear weapons systems are defined as systems not deployed on U.S. soil, excluding ICBM-equipped submarines. Nuclear systems are now integrated into virtually every part of the U.S. defense system. The most publicized nonstrategic components of the U.S. nuclear arsenal—tactical nuclear forces (**TNF**)—are located in Europe. Tactical nuclear forces exist elsewhere as well. Since the U.S. Navy is equipped with nuclear war-fighting capability, anywhere that naval ships are located, e.g., in the Mediterranean Sea, there is TNF capability. The tactical systems include weapons with a capability of carrying out (it is claimed) many of the functions—though with far greater firepower—of conventional systems. Examples are defending troops, destroying enemy gun emplacements, and attacking submarines with nuclear depth charges.

Present planning in the United States and in NATO assumes that the European frontier is a prime candidate for invasion. This perception derives from the fact that World War I and World War II started in Europe. Probably the strongest memory that drives this thinking is of the Berlin blockade, when the Soviet Union closed off land access to Berlin and the city was supplied by airlift for several months. The prospect of new tensions associated with the isolated position of Berlin is very real. Such tensions triggered the nuclear war depicted in the television presentation *The Day After* (ABC television, 1983).

The United States and the Soviet Union each have perhaps 10,000 tactical nuclear weapons, though the uncertainty is large for both superpowers. Both powers have fully integrated tactical nuclear weapons into their military systems. This integration may inhibit the ability to fight conventional wars and may simultaneously increase the risk of nuclear war.

There are several reasons for this. One is that commanders who are about to be overrun will have strong incentive to use nuclear weapons before they can be captured ("use 'em or lose 'em"). Another is that there will be strong incentive for a commander to use all weapons at his command in order to accomplish assigned missions. Accordingly, full scale integration of nuclear weapons into the military places very heavy burdens on command and control systems and on permissive action links (PALs).

All nuclear weapons in the Warsaw Pact nations (the U.S.S.R., Albania, Bulgaria, Czechoslovakia, the German Democratic Republic, Hungary, Poland, and Romania) are directly controlled by the U.S.S.R. The Center for Defense Information estimates there are about 6000 Warsaw Pact nuclear weapons and 4500 delivery vehicles. Tactical nuclear weapons supplied by the United States to **NATO** (the United States, Belgium, Canada, Denmark, West Germany, France, Iceland, Italy, Luxembourg, The Netherlands, Norway, Portugal, Spain, Turkey, and the United Kingdom) are controlled by the United States. Britain and France have their own strategic and tactical nuclear weapons which are under their national control. Norway and Denmark do not permit nuclear weapons on their territory in peacetime. According to the Center for Defense Information, in 1984 there were some 6000 tactical nuclear weapons and about 3800 delivery vehicles (aircraft, missiles, and howitzers) under NATO command. The average yield of these tactical weapons is estimated to be 100 kilotons for bombs and 20 kilotons for missiles. These tactical weapons are small compared to strategic weapons, but not compared to the bombs used at Hiroshima and Nagasaki.

The French strategic nuclear arsenal *(force de frappe)* consists of five nuclear-powered submarines, each with 16 SLBMs; 18 intermediate-range ballistic missiles; and over 50 aircraft with the capability of reaching the Soviet Union. Britain's strategic nuclear capability consists of four nuclear submarines, each carrying 16 Polaris A-3 triply MRVed missiles.

Europe is today by far the most heavily armed major area in the world. It is also an area in which major change is likely to occur in the next decade. At the end of World War II the armies of the Allied Powers swept through Europe and Germany. Forces from the East and the West met in Berlin, which even now remains partitioned. The Soviet Union today maintains control over a band of nations sweeping through Eastern Europe, which serves as a buffer zone. From north to south these are Poland, East Germany (which does not actually abut the Soviet Union), Czechoslovakia, Hungary, Rumania, and Bulgaria. These nations, together with the Soviet Union itself are known collectively as the Warsaw Treaty Organization **(WTO).** The northern and southern ends of the Soviet Union protective belt are not under the same control as the rest. Finland has managed to maintain a high degree of independence, though it is committed to support the Soviet Union against any invasion from the north. At the southern end of the band is Yugoslavia, which while a communist country is politically independent of both east and west.

The NATO nations consist of most nations of Western Europe except for France, plus the United States and Canada. Ireland, Switzerland, and Austria are not a part of NATO. Nor is France, though it is a part of NATO's political structure. NATO was established to offset the massive WTO forces, and to deter a possible invasion of Europe. The NATO forces are organized in a complex structure headed by an

American officer (SACEUR, the Supreme Allied Commander for Europe), with the second in command always being European.

The militarization of Europe stems from a variety of factors. NATO is worried about a possible invasion. The Soviets, however, remember that they have often been invaded from Europe: by Napoleon, and twice by Germany. Much of their policy is based on their memories of the grief they suffered at the hands of Europeans. Unlike NATO, the Soviet Union needs forces in Eastern Europe to maintain control over their WTO allies, whose loyalty to the Soviet Union is at best dubious. There must thus always remain questions in the minds of Soviet leaders as to which way their WTO allies are likely to shoot, should war break out.

Both the WTO and NATO rely on both conventional and nuclear weapons. Control of nuclear weapons remains in the hands of the Soviets and the Americans, respectively. Nuclear weaponry in Western Europe is complicated by the British and French nuclear arsenals. British nuclear weapons are integrated into NATO planning. Since France is not a part of NATO, integration of both the nuclear and nonnuclear forces is less comprehensive and is based on tacit understandings rather than treaties.

Germany occupies a special place. Germany is divided into East Germany under Soviet control and West Germany. The policy of West Germany has long been to seek reunification, a goal opposed not only by the Soviets but also by many West Europeans who remember their history.

The INF agreement (Chapter 2) has led to important reductions in the nuclear arsenals in Europe. Major changes appear possible. A major part of the debate in Europe has related to the willingness of the United States to stand together with the rest of NATO in case of attack. Europeans worry that the United States (which has absolute veto power over all nuclear weapons except those of the French and British) may lack the will to support Europe in the event of a war. According to this view, a major policy of the Soviet Union is to introduce tensions which will weaken U.S. "resolve."

The most important considerations for the evolution of the military situation in Europe are the impacts of glasnost and perestroika on the Soviet satellite nations, and the impact of changing perceptions of the Soviet threat in Western Europe. It is quite conceivable that the threat of war in Europe will be taken ever less seriously, and that a major restructuring of the entire set of European arsenals—both east and west—will emerge. A major theme of debate is the prospect for less threatening arsenals, designed for defensive rather than offensive purposes. These weapons systems would be nonnuclear, and would be structured into systems often described as "Non-Offensive-Defense," or NOD. We discuss some of the NOD possibilities in Chapter 6.

Whatever occurs in Europe, including the elimination of most or even all European nuclear weapons, there will always remain the risk that any European conflict might quickly become nuclear. Even with tactical and battlefield weapons removed, strategic weapons will remain. Most of these weapons (e.g., ICBMs, SLBMs, SLCMs, and ALCMs) could be rapidly retargeted to attack European targets.

The effects of even a few large nuclear explosions in Europe would be far more devastating than the effects of all wars ever fought there. Thus even a nonnuclear

Europe would not be a Europe likely to again see the kinds of aggression which have occurred so often in the past. The risks have become too great.

3-6 NEW NUCLEAR WEAPONS

Under the Reagan administration there was a substantial modernization of nuclear weaponry. The unratified SALT II agreement, which had limited the numbers of strategic nuclear weapons, was abandoned as additional B-52 bombers and missile-carrying submarines were deployed. However, the INF agreement represented a start toward decreasing one category of weaponry.

New nuclear weapons systems are being developed. The B-1 bomber is designed to fly at low altitudes so as to be able to escape enemy radar more readily. A bomb to be dropped from a low-flying aircraft must have characteristics quite different from those of one designed to be dropped from high altitudes. In particular it must have much greater shock resistance, since it may well hit the ground at high speed, or even crash into a building. Bombs designed for dropping at low altitude must also have built-in delays so as to permit the delivery aircraft to escape.

Research is being done on **deep-penetrator** warheads. These are designed to dig into the earth before detonating. Detonations underground are better coupled into the earth, and hence more damage can be achieved with a given amount of explosive energy. Deep penetrations might be used for destruction of hardened targets, including the command centers the Soviets are reportedly deploying in and around Moscow. Underground detonation also leads to reduction in radioactivity releases, and hence the deep penetrator may be viewed as a weapon which makes nuclear war fighting more feasible.

A warhead is under development for use on the Midgetman missile, a proposed single-warhead mobile missile which was strongly recommended in the Scowcroft Report (1983).

Other new weapons systems include warheads for cruise missiles, nuclear depth charges for attacking submarines, and new artillery shells with increased range.

What lies further ahead? A primary focus is development of ''directed energy weapons.'' These focus the energy of a nuclear explosion and convert the energy into specific forms. The most discussed example is the x-ray laser, which has received a great deal of attention in conjunction with the Strategic Defense Initiative (see Chapter 20). The x-ray laser would produce intense beams of soft x-ray radiation. One can envisage new weapons which would produce intense beams of many types of radiation. An example might be a weapon designed to maximize the effects of electromagnetic pulses (see Chapter 17).

Each of these new systems needs to be examined in the context of whether it is likely to prove stabilizing or destabilizing. For example, it may be in the interest of the United States to assure that Soviet command centers remain operable so that negotiations can be carried out in the event of war.

We conclude this section with an observation we believe has not received sufficient attention. Nuclear weapons technology is quite mature. The destructiveness of nuclear weapons is so great that defensive technology lags far behind, perhaps hope-lessly far behind. While it is impossible to think of every new technology which might be developed, this does not mean that technological developments can't be anticipated at all. We suggest that there are no new nuclear technologies now on the horizon with the potential to totally change the nuclear balance. This includes the x-ray laser and other third-generation weapons. Because of this plateau in nuclear technology, the present time may be superbly well suited to slowing down research in nuclear weapons technology and developing agreements and procedures that will allow the United States and the Soviet Union to significantly reduce the number of nuclear weapons in their arsenals, and to decrease the risk of planned or accidental events which would unleash nuclear forces that could well destroy both societies.

3-7 PROBABILITY AND ACCURACY-YIELD TRADE-OFF: TECHNICAL DETAILS

Many situations can be described using concepts of probability. A simple example is the toss of a coin. If the toss is fair, it is equally likely to come up heads or tails. If the coin is tossed many times, on the average there will be as many heads as there are tails. This does not mean that there will always be equal numbers of heads and tails. (Obviously, after an odd number of tosses there can't be.) Every once in a while there will be long sequences or runs of heads, or of tails. The occurrence of such series is not predictable, but it is to be expected. Despite the belief by some gamblers in runs of bad or good luck, the chance that the next coin toss will be a head or a tail is not affected in any way by what has occurred previously. Expressed in somewhat more technical language, the probability of a head (or a tail) on any flip of a fair coin is independent of all previous flips. In random events there is no memory.

There are many examples in which probability provides a good way of describing certain properties of systems. Examples are the distribution of cards in a well-shuffled deck, the numbers which are drawn in bingo, a state lottery, or Keno, and the chance that one's next child will be a girl. The expected probability distributions depend on the particular process being described. Thus the chance of drawing a club from a deck of cards is one-fourth, and the chance of rolling a two with a pair of dice is one in 36. Details of probability calculations quickly become complicated.

Probabilities are defined so that the chance of all possible outcomes is unity (100 percent). If the probability of heads and tails is equal, then the probability of each must be 50 percent, or 0.5.

What is the probability of three heads in a row? The probability of the first head is one-half. The probability of the second head is also one-half. Hence the probability of two heads in a row is one-half times one-half, or one-quarter. Similarly, the prob-ability of three heads in a row is one-half cubed, or one-eighth. The probabilities of all other possible events must therefore be seven-eighths. You might try to work out what the other possibilities are. One example is head, head, tail. Another is tail, head, head. And so on.

The situation with missiles is similar. Each missile is assumed to have a certain probability of destroying a target. This probability is determined by the design of the missile, the warhead, the aiming system, and the hardness of the target. Let's consider what happens if several missiles are fired at the same target.

We want to know the probability that the target is destroyed. The probability that the target is destroyed after several missile shots is one minus the probability of its surviving. Suppose the probability of its surviving a single ICBM is 0.1 (10 percent). Then the chance of surviving two ICBMs is $(0.1)(0.1) = 0.01$ (1 percent). The chance of its *not* surviving (i.e., being destroyed) is one minus the probability of its surviving. That is, the probability of destruction is $1 - 0.01 = 0.99$ (99 percent). This shows why it is usual to target several ICBMs on critical targets. The chance of destruction increases rapidly with the number of ICBMs assigned to a target.

These arguments are correct only if the probabilities are *independent*. If something affects all the ICBMs, the probabilities are not independent, and the analysis given here is incorrect. One example of this would be an aiming error in which the wrong target coordinates are entered into the guidance computer. Others would be shifts during the reentry phase due to winds or fratricide.* Such errors, which are common to all the ICBMs, are sometimes called "common mode" errors.

Many random processes are described by the so-called normal distribution sketched in Figure 3-9. Normal distributions are often applicable to situations where some particular outcome is most likely, and the likelihood of other outcomes decreases as one moves away from the most likely result. Shooting at a target is an excellent example. The normal distribution is described by the equation:

$$P(R) = e^{-R^2/2S^2} \qquad (3-2)$$

Here $P(R)$ is the probability of hitting outside a circle of radius R, R is the distance from the most likely point, S is a parameter that characterizes the distribution, and $e = 2.71828$ is the base of the napierian logarithms. The probability of finding a dart further away than a distance $R = S$ (S is the size of the distribution) is $P(R = S) = e^{-1/2} = 0.6$. The probability drops off very slowly for values of $R \ll S$, and very fast for $R \gg S$. The probability of finding a dart further away than $3S$ is $P(R = 3S) = e^{-9S^2/2S^2} = e^{-9/2} = 0.011$, or about 1 percent.

While the normal distribution is mathematically convenient, it does not always describe reality. In practical tests of weapons, for example, the "tails" of the distributions are much broader. Experiments are required to characterize the actual distribution.

The probability of finding a dart inside a circle of radius R is

$$P(\text{inside}) = 1 - (\text{probability of finding dart outside circle of radius } R) \qquad (3-3)$$
$$= 1 - P(R)$$

In the missile case, the probability we are concerned with is the probability of survival

---

*Fratricide refers to the destruction of one warhead by another.

following attack. The survival probability $P(R)$ is unity if the attacking missile hits a long way off (large R) and zero if $R = 0$ (direct hit). In an attack on a hardened target the quantity of interest is the kill probability, which is the probability that a missile will hit within the critical radius required to produce a high enough overpressure to destroy the target. The kill probability P_{kill} is then:

$$P_{kill}(R) = 1 - P(R) = 1 - e^{-R^2/2S^2} \tag{3-4}$$

The smaller S is, the more accurate the missile and the greater the kill probability.

Consider a silo hardened to withstand an overpressure of H psi. An empirical formula for the overpressure produced by a weapon of yield Y megatons exploded at ground level is, approximately:

$$p_o = 23.4Y/R^3 + 15.8(Y/R^3)^{1/2} \tag{3-5}$$

Here Y is the yield in megatons and R is the range in miles. At low pressures, which are important for damage to cities, both terms are often needed, as well as corrections for the mach stem effect. (For more detail, see Chapter 13.) For high pressures (above a few hundred psi) the first term is much greater than the second. For a 1-megaton weapon at a distance of 0.25 mile, $Y/R^3 = 64$. The first term equals 1500 psi and the second term equals 126 psi, which is less than 10 percent of the first and can be ignored. The total pressure is 1500 psi, which is typical of the blast resistance of today's missile silos. Ignoring the second term, solving for the radius R, and replacing the pressure p_o by the silo hardness H yields

$$R = 2.9\left(\frac{Y}{H}\right)^{1/3} \qquad \text{psi} \tag{3-6}$$

The survival probability is $P = e^{-R^2/2S^2}$. The kill probability is then

$$P_{kill} = 1 - e^{-R^2/2S^2} \tag{3-7}$$
$$= 1 - e^{-Y^{2/3}/(0.24H^{2/3}S^2)}$$

Usually the parameter S (which is generally used to characterize the normal distribution function) is replaced by the closely related quantity, circular error probable (CEP), the distance for which the probability is 50 percent that a missile will hit inside a circle of radius $R = $ CEP. It can be shown (Tsipis, 1983) that $S = 0.85$ CEP. It is usual also to collect the variables which are under the control of the attacker into a single quantity called the kill ratio K. By definition,

$$K = Y^{2/3}/\text{CEP}^2 \tag{3-8}$$

Combining the above, the kill probability becomes

$$P_{kill} = 1 - e^{-K/0.17H^{2/3}} \tag{3-9}$$

The dimensions are important here: yield is in megatons, CEP is in miles, and hardness is in psi. Remember that the equation was derived under the assumption of high values of hardening. It should not be applied to targets hardened to less than about 300 psi.

Examples What is the probability of destroying a silo hardened to 2000 psi using a 1-megaton warhead on a missile with a CEP of 300 meters? Convert 300 meters to 0.19 miles. The kill ratio is

$$K = \frac{1^{2/3}}{(0.19)^2} = 27.7$$

The kill probability is

$$P_{\text{kill}} = 1 - e^{-1.02} = 0.62 \text{ or } 62 \text{ percent}$$

If the silo is only hardened to 1000 psi, the kill probability increases to

$$P_{\text{kill}} = 1 - e^{-1.55} = 0.78 \text{ or } 78 \text{ percent}$$

If the accuracy of the attacking missile is improved to a CEP of 200 meters (0.125 miles), the kill probability increases to $P_{\text{kill}} = 0.97$ (97 percent).

Suppose the silo is attacked with two missiles. The two-hit kill probability $P_{\text{kill}, 2}$ is 1 minus the probability of surviving two hits, so $P_{\text{kill}, 2} = 1 - P^2$. The kill probability with an N-missile attack is

$$P_{\text{kill}, N} = 1 - P^N = 1 - (1 - P_{\text{kill}})^N$$

If, in the 1000-psi case, the missile reliability is denoted by $M_{\text{rel}}(0 \leq M_{\text{rel}} \leq 1)$, then the kill probability is reduced to $M_{\text{rel}} \times P_{\text{kill}}$. This means that the survival probability is $1 - M_{\text{rel}}P_{\text{kill}}$. The probability of surviving an N-missile attack is $(1 - M_{\text{rel}}P_{\text{kill}})^N$, and the probability of not surviving an N-missile attack where each missile has reliability M_{rel} is

$$P_{\text{kill}}(M_{\text{rel}}) = 1 - (1 - M_{\text{rel}}*P_{\text{kill}})^N \tag{3-10}$$

3-8 SUMMARY OF THE NUCLEAR CAPACITIES OF THE MAJOR POWERS

Tables 3-7 to 3-11 summarize the compositions of the strategic forces of the nuclear powers. The tables are taken from Part I, chapter 1 of the 1987 SIPRI Yearbook. This chapter is authored by the staff of the Nuclear Databook Project. Because data are continually being updated, there are minor discrepancies between these data and those shown elsewhere in this chapter. Not surprisingly, uncertainties about Soviet and Chinese nuclear arsenals are far greater than those about U.S., British, and French arsenals.

It is important to bear in mind that uncertainties abound. The data which go into development of these tables come from a wide variety of sources, most of them relating in one way or another to the United States intelligence community. Data released to the congress and the public may be intentionally biased by the intelligence sources. There are many reasons why the best available classified information also contains inaccuracies.

In assigning numbers of warheads to Soviet missiles it is usual to assume each can carry the maximum number at which tests have ever been observed. There is no independent way to determine how many MIRVs are actually deployed.

TABLE 3-6
Plans for additions and replacements to the U.S. nuclear stockpile, 1983–1992

No. to be built	DOE designation	Weapons system (date operational)	War-fighting purpose
560	W-84*	Ground-launched cruise missile (1983)	Highly accurate intermediate-range missiles for deployment in Europe.
2500	B-83*	Bomb (1984)—to replace B28 and B43 bombs	High-yield bomb (1 mt) with improved very low level delivery capability. Major gravity weapon for B-1. It will be capable of destroying "hardened Soviet ICBM silo and launch complexes, comamnd, control, communication installations, and nuclear storage sites," according to DOD.
758	W-80-0*	Sea-launched cruise missile (1984)	Planned for close-in attacks as well as a "strategic reserve" for protracted wars. First-strike potential against coastal targets.
3500	W-80-1*	Air-launched cruise missile (1982)—assumes both versions	1500-mile version to be used in standoff role, longer range "stealth" version under deployment. B-52, B-1B launch platforms.
800	W-79-1*	8-inch artillery (1982)—neutron weapon	Planned for battlefield use. Assumes that "collateral damage" will be lessened.
1440	W-76*	Trident C-4 SLBM (1979)—For six Trident subs (MIRV $\times$ 8) plus spares for possible uploading to 10 warheads per missile	Longer-range, higher-accuracy missile than C-3 SLBM.
1000	B-61 Mod 3* B-61 Mod 4*	Bomb (1976)	Variable-yield modern strategic and tactical bomb.
1055	W-87	MX ICBM (1986)—for 100 missiles, yield about 300 kt	Prompt hard target kill potential (CEP about 400 feet). First strike potential.
1440	W-87	Trident II SLBM (1989)—for six Trident subs MIRV $\times$ 10, yield 475 kt	Prompt hard target kill potential (CEP about 400 feet). First strike potential.
1000	W-82	155-mm artillery (mid-80s)—neutron weapon to replace W-48	Planned for battlefield use. Assumes that "collateral damage" will be lessened.
500	W-81	Standard Missile 2 (1968-87)—antiaircraft weapon to replace Terrier and for Aegis systems	Antiaircraft missile for nuclear war at sea.
1650	W-?	Antisubmarine warfare weapon (late 1980s)—to replace ASROC and SUBROC	Nuclear depth charge for antisubmarine use by surface ships and submarines

*Being produced.

Source: Center for Defense Information; *The Defense Monitor.*

TABLE 3-7
U.S. strategic nuclear forces, 1987

Weapon system				Warheads		
Type	No. deployed	Year deployed	Range (km)	Warhead × yield	Type	No. in stockpile
ICBMs[a]:						
Minuteman II	450	1966	11,300	1 × 1.2 Mt	W-56	480
Minuteman III (Mk 12)	240	1970	13,000	3 × 170 kt	W-62	750
Minuteman III (Mk 12A)	300	1979	13,000	3 × 335 kt	W-78	950
MX	10	1986	11,000	10 × 300 kt	W-87	110
Total	1,000					2,290
SLBMS:						
Poseidon	256	1971	4,600	10 × 50 kt	W-68	2,750
Trident II	384	1979	7,400	8 × 100 kt	W-76	3,300
Total	640					6,050
Bombers:						
B-1B	18	1986	9,800	8–24	[b]	250
B-52G/H	263	1955	16,000	8–24[b]	[b]	4,733
FB-111	61	1969	4,700	6[b]	[b]	360
Total	339					5,343
Refueling aircraft:						
KC-135	615	1957	. . .	. . .	. . .	. . .

[a] The four Titan II ICBMs remaining at December 1986 are scheduled to be deactivated by mid-1987.

[b] Bomber weapons include six different nuclear bomb designs (B-83, B-61-0, -1, -7, B-57, B-53, B-43, B-28) with yields from sub-kt to 9 Mt, ALCMs with selectable yields from 5 to 150 kt, and SRAMs with a yield of 200 kt. FB-111s do not carry ALCMs or B-53 or B-28 bombs.

Source: SIPRI, 1987.

One frequently used measure of the capabilities of the superpowers is the total megatonnage or total equivalent megatonnage (EMT) in their arsenals. We believe this measure is virtually meaningless, except in special circumstances. One way to understand why is to calculate the EMT of the United States' strategic arsenal using the data in Table 3-6. The calculations for the ICBM and SLBM legs of the triad are clear enough. However, the weapons configuration of the bomber leg can be varied enormously. Bombers can carry bombs with yields ranging over more than an order of magnitude (factor of ten) in yield. They can also be configured to carry ALCMs. Taking these options into account can readily change the total EMT calculated for the bomber leg by large factors.

Figure 3-12 shows the total megatonnage in the United States nuclear weapons stockpile. Development of this curve required assembling data from several sources. Clearly no similar data are available for the Soviet Union. The rapid drop in megatonnage in 1961 resulted from withdrawal of B-36 bombers carrying very large bombs. The overall drop in the post-1960 period reflects primarily a move toward MIRVing, and the reduction in megatonnage required for a given kill level made possible by improvements in accuracy.

TABLE 3-8
Soviet strategic nuclear forces, 1987

Weapon system					Warheads	No. in
Type	NATO code name	No. deployed	Year deployed	Range (km)	Warhead × yield	stockpile[a]
ICBMs:						
SS-11 Mod. 1	Sego	28	1966	11,000	1 × 1 Mt	29 – 56
Mod. 2		360	1973	13,000	1 × 1 Mt	380 – 720
Mod. 3		60	1973	10,600	3 × 250–350 kt (MRV)	190 – 360
SS-13 Mod. 2	Savage	60	1972	9,400	1 × 600–750 kt	63 – 120
SS-17 Mod. 2	Spanker	150	1979	10,000	4 × 750 kt (MIRV)	630 – 1,200
SS-18 Mod. 4	Satan	308	1979	11,000	10 × 550 kt (MIRV)	3,200 – 6,200
SS-19 Mod. 3	Stiletto	360	1979	10,000	6 × 550 kt (MIRV)	2,300 – 4,300
SS-X-24	Scalpel	. . .	1987?	10,000	7–10 × 100 kt (MIRV)	. . . – . . .
SS-25	Sickle	72	1985	10,500	1 × 550 kt	76 – 140
Total		1,398				6,900 –13,000
SLBMs:						
SS-N5	Sark }	39	1963	1,400	1 × 1 Mt	41 – 47
SS-N-6 Mod. 1/2	Serb }	288[b]	1967	2,400	1 × 1 Mt	450 – 520
Mod. 3			1973	3,000	2 × 200–350 kt (MRV) }	
SS-N-8	Sawfly	292	1973	7,800	1 × 800 kt–1 Mt	310 – 350
SS-N-17	Snipe	12	1977	3,900	1 × 1 Mt	13 – 14
SS-N-18 Mod. 1/3	Stingray }	224	1978	6,500	3–7 × 200-500 kt }	710 – 1,900
Mod. 2			1978	8,000	1 × 450 kt–1 Mt }	
SS-N-20[c]	Sturgeon	80	1983	8,300	6–9 × 350-500 kt	500 – 860
SS-N-23[c]	Skiff	32	1986	7,240	10 × 350-500 kt	340 – 380
Total		967				2,400 – 4,100

						Low – High
Bombers:						
Tu-95	Bear A/B/C/G	100	1956	8,300	2–4 × bombs/ASMs	280 – 560
Tu-95	Bear H[d]	40	1984	8,300	8 × AS-15 ALCMs	320 – 640
Total[e]		140				600 – 1,200
Refuelling aircraft:[f]		140–170				
ABMs						
AMB-1B	Galosh Mod.	32	1986	320	1 × unknown	32 – 64
ABM-3	Gazelle	68	1985	70	1 × low yield	68 – 140
Total		100				100 – 200

[a] Figures for numbers of warheads are low and high estimates of possible force loadings (including reloads). Reloads for ICBMs are 5 and 100 percent; and for SLBMs 5 and 20 percent extra missiles and associated warheads. Half the SS-N-6s are assumed to be Mod. 3s, and SS-N-18 warheads are assumed to be 3 or 7 warheads. Bomber warheads are force loadings and force loadings plus 100 percent reloads. It is assumed that 40 Bear Gs are now deployed (4 warheads each). All warhead total estimates have been rounded to two significant digits. Warhead estimates do not include downloading for single-warhead SS-17 Mod. 2, SS-19 Mod. 2 or SS-18 Mod. 1/3 missiles, which could be deployed, nor lower estimates for the SS-18 force, which could still include some Mod. 2 missiles with 8 or 10 warheads.

[b] It is not known whether the Soviet Union has already removed—or is planning to remove—from operational service an additional one or two Yankee Is during 1986 to make room for additional Typhoon and Delta IV Class submarines which may have entered sea trials. Alternatively, the U.S.S.R. may have decided to wait to make these withdrawals until the United States exceeds the SALT limits.

[c] An additional Typhoon (20 SS-N-20 missiles) and Delta IV (16 SS-N-23 missiles) may be on sea trials and are thus included in the force totals. See note b.

[d] It is believed that, as of mid-1986, three squadrons of 12 Bear H aircraft each were in service. An additional squadron may have entered the operational force by the end of 1986.

[e] Excludes 30 MYA-4 Bison bombers which are under dispute. The United States believes that they remain SALT-accountable, while the U.S.S.R. claims that they have been converted to refueling tankers. Here they are included in the refueling aircraft totals.

[f] Includes Badger and Bison A bombers converted to aerial refueling and 15 confirmed new Bison conversions, with 30 possible new Bison conversions claimed by the U.S.S.R.

Source: SIPRI, 1987

TABLE 3-9
British nuclear forces, 1987[a]

| Weapon system | | | | Warheads | | |
Type	No. deployed	Year deployed	Range (km)	Warhead × yield	Type	Max. no. in stockpile
Aircraft:						
Buccaneer S2	25	1962	1,700	1 × bombs	WE-177	30
Tornado GR-1	190	1982	1,300	1 × bomb	WE-177	195
SLBMs:						
Polaris A3-TK	64	1982	4,700	2 × 40 kt	MRV	128
Carrier aircraft:						
Sea Harrier	23	1980	450	1 × bombs	WE-177	25
ASW helicopters:						
Sea King HAS 2/5	61	1976	—	1 × depth bombs	?	61
Wasp HAS 1	22	1963	—	1 × depth bombs	?	22
Lynx HAS 2/5	75	1976	—	1 × depth bombs	?	75

Source: SIPRI, 1987.

TABLE 3-10
French nuclear forces, 1987

Weapon system				Warheads		
Type	No. deployed	Year deployed	Range (km)	Warhead × yield	Type	No. in stockpile
Aircraft:						
Mirage IVP/ASMP	18	1986	1,500	1 × 300 kt	TN 80	80
Jaguar A	45	1974	750	1 × 6–8/30 kt	ANT-52	50
Mirage IIIE	30	1972	600	1 × 6–8/30 kt	ANT-52	35
Refuelling aircraft:						
C-135F/FR	11	1965	...	...	...	...
Land-based missiles:						
S3D	18	1980	3,500	1 × 1 Mt	TN-61	18
Pluton	44	1974	120	1 × 10/25 kt	ANT-51	70
Submarine-based missiles:						
M-20	64	1977	3,000	1 × 1 Mt	TN-61	64
M-4A	16	1985	4,000–5,000	6 × 150 kt (MIRV)	TN-70	96
M-4 (modified)	16	1987	6,000	1–6 × 150 kt (MIRV)	TN-71	<96
Carrier aircraft:						
Super Etendard	36	1978	650	1 × 6–8/30 kt	ANT-52	40

Source: SIPRI, 1987.

TABLE 3-11
Chinese nuclear forces, 1987

| Weapon system | | | | Warheads | |
Type	No. deployed	Year deployed	Range (km)	Warhead × yield	No. in stockpile
Aircraft:					
Il-28 Beagle (B-5)	15–30	1974	1,850	1 × bombs	15–30
Tu-16 Badger (B-6)	100	1966	5,900	1–3 × bombs	100–130
Land-based missiles:					
CSS-1 (DF-2)	40–60	1966	1,100	1 × 20 kt	40–60
CSS-2 (DF-3)	85–125	1972	2,600	1 × 2–3 Mt	85–125
CSS-3 (DF-4)	~10	1978	7,000	1 × 1–3 Mt	20
CSS-4 (DF-5)	~10	1980	12,000	1 × 4–5 Mt	20
Submarine-based missiles:					
CSS-N-3	26	1983	3,300	1 × 200 kt–1 Mt	26–38

Source: SIPRI, 1987.

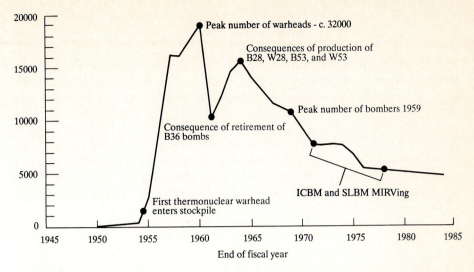

FIGURE 3-12

Total megatonnage of U.S. nuclear weapons stockpile, 1950–1984. *Note:* The curve showing the relative megatonnage by year was supplied by DOE. The vertical scale was added by the authors by scaling the relative values for end FY 1960 to 19000 megatons. The uncertainty in this scaling is estimated to be less than 10%. (Source: Nuclear Weapons Databook, Volume II.)

TABLE 3-12
The United States–Soviet Union strategic balance

Delivery systems	Area destroyable, mi²
U.S.	
ICBMs	44,300
Submarines	24,800
Bombers	54,200
Total	123,300
U.S.S.R.	
ICBMs	139,800
Submarines	36,600
Bombers	12,200
Total	188,600

The area each can destroy, in square miles, assuming 30 square miles/EMT

Source: D. W. Hafemeister and D. Schroeer (eds.), *Physics, Technology, and the Nuclear Arms Race*, Proceedings of the American Institute of Physics Conference 104, Appendix E, New York, 1983.

Finally, one must be careful not to be drawn too far into "bean-counting" analyses of capabilities. Single numbers, or even a few numbers, may not accurately represent the actual capabilities of the systems being described. This is a large problem with nuclear weapons themselves, and becomes much more difficult when one attempts to assess the reliability of delivery systems, the capability of troops, and the vast numbers of factors which, taken in toto, represent the military capability of a nation.

Table 3-12 expresses the destructive power in terms of land area that could be destroyed if targeting were designed to maximize land area (i.e., no multiple targeting, or the "cookie-cutter" approach), assuming 30 square miles destroyed per EMT corresponding to about 10 psi overpressure. This table make very clear the ability of any leg of the U.S. strategic triad to destroy all the major and most of the secondary cities in the Soviet Union, and vice versa.

QUESTIONS

1. Write a short statement clarifying your understanding of the difference between tactical and strategic weaponry.
2. How do you think the Soviet view of the United States arsenal might differ from the United States view of the Soviet arsenal? Identify some reasons why the Soviet arsenal might reasonably be expected to have a different composition than that of the United States.
3. Can you identify some possible weapons system the U.S.S.R. might build that might overcome the synergistic effects that make the U.S. bomber and land-based ICBM system supportive of each other?
4. Compare the strategic balance between the United States and the Soviet Union as given in Table 3-3 with the balance as given in the tables in Section 3-8. Identify some discrepancies you think might be significant. If you think none of the discrepancies are significant, explain your reasoning.
5. Define bias error and give a list of possible sources of error. Try to identify some sources not included in the list in the text.
6. Make a list of problems you can identify that might fall into the general category of "fratricide effects." Try to expand the list beyond the factors discussed in the text.

PROBLEMS

1. Calculate the EMT of the following weapons: (a) 100 Mt; (b) 10 Mt; (c) 1 Mt; (d) 100 kt; (e) 10 kt; (f) 1 kt.
2. Calculate the CEP required to achieve a 90 percent single-shot kill probability on a silo hardened to 2000 psi with the following size warheads: (a) 1 kt; (b) 10 kt; (c) 100 kt; (d) 1 Mt; (e) 10 Mt.
3. Repeat Problem 2 using the assumption that the warhead reliability is 95 percent.
4. Repeat Problem 2, but allow two shots rather than only one.

KEY WORDS

ALCM air-launched cruise missile ("alcom").

bus the part of a booster assembly carrying the MIRV warheads. After the bus is launched into space by the booster, the warheads are individually launched.

CEP circular error probable. A measure of the aiming accuracy of a missile or other weapon.

cruise missile a low-flying pilotless aircraft capable of delivering nuclear or conventional weapons at subsonic speeds. The wings are small, so the cruise must be given a moderate speed by its launching device.

deep penetrator a warhead now under development designed to penetrate several meters into the earth before exploding. The device couples its energy into the ground more efficiently than existing nuclear weapons. It would be useful in attacking command structures or hardened targets. Some argue that the deep penetrator is an example of a highly destabilizing weapon.

EMT equivalent megaton, defined as the yield expressed in megatons, raised to the two-thirds power.

flexible response a policy doctrine emphasizing the ability to respond to threats selectively, using a carefully chosen level of force, ranging from conventional weaponry through tactical nuclear weapons to strategic systems.

footprint the region within which a set of warheads from a MIRVed missile can be targeted.

fratricide the damaging influence of one attacking warhead on a later arriving warhead. The dust or wind raised by a first bomb may damage a second one.

GLCM ground-launched cruise missile ("gliccom").

hardened reinforced (usually with steel and concrete) so as to be able to withstand the blast of a nearby nuclear or conventional explosion. Hardening is expressed in the terms of the blast overpressure (in pounds per square inch) which an object can withstand.

ICBM intercontinental ballistic missile.

kill ratio a measure of the ability of a particular weapon system to attack a target. Kill ratio depends on weapon yield and accuracy of the delivery system.

LOW Launch on warning. The policy of launching weapons upon warning that an attack may be underway, before the attacking weapons have actually detonated.

MAD Mutually assured destruction. The capability of two superpowers to destroy each other.

MaRV maneuverable reentry vehicles. MaRV warheads can be aimed during reentry or final approach phase, thereby allowing improved accuracy.

megaton 1000 kilotons. A unit of explosive energy. One megaton is the energy that would be released in the explosion of one million tons of TNT explosive.

MIRV multiple independently targeted reentry vehicle.

NATO North Atlantic Treaty Organization. Most of the nations of Western Europe, plus the United States and Canada.

normal distribution a bell-shaped curve describing the distribution of events, such as the spread of shots aimed at a particular point.

SLBM submarine-launched ballistic missile. A missile (possibly MIRVed) launched from a submarine.

SLCM submarine-launched cruise missile ("sliccom").

TNF tactical nuclear forces. Nuclear weapons of relatively "small" yield in the kiloton range to be used on the battlefield or at sea.

WTO Warsaw Treaty Organization. The nations of Eastern Europe, plus the Soviet Union.

CHAPTER
4

NUCLEAR WEAPONS POLICY OF THE UNITED STATES

O wad some Pow'r the giftie gie us
To see oursels as others see us!
It wad frae monie a blunder free us,
*   An' foolish notion.*

Robert Burns, "To a Louse," ca. 1786

One man's word is no man's word. We should quietly hear both sides.

Goethe

Important Principles may and must be flexible.

Lincoln, speech 1865

4-1 THEMES

The uses of war in resolving international conflict have been fundamentally changed by the advent of nuclear weapons. In the four decades since nuclear weapons were developed, the strategic nuclear policies of the superpowers (and other nuclear states) have created a situation of unprecedented peril. Nuclear weapons orders of magnitude more powerful that those used against Japan have been developed and can be delivered by the thousands in a few minutes' time.

The United States and the Soviet Union together can deliver about a million Hiroshimas of destructive energy. Such destruction is the potential inherent in any United States–Soviet confrontation. Unless political methods can be developed to contain this threat, our civilizations and the global ecosystem itself remain in great danger.

Strategic nuclear policy can never be fully rational as long as it involves two or more nations that both possess an appreciable number of nuclear weapons. The distinction between means and ends is meaningless. In the past, winners could dominate losers, bending them to their will, but extensive nuclear war amounts to mutual extermination.

Six possible objectives of a nuclear weapons policy of the United States have been described as follows (Carnendale et al., 1983):

1. *Basic deterrence*. Deter a nuclear attack by the Soviet Union on the United States.
2. *Extended deterrence*. Deter a nuclear or conventional attack on allies of the United States.
3. *Crisis stability*. Minimize the incentives for either side to strike first in an international crisis.
4. *War fighting, damage limitation, escalation control*. If deterrence fails, help defeat nuclear or conventional attacks on the United States or its allies and minimize damage to them.
5. *War termination*. If deterrence fails, help terminate conventional or nuclear war in a manner least damaging to United States security and to the security of the allies of the United States.
6. *Bargaining chip, arms control support*. Provide support for United States policies in arms control negotiations and be amenable to limitation by arms control agreements.

DETERRENCE

To this list might also be added a nonnuclear defense posture and a nonoffensive defense or, otherwise stated, a nonprovocative defense (Forsberg, 1984). The former has the long-term goal to place less and less reliance on nuclear weapons and eventually not to rely on them at all. This policy is viewed by some as making the world safe for conventional wars between the superpowers. Nonoffensive defense or nonprovocative defense advocates argue for a defense policy that is truly defensive and nonthreatening. For example, armaments that could be used offensively, such as tanks and bombers, would be reduced and eventually eliminated by agreements among the superpowers and others. See Chapters 6 and 26 for further discussion of the possible reduction in nuclear weapons by a change in nuclear policy. These policies are a departure from that of deterrence and have recently received increased attention.

In this chapter we review the evolution of United States nuclear weapons policy. In the four decades since 1945 the emphasis of policy has shifted considerably, but for much of this period each of the goals listed above has played a role.

4-2 EARLY NUCLEAR WEAPONS POLICY: WORLD WAR II AND THE IMMEDIATE POSTWAR PERIOD

In the Roosevelt administration of the 1940s it was assumed that nuclear weapons would be used after they had been successfully developed. President Truman did not really have to make a decision on whether or not to use nuclear weapons against Japan; the decision had, in effect, been made for him. Although some scientists from the Manhattan Project proposed a demonstration explosion, their arguments were not persuasive enough to alter previous de facto policy—and so the bombs fell against two defenseless cities and the war against Japan ended.

In the immediate postwar period, the United States, led by James Byrnes, secretary of state under Truman, tried a policy known as "atomic diplomacy" in dealing with the war-devastated Soviet Union. Nuclear weapons were by no means the only military force available to the United States, but the fact that the United States had a monopoly on such weapons was used in an effort to force the Soviets to accept U.S. nuclear dominance. The U.S.S.R. was unwilling to accept this, and the first major post-World War II conference, the Moscow conference of 1945, was—probably inevitably—a failure. According to Senator Henry A. Jackson,* the United States did use atomic diplomacy successfully at least once during that period—in forcing the Soviet Union to withdraw from Iran in 1946.

For a brief period before the Cold War began in earnest the United States recognized that our nuclear monopoly would not last forever and that our security might be best served by having all fissionable material under United Nations control. This idea was embodied in the Oppenheimer-Baruch proposal, which was presented to the United Nations but was condemned by the Soviet Union as an attempt by the United States to maintain de facto its nuclear monopoly.

Time Magazine, Jan. 28, 1980.

In 1949 the Western world was profoundly shocked when the Soviet Union exploded its first atomic bomb. Truman had difficulty believing, even with the evidence of airborne radioactivity and other intelligence before him, that "those Asiatics" could have developed an atomic bomb so soon. That they were able to do so was in part because of effective espionage (see Chapter 2) and the knowledge that an atomic bomb was possible. The most important point to be made is, however, that any industrial nation can produce nuclear weapons once it has certain technology and it decides to make the commitment to do so. It should also be noted that the Soviets had a strong nuclear physics research effort in the 1930s. Soviet physicists developed the first cyclotron in Europe (in Leningrad) and were working seriously on fission in 1939. The Soviet bomb project grew naturally out of these early beginnings.

Even during the period of atomic diplomacy the United States recognized that its nuclear monopoly would not last indefinitely and that inevitably we would have to deal with the possibility of retaliation with nuclear weapons. Bernard Brodie, sometimes called the father of nuclear strategy, wrote in 1946:

> The first and most vital step in any American security program for the age of atomic bombs is to take measures to guarantee to ourselves in case of attack the possibility of retaliation in kind. The writer is not for the moment concerned about who will *win* the next war in which atomic bombs are used. Thus far the chief purpose of our military establishment has been to win wars. From now on its chief purpose must be to avert them. It can have no other useful purpose.

In the same paper Brodie recognized that there are upper limits to the number of conceivably useful nuclear weapons:

> The number of critical targets is quite limited. . . . That does not mean that additional hits would be useless but simply that diminishing returns would set in early; and after the cities of, say, 100,000 population were eliminated, the returns from additional bombs would decline drastically. . . . If 2000 bombs in the hands of either party is enough to destroy entirely the economy of the other, the fact that one side has 6000 and the other 2000 will be of relatively small significance.

Here Brodie asked for the first time the crucial question, "How much is enough?" One of the best-known responses was that of then Secretary of Defense Robert McNamara in the 1960s (see Section 3-2). He concluded that a few hundred megatons delivered on selected targets are more than adequate to destroy the Soviet Union as a functioning society.

4-3 THE 1950s

Nuclear Threats

The beginning of the 1950s saw the start of the Cold War. The Soviet Union had invaded Czechoslovakia and was threatening Berlin. China, under the leadership of Mao Zedong, had become communist. The Sino-Soviet alliance appeared monolithic and sinister to the U.S. government. It was the opinion of many that the communist nations were bent on world domination and that communism had to be contained.

When South Korea was invaded by North Korea, the United States went to its support with U.N. participation (made possible by a Soviet boycott of the U.N. Security Council). Once U.N. forces had reached the Yalu River, the Chinese entered the conflict from their side of the Yalu in Manchuria. The war resulted in a stalemate. General Dwight D. Eisenhower was elected President with the promise to "end the war in Korea." In Eisenhower's memoirs (*Mandate for Change,* vol. I), he reveals that he made a nuclear threat against the Chinese in 1953. This was regarded by Eisenhower and his vice president, Richard Nixon, as critical to the successful negotiations that ended the Korean War.

Nuclear diplomacy was also considered in Vietnam in 1954. Richard Nixon's memoirs confirm French Prime Minister Georges Bidault's account of high-level consideration of a proposal calling for the United States to give three atomic weapons to the French to be used for the relief of French forces surrounded at Dienbienphu. (The United States had logistically supported the French effort to preserve France's prewar colonial position as part of western Cold War policy of containing communism. The "domino theory" held that if Vietnam should fall to the communists, then all of Southeast Asia, Indonesia, and the Philippines would also eventually fall.) The weapons were not provided, however, and the final French defeat occurred at Dienbienphu. Shortly thereafter the French withdrew, and the United States took over the struggle.

Daniel Ellsberg (1980), a high-level national security analyst during the administrations of four different presidents, asserts that atomic diplomacy has been considered frequently. He writes:

> What I discovered, going back to Truman . . . is that every president has seen serious recommendations of the Joint Chiefs of Staff of plans involving the initiation of nuclear warfare under certain circumstances. More significantly, at least four presidents have secretly authorized advanced preparations for such first-use, or have threatened adversaries with U.S. first use in an ongoing crisis.

In the case of Quemoy and Matsu, two islands off the coast of mainland China that had long been occupied by Taiwanese forces during the Eisenhower era, the idea of using nuclear weapons was openly approved by Congress. According to Quester (1970), this served as a warning to the Chinese:

> . . . The President (Eisenhower) did request and receive from Congress authority to defend Quemoy and Matsu if the threat to the islands seemed to embody a threat to Taiwan; and statements were issued that the administration in fact did now see the threats to be so coupled that tactical nuclear weapons would be used if needed for the defense of the islands.

According to Ellsberg, there were contingency plans to use nuclear weapons during the Cuban missile crisis. However, basically because neither side wanted a confrontation that could have led to nuclear war, the use of a naval blockade and nonnuclear diplomacy prevailed.

H. R. Haldeman, the special executive assistant to President Nixon who was involved in the Watergate scandal, wrote (1978) of a proposed nuclear approach to ending the war in Vietnam:

The threat was the key, and Nixon coined a phrase for this theory which I'm sure will bring smiles of delight to Nixon-haters everywhere. We were walking along a foggy beach after a long day of speech-writing. He said, ''I call it the Madman Theory, Bob. I want the North Vietnamese to believe I've reached the point were I might do *anything* to stop the war. We'll just slip the word to them that, 'for God's sake, you known Nixon is obsessed about communism. We can't restrain him when he's angry—and he has his hand on the nuclear button'—and Ho Chi Minh himself will be in Paris in two days begging for peace.''

Nixon had conceived the ''Madman Theory'' as the way to do it. Henry (Kissinger) perfected the theory and carried it to the secret series of Paris peace talks: A threat of egregious military action by an unpredictable U.S. president who hated communism, coupled with generous offers of financial aid. Henry arrived at the peace negotiations fully expecting his plan to be successful.

But there the theory—and Nixon and Kissinger's hopes for peace in Nixon's first year—crumbled. Henry found the North Vietnamese absolutely intractable. They wouldn't even negotiate. And the reason was clear. No threat and no offer could obscure one great fact known to the world at large. The American people had turned against the war. The young were saying they wouldn't fight it. The response to Eugene McCarthy's Democratic primary campaign in 1968 convinced the North Vietnamese that it was only a matter of time before the U.S. would *have* to pull out, no matter what. So why negotiate?

Massive Retaliation

In the early 1950s U.S. authorities believed that we had such a large nuclear advantage—in both numbers of weapons (thousands, versus some 50 at the beginning of the decade) and the means to deliver them—that a doctrine of *massive retaliation* was possible. As expressed by Secretary of State John Foster Dulles (1954), the policy states that in order to deter or counter aggression, the United States would ''depend primarily upon a great capacity to retaliate instantly by means and at places of our own choosing.'' This policy was to be short-lived. Even though we had strategic superiority in nuclear weapons and delivery systems [via the aircraft of the Strategic Air Command (SAC)], the Soviet Union was soon in a position to retaliate effectively.

Implicit in the doctrine of massive retaliation is the concept of *deterrence*. Deterrence is a means of preventing another nation from taking certain actions. For it to function the adversary needs to know what response will occur. Credibility is important—the opponent must believe the deterrer's intent. There are always risks, a major one being that loss of credibility will lead to nuclear destruction.

Tactical Nuclear Forces in Europe

Nuclear weapons were introduced in Europe in the late 1940s when American bombers were deployed in Britain. At that time bombers did not have the range to reach the Soviet Union from the United States. By the early 1950s the United States had developed smaller nuclear weapons for battlefield use (**tactical nuclear weapons**), which were deployed as part of NATO forces. According to Solly Zuckerman (1982), chief scientific adviser to the minister of defense for the United Kingdom:

At the NATO conference held in Lisbon in 1952, force levels had been set for the alliance at 96 divisions, partly in order to obviate the danger of nuclear war by making it possible to offer a conventional defense to a Soviet attack. But by 1954 it had become apparent that these divisions were never going to materialize, and the NATO Council decided that "tactical nuclear weapons" should be used to redress any disparity in numbers of men that might occur between the West and the U.S.S.R.

The beginning of tactical nuclear weapons deployment may be traced to a study in 1951 in which J. R. Oppenheimer played an important role. It provided the basis for the council's decision in 1954.

Tactical nuclear weapons were allowed because members of NATO were not able or willing to bear the burden of conventional arms. It was cheaper and politically easier to "go nuclear" to contain the perceived threat of a Soviet invasion of Western Europe.

By the end of the decade the Soviets too had introduced nuclear weapons on their side of the East-West boundary. By 1983 there were 10,000 to 15,000 nuclear weapons in Europe, with yields ranging from about 1 kiloton to 1 megaton (Holloway, 1983).

The presence of tactical nuclear weapons in Europe creates serious problems of instability. These are discussed in Section 4-4.

4-4 THE 1960s: COUNTERFORCE OR NUCLEAR USE THEORIES (NUTS) AND MUTUAL ASSURED DESTRUCTION (MAD)

At the end of the 1950s the United States faced a new challenge to its security: the intercontinental ballistic missile. The U.S. response to the Soviet Union's launching in 1957 of the world's first satellite, Sputnik, was first dismay, then action. The response was aggravated by Soviet Premier Nikita Khrushchev, who implied (erroneously) that the Soviet Union's capability for putting a satellite in orbit had already been translated into intercontinental nuclear arms. The "missile gap" became a useful political device for increasing procurements for U.S. armed forces.

United States space programs were fueled by the insecurity generated by Sputnik. The crash programs for missile development led to bitter interservice rivalries which still exist (York, 1970). The rivalries in turn generated different self-serving strategic nuclear policies, each of which gained its advocates and constituencies in Congress. Successive administrations, including the present administration, have been forced to respond to these groups.

In the late 1950s the Air Force was facing an internal threat: the Navy's new Polaris submarine. Unlike Strategic Air Command (SAC) bombers, which sat on airfields that were increasingly being seen as vulnerable to attack, Polaris moved underwater, undetected. Its SLBMs traveled at hypersonic speeds in ballistic trajectories and were invulnerable to Soviet air defenses. Polaris could destroy Soviet cities just as easily as the bombers. Since SAC's war plan called for hitting urban and military targets simultaneously—with an emphasis on destroying industrial plants in enemy cities—SAC seemed in danger of obsolescence.

The Air Force needed a new strategy. An Air Force-funded think tank, the RAND Corporation, proposed a counterforce–no–cities approach. By emphasizing precision strikes on military targets the Air Force had found a strategy which the Navy could not match.

The Navy developed its own nuclear strategy: an up-dated version of Brodie's (1946) earlier ideas. The idea was that an enemy would be deterred from striking first if the cost would be the loss of its urban-industrial society as a result of hits by surviving U.S. second-strike weapons. The best way to accomplish such deterrence, it was argued, was by undetectable nuclear-armed submarines, most of which would be at sea at any time. The Navy pointed out that no matter how many weapons the Soviets built, the United States would be secure (i.e., able to counterattack) as long as the submarines were there. Moreover, the Navy argued, further building of bombers and land-based missiles would be more likely to guarantee a continuing arms race.

When President John F. Kennedy took office in January 1961, his Secretary of Defense, Robert McNamara, brought to Washington ideas of cost analysis which he had implemented as president of the Ford Motor Company. His concept of "finite deterrence" was at first intended to provide a way to establish fiscal control on the military. But the concept had wider application.

The nation's master plan for strategic defense coordinated all nuclear forces through the *single integrated operational plan,* or **SIOP**. When Robert McNamara became Secretary of Defense he found that the SIOP allowed the President virtually no nuclear options against threats other than a full-scale attack. The Air Force counterforce–no–cities idea offered the prospect of options. These options have sometimes been called *nuclear use theories,* or NUTs. Military targets could be identified using spy planes and satellite surveillance. Then accurate land-based missiles and SAC bombers could destroy them while minimizing collateral damage to cities.

By May 1962 the counterforce idea became official Defense Department policy. However, at the same time McNamara cut the Air Force budget heavily, eliminating the B-70 bomber, cruise missiles, and several other programs. The Air Force had won the policy battle, but lost the budget war. Intense pressure was put on McNamara. He responded by developing a new measure of nuclear adequacy, *assured destruction* (later to be termed *mutual assured destruction,* or **MAD**). This gave each service an important role in nuclear strategy. Thus was born the idea of the *strategic triad—* deterrent capability in land-based missiles, nuclear bombs dropped from aircraft, and submarine-based missiles—which remains the mainstay of U.S. strategic posture.

4-5 RECENT NUCLEAR WEAPONS POLICY: THE 1970s AND 1980s

Strategic Weapons

United States nuclear policy is a result not only of internal factors but also of a complex dynamic interplay between ourselves and the Soviet Union. During the late 1960s the Soviet Union produced large numbers of strategic missiles in an effort to catch up with the United States. The United States responded in several ways. Land-based missiles were augmented by developing **MIRVs**, multiple independently targetable reentry vehicles which permit installation of several warheads, each capable of independent aiming, on each booster rocket. The primary land-based missiles, the Minutemen, were provided with three warheads each. Aiming accuracy was also substantially improved. These developments were justified by an alleged need to saturate anticipated Soviet ABM defenses.

By the end of the 1960s however, the Soviets had built so many ICBMs in hardened silos (about 1400) that the improved U.S. weapons were insufficient in principle to destroy all the Soviet missiles. Therefore in 1973 the Air Force asked for a new missile, the MX, which would have 10 warheads instead of 3 and have improved accuracy. It was argued that 200 MXs, or 100 MXs combined with 550 improved Minuteman III missiles, would make counterforce viable again—assuming that strategic missile forces would be limited by the SALT agreements to approximately the number then existing.

In the 1970s the Navy also equipped its submarines, Poseidon and Trident I, with MIRVs. Because one Poseidon submarine had 16 missiles, each with 10 MIRVed warheads, the Navy soon exceeded the requirements set up for deterrence under the strategy of the McNamara era. Improved aiming accuracy allowed the Navy to shift from pure "city busting" to a "silo busting" capability. Thus the Navy for the first time joined the counterforce policy position. The cornerstone of its new role is the Trident II missile. Trident submarines are now (1988) being commissioned by the U.S. Navy at the rate of about one per year. The Trident submarine has 24 missile launchers so that it can fire up to 240 highly accurate warheads (see Chapter 3).

However, as early as 1960 some strategists [e.g., Thomas Schelling (1960)] recognized that the growing number of **counterforce** warheads would make it difficult for the Soviets to distinguish between a counterforce strike and an all-out countervalue, or city-targeting, attack. Indeed, by the late 1960s the United States would have had to use 2000 warheads to eliminate about 1000 Soviet missiles—assuming that, for reliability, two U.S. missiles were targeted on each Soviet missile. There is considerable doubt that in the heat of nuclear battle the Soviets could or would distinguish a 2000-warhead counterforce strike from an attack on cities. The same is true of the United States.

One proposed solution to the all-out counterforce dilemma was to fire small-scale warning strikes, avoiding Soviet cities. This is the concept of "limited nuclear war." It is assumed that the Soviets would also elect to keep the conflict limited, presumably replying in kind. This may not be their intent (see below).

As a strategist for the RAND Corporation, James Schlesinger embraced the limited counterforce idea. When he became Secretary of Defense he determined to make it policy. The result was a series of national security decision memoranda, culminating in 1980 with President Carter's Presidential Directive 59. Small-scale counterforce policy was more recently elaborated by Secretary of Defense Caspar W. Weinberger as the 1982 "defense guidance" plan.

During testimony to Congress on limited counterforce policy, Schlesinger was questioned closely regarding casualties that would result from a counterforce exchange. Not satisfied with the response, the congressional committee authorized a study to be made of various nulcear war scenarios with casualty and damage estimates (Office of Technology Assessment, 1980). For a Soviet counterforce attack on United

States ICBMs alone, the casualty estimate ranges from 2 million to 20 million people—the large uncertainty resulting from the difficulty of estimating fallout casualties (see Chapter 16).

These casualty estimates were controversial, and have led to intense debate over whether counterforce strategy can be distinguished from countervalue in the heat of nuclear battle. Entirely new analyses undertaken several years after the OTA report concluded that if anything the situation is worse than OTA estimated (von Hippel et al., 1988; Daugherty et al., 1986; Levi et al., 1987). The more recent work examined an attack on the major strategic targets in the United States and the Soviet Union. The targets considered were long-range ballistic missiles, long-range bomber bases, naval bases, command and control centers and early warning radars, nuclear weapons storage sites, and intermediate-range missile and bomber sites.

The studies concluded that a major counterforce attack on the United States would lead to 12 to 27 million deaths, and a counterforce attack on the Soviet Union would lead to 15 to 32 million deaths. The ranges of deaths depend on assumptions regarding the attack pattern and varying assumptions about the severity of fires. The populations most at risk are those located in the vicinity of or downwind of major strategic targets. In the United States these regions are predominantly around the ICBM sites in the north central part of the nation (as far downwind as Chicago) and in California. The region around San Francisco, including our home base of Davis, is particularly vulnerable. Even with a high-quality fallout shelter survival in the San Francisco area would be unlikely (see also Chapter 16 on fallout and Chapter 21 on civil defense).

The Soviet Union would be damaged primarily in the western region, and the devastation would be particularly heavy in major western cities including Moscow, Leningrad, and Kiev.

We find it impossible to imagine how a war which killed 10 percent or more of the population could possibly be called "limited." "Flexible response" is a concept which is militarily attractive but would lead to a major disaster in its own right, as well as entailing the risk of escalation to full-scale nuclear war.

Tactical Nuclear Weapons

The wisdom of employing massive numbers of tactical nuclear weapons in Europe is being increasingly questioned.

Former high officials of the U.S. government (McGeorge Bundy, George Kennan, Robert McNamara, and Gerald Smith) are now saying that "no first use should be given careful consideration" (Bundy, 1982). They are concerned that with the proliferation of nuclear weapons down to the battlefield level, the risk of nuclear war as a result of accident or of escalation of a local conflict on the East-West border is becoming too great. It is likely that tactical nuclear weapons would be overrun in any sudden attack. If they were used, they could trigger Soviet nuclear response. Since use would most likely be largely on western territory, tactical nuclear weapons might destroy much of what they were used to defend.

In February 1983 several former defense leaders of the United States, Great Britain, and the Federal German Republic supported the no-first-use idea. They stated:

''Nobody has ever suggested how to limit a nuclear war once it's started, and nobody has ever suggested that an unlimited nuclear war will do other than destroy Western civilization.''* The no-first-use idea was rejected by the Reagan administration with the statement by State Department spokesman Alan Romberg that ''we believe that a no-first-strike pledge would undermine deterrence and increase the risk of Soviet conventional aggression against our European allies.''

In July 1988 the Reverend Jesse Jackson called for abandonment of the first-use policy of NATO in a major statement at the Convention of the Democratic Party.

If a no-first-use policy were actually decided upon, it would require a major review of NATO strategy. In December 1988 President Gorbachev, in a major speech at the United Nations, stated that he would unilaterally reduce Soviet troops and weapons. Should these reductions be put into effect it is certain that NATO will be under major pressure to reduce similarly. Reductions in both manpower and nuclear weaponry will be intensively discussed.

Theater Nuclear Force Weapons

Theater nuclear force (TNF) weapons are those located outside the United States which have a range of over 100 kilometers and which would be used in some ''theater'' of operations. Their maximum range, about 5000 kilometers, is considerably less than that of strategic missiles, which can travel distances of up to 10,000 kilometers. The above definition is somewhat arbitrary, and the distinction between them and tactical weapons is sometimes blurred. These weapons have also been termed intermediate nuclear forces (INF), and the 1988 INF Treaty provides for destruction of all such weapons by the United States and U.S.S.R. as well as ground-launched cruise missiles. (See Chapter 2 for a list of theater weapons to be destroyed under the INF Treaty.)

The Soviets regarded the Pershing II and cruise weapons as particularly threatening. They claimed that these missiles were really strategic in nature since they had ranges sufficient to reach the Soviet homeland. The range of the Pershing II was 1100 miles and of the cruise missile 1500 miles. It was also possible to increase the range of the Pershing II without too much difficulty. Since this new generation of missiles was more accurate, and time from launch to target for the Pershing II missiles was only about 10 minutes, it was conceivable that the Soviets would have been forced into a launch on warning (LOW) mode for their threatened missiles. Such a decision would have carried grave risks of accidental nuclear war. The security of the United States and Europe would have been dependent on the reliability of Soviet electronics (which is not noted for technical excellence).

4-6   POLICY ISSUES

The nuclear weapons policy of the United States, as delineated in the current single integrated operational plan, SIOP-6, prepared by the Reagan administration, is in-

---

San Francisco Chronicle, Feb. 2, 1983, p. 10.

tended to "create a capacity to fight and 'prevail' in a nuclear war." The current policy emphasizes the need to be able to fight a protracted nuclear war and to have enough resilience and flexibility of response so that even after a major first exchange the United States would have power to bargain.

According to Arkin (1983):

> "Protracted," "enduring," and "flexibility" are the new elements of the policy. SIOP-6 contains a larger number of pre-selected target options—limited war target sets—than any previous plan. This will provide practically unlimited capability to use nuclear weapons to any tactical advantage in a war. And through a combination of new, more accurate, and survivable weapons, and massive upgrading of command, control, communications and intelligence (C-cubed-I) machinery, the intent is to implement a policy that ensures limitation and control. . . . Assured and massive retaliation to an attack is no longer the centerpiece of U.S. deterrence policy.
>
> The adoption of war fighting, along with the notion of prevailing (in a nuclear war) breaks with the single policy of deterrence. The termination of hostilities on terms "favorable to the United States," as Weinberger's Consolidated Guidance requires, is the new strategy based on the new belief that the ability to fight a war with nuclear weapons is what deters, and that limitations are possible and controllable.

Such a strategy is intended to provide the capability of using nuclear weapons in a limited way to achieve tactical advantages. These objectives place enormous emphasis on the ability to survive second- and even third-strike attacks, particularly on command, control, communications, and intelligence (C-cube-I) requirements. SIOP-6 can be described as one version of a nuclear use theory.

Opinions vary widely as to the practical utility of limited restrained use of nuclear weapons. Lifton and Falk (1983) argue that "our dependence on nuclear weapons, the disease of 'nuclearism,' undermines our national security, destroys political legitimacy, and psychologically impairs the future." They argue that the premises of nuclear use theory are wrong—that the possibility of recovery from a nuclear war is illusory, and crucial assumptions about human behavior in relation to nuclear weapons are false. In the same vein, George Kennan, former ambassador to the Soviet Union and architect of some of our Cold War policies early in the nuclear arms race (among these the policy of containing communist expansion), now states that "nuclear weapons are not weapons, they are an obscenity" (Kennan, 1981).

As is evident from the discussion of counterforce, nuclear utilization theories are not really new. However, the development of new weapons systems, with more accurate and effective weapons has made and will continue to make such theories appealing to some nuclear advisers—especially in view of the inherent difficulties with MAD strategies. Other strategists will continue to oppose nuclear utilization. When General David C. Jones retired as chairman of the joint chiefs of staff in 1982, he said: "If you try to do everything to fight a protracted nuclear war, then you end up in a bottomless pit. . . . I don't see much chance of nuclear war being limited or protracted. In defense, we are in the priority business. We can't do everything. I personally would not spend a lot of money on protracted nuclear war."

A sobering admission of SIOP-6 is that there are 60 "military" targets within the city of Moscow alone and 40,000 in the entire Soviet Union. The only distinction between all-out counterforce and the "massive retaliation" of Dulles's time is that a present-day counterforce attack would be much more massive.

For counterforce to succeed both sides would need communication facilities that could keep leaders informed on what targets had been hit and what weapons remained (see Chapter 5). This system would have to function in a chaotic environment created by the nuclear strike: blast, radiation, and electromagnetic pulse. In fact, in some strategies the command and control centers are priority targets. In "decapitation" scenarios, for example, the top political and military leaders are the targets of the first salvo. This would, of course, make a "rational" conduct of the nuclear exchange even more dubious. It is far from clear how such a nuclear war, once begun, could be stopped.

A major difficulty with the restrained counterforce policy is that the Soviet authorities have given no assurance that they will wage nuclear war in this fashion. According to one military analyst (Douglass, 1982):

> Unfortunately, neither counterforce targeting nor mutual restraint are concepts that one encounters in Soviet military thought, except as treated in their analyses of U.S. concepts. This is not to say that the Soviets are not interested in limiting damage. They most certainly are. But in Soviet strategy one limits damage by destroying the enemy's forces. . . . Gradualism does not appear to be a Soviet concept. . . . . The possibility of achieving strategic results at the start of a war is the essence of the revolution in military strategy brought about by nuclear weapons. Accordingly, Soviet doctrine calls for constant readiness to deliver nuclear strikes and the attainment of victory in the shortest possible time.

One difficulty in formulating nuclear strategy is that the results rest substantially on each side's *perceptions* of the opposing side, not on the actual intent. Thus if the United States pushes nuclear use policies too far it will begin to look to the Soviets very much as if we are preparing a first-strike capability. For example, the accurate MX missile with its 10 warheads is presumably intended for implementation of a nuclear utilization strategy, but sufficient numbers of MX missiles, along with other missiles, might be viewed by the Soviets as a weapons system to be used for a preemptive first strike. The argument for a first-strike use is strengthened because the MX itself is vulnerable to ICBM attack and the Soviets might assume that the only reason the United States has so many MXs is that it is indeed planning for a first strike. The reality might be otherwise, but it is the Soviet *perception* that is important. The converse argument can be made about concern in the United States about accurate Soviet SS-18's, which also could be perceived as having first-strike capability.

One Soviet response might be to increase the number of their missiles. Another response, cheaper but much more dangerous, would be to launch on warning so that U.S. missiles would hit empty silos. In an extreme case, say an international crisis with great tension, the Soviets might resort to a preemptive first strike in order to avoid losing their missiles as a result of our (perceived) first strike. A former design engineer for the Polaris and Trident missile system, Robert Aldridge, takes the position that the Pentagon *actually is* preparing a first-strike capability (Aldridge, 1983). It is inevitable that perception and reality are intertwined.

A radical departure from present nuclear policy was proclaimed by President Reagan in his address to the nation in March 1983 in which he called for a ballistic missile defense that would "make nuclear weapons impotent and obsolete." With this his administration launched the Strategic Defense Initiative or **SDI**, dubbed "star wars" by some critics. Reagan's vision of an impenetrable shield, if feasible, would indeed make possible a new defensive nuclear policy to replace deterrence. However, there are at this time immense technical difficulties and serious international political realities that make it doubtful whether Reagan's vision of defending the U.S. population could be eventually realized—even if the United States would be willing to commit itself to the expenditure of about a trillion dollars that would probably be required. (See Chapter 20 for a more detailed discussion of ballistic missile defense.)

4-7 MORALITY

The prospect of killing and maiming hundreds of millions of our fellow human beings in a nuclear war brings with it profound moral questions.

Under what conditions might it be moral to engage in nuclear war? Consider the statements below [Mahedy (1983) and the National Conference of Catholic Bishops (1983)]:

1. The war is for a good cause.
2. The direct effect of the war is morally acceptable.
3. The intentions of the wager of war are good; only the side effects are harmful.
4. The good effect is greater than the bad effect.

The strategic bombing concepts developed in Britain and the United States in the 1930s set the stage for the erosion of these "justifications," and in World War II the erosion continued. Enemy cities came to be thought of as part of the war machine. Such thinking approaches abandonment of all moral principles of warfare.

Mahedy asserts that thermonuclear war is immoral because it means total and indiscriminate killing. He also views a counterforce war as immoral because of the large number of people that would be killed by "side effects."

In 1983 the National Conference of Catholic Bishops published the results of months of deliberations on the morality of nuclear war and nuclear weapons policies. Their conclusions are as follows:

1. Counter Population Use (Countervalue): Under no circumstances may nuclear weapons or other instruments of mass slaughter be used for the purposes of destroying population centers or other predominantly civilian targets. Retaliatory action which would indiscriminately and disproportionately take many wholly innocent lives, lives of people who are in no way responsible for reckless actions of the government, must also be condemned.
2. The Initiation of Nuclear War: We do not perceive any situation in which the deliberate initiation of nuclear war, on however restricted a scale, can be morally justified.

Nonnuclear attacks by another state must be resisted by other means. Therefore a serious moral obligation exists to develop nonnuclear defensive strategies as rapidly as possible. In the letter we urge NATO to move rapidly toward the adoption of a ''no first use'' policy, but we recognize this will take time to implement and will require the development of an adequate alternative defense posture.

3. Limited Nuclear War: Our examination of the various arguments on this question makes us highly skeptical about the real meaning of ''limited.'' One of the criteria of ''just war'' teaching is that there must be reasonable hope of success in bringing about justice and peace. We must ask whether such a reasonable hope can exist once nuclear weapons have been exchanged. The burden of proof remains on those who assert that meaningful limitation is possible. In our view the first imperative is to prevent any use of nuclear weapons and we hope that leaders will resist the notion that nuclear conflict can be limited, contained or won in any traditional sense.

4. On Deterrence: In current conditions ''deterrence'' based on balance, certainly not an end in itself, may still be judged morally acceptable. No use of nuclear weapons which would violate the principles of discrimination and proportionality may be intended in a strategy of deterrence. Deterrence is not an adequate strategy as a long-term basis for peace; it is a transitional strategy justifiable only in conjunction with resolute determination to seek arms control and disarmament.

These views have inevitably proved controversial. Thus Wohlstetter writes (1983):

The danger of Soviet aggression is more likely to be lessened by a Western ability to threaten the military means of domination than by a Western ability to threaten bystanders. First, the Soviets value their military power, on the evidence, more than the lives of bystanders. Second, Western non-suicidal threats against legitimate military targets are more credible than threats to bring about the destruction of civil society on both sides. The latter have a negligible likelihood of being carried out by Western leaders, and therefore cannot be relied on to dissuade Soviet intimidation or aggression. Finally, it is even more absurd and dangerous to suppose that the only way to dissuade the U.S.S.R. from unleashing aggression is to help the Soviets threaten our civilians by leaving them defenseless and by leaving us no choices other than capitulation or an uncontrollable destructive offense against Soviet cities that would invite reciprocal destruction of our own civil society.

Only some widely prevalent but shallow evasions and self-befuddlements, and not any deep moral dilemma or basic paradox, force us to threaten the annihilation of civilians in order to prevent nuclear or conventional war. The bishops are clear about rejecting the actual use of nuclear weapons to kill innocents. About *threats* to kill innocents, they are much less clear.

For a rebuttal of Wohlstetter's views see Draper (1983).

Since the use of offensive nuclear weapons would be genocidal, is reliance on such weapons basically immoral? To what, if any, extent are technologies intrinsically moral or immoral? What moral questions are involved in the production by a U.S.–U.S.S.R. nuclear exchange of a nuclear winter and global fallout to impact noncombatant nations (see Chapter 19)? These are issues with which a long-range nuclear weapons policy must grapple.

4-8 LONG-TERM NUCLEAR WEAPONS POLICY

Not only have the peoples of the superpowers developed the capability of destroying each other's nations but they have also created the possibility of a catastrophic blow to the ecosphere and the destruction of much of human life on earth (see Chapter 19). To a considerable degree we have stumbled into this morass unwittingly. Most strategic planning focuses on weapons systems for the next year, or the next decade. There is little attention to the question: "Where is our nuclear policy leading us?"

Will a policy of deterrence really serve us well in the long run? Will there be nuclear stability for the next decade, the next 50 years, the next 500 years? Will there be no miscalculation or accident—that might well result in unprecedented catastrophe? Perhaps it would be wise to reexamine our assumptions about the security provided by offensive nuclear weapons.

Jonathan Schell (1984) has called for abolition of all nuclear weapons (not just enough for minimum deterrence). He labels this concept "weaponless deterrence." He envisions a nuclear-weapons-free but conventionally armed and nuclear-capable world of sovereign and independent states linked together by an agreement in which nuclear weapons are abolished. He argues that such a world, while not without conflict, would be a positive step away from the nuclear abyss. It would provide at least an alternative to the choice of nuclear genocide on the one hand and the possibility of world tyranny by one nation on the other.

In *Weapons and Hope* Freeman Dyson (1984) offers the concept of "live and let live" as a possible way of escape from our nuclear predicament. He envisions a deliberate process in which we move away from nuclear weapons of all sorts toward a defensive posture based on nonnuclear weaponry. Nuclear weapons in his view are to be regarded as useful only for bargaining away in arms control negotiations. Such bargaining would be conducted with vigor and patience in an atmosphere of increasing trust as nuclear weapons were in fact negotiated away.

Dyson argues that if strategic nuclear weapons could be reduced by a factor of 30 to 100, it might be possible to develop a terminal defense (not a "star-wars" defense) against nuclear attack (see Chapter 20). Such a defensive system would presumably be constructed in a nonthreatening manner over a long period of time so that the Soviets would have the opportunity to build a similar defense.

Thus, Dyson argues, a combination of serious and patient arms control negotiations and defense technology can free the world from the omnipresent specter of nuclear catastrophe.

To the present authors it seems that at the current level of nuclear armament a deployed defense system would be destabilizing, as it might be perceived as part of a first-strike capability. Further, such a defense is technically very doubtful in any case (see Chapter 20).

Too often policies have evolved to deal with advances in technology when, ideally, goals and values should first be defined and then technological advances employed to achieve these goals. Growing public dialogue over such matters may lead to a larger role for moral and ethical principles, although to date these considerations have had little or no effect on either policy or technical choices.

President Gorbachev in his address to the United Nations General Assembly December 7, 1988, announced a major shift in Soviet military policy. If it is carried out in practice, it will indeed be a serious change toward "live and let live" rather than confrontation between the Soviet bloc and NATO. He stated that the Soviet Union would unilaterally reduce 500,000 troops and 5000 tanks that face NATO. He also stated that military forces in Eastern Europe would be restructured so that they are clearly intended for defensive purposes only—a step toward nonoffensive defense. For example, he stated that temporary bridges would be removed from these forces. These are used in offensive operations to bridge streams and rivers in which the defense has destroyed normal crossing points in order to delay the attack.

These changes in Soviet military policy will require the United States and its allies to get their own strategic thinking in order. What are the minimum U.S. forces required in Europe? Can further reductions in conventional forces be made by mutual agreement between the Warsaw pact and NATO so that the "first use" policy for tactical nuclear weapons by NATO can be abandoned? Do we really have to modernize nuclear weapons in NATO as is presently being planned? How many nuclear-tipped air-borne and sea-launched cruise missiles will be needed to defend Europe (since land-based cruise missiles are now outlawed by the INF Treaty)? Can NATO also begin to restructure for nonoffensive defense?

Responding to this new "perestroika" of Soviet leaders will require imagination and prudence. Imagination, because the United States and its allies are being asked to entertain the thought that East-West relations can be significantly different and greatly improved over the sometimes bitter relations of the last 40 years. Prudence, because the effect of actions either taken or not taken can result in unintended and unwelcome consequences.

QUESTIONS

1. What is deterrence?
2. Define: MAD, NUTs, SIOP, LOW, MIRV, ICBM, SLBM.
3. Distinguish between strategic nuclear weapons, theater nuclear weapons, and tactical nuclear weapons.
4. What was the policy of massive nuclear retaliation and why was it short-lived?
5. What is counterforce strategy? Countervalue?
6. Discuss the moral issues of nuclear policy.
7. Discuss present nuclear policy (SIOP-6).
8. Why did McNamara devise the MAD policy?
9. What are the basic inconsistencies of any counterforce strategy?
10. What are the difficulties with the MAD policy?
11. How does Joseph Douglass describe Soviet nuclear policy?
12. What are the basic goals of nuclear policy as given by the Harvard study group? What is your own ranking of the importance of these goals?
13. Why does the United States not agree to a no-first-use policy as the Soviets have suggested?
14. How many military targets are in Moscow according to SIOP-6?

15. According to OTA, how many people in the United States would be killed by a Soviet counterforce strike on U.S. military targets?
16. Discuss perceptions as a factor in nuclear policies.
17. Discuss possible alternatives to reliance on offensive nuclear weapons.
18. Discuss the impact of the INF Treaty on nuclear weapons policy.
19. How would nonoffensive defense affect our present nuclear weapons policy?

KEY WORDS

Counterforce   a targeting policy for nuclear weapons which confine attacks to military targets.

MAD   mutually assured destruction. The doctrine of minimal deterrence in which each side can cause unacceptable damage to the other in a retaliatory nuclear strike.

MIRV   multiple independently targetable reentry vehicles. MIRVing permits individual warheads contained on a single rocket to be targeted independently.

SDI   strategic defense initiative, also called "star wars" by some critics. Originally proposed as a missile defense to shield the U.S. population from nuclear attack.

SIOP   single integrated operational plan: a coordinated plan for the nuclear forces involving strategic defense.

tactical nuclear weapons   nuclear weapons of relatively "small" yield in the kiloton range to be used on the battlefield or at sea.

CHAPTER
5

COMMAND, CONTROL, COMMUNICATION, AND INTELLIGENCE: C-CUBE-I

The era of armaments has ended and the human race must conform its actions to this truth or die.

President Dwight D. Eisenhower, 1956

5-1 THEMES

All nuclear weapons systems consist of three relatively distinct components, all of which must function reliably if the system is to be effective. These are (1) the warheads, the nuclear weapons themselves; (2) the weapons platforms, the systems designed to deliver the warheads to an intended target; and (3) the control and communications systems which provide instructions on where the weapons platforms are to deliver their munitions. The general name for the systems that accomplish the last of these tasks is *command, control, communications,* and *intelligence,* or **C-cube-I** (C^3I).

There is conflict inherent in these control systems. On the one hand, they must be capable of providing the means for launching nuclear weaponry when this is desired. On the other, they must be extremely resistant to accidents which might lead to inadvertent launch.

The complexity of C-cube-I systems and the vulnerability of major elements makes these systems among the most critical parts of nuclear arsenals. C-cube-I systems are increasingly becoming the most critical part of our nuclear arsenals, and the parts most likely to lead to catastrophic error. Consequently, it is essential that much more attention—and money—be devoted to these systems in the future than in the past.

5-2   SURVEY OF C-CUBE-I

C-cube-I systems cover a vast range of capabilities, which are best discussed by breaking them down into subcategories:

Command systems convey specific instructions on how weapons and weapons systems are to be deployed and what strategies and tactics are to be carried out. An example of a command would be the process by which an instruction by the President to place the Pacific Fleet at a particular stage of alert is relayed through the military hierarchy to the fleet commander and finally to each local ship commander.

Control systems assure that devices respond in accordance with commands. They include such things as the mechanical controls that couple a pilot's wheel on a ship to the rudder and the control stick on an airplane to the ailerons and other control surfaces. They also include the control systems that make it impossible to launch a missile without explicit approval from high levels, as well as such technical controls over nuclear weapons as the *permissive action links* (PALs) which have existed for European missiles for several decades and which are a key element of the weapons security program. PALs are locking devices that prevent missiles from being armed without specific instructions from higher command authority. The details are secret, but it is presumed that they can operate using either code words or numbers which act like codes for combination locks or using coded electrical signals that activate directly a locking device on a weapon.

Communications systems are normal channels for communicating information. They include voice and video channels using radio waves, as well as digital channels that may transmit intelligence for display on readout panels. The same channels used for general communications can be used for carrying command and control information.

Intelligence is information used as input to tactical and strategic decisions. Intelligence includes slowly gathered information obtained by spies, by analysis of enemy publications, etc. It also includes information gathered rapidly by, for example, outer-space sensors designed to detect nuclear explosions or rocket launches. Intelligence information is transmitted over communications channels.

The term *C-cube-I* is generally applied to military systems only, though occasionally it is used in reference to such civilian systems as civil defense and natural disaster response. Military C-cube-I capability must function throughout every military-related activity—in peacetime, during periods of tension, and in war. It must be reliable in the face of explicit enemy attempts at interference, and under the disruptive conditions of battle. The types of activities which C-cube-I comprises include the provision of:

Intelligence about enemy plans for weaponry, such as R & D programs and weapons testing

Intelligence about enemy weapons production and deployment

Information on the location and state of readiness of friendly and enemy troops and logistical support systems

Instructions to all elements of the military system regarding how to deploy weapons and what state of readiness to be in

Battlefield instructions, before, during, and after engagements

Damage assessment both to personnel and to equipment

Instructions regarding postaction recovery

C-cube-I systems contain an inherent internal contradiction. The problem is analogous to a trigger on a pistol. If the trigger is too tight, the gun is hard to fire. If it is too loose (a hair trigger), there is a risk that the gun will go off inadvertently, for instance, as it is being pulled from its holster. Nuclear weapons system control has the same problem. The weapons must be maintained under tight control so that they cannot be launched by accident or stolen by terrorists. This is called **negative control**. However, command authorities must be able to release the weapons systems when this is desired (**positive control**).

In peacetime there is heavy emphasis on negative control. If tensions increase, the military system shifts increasingly in the direction of positive control. In the United States one way in which this is accomplished is through a series of DEFCON (defense condition) levels. In peacetime the military is normally in DEFCON 5, the lowest state of readiness (the Strategic Air Command is an exception—its normal condition is DEFCON 4). As tensions increase, the military moves to lower DEFCON levels, ultimately reaching a state of highest readiness, known as DEFCON 1, or "cocked pistol." While details of the various DEFCON levels are obviously and necessarily highly classified, some indication of what is involved is found in the movie *War Games,* which also included some extremely realistic sequences accurately portraying the NORAD battle headquarters deep inside Cheyenne Mountain, Colorado.

As higher states of readiness are reached, control of nuclear weapons is probably shifted from central command to field officers. This is particularly important for nuclear weapons in Europe, which are stockpiled in central warehouses. To be used in time of attack, these weapons must be moved to the field.

A serious but intrinsic problem with high-readiness states is that authority becomes more diffused, which means there are more individuals in positions to mistakenly approve of a launch. These concerns have lead some analysts to believe that there is today far greater risk of accident through failure of C-cube-I systems than through failure of the warheads or the delivery systems. If military officers believe that there is serious risk that their control capabilities may be destroyed in a preemptive attack, this is likely to give them a bit more "trigger itch" and increase the chance of too-early launch. It is sometimes asserted that Soviet command structures may maintain closer control over the nuclear weapons command chain than do United States structures.

Awareness of this kind of problem has led in recent years to major investments in improving the reliability of C-Cube-I systems. Among the many ways in which this is accomplished is through use of **fiber optic** communication links, multiple satellites and spare satellites, and high levels of system redundancy.

5-3 THE STRUCTURE OF C-CUBE-I SYSTEMS

C-cube-I systems are not new; they have always been an essential part of every effective military system. However, technical advances have placed new requirements on such systems and at the same time have made possible functions that were undreamed of only a few years ago. Anyone who watches the news knows of the black bag (informally called the ''football'') which accompanies the President wherever he goes and which contains the secret codes which are used to authorize use of nuclear weapons. NORAD headquarters, in a mountain in Colorado, contains linkages to every aspect of the military system. The large-screen displays used in NORAD headquarters have become familiar through movies such as *War Games*.

The C-Cube-I structure has at its center the National Military Command Authority, which consists of the President and the Secretary of Defense supported by the joint chiefs of staff. The primary National Military Command Center is in Washington, D.C.; secondary centers are located aboard special aircraft and in hardened sites such as NORAD. Communications links use many different technologies, such as telephone lines, fiber-optic links, and microwaves that are relayed through land-based and satellite stations. Encryption techniques are included, with a variety of levels of security available. Digital as well as voice data are handled.

An important C-cube-I component is the Minimum Essential Emergency Communication Network (MEECN), which is intended to coordinate nuclear forces in time of attack. MEECN systems cover the entire electromagnetic spectrum from the extra low frequency (**ELF**) systems used for communicating with submerged nuclear submarines through super high frequency satellite communications systems.

Satellite Communications

The capabilities of some of the modern communications systems are remarkable. The **NAVSTAR** system includes 24 satellites in 12-hour orbits over every part of the world. The satellites are inclined at 63 degrees to the earth's axis at a height of 18,668 kilometers above the earth's surface. They transmit short-wavelength (L-band) timing signals which can be received by devices small enough to be carried by a foot soldier yet precise enough to specify location to within ± 10 meters (in three dimensions) and speed to within ± 0.1 meters per second at any point on the surface of the earth. This capability means that a battlefield commander can have a field readout device that will specify precisely the position of personnel and equipment. Compare this with the situation in Napoleon's time, when information on troop location had to be delivered by horse, which not infrequently took days.

One difficulty with modern communication is that commanders may be deluged with so much information from such a variety of sources that sifting out the essential information in a timely manner can be a formidable task.

Inertial navigation guidance systems are essential to many weapons delivery systems. An example of this technology is a new system designed for use on B-52 bombers: the Standard Precision Navigator/Gimballed Electrostatic Aircraft Navigation System. It uses an electrostatically suspended gyroscope with a rotor made of beryllium metal spinning at 700 revolutions per second. The support system is so friction-free that the decay time constant (time for the system to slow down) is 5 to 10 years. The navigation system is accurate to ± 0.16 kilometers per hour, or 4 centimeters per second (*IEEE Spectrum,* January 1982). The NAVSTAR or other external reference system is used for confirmation.

Missiles launched from submarines have traditionally been less accurate than land-based missiles because of uncertainties in the location and speed of the missile as it leaves the launch vehicle. However, NAVSTAR permits correction of on-board information once the missile is in flight. Optical systems coupled with on-board computers also permit precise navigation by sighting on stars.

In recent years synthetic-aperture optical and radar systems have been developed that permit large antennas to be electrically focused at high speed. This capability is essential if a system is to track large numbers of missiles simultaneously. Systems capable of keeping track of hundreds of objects simultaneously have been built.

5-4 THREATS TO C-CUBE-I SYSTEMS

Electromagnetic Pulse (see Chapter 17)

A critical element in any system designed to operate in a nuclear-war environment is its ability to continue to function in highly adverse situations involving blast, radiation, and electromagnetic pulse (EMP). Early transistors were extremely vulnerable to radiation and to EMP. Amorphous systems now being developed are hardened to radiation and are far less vulnerable to EMP. Whether these systems will work under actual nuclear battlefield conditions is, of course, unknown and unknowable, though simulations of many aspects are routine.

Antisatellite Weapons (ASAT)

In peacetime satellites are useful to both superpowers in providing information about the other's military forces and operations. This promotes stability because it decreases surprises. Satellites are invaluable in providing verification of arms control treaties. They are thus essential to confidence-building measures and for defusing a crisis situation.

Satellites are, however, particularly vulnerable to EMP, especially system-generated EMP (SGEMP) due to nuclear explosions above the atmosphere (see Chapter 17). Because of this, a major theme of current R & D is the protection of satellites. Satellites can also be attacked by using a co-orbital interceptor which explodes in a swarm of pellets when it is sufficiently close to its target or by using a high-altitude rocket, launched from high-flying aircraft, which makes a direct impact.

According to Garwin et al. (1984):

> The parts of the C-cube-I system essential to the strategic forces of each side are largely immune to ASAT attack for this time being . . . this is [because] all ASAT weapons currently deployed or undergoing field tests have a maximum altitude of several thousand kilometers or less. Hence they could attack satellites only in low orbits or highly elliptical ones. Since early-warning, navigation, attack-assessment and communications satellites essential to the U.S. strategic forces are all in very high orbits, they are not at risk in the near term. The U.S.S.R. faces a somewhat greater potential threat, since some of its essential communication satellites and all its early-warning satellites are currently in highly elliptic Molniya orbits.

However, the same authors are of the opinion that "the ability to destroy low-orbit satellites promptly could inflame a political crisis or a minor conflict that might otherwise have been resolved by diplomacy had there been no ASAT weapons." They argue that a treaty banning ASAT weapons would be advantageous to both superpowers and that in the absence of such a treaty "there would be a serious risk that an unrestrained competition in space weapons could spawn grave crises and even armed conflict."

5-5 COMMUNICATION DURING A CRISIS OR CONFLICT

Communication with Submarines

Because of the high electrical conductivity of salt water, electromagnetic signals (radiowaves) do not easily penetrate the ocean. Thus deeply submerged submarines cannot maintain direct contact with land stations. Two approaches can be used to address this problem. Submarines can travel close to the surface, where they can pick up long-wave radio broadcasts, or they can trail a long wire or float a buoy close to the surface which can detect higher-frequency broadcasts. An extremely low frequency facility (ELF) has been built in the northern United States to enhance communication with submarines.

Because of the isolation of nuclear submarines permissive action links (PALs) are not feasible. That is, submarine crews have the technical capability to use their weapons independently of any external authority, though to accomplish this requires the collaboration of several crew members. Because of the procedural requirement that several officers must agree before missile launch can occur, the crew can in this instance override the submarine commander. Submarines are thus the only place in the military where mutiny is officially sanctioned.

Nuclear submarines have the capability to remain hidden for long periods of time (months). They are not vulnerable to destruction in a first-strike attack. Thus the communication needs are quite different from those for a land-based missile system, which must be capable of launch within a few minutes of warning of an impending attack.

One approach to the problem of adequate submarine communication is the development of a satellite employing blue-green laser light. Blue-green light penetrates seawater better than other colors do, and therefore offers the possibility of communication without the need for the submarine to surface completely. Modulation of this light beam would be used to transmit information.

Air Force Communications

The U.S. Air Force is establishing an elaborate communications network called the Air Force Satellite Communications Network, or AFSATCOM. This is designed to operate during an extended nuclear war to provide information in a continuous loop of information and action ("strategic connectivity" in Pentagon jargon). Its purpose is to provide communications both during and after attack to aid in organizing surviving forces (Karas, 1983).

The air-breathing leg of the strategic triad—currently B-52 bombers—is set up so that a large portion of the planes can become airborne within a few minutes of a warning signal. This means they can be in the air before short-range submarine-launched missiles can destroy them on the ground. However, if the planes are to proceed to target, there must be a reliable means of communicating this information to them. There should also be a reliable means for calling them back should such a decision be made. A communications system that failed to permit one bomber to be called back was used in Stanley Kubrick's 1963 film *Dr. Strangelove, or How I Learned to Stop Worrying and Love the Bomb*. The results in that case were disastrous.

ICBM Systems

ICBM systems are currently designed so that they cannot be called back or interfered with once launched. This has the advantage of preventing an enemy from defeating the missiles by learning how to operate the system. It also prevents any possibility of recovery from an erroneous launch. It has been proposed at various times that missile control systems be arranged so that missiles are (1) launched on a LOW system; (2) launched under actual attack (i.e., after some damage has been sustained); (3) armed in flight using a secure and highly redundant radio linkage; and (4) disarmed in flight using a secure and highly redundant radio linkage. The last two approaches provide flexibility because missiles could be launched before being absolutely sure that an attack had begun, since there would be an opportunity to recover. Each of these control systems has many political and technical risks associated with it.

Communication During Nuclear War

The extremely chaotic environment that would result after any nuclear explosion—including even a "small" field weapon of the type deployed in Europe—makes it difficult to predict how the C-cube-I system would respond. This leads to the question of whether it is technically possible to design a C-cube-I system that would provide enough redundancy to operate under nuclear war conditions. If C-cube-I did not operate effectively, decisions might well revert to the local commander level, at which point it is hard to see how escalation could be avoided. It is this kind of consideration that has led many analysts to be dubious about the possibility of limiting any nuclear war. This concern applies to use of battlefield weapons as well as to any attempt at a "surgical strike" on military targets with strategic weapons.

5-6 HOT-LINE SYSTEMS

The hot line between the United States and the Soviet Union was installed after the Cuban missile crisis so as to minimize risks of confusion due to lack of information. Such a system might play a critical role if an unanticipated nuclear explosion were to occur in the United States, the Soviet Union, or Europe. Such an explosion might be the result of an accident or of sabotage by one of the developing nations or a terrorist group, or might be part of a real attack by one of the nuclear powers. Whatever the origin of any such explosion, a reliable communications system will be a critical element in preventing escalation.

Hot-line systems might also be essential in bringing any nuclear war to a halt. It is difficult to imagine how such a communications system could be made reliable, since there are both technical problems (how to maintain it in a nuclear attack environment) and command problems (knowing who has authority if the national capitals have been destroyed) involved in its use. The attempt, however, should be made. The existing hot line is potentially useful, but work needs to be done on making it more responsive to fast-changing crisis situations. In 1984 the Nuclear Negotiation Project of the Harvard Law School proposed a broadened scheme for crisis control between the Soviet Union and the United States. Both Moscow and Washington would have terminals of an augmented communications network which would be jointly staffed by United States and Soviet military personnel. Working together on a daily basis, staff at these crisis control centers would, it is surmised, develop mutual confidence and understanding which could prove critical in an emergency. This could be extremely important in a time of crisis when one considers the short delivery time of strategic nuclear weapons and the rapidity of communications within each nation (Ury and Smoke, 1984).

5-7 STRATEGIC SYSTEM STABILITY INCLUDING C-CUBE-I

The C-cube-I characteristics of different weapons systems differ. The difference in the control of submarines and of aircraft was discussed in Section 5-5. One's assessment of the reliability of control systems for the different weapons systems can strongly influence one's view of which weapons systems are the most stabilizing or most destabilizing. This is an area where the views of the Soviet military and of the U.S. military appear to differ considerably.

The United States is comfortable with the control of SLBM carrying submarines and considers these systems among the most stabilizing parts of the strategic arsenal. The Soviet Union appears to be far more doubtful about the submarines, and considers land-based missiles (especially the modern mobile land-based missiles such as the SS-24 and SS-25) to be more stabilizing than submarines (IMEMO, 1988).

The United States and the Soviet Union also may have differing views about cruise missiles. In the United States it is often argued that since cruise missiles have a long flight time, there is warning of attack. Therefore, cruise missiles are relatively stabilizing. A counter view is that cruise missiles can be built with "**stealth**" technology so as to be difficult to detect. (Stealth techniques include designs which are very difficult to detect using radar or using heat signatures.) Cruise missiles might be launched from offshore submarines. They could fly low and deliver an attack on many different military systems almost simultaneously with very little warning.

Both the United States and the Soviet Union would be vulnerable to such cruise missiles. However, the United States has much more accessible coastline than does the Soviet Union and also has major cities on the coasts. The United States would therefore be much more vulnerable to offshore attack by cruise missiles than the Soviet Union.

These considerations make it useful to find ways to examine the stabilizing characteristics of various weapons systems, taking account of both delivery system and C-cube-I characteristics. One simple but useful way to accomplish this has been proposed by Soviet analysts (IMEMO, 1988). Tables 5-1 and 5-2 show the approach. The approach assumes that each weapons system can be characterized by a number of parameters, which can be ranked on a scale from 1 to 6. The individual ratings are then multiplied together to obtain an overall index. The idea that a useful index can be generated by a technique so simple as multiplication is subject to considerable question.

Despite the shortcomings of this multiplicative approach, it does have the great virtue that its simplicity allows it to be easily understood and makes it easy to carry on a discussion of major issues involving the stabilizing and destabilizing characteristics of weapons systems combined with their command and control systems.

Table 5-1 examines characteristics of key weapons systems in each leg of strategic triads. The table takes note of some major systems differences. Thus land-based ICBMs are considered in terms of single warhead, multiple warhead, stationary, and mobile. Each major system is evaluated in terms of a number of key technical parameters, such as hard target kill capability and recallability. The individual rankings are assigned subjectively. You should examine the table closely and assign your own. A final tally is made by multiplying the individual rankings. This final ranking is then scaled such that the most stabilizing weapon system (the one with the lowest product) is normalized to unity.

Table 5-2 uses the results of Table 5-1 as a starting point. It introduces several parameters which are specific to the command and control systems. A grand ranking is obtained by multiplying all the numbers together, and again scaling to unity for the system with the lowest number. Inspection of the tables shows that there is a change in ranking when command and control systems are included. In particular, the SLBM systems are found to be less stabilizing, and cruise missiles are found to be more stabilizing.

TABLE 5-1
Relative destabilizing effect of strategic systems by U.S. standards*

Weapons systems	Hard target kill probability	Vulnerability	Flight time	Destabilizing effect	Relative destabiliz- ing effect
ICBMs					
Fixed:					
MRVed	6	4	4	96	9.6
Single-warhead	3	4	4	48	4.8
New type single-warhead	4	4	4	64	6.4
Mobile:					
MRVed	5	3	4	60	6.0
Single-warhead	3	2	4	24	2.4
SLBMs					
Single-warhead	1	2	5	10	1.0
MRVed	3	1	5	15	1.5
MRVed new type	5	1	5	25	2.5
Heavy bombers:					
With gravity bombs	4	4	1	16	1.6
With ALCMs	5	3	1	15	1.5
Stealth type	5	3	1	15	1.5
Cruise missiles:					
SLCMs	5	2	2	20	2.0
GLCMs	5	3	2	30	3.0

Table 5-1. A simple means of assessing the stabilizing characteristics of major weapons systems. Systems are rated on a scale of 1 to 6 using the criteria shown in the columns. The final score is the product of the individual ratings, normalized to unity for the most stabilizing system. *Source:* IMEMO, 1988.
*All the estimates have been made with due account of the point of view of some leading U.S. experts: Andrew Goldberg, Albert Carnesale, George William Rathjens, and John D. Steinbruner.

To assess the destabilizing effect of a given weapon system we established a six-point scale where 1 is "very low effect," 2 "low," 3 "sufficiently low," 4 "questionable," 5 "high," 6 "very high." The points were established on the basis of expert assessments in accordance with each index and a corresponding weapon system. The lowest point was given: for the hard-target kill probability (HTKP)—if a system cannot destroy hardened targets: for the vulnerability—if a system is highly survivable (for aircraft account was taken of the vulnerability on airfields and in flight, which is affected not only by the capability for takeoff of aircraft on alert but also by the capability to penetrate air defense viewed as a destabilizing factor); for the flight time—for "slow flying" systems. The destabilizing effect of a given system was calculated as a product of three main indices: HTKP, vulnerability and flight time with the account taken of the mutually strengthening effect of destabilizing characteristics (i.e., the general stability is a product rather than a sum of the indices). Thus, we view a system with the highest aggregate index as the most destabilizing one.

The relative destabilizing effect shows to what extent a given weapon system negatively affects strategic stability in comparison with a system with the lowest index of the destabilizing effect calculated according to the following formula:

$$D = \frac{H \times V \times F}{d_{min}}$$

where H is HTKP; V is vulnerability; F is flight time; and d_{min} is the minimum index of destabilizing effect in the suggested list of weapon systems (in this case they are single-warhead SLBMs having 10 conventional points, i.e., $d_{min} = 10$).

TABLE 5-2
Comparative destabilizing effect of strategic systems with account taken of C³I*

Weapon system	Destabilizing effect by U.S. standards	Reliability of two-way communications[a]	Provocative effect of combat alert[b]	Probability of engagement in conventional conflict[c]	Threat to key C^3I[d] elements	Attack warning time[e]	Destabilizing effect[f]	Relative destabilizing effect[g]
ICBMs								
Fixed:								
MRVed	96	1	2	1	5	3	2,880	5.0
Single-warhead	48	1	1	1	4	3	576	1.0
New type single-warhead	64	1	1	2	4	3	1,536	2.7
Mobile:								
MRVed	60	2	3	1	5	3	5,400	9.4
Single-warhead	24	2	2	1	4	3	1,152	2.0
SLBMs								
Single-warhead	10	6	3	5	4	5	18,000	31.3
MRVed	15	5	4	4	5	5	30,000	52.1
MRVed new type	25	5	4	4	5	5	50,000	86.8
Heavy bombers:								
With gravity bombs and SRAMs	16	3	4	4	1	1	768	1.3
With ALCMs	15	3	4	4	3	3	6,480	11.3
Stealth type	15	3	5	4	4	4	14,400	25.0
Cruise missiles:								
SLCMs	12	6	4	5	5	5	60,000	104.2
GLCMs	20	2	3	4	4	4	28,800	50.0

Table 5-2. The first column is the results from Table 5-1. Other columns take into account command and control attributes of the weapons systems. The final tally is obtained by multiplying the individual ratings, and normalizing to unity for the most stabilizing system. The rankings shown represent a Soviet view of the world. Your own views will undoubtedly differ. *Source:* IMEMO.

*All the estimates have been made with due account of the point of view of some leading U.S. experts: Andrew Goldberg, Albert Carnesale, George William Rathjens, and John D. Steinbruner.

Weapons characteristics which could have a stabilizing or destabilizing effect in a crisis situation are as follows:

a. Reliability of two-way communications, which ensures compatibility of negative and positive control: ensuring the capability of weapons to deliver a retaliatory strike without the delegation of authority beforehand and the physical ability to use nuclear arms.

b. Provoking effect of placing strategic forces on high readiness (e.g., takeoff of strategic aircraft, which was already mentioned; ordering SSBNs to leave bases; deconcentration of mobile land-based missiles, etc.).

c. Probability of engagement in conventional conflict, first of all SSBNs, especially in the light of a new U.S. concept of sea operations which envisages active search for and destruction of SSBNs at the early stages of a conflict.

d. Threat of strategic nuclear forces to key C³I elements (radars, command posts, and communications centers).

e. Attack warning time: this index (contrary to a more narrow criterion of flight time) has a decisive influence upon all activities to prepare a retaliatory strike or launch-on-warning.

f. Destabilizing effect is calculated as a product of points given to various weapon systems as regards each specific characteristic, including the value of that effect by the U.S. standards (see Table 5-1).

g. Relative destabilizing effect is calculated similarly to that in Table 5-1.

Calculation formula:

$$D = \frac{D_{VS} \times R \times P \times C \times T \times W}{d_{min}}$$

where D_{VS} = destabilizing effect by the U.S. standards

R = reliability of two-way communications

P = provocative effect of combat alert

C = probability of engagement in conventional conflict

T = threat to key C³I elements

W = attack warning time

d_{min} = minimum value of destabilizing effect in the suggested list of weapon systems (in this case these are fixed single-warhead ICBMs of the existing types with 576 points, i.e., d_{min} = 576).

Source: IMEMO.

As noted, this ranking system is simplistic, and the values in the table represent a Soviet view of the world. The approach does not take into account synergistic effects between different weapons systems. It also fails to include the implications of different numbers of weapons and weapons systems in the different legs of the triads. It does offer a simple way of looking at a complex set of issues, and it could readily be modified to respond to these and other concerns.

Despite the simplicity of the approach shown here, it does make the important point that the warheads and delivery systems should not be considered outside of the context of the characteristics and capabilities of their command and control systems. It appears likely that the next years of change in nuclear weaponry will make the command and control systems even more important than today. Because of the high reliability and relative invulnerability of delivery systems, it appears to us likely that in the next few years command and control systems will be the most critical components in terms of assuring that nuclear weapons are not released by accident.

QUESTIONS

1. List some of the considerations you would want to take into account if you were responsible for devising a C-cube-I system that would operate in the aftermath of an unanticipated nuclear attack on Washington, D.C.
2. What are some of the elements that should go into a C-cube-I system designed to prevent unintended escalation following use of a few battlefield nuclear weapons in Europe?
3. What kind of instructions might you give to a commander of a nuclear submarine regarding decision making during a nuclear attack if communications with the Pentagon were severed?
4. What are some of the advantages and problems of a missile control system that relies on some means for arming or disarming the missiles once they have been launched?
5. Should the United States attempt to design a weapons system specifically in order to destroy Soviet C-cube-I systems? Under what circumstances might we wish to ensure that certain elements of a Soviet C-cube-I system remained intact?
6. Discuss the use of satellites for military communications.

KEY WORDS

ASAT antisatellite system. An antisatellite system is one capable of damaging or destroying a satellite.

C-cube-I command, control, communication, and intelligence. Sometimes written C^3I.

ELF extra low frequency communications channels. ELF signals propagate better through sea (salt) water than do high frequencies, and so are useful for communicating with submarines.

fiber optics transmission of communications signals through small glass fibers. Fiber optics provides the ability to move very large amounts of information (high band width) and high security against electromagnetic pulse. Like all physical linkages, the fibers are vulnerable to blast.

NAVSTAR   A precise global positioning system making use of satellites.

negative control   a system to assure that weapons will not be launched unless an order to launch is given. Compare positive control. Provides safety against "trigger itch."

positive control   a system to assure that weapons can be launched when the order to launch is given. Compare negative control.

stealth technology   aircraft, cruise missiles, etc., designed so as to be very difficult to detect from their radar, thermal, or other signatures. Stealth systems can sneak into enemy territory with low risk of detection. Even if detected, they are hard to track.

CHAPTER
6

CONVENTIONAL
WEAPONS

As far as sinking a ship with a bomb is concerned, you just can't do it.

Rear-Admiral Clark Woodward, 1939

6-1 THEMES

Advances in nonnuclear military technology are interacting strongly with the evolution of the nuclear arms race. In many circumstances policy objectives can be achieved more effectively with conventional weapons than with the threat of nuclear weapons. This is clearly the case in third world conflicts, such as in Central America, Grenada, or Afghanistan, where nuclear weapons have no role whatsoever. A nonnuclear defense of Western Europe may also be possible, and perhaps highly desirable. At some time in the future, if nuclear arsenals are dramatically reduced, nonnuclear strategic defense may be achievable (see Chapter 20).

6-2 MILITARY OBJECTIVES

The role of the military is to accomplish national policy objectives that cannot be achieved using purely political methods. Military techniques fall into five broad categories: (1) having the will and ability to use military power; (2) being able to destroy specific pieces of military hardware such as aircraft, ships, gun and missile installations, etc.; (3) being able to incapacitate personnel so that they cannot operate military weaponry; (4) being able to destroy the effectiveness of C-cube-I systems, which largely determine the success of military actions; and (5) being able to interfere with support systems, without which the fighting elements of a military system cannot function.

120

To destroy large regions, nuclear weapons have no equal. However, if one believes that nuclear weapons cannot be used for war fighting because of the risks of escalation, then their use is limited to intimidation. This has been the case in recent decades. Nuclear bombs have not been used in warfare since 1945, yet there have been large numbers of armed conflicts: the Korean war, the war in Vietnam, the Soviet invasion of Afghanistan, the conflicts in the Falklands, Nicaragua, and Grenada, and the complex of wars in the Middle East are examples. And there is no end in sight.

Many of the wars fought in recent decades have involved guerrilla action in which relatively informal armies have operated throughout a large territory, attacking more organized troops at times and places of the guerrillas' choosing. When the guerrillas are defending their home territory, they try to obtain support from the local populace. This makes it difficult or impossible to distinguish troops from civilians, which virtually assures that there will be attacks on civilians—as happened in Vietnam and Afghanistan—and as is now happening in Central America. In this kind of situation, large concentrations of firepower may be incapable of achieving military ends. The destructiveness of modern weaponry, central to thinking about nuclear war, is increasingly relevant to nonnuclear war as well. Military and political planning need to recognize the limits of military power.

6-3   THE EAST-WEST STANDOFF

We are living in a new era in human experience—one in which the prospect of nuclear war has an effect on every international decision made by a nuclear power—and on decisions made by many nonnuclear powers as well. One unprecedented result is the reluctance of the United States and the Soviet Union to place themselves in situations in which their troops may come into direct conflict. The risk that such a conflict could escalate into nuclear confrontation has been too great to permit it to occur, except under extreme provocation. Instead, there has been a gradual evolution of lines of demarcation. Much of the world is divided into areas which are clearly under the control either of the west (Western Europe, North America) or of the Soviet bloc (Eastern Europe). Thus the United States has been supportive of anti-Soviet revolt in Hungary and Poland and complained bitterly about Soviet policy in Afghanistan, but has not physically intervened in any way. Similarly, the Soviet Union attempts to foment revolution in South America, but has refrained from sending Soviet troops. When the United States was mired in Vietnam, the Soviets provided massive military aid, but studiously avoided placing Soviet troops in any situation in which they might directly confront United States troops.

The last direct military confrontation between the United States and the Soviet Union was the missile crisis in Cuba in 1962 (see Chapter 2). The stress of that event was so great that both nations have since acted relatively conservatively, attempting to keep out of each other's territory.

In avoiding direct confrontation, both the United States and the Soviet Union have relied on ''proxy'' nations or organizations to advance their interests. Among the many examples of this are the Soviet support for revolutionary armies in Africa and South America, and United States support for authoritarian governments in Central America and Africa. In the Middle East, one of the most sensitive "powder keg" areas of the world, both the United States and the Soviet Union provide massive military support to various armies—but both have been sensitive to the risk of direct involvement of their own troops.

6-4 NONNUCLEAR FORCES

The only kind of war that a nation can realistically imagine fighting in a nuclear era is nonnuclear. Therefore, nuclear powers must be prepared to fight a wide variety of nonnuclear wars. The United States has over 2 million soldiers, sailors, and marines and two-thirds of a million reservists capable of providing military support anywhere in the world. Because of Europe's strategic importance, the largest single concentration of U.S. troops overseas is there. About one-half million troops (plus dependents) are stationed overseas (Table 6-1).

The total number of NATO troops in central Europe is about 1.9 million: this includes 900,000 in the Federal Republic of Germany, 360,000 in the United Kingdom, 220,000 in the Netherlands, 112,000 in Belgium, 123,000 in Denmark, 3000 in Canada, and 600 in Luxembourg. France, which is not part of NATO, has 600,000 troops. Warsaw Pact troops are comparable in number to those of NATO and France, although there are significant differences and the details of the balancing are controversial.

The balance of weaponry is complex, and there is much controversy over whether or not the WTO could mount a successful attack on NATO. Tables 6-1 through 6-3 present illustrative data comparing the various forces. Table 6-2 shows comparisons of numbers of key pieces of military hardware. The WTO is ahead in many areas. However, these ratios don't tell the full story. First, nuclear weapons are

TABLE 6-1
Comparison of forces of the WTO, NATO, and China

	Warsaw Pact	NATO	China
Troops*	5 million	5.5 million	3.2 million
Main battle tanks	68,700	31,200	12,050
Antitank missiles	Unavailable	400,000	Unavailable
Other armored vehicles	77,400	65,300	2,800
Helicopters	6,000	14,200	500
Combat aircraft	11,400	12,900	6,200
Diesel attack submarines	147	124	114
Nuclear attack submarines	131	115	3
Major surface warships	306	537	53

*Excludes all reserves and paramilitary troops; 1.5 million Soviet construction, command, and support troops; and 2 million civilian employees in NATO nations.
Source: Center for Defense Information.

TABLE 6-2
Examples of the numbers of key military equipment in the WTO and NATO, and their ratios

	Warsaw Pact	NATO	Pact-to-NATO ratio
Main battle tanks	53,100	28,200	1.88:1
Antitank guided weapons launchers	30,800	24,600	1.25:1
Artillery	44,000	22,200	1.98:1
Other armored vehicles	60,000	39,800	1.51:1
Attack helicopters	1,250	1,480	0.84:1
Combat aircraft	7,120	6,100	1.17:1

NATO: Belgium, Canada, Denmark, France, FRG, Greece, Iceland, Italy, Luxembourg, Netherlands, Norway, Portugal, Spain, Turkey, U.K., U.S.

Warsaw Pact: Bulgaria, Czechoslovakia, GDR, Hungary, Poland, Romania, U.S.S.R.

In many key areas the WTO is numerically ahead. This superiority does not mean that NATO is necessarily inadequately defended.

Source: Center for Defense Information.

in the background, and if brought into play would change any battle in large and poorly understood ways. Second, even in a conventional attack it is generally held that the offense must have a substantial local margin of superiority over the defense to invade successfully.*

The United States has a fleet of more than 6000 tactical and combat aircraft, which is supplemented by about 3500 non-United States NATO aircraft and about 1200 aircraft belonging to Pacific allies. Aircraft and gunship helicopters are capable of quickly delivering enormous firepower, but they are growing increasingly vulnerable to ground-based missiles. The reliability of air systems for difficult missions was brought into question by their poor effectiveness against guerrilla troops in the Vietnam war and by the failure of the U.S. mission to rescue the hostages held in the U.S. embassy in Teheran. In contrast, the Israeli air force has demonstrated its ability to destroy targets with precision and with limited loss—for example, the Iraqi Osiraq nuclear reactor (a potential source of fuel for nuclear weapons) and Syrian and Palestinian missiles sites.

The U.S. Navy is the largest in the world in terms of number of personnel and tonnage. It is supported by the navies of other NATO and ANZUS (Australia, New Zealand, and the United States—the Pacific analogue of NATO) nations. The United

*The idea of local margin of superiority captures the concept that an attacker will concentrate firepower at the points where he intends to break through. In Europe this might be at six or eight concentration points each of 5 or 10 kilometers width, at various points along the 800-kilometer border between the WTO and NATO.

TABLE 6-3
Distribution of U.S. military personnel around the world, as of 1984

	Personnel, Thousands
U.S. territory	1639
Germany	251
Other Europe	82
South Korea	40
Japan and Ryukyus	46
Other Pacific	17
Pacific, afloat	19
Miscellaneous	49
Total	2143

Source: U.S. Department of Defense.

States has numerous bases around the world to provide support facilities. The Soviet navy, in contrast, must cope with the annual freezing of three of its five major bases and with the prospect of having their fleet bottled up in narrow seas and channels: the Dardanelles, Skagerrak, Gibraltar, and the Sea of Japan. Table 6-4 gives a comparison of U.S. and Soviet navies as of 1984.

Superpower navies have two distinct roles. Nuclear-missile-carrying submarines are a part of strategic defense, while surface ships and other submarines can be used in a conventional way. Meanwhile, the role of large surface ships in modern warfare is highly debatable. As the accuracy and firepower of guided munitions increase, the ability of large ships—particularly aircraft carriers—to survive attack is being called into question. Cheap "smart" missiles can be fired in large numbers, and may be able to overwhelm even the most elaborate defenses.

The British experience in the Falkland Islands conflict was particularly disturbing. A British frigate was sunk by a single Exocet missile, fired from a French Super Etendard aircraft. In this case, the heat-seeking missile was able to approach and destroy the frigate without being detected by its radar. Some reports maintain that the frigate's electronic system was not in correct operational condition so that the sinking might have been avoided. The power of nonnuclear offensive weapons was clearly demonstrated, however.

Some naval officers have used the Falklands Islands experience to justify additional large ships capable of bringing heavy firepower to remote regions of the world relatively quickly. The debate over the advantages of expensive, heavily defended weapons platforms (ships, tanks) as contrasted with small, relatively cheap, highly maneuverable weapons will continue, probably until the next war occurs—which will provide some "ground truth." In our judgment advances in cheap munitions and guidance systems are coming so fast that the large systems are likely to prove ever less cost-effective.

TABLE 6-4
Comparison of Soviet and United States navies

Naval order of battle	U.S.	U.S.S.R.
Nuclear aircraft carriers	4	
Conventional aircraft carriers	9	
Helicopter and V/STOL carriers	12	5
Carrier-based aircraft	1,407	126
Battleships	2	
Guided missile cruisers	19	33
Gun-armed cruisers		9
Guided missile destroyers	37	46
Gun-armed destroyers	38	25
Guided missile frigates	40	32
Gun-armed frigates	59	163
Nuclear ballistic missile submarines*	35	66
Diesel ballistic missile submarines*		15
Nuclear attack submarines†	93	122
Diesel attack submarines†	4	173
Total tonnage	3,503,509	2,826,334
Naval personnel	553,329	467,000
Number of marines	199,500	14,500
Number of overseas bases	44 + 6 Marine	

*United States submarines carry over 5500 warheads; Soviet submarines carry approximately 2500.

†Including torpedo-armed cruise missile.

Source: Center for Defense Information, 1984.

6-5 NONNUCLEAR WEAPONS SYSTEMS

Modern technology is rapidly changing the characteristics of nonnuclear military systems. The changes are occurring in virtually every area, and so any attempt to categorize them will inevitably prove incomplete. The single most important technological developments in the transformation of nonnuclear weapons have been the transistor and its derivative, the integrated chip. Transistors and integrated chips have made it possible to incorporate a large amount of intelligence into individual weapons systems. Thus, aircraft using satellite or inertial navigation are able to largely fly themselves and find targets even in zero visibility conditions. No longer must soldiers or pilots track a target. They need identify it only once, and so instruct their weapons. After that, computers take over and lead the weapon to its target ("fire and forget"). Missiles equipped with heat-seeking sensors do not even need to be aimed; pointing them in the general direction of a target is all that is required.

Fiber-optics technology has permitted development of short-range munitions having ranges of about 10 kilometers which can be accurately guided by soldiers hidden in hardened bunkers. Fiber-optics fibers transmit detailed video information to the control point. These relatively cheap weapons may be especially effective against tanks, since they can strike from above. They are also promising against gunship helicopters.

Navigation

Cruise missiles, equipped with either conventional or nuclear warheads, achieve precision guidance with terrain-matching radar. A map of the territory over which the missile is to travel is built into an on-board computer's memory. The missile then uses a television camera or radar to observe the ground over which it is flying. This information is supplemented with inertial guidance.

The increased accuracy of navigation available with inertial systems and with satellites means that conventional weapons may achieve goals previously possible only with nuclear weapons. For example, the NAVSTAR ground positioning system is able to specify position in three dimensions to within 10 to 30 meters, at any point on the earth's surface. This kind of precision means that a cruise missile or other delivery system armed with advanced nonnuclear warheads could destroy a hardened target—perhaps even a land-based ICBM.

Tank Warfare

There have been enormous advances in the amount of destruction achievable with a given amount of high explosive. Shaped charges are widely used—for example, a light antitank weapon that can be carried by a couple of soldiers can launch a missile capable of piercing a number of inches of steel and destroying any tank from a considerable distance. These weapons, known as precision-guided munitions (PGMs), are guided to their targets by lasers or other tracking devices. Weapons of this sophistication are advantageous since progress is being made in armoring tanks with composite layers of material (e.g., the British Culham armor) that will stop all but a highly specialized projectile.

Warsaw Pact tanks deployed in Europe reportedly are being protected with a material (Permali) that contains light elements that absorb neutrons; this improves the ability of these tanks to function where neutron bombs (enhanced radiation weapons) are used. Permali has only 17 percent of the weight of normal armor for the same thickness. The low-density material not only absorbs neutrons but also destabilizes armor-penetrating shells and missiles, thus providing some additional protection against modern antitank weapons (Zimmerman, 1983).

An example of the power of modern light antitank weapons is the AL-300 Jupiter shoulder-launched rocket system.* A French-German consortium developed and is marketing this weapon—a single-shot disposable launching system fired much like a rifle. The entire system weighs 12 kilograms, and the rocket itself weighs only 3.5 kilograms. The rocket is launched at a velocity of 150 meters per second and maintains its speed with in-flight propulsion, so that it can hit a target at a range of 300 meters in 1.5 seconds. The 115-millimeter-diameter warhead is able to penetrate more than

---

Aviation Week and Space Technology, May 2, 1983.

80 centimeters of armor plate, which means it can turn the interior of a tank into an inferno. The device has negligible muzzle flash and makes no more noise than a pistol shot, so troops using it cannot be readily detected.

Antitank weapons can also be equipped with thermal or microwave sensors that can detect a tank column (Walker, 1981). The military community has long argued over whether tanks are becoming obsolete. While we tend to believe that they are, a compelling argument to the contrary is given by Luttwak (1987).

Sensors

Weapons can be made much more effective with the aid of sensors. Advanced infrared sensors have made it possible to see clearly even in total darkness. Television cameras can be used to monitor battlefields remotely, thereby separating the intelligence function from the attack weapons. The flash from a rifle or other weapon gives its location, after which it can be attacked. Sensors give no sign, and small weapons (such as antitank missiles) can be widely dispersed.

The Submunitions Revolution

Another change in recent years has been the "submunitions revolution" (Keegan, 1983). For example, innovations in design have made it possible to develop shells, rockets, and bombs that release destructive energy over extremely large areas. In the past, a blast effect might cover a radius of 50 yards. Modern bombs or rockets may contain miniaturized devices that vastly extend this danger zone. These can be composed of materials which react chemically with the steel of tank armor, burning their way through. Or they can be filled with *flechettes,* fin-stabilized needles that disperse in a dense lethal cloud which kill anyone in the vicinity. The scatter pattern of some of these devices can cover an area as large as 300 by 1000 meters, and a plane carrying eight such units can cover an area of almost 8 square kilometers. Further, many of the bomblets fail to detonate after hitting the ground, which makes the area hazardous to enter afterward.

A central debate is over whether changes of this type are shifting the advantage in nonnuclear war fighting to the defense. If so, this should be a stabilizing factor in international relations since it increases the cost of an attack.

Chemical Weapons

By treaty (1925 Geneva Protocol) chemical weapons may be stockpiled but not used except in response to attack. New varieties of chemical weapons are extremely lethal; microscopic amounts of them can incapacitate persons within moments. The International Institute for Strategic Studies has grouped chemical agents in military inventories into the following categories:

Irritants These include tear gas and sneezing agents. They are temporarily incapacitating but relatively harmless.

Incapacitating agents These cause disorientation, mental disturbance, and sleepiness. Recovery occurs without medical treatment.

Vomiting agents Vomiting agents are solids which, when heated, form aerosols. They cause severe headache, pain, nausea, and vomiting. Effects last for one-half hour to several hours.

Choking agents These cause pulmonary edemas.

Blood agents Blood agents are absorbed through the lungs and are extremely volatile. They disperse rapidly, permitting attackers to enter an area without protection.

Blister agents These attack protein enzymes and coenzymes, causing inflammation, blisters, and tissue destruction.

Nerve agents Nerve agents, which are highly toxic, are odorless and colorless. They react with the enzyme cholinesterase to permit acetylcholine to accumulate. This causes loss of nervous control. Agents include tabun, sarin, and soman. Lethal doses are of the order of a few milligrams and death can occur within about 15 minutes of exposure.

Weapons have recently been developed which overcome many of the risks of accident associated with stockpiling chemical weapons. These weapons, known as *binary weapons,* contain two chemicals, each of which is harmless by itself. A membrane in the shell which separates the two chemicals is ruptured after firing.

The United States maintains a large stockpile of chemical weapons. According to the Stockholm Institute for Peace Research (1982) the U.S. stockpile of "serviceable and ready-to-use poison-gas munitions amounts to some 70,000 tons." Mustard and nerve gases that are bulk-stored add another 200,000 tons. Most of the material is located in the United States, but there are at least two other depots—in the Federal Republic of Germany and on Johnston Island in the Pacific.

A factory for binary nerve-gas munitions is being constructed. The capacity is to be 20,000 rounds of 155-millimeter shells per month. Five-hundred-pound binary spraybombs ("Big-Eye" bombs) for aerial use would also be available at roughly the same time. Binary weapons are being prepared for use in a wide range of weapons platforms, including ground-launched cruise missiles (GLCMs).

The French are believed to have some hundreds of tons of chemical weapons stockpiled. There is virtually no information on Soviet chemical arsenals, though it is generally assumed that they exist. Estimates range from less than 30,000 tons to more than 700,000 tons, leading to a commonly quoted average of 350,000 tons. This figure has little or no reliability.

Iraq may have used chemical weapons in its war with Iran. Both sides used chlorine and mustard gas in World War I. Italy used chemical weapons on Ethiopian targets and Japan on Chinese targets in the 1930s.

Biological Weapons

The 1972 biological warfare convention signed by the United States, the Soviet Union, and most other powers precludes the use of biological weapons in war. This is an interesting example of a unilateral action by one superpower that produced an arms control agreement. President Richard M. Nixon first declared that the United States would not develop new biological weapons and would destroy all existing stockpiles. This declaration led to the treaty.

In the early 1980s the United States accused the Soviet Union of using toxins (by-products of certain biological processes) in Afghanistan and providing them to Cambodia. The Soviet Union denies this, and the matter is unresolved. The existence of the biological warfare treaty has served to make both the United States and the Soviet Union wary of officially using such weapons.

Chemical and biological weaponry is singularly difficult to control. The manufacturing facilities are cheap, and equipment can be readily purchased. Terrorism using chemical and biological techniques appears far easier than nuclear terrorism. The possibilities are laid out in disturbing detail by Livingstone and Douglas (1984).

6-6 SOME CAVEATS

It is indisputable that modern nonnuclear military systems have destructive power far in excess of anything known in the past. The very nature of war, however, means that equipment must often be used under circumstances very different from those for which it was designed, and frequently under extremes of adversity. There have been many instances of elaborate weapons that failed to deliver under combat conditions. Military design often leads to complicated systems that, when put to the test, do not perform. Fallows (1981) documents a number of instances. The M-16 rifle is one example among many of a weapon that performed poorly. The story given below is an abridged version of Fallows's detailed account.

During the war in Vietnam, between 1965 and 1969, U.S. soldiers were equipped with a rifle, the M-16. According to Fallows, their superiors knew the M-16 would fail when put to the test. The M-16 was based on the Armalite Company's AR-15, a highly reliable weapon. The AR-15 used a high-velocity but small-caliber (0.22-inch) bullet (as compared to the then-standard 0.30-inch caliber used in the M-1 rifle of World War II), which was designed so that on entering the body it would become unstable and tumble, producing enormous internal damage. But the AR-15 had been developed outside the military bureaucracy, which made it unpopular.

In the course of much bureaucratic infighting, the AR-15 concept was accepted but the weapon was "militarized." The weight was increased. A bolt closure was added to permit a soldier to ram a cartridge in manually in the event of a misfire. The "twist" (rifling) of the barrel was increased from one in 14 inches to one in 12 inches, thereby increasing the spin rate—but at the same time making the bullet more stable after entering a target and decreasing the lethality. Finally, and most important, the powder was changed from the IMR (improved military rifle) powder used by the Armalite Company to military standard ball powder. The ball powder, unfortunately, tended to leave a residue inside the chamber that made the rifle more likely to jam. It also caused the rate of fire to increase from 800 to 1000 rounds per minute. This caused vibrations and loss of reliability.

Despite all this, the gun was delivered to Vietnam. The instructions read, "This rifle will fire longer without cleaning than any other known rifle." The claim was simply not true. All too often the M-16 did not operate properly. Lives were lost when soldier's weapons failed to work at critical moments. Letters were sent home and to members of Congress. One read, in part, "Yesterday, we got in a big one. . . . The day found one Marine beating an NVA (North Vietnam Army) with his helmet and a hunting knife because his rifle failed—this can't continue—32 of about 80 rifles failed yesterday." [Quoted by Fallows (1981).]

Eventually, congressional hearings led to pressure on the military. The reliability problem was solved by slowing the firing rate—through a modification of the mechanical "buffer" in the rifle. The rifling was not changed, nor was the powder. The rifle is still in use, and is still heavier and less deadly than the original AR-15. The bureaucracy won out.

The lessons from this story are important. These same kinds of problems have occurred numerous times with very high technology systems—such as the F-16 fighter aircraft (Fallows, 1981). The needs of bureaucracies, and the rewards that go to those who never challenge the system, have repeatedly led to military systems that do not do in practice what is claimed in theory. A healthy suspicion about the reliability of military (as well as other) complex systems is justified. With military systems in particular, equipment is necessarily placed in service having never been tested in combat conditions. Modern military systems are vastly more powerful than ever before, but common sense requires some skepticism about their actual performance in war environments and unanticipated situations.

6-7 THE FUTURE OF NATO: NONOFFENSIVE DEFENSE

The primary area of east-west standoff is in Europe. Along an 800-kilometer border, the forces of the Warsaw Treaty Organization (WTO) are arrayed against those of the North Atlantic Treaty Organization (NATO). The Soviet Union, long fearful of invasion from Europe, remembers how it suffered from wars with Napoleon and two invasions by Germany. It has buffered itself from Europe, using a series of Soviet-controlled nations which, taken together, constitute the WTO (see Chapter 3).

Europe is probably the most heavily armed region of the world. The weaponry is of all types, both nuclear and conventional. Should war break out in Europe, it is likely to prove exceedingly destructive. The limited experience which exists with modern conventional weaponry shows that in conflict it is used up extremely fast, and that it is exceedingly destructive of both military and civilian property and persons. This was demonstrated unambiguously in Vietnam, in Afghanistan, and in the several wars between Israel and the Arab states.

The European situation is politically complex. Many European nations have strong peace parties, which would like to see major reductions in military expenses. The United States presently supplies a substantial part of the military support in Europe—far more than its proportionate share based on gross national product. Yet European nations have proved unwilling to increase their contribution to the defense of NATO.

The military balance is complex and difficult to evaluate. The WTO is far ahead in some areas, most notably main battle tanks. But the WTO must concern itself with the advanced technologies of the west.

NATO is fundamentally structured as a defensive organization. The Soviet Union asserts that the WTO is purely defensive, but this assertion is disbelieved in much of the west. (For an excellent and authoritative Soviet analysis, see IMEMO, or *The Disarmament and Security Yearbook,* USSR Academy of Sciences, 1987.)

NATO concerns about inadequate conventional weaponry to repel a WTO invasion have led to a controversial policy that NATO reserves the right to use nuclear weapons first, should this be necessary. Such a policy may be stabilizing (Luttwak, 1987), but it is inevitably controversial. However, should war occur in Europe, it would almost certainly take place in western land areas, which would suffer horribly (see also Chapter 4).

Consequently, NATO has developed a strategy of carrying the battle to the enemy. NATO forces are structured for rapid deep penetration into enemy territory. These strategies make use of highly mobile air and land systems. They are known as FOFA (Follow on Forces Attack) and as Air/Land Battle. Not surprisingly, the WTO nations see these strategies as aggressive.

There are several reasons to believe that the military situation in Europe is ripe for change. The Stockholm Accords established a procedure whereby major military maneuvers are announced long in advance, and under which maneuvers are observed by representatives from the other side. The INF agreement has started the process of removal of nuclear weapons and has begun a new era of on-site inspection. The Soviet Party Congress of 1987 made it clear that glasnost and perestroika are leading to significant changes in the Soviet Union, though the implications of these changes for Europe are yet to become clear. For example, President Gorbachev, in an address to the United Nations in December 1988 offered significant reductions in tanks and personnel as well as some offensive equipment, such as bridging facilities useful for in WTO forces on attacker. Finally, there is within Europe a growing sense that the Soviet Union is no longer a major threat, and that military expenses need to be reduced.

One of the most interesting areas under exploration is the concept of nonoffensive defense, or NOD (Boserup, 1986; Ahfeldt, 1983; Lucas, 1988; Defending Europe, 1983).* NOD is under active discussion in many parts of Europe but has not yet received much U.S. attention. The idea is conceptually simple, though very complex in practice. It is to move toward force structures with reduced capability for highly provocative acts. Such forces are basically defensive in character. Forces are intentionally designed with low mobility and short range. The example mentioned above of a fiber-optic controlled missile is illustrative. Such a device is highly effective, but the range is unambiguously limited by the fiber's length. Other approaches

---

*See numerous articles in, for example, the *Bulletin of Peace Proposals* and the *Journal of Peace Research.* Also the *ADIEU Report,* published by the University of Sussex (England).

to limiting mobility involve restrictions on fuel depots for tank resupply, reductions in numbers of gunship helicopters, and an absence of troop training in operations extending over long distances.

Beyond this, there are numerous new technologies which can make certain regions extremely difficult to cross. Such "islands of fire" would be loaded with munitions and remote sensing. WTO and NATO armed zones could be separated by a demilitarized zone along the entire WTO/NATO border.

NOD planning is complicated considerably by the view of West Germany that the division of Germany into East and West is temporary. Thus West Germany is opposed to any moves in the direction of making this division permanent, as would be implied by the kind of system described here.

A further problem is the memory in Europe of the failure at the outset of World War II of the Maginot Line. However, in that situation Hitler moved around the line, rather than through it.

The present situation differs fundamentally from the past in that the threat of escalation to nuclear war always looms in the background. Even if all nuclear weapons are removed from Europe, both the United States and the Soviet Union will retain strategic nuclear weapons, which could easily be targeted on Europe should this be deemed desirable.

Should tensions between the two superpowers decrease, Europe is a prime candidate for major changes. The expenditures on military wherewithall in that theater are enormous, according to one estimate amounting to half the world's military expenditures (Dean, 1987). Even a modest relaxation in tensions could lead to substantial savings.

There is also precedent for change. The INF treaty is one example, discussed in Chapter 2. Of particular interest for the future of conventional weapons control is the Stockholm Accord on Confidence Building and Security Building Measures (CSBMs) (SIPRI Yearbook, 1987). Although not a formal treaty, the accord was signed by 35 nations. Its many provisions call for notification of certain military activities up to 2 years in advance, and permit observers during troop exercises.

Even if tensions between the superpowers should not decrease, pressures for change are building within Europe. Over the next decade, the European theater may well prove the most interesting place to watch.

For more details on the future of NATO, conventional defense in general, and nonoffensive defense (NOD), see the following articles: Defense and Disarmament Alternatives (1988), *Bulletin of the Atomic Scientists* (1988), Golden et al. (1984), ESECS (1983), Kelleher and Mattox (1987), Nye et al. (1988), European Security (1988), Gates (1987), and Ahfeldt (1983).

QUESTIONS

1. Why are conventional arms important to consider in connection with the nuclear arms race?
2. Approximately how many troops did the United States have overseas at the beginning of the 1980s?

3. What is the difference between chemical and biological warfare?

4. Discuss the advantages and disadvantages of the use of tactical weapons (neutron bombs) or conventional weapons against a tank assault.

5. Design a terrorist attack on the White House using chemical or biological weapons.

6. Discuss several new types of conventional weapons. Use *Aviation Week* as a source.

7. How might nuclear weapons be used in a "Vietnam" (guerrilla) type of war? Under what conditions (if any) might their use be justified militarily? Politically?

8. What are some of the practical difficulties with using chemical or biological weapons in a tactical war-fighting situation?

9. What is NOD? Discuss.

PART

II

TECHNICAL
BACKGROUND

But in physics I soon learned to scent out the paths that led to the depths, and to disregard everything else, all the many things that clutter up the mind, and divert it from the essential. The hitch in this was, of course, the fact that one had to cram all this stuff into one's mind for the examination, whether one liked it or not.

Albert Einstein

Part 2 (Chapters 7 to 18) contains technical and scientific material needed to understand how nuclear weapons work and what happens when they are exploded. The material in this section provides one with important perspectives on the destructiveness of nuclear weaponry. Without such background one may miss the macabre humor of a newspaper caption to a photograph showing the destruction produced by a chemical explosion reading, "500 pounds of high explosive went off with megaton force." The headings in Chapter 7 are the titles of Chapters 8 through 18.

SUMMARY OF
PART TWO:
MAJOR
TECHNICAL
CONCEPTS

INTRODUCTION TO PHYSICS

Physics has proved extremely successful in providing methods for understanding and manipulating the physical world. Physics is grounded in an experimental view of the world. Theories are of interest only if they can be tested. Basic concepts are developed that can be used to understand a wide variety of phenomena. Examples are force and energy. *Energy*, measured in units of joules, is the ability to do work. A force moving an object over a distance does work, while a stationary force does not. *Pressure* is force per unit area. It is measured in units of newtons per meter squared (or newtons per square meter, abbreviated N/m^2 in the SI system, or in units of pounds per square inch (psi) in the U.S. system.

Because of the enormous range in the sizes of the numbers that occur in nuclear physics, *exponential notation* is often used. With exponential notation, numbers are expressed as powers of 10. For example,

$$1000 \text{ tons } = 10^3 \text{ tons } = 1 \text{ kiloton } = 0.001 \text{ megaton } = 10^{-3} \text{ megaton}$$

Order-of-magnitude (rough) estimates are often quite adequate for understanding important effects in nuclear physics. It is important to understand the difference between a 1-kiloton bomb and a 1-megaton bomb, but the difference between the effects of a 1-megaton bomb and a 1.1-megaton bomb are rarely significant.

Sometimes accuracy is important. An ICBM which travels 10,000 miles and hits within 100 meters has an aiming accuracy of about 6 parts in a million. A ball with this accuracy, thrown the length of a football field, would hit within 0.02 inch (0.5 millimeter) of the designated spot.

ENERGY—AN INTRODUCTION TO NUCLEAR PHYSICS

The yield of nuclear weapons is measured by the energy released in the explosion. The energy release of nuclear weapons is measured in units of the energy released from 1000 tons, or 1 kiloton (kt), of TNT (4.2×10^{12} joules). For thermonuclear bombs the yield is often measured in megatons (Mt) of TNT. One megaton is equal to 1 million tons or 1000 kilotons. The energy released by the Hiroshima bomb was about 15 kilotons. The largest bomb ever tested (a Soviet weapon) released about 60 megatons.

The energy release in a Hiroshima-size (15-kiloton) bomb is roughly equal to the energy that would be released if all the automobiles in the United States (over 100 million of them) were accelerated to a speed of 60 miles per hour and simultaneously crashed into each other. A 1-megaton explosion would release 67 times more energy.

The origin of the energy released by nuclear bombs is expressed by Einstein's famous relation $E = mc^2$, where m is mass and c is the speed of light. Mass is an equivalent form of energy, and one can be converted to the other. Because the speed of light is a large number (about 300,000 kilometers per second, or 186,000 miles/sec), a small amount of mass converts into an enormous amount of energy. One gram of matter, if converted entirely into energy, would give an energy release equivalent to about 20 kilotons of TNT, which was the yield of the bomb that destroyed Nagasaki.

Fission of uranium or plutonium nuclei provides a practical means by which the potential in Einstein's relation can be realized. In a fission explosion a small fraction (about 0.1 percent) of the uranium or plutonium mass is converted into energy. Fusion of tritium and deuterium nuclei to form helium also produces nuclear energy. This is the reaction of the thermonuclear bomb.

Tritium and deuterium are special forms [called *isotopes*, meaning "same place" (in the periodic table of the elements)] of hydrogen. All isotopes of hydrogen contain one proton in the nucleus. The deuterium nucleus also contains a neutron, while tritium contains two neutrons. A neutron has almost the same mass as a proton.

Uranium 235 (^{235}U) has 92 protons and $235 - 92 = 143$ neutrons in its nucleus. Uranium 238 (^{238}U) is an isotope of uranium with $238 - 92 = 146$ neutrons.

The most stable element is iron. Energy is released when heavier elements are split (e.g., fission of ^{235}U or ^{239}Pu), or when lighter elements are fused together (e.g., fusion of deuterium and tritium to form helium). The energy release in nuclear processes is measured in a tiny unit called the *electron volt* (eV). About 200 million electron volts, or 200 MeV, are released when a single ^{235}U or ^{239}Pu nucleus fissions. The release of 10 kilotons of energy requires that about 1.3×10^{24} nuclei fission. This many ^{235}U or ^{239}Pu atoms have a mass of about 500 grams. One electron volt equals 1.6×10^{-19} joules.

RADIOACTIVITY

The process in which nuclei spontaneously change into others is called *radioactivity*. Fission (splitting) of heavy elements into lighter ones can occur spontaneously or can be induced by neutrons. The latter is the source of the fissions in a fission bomb. Three types of process are important in nuclear weaponry: alpha decay, beta decay, and fission.

In *alpha decay* a nucleus spontaneously emits a helium nucleus which contains two protons and two neutrons. Alpha particles occur in the spontaneous decay of some heavy elements (e.g., plutonium) and therefore occur in fallout. Protection from alpha particles can be provided by thin layers of cloth or metal. However, bits of radioactive material which emit alpha particles lodged in the lungs or bone marrow can cause cancer. This is the primary reason why plutonium is extremely hazardous.

In *beta decay*, beta particles, which are electrons, are emitted by isotopes which are produced during fission. Like alpha particles, beta particles are easily shielded against unless the beta-emitting material is ingested.

After alpha or beta decay the resulting nucleus is often in an excited state. It rapidly decays further to its most stable, or ground, state by emitting energetic light rays (electromagnetic radiation) called *gamma rays*. Gamma rays are much more penetrating than alpha or beta rays, and hence it is more difficult to provide shielding protection from them.

Fission occurs when an element splits into two lighter elements. The fission products of a nuclear explosion are themselves extremely radioactive, emitting beta rays and gamma rays, which are important in fallout (see Chapter 16).

Shielding from nuclear radiation focuses heavily on protection from gamma radiation and from neutrons. The fission process also releases neutrons; typically two or three neutrons are released each time a uranium or plutonium nucleus fissions. These neutrons can cause further fission if they hit other uranium or plutonium nuclei, giving rise to a chain reaction, or they can escape and hit people or objects.

Neutrons are important near an bomb blast, but they do not occur in fallout. They are uncharged and are hard to shield against. In large bombs the effects of blast and heat dominate the effects of neutron radiation, but in small bombs neutron effects can be important (e.g., in the neutron, or enhanced-radiation, bomb).

ON THE BUILDING OF BOMBS

Fission Bombs

In a fission bomb it is necessary to have a *chain reaction*. A chain reaction refers to a process in which neutrons released in fission produce additional fissions in at least one further nucleus. This nucleus in turn produces neutrons, and the process repeats. If, for example, each neutron produces a fission which releases two more neutrons, then the number of fissions doubles in each generation. In that case in 10 generations there are $2^{10} = 1024$ fissions and in 40 generations about 1 trillion fissions.

In a fission bomb each generation takes about $1/100,000,000$ (10^{-8}) second. After about 80 generations so much energy has been released that the bomb blows itself apart and the chain reaction ceases. But by then there have been a trillion trillion, or 10^{24}, fissions and ten kilotons of TNT energy equivalent released in a Hiroshima-sized bomb.

A chain reaction can occur only if enough fissionable materials, in the proper geometry, are present. A sphere has the minimum possible surface area for a given mass, and hence minimizes the leakage of neutrons. A mass of material arranged so that as many neutrons are produced by fission as leak out is called a *critical mass*. To build a bomb one must have a mass larger than the critical mass and must hold it together long enough for the desired energy release to occur.

Natural uranium cannot be used to make bombs. It is composed predominantly (99.3 percent) of ^{238}U, which mostly absorbs neutrons without fissioning. The uranium must be enriched in the fissionable isotope ^{235}U from the natural concentration of 0.7 percent to more than 90 percent. This requires an elaborate process called *isotopic separation*, or *uranium enrichment*.

Plutonium 239 can also be used to make a fission bomb. Plutonium is unstable and does not exist in nature. It can be produced in nuclear reactors by means of neutron capture in ^{238}U (and subsequent radioactive decay).

Two types of fission bombs have been developed. In the gun-type bomb one piece of material is shot from a gun at another piece. The combined mass exceeds the critical mass. This method works with ^{235}U but not with ^{239}Pu. A gun-type ^{235}U bomb was used on Hiroshima.

Plutonium 239 has a relatively high spontaneous fission rate and plutonium 240, which is also produced in the reactor, has an even higher rate. They therefore spontaneously produce neutrons. Thus if a gun-type weapon were used with ^{239}Pu, the weapon would detonate prematurely. A faster assembly process, called *implosion*, is needed. In this method the plutonium is squeezed to abnormal density by a chemical explosion, after which the nuclear reaction is initiated. The first nuclear explosion at Alamogordo and the bomb that devastated Nagasaki used plutonium and the implosion technique.

Thermonuclear Bombs

A thermonuclear bomb uses the fusion of two light nuclei, such as tritium and deuterium, to produce an energy release. The size of a thermonuclear bomb is not limited by critical-mass considerations. In order to initiate the thermonuclear reaction, a "match" in the form of a fission bomb is needed. Normally a thermonuclear bomb is surrounded by a natural uranium jacket, which increases its yield. About 50 percent of the energy release of a typical thermonuclear weapon comes from the fission of the uranium jacket. These bombs therefore release an enormous amount of fission products as radioactive fallout.

The "secret" of the hydrogen bomb was the invention of a technique by which gamma radiation for the igniting fission bomb (called the *primary*) was used to compress and ignite the material in the fusion part of the weapon (the *secondary*).

THE IMMEDIATE EFFECTS OF
NUCLEAR WEAPONS

The immediate effects of nuclear weapons are blast, thermal radiation (heat), initial nuclear radiation, and the electromagnetic pulse (EMP). The only effect nuclear weapons have in common with ordinary bombs (chemical explosives) is blast, or overpressure. All the other effects are peculiar to nuclear bombs.

The effects of blast, thermal radiation, gamma rays, and neutrons for a 1-kiloton fission weapon exploded 600 feet above the ground as a function of the distance from ground zero are compared in Figure 7-1. The altitude is selected so as to maximize the area experiencing an overpressure of more than 20 psi (a pressure that will demolish all buildings not specially hardened). As the curves approach ground zero, they are drawn with heavier symbols when it is estimated that casualties from the effect would be 50 percent or greater. For example, 50 percent casualties would occur at neutron or gamma-ray doses of 400 rad (radiation absorbed dose). At 1000 rad mortality approaches 100 percent.

Extremely high gamma ray and neutron exposures are possible near ground zero since there is little atmosphere to absorb the radiation. For small nuclear weapons this radiation exposure is a major cause of casualties. The figure shows that the initial nuclear radiation is the most important cause of death for a 1-kiloton fission bomb. The 50 percent mortality point at 400 rad is at about 2700 feet from ground zero for either neutrons or gamma rays considered separately. Since a person would be exposed to both neutrons and gamma rays, the 200-rad point, at 3100 feet, in fact represents a *total* radiation dose of 400 rad.

At a distance of 2100 feet for a 1-kiloton bomb, indirect pressure effects, moving debris and the like, and burns from thermal radiation will kill half of those exposed. At this distance the radiation doses from gamma rays and neutrons are about 1100 and 1300 rad, respectively. The letters refer to blast effects discussed in Table 13-2. Thermal radiation of 6 calories per square centimeter produces third-degree burns in 50 percent of the population and second-degree burns for the remaining 50 percent (see Chapter 14). If individuals with such burns are not treated in a special burn facility, shock and death are likely.

In the neutron bomb or enhanced radiation warhead (ERW) (see Section 11-4) a small hydrogen bomb is produced without the usual U238 jacket. The neutron yield is about six times greater than for a fission bomb of the same yield. Furthermore the neutrons from the thermonuclear reaction are of higher energy and are less attenuated by the air between bomb burst and target (Kaplan, 1979). The neutron dose delivered by a 1-kiloton neutron bomb is shown in Figure 7-1.

Figure 7-2 summarizes the effect of a 1-megaton thermonuclear bomb whose yield is 50 percent fission. The scale of the abscissa is 10 times that of Figure 7-1. The burst height, 6000 feet, is also 10 times that of Figure 7-1.

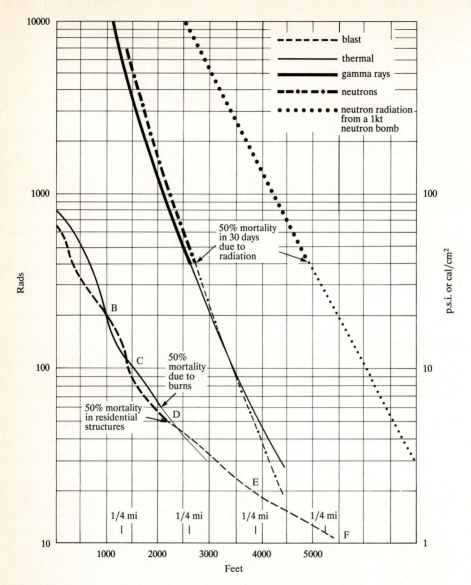

FIGURE 7-1
Comparison of blast, thermal, and initial nuclear radiation from a 1-kiloton fission bomb exploded at an altitude of 600 feet as a function of the distance from ground zero. Also shown is the neutron radiation from a 1-kiloton neutron bomb on the same scale. Note that the neutron radiation from the neutron bomb is less attenuated by the atmosphere since it has higher initial average kinetic energy.

The thermal effect is the dominating feature at large distances from the explosion. At about 6 miles from ground zero there is 50 percent mortality for burns. Close in, the blast effect also becomes important, with 50 percent mortality from blasts

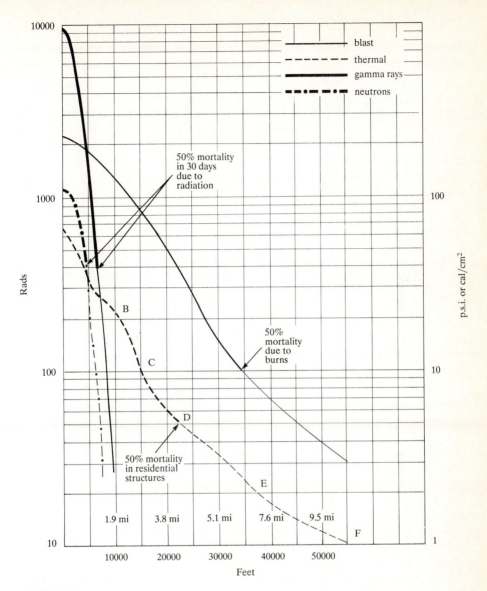

FIGURE 7-2
The effect of a 1-megaton thermonuclear bomb whose yield is 50 percent fission.

occurring at about 4 miles from ground zero. The initial nuclear radiation is very large close to ground zero, but because of atmospheric absorption it rapidly decreases with distance. Its effective range is about 1.4 miles from ground zero. However, at that distance the blast effect is 25 psi and the thermal effect is 200 calories per square centimeter, which would kill everyone in open areas.

ELECTROMAGNETIC PULSE (EMP)

As far as we know, the EMP does not affect people directly, but can induce a pulse of high voltage and currents in power lines and telephone lines, thereby causing electric power interruption and incapacitating communications and electronic devices, such as computers. Military electronic installations are, at least in some areas, "hardened" against EMP, but civilian systems relying on electricity or electronics would be extremely vulnerable. A 1-megaton bomb exploded 500 kilometers over Nebraska would probably shut down the entire nations's electrical grid and telephone system. Electronic apparatus could be damaged because of voltage surges on the electric power grid or directly through electric induction of voltage within equipment by the electromagnetic wave of the EMP.

FALLOUT

Many neutrons are emitted during the explosion of fission or fusion bombs. This means that they spontaneously emit radiation in the form of electrons or gamma radiation. Heavy nuclei, such as uranium or plutonium, emit alpha particles as well.

Accompanying fission and fusion are many free neutrons. These can be captured by the nuclei of ordinary materials, rendering these materials radioactive (neutron-induced radioactivity). When a nuclear weapon explodes, large amounts of radioactivity are released into the environment from fission products and from neutron-induced radioactivity in the weapons material (and, in the case of a ground burst, in soil). This gives rise to *fallout*, which can be a significant after-effect of a nuclear explosion. Vaporized soil particles and weapons components drift to the earth's surface in a pattern dependent on the vagaries of local wind patterns, precipitation, and particle size and density.

If the United States were attacked with 2500 megatons of fission yield and the resultant fallout were spread uniformly over the area of the U.S. (excluding Alaska), then the average radiation exposure for unshielded persons would be about 10,000 rad. This would kill anyone exposed to it. This estimate is unrealistic because not all the fallout would be on the ground within one hour, as is assumed in this calculation. Some regions would receive much more and some much less than the average radiation exposure in an actual nuclear war, but the amount of fallout is so large that it would clearly be an extremely serious problem. The long-term effect of such fallout would affect the entire northern hemisphere and perhaps the southern hemisphere as well.

BIOLOGICAL AND MEDICAL EFFECTS OF RADIOACTIVITY, GAMMA RAYS, AND NEUTRONS FROM NUCLEAR WEAPONS

Radiation levels are often measured in the unit radiation absorbed dose (rad). Four hundred rad causes death in 50 to 70 percent of normal adults in 30 days as a result of damage to body cells. Nonlethal levels of radiation can cause diarrhea and vomiting and lower an individual's resistance to infection. Exposure to radiation also involves an increased risk of cancer. About 200 cases of cancer will appear each year in a population of 1 million persons exposed to 1 rad.

Since neutrons and alpha particles can produce relatively more biological damage than beta rays or gamma rays per rad, the *rem* (*roentgen equivalent mammal*) is used in measuring neutron or alpha-particle radiation effects. For beta rays and gamma rays the rem and the rad are almost identical.

Whole-body exposure to external radiation, usually gamma rays, or ingestion of radioactive material can cause biological damage. Ingestion of radioactive material will also expose internal organs to additional radiation.

Radiation damages the reproductive genetic material in the body. This can produce degenerative diseases in offspring and other anomalies that lead to "genetic death."

CHAPTER
8

INTRODUCTION
TO PHYSICS

Words mean exactly what I choose them to mean; neither more nor less.

The Red Queen in *Alice in Wonderland*

8-1   THEMES

Twentieth-century science—particularly physics—has made possible many new technologies, including the development of atomic weapons and the systems for delivering these weapons. This chapter discusses the world view of physics, that is, its conception of reality. It introduces the idea of scientific observation and measurement and explores the reasons why numbers play such an important role in physics.

Some of the key concepts of physics are introduced—distance, velocity, time, force, mass, and pressure—together with some of the relations among these quantities. Units are reviewed, including the British system used in the United States and the metric system used in most of the rest of the world (the Système Internationale, or SI). Exponential notation for dealing with very large and very small numbers is introduced.

8-2   WHAT IS PHYSICS?

The development of atomic weapons was possible only because of spectacular advances in understanding the physical world. Discoveries in the nineteenth century about electromagnetic radiation and heat led in the early twentieth century to Einstein's work on the equivalence of mass and energy and the theory of relativity, to quantum mechanics, and to many discoveries about the structure of atomic nuclei.

Physics has proved phenomenally successful in providing techniques for manipulating the physical world, techniques which are collectively known as *technology*. Nuclear weapons, transistors, computers, rockets, and high-speed airplanes are examples of technological systems which are applications of physics.

Despite the apparent complexity of physics, many of the most important ideas can be easily grasped. The essential ideas can be expressed in words, and understood without recourse to mathematics, though the language of mathematics is essential if the ideas are to be explored in depth or applied in complex situations.

One of our primary goals is to provide you with key concepts of physics that are relevant to the arms race. Readers with no knowledge of physics can use the text effectively by passing over the more technical discussions, while those with deeper interests will find available supplementary material which will expand considerably their insight and understanding.

The methodology of physics emphasizes precise formulations of concepts, generally (though not always) through the use of equations. Experiments are performed to test the concepts against the reality of the physical world. These experiments are usually designed so as to yield numerical results. Numbers thus assume a special role in physics.

Physics focuses on development of unifying principles, such as Newton's laws, that serve to unite many different ideas into generally simple frameworks. These are called *theories*. Because of the importance of theories in the scientific description of the world, we need to be quite clear about what theories are and what they are not.

The philosopher Karl Popper has examined the meaning of the term *theory* in the context of modern science. His best-known contribution is the idea of *falsifiability*. A theory about the real world must be of such a character that it can be proved wrong. (Popper points out that a theory can never be proved correct—there is always an alternative theory that may be as good or better). A true theory must produce predictions that can be tested in the world of experience is such a way that the results could prove the theory wrong. Since our ability to investigate the world keeps improving, a concept can, over time, achieve the status of a theory. For example, the Greek philosopher Democritus described matter as being composed of tiny atoms with hooks connecting them together. The idea sounds a great deal like modern atomic theory. Yet there was no way, in Democritus's time, to *test* the idea. It therefore was not a theory in the modern sense.

An example of a question that does not (currently, at least) fit into the scientific framework is: "How many angels can dance on the head of a pin?" No theory of angels and pins can yield *testable* predictions. Theory in science is totally dependent on observations in the external world.

Einstein's theory of relativity is a good example of a set of theoretical ideas which could be and were tested. His theory predicted results of experiments that had not previously been performed—a fact that caused it to be taken very seriously. Einstein's theory explained everything that earlier theories had explained (an essential requirement), and much more besides. It thus replaced Newtonian mechanics, although that method is still widely used in those domains where there are negligible relativistic effects.

The most useful theories apply to many situations. They allow successful generalizations. It is the conciseness of theoretical physics—the ability of a few ideas or equations to encompass the results of many different physical situations—that make physics so useful. Once one understands the general principles it is possible to predict the results of many different experiments and experiences. In this book we examine some of the unifying principles of physics that are relevant to understanding technical aspects of the arms race.

As we have said, every concept in physics must be traceable back to "observables," quantities which can be observed and measured. In many of the situations we are concerned with in this book, the units and quantities involved will be familiar from everyday experience. In others, they will be less familiar. Force and distance are examples of concepts that are relatively familiar, while electric and magnetic fields are less familiar because they cannot readily be experienced with the unaided human senses.

As your familiarity with physics grows, you can expect to become increasingly comfortable with new concepts. Ideas that were once obscure will become familiar. This expansion of your horizons is one of the primary goals of this book. The new knowledge should allow you to discern patterns of meaning in the world around you where formerly you saw none.

8-3   DEFINITIONS

The spectacular ability of physics to explain the universe is largely due to precise definition of terms. This may seem a curious assertion, but think about it for a moment. In many aspects of life we use terms that are highly ambiguous.

For example, consider the term *green*. Is this precisely defined? Probably not, if what you are referring to is your perception of the color green. Your perception is very likely quite different from mine. For example, I might be partially color-blind, and barely able to distinguish red from green. You, on the other hand, may be extremely sensitive to colors and able to distinguish far more color gradations than the normal person. In a simple situation with a highly saturated color and not too many gradations, we may both agree that the word green appropriately describes a particular object's color ("Please bring me the green book." "The dollar bill is green."). In more complicated situations you may talk of variations in greenness that I am unable to perceive.

What does the physicist mean by *green* or *red*? Surprisingly, the words for colors are not terms that are commonly used in a technical sense in physics. They are usually defined in the context of a particular situation. The light from the sun is composed of a broad spectrum of frequencies—from the very short wavelengths of the far ultraviolet to the very long wavelengths of the infrared. The wavelengths in the vicinity of 0.7 micrometer (a micrometer is a millionth of a meter) appear to us as red, while those in the vicinity of 0.5 micrometer appear to us as blue. There is a range of wavelengths, though, and no unique definition is given to the names *red* or *blue*. Green light has a slightly longer wavelength than blue light, 0.55 micrometer. A helium-neon laser emits radiation with a well-defined wavelength which appears red. This radiation is close to monochromatic, but for many experiments the spread of frequencies (deviation from monochromaticity) of even this laser light is important.

Ambiguities in interpretation are typical of words used in normal experience. We are used to this and adjust to it. Such ambiguity is intolerable in physics. Physicists expend considerable effort in specifying precisely the definitions of concepts. We approach the world in exactly the opposite way from Lewis Carroll's Red Queen. (Remember, though, that Lewis Carroll was a professor of logic, and knew exactly what he was up to. When his words were ambiguous, it was never an accident.) Precise definitions of the meanings of words minimize ambiguity and contribute a great deal to the ease with which scientific dialogue crosses national and cultural boundaries.

The literature of the arms race includes many technical words. We will begin with a few from physics. Later on we will leave it to you to assure yourself that you know what these key words mean. In this way we will be able to keep our discussions sharp and precise so that differences of opinion will relate to substantive issues rather than to confusion over what words mean.

8-4 OBSERVABLES

Distance, speed, acceleration, force, pressure, and time are terms that are routinely used in ordinary conversation. They are also important concepts in understanding the operation of ballistic missiles and the processes which go on inside an atomic bomb.

We will consider distance and time to be intuitive concepts. Their fundamental definition is quite difficult, and over the years has occupied many physicists. Until a few years ago the fundamental definition of distance was based on the separation of two scratches on a platinum-iridium bar located in a climate-controlled vault in Paris. By arbitrary definition this bar was precisely 1 meter long. All other distances were referenced to this standard meter. Time was based on astronomical observations of the transit of stars over Greenwich, England. Today, time is based on atomic transitions in "atomic clocks," and distance is defined in terms of the ratio of the speed of light (which is very accurately known) to a measured time for the light to move from one point to another.

Speed is a distance divided by the time required to traverse it. Speed may be measured (for example) in miles per hour, kilometers per hour, or feet per second. Any quantity which describes the speed of an object must have dimensions of *distance* divided by *time*, though the units may vary. The term **velocity** is often used synonymously with speed, and we shall do so. (Technically the two terms have different meanings, velocity referring to a vector quantity which includes direction as well as speed.) A missile which covers a distance of 5000 miles in half an hour moves at a speed of 10,000 miles per hour, or (5000 miles)/(30 minutes) = 167 miles per minute, or 2.78 miles per second.

Acceleration is the rate of change of speed. If a missile achieves a speed of 10,000 miles per hour in 5 minutes, its acceleration is 2000 miles per hour per minute. If a car speeds up from 10 to 60 miles per hour in 30 seconds, then the acceleration is 50 miles per hour in 30 seconds, or 1.67 miles per hour per second.

Force is a push on an object by some other agency. The more *mass* (or number of elementary constituents, such as atoms) an object has, the more force is needed to give the object a certain *acceleration*. A fundamental relationship between force, acceleration, and mass is expressed by *Newton's second law*, which states that the force needed to produce a given acceleration is proportional to the mass of the object.

A bullet is accelerated by an applied force produced by expanding gases from the burning gunpowder; a building may be knocked down by the force of air pushing against it after a nuclear explosion. The force which drives a rocket forward is produced by reaction against the burned fuel expelled from the rocket's nozzle.

Pressure is the force upon a unit area (measured perpendicular to the area). A common occurrence of pressure is in tire inflation. A typical inflation pressure is 30 psi (pounds per square inch), or 2 kilograms per square centimeter. A person would be severely knocked about by a force of 6000 pounds applied to his or her body. What pressure is needed to produce this force? If we assume the area of the person's body facing a blast is about 10 inches wide by 60 inches tall, or 600 square inches, then the pressure is the force divided by the area, or 6000 pounds divided by 600 square inches, which equals 10 psi. Blast pressure this high will destroy almost any building not specially reinforced.

8-5   NUMERICAL CONSIDERATIONS

Units

Just as the people of the world speak different languages, the laws of physics have been formulated using many systems of units. The speedometer of an American car is calibrated in miles per hour. Generally there is another scale, calibrated in kilometers per hour, which is the unit in common use in much of the world outside the United States. Many other units for speed exist. Meters per second, knots (nautical miles per hour), feet per minute, furlongs per fortnight, and microns per nanosecond are a few.

Two different kinds of units are now in common use in physics: U.S. Customary, or "British," units and SI units. U.S. Customary (USC) units are those you are most familiar with—inches, feet, gallons, and acres. The initials *SI* stand for the French words *Système Internationale*, which is the metric system in use in most parts of the world. Some SI units are in common use in the United States—for example, seconds, watts, kilowatts—but the United States has been very slow in converting. In arms-race matters we tend to jump back and forth from British to SI units, and therefore you need to become familiar with both.

To give an indication of how confused the situation sometimes gets, let's consider the design of a nuclear reactor. The nuclear parts of the system were developed by physicists, who prefer SI units, so these parts of all reactors made in the United States have their dimensions specified in millimeters, centimeters, and meters. The nonnuclear parts of the reactors were designed by engineers, who generally prefer British units, and the dimensions of these parts are expressed in mils (thousandths of an inch), inches, feet, or (rarely) yards.

Conversion Factors

Conversion factors are numbers that are used to convert from one unit to another. A simple example is:

$$1 \text{ inch} = 2.54 \text{ centimeters} \qquad (8\text{-}1)$$

First, note that (8-1) is an equation. That is, it expresses an equality. When an equation is read as a sentence, the equals sign becomes the verb. Equations (8-1) is read as "one inch equals two point five four centimeters."

Now divide the left and the right sides of Eq. (8-1) by 1 inch. The result is

$$1 = \frac{2.54 \text{ centimeters}}{1 \text{ inch}} \qquad (8\text{-}2)$$

If this example is clear to you, you should have no trouble with the conversion factors that will arise later on.

In Eq. (8-2) the left and right sides of the equation have been divided by the same factor. By one of the basic laws of algebra, the equality remains ("when equals are divided by equals, the results are equal"). The curious thing about Eq. (8-2) is that the left-hand side is exactly 1 (unity). Expressions for conversion factors can always be written so that one side is unity. This is a very convenient way to write them for purposes of calculations and also for checking answers. Now, let's use this procedure to do a simple conversion.

Professor Jungerman is about 70 inches tall (see Figure 8-1). How many centimeters tall is he? If we multiply his height in inches times the conversion factor (1 inch = 2.54 centimeters), we find that his height in centimeters is

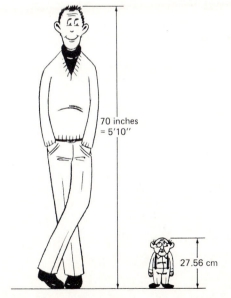

70 inches
= 5'10"

27.56 cm

FIGURE 8-1
Remembering numbers.

$$(70 \text{ inches}) \times (2.54 \text{ centimeters/inch}) = 177.8 \text{ centimeters} \qquad (8\text{-}3)$$

Notice several features of this equation. To start with, the second set of parentheses is just the expression from Eq. (8-2), which is equal to 1, or unity. An algebraic expression is never changed by multiplying by unity. Also, the dimension "inches," occurring in the phrase "70 inches," is exactly canceled out by the dimension "inches" in the denominator of the second term. The upshot is that the dimensions on the right-hand side of the equation (centimeters) are identical with those on the left-hand side. This dimensional equivalence is always true in a conversion of units, and this fact provides an important and very useful test on whether the factors introduced in a complicated set of conversions are dimensionally consistent. Of this, more later.

If one is not careful to maintain dimensional consistency when converting units, it is easy to get the numerical factors wrong. Suppose you inadvertently write

$$\frac{70 \text{ inches}}{2.54 \text{ centimeters/inch}} = 27.56 \text{ square inches/centimeter} \qquad (8\text{-}4)$$

In this (erroneous) example the inches do not cancel out, an immediate indication that something is wrong. Of course in this case we have enough feeling for the units to realize at once that something is wrong. If Professor Jungerman were in fact 27.56 centimeters tall, he would have a hard time looking over the lecture table. But in more complicated situations our intuition, which works pretty well for centimeters and inches, will quickly run into trouble. Careful attention to units will help considerably.

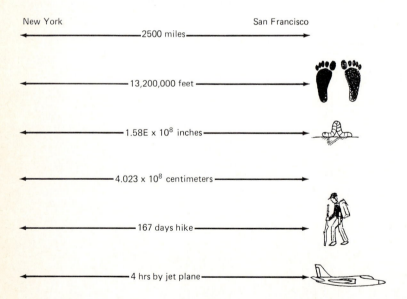

FIGURE 8-2
Illustration of conversion factors, exponential notation, and significant figures.

Remembering Numbers

It is much easier to remember small numbers than large ones. The distance from Davis, California, to Sacramento, California, is about 13 miles—which is easy to remember. If we use feet instead of miles, the distance is 68,640 feet, which, even if we round to 70,000 feet, is still much harder to remember than the number 13. If we use inches, we have to deal with a quite large number, 823,680—impossible for most of us to remember easily. Figure 8-2 is illustrative as well.

Systems of units deal with the problem by introducing various units such that almost any number of interest can be expressed as a number somewhere in the neighborhood of 0.1 to 100.

Powers of Ten—Metric Prefixes and Exponential Notation

The domain of physics ranges from the inconceivably small to the spectacularly large—from the internal workings of the nucleus to the structure of the universe. The prefixes listed in Table 8-1 are one way of making very large and very small numbers manageable. Another commonly used approach is to express numbers using *base-10*, or *exponential notation*.

In this system a value is expressed as a number between 1 and 10, multiplied by 10 to some power (see Table 8-1). There are a variety of ways to represent a number in exponential form. Here are some of them.

$$123456 = 1.23456 \times 10^5 = 1.23456 \times 10^\wedge 5 = 1.23456E + 5 \qquad (8\text{-}5)$$

The notations $10^\wedge 5$ and $E + 5$ are convenient if the printing system doesn't handle superscripts. This is often the case with computer printers. The $+$ sign in the last expression is arbitrary; one can equally well write $1.23456E5$.

Numbers less than unity are represented using negative exponents:

$$0.000123456 = 1.23456 \times 10^{-4} = 1.23456 \times 10^\wedge(-4) = 1.23456E\text{-}4 \qquad (8\text{-}6)$$

With negative exponents the negative sign is of course mandatory.

TABLE 8-1
Metric prefixes

Prefix	Size	Length	Volume	Volatage	Power
nano	billionth	nanometer	nanoliter	nanovolt	-9
micro	millionth	micron	microliter	microvolt	-6
milli	thousandth	millimeter	milliliter	millivolt	-3
centi	hundredth	centimeter	centiliter	centivolt	-2
deci	tenth	decimeter	deciliter	decivolt	-1
kilo	thousand	kilometer	kiloliter	kilovolt	$+3$
mega	million	megameter	megaliter	megavolt	$+6$
giga	billion*	gigameter	gigaliter	gigavolt	$+9$

*In Europe a billion is 1 followed by 12 zeros, rather than 9, as in the United States; that is, it is a million million rather than a thousand million.

Negative numbers have minus signs in front, as usual $(-0.000123456 = -1.23456 \times 10^{-4})$. Note that whenever we write a number that begins with a decimal point, we precede the decimal with a zero (0.0123). This is not strictly necessary but it is helpful for clarity. Sometimes the decimal point is hard to read, and numbers like .12 come out looking like 12. Writing it as 0.12 overcomes the problem, since even if the decimal point is illegible (0 12), we can figure out where it belongs.

Orders of Magnitude: Back-of-the-Envelope Calculations

Many aspects of the arms race can best be understood using numerical examples. Frequently in the course of manipulating numbers one will obtain numbers that have many digits, for example, on the readout of a hand-held calculator. How many of these digits matter?

The general rule is to avoid carrying along more numbers than are needed. The additional numbers are confusing and imply a precision that usually is not present. The quantity of decimal places needed will depend on just what the problem is, which means that each case will require individual assessment.

Suppose I want to know, roughly, how many dollars are spent per capita on defense. It may be sufficient for me to know that the annual Department of Defense budget is about $300 billion, and that there are about 220 million Americans. From this I might calculate

$$\text{DOD budget/capita} = \frac{\$300 \text{ billion/year}}{220 \text{ million people}}$$

$$= \$1363.63/\text{capita/year} \qquad (8\text{-}7)$$

This answer is, however, misleading, since the starting numbers were so approximate. The final result is probably not even accurate to within $100 per capita. Thus it would be better to round off and say that the military expenditure per capita is about $1400 per year. More digits than that would be not only hard to remember, but misleading.

Situations in which rough estimates are quite adequate come up so frequently in physics that they have been given a special name. They are called *order-of-magnitude* calculations—which means they are accurate to within about a factor of 10. Often the phrase *order-of-magnitude* is used in the looser sense of *approximately*.

For many calculations we will want to know results only to within an order of magnitude or so. It is important to know that it would take about a 1-megaton bomb to devastate the San Francisco Bay region and that a 1-kiloton bomb would cause a major disaster but not destroy the city. On the other hand, there is nothing useful you can say (in fact there is not much that anyone can say) about the difference between the effect of a 1-megaton bomb and a 1.5-megaton bomb on a large city, since there are so many factors that simply can't be known.

Of course, a high level of accuracy is sometimes quite important. If you are a general in charge of targeting a Soviet missile emplacement and you know that your warhead has a kill radius of 300 meters (i.e., it can destroy a hardened missile silo only if it hits within 300 meters), then you absolutely must have navigational precision good to that level of accuracy. How accurate is that? It means you must know the distance to an accuracy of 300 meters. If the target range is roughly 4000 miles

$$4000 \text{ miles} \times \frac{1}{0.621 \text{ mile per kilometer}} \times 1000 \text{ meters per kilometer}$$

$$= 6.44 \times 10^6 \text{ meters}$$

the distance must be known to within a fractional accuracy of

$$\frac{300 \text{ meters}}{6.44 \times 10^6 \text{ meters}} = 4.7 \times 10^{-5}$$

Expressed as a percent (percent means "per hundred," so 1 percent means 1 in 100), this is

$$(4.7 \times 10^{-5}) \times 100 = 4.7 \times 10^{-3} \text{ percent}$$

or, roughly, $5 \times 10^{-3} = 0.005$ percent. The fact that this kind of accuracy can be achieved is impressive; modern missile targeting requires the very best of high technology. By way of comparison, let us see how accurately we would have to measure the length of a football field to specify it to 0.005 percent (*Answer*: (100 meters) × (0.005 percent) × (1/100) = 0.005 meters = 0.5 centimeters.)

Significant Figures—A Useful Rule

A *significant figure* is any figure that is known to be accurate. Thus 2.234 has four significant figures, as does 2.034; 2.00 and 124,000,000 (1.24×10^8) both have three significant figures. In mathematical computations, a common rule is to include in the answer only as many significant figures as are contained in the least accurate factor. For example,

$$1.24 \times 10^8 \times 12 = 1.5 \times 10^9$$

The factor 12 has only two significant figures; therefore, the answer should have only two significant figures.

8-6 ARITHMETIC WITH EXPONENTIALS

Many of the most interesting numerical problems in the arms race involve multiplying, dividing, adding, and subtracting numbers. Exponential notation is especially useful in multiplication and division. The rules are simple but important.

Multiplication

To multiply numbers in exponential format, multiply the mantissas (the part of the number in front of the exponent) and add the exponents. Then shift the decimal point so that there is just one figure in front of it. Don't forget to drop insignificant digits.

Examples

$$(1.5 \times 10^4) \times (2 \times 10^6) = 3 \times 10^{10} \qquad (8\text{-}8a)$$

$$(3.5 \times 10^3) \times (8 \times 10^{-5}) = 28 \times 10^{-2} = 2.8 \times 10^{-1} = 0.28 \qquad (8\text{-}8b)$$

$$5.56 \times 10^7 \times 6.87 \times 10^{-2} = 3.82 \times 10^6 \qquad (8\text{-}8c)$$

Division

To divide numbers in exponential format, divide the mantissas and subtract the exponent of the denominator from the exponent of the numerator.

Examples

$$\frac{1.5 \times 10^4}{2 \times 10^6} = 0.75 \times 10^{-2} = 7.5 \times 10^{-3} \qquad (8\text{-}9a)$$

$$\frac{1.234 \times 10^{-5}}{5.65 \times 10^6} = 2.18 \times 10^{-12} \qquad (8\text{-}9b)$$

Addition and Subtraction

The main point to remember in addition and subtraction of numbers expressed in exponential format are:

1. Adust the exponents to be the same if you possibly can.
2. If one number is very much smaller than the other, it can generally be neglected since including it in the calculations will not significantly affect the answer.

Examples

$$1.24 \times 10^5 + 2.21 \times 10^3 = 1.24 \times 10^5 + 0.0221 \times 10^5 = 1.26 \times 10^5 \qquad (8\text{-}10a)$$

$$1.24 \times 10^5 + 2.23 \times 10^{-3} = 1.24 \times 10^5 + 0.0000000223 \times 10^5 \times 10^5 = 1.24 \times 10^5 \qquad (8\text{-}10b)$$

In Eq. (8-10a) the 1 in the expression 2.21×10^3 was dropped. This is an example of the use of the guideline that the number of places to be considered significant should be equal to the number of significant figures in the least accurate number given. In Eq. (8-10b) the entire second number was dropped because it was so small that it would have made no significant contribution to the result.

8-7 POWERS AND ROOTS

Sometimes the variable appears in the exponent:

$$y = a^x \qquad (8\text{-}11)$$

Here a is considered to be a constant, called the *base*, and x is the variable. If $a = 10$, we have a base-10 system. In the last few sections we have used the base-10 system for representing numbers. Other bases are sometimes encountered. Computers often use a binary system, which makes use of base 2. (The irrational number $e = 2.718281 \ldots$ is sometimes encountered. See Section P8-7.)

Examples

If $x = 5$, then $2^x = 2 \times 2 \times 2 \times 2 \times 2 = 32$.
If $x = 12$, then $2^x = 4096$.
If $x = \frac{1}{2}$, then $2^x = 1.414$.
If $x = \frac{1}{4}$, then $256^x = 4$.

Quantities can be raised to fractional powers. We can express the fact that the square root of 4 is 2 by writing $4^{0.5} = 2$. The fractional exponent $0.5 = \frac{1}{2}$ is called a square root; the fractional power $\frac{1}{3}$ is called a cube root; and so on. Many pocket calculators can raise numbers to an arbitrary (positive) power. Convince yourself that

$$16^{0.5} = 4$$
$$8^{1/3} = 2$$
$$10000^{1/4} = 100^{1/2} = 10$$

ADDITIONAL PHYSICS SECTION

This section begins a procedure, used throughout the book, of offering additional technical material that explores in more depth some of the ideas introduced in the first part of the chapter. This was done previously in Chapter 3. The material included here will be helpful in understanding the additional physics sections in later chapters, but is not required for reading the main sections of the book. Each main heading has the same number as the section in the chapter to which the material applies.

Summary

If the velocity is v and is constant and the time is t, the distance traversed is

$$d = vt$$

In nonuniform motion v may be variable. One can then speak of an average velocity so that the distance d would be transversed in the time t if the actual velocity were the average instead of one that is changing.

A special case of variable velocity is that of constant acceleration. In this case increase in speed is proportional to time and we have

$$v = at \qquad \text{where } a = \text{acceleration}$$

This equation also defines average acceleration as being

$$a = \frac{v}{t}$$

In the SI system, the unit of acceleration is meters per second per second, or meters per second squared (m/s²); in the British system, it is feet per second per second, or feet per second squared (ft/s²).

A special acceleration is that due to gravity. The symbol for this is g, which is numerically equal to about 32 ft/s², or 9.8 m/s².

If we wish to calculate the distance gone under constant acceleration, the expression

$$d = \tfrac{1}{2}at^2$$

can be used.

The agency for producing acceleration of a mass is a **force**, and the acceleration is proportional to the force. The constant of proportionality is mass, M. This gives us Newton's second law:

$$F = Ma \qquad \text{where } F = \text{force}$$

The unit of force in the SI system is called the *newton*, the basic units, or dimensions, of which are kilogram-meters per second squared (kg · m/s²).

Pressure (P) is defined as the force per unit area or

$$P = \frac{F}{A} \qquad \text{where } A = \text{area}$$

In our discussions of blast pressure, we will use the British unit *pounds per square inch*, or psi.

P8-4   QUANTIFICATION OF PHYSICS OBSERVABLES

For constant velocities the relationship between distance, velocity, and time can be written in the form of a mathematical equation:

$$d = vt \qquad\qquad\qquad\qquad \text{(P8-1)}$$

Read as a sentence this equation is: "The distance traveled is equal to the velocity times the time." Since we have placed considerable emphasis on units, a good way to begin to discuss the equation is to verify that the units are consistent. To do so, rewrite Eq. (P8-1) with units included. Begin with SI units.

$$d(\text{m}) = v(\text{m/s}) \times t\,(\text{s}) \qquad\qquad \text{(P8-2)}$$

Note that the seconds cancel on the right-hand side, so that the equation is dimensionally consistent. Verify that the units are also consistent if distance is measured in miles, velocity in miles per hour, and time in hours. The relationship $d = vt$ is plotted

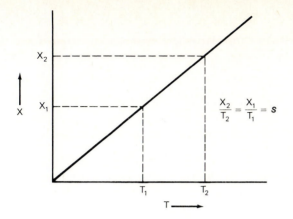

FIGURE 8-3
A plot of distance versus time at constant velocity.

as a graph in Figure 8-3. The ordinate d is given as a function of the abcissa t. The slope of the line is the velocity, v.

Now, what happens if we happen to have units that do not cancel out? Consider a missile traveling at 10,000 mi/h. How far does it go in 2.000 min? An equation one might write down is

$$d = v(\text{mi/h}) \times t(\text{min})$$
$$= 10,000 \ (\text{mi/h}) \times 2.000 \ (\text{min}) \qquad \text{(P8-3)}$$

The units don't cancel. What do we do? Start by noting that both "hour" and "minute" are time dimensions. The problem is that the units are different. We need a conversion factor to convert from hours to minutes. This factor is

$$1 \ \text{hr} = 60 \ \text{min} \qquad \text{(P8-4)}$$

or

$$1 = \tfrac{1}{60} \ \text{h/min} \qquad \text{(P8-5)}$$

Using this conversion factor (P8-3) becomes

$$d = (10,000 \ \text{mi/h}) \times (2.000 \ \text{min}) \times (\tfrac{1}{60} \ \text{h/min})$$
$$= 333.3 \ \text{mi} \qquad \text{(P8-6)}$$

The units and the dimensions are now consistent. Be very sure that in each of your calculations the units and dimensions are consistent. It should be obvious that if they aren't, your answers are likely to be nonsense. If your calculations relate to things you are familiar with—like walking, riding in a car, or riding a bike—you will probably intuitively recognize your errors and go back to see what was wrong. In most of our examples you will not have much intuition to draw on, so you should be sure that you do the calculation correctly.

> **Example.** The distance from an offshore submarine launch site to Moscow was 2000 mi. The rocket travels at an average speed of 8000 mi/h. How many minutes does it travel from liftoff to impact?

Solution

$$t = (2000 \text{ mi}) \times (60 \text{ min/h})/(8000 \text{ mi/h})$$
$$= 15 \text{ min}$$

This doesn't allow much time for warning.

Nonuniform Motion

In our previous examples, we assumed that the velocity was constant. When this is the case, the simple equation (P8-1) is correct. In most real situations, however, the velocity is changing with time. This is certainly the case with a missile, which goes slowly during launch and very rapidly on the final descent trajectory.

The typical velocity pattern of an ICBM is given in Figure 8-4. The velocity given is approximate only, but some principle features can be seen. In this schematic picture the missile starts from rest (0 velocity) and accelerates uniformly for 5 min. It then coasts upward above the atmosphere, losing some velocity. It then begins its descent, gathering velocity as it falls with uniform acceleration. As the missile reenters the atmosphere, there is a braking action due to air friction. Since the flight for a 6000-mile trajectory is about 0.5h, the average horizontal velocity is about 12,000 mi/h. When the vertical velocity is added to this as the missile falls, the total velocity reaches about 20,000 mi/h, as shown in the figure. This high velocity makes interception of such missiles at the target area extremely difficult, especially if many are fired simultaneously.

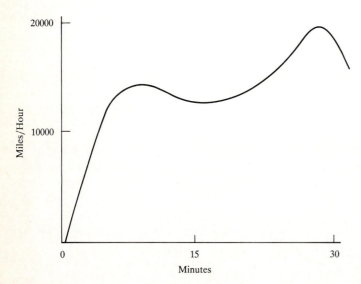

FIGURE 8-4
Velocity of an ICBM as a function of time from launch.

Acceleration

If the velocity of an object changes, the object accelerates. Acceleration is the rate of change of velocity. It can be positive, in which case the velocity is increasing, or negative, in which case the velocity is decreasing. A car approaching an intersection might slow (decelerate) from 60 to 20 mi/h in 10 s. The acceleration, or deceleration in this case, is the change in velocity (final velocity minus initial velocity) divided by the elapsed time:

$$\frac{20 \text{ mi/h} - 60 \text{ mi/h}}{10 \text{s}} = -4 (\text{mi/h})/\text{s}$$

The negative sign indicates that the car is decelerating. The constant velocity we assumed in the discussion of the equation $d = vt$ does not apply here. For our examples we will generally use either a constant velocity approximation or a constant acceleration approximation. To deal with varying velocities and accelerations requires the use of calculus.

As we have said, the standard unit for acceleration in the SI system is meters per second per second, or meters per second squared (m/s^2). Other scale factors can be used, such as kilometers. Thus:

$$(1 \text{ km/s}^2) \times (10^3 \text{ m/km}) = 1000 \text{ m/s}^2 \qquad \text{(P8-7)}$$

Example. A missile enters the earth's atmosphere moving at 20,000 mi/h. As it passes through the atmosphere, the nose is eroded (ablated). The friction that causes the ablation is a retarding force and produces a deceleration. After 0.3 min, the missile is moving at 18,000 mi/h. What is the acceleration in m/s^2? Note the need to do some conversion of units in this problem.

Solution

$$a = \frac{(18,000 \text{ mi/h} - 20,000 \text{ mi/h})}{0.3 \text{ min}} \times \frac{(1600 \text{ m/mi})}{(60 \text{ sec/min})(3600 \text{ sec/h})}$$

$$= -49 \text{ m/s}^2$$

Newton's Second Law

Sir Isaac Newton was the first person to understand and quantify the relationship between forces applied to a body and the resulting acceleration. Newton's second law states that the application of a force leads to acceleration. The constant of proportionality is the mass.

As is usual in physics we will use symbols to express Newton's idea precisely. Consider a body of mass M kg. Apply a force F. In the SI system force is measured in newtons (N). (A force of 1 N is equal to that exerted by a weight of 0.225 lb.) The body will accelerate uniformly with an acceleration a m/s^2. The equation that states this is

$$F = Ma \qquad \text{(P8-8}a\text{)}$$

or

$$F \text{ (newtons)} = M \text{ (kg)} \times a \text{ (m/s}^2) \tag{P8-8b}$$

The constant of proportionality between force and acceleration is the *mass*. For a given force the larger the mass the smaller the acceleration.

In this equation the mass is expressed in kilograms and the acceleration (measured in m/s²) is produced by a force measured in newtons.

It is important to note that Eq. (P8-8a) says that if there is no force, there is no acceleration. That is, the velocity remains unchanged. At first this seems contrary to our experience, since objects set into motion in our daily lives come to rest. However, there is a force acting in such cases, namely, the force of friction. Where there is very little friction, such as in a satellite's orbit, the velocity continues undiminished. If there were no gravity present, the satellite would proceed at constant velocity into space. *Gravitational force* keeps the satellite in a circular path.

The law of gravity states that any two bodies with mass are attracted toward each other. The earth has a very large mass, and it exerts a substantial gravitational attraction on a person. The mass of the moon is much less than that of the earth, so the acceleration force exerted on a person standing on the surface of the moon is much less than on a person standing on the earth. A person standing on the moon weighs only about one-sixth as much as the same person weighs on the earth.

Because on the earth we so often deal with acceleration due to gravity, it has been given a special symbol, g. We can determine g experimentally. The key to one method is found in the equations relating velocity, acceleration, and time when the acceleration is constant:

$$v = at \tag{P8-9}$$

For the acceleration we use the acceleration due to gravity. That is, we drop an object and see how quickly it speeds up. Replacing a by g and solving for g, we get

$$g = \frac{v}{t} \tag{P8-10}$$

All you need do is measure the velocity of a dropped object after it has fallen for a time t. A typical result is that a dropped object will be moving at about 98 m/s after falling for 10 s (in this time it falls about 500 m). From this data we calculate the acceleration at the earth's surface due to gravity to be

$$g = 9.8 \text{ m/s}^2 \tag{P8-11}$$

The force on a 100-kg person (220 lb) in the gravitational field at the earth's surface is

$$F = mg = (100 \text{ kg}) \times (9.8 \text{ m/s}^2) = 980 \text{ N} \tag{P8-12}$$

The force exerted by gravity on a mass M has a special name. It is the **weight** of the mass. Weight in the British system is expressed by the unit pound-force (lbf).

There is a simple way to relate the acceleration due to the earth's gravity to acceleration due to changing velocity. Imagine a plumb bob held in an automobile.

While the car is at rest or in uniform motion, the plumb bob hangs straight down. As the car is braked to a halt, the plumb bob swings forward. When the plumb bob is at exactly 45 degrees, the force due to the deceleration is exactly equal to the acceleration due to gravity, or 9.8 m/s². A person sitting in the car is pushed forward with an acceleration equal to that of gravity, or 1 g.

When an object is dropped from rest, it acquires velocity as a result of acceleration caused by gravity. In the first second of acceleration, the object starts from zero velocity and at the end of the first second it has a velocity of

$$v = gt = (9.8 \text{ m/s}^2) \times (1 \text{ s}) = 9.8 \text{ m/s} \qquad \text{(about 10 m/s)}$$

If we want to know how far the body fell in the first second, it is important to remember that the *average* velocity (v_{av}) should be used:

$$v_{av} = \frac{\text{initial velocity} + \text{final velocity}}{2} \qquad \text{(P8-13)}$$

The average velocity in this case is 5 m/s, and therefore in 1 s the object would fall a distance

$$d = (5 \text{ m/s}) \times (1 \text{ s}) = 5 \text{ m}$$

In general, we can state that the distance fallen d is given by the average velocity multiplied by the time interval:

$$d = v_{av}t \qquad \text{(P8-14)}$$

So, for example, if we wish to know how far a body will fall during the 1-s interval between the ends of the first and of the second seconds, we first calculate the average velocity in that interval: $v_{av} = (10 + 20)/2 = 15$ m/s. An object with this velocity will fall 15m in the second second and 15 m + 5 m = 20 m in the first two seconds. A more general expression for the distance traveled by the end of t seconds is

$$d = \tfrac{1}{2}gt^2 \qquad \text{(P8-15)}$$

Figure 8-5 illustrates a famous experiment alleged to have been conducted at the leaning tower of Pisa by Galileo in the seventeenth century. It demonstrated that the time it takes for objects to fall from a given height is independent of their mass.

Units of Force—The Horrors of the British System

One unit we used above to quantify force was the pound-force (lbf). Sometimes the abbreviated term *pounds* is used. In keeping with our physics background we will generally use the SI unit, the newton, so-called for obvious reasons. (The "n" in newton isn't capitalized. Once one has achieved sufficient fame to become a unit, one is no longer a name! So too with volt, ohm, ampere, watt, coulomb, weber, gauss, and many more.)

In contrast to the SI distance units meters, newtons are quite unfamiliar to most of us. We use them for two reasons. One is that they are in standard use in the

FIGURE 8-5
An object is dropped from the Tower of Pisa.

scientific community. The second reason is that the historical development of the British system led to some horrible notation and some very bad definitions, which make it confusing to carry out force calculations using those units.

The complexity of the British system is so great that we will adopt a rather roundabout procedure for calculating forces. If the calculation has been stated in SI units, there is no problem. If it has been specified in British units—pounds or pound-force— we will convert everything to newtons. If the final answer needs to be specified in British units, we will convert back again!

Pounds, Kilograms, and Tons

The gravitational force (weight) on a 1-kg mass is about 2.2 lbf.

$$1 \text{ kg weight} \approx 2.2 \text{ lbf}$$

$$1 \text{ pound} \approx \frac{1}{2.2} \text{ kg} = 0.454 \text{ kg} = 454g$$

Sometimes weights or forces will be given in tons. In the SI system a ton (sometimes called a metric ton) is always equal to the weight of a 1000 kg mass.

In most of your calculations, you should convert pounds (or tons or ounces, if they occur) into kilograms and then proceed using the SI system. If necessary, convert back to British units at the end of the problem.

Calculation of Pressure

Example 1. What is the force on a wall of a house that has dimensions of 10 ft by 15 ft if the overpressure on the wall is 4 psi (see Fig. 8-6)? Here psi really refers to pounds-force per square inch.

Solution. In equation form the pressure is calculated as

$$P = \frac{F}{A} \tag{P8-16}$$

where P = pressure
F = force
A = area

We begin by expressing the area in square inches:

$$A = (10 \text{ ft}) \times (15 \text{ ft}) = 150 \text{ ft}^2$$
$$(150 \text{ ft}^2) \times (12 \text{ in/ft})^2 = 21,600 \text{ in}^2$$

Next, multiply the area by the force:

$$F = PA = (4 \text{ psi}) \times (21,600 \text{ in}^2) = 86,400 \text{ lbf}$$

Note that the units come out correctly. This force is also equal to 43 tons (2000 lbf/ton). It is certainly sufficient to demolish an ordinary house.

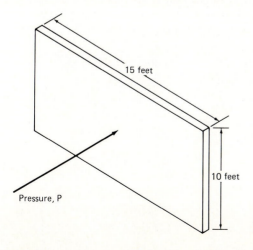

15 feet

10 feet

Pressure, P

FIGURE 8-6
A pressure wave is incident on the wall of a house, creating a force on the structure.

Example 2. What is the blast force on a person exposed to a 1-Mt explosion 5 mi from ground zero?

Solution. A 1-Mt nuclear weapon burst at 6000 ft will give a short-duration overpressure of about 4 psi in the horizontal direction at 5 mi from ground zero. We can estimate the force that a person standing upright 5 mi from the explosion would experience. Suppose such a person were rectangular (for ease of calculation), having dimensions of 10 in wide by 70 in high. The person's area is then 10 in × 70 in, or 700 in². Then the force exerted by the blast pressure is

$$F = PA = (4 \text{ lb/in}^2) \times (700 \text{ in}^2) = 2800 \text{ lbf}$$

A force greatly exceeding the weight of a person will move that person around. In fact, for a person weighing 140 lb the above force is 20 times the force of gravity, or $20g$. The above force is not only sufficient to knock the person down, but also to give her or him considerable velocity (see Glasstone, Chap. 12). This is the origin of some blast injuries.

Pressure is an important quantity in designing structures to resist blasts. In Chapter 13 we examine design criteria for structures that are used to protect missile silos against attack and discuss the effects of pressure on urban structures.

P8-7 EXPONENTIALS: BASE *e*

A number occurring naturally in physics is 2.718281 . . . (the dots indicate that the number continues indefinitely when expressed as a decimal). This number is so common in physics that it has been given a special symbol, *e*. It is called an irrational number, meaning that it cannot be expressed exactly as a continuing fraction. Pi, the ratio of the circumference to the diameter of a circle, is also an irrational number.

The quantity *e* occurs in processes in which the rate of change of a quantity is proportional to the amount left of the quantity. For example, the rate of radioactive decay, or radioactivity, of a given material is proportional to the number of radioactive atoms remaining (see Chapter 10) in that material. The absorption of gamma rays in matter is another example, since the number of gamma rays absorbed in a small thickness of material is proportional to the number entering it.

The quantity *e* is also found in the discussion of the probability of hitting a target given a specified missile targeting accuracy.

Example. Evaluate $y = e^x$, where $x = 3$.

Solution. Using a calculator, we find $y = 20.0855$.

QUESTIONS

1. Distinguish between speed and velocity.
2. Are "kilograms" a measure of mass or force?
3. Define acceleration.
4. What determines how much mass an object has?

5. How is acceleration related to force and mass?
6. How is weight related to mass?
7. Discuss the difference between technology and physics.
8. Discuss falsifiability as a measure of a theory in physics.
9. How many centimeters are there in an inch?
10. Express (1.5E5) in ordinary numerical notation.
11. What is 1.0×10^{-3} multiplied by 2.0×10^5?
12. Define pressure.

PROBLEMS

1. An intercontinental ballistic missile is rated as Mach 25. This means that it enters the atmosphere at 25 times the speed of sound at sea level, which is about 1100 ft/s. What is the velocity of the missile in miles per hour? (5280 ft = 1 mi). Give the answer to two significant figures.
2. How far does an object released from rest fall between the end of the second second and the end of the third second after it is released?
3. A car accelerates uniformly from rest to 60 mi/h in 10 s. What is the acceleration in miles per hour per second?
4. How far does the car in Problem 3 go?
5. If a woman has a mass of 60 kg what is her weight (in newtons)?
6. How much would the woman weigh on the moon where gravity is one-sixth of that on the earth? Would her mass change?
7. The nuclear chain reaction (fission) that produces the explosion of an atom bomb occurs in 1 μs $(1 \times 10^{-6}$s). If the speed of the bomb fragments and vaporized components is 3×10^5 m/s, how far do the components disperse during the nuclear explosion phase? (Assume that the components start from rest and are uniformly accelerated.)
8. How much force is required to give a missile with a mass of 10 tons (10,000 kg) a velocity of 1 km/s in a time period of 100 s?
9. Assume that thunder and lighting occur simultaneously and that light travels almost instantaneously. If you hear the thunder 10 s after you see the lightning, how far away is the thunderstorm? (Assume that the speed of sound is 1100 ft/s.)
10. The cruising speed of a Boeing 747 is 600 mi/h. If the air distance from New York to Los Angeles is 2500 mi, how long will the trip take?
11. A rocket accelerates with an average acceleration (i.e., equivalent to a uniform acceleration) of 20 m/s² for 5 min. What is the magnitude of its final velocity in meters per second? What is this velocity in feet per second?
12. An object is dropped from a bridge into a river below and a splash is seen 4 s later. What is the height of the bridge above the water?
13. In Problem 12 what is the velocity of the object just as it strikes the water?
14. A bullet whose mass is 10 g strikes a tree and stops in 10 cm. If the original velocity of the bullet is 200 m/s, what is the average force on the bullet exerted by the tree?
15. If a 20-N force is applied to a mass of 100 kg, how long does it take to achieve a velocity of 25 m/s?
16. How far has the mass in Problem 15 gone by the time is has achieved a velocity of 25 m/s?

17. Express the following numbers in exponential notation: (*a*) 0.00345, (*b*) 123.456, (*c*) 1000, (*d*) 0.00000093.

18. Express the following numbers without using exponential notation: (*a*) 123 $\times$ 10^6, (*b*) 123 $\times$ 16^{-6}, (*c*) 0.00345 $\times$ 10^3, (*c*) 123.000123 $\times$ 10^9.

19. Assume that the following numbers are valid to within 10 percent. Round them off so that only significant digits are included: (*a*) 12345, (*b*) 0.00765, (*c*) 123 $\times$ 10^6, (*d*) 1.5 $\times$ 10^{-8}, (*e*) 9.7 $\times$ 10^{10}.

20. What is wrong with the following conversion? 1 year contains Z seconds. Therefore, Z is given by

$$Z = (365 \text{ days/yr}) \times (1/24 \text{ h/day}) \times (60 \text{ min/h}) \times (60 \text{ s/min})$$
$$= 54750 \text{ s/yr}$$

21. Carry out the following operations and round the results to two significant figures: (*a*) (45 $\times$ 10^5)/(6.5 $\times$ 10^4), (*b*) 123.456/(8 $\times$ 10^{-5}), (*c*) 154.7 + 0.000456, (*d*) $-65.99 - (976 \times 10^{-1})$.

22. Evaluate the following expressions: (*a*) $\frac{6}{5} + \frac{7}{6} + \frac{8}{9}$, (*b*) 6/(5 + 7)/6 + $\frac{8}{9}$, (*c*) 6/(5 + 7)/(6 + 8)/9, (*d*) 6/(5 + 7)/(6 + 8)/9).

23. Evaluate the following expressions: (*a*) 2^8, (*b*) 2^{-8}, (*c*) 8^2, (*d*) 8^{-2}, (*e*) 8$^{1/2}$, (*f*) 8$^{-1/2}$, (*g*) 2$^{1/8}$, (*h*) 2$^{-1/8}$, (*i*) 1/2$^{-1/8}$ (*j*) 1/2$^{1/8}$. Explain why several of the answers are equal.

24. In driving from Davis to San Francisco (80 mi) I travel 40 mi at 60 mi/h and 40 mi at 30 mi/h. What is my average velocity? If I travel 50 mi at 60 mi/h and 30 mi at 30 mi/h, what is my average velocity. [*Note*: Why is it wrong to average the two speeds directly? That is, why is it *not* true that $\bar{v} = (\hat{v}_1 + v_2)/2$?]

25. An accelerating missile has the following velocities at the indicated times. Approximately how far will it have gone at the end of 30 s?

Time, *s*	Velocity, **mph**
5	50
10	200
15	400
20	800
25	1400
30	2400

26. (*a*) How long does it take a weight to drop to the ground from the top of a building that is 100 ft. tall; (*b*) How long does a climber who slips off the face of El Capitan (Yosemite valley) have to review his life (exposed face height about 3000 ft)?

27. Give the force exerted on a wall of a supermarket that is oriented perpendicular to the blast wave of a 1 Mt nuclear explosion under the following conditions: The wall is 100 ft long and 20 ft high and is located 5 mi from ground zero. The overpressure is 4 psi. Give your answer in tons.

28. A rock is hurled upward at an initial velocity of 20 m/s. If air resistance is neglected, how high will the rock rise?

29. How much force does it take (in newtons) to lift a car with a 1000-kg mass?

30. A horizontal force of 100 N is applied to a body of mass 20 kg which is initially at rest on a frictionless surface. Calculate the acceleration of the mass.

31. If a missile is traveling at 100 km altitude and has a horizontal velocity of 2 km/s, what is its impact velocity, neglecting air friction?

KEY WORDS

velocity   the change in distance in a certain time, or the distance traversed divided by the elapsed time.

acceleration   the change in velocity in a certain time, or the change in velocity divided by the elapsed time.

force   the physical means by which an acceleration is produced. According to Newton's second law, force is the product of an object's mass and the acceleration produced by the force. If there is no force, the acceleration is zero and the velocity does not change.

weight   the attraction of gravity (usually that of the earth) for a mass. It is equal to the object's mass multiplied by the acceleration of gravity g.

pressure   force divided by the area over which the force acts. Usually expressed as pounds per square inch.

CHAPTER
9

ENERGY—
AN INTRODUCTION
TO NUCLEAR
PHYSICS

only the earth endures, but it endures forever

Thomas Wolfe

9-1   THEMES

The concept of energy (particularly nuclear energy) is introduced. Einstein's equation $E = mc^2$ is introduced and used to calculate the amount of mass converted to energy in atomic bombs and fusion bombs. Atomic number, mass number, and isotope are defined, and the symbols conventionally used to refer to them are given.

9-2   OVERVIEW

What is meant by a "1-megaton" nuclear explosion? To understand this we need the concept of *energy*. A nuclear weapon with a yield of 1 megaton releases as much energy as is contained in 1 million tons of TNT. A 10-kiloton, or nearly Hiroshima-sized, explosion releases the energy equivalent of 10,000 tons of TNT. A standard railroad hopper car holds about 100 tons, so the amount of TNT to produce a Hiroshima-sized explosion would require a 100-car train. (A modern 100-megawatt coal-fired power plant requires a 100-car trainload of coal each day.) One megaton is 100 times more than that, an amount of energy so large that it is almost impossible to imagine.

   Energy may be defined as the capability of doing work. Energy exists in many different forms: mechanical, electrical, nuclear, heat, thermal radiation, and even as mass (see below). Mechanical energy can be in the form of **kinetic energy** (energy due to motion) or **potential energy** (energy due to position). Energy can be transformed from one form to another. For example, a raised object at rest has potential energy only, but when it is released its potential energy is transformed into kinetic energy. Einstein showed that mass and energy are in certain ways interchangeable. Mass can be converted to energy, and energy to mass.

Energy (in its broad sense, including mass) is never lost or created. This universal observation is so profound and so important that it has been elevated to the status of a law: *the law of conservation of energy*. (This law is sometimes called the law of conservation of mass-energy to stress that mass is a form of energy.)

9-3   ENERGY UNITS

The energy released in the fission of single uranium nucleus, or the fission of two light nuclei such as deuterium and tritium (see Sections 9-6 and 9-7), is very tiny by macroscopic standards. Vast numbers of nuclei must undergo fission or fusion to produce the energy released in a nuclear explosion. To describe these different processes requires both large and small energy units.

In the SI system of units the basic energy unit (or work unit, since work and energy are identical) is the *joule* (J). This is a "human scale" unit. Work carried out at a certain rate is *power*. One joule of work expended every second produces exactly one *watt* of power. That is, a watt is a joule per second. A typical light bulb consumes energy at a rate of 100 watts, or 100 joules per second. A person working very hard can produce about 100 watts continuously throughout an 8-hour day. One horsepower is equal to 746 watts, which is a rate of energy consumption of 746 joules per second.

The energy release in a 1-megaton explosion is 4.72 quadrillion joules:

$$1 \text{ megaton (Mt) TNT} = 4.18 \times 10^{15} \text{ joules} \tag{9-1}$$

Hence

$$1 \text{ kiloton (kt) TNT} = 0.001 \text{ megaton} = 4.18 \times 10^{12} \text{ joules}$$

The unit of energy commonly used in discussing nuclear reactions is the electron volt (eV). An electron volt is the amount of energy a unit charge (as on an electron) would gain in falling through an electrical potential difference of 1 volt (see Chapter 12). It takes about 6000 quadrillion election volts to make 1 joule (1 electron volt $= 1.6 \times 10^{-19}$ joules). The electron volt is so tiny that it cannot be detected directly by a human being. The energy released in a single atom or molecule in a chemical reaction is typically of the order of a few electron volts.

In nuclear fission or fusion reactions, the energy released is millions of times larger than the energy released in chemical reactions. It is measured in units of millions of electron volts (MeV). One MeV is one million electron volts.

$$1 \text{ MeV} = 1 \times 10^{6} \text{ electron volts} = 1.6 \times 10^{-13} \text{ joules} \tag{9-2}$$

Even though the energy release in a nuclear fission reaction is large compared to the energy release in a chemical reaction, it is still extremely small compared to that released in a bomb. A nuclear explosion requires enormous numbers of nuclear reactions: about 10^{26} nuclear fissions (one hundred billion quadrillion fissions) are required to release 1 megaton of energy (see Section P9-6).

9-4 MASS AS A FORM OF ENERGY

A consequence of the special theory of relativity of Einstein (1905) is that mass and energy are equivalent quantities. The equivalence is expressed by Einstein's famous equation

$$E = mc^2 \qquad (9-3)$$

where E = energy, joules
  m = mass, kilograms
  c = speed of light, 3×10^8 meters per second

Because the speed of light is so large, the conversion of just a small amount of mass produces a large quantity of energy. If a 1-gram mass of uranium (which is about the size of an aspirin tablet) were converted into energy, it would produce:

$$(0.001 \text{ kilograms}) \times (3 \times 10^8 \text{ meters per second})^2$$

$$= 9 \times 10^{13} \text{ kilogram-meters squared per}$$
$$\text{second squared (kg} \cdot \text{m}^2/\text{s}^2)$$

$$= 9 \times 10^{13} \text{ joules}$$

Since there are 4.18×10^{12} joules per kiloton, the TNT equivalent of the conversion of 1 gram of mass to energy is $(9 \times 10^{13}$ joules$)/(4.18 \times 10^{12}$ joules per kiloton$)$ = 22 kilotons of TNT. This is about the energy released by the Nagasaki bomb. Einstein's equation does not tell us how to convert mass into energy or vice versa, but it does tell us quantitatively what the energy release would be.

Chemical processes change a very small amount of mass into energy per chemical reaction (typically 1 ten-billionth is changed). (Chemists often talk about the conservation of mass in chemical reactions. While not strictly correct, the approximation is accurate enough for many purposes.) In contrast, in nuclear reactions in nuclear bombs about 0.1 percent of the mass is converted into energy. This is the origin of the awesome power of nuclear weapons.

When a nuclear weapon explodes, the nuclear energy is released chiefly in the kinetic energy (energy of motion) of the fission fragments. This kinetic energy is mostly converted to thermal energy (heat energy). The resulting fireball is many times brighter than the sun and radiates electromagnetic energy. The rapidly expanding fireball produces a pressure wave.

9-5 NUCLEAR CONSTITUENTS

Atomic nuclei are made of neutrons and protons. These have almost the same mass, but one proton carries one positive unit of electrical charge (an electron carries one

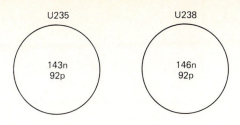

FIGURE 9-1
Nuclei of uranium 235 and uranium 238 are shown schematically with their neutron and proton numbers indicated.

negative unit), whereas the neutron is electrically neutral. Neutrons or protons are described as **nucleons**. The nuclear constituents are bound together through nuclear binding forces which are far stronger than the electrical forces which hold atoms together.

Nuclei of the same chemical element have the same number of protons. The number of protons in a nucleus is called the **atomic number** and is denoted by the symbol Z. Uranium has an atomic number of 92 since it has 92 protons in its nucleus. Nuclei that have the same number of protons but a different number of neutrons are called *isotopes*. The number of neutrons in the nucleus is denoted by the symbol N. Two important isotopes of uranium are uranium 235 and uranium 238. The former has $235 - 92 = 143$ neutrons in its nucleus, and the latter has $238 - 92 = 146$ neutrons in its nucleus. The total number of nuclear constituents (neutrons plus protons) is called the **mass number** (symbol A).

It is always true that the nuclear mass number A is given by

$$A = N + Z \tag{9-4}$$

Thus A is 235 for uranium 235 and 238 for uranium 238. Figure 9-1 gives a schematic picture of these two uranium nuclei. In actual fact, nuclei are approximately spherical in shape, but are exceedingly tiny, a uranium nucleus being only about 2×10^{-14} meters (20 quadrillionths of a meter) in diameter.

The symbolic notation used for nuclei consists of the symbol for the element, with the mass number appearing to the left of the symbol, as a superscript, and the atomic number to the left of the symbol, as a subscript; for example,

$$^{238}_{92}\text{U} \qquad ^{235}_{92}\text{U}$$

9-6   ENERGY RELEASE FROM NUCLEAR FISSION

When a nucleus of a uranium 235 atom captures a neutron, it has a high probability of fissioning into two fragments of unequal mass. The sum of the masses of the fragments is slightly less than the mass of the original nucleus. The missing mass has been converted into energy. The Einstein relation $E = mc^2$ tells us that energy will be released. (Here m is the loss of mass that occurs when the $^{235}_{92}\text{U}$ fissions.) The energy release is approximately 200 MeV per fission of each nucleus. About one one-thousandth (0.1 percent) of the mass of the uranium atom is actually converted into energy. Complete fission of 57 grams of uranium converts approximately 0.057 gram of mass (0.001×57) to energy, yielding an energy release of 1 kiloton.

Although each fission releases only 200 MeV $\times$ 1.6×10^{-13} joules per MeV, or 3.2×10^{-11} joules of energy, there are an enormous number of fissions if 57 grams of uranium are fissioned to release an energy of 1 kiloton of TNT: about 1.3×10^{23}! The product of the energy release per fission and the number of fissions is about 4.2×10^{12} joules, or 1 kiloton of TNT equivalent.

In an explosion the bomb blows itself apart ("disassembles" in the jargon of nuclear bomb builders) before all uranium atoms have been fissioned. A fission bomb typically contains several kilograms of uranium 235 or plutonium 239. The enormous energy released separates the bomb's constituents in a few millionths of a second (microseconds) and begins to form a fireball.

9-7 ENERGY RELEASE FROM NUCLEAR FUSION

Nuclear energy can also be released by the *fusion* of two nuclei. This is possible because the fusion products for nuclei of small atomic number have less mass than the combined mass of the original nuclei that are fused. In the hydrogen bomb this is accomplished in part by fusing together the nuclei of two hydrogen isotopes, deuterium and tritium, to form a nucleus of helium and a neutron.* Deuterium is the name given to the isotope of hydrogen which has one neutron and one proton. Normal hydrogen has a nucleus of just a proton so the deuterium nucleus has about twice the mass of an ordinary hydrogen nucleus. Tritium is an isotope of hydrogen with two neutrons and one proton in this nucleus. It therefore has about 3 times the mass of an ordinary hydrogen nucleus.

The fusion of deuterium (the isotope of hydrogen with nuclear mass $A = 2$) and tritium (the isotope of hydrogen with nuclear mass $A = 3$) to form helium and a neutron with a release of energy may be written:

$$\,^2_1\text{H} \;+\; \,^3_1\text{H} \;\rightarrow\; \,^4_2\text{He} \;+\; \,^1_0 n \;\; + 17.6 \text{ MeV}$$

deuterium + tritium $\rightarrow$ helium 4 + neutron +   energy

In this nuclear reaction the sum of the atomic numbers on one side of the equation is equal to the sum of the atomic numbers on the other side: $1 + 1 = 2 + 0$. This expresses the fact that nuclear charge is a conserved quantity. If a charged particle such as an electron is part of the reaction products (as in radioactivity), the number of protons can change but the overall charge is conserved. Similarly, the total number of neutrons and protons, or the mass number, is conserved so that in the above equation

---

*Energy in a hydrogen bomb is also released from the fission primary, which serves as the match to ignite the deuterium and tritium, and from the fission of uranium which surrounds the thermonuclear part of the bomb. See Chapter 11.

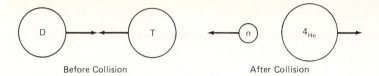

FIGURE 9-2

Deuterium and tritum nuclei are given enough kinetic energy to permit them to fuse when they collide. A nuclear reaction takes place in which energy is released and the reaction products ^{4}He and a neutron are formed.

the sums of the superscripts on both sides are equal $(2 + 3 = 4 + 1)$. This reaction is shown schematically in Figure 9.2.

In the nuclear reaction shown in Figure 9-2, 17.6 MeV is the energy released. In a hydrogen bomb (in contrast to a fission bomb) there is no limit to the amount of fusible atoms one can use. This is because a fusion reaction is not a chain reaction, as is a fission reaction. There is no critical mass, which occurs when two subcritical pieces are assembled. The process of fusion is similar to that involved in the explosion of dynamite by a percussion cap. The amount of dynamite that is exploded depends only on how much dynamite is in the vicinity of the percussion cap. In a hydrogen bomb, a fission bomb becomes the percussion cap (see Chapter 11).

ADDITIONAL PHYSICS SECTION

Summary

In the following expressions for work and energy, energy is measured in joules, mass in kilograms, and distance in meters.

$$E = F \times d$$

where E = energy, joules
F = force, newtons
d = distance, meters

Kinetic energy KE $= \frac{1}{2}Mv^2$
$= \frac{1}{2}$ (mass $\times$ velocity squared)

Gravitional potential energy PE $= M \times g \times h$
$=$ mass $\times$ acceleration of gravity $\times$ height

A mole is the mass in grams with the numerical value equal to the mass number of an isotope. Thus 1 mole of ^{235}U weighs 235 g. There are 6.02×10^{23} atoms in 1 mole. (This quantity is called Avogadro's number.) Hence 235 g of ^{235}U and 2 g of deuterium (^{2}H) each contain 6.02×10^{23} atoms.

P9-2   ENERGY

Mechanical energy is produced when a force acts through a distance (d) in the direction of the force:

$$E\text{(joules)} = F\text{(newtons)} \times d\text{(meters)} \tag{P9-1}$$

If the force is due to gravity, then, from Newton's law,

$$F\text{(newtons)} = M\text{(kg)} \times g\text{(m/s}^2\text{)} \quad \text{(the object's weight)}$$

where $g = 9.8$ m/s^2 is the acceleration due to gravity (see P8-1).

   If a missile has a mass of 20 tons (18,000 kg), the mechanical energy required to lift it 1 km (1000 m) above the earth in its flight is (see Figure 9-3):

$$E = Fd = Mgd = (18{,}000 \text{ kg}) \times (9.8 \text{ m/s}^2) \times (1000 \text{ m})$$
$$Mgd = 1.8 \times 10^8 \text{ kg} \cdot \text{m}^2/\text{s}^2 \tag{P9-2}$$
$$= 1.8 \times 10^8 \text{ J}$$

Kinetic Energy

One form of mechanical energy is **kinetic energy**. If a car with a mass (M) of 1000 kg is pushed with a force of 100 N, it will accelerate and work will be done on it. The work done by the applied force goes into the energy of the car's motion and is called the *kinetic* energy (sometimes called the kinetic energy of motion). Kinetic energy is energy that an object contains by virtue of its motion. This is illustrated in Figure 9-4. When the car, which is initially at rest, accelerates, it acquires a velocity (v). There is a kinetic energy associated with this speed:

$$\text{KE} = \tfrac{1}{2}Mv^2 \tag{P9-3}$$

Note that the units of kinetic energy are kg $\cdot$ m^2/s^2 (kilogram-meters squared per second squared), or J (joules). Note also that the kinetic energy depends on the square

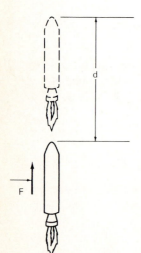

FIGURE 9-3
A missile is lifted in the earth's gravitational field. This requires that work done on it be equal to its mass times the acceleration of gravity times the height—all in consistent units.

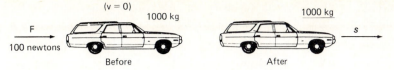

FIGURE 9-4
When a force is applied to a body and the body moves in the direction of the force, work is done. A force that does not lead to motion does not work.

of the velocity. This means that a car that is going 60 mi/h has four times the kinetic energy as one going 30 mi/h (and therefore can do four times as much damage, not twice as much).

Using the law of conservation of energy, we may write

$$\tfrac{1}{2}Mv^2 = Fd \qquad \text{(P9-4)}$$

In words: "One-half the mass (in kilograms) times velocity (in meters squared per second squared) is equal to the force (in newtons) times distance (in meters)."

Since mechanical quantities are involved here, this is an example of the law of conservation of mechanical energy. More generally we can convert virtually any form of energy into another. Other forms include heat energy, nuclear energy, chemical energy, and electrical energy.

We can calculate the kinetic energy acquired by the car if we know the distance through which the force acts. If this distance is 10 m, the kinetic energy is [by Eq. (P9-1)]

$$KE = (100 \text{ N}) \times (10 \text{ m}) = 1000 \text{ N} \cdot \text{m} \qquad \text{(or 1000 J)}$$

We can develop some understanding of why the kinetic energy should be $\tfrac{1}{2}M \times v^2$ by noting that the distance traveled under steady acceleration is given by the *average* velocity multiplied by the time in whch the acceleration acts. For uniform (constant) acceleration starting from zero velocity ($v = 0$) and accelerating to velocity v, the average velocity is $(0 + v) = \dfrac{v}{2}$. Thus the distance traveled is $d = (v/2)t$. The kinetic energy is given by the product Fd, and F is equal to the mass multiplied by the acceleration (v/t) (Newton's law; see Chapter 8). From Chapter 8 we know that the velocity is the acceleration times the time. Hence the acceleration is

$$a = \frac{v}{t}$$

Therefore, the product Fd is

$$\frac{Mv}{t} \times \frac{vt}{2} = \tfrac{1}{2}Mv^2$$

Potential Energy

Another form of mechanical energy is **potential energy**. This is the energy contained in a system by virtue of its position. If we lift a mass M against the force of gravity, then we are doing work. To overcome gravity we must supply a force equal to the mass multiplied by g, the acceleration due to gravity. If the mass is lifted a height h against gravity, then the force Mg acts through a distance h, given as a potential energy:

$$PE = Mgh \tag{P9-5}$$

This equation states that the potential energy equals the mass M (in kilograms) times the acceleration of gravity g (in meters per second squared) times height h (in meters). The final dimensions are

$$(kg \cdot m/s^2) \times (m) = kg) \, m^2/s^2 d = J$$

Since energy is conserved, nuclear energy can be transformed into mechanical energy and mechanical energy can in turn be transformed from kinetic energy to potential energy and vice versa. In the British system of units, energy is expressed in British thermal units (Btu) (1 Btu equals 1055 J). Sometimes energy is expressed by a mixed unit, the *calorie*. One calorie equals 4.2 joules. Formerly, the term *Calorie* (capital C) denoted 1000 calories (lowercase c), or 1 kilocalorie. The calories appearing on food containers (often written with a lowercase c) are always kilocalories.

Example 1. How many kilocalories will be used by a 100-kg (220-lb) climber hiking up Mount Whitney? The vertical height from the Lone Pine roadhead is roughly 1 km (1000 m).

Solution. The energy needed is $Mgh = (100 \text{ kg}) \times 9.8 \text{ m/s}^2) \times (1000 \text{ m}) = 1 \times 10^6$ J. There are 4.2 joules per calorie, or 4200 joules per kilocalorie. Thus the food energy required is about $(10^6 \text{ J})/(4200 \text{ joules per kilocalorie}) = 240$ kilocalories (240 Calories). This is roughly the energy in two individual packages of oatmeal. Since the hiker is not 100 percent efficient, the actual energy requirement will be substantially greater.

Example 2. A 1-kt bomb is exploded under an aircraft carrier of the Nimitz class (loaded) which has a mass of 90,000 tons. (The cost of such a carrier is currently $2 billion, or about $10 per pound. This is twice as expensive as a compact car, which weighs about one ton and costs about $10,000!) How high would the carrier be lifted if 10% of the nuclear energy were converted to kinetic energy? (see Figure 9-5). (*Note*: This in an unrealistic problem because only a small part of the nuclear energy would actually be available as kinetic energy—probably only a few percent. However, one could equally well assume a 10-kt bomb at 1 percent efficiency of conversion or a 100-kt bomb at 0.1 percent efficiency rather than a 1-kt bomb at 10 percent efficiency.)

Solution. By the law of conservation of energy:

$$Mgh = 0.1 \times 1 \text{ kt} = 4.18 \times 10^{11} \text{ J} \tag{P9-6}$$

It is important to be sure that the units in the calculation are consistent. If the energy is in joules, then the mass must be in kilograms and the lengths in meters. A 1-ton mass is 2000 lb, and 1 lb $= 1/2.2$ kg, so there are about 900 kg/ton. The carrier therefore has a mass of $(900 \times 90,000)$ kg $= 8.1 \times 10^7$ kg. Since $PE = Mgh$ we know that

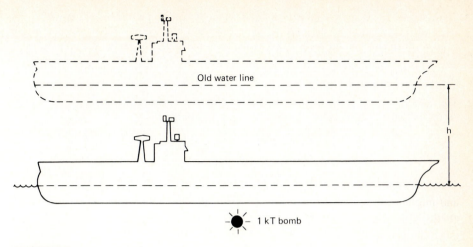

FIGURE 9-5
An aircraft carrier of the Nimitz class is lifted vertically a distance h against the pull of gravity by the explosion of a 1-kiloton atomic bomb beneath it.

$$h = \frac{PE}{Mg} \qquad (P9\text{-}7)$$

Then

$$h = \frac{1 \text{ kt}}{Mg} \times 0.01 = \frac{4.18 \times 10^{12} \text{ J} \times 0.1}{(8.1 \times 10^7 \text{ kg}) \times (9.8 \text{ m/s}^2)} = 527 \text{ meters}$$

and

$$(527 \text{ m}) \times (3.18 \text{ ft/m}) = 1730 \text{ ft}$$

Here the factor 9.8 m/s^2 is g expressed in SI units. Often we will assume that g is 10 m/s^2 in order-of-magnitude calculations.

We can use the law of conservation of mechanical energy to find the initial speed of the carrier:

$$\begin{aligned}
\tfrac{1}{2}Mv^2 &= Mgh \\
&= (8.1 \times 10^7 \text{ kg}) \times (9.8 \text{ m/s}^2) \times (527 \text{ m}) \qquad (P9\text{-}8) \\
&= 4.18 \times 10^{11} \text{ J}
\end{aligned}$$

This energy is just one-tenth the original energy of the 1-kt nuclear explosion, as we assumed. We can use (P9-8) to solve for the velocity of the ship:

$$\begin{aligned}
\tfrac{1}{2} Mv^2 &= Mgh \\
&= \frac{Mgh}{\tfrac{1}{2}M} = \frac{2Mgh}{M} = \frac{2(4.18 \times 10^{11})}{8.1 \times 10^7}
\end{aligned}$$

from which we find

$$v = 102 \text{ m/s} \qquad \text{(about 230 mi/h)}$$

If this velocity were achieved in, say, 0.5s, the acceleration would be (102 m/s)/0.5 s = 204 m/s², or about 20 g (20 × the acceleration of gravity). (The conversion to g is done by dividing the acceleration by the acceleration due to gravity, 9.8 m/s².)

In this example we might also ask what force is exerted on the carrier. The force can be found from the acceleration and the carrier's mass. The acceleration is the final speed, 102 m/s, divided by the time to attain it, assumed to be 0.5 s. Therefore, the acceleration is 204 m/s², and the force is

$$F = (8.1 \times 10^7 \text{ kg}) \times (204 \text{ m/s}^2)$$
$$= 1.65 \times 10^{10} \text{ N}$$

Since a force of 10 N corresponds to about 2.2 lbf, this amounts to about (1.65 × 10¹⁰ N) × (2.2 lbf/10 N) = 3.6 × 10⁹ lb, or 1.8 million tons (about 20 times the carrier's normal weight).

P9-6 ENERGY RELEASE FROM NUCLEAR FISSION—AVOGADRO'S NUMBER

The basic concept behind obtaining energy from nuclear fission is

Total energy = energy release per fission × large number of fissions

Suppose that a bomb contains 5 kg of $^{235}_{92}$U and that 10 percent of it fissions in a nuclear explosion. How much energy will be released? In order to calculate this we need to know how many uranium atoms there are in 5 kg of uranium.

The key to calculating the number of atoms is found in the mass number. In ^{235}U there are 235 protons and neutrons. If we know the mass of an individual proton and neutron, then the number of protons and neutrons can be found by dividing their individual masses into the total mass of the element or isotope. This kind of calculation is done very often in science. To make it simple we use the concept of a *mole*. The **mole** of a substance is the mass (in grams) corresponding numerically to the mass number of the element. Thus the mole weight of ^{235}U is 235 g, and the mole weight of ^{238}U is 238 g. The advantage of the mole-weight concept is that 1 mole weight (often called *gram-molecular weight*) contains the same number of nuclei, regardless of the mass number.

There are just 6.023 × 10²³ nuclei contained in 1 mole of any substance. This number is so important and so often used that it is given a special name: **Avogadro's number**. One mole of uranium 235 has a mass of 235 g. Hence 235 g of uranium 235 contains 6.023 × 10²³ uranium atoms. In our example we assume we start with 5 kg of ^{235}U and fission 10 percent of it. The mass of the ^{235}U fissioned is therefore 5 kg × 0.10 = 500 g. 500 g is 500/235 = 2.13 moles. The number of ^{235}U nuclei fissioned is therefore (2.13 moles) × (6.023 × 10²³) = 1.3 × 10²⁴ fissioned ^{235}U nuclei.

If each nucleus of the atom releases 200 MeV when it fissions, the total energy release is

$(1.3 \times 10^{24} \text{ fissions}) \times (200 \text{ MeV/fission})$
$$\times (1.6 \times 10^{-13} \text{ J/MeV}) = 4.1 \times 10^{13} \text{ J}$$

Since there are 4.2×10^{12} J/kt, the energy released in this example is approximately equivalent to 10 kt of TNT.

P9-7   CALCULATION OF THE ENERGY RELEASED IN A FUSION BOMB

Suppose that a fusion bomb is composed of 100 kg of deuterium ^2_1H (1 mole = 2g) and 150 kg of tritium ^3_1H (1 mole = 3 g), and the 10 percent of the material in the bomb fuses in the explosion. What is the energy release?

The total mass involved in the fusion reactions is $0.1 \times (100 \text{ kg})$, or 10 kg, of deuterium and 0.1×150, or 15 kg, of tritium. If we use the deuterium to measure the number of reactions, we have

No. of reactions $= (10 \text{ kg}) \times (1000 \text{ g/kg}) \times (6.023 \times 10^{23} \text{ nuclei/mole})$
$$\times (0.5 \text{ mole/g})$$
$$= 3.01 \times 10^{27} \text{ reactions}$$

Each reaction releases 17.6 MeV of energy. Since there are 1.6×10^{-13} J/MeV, each reaction releases $17.6 \times 1.6 \times 10^{-13} = 2.82 \times 10^{-12}$ J. The total energy released is then the product of the energy released by the individual reaction multiplied by the number of reactions:

Total energy released $= (2.82 \times 10^{-12} \text{ J/reaction}) \times (3.0 \times 10^{27} \text{ reactions})$
$$= 8.5 \times 10^{15} \text{ J}$$
$$= 2 \text{ Mt}$$

P9-8   THE AVERAGE BINDING ENERGY PER NUCLEON

Figure 9-6 shows the average **binding energy per nucleon** for nuclei with mass numbers from hydrogen to plutonium. This curve demonstrates that nuclei in the vicinity of iron in atomic number are the most tightly bound. The binding energy is nearly 9 MeV per nucleon. This means that on the average 9 MeV must be expended to extract a nucleon from this nuclei. They are therefore more stable than other nuclei for which the binding energy per nucleon is less—for example, uranium, which has a binding energy per nucleon of about 7.5 MeV. When a uranium or plutonium nucleus undergoes fission, the fission fragments are likely to be formed in the region of mass number 90 for the light fragment and about 140 for the heavy fragment (see Section 10-5). The binding energies per nucleon are about 8.8 MeV and 8.4 MeV respectively. Therefore, there is roughly an average binding energy of about 1 MeV per nucleon between the original uranium nucleus and its fragments. Since there are about 200

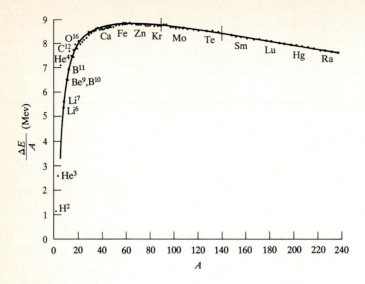

FIGURE 9-6

The average binding energy per nucleon for a number of nuclei. The smooth curve is from the semiempirical mass formula. Source: From R.B. Leighton, *Principles of Modern Physics,* McGraw-Hill Book Company, New York, 1959. The figure is reproduced here by courtesy of Professor Leighton.

nucleons involved, the energy that becomes available because of the increased binding energy of the fragments is about 200 MeV.

As nuclei contain more and more protons, the repulsive forces from their positive charges lower the binding energy (see Chapter 12 for a discussion of forces between electrical charges). For this reason the value of the binding energy per nucleon shows a steady decline as the mass number increases beyond the iron region.

For nuclei of low mass number there are not sufficient nucleons present in the nucleus for the nuclear forces to be used up or to saturate. Saturation begins to occur for helium 4 or the alpha particle. Therefore, if hydrogen isotopes can be fused to form helium, again there will be energy released as the more stable helium nucleus is formed (see Problem 20). Here the energy released per nucleon is larger than in the case of fission. In the reaction during which deuterium and tritium are fused to form helium 4, 17.6 MeV is released, or over 4 MeV per nucleon. However, the energy released per event is much less than for fission.

QUESTIONS

1. How much energy is contained in 1 Mt of TNT?
2. Discuss the release of energy by fission and fusion reactions, describing their similarities and differences.
3. What are the constituents of a chemical element?
4. Define isotope.

5. What is the relation between the atomic mass number, the atomic number, and the number of neutrons in a nucleus?

6. What does $E = mc^2$ mean?

7. Define electron-volt.

8. What nuclei are fused in the nuclear reaction of a hydrogen bomb?

9. How many protons and how many neutrons are contained in the nucleus of plutonium 239 (element 94)?

PROBLEMS

1. The nuclear chain reaction that produces the explosion of an atom bomb occurs in about 0.5 μ s. If the speed of the bomb fragments or vaporized components is 3×10^5 m/s, how far do the components disperse during the nuclear explosion phase? (Assume the components start from rest and are uniformly accelerated.)

2. How much energy (in joules) is released in the total conversion of 10 g of mass of energy? How many megatons TNT equivalent are released?

3. How many grams of mass would have to be converted to energy (at 100 percent efficiency) to lift a 1-ton car to a height of 100 mi?

4. A rocket of 2000 kg mass is fired and reaches an altitude of 3000 m (about 10,000 ft). At this point it has zero velocity. How much energy in joules was required of the rocket fuel?

5. What is the velocity of the rocket in Problem 4 as it strikes the earth?

6. Calculate the kinetic energy of a 4000-kg missile moving at 4500 m/s (10,000 mi/h). Note: this is roughly the reentry velocity of some ICBMs.

7. Calculate the kinetic energy of a neutron (mass = 1.67×10^{-27} kg) if it is moving at a velocity of 1.0×10^8 m/s. Give your answer in MeV.

8. Calculate the potential energy change involved in lifting a 50-kg mass 100 m.

9. A rock is hurled upward at an initial velocity of 20 m/s. If air resistance is neglected, how high will the rock rise?

10. If a 20-kt nuclear weapon is exploded under a cruiser of 20,000 tons, how high will the cruiser be lifted into the air if the bomb delivers 10 percent of its energy to the initial kinetic energy of the cruiser?

11. How many joules of energy are there in a 20-kt nuclear weapon when exploded?

12. How much force does it take (in newtons) to lift a car with a mass of 2000 kg?

13. A nuclear explosion creates an overpressure of 15 psi (this would momentarily double atmospheric pressure). What is the overpressure in newtons per square meter?

14. In Problem 13 what would be the force on a person 1.5 m in height and 0.2 m wide (a rectangular simplification of the person's upright area, which would be exposed to a blast)?

15. A horizontal force of 100 N is applied to a body of mass 20 kg which is initially at rest on a frictionless surface. Calculate the acceleration of the mass.

16. In Problem 15 find the total work done by the applied force after 10 s have elapsed.

17. How much work would be required to lift a 1000-kg missile through a vertical distance of 2 m?

18. If a missile is traveling at 100 km altitude and has a horizontal velocity of 2 km/s, what is its impact velocity, neglecting air friction?

19. If an electron and a positive electron (positron) come together, their masses are entirely converted into two gamma rays of energy (to conserve momentum). Calculate the energy

of one of these gamma rays in MeV. (The masses of the electron and positron are both 9.11×10^{-28} g.)

20. Calculate the energy release (in MeV) in the fusion reaction:

$$^2_1H + ^2_1H \rightarrow ^3_2He + ^1_0n$$

The masses are:

$$^2_1H = 2.014102 \text{ amu}$$
$$^3He = 3.016029 \text{ amu}$$
$$^1_0n = 1.009665 \text{ amu}$$

21. Assume that a 1-kt bomb is exploded deep in the ocean. The ambient ocean temperature is 10°C. Calculate the mass of water that would be raised to the boiling point (100°C). (Assume that the temperature of the water surrounding the heated water does not change. The heat capacity of water is 4.2 J/gm-K.)

22. A watt is a unit of power equal to 1 joule per second. What is the number of kilowatt-hours given by a 1-kt nuclear explosion? (Home consumption is about 500 kWh/month, for example.)

23. Using the definition of a watt given in Problem 22, show that 1 kWh is equal to 3.6×10^6 J.

KEY WORDS

atomic number   the number of protons in a nucleus.

Avogadro's number   the number of atoms or nuclei contained in one mole. It is numerically equal to 6.023×10^{23}.

binding energy per nucleon   the energy required to remove a nucleon from a nucleus. In the region of iron in the periodic table the binding energy per nucleon is greatest, over 8 MeV.

energy   energy is the capability of doing work. It is the product of the force multiplied by the distance through which the force acts.

kinetic energy   energy possessed by an object in motion. It is numerically equal to one half of the product of the mass and the square of the object's velocity.

mass number   the number of protons and neutrons in a nucleus or the total number of nucleons in a nucleus.

mole   the mass in grams corresponding to the mass number of the element. For example, one mole of uranium-238 is 238 grams.

nucleon   refers to either a proton or a neutron, a nuclear constituent.

potential energy   energy possessed by an object because of its position, usually in the gravitational field of the earth. The higher an object is the greater is its potential energy, which is equal to the product of its weight and height.

CHAPTER
10

RADIOACTIVITY

10-1   THEMES

Radioactivity results when a nucleus changes from one form to another in order to reach a more stable configuration. These spontaneous changes can occur in a variety of ways. For example, a nucleus can decay by changing one of its neutrons into a proton with the simultaneous emission of an electron (beta decay), by emitting a helium nucleus (alpha decay), or by spontaneously fissioning (splitting) into two fragments. Sometimes after radioactive decay the daughter nucleus is either radioactive or left in an excited state. This means that it will eventually decay again. The average time required for the decay is proportional to the *half-life*. (It is actually equal to 1.44 times the half-life.)

After fission occurs, the fragments are intensely radioactive and give rise to *fallout* when mixed with the debris of a bomb burst (see Chapter 16). In this chapter we examine some of the characteristics of these fission products and discuss ways of shielding from the effects of beta rays and gamma rays.

10-2   BETA DECAY

Radioactivity is the spontaneous transformation of one nucleus into another. The stable isotopes of the elements plotted by neutron number versus proton number form a *line of stability*. See Figure 10-1. The stable nuclei are shown in black in the figure. Notice that as the atomic number (number of protons) in the nucleus increases, a larger number of neutrons leads to more stable nuclei. In these heavy nuclei, the positively charged protons repel each other. Neutrons, on the other hand, have no charge and hence no coulomb repulsion from each other or from protons. Therefore, heavy nuclei in which the number of neutrons exceeds the number of protons are more stable than those with equal numbers of neutrons and protons.

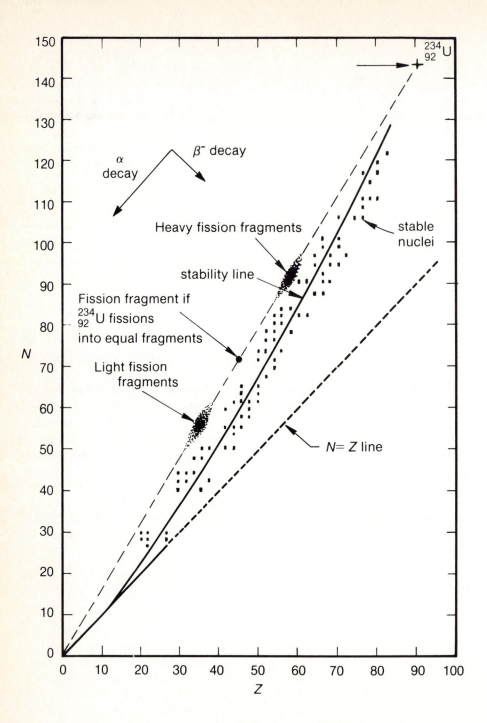

However, when a nucleus has too many neutrons, it will spontaneously change a neutron into a proton. The subsequent nucleus is sometimes called the *daughter nucleus* and the original nucleus the *parent nucleus*. The daughter nucleus may also be unstable (i.e., radioactive) and itself change another neutron into a proton in an effort to reach the line of stability. This is shown as an arrow on the left-hand side of the stability line in Figure 10-1. The transformation of a neutron into a proton is called **beta decay,** so-called because when the transformation occurs, a beta particle, or electron, is emitted. Note that in beta decay the total number of neutrons plus protons remains constant. The sum of the two is termed the mass number A. That is

$$A = N + Z \qquad (10\text{-}1)$$

where A is the mass number, N is the number of neutrons, and Z is the atomic number. An example is the beta decay of tritium, an isotope of hydrogen containing one proton and two neutrons. The nuclei of two *isotopes* of an element have the same number of protons (the same atomic number) but different numbers of neutrons and hence different mass numbers A. Different isotopes behave almost identically in chemical reactions.

The tritium beta-decay process is written as follows:

$$\underset{\text{tritium}}{{}^{3}_{1}\text{H}} \xrightarrow{\text{12 yr}} \underset{\text{helium 3}}{{}^{3}_{2}\text{He}} + \underset{\text{electron}}{{}^{0}_{-1}e} + \underset{\text{antineutrino}}{{}^{0}_{0}\bar{\nu}} \qquad (10\text{-}2)$$

The **antineutrino,** $\bar{\nu}$, has a mass of zero, or nearly zero, and has no charge.*

10-3   ALPHA DECAY

Another type of radioactivity is *alpha decay*. Alpha decay, which occurs in heavy nuclei such as uranium or plutonium, is another mechanism (see beta decay above) by which nuclei spontaneously rid themselves of protons, which repel each other, and

---

*This particle is necessary in order to conserve energy in the beta-decay process. It is observed that the beta particles are emitted with a spectrum of energies up to a maximum value. At the maximum value energy is conserved without introduction of the antineutrino, but at other values it is necessary to include the antineutrino, which carries off the extra energy. The antineutrino was experimentally observed in the 1950s, about two decades after it was postulated.

FIGURE 10-1
Stable isotopes of the elements. The stable isotopes form a line of stability (squares in black) when plotted by neutron number versus proton number. There are no stable nuclei above bismuth (element 83). Note also the fission product nuclei in the region of elements 38 and 55. Unstable nuclei formed in fission beta-decay to the stability line, emitting on the average about four beta particles. Uranium 234 is shown as the nucleus undergoing fission on the assumption that uranium 235 has captured a neutron forming a uranium 236 nucleus in an excited state. It then emits two neutrons becoming uranium 234. The uranium 234 in turn is shown splitting either into two equal fragments or, what is much more likely, into two unequal fragments.

thereby increase their stability. There are no stable nuclei with atomic numbers greater than 82 (Pb, lead). See Figure 10-1. In alpha decay a helium nucleus (called an alpha particle) is ejected spontaneously. For example, plutonium 239 decays by alpha-particle emission as follows:

$$\underset{\text{plutonium 239}}{^{239}_{94}\text{Pu}} \xrightarrow{\text{24,000 yr}} \underset{\text{uranium 235}}{^{235}_{92}\text{U}} + \underset{\substack{\text{helium 4} \quad \text{(alpha particle)}}}{^{4}_{2}\text{He}} \tag{10-3}$$

10-4   HALF-LIFE

The fundamental law of radioactive decay is that each radioisotope decays at its own characteristic rate, which is governed by the *half-life* of the substance. The **half-life** of a substance is the time it takes for one-half the nuclei to decay. In addition, the number of nuclei that decay in a given time is proportional to the number of nuclei available for decay at that time. For example, in the beta decay of tritium, Eq. (10-2), the half-life is about 12 years. If we start with, say, 10 kilograms of tritium, in 12 years half will have decayed, leaving 5 kilograms; in 24 years, 2.5 kilograms will remain; in 36 years, 1.25 kilograms will remain; and so on. Since the radioactivity is proportional to the number of nuclei, it will also decay in the same manner.

In the case of plutonium 239, the half-life is 24,000 yr. This relatively short half-life (uranium 238 has a half-life of 4.5 billion years, for example) is one reason why plutonium is an extremely dangerous substance. If plutonium particles are inhaled, they may lodge in lung tissue and emit alpha particles over the lifetime of the person. These highly ionizing particles are carcinogenic in the lung. *Pulmonary ingestion of as little as 1 microgram of plutonium or less is a serious health hazard.*

The intensity of radioactivity of a substance depends on the number of disintegrations per second. A given number of grams of an isotope with a very long half-life will have fewer disintegrations per second than an isotope with a shorter half-life, and be less immediately dangerous. The long-lived isotope will, however, be around for a much longer time and will therefore present long-term problems. Further discussion of half-life will be found in Section P10-4.

10-5   FISSION PRODUCTS

When a nucleus of uranium fissions, the fission fragments are too neutron-rich for the atomic number region in which they find themselves (Z in the range from 30 to 60). Fission fragments are therefore intensely radioactive, emitting beta particles (electrons) spontaneously. On the average about four beta decays are required for the nucleus of a fission fragment to reach the stability line. This is shown in Fig. 10-1 for the case of fission of uranium 234 dividing into two equal fragments.

Fission is induced in uranium (or plutonium) by capture of a neutron in the following nuclear reaction:

$$^{235}_{92}\text{U} + {}^{1}_{0}n \rightarrow \text{fission} + 2 \text{ or } 3\ {}^{1}_{0}n \tag{10-4}$$

The fact that several neutrons are released in each fission is one of the key factors leading to the possibility of a chain reaction. In the chain reaction that produces a nuclear explosion the two or three neutrons released from each fissioning nucleus in the reaction above produce fission in additional uranium nuclei, which in turn produce more neutrons, and so on through about 80 generations (see Chapter 11). In the fission process a nucleus is much more likely to split asymmetrically than symmetrically. The observed distribution of fragments is shown in Figure 10-2.

One of the most prominent light fission fragments is strontium 90. Strontium 90 is a dangerous constituent of fallout for the following reasons:

1. It is produced in abundance (near the mass number where fission often occurs). (See Figure 10-1.)
2. It is chemically like calcium and therefore a bone seeker. Radioactivity in the bones can lead to bone cancer, particularly in children and infants, who have a high metabolic rate in the bone.
3. It has a long half-life, 28 yr, so that it remains in the ecosystem (and therefore in people) for one to two human generations.

On the high-mass-number side of the distribution of fission fragments, a nucleus that is highly likely to be formed is iodine 131. This isotope, which has a half-life of about 8 days, is a dangerous short-term hazard because of the uptake of iodine by the thyroid gland (see Chapter 18).

If we consider all possible fission products, we find that over 300 different radioactive nuclei are formed, with a variety of half-lives. Because of the complexity of the beta and gamma ray spectra associated with each radioactive nucleus a great variety of beta- and gamma-radiation energies are emitted from fission products. Therefore, radioactive fallout, which consists chiefly of fission products, does not decay exponentially with time, but decays inversely proportional to the time (see Chapter 16).

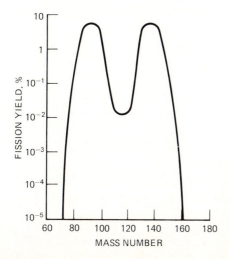

FIGURE 10-2
The mass distribution of fission fragments. It is unlikely (by about 2 orders of magnitude) that a nucleus undergoing fission induced by neutrons of a few MeV will divide into two equal (symmetric) fragments.

10-6 GAMMA RADIATION

It often happens that beta decay leaves the daughter nucleus in an *excited* state. This means that the energy level in the nucleus is higher than it is in the normal, or ground, state. This state changes within a very short time (on the order of 10^{-12} second) to the ground state of the daughter nucleus as a result of the emission of electromagnetic radiation, or photons (see Chapter 12). Electromagnetic radiation that is nuclear in origin is called *gamma radiation*. **Gamma radiation** is just like visible light except that it is more energetic. Gamma radiation has typically about a million times more energy in one of its light quanta, or photons, than visible light.

Gamma rays are the most difficult to shield against, and they are the major factor in doses of radiation from radioactive fallout, or external radiation, as distinct from doses incurred by ingesting radioactive material.

10-7 RADIATION UNITS

A unit of radioactivity often used is the *curie*. Technically, one curie is the radioactivity of one gram of radium in equilibrium with its decay products. However, for our purposes the curie will be defined as 3.7×10^{10} disintegrations per second. Recently a new measure of radioactivity has been adopted, the "becquerel." 1 becquerel = 1 disintegration per second.

One rad (radiation absorbed dose) is equal to the absorption of 0.01 joule of radiation energy per kilogram of tissue, or 100 ergs per gram of tissue.

A normal human adult exposed to 400 rad of radiation has a 50 percent chance of death within 30 days. For children, the aged, or the infirm, the fatal dosage is lower (see Chapter 18).

10-8 SPONTANEOUS FISSION

Spontaneous fission, like alpha and beta decay, is a form of radioactivity in which a nucleus spontaneously transforms into some other nucleus. There is a certain probability that a heavy nucleus such as uranium or plutonium will spontaneousiy fission. The spontaneous fission rate is quite low compared to the rate of alpha decay, typically by several orders of magnitude. Nevertheless, spontaneous fission is important in nuclear weapons design. Plutonium 240, for example, if present in sufficient quantity, can cause an atomic bomb to "fizzle" because of the uncontrolled neutrons released from the spontaneous fission. In other words, the neutrons produced by random spontaneous fission may cause premature initiation of the chain reaction—before the fissioning mass is assembled to optimum size. (The design of nuclear weapons is discussed in more detail in Chapter 11.)

10-9 SHIELDING AGAINST BETA AND GAMMA RADIATION

Beta rays have fairly well-defined ranges that are determined by their energy. The most energetic ones, from fission products, can be stopped by 2 or 3 centimeters of wood (denser material can be thinner). Gamma rays, on the other hand, are attenuated exponentially; that is, one-half of them are removed after going through a certain distance of a specified material. For 1-MeV gamma rays shielded by lead, this distance, known as the **half-value thickness,** is about 1 centimeter. With exponential attenuation there is no definite range: *some* gamma radiation will pass through any given thickness of absorber. However, if the absorber is made thick enough, the fraction passing through can be small enough to be negligible.

10-10   RADIOACTIVITY FROM NEUTRON CAPTURE

Neutrons, which have no electric charge, induce nuclear reactions more readily than charged particles. This is because they do not have to overcome the coulomb repulsive force produced on a positively charged particle as it approaches the nucleus. When a neutron is captured by a nucleus, the mass number of the nucleus increases by 1 but the proton number stays the same. Therefore, a new isotope, often radioactive, of the element is formed. For example, a neutron may be captured in ordinary sodium (sodium 23) to produce sodium 24:

$$\ce{^{23}_{11}Na} \ +\ \ce{^{1}_{0}n}\ \rightarrow\ \ce{^{24}_{11}Na} \tag{10-5}$$

sodium 23 + neutron → sodium 24

The sodium 24 then decays by beta emission, with a half-life of 15 hours:

$$\ce{^{24}_{11}Na} \xrightarrow{15\,h} \ce{^{24}_{12}Mg}\ +\ \ce{^{0}_{-1}e}\ +\ \ce{^{0}_{0}\bar{\nu}}\ +\ \text{gamma ray} \tag{10-6}$$

sodium 24→magnesium 24 + beta + antineutrino + 1.38-MeV gamma ray

Neutron capture contributes to radioactivity in the vicinity of a nuclear explosion because it produces enormous numbers of beta and gamma rays.

ADDITIONAL PHYSICS SECTION

Summary

In this section the concepts of half-life and mean life are explained in more detail. Nuclear forces are also discussed briefly. An actual fission chain is given for the case leading to the prominent fallout product strontium 90, illustrating the beta decay process to nuclear stability. An example is given in detail of the energy produced in the fission process for both the fission fragments and their subsequent beta decay.

Some detail of the beta and gamma spectra is given in order to show the complicated nature of the fission products and to illustrate how gamma rays originate. Shielding from beta and gamma rays is also discussed. Finally, an estimate is made of the radioactivity produced beneath a 1-kt fission bomb by neutron capture.

P10-2   BETA DECAY AND NUCLEAR FORCES

One might ask why a nucleus should change one of its neutrons spontaneously into a proton (beta decay). Since the electrical force between the like-charged protons is repulsive (see Chapter 12), a greater binding energy might be achieved by having nuclei made up of only neutrons, for example. The answer to this question lies in the nature of the nuclear force. Nuclear forces are responsible for the fact that nuclei are formed, even in opposition to the repulsive electrical forces produced between protons.

Nuclear forces are short-range, very strong, attractive, and exist appreciably only within nuclei. The nuclear forces between a neutron and another neutron, a proton and another proton, or between a neutron and a proton are approximately equal. Both neutrons and protons obey the **Pauli exclusion principle.** This principle states that identical particles (such as neutrons or protons) that obey it cannot be in the same quantum state. That is, a neutron or a proton has to have a unique quantum state in the nucleus.

When a quantum state is filled, say by a neutron, the next neutron added to the nucleus cannot occupy the same state and generally finds itself in a higher quantum state. This higher state has higher energy, and so the binding energy of this next neutron to the nucleus is reduced. When an excess of neutrons is added to the nucleus, the binding energy of the neutrons is reduced so much that the nucleus is able to form a lower-energy state by changing a neutron into a proton (beta decay). A heavy nucleus undergoing fission splits into fragments that have an excess number of neutrons (see Figure 10-1). These fragment nuclei then seek stability by the beta-decay process.

The Pauli exclusion principle, if acting alone, would produce nuclei that had an equal number of neutrons and protons. This is in fact the case for light nuclei such as carbon and oxygen (see Figure 10-1). However, as protons are added to form heavier and heavier elements, the loss in nuclear binding energy due to the electrical repulsive forces between these protons becomes sufficient that the overall binding energy is greatest if there are more neutrons than protons. For example, uranium 238 has 92 protons and 146 neutrons. The stability curve for the nuclei (Figure 10-1) is generated by plotting N versus Z for the nuclei that have the greatest binding energy.

P10-4   HALF-LIFE AND MEAN LIFE

The fundamental law of radioactive decay is that the number of atoms that decay in a unit of time is proportional to the number of atoms present. The constant of proportionality is called the **decay constant,** λ. In the language of the calculus if N is the number of atoms present and dN/dt is the rate of change of those atoms with time, or radioactivity, then the law of radioactive decay is:

$$dN/dt = -\lambda N \qquad \text{(P10-11)}$$

Equation (P10-1) can be integrated to give the exponential law that governs radioactive decay:

$$N = N_0 e^{-\lambda t} \qquad \text{(P10-12)}$$

where N_0 is the number of atoms originally present. From this equation it can be seen that in a time equal to $1/\lambda$ the number of atoms present falls to $1/e$ or about 37 percent of the original number ($e = 2.7183$).

Since Eq. (P10-11) tells us that the radioactivity is proportional to the number of atoms, it is also true that the radioactivity, or rate of change of the number of atoms with time, will also obey an exponential decay law:

$$dN/dt = (dN/dt)_0 e^{-\lambda t} \qquad (P10\text{-}13)$$

Stated in words: the radioactivity, dN/dt, present at time t is related to the radioactivity at time zero $(dN/dt)_0$ by multiplication by the exponential factor $e^{-\lambda t}$. One can ask when the radioactivity will be one-half of its original value. This time occurs when $e^{-\lambda t_{1/2}} = \frac{1}{2}$. This defines the half-life, $t_{1/2}$. $t_{1/2}$ can be found explicitly by taking the natural logarithm of the above equation:

$$t_{1/2} = \ln 2/\lambda = 0.693/\lambda \qquad (P10\text{-}14)$$

In terms of the half-life Eq. (P10-13) can be written:

$$\text{Radioactivity} = dN/dt = (dN/dt)_0 (1/2)^{t/t_{1/2}} \qquad (P10\text{-}15)$$

Or, stated in words, the radioactivity (or also the number of atoms present) at time t is equal to the radioactivity (or the number of atoms) at time 0 multiplied by one-half to the power of the elapsed time t divided by the half-life. Thus in an elapsed time equal to one half-life the radioactivity decreases by a factor 2, and in two half-lives by a factor 4, and in general in n half-lives by a factor 2^n.

The average or mean time required for a decay to take place is obtained by integrating (P10-3) to infinite time and is found to be equal to $1/\lambda$. This quantity is called the **mean life** and is equal to $t_{1/2}/\ln 2 = 1.443 \, t_{1/2}$.

The exponential curve generated by Eqs. (P10-13) or (P10-15) is illustrated in Figure 10-3 for the case of the decay of tritium, which has a half-life of 12.3 years. The values of the activity, or equally the number of atoms, is shown for several half-lives, and the mean life is also illustrated.

P10-5 AN ACTUAL FISSION CHAIN FORMED FROM UNEQUAL MASS FRAGMENTS AND A CALCULATION OF THE ENERGY RELEASED IN THE FISSION THAT FORMED THEM

The maxima in the distribution of fission fragments occur at mass numbers of about 95 and 140, rather than at 118, as would be expected if the fragment distribution were symmetric. The actual situation can be described as follows:

$$^{235}_{92}\text{U} + ^{1}_{0}n \rightarrow ^{236}_{92}\text{U} \rightarrow X + Y + 2 \text{ or } 3 \text{ neutrons} \qquad (P10\text{-}16)$$

The sum of the atomic numbers of X and Y must equal 92, the number of protons in uranium. Figures 10-1 and 10-2 show the unstable fission-fragment nuclei in the vicinity of atomic numbers 35 and 55. For symmetric fission (which occurs rarely),

Amount of tritium
remaining

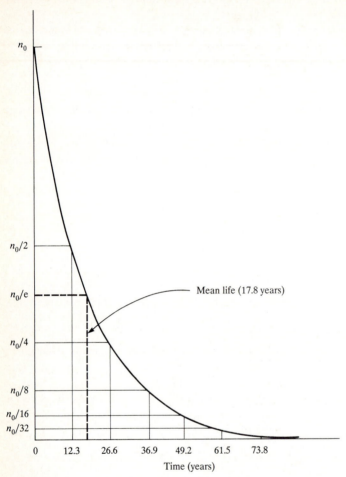

FIGURE 10-3

The amount of radioactive tritium as a function of time. n (subzero) is the number of tritium atoms initially, or alternately the amount of radioactivity initially ($t = 0$). Tritium is an isotope of hydrogen which has a half-life of 12.3 years and is used in thermonuclear bombs. In a time equal to the half-life the radioactivity is reduced to one-half of its initial value. Shown also is the mean life, which is the time for the radioactivity to decay to $1/e$ of its original value.

X = Y = element 46 = palladium. A probable combination is X = element 37 = rubidium, and Y = element 55 = cesium. We choose X = element 37 = rubidium, and Y = element 55 = cesium. If we assume that 2 neutrons are emitted, then the fragments X and Y have a total mass of 234. We choose arbitrarily 90 for the mass of the rubidium and 144 for the mass number of cesium. Other pairs of mass numbers are also possible as well as other pairs of elements as long as the atomic numbers of the fragments add to 92, the original atomic number of the uranium 236 parent nucleus. The mass numbers of the fragments total 234 since two neutrons are emitted.

$$^{236}_{92}U \rightarrow \, ^{90}_{37}Rb + \, ^{144}_{55}Cs + 2^{1}_{0}n \tag{P10-7}$$

The cesium 144, that is the heavy fragment of this pair, has a half-life of about one second and decays by a series of six beta emissions forming radioactive isotopes of mass number 144 in turn of barium, lanthanum, cerium, and praseodymium, which beta-decays to stable neodymium.

We now follow the decay of the $^{90}_{37}Rb$ nucleus that seeks stability by emission of three beta particles with accompanying gamma rays and antineutrinos.

$$^{90}_{37}Rb \xrightarrow{\text{2.6 min}} \, ^{90}_{38}Sr + \underset{\text{6.3 MeV}}{_{-1}^{0}e} + \underset{\text{antineutrino}}{_{0}^{0}\overline{\nu}} \tag{P10-8}$$

$$^{90}_{38}Sr \xrightarrow{\text{28 yr}} \, ^{90}_{39}Y + \underset{\text{0.55 MeV}}{_{-1}^{0}e} + \underset{\text{antineutrino}}{_{0}^{0}\overline{\nu}} \tag{P10-9}$$

$$^{90}_{39}Y \xrightarrow{\text{64 h}} \, ^{90}_{40}Zr + \underset{\text{2.3 MeV}}{_{-1}^{0}e} + \underset{\text{antineutrino}}{_{0}^{0}\overline{\nu}} \tag{P10-10}$$

The strontium 90 fission product is particularly dangerous because of its long half-life and because it is deposited in the bone. It also gives rise to a daughter, yttrium 90, which has a very energetic beta ray that will produce additional biological damage at the site of the strontium 90.

The energy given to the fission fragments can be calculated from the masses of the initial nucleus and its fragments.* The released energy arises from the coulomb repulsion of the positively charged fragments which gives them large kinetic energies (on a nuclear scale) as they fly apart. See Chapter 12 for a discussion of the repulsive force between particles of similar electric charge, in this case the nuclear protons.

The energy released in forming the fission fragments will be the mass difference between the left-hand side of Eq. (P10-7) and its right-hand side multiplied by the square of the velocity of light according to Einstein's equation $E = mc^2$. The following are the masses involved:

> Uranium 236: 236.045663 amu (atomic mass units)
> Rubidium 90: 89.914752 amu
> Cesium 144: 143.931108 amu
> Neutron: 1.008665 amu

An *atomic mass unit* is equal to 1.661×10^{-27} kg. If, for example, the mass of the neutron were exactly its mass number, 1.000, then the neutron mass would be

---

*The masses were calculated from mass excesses that were calculated by G. T. Garvey et al., *Review of Modern Physics*, Vol. 41, No 4, pp. S1–S80, 1969.

1.661×10^{-27} kg. The mass of the neutron is in fact a little larger. One can see from the above numbers that uranium 236 has an excess of mass over its mass number, whereas rubidium 90 and cesium 144 have a deficiency, since they have more binding energy (see Figure 9-10).

Adding up the masses on the left-hand side taking into account that two neutrons are emitted, the total mass after fission of the uranium 236 is 235.863190. It is necessary to keep so many significant figures (see Chapter 8) here because when 235.863190 is subtracted from 236.045663 to find the mass difference three significant figures are lost. This difference is in fact 0.182473. The energy released to form the fragments is therefore:

$$E = (0.182473 \text{ amu} \times 1.661 \times 10^{-27} \text{ kg/amu}) \times (2.99793 \times 10^8)^2 \text{ J}$$

(Here we take a more exact velocity of light than usual because of the significant figures in the calculation.)

$$= 2.7240 \times 10^{-11} \text{ J}$$
$$= 2.7240 \times 10^{-11} \text{ J} \times 1 \text{ MeV}/(1.602 \times 10^{-13} \text{ J}) = 170.0 \text{ MeV}$$

This result is in accord with Table 11-2, which shows the distribution of fission energy. Here we have calculated only the energy associated with the kinetic energy of the fission fragments. The masses of the rubidium 90 and cesium 144 isotopes are still larger than the same mass numbers for stable nuclei. These isotopes then beta-decay to reach stability, changing their excess neutrons into protons spontaneously. In so doing they will release additional energy in the form of beta and gamma rays from the fission products and their accompanying antineutrinos. We now calculate this additional energy release by finding the difference in mass between rubidium 90 and the stable nucleus it reaches after three beta decays, zirconium 90. Similarly we calculate the energy release for cesium 144 and the stable nucleus it reaches, neodymium 144, after six beta decays.

The new masses needed are:

Zirconium 90:	89.904625 amu
Neodymium 144:	143.91004 amu

The beta decay of rubidium 90 then releases an atomic mass unit difference of 89.914752 − 89.904625 amu or 0.010095 amu. Using the direct energy conversion that $1 \text{ amu} \times c^2 = 931.2 \text{ MeV}$, this is equivalent to 9.43 MeV. If we are interested in the energy release in MeV, the use of direct conversion from amu to MeV avoids calculation of the difference in nuclear masses in kilograms as in the previous example. Similarly the beta decay of cesium 144 releases a difference of 143.91004 amu = 143.931108 amu or 0.021068 amu. This is equal to 19.62 MeV. The total energy released in the beta decay processes from both fragments is therefore 29.05 MeV. This total includes the energies of all the electrons, antineutrinos, and gamma rays emitted. This figure compares favorably with the typical value of 23 MeV found in Table 11-2.

Therefore, the total energy released, including both kinetic energy of the fission fragments and their subsequent beta decay, is 170.0 MeV + 29.05 MeV = 199.1

MeV. This total energy release is the value for this particular choice of fragments and is close to the typical value of 200 MeV often cited as the energy released in fission (see Table 11-2).

P10-6 GAMMA RADIATION

Figure 10-4 shows a typical case of gamma emission from the fission fragment krypton 90. Rubidium 90 is sometimes formed directly in the fission process and is sometimes a daughter of krypton 90. Twenty-nine percent of the time krypton 90 emits one beta group to the ground state of rubidium 90, but 63 percent of the time the beta emission is to an excited state of rubidium 90. This state subsequently decays by emitting several gamma rays. The major decay is by a series of gamma rays that are emitted sequentially as the rubidium 90 nucleus deexcites from the nuclear level at 1.780 MeV, to another at 0.661 MeV, to another at 0.122 MeV, and finally to the ground state.

   The gamma rays that are given off have energies that are equal to the difference in the nuclear energy levels, namely, 1.119, 0.539, and 0.122 MeV. There is also an appreciable gamma radiation of 1.780 MeV that corresponds to a transition directly from the 1.780-MeV level to the ground level of ^{90}Rb, which in turn beta-decays (half-life = 153 s) to the bone-seeker ^{90}Sr.

   There are also on the order of a dozen more beta groups that collectively make up the remaining 8 percent of the beta transitions of ^{90}Kr. They populate other nuclear levels, giving rise to gamma rays in small abundance that range in energy from 0.107 to 3.88 MeV. The example of ^{90}Kr illustrates the fact that it is usual to have many gamma rays of a variety of energies associated with the beta decay of fission products.

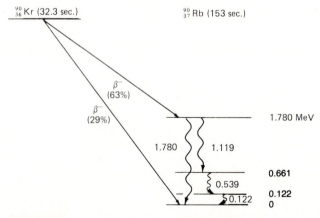

FIGURE 10-4

Formation of gamma rays by nuclear deexcitation. In the figure two groups of beta particles are emitted by the radioactive nucleus, ^{90}Kr. One group (29 percent of the time) goes directly to the ground state of the daughter nucleus, ^{90}Rb. The second group (63 percent of the time) populates an excited nuclear state in ^{90}Rb. This excited state very quickly (1 × 10^{-12} seconds) deexcites itself to the ground state of ^{90}Rb, emitting several gamma rays.

P10-9   SHIELDING FROM BETA AND GAMMA RADIATION

Very roughly, the *range* of the electrons in beta radiation, in centimeters, is 0.5 times the energy of the electrons, in MeV.

$$\text{Range (cm)} = 0.5 \times \text{MeV energy} \qquad \text{(P10-17)}$$

This expression is approximately true for electrons with energies of 1 MeV or greater. It is also valid for absorbers that have unit density, for example, water, with a unit density of 1 g/cm^3. When yttrium 90 disintegrates, it emits electrons with energies up to 2.3 MeV. Yttrium 90 is created in the disintegration of strontium 90, and so there is one yttrium 90 disintegration associated with every strontium 90 disintegration. For the strontium 90 constituent of fallout, how much material of unit density will it require to stop the beta rays? Using Eq. (P10-16),

$$\text{Range} = 0.5 \times 2.3 \text{ MeV} = 1.2 \text{ cm} \qquad \text{(P10-18)}$$

In the case of gamma rays there is no definite range, but an exponential absorption. That is, the probability of the gamma ray being absorbed is proportional to the thickness of the absorber. This leads to the concept of *half-value thickness*. The half-value thickness is the thickness of material required to reduce the number of gamma rays by one-half. The half-value thickness of a lead absorber being used to shield against 1-MeV gamma rays is about 1 cm (Glasstone and Dolan, 1977, section 8.38).

A source of cobalt 60 emits gamma rays of 1.33 MeV and 1.17 MeV in equal abundance. If 100 gamma rays of cobalt 60 impinge on a lead shield 1 cm thick, about 50 will pass through the lead and about 50 will be absorbed. If we add a second lead sheet, also of 1 cm thickness, the 50 gamma rays entering the second sheet will be attenuated to 25. Each half-value thickness (1 cm in this case) reduces the gamma-ray intensity by a factor of 2.

> **Example.** According to Glasstone: "At a distance of 1 mile from a 1 Mt explosion the initial nuclear radiation would probably prove fatal to exposed human beings even if surrounded by 24 inches of concrete" (1977, p. 325). Let's check this statement. Figure 15-2 shows that an unshielded person would receive about 30,000 rad at 1760 yd (1 mi) from a 1-Mt explosion.
>
> Glasstone gives the tenth-value thickness (in inches) for fission-product gamma rays in concrete as 11. Thus 11 in of concrete would afford a 10-fold reduction in intensity and 22 in would give a 100-fold reduction in intensity. Therefore, after passing through 22 in of concrete the radiation dose would be 300 rad. The extra 2 in of concrete would reduce this figure to 190 rad.
>
> However, gamma rays produced by capture of neutrons by the nitrogen in the air require a tenth-value thickness of 16 in. Glasstone suggests that the higher of these figures (i.e., 16) be used generally because it is safer to be conservative. Using a tenth-value figure of 16 in for concrete, we obtain a 10-fold reduction for the first 16 in and an additional reduction of $10 \times 10^{-0.5}$ for the next 8 in, or 3.16. Thus the overall reduction factor is $10 \times 3.16 = 31.6$.
>
> In this case the radiation dose is the unshielded value (30,000) divided by the reduction factor (31.6). This is 949 rad, a fatal dose. When one considers also that the

direct effect of neutrons on those persons within the shielded area has been neglected, then Glasstone's statement that the exposure "would probably prove fatal to a large proportion of human beings" is correct.

P10-10 RADIOACTIVITY FROM NEUTRON CAPTURE

To calculate the radioactivity induced by a 1-kt bomb at 100 meters by neutron capture we first need to find the number of neutrons such a bomb would release. This is calculated as follows:

1. There are 4.18×10^{12} J/kt
2. Each fission releases 200 MeV
3. There are 1.6×10^{-13} J/MeV
4. Each fission gives 2.5 neutrons on the average. About 1.5 are needed to keep the chain reaction going. This leaves 1 free neutron per fission.

Using (1) and (2), we calculate the number of joules released per fission:

$$(200 \text{ MeV/fission}) \times (1.6 \times 10^{-13} \text{ J/MeV}) = 3.2 \times 10^{-11} \text{ J/fission} \quad \text{(P10-19)}$$

If we now divide the number of joules per fission into the number of joules available in a 1-kt bomb, we obtain the number of fissions in a 1-kt bomb:

$$N = \frac{4.18 \times 10^{12} \text{ J/kt}}{3.2 \times 10^{-11} \text{ J/fission}}$$
$$= 1.3 \times 10^{23} \text{ fissions/kt} \quad \text{(P10-20)}$$

We can calculate roughly the number of neutrons per square meter at a range of 0.1 km from the explosion as follows. First we find the number of square meters in a sphere 0.1 km in radius. The area of a sphere is $4\pi r^2 = 4(3.14) \times (100 \text{ m})^2 = 1.2 \times 10^5 \text{ m}^2$. The 1.3×10^{23} neutrons will be distributed over this area, neglecting reflections and absorption in the air. Then the **neutron fluence,** f (the number of neutrons passing through 1 m^2), at a range of 0.1 km may be calculated:

$$f = \frac{1.3 \times 10^{23} \text{ fissions/kt}}{1.2 \times 10^5 \text{ m}^2} = 1.1 \times 10^{18} \text{ neutrons/m}^2$$

Example: Advanced calculation. How much induced radioactivity will be produced from a 1-kt bomb?

Solution. To be specific, we calculate the radioactivity formed from the sodium in the soil. First of all, soils vary in sodium content, typically from 1 to 10 percent by weight. Assume the sodium level is 2 percent and the soil density is 3 g/cm^3. Therefore, the density of sodium is 0.06 g/cm^3. We further assume an effective soil depth of 20 cm. (Gamma rays produced at greater depth from the decay of the sodium 24 will not escape from the earth into the air because of the shielding of the earth.) The thickness of sodium presented to the neutrons is then $(20 \text{ cm}) \times (0.06 \text{ g/cm}^3) = 1.2 \text{ g/cm}^2$. The number of atoms of sodium per square centimeter is the sodium thickness t:

$$t = 1.2 \text{ g/cm}^2 \times \frac{6 \times 10^{23} \text{ atoms/mole}}{23 \text{ g/mole}} = 3 \times 10^{22} \text{ atoms/cm}^2 \qquad (P10\text{-}21)$$

The number of sodium 24 atoms produced per square meter is

$$\text{No. of sodium 24 atoms/m}^2 = stf \qquad (P10\text{-}22)$$

where s is the cross section for the neutron-capture process. We shall assume that it is $1.0 \times 10^{-26} \text{ cm}^2$. Then

$$\begin{aligned} stf &= (1.0 \times 10^{-26} \text{ cm}^2) \times (3 \times 10^{22} \text{ atoms/cm}^2) \\ &\quad \times 1.1 \times 10^{18} \text{ neutrons/m}^2) \qquad (P10\text{-}23) \\ &= 2.4 \times 10^{14} \text{ sodium 24 atoms/m}^2 \end{aligned}$$

The disintegration rate DR is equal to the product of the number of atoms present multiplied by 0.693 and divided by the half-life:

$$\begin{aligned} \text{DR} &= \frac{(3.3 \times 10^{14} \text{ atoms/m}^2) \times 0.693}{15 \text{ h} \times (3600 \text{ s/h})} \qquad (P10\text{-}24) \\ &= 4.3 \times 19^9 \text{ (disintegrations/s)/m}^2 \end{aligned}$$

Since one curie corresponds to 3.7×10^{10} disintegrations/s, the radioactivity is 0.12 curie/m². A very rough estimate of what the radiation dose from this would be can be calculated as follows. A point source of 1 curie of radium gives about 1 rad/h at 1 m. The equivalent point source for 0.12 curie/m² is

$$4\pi \times (1 \text{ m}^2) \times (0.12 \text{ curie/m}^2) = 1.4 \text{ curies (per kt)} \qquad (P10\text{-}25)$$

The radiation field is thus about 1.4 rad/h from sodium 24 for a 1-kt bomb. This number is very approximate because the radiations from radium and from sodium 24 are quite different. Nevertheless the calculation shows that neutron-induced radioactivity can be significant.

QUESTIONS

1. In beta decay, how is the final nucleus related to the original nucleus in terms of the number of neutrons and protons?
2. Why is an antineutrino needed in beta decay?
3. In alpha decay, how is the final nucleus related to the original nucleus in terms of the number of neutrons and protons?
4. Why is radioactive fallout not governed by the exponential decay law?
5. Where do gamma rays come from?
6. What is meant by the half-life of a radioactive substance?
7. What is a curie? A rad?
8. How many rads exposure will produce a 50 percent chance of death to a normal adult person?
9. What is spontaneous fission? Why is it important?
10. Describe how radioactivity is produced by neutron capture.

PROBLEMS

1. $^{131}_{53}I$ is a prominent constituent of radioactive fallout. It decays by beta emission, with a half-life of about 8 days. What is the decay-product nucleus? Complete the nuclear equation below:

$$^{131}_{53}I \rightarrow ? + _{-1}^{0}e + _{0}^{0}\bar{\nu}$$

2. When tritium beta-decays to helium 3, what is the maximum energy of the beta particle emitted (when the antineutrino has zero energy)? The atomic mass of helium 3 is 5.008314×10^{-27} kg; the atomic mass of tritium is 5.008347×10^{-27} kg. If atomic masses are used, the mass of the created electron is automatically taken into account (see Problem 11). Give your answer in MeV (1 MeV $= 1.6 \times 10^{-13}$ J). Assume the velocity of light is 3.0×10^{8} m/s.

3. Plutonium 239 has a half-life of 24,000 yr. Assume that in a global nuclear exchange 10,000 4-kg plutonium bombs are exploded. Only 50 percent of the plutonium is actually fissioned, the remainder being vaporized during the explosion.
   (*a*) How much plutonium is vaporized into the environment initially?
   (*b*) How much plutonium remains in the environment after 48,000 yr?
   (*c*) How much plutonium remains in the environment after 96,000 yr?

4. The radiation level outside a fallout shelter is 1000 rad/h (400 rad will produce 50 percent mortality). What would be the thickness of concrete required to reduce the radiation level within the shelter to 1 rad/h? Assume the tenth-value thickness for concrete is 11 in.

5. If 1000 gamma rays enter perpendicularly into 2 cm of lead shielding, approximately how many emerge into the shielded region assuming the half-value thickness of lead for these particular gamma rays is 1 cm?

6. When ^{238}U decays by alpha-particle emission, what nucleus is formed?

7. In Fig. 10-3, if the beta rays to the ground state of rubidium 90 have a maximum energy of 4.39 MeV, what is the maximum energy (antineutrino energy $= 0$) of the beta radiation to the excited state of rubidium 90 at 1.78 MeV?

8. The sun's energy is produced by fusion energy in a complex series of nuclear reactions the net result of which is that four hydrogen nuclei are fused to form one helium 4 nucleus. It is estimated that the sun "burns" about 6×10^{11} kg of hydrogen per second in this process. Calculate the power released by the sun in watts (joules per second). The mass of hydrogen is 1.007825 atomic mass units, and the mass of helium 4 is 4.002603 atomic mass units (1 atomic mass unit is 1.66×10^{-27} kg). Assume the velocity of light to be 3.0×10^{8} m/s.

9. Estimate the density of a uranium nucleus in kilograms per cubic meter. Assume that the nucleus is spherical, with a radius of 8×10^{-15} m, and that it contains 238 atomic mass units, each of which is 1.66×10^{-27} kg. [The volume of a sphere is $(4/3)\pi r^3$.]

10. The isotopic abundance of ^{235}U is 0.7 percent. Its half-life is about 700 million years. What would have been the isotopic abundance of ^{235}U 1.4 billion years ago? The half-life of ^{238}U, which is 99.3 percent of the isotopic abundance now, is $4\frac{1}{2}$ billion years. Therefore, its change in the last billion years can be neglected in this problem as a rough approximation.

11. When strontium 90, a major long-lived constituent of fallout, decays, it emits a beta particle and forms yttrium 90. If the mass of an atom of strontium 90 is 89.90775 atomic mass units and that of yttrium 90 is 89.90716 atomic mass units, calculate the maximum energy of the beta radiation from strontium 90 (1 atomic mass unit is 931.5 MeV). The electron's

mass need not be considered in this problem. This is because strontium is element 38, and hence has 38 electrons surrounding its nucleus, whereas the corresponding number for atomic yttrium is 39. Since *nuclear* masses are involved in beta decay, the electron number, including the beta particle, automatically balances if *atomic* masses are used.

12. Give the series of nuclear reactions that begin with the capture of a neutron by ^{238}U and lead by beta decay to ^{239}Pu. This is the process by which plutonium is produced in a nuclear reactor.

13. If ^{131}I is produced in 7 percent of fissions, how many atoms of ^{131}I are produced in the fission of 1 g of plutonium (about the number of fissions in the Nagasaki bomb)? Remember: there are Avogadro's number of atoms in 1 mole of a substance; 1 mole is the gram-molecular weight or, in the case of ^{239}Pu, 239 g.

KEY WORDS

antineutrino a particle with very little or no mass and no electric charge which is emitted along with an electron in beta decay.

beta decay the process taking place within a nucleus in which a neutron changes into a proton. Beta decay therefore increases the atomic number by one.

decay constant the number of radioactive atoms decaying per unit time is proportional to the number of such atoms present. The constant of proportionality is the decay constant. It is also the reciprocal of the mean life.

gamma radiation electromagnetic radiation of high frequency emitted from nuclei when they decay from excited states.

half-life the time in which a given amount of radioactivity will decay to one-half its initial value. It is also the time for the number of radioactive atoms to be one-half their initial value.

half-value thickness the thickness of shielding that will reduce radiation to one-half of its incident value.

mean life the average time required for a radioactive atom to decay. The mean life is approximately 1.44 times as long as the half-life.

neutron capture the process in which a neutron is absorbed by a nucleus thereby creating a new nucleus with a mass number one greater than the original nucleus.

neutron fluence the number of neutrons per unit area. In the MKS system, the number of neutrons per square meter.

nuclear forces the forces which hold nuclei together. Nuclear forces are strong and short-range and can overcome the repulsive forces of the protons for distances of nuclear dimensions (about 10^{-14} to 10^{-15} meters).

Pauli exclusion principle a principle of quantum theory that states that certain particles, such as neutrons and protons, cannot occupy the same quantum state.

CHAPTER
11

ON THE
BUILDING
OF BOMBS

When we try to pick out anything by itself, we find it connected to everything in the universe.

John Muir

11-1 THEMES

This chapter is a tutorial on how atomic bombs and H-bombs work. It isn't detailed enough to tell you how to make your own bomb. It does go far enough so that after reading it you should be able to tell your friends how a nuclear bomb works. It tells why ^{235}U and ^{239}Pu are the best materials for building a **fission bomb,** what a **neutron bomb** is, why a **fusion bomb** needs a fission **trigger**, and what the secret of the H-bomb is.

11-2 INTRODUCTION

Most of you will never try to build an atomic bomb. Yet some technical background on how nuclear weapons work is essential information for anyone who intends to be a responsible member of late-twentieth-century society. While it is possible to discuss nuclear weapons policy in terms only of the destructive potential of nuclear war, some understanding of basic nuclear technology is essential for assessing such matters as nuclear proliferation and theft of weapons. Fortunately (or unfortunately) only a few concepts are needed in order to understand the basic issues. Secondary concepts abound, which are important in terms of detailed technical matters, but you need grasp only a few key ideas in order to discuss the most important aspects of nuclear weaponry.

The construction of the first atomic bombs—those used for the Trinity test and those dropped on Hiroshima and Nagasaki—was a technical tour de force. Many technical questions had to be identified and answered. But the most significant question—one that no one could address before the fact—was: Could an atomic bomb be built?

As the Manhattan Project moved toward its climax, the scientists came to a curious and mixed conclusion on this question. They decided that the reliability of plutonium weapons could not be assured without a test, while that of a uranium bomb could be. Accordingly, a plutonium device was tested (the Trinity test at Alamogordo), but the first nuclear device detonated over a human population, at Hiroshima, was an untested uranium design.

The Hiroshima and Nagasaki weapons utilized the *fission* of heavy nuclei: heavy nuclei of uranium or of plutonium were split apart (fissioned) with an attendant release of energy. Fission-type weapons were the only kind of atomic weapon that existed from 1945 to 1951. In 1951 the United States learned how to release nuclear energy by joining light nuclei together in a *fusion* reaction—leading to a type of weapon now known as the H-bomb. In an H-bomb light isotopes of hydrogen such as deuterium and tritium are fused together to form heavier elements, particularly helium. To achieve the extremely high temperatures needed, an H-bomb uses an A-bomb as a ''match.'' Thus all H-bombs built to date use A-bombs as internal parts. The first thing one needs to understand, then, is how an atomic bomb works.

11-3   ATOMIC BOMBS

Atomic bomb is a generic term used in reference to devices that release nuclear energy through fission, or the breaking up of heavy nuclei into lighter ones.

In Chapter 10 we discussed the stability of the elements. The most stable element in the universe is iron, with an atomic weight of about 56 atomic mass units. Elements much lighter than iron give up energy when they are joined together (fused) into heavier elements. Heavy elements, on the other hand, give up energy when they are broken apart. The very heaviest elements, uranium and plutonium, are particularly good candidates for fission. The fission fragments that result when heavy atoms are broken apart are themselves elements, and they tend to be those in the middle of the periodic table (see Figure 10-1). The best isotopes for bomb building are uranium 235 and plutonium 239.

Introduction to Atomic Bomb Building

What are the properties of uranium that make it suitable for a weapon? First, it must split (fission) when hit by a neutron. Then, when it splits, it must do at least three things:

1. It must release more than one neutron. That is, the neutron that hits the uranium nucleus must produce more than one ''secondary'' neutron. The larger the number of neutrons produced, the better. In typical fission reactions every neutron that causes a fission produces two or three secondary neutrons.

2. There must be a net energy release when the nucleus splits apart. This energy is mostly in the form of kinetic energy of fission fragments.

3. When all competing avenues (such as neutron capture or escape) are taken into account, at least one neutron must be left (out of the two or three) to start the next generation of fissions.

If all these requirements are met, one has a **critical mass**.

The fission reaction may be written schematically:

Neutron + fissionable nucleus → fission fragments + 2 or 3 neutrons

Fisson Generations and Total Number of Fissions

Imagine a ball of uranium 235 about the size of a baseball. Suppose that a neutron suddenly appears. This neutron could come from spontaneous fission of a uranium atom, or it could be introduced by some sort of neutron generator. The neutron will travel for a while through the material, and eventually, if it doesn't escape from the ball, it will hit a uranium 235 nucleus. This nucleus fissions, splitting into two fast-moving fission fragments and simultaneously releasing several more neutrons. Each of these neutrons now goes through the same process, traveling through the material for a while, then either escaping or colliding with a uranium atom, inducing a fission, and releasing still more highly energetic fission fragments and neutrons.

If each fissioning uranium atom releases just two neutrons (the actual number averages about 2.5), there will be a rapid increase in the number of neutrons and in the number of fissioned uranium atoms. Each doubling of the number of neutrons is called a **generation.** The sequence looks like that shown in Table 11-1. This kind of growth process—where at equal time intervals the thing that is growing doubles—is called **exponential growth**. The term is often used in informal conversation simply to mean "fast growth." The scientist has a much more precise definition—as illustrated in Table 11-1. The numbers go up very rapidly indeed.

The total number of fissions at any stage is the sum of all the fissions that have taken place up to that point. This is 3 in the second generation, 7 in the third, 15 in the fourth, etc. The total number of fissions that takes place in the most recent generation is exactly equal to all those that have taken place in *all* preceding generation, plus 1. (When the numbers get large, as they do in a hurry, we can forget the 1.)

Since the last generation produces as many fissions—and hence as many fission fragments and as much energy release—as all preceding generations put together, in the early generations very little seems to be going on. Once the reaction gets far advanced, things happen fast.

There is a story about a king of an ancient land, who rewarded his loyal scientist-astrologer by granting a single wish. The advisor asked for very little—just a single grain of wheat for the first square of a checkerboard, two grains for the second square, four for the third, and so on until all 64 squares were filled. The king agreed readily, thinking the request modest.

But the number is vast. Look at Table 11-1. There would be 9.2×10^{18} grains on the last square, and almost 2×10^{19} grains (or 20,000 quadrillion grains) on the board. Suppose each grain weighed 1 grain. (A grain is a unit of weight, roughly equal to the weight of a grain of wheat, that is used today for specifying the weight of some pharmaceuticals. It weighs 0.0648 gram, and there are about 7000 grains to the pound.) The total weight of the wheat would be

$$2 \times 10^{19} \text{ grains} \times \frac{1}{(7000 \text{ grains/pound}) \times (2000 \text{ pound/ton})}$$
$$= 1.3 \times 10^{12} \text{ tons (or 1.3 trillion tons)}$$

The world wheat crop in 1980 was only about 439 million tons. As the story goes, once the king realized what was going on he had the sage beheaded. One can get too clever!

Another story concerns a lily pond in one corner of which is a small lily pad. This lily pad grows so fast that the area it covers doubles each day. It takes 100 days for the pond to be completely covered. The question: How many days before the pond is completely covered is it half covered?

A frequently used lecture demonstration of the chain reaction consists of a large, transparent box containing 50 or so set mouse traps. On each mouse trap are placed two table tennis balls. The demonstration is started by dropping a single ball into the box. Pandemonium ensues. The first trap releases two balls; these each set off two more, etc. In a second or so all the traps are sprung. Imagine the care needed to set up this demonstration!

TABLE 11-1

Generation	Fissions in the generation
1	$2^0 = 1$
2	$2^1 = 2$
3	$2^2 = 2 \times 2 = 4$
4	$2^3 = 2 \times 2 \times 2 = 8$
5	$2^4 = 2 \times 2 \times 2 \times 2 = 16$
6	$2^5 = 2 \times 2 \times 2 \times 2 \times 2 = 32$
10	$2^9 = 512$
11	$2^{10} = 1024$
20	$2^{19} = 5.2 \times 10^5$
30	$2^{29} = 5.3 \times 10^8$
40	$2^{39} = 5.5 \times 10^{11}$
64	$2^{63} = 9.2 \times 10^{18}$
70	$2^{69} = 5.9 \times 10^{20}$
80	$2^{79} = 6 \times 10^{23}$
81	$2^{80} = 1.2 \times 10^{24}$
82	$2^{81} = 2.4 \times 10^{24}$

Critical Mass

The minimum mass required to produce a chain reaction is called the *critical mass*. A critical mass will just barely sustain a chain reaction because the number of neutrons being absorbed or escaping will be exactly equal to those being produced. The rapid buildup of neutrons necessary for an explosion requires a substantially larger mass. The critical mass for a given chain reaction depends on the isotope involved, the geometry of the device being used, the material surrounding the fissionable material, and the purity of the fissionable material. Thus the minimum mass to make a bomb cannot be exactly quantified but depends on the materials involved and the ingenuity of the designer.

A baseball-sized piece of ^{235}U or ^{239}U weighs nearly 10 kilograms, and is more than enough for a critical mass. If the material is impure (e.g., low-enrichment ^{235}U containing other isotopes of uranium), more material may be needed. In testimony before the Nuclear Regulatory Commission (1984) discussing safeguard requirements for highly enriched uranium, Theodore Taylor, who was one of the physicists who worked at Los Alamos, indicated that amounts of ^{235}U as small as 1 kilogram are significant quantities. He did not state that anyone could build a bomb with 1 kilogram of ^{235}U, but did suggest that this is roughly the amount that a *good* designer would need.

One kilogram of ^{235}U occupies a volume of only about 50 cubic centimeters; this corresponds to a sphere less than 2 inches in diameter. It is clear that the problems involved in safeguarding materials are vast.

How Long Does an Atomic Bomb Explosion Take?

How many generations occur in an atomic bomb explosion? We already know enough to calculate this; it only requires putting together some puzzle pieces. We know from Chapter 9 that each time a uranium atom fissions, there is an energy release of about 200 MeV. The energy is emitted in several forms; these are listed in Table 11-2. Most of this energy remains in the bomb and serves to heat it. Now 200 MeV is not a very large number, by macroscopic standards. It is only 3.2×10^{-11} joule [see Eq. (P11-1)]. But when there is a very large number of fissions, the resulting energy is

TABLE 11-2
Distribution of fission energy

	MeV/fission
Kinetic energy of fission fragments	165
Instantaneous gamma-ray energy	7
Kinetic energy of fission neutrons	5
Beta particles from fission products	7
Gamma rays from fission products	6
Neutrinos from fission products	10
Total energy per fission, MeV	200

large. The release of nuclear fission energy is the result of a very large number of events, each of which releases a minuscule amount of energy.

The energy release in a bomb of the type dropped on Hiroshima is roughly 10 kilotons. By definition the energy release in a 1-kiloton explosion is 1×10^{12} calories $= 4.2 \times 10^{12}$ joules. Thus the energy release in a 10-kiloton explosion is 4.2×10^{13} joules. Hence the total number of fissions required to release 10 kilotons is

$$N = \frac{4.2 \times 10^{13} \text{ joules}}{3.2 \times 10^{-11} \text{ joule/fission}}$$

$$= 1.3 \times 10^{24} \text{ fissions}$$

Now look at Table 11-1. This number of fissions occurs in the eighty-first generation. But the energy released in the eighty-first generation is equal to all the energy released in all previous generations. So we require one less generation; thus,

$$80 \text{ generations} \approx 10\text{-kiloton energy release}$$

Most of the energy comes out in the last few generations. By adding up the numbers in Table 11-1 (plus a few that you'll have to calculate yourself) you can show that 99.9 percent of all the energy released is released in the last 10 generations.

How long does this process take? The neutrons released travel at speeds of about 10 million meters per second, or roughly 3 percent of the speed of light. The characteristic time for a generation is, roughly, the time it takes a neutron to cross the diameter of the ball of ^{235}U. (If neutrons escape most of the time, there will be no sustained reaction; if no neutrons escape, there is extra uranium present and the bomb can be made smaller.) Suppose we have a ball of uranium that is roughly baseball-sized, with a diameter of about 10 centimeters (0.1 meter). The time t it will take for a neutron to cross the sphere is

$$t = \frac{0.1 \text{ meter}}{1 \times 10^7 \text{ meters/second}} = 1 \times 10^{-8} \text{ second}$$

that is, about a hundred-millionth of a second. The complete process of bomb explosion, from the release of the first neutron to the total energy release, is about 80 times this number, or roughly 100 hundred-millionths of a second, or a *microsecond*. Since 99.9 percent of the energy is released in the final 10 generations, the important macroscopic energy-release processes take place in about one-tenth of a microsecond.

The characteristic time for a generation—a hundred-millionth of a second—is so important to weapons design that the physicists working in Los Alamos during World War II gave it a special name, the *shake* ("as fast as the shake of a lamb's tail"). One shake equals 1×10^{-8} second, or 0.01 microsecond.

Mechanisms of Neutron Loss

If too many neutrons are lost (fail to produce more neutrons through fission), the exponential growth process cannot occur. The most important loss mechanisms are leakage and internal absorption of neutrons.

LEAKAGE. One may have the right fissionable material, but have so little of it that most of the neutrons released escape before they can produce another fission. This phenomenon is called **neutron leakage**. The best possible shape for minimizing leakage is a sphere. A sphere has the least surface area for a given mass. If one has just enough material for a spherical critical mass, but spreads it out into some other shape, more neutrons will leak out, and the mass will not be critical.

One important way to reduce the amount of mass needed is to surround the fissionable material with a **reflector**, which reflects some of the escaping neutrons back into the fissionable material. Beryllium is often used for this purpose.

ABSORPTION. The fissionable material may contain impurities which absorb some of the neutrons. These impurities may occur naturally, or they may be placed in the system by design. Natural uranium consists of several isotopes, the most abundant of which is ^{238}U (99.3 percent). With ^{238}U there is a high probability that the isotope will either capture or scatter a neutron inelastically. If a neutron is captured, it disappears and is no longer available to induce fission. If a neutron is scattered inelastically, the emergent neutron may have an energy below the threshold for fission in ^{238}U, which is about 1 MeV. In technical terms, we say that the ^{238}U has a large **cross section** for neutron absorption and inelastic scattering. In ^{235}U, on the other hand, capture and inelastic-scattering processes are much less probable than fission, so fission is more likely when ^{235}U is struck by an energetic neutron from a previous fission.

The natural concentration of ^{235}U in uranium is only 0.7 percent. In order to produce a critical mass it is necessary to increase this concentration. The desirable concentration depends on many things, but a concentration of ^{235}U of over 90 percent is typical of weapons-grade uranium. Lower concentrations of ^{235}U will support chain reactions, but are difficult to use in bombs. The uranium used in commercial reactors in the United States is enriched in ^{235}U to about 3 percent. Most reactor-grade uranium cannot be used for bombs. Some research reactors use fuel rods enriched in ^{235}U to 93 percent, and these reactors are a good source of bomb material (see Taylor, 1984). Chapter 23 examines this issue in more detail.

Accidents Involving Critical Assembly

A nearly critical mass of a fissionable material can be very dangerous to have around. Critical-assembly accidents have occurred, with tragic consequences.

One of the first persons to die as a result of neutrons coming from a critical mass of fissionable material was Louis Slotin. Slotin was a young physicist who worked at Los Alamos during the early 1940s. His job was to determine critical masses. He used the simple approach of taking two small chunks of ^{235}U, each less than the critical mass, and slowly moving them together. He used a counter to monitor neutrons leaking from the assembly. As the two chunks were brought closer and closer together, the signal in the counter got larger and larger. The idea of the experiment was to determine the precise mass of material needed in order for the system to "go critical." Slotin's chunks were resting on a bench top. He used a screwdriver to move them around and hold them apart. One day the screwdriver slipped, the chunks moved together, and the counter went berserk. He knew at once that he had received an enormous dose of radiation. Instead of running from the room, he reached to the table and pried the chunks apart. Slotin had received a lethal dose of radiation, and a few days later he died. Slotin Field at Los Alamos is a memorial to him.

In 1960, when one of us (P.C.) was working at Los Alamos, a similar event occurred. Chemical reactions involving plutonium were being carried out using a large vat which was a part of a processing plant. One day an error was made and too much plutonium was allowed to accumulate. Some of it was in an insoluble form and settled to the bottom, where it spread out in a noncritical layer. When a technician turned on a stirring motor to mix the material, there was a blue flash and radiation alarms went off all over the building. The technician turned off the motor and collapsed. Within a few days he had died of radiation exposure. The stirring had changed the shape of the plutonium solids resting in the bottom of the vat, causing a critical mass to develop. The blue flash was Cerenkov radiation in the water in the vat. (Cerenkov radiation occurs when gamma rays emitted during nuclear fission pass through water. The same radiation is visible around water-moderated reactors and around spent fuel rods from reactors when these rods are stored under water.)

Richard Feynman (1985) humorously describes his experience during World War II of being sent to Oak Ridge, Tennessee, to review the gaseous diffusion facility. The people running the plant did not know why they were making enriched ^{235}U, and inadvertently stacked their product in a dangerous configuration, but fortunately one that did not go critical.

Bomb Assembly and Initiation

Safety requirements dictate that devices not have critical masses until the precise moment when the bomb is to explode. In fact, it is not possible to maintain a critical mass for very long at all, since there are always stray neutrons around and a single neutron can initiate a chain reaction. Stray neutrons arise from two sources: (1) spontaneous fission within the nuclear material itself, and (2) external sources such as cosmic ray interactions and radioactivity in building materials and the ground.

In setting off a bomb, neutrons are introduced at the right moment in a process called **ignition**. The device that produces the ignition of neutrons is called the **initiator.**

To prevent spontaneous detonation, a bomb is maintained in a noncritical configuration until just before it is to be detonated. It is then rapidly assembled. At just the critical instant, a source of neutrons initiates the chain reaction. The following discussion of the assembly process will help you to understand the differences between uranium and plutonium bombs. It will also lead to some understanding of the security procedures needed to prevent accidental detonation of nuclear weapons.

Assembly Speed: Uranium 235 versus Plutonium 239

What is the difference between pure ^{235}U and pure ^{239}Pu? The atomic numbers are 92 and 94 and the atomic weights are 235 and 239, respectively. The important difference for bomb making, though, is that the two isotopes have very different **spontaneous fission rates.** "Spontaneous fission rate" is the probability per second that a given atom will fission spontaneously—that is, without any external intervention.

^{239}Pu has a very much higher spontaneous fission rate than does ^{235}U. In fact, ^{239}Pu is more unstable against all modes of decay than is ^{235}U. Thus ^{235}U lives longer. The **half-life** of an element is inversely proportional to the decay rate. The half-lives of ^{235}U and ^{239}Pu are very different: 0.704 billion years and 24,390 years, respectively. This is why no ^{239}Pu is found in nature (see Table 11-4).

> **Aside: Isotopic Dating** The spontaneous decay rates, due principally to alpha decay, of ^{235}U, which is now 0.7 percent abundant, and ^{238}U, which is now 99.3 percent abundant, are very different. The half-life of ^{238}U is 4.5 billion years. The result of this is that as time passes, the ratio of the two abundances changes. One can extrapolate these ratios back into geologic time to the early history of the universe. The ratio of the two isotopes thus provides a clock which can be used to date ancient minerals, meteorites, and other materials. In using this clock, one must be careful to search for other mechanisms that might fractionate the different isotopes, leading to changes in the relative abundance having nothing to do with age. The usual way to perform this kind of check is by dating with several different elements which are known to have different fractionation characteristics. Rocks known to be the same age are generally found to have the same isotopic abundances of ^{235}U and ^{238}U. One important exception is found in Gabon (Africa), where, in one uranium mine, the concentration of ^{235}U is significantly lower than the concentration in any other natural uranium ever mined. Careful research led to the conclusion that about 2 billion years ago a natural nuclear reactor operated for 1 or 2 million years. At that time there was a much greater relative abundance of ^{235}U. Thus the conditions for a reactor to operate were much less stringent than they are with natural uranium as it exists today. The operation of the reactor depleted the rock in ^{235}U and altered the ratio of ^{235}U to ^{238}U. The decay products have moved only a few centimeters over this time. This stability is used as an argument that radioactive materials can be disposed of satisfactorily in suitably chosen rock formations for the very long times required for them to decay to safe levels.

Once a bomb is assembled and has a mass larger than the critical mass, any neutron that is introduced into it is likely to start a chain reaction. The important consideration is assembling a bomb is that *the assembly must take place in a short time compared to the time between the arrival of neutrons*. Since plutonium fissions spontaneously much faster than does uranium, there are more stray neutrons around in a plutonium reaction. Thus a ^{239}Pu bomb must be assembled much faster than a ^{235}U bomb. The spontaneous fission rate of ^{240}Pu is forty thousand times greater than ^{239}Pu. It is made in the reactor along with ^{239}Pu and greatly enhances the overall spontaneous fission rate of plutonium made in practice (see Section P11-3).

Little Boy: A Gun-Type Bomb

Little Boy, the bomb detonated at Hiroshima on August 6, 1945, was a gun-type bomb using ^{235}U. In essence, it consisted of a gun that fired one mass of ^{235}U at another. Each mass separately was less than the critical mass. A crucial design requirement was that the two pieces had to be brought together in a time shorter than the average time between the appearance of spontaneous neutrons. A gun could fire the uranium at speeds of a few millimeters per microsecond, which is fast enough.

Once the two pieces of fissile material are brought together, the initiator introduces a burst of neutrons and the chain reaction begins, continuing until the energy released becomes so great that the bomb simply blows itself apart and there is no longer a critical mass. This is called *disassembly*.

The bomb designers at Los Alamos were so sure that Little Boy would work that they didn't believe a test was necessary. Their confidence was justified when it exploded over Hiroshima.

The shape of a gun-type bomb is determined by the gun. Because the shape gives away important information, photographs of Little Boy remained classified for many years. Today many models and photographs of nuclear weapons are available, though not for the latest devices. Some of the best models are to be seen in the weapons museums at the Los Alamos Scientific Laboratory and at the Kirtland Air Force Base at Albuquerque, New Mexico. Many photographs are included in the *Nuclear Weapons Data Book* (Cochran, 1984).

Since the ^{235}U bomb was relatively straightforward to manufacture, one might ask why there was any interest at all in a ^{239}Pu bomb. The answer is that at that time, facilities for isotopically enriching uranium in ^{235}U were being developed only gradually, and there simply wasn't enough available. ^{239}Pu, which was being produced in reactors, was much more easily obtained. Later, as gaseous diffusion plants began to operate, a much larger amount of ^{235}U became available.

Fat Man: An Implosion Bomb

The rapid spontaneous fission of plutonium necessitated that a very different type of bomb be designed. A gun-type bomb would not be fast enough to work reliably. Before the bomb had been fully assembled, a few stray neutrons would probably be emitted, and these would start a premature chain reaction—leading to a great reduction in the destructive energy released or possibly a total fizzle.

The solution was found in a bomb design based on *implosion*. An implosion-type design will work equally well with ^{235}U and plutonium, but *must* be used with plutonium. In an implosion design the fissionable material is formed into a single sphere, with a mass less than critical. The sphere is surrounded by very carefully arranged layers of high explosive. At the proper time the explosive is symmetrically detonated. The force of the resulting shock wave compresses the nuclear material into a much smaller volume. As the density increases the distance a neutron has to go to initiate the next fission decreases, so the fraction lost through the surface decreases. The surface to mass ratio decreases and the material becomes supercritical (see Figure 11-1). Assembly can be accomplished far more rapidly with explosive compression than with a gun, so the problems caused by the high spontaneous fission rate of plutonium can be circumvented.

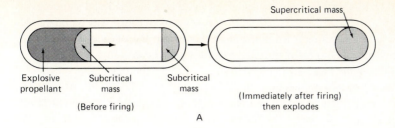

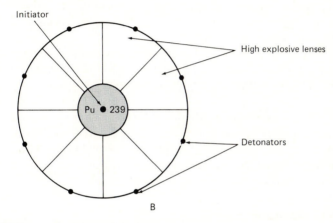

FIGURE 11-1
Schematic diagram of a gun-type fission bomb (above) and an implosion-type bomb (below).

The requirements for the high explosives used in implosion bombs are critical. The explosive must produce an extremely precise shock wave which will collapse and compress the nuclear material symmetrically so as to achieve a critical mass and sustain it for enough generations for the design energy to be released. Symmetrical compression is accomplished using shaped charges and **explosive lenses**.

Development of the precisely shaped high explosives to accomplish this task was one of the major research projects at Los Alamos. Espionage led to the transmission to the Soviets of details of the construction of explosive lenses, and ultimately to the Julius and Ethel Rosenberg and Klaus Fuchs trials (see Chapter 2).

You might think that a high explosive "explodes." Actually, the material burns quickly. The burning can be precisely controlled by careful design and quality control. In an implosion bomb the role of the high explosive is to produce a large symmetrical shock wave that compresses the fissionable material in the core. But to produce an inward directed force, the explosion must have something to push outward against. That something is material which is pushed (accelerated) outward by the burning of the high explosive. The process is called **inertial containment**. (This same term is used for a type of confinement occurring in one type of fusion power system.)

To visualize this process, imagine yourself holding a baseball and standing on a skateboard. If you throw the baseball north (say), the skateboard will be propelled south. The law of conservation of momentum requires that the mass of the baseball times its velocity be equal to the mass of you and the skateboard times your velocity. The faster you throw the baseball, the faster you will move the other way.

The balancing of two momentums in this way is also the key to the jet airplane and the rocket. The jet engine expels hot air at high speed behind it; the momentum of the hot air moving backward must balance against the momentum of the aircraft moving forward. Similarly the burned fuel expelled by a rocket backward must balance against that of the rocket moving forward. According to Newton's law, the force on an object is the rate of change of the momentum.* One can think of either a jet engine or a rocket as analogous to a person standing on a skateboard throwing one ball after another. The more balls thrown, and the faster they are thrown, the faster the board will move. (See Section P11-5.)

The explosive material in the bomb is arranged so that some of it moves inward to compress the nuclear material while at the same time some moves radially outward to conserve momentum. The process involves the following steps:

1. The high explosive is ignited. Typically there will be a number of ignition points so that the implosion starts simultaneously from many different points on the bomb and is thereby made more symmetrical. (Note that the multiple-point ignition is extremely important for safety. A bomb which could be set off by detonating the high explosive at a single point is called a **one-point-safe** bomb. Such a bomb would clearly be very unsafe from the point of view of accidents; for example, it could explode if dropped during loading. A major goal of weapons design is to assure that bombs are *not* one-point-safe. Ideally, they should be three or more points safe. Another goal of modern weapons design is to increase safety by using explosives that are very difficult to ignite. In the latest generation of warheads—such as those intended for use on the MX missile—the explosives are so insensitive that they will not explode even when hit by a rifle bullet.)

2. The burning produces two effects. On the outside of the bomb, material begins to move outward, providing momentum to counterbalance other material moving inward to start compression of the fissile material. At the same time a **compressional shock wave** begins to move inward. The shock wave moves faster than the speed of sound in the medium and creates a large rise in pressure. (It is the pressure rise that gives rise to the sonic boom you hear when a supersonic airplane passes by, producing a shock wave in the air.) The shock wave impinges on all points on the surface of the sphere of fissile material in the bomb core at the same instant. This starts the compression process.

3. As the core density increases, the mass becomes critical (just able to sustain a chain reaction), and then supercritical (where the chain reaction grows exponen-

---

*Momentum is defined as mass times velocity. In a typical situation in which the exhaust velocity is constant, it is the change in mass with time which produces the propulsive force.

tially). When the density has reached the maximum, the time is ripe for **initiation.** Remember that the assembly process was designed to go so quickly that there would be a negligible chance for any neutrons to appear as a result of spontaneous fission. As with the gun-type bomb, an initiator is used to introduce neutrons at the critical moment, and the chain reaction begins. A good initiator produces many neutrons, so many early generations of exponential growth are bypassed.

4. The chain reaction continues until the energy generated inside the bomb becomes so great that the internal pressures due to the energy of the fission fragments exceed the implosion pressure due to the shock wave. This will happen during the last ten generations or so, when most (99.9 percent) of the fission energy is released. In the very last generation, half of the total energy of the explosion is released and the bomb starts to come apart (**disassemble**). There is no longer a critical mass.

5. As the bomb disassembles, the energy released in the fission process is transferred to the surroundings.

A schematic representation of a gun-type type bomb is reproduced in Figure 11-2, which is taken from a Soviet text on atomic energy.

Initiators

An initiator is a device that produces neutrons at just the right instant, when the assembly process has reached the stage at which the fissile material is compressed into a supercritical mass. As noted, the fissile material itself produces so few neutrons spontaneously that there is only a small chance that even one will be emitted during assembly. The initiator is designed to produce a burst of neutrons at that instant which will lead to maximum energy release. The initiator can be an internal device, located inside the bomb so that the compressional shock wave sets it off automatically, or it can be an external device, which is triggered electrically or mechanically. Section P11-3 describes the design of one kind of initiator. If a neutron generator produces 1×10^{20} neutrons, then about 66 generations are bypassed (since 1×10^{20} is approximately equal to 2^{66}).

Tamper

The mass of ^{239}Pu or ^{235}U required for criticality can be reduced by installing a neutron reflector around the fissionable material of the bomb, inside the explosive lens. A neutron reflector can serve a dual purpose; in addition to reflecting neutrons it can serve as material for the outward-moving explosion to push against. This "tamping" action led to the term **tamper** being used for a neutron reflector surrounding an explosive. Beryllium is often used for tampers.

Boosted Primaries

Military requirements for nuclear weapons place safety first. Following this obviously essential requirement come specific military needs, among which is compactness and

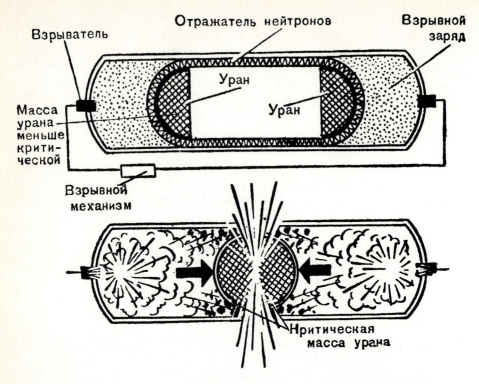

Схема устройства атомной бомбы. Два слитка урана с некритической массой и относительно безопасной формы (полушария), выстреленные навстречу друг другу, мгновенно соединяются вместе, образуя критическую массу наиболее благоприятной формы (шар).

FIGURE 11-2
A highly schematic representation of a gun-type bomb taken from a Soviet book on atomic energy. Many of the basic features are included, but many are missing. What are the main missing essentials?

robustness. Modern warheads are remarkably robust. They can be fired from field artillery, and dropped from low-flying aircraft such as the B-1 bomber. A secondary but nevertheless important military requirement is that nuclear weapons use the least possible quantities of uranium or plutonium. Boosted primaries provide one way of saving such special nuclear material. They also make it possible to build smaller weapons.

As noted above, the energy release in the primary is determined by how rapidly the chain reaction builds up. At early stages in the chain reaction the number of neutrons is small. A way to help the reaction build up rapidly and simultaneously cut down on the amount of U or Pu is through boosting. A small quantity of tritium and deuterium is placed inside the primary. After implosion the initiator is fired, bombarding the core region with neutrons. Some of these neutrons interact with the deuterium and tritium, heating it, driving nuclear reactions, and producing copious quantities of additional neutrons. This increases the yield for a given size. The reasons that tritium is used, rather than the lithium [which is used in the secondary, see Eq. (11-2)] is that the temperature required for production of neutrons is lower for tritium. The inclusion of radioactive tritium (half-life about 12 years) within the primary means that the primary characteristics change over time.

Hence stockpile maintenance requires continued tritium production. One proposal for slowing the nuclear arms race is based on limiting tritium production (Mark et al., 1988; Sutcliffe, 1988). The United States operates several large reactors for tritium production for this purpose. These reactors are aging, and do not meet environmental standards. The cost of maintaining or replacing them will require billions of dollars. This is an expensive aspect of the nuclear arms race which only rarely receives public attention.

11-4   H-BOMBS

The original atomic bombs were based on the idea of energy release through the fission of heavy elements, particularly ^{235}U and ^{239}Pu. Even while the Manhattan Project was under way, it was clear that bombs based on fission had to be limited in size. A fission weapon must be assembled into a critical mass and held together long enough for energy release to occur, and the task of holding it together gets more and more difficult as the size increases. Undoubtedly, ingenuity could have led to great improvements, but scientists knew that the energy of fission bombs would be dwarfed by that of fusion weapons.

The idea of energy release from fusion of light atoms goes back to the work of Hans Bethe and his colleagues on the origin of the sun's energy. Bethe developed the idea that solar energy comes from the fusion of hydrogen nuclei in the core of the sun. This was confirmed through many experiments, and Hans Bethe received the Nobel prize for the discovery.

Among the scientists working on the Manhattan Project, Edward Teller was the most outspoken advocate of work on the fusion concept. Oppenheimer, though he believed that the fusion process held promise, also thought that the technical difficulties of building a fusion bomb were much greater than the difficulties of building a fission bomb. Because of what was felt to be an urgent need to develop atomic weaponry—a sense of urgency that was aggravated by the fear, later found to be unjustified, that Hitler's Nazi Germany might be working on an atomic bomb—no work on the fusion concept was undertaken until after the end of World War II (see Chapter 2).

In 1950 a major H-bomb development program was undertaken. This led to the first true thermonuclear explosion (the Mike shot, detonated on Eniwetok Atoll in the South Pacific) in 1952 and to the rapid augmentation of the U.S. arsenal of fission weapons with fusion bombs.

Fusion bombs may be likened to combustible material ignited with a match. The combustible material is an isotope of hydrogen—typically deuterium or tritium, which are hydrogen isotopes with atomic mass numbers of 2 and 3, respectively. (The letters "D" and "T" are often used to denote deuterium and tritium). The match is a fission bomb. Someday fusion bombs might be ignited using lasers, and fission primaries may not be needed, but this is not presently possible.

A fundamental nuclear reaction that gives rise to energy release through fusion is the D-T reaction:

$$^2_1H + ^3_1H \rightarrow ^4_2He + ^1_0n + 17.6 \text{ MeV} \tag{11-1}$$

$$\text{Deuterium} + \text{tritium} \rightarrow \text{helium-4} + \text{neutron} + \text{energy release}$$

The neutron produced in this reaction carries with it a kinetic energy of 14 MeV, and the helium 4 carries a kinetic energy of about 3 MeV, for a total energy release of 17.6 MeV. This may be compared with the energy release of about 200 MeV from a single ^{235}U or ^{239}Pu fission event. However, since the mass of the hydrogen isotopes is much less than that of the heavy elements involved in the fission process, the energy release per unit of mass is about four times larger in a fusion than in a fission reaction. To release an energy of 1 megaton, 57 kilograms of ^{235}U or ^{239}Pu would have to be fissioned, whereas only 14 kilograms of tritium and deuterium would have to be fused. The total mass converted to energy, 46 grams, is the same in both cases and is given by Einstein's relation $E = mc^2$.

A simple demonstration of nonnuclear fusion with a barrier is easy with water droplets. Put a couple of drops of water on the surface of a clean pan coated with a nonstick material. Roll them around. You will notice that if they bump into each other gently, they will not fuse together, but if they bump together hard, they become a single droplet. The force preventing them from fusing is called *surface tension*. The total surface-tension energy after the two droplets are fused is less than that of the two of them separately because of two factors. (1) The surface to volume ratio for the single droplet is smaller than for the two droplets. (2) The binding energy between one water molecule and another water molecule is greater than that between a water molecule and air.

The trick in making a thermonuclear device is to heat the hydrogen isotopes enough so that fusion will occur (the Coulomb barrier preventing their fusing is overcome) and then to hold them at this high temperature long enough for the desired energy release to occur. It was clear from the beginning that a fission explosion might be a good way to provide the heat. The difficulty was to get the heat to the right place, for a long enough time. It was this problem that the physicist working on the H-bomb set out to solve.

The Oppenheimer Controversy

The approach that was eventually developed remains classified to this day. However, some information on it does exist. The critical idea was developed by Edward Teller and Stanislaw Ulam. When Robert Oppenheimer heard about the idea, he described it as so "technically sweet" as to be irresistible. The term "technically sweet" has become a favorite among physicists in describing particularly exciting new concepts. It raises many philosophical questions relating to the idea of a "technological imperative"—the inability of a society to resist building something that is technologically attractive, even if highly adverse impacts on the society are suspected.

The ethical and personality issues raised in the debate over the development of the H-bomb in the 1950s have been extensively documented and discussed. (See Chapter 2 for some of the background.) The debate occurred during the height of the ''McCarthy era'' of repression and ''red baiting,'' and many of the opinions aired did not reflect well on democracy. Insights into the climate of opinion of those times can be found in histories of the H-bomb (see, for example, York, 1975).

The Progressive Article

The details of H-bomb construction remain secret. However, in 1979 investigative reporter Howard Morland wrote a highly controversial article for *Progressive Magazine* which provides basic understanding of how an H-bomb might be built. The federal government attempted to suppress the information. It took *Progressive Magazine* to court, but after much litigation the article was published. An interesting aspect of the hearings on the article was that the defendant refused to look at key documentation and had to work through his lawyers. The reason for this was that Morland refused to accept any security clearance whatsoever on the grounds that this could limit his abilities to undertake investigative reporting in the future.

Whether Morland was acting in the public interest as he claimed or was releasing material that could prove helpful to enemies of the nation remains a matter of debate. The secrecy sought by the government was probably not significant in terms of enemies, but it would have perhaps retarded the open discussion that is the essence of democratic society. This was the view of the courts. We draw heavily upon Morland's article here. Figure 11-3 shows Mr. Morland with his H-bomb model.

FIGURE 11-3
Howard Morland's model of an H-bomb warhead. A warhead this size produces an explosion 20 times more powerful than the Hiroshima bomb. Such warheads are carried by the MX Trident, Minuteman, and cruise missiles. Washington, D.C., July 10, 1983. *Source:* Robert Del Tredici, *At Work in the Fields of the Bomb,* New York, Harper & Row, Inc., 1987.

The H-Bomb: General Principles

The first proof that energy could be released by fusing of light nuclei occurred in 1951, at Eniwetok Atoll in the South Pacific. The device exploded was not really a bomb, but rather an elaborate experiment involving very complicated apparatus for liquifying deuterium. The next step was to move from the isotopes of hydrogen, which required cryogenic apparatus, to something more practical. The successful approach made use of lithium deuteride, a compound which is stable.

The system works as follows. A fission bomb, called the **primary**, produces a flood of radiation including a large number of neutrons. This radiation impinges on the thermonuclear portion of the bomb, known as the **secondary.** The secondary consists largely of lithium deuteride. The neutrons react with the lithium in this chemical compound, producing tritium (hydrogen-3) and helium-4:

$$\ce{^6_3Li} + \ce{^1_0}n \rightarrow \ce{^3_1H} + \ce{^4_2He} \tag{11-2}$$

Lithium-6 + neutron → tritium + helium-4

This reaction produces the tritium on the spot, so there is no need to include tritium in the bomb itself. At the extremely high temperatures which exist in the bomb, the tritium fuses with the deuterium in the lithium deuteride according to the reaction given in Eq. (11-1).

The yield can be boosted by placing near the lithium deuteride a material such as ^{238}U that fissions to release energy. (Any isotope could be used which fissions when irradiated by high-energy neutrons. ^{238}U has the advantage of being cheap and abundant.) The ^{238}U also releases several neutrons each time it fissions, so there is a synergistic relationship between the neutrons produced in the ^{238}U and the reactions in the lithium deuteride. Fission in the jacket material can account for a large part of the energy release in an H-bomb.

Since many fission products result from the fission of ^{238}U, the final explosion results in a great deal of radioactivity—even though the fusion process itself does not produce much. Techniques have been developed for reducing the amount of fissionable material required. These led to the concept of the neutron bomb, which is discussed below.

The Real Secret of the H-Bomb

The above description of the H-bomb overlooks some important effects. How do you build a bomb that will maintain the high temperatures required for thermonuclear reactions long enough to obtain the desired energy release? How do you keep the bomb from blowing itself up prematurely? This was the technical difficulty that made Oppenheimer and other experts dubious on technical grounds about the "super." (Oppenheimer also was dubious on ethical grounds.) This was the problem that Edward Teller and Stanislaw Ulam overcame.

The nub of the problem, as described by Morland (1979), was that the shock waves produced by the primary (A-bomb) would propagate too slowly to permit assembly of the thermonuclear stage before the bomb blew itself apart. Teller and

Ulam noted that the gamma radiation from the primary propagates at the speed of light, so the time decay problem could be solved if radiation, instead of shock waves, could be used for compression.

To accomplish this, Teller and Ulam introduced a gamma-ray absorbing material to capture the momentum of the gamma radiation and use it to produce compression of the lithium deuteride. Figure 11-4 shows a conceptual way to accomplish this.

In Figure 11-4 the primary is shown as a sphere surrounded by explosives that produce a spherically symmetrical shock wave. A reflector is located above the sphere to direct as large a fraction as possible of the emitted radiation downward. The secondary is arranged in the form of a cylinder, the length of which is related to the desired yield. A neutron-producing material such as ^{238}U is located along the axis of this cylinder. Lithium deuteride surrounds this core. Shielding material between the primary and the secondary is used to prevent radiation from the primary from directly hitting the core material in the cylinder and producing premature heating. The next layer is a gamma absorber, intermixed with a light material such as plastic foam to transmit momentum to the core. (The gamma absorber and the plastic foam act somewhat like the piston and the steam in a steam engine.) The outer jacket of the bomb is a highly dense material, such as more ^{238}U, which provides momentum balance and also produces extra neutrons, thereby substantially increasing the total energy yield (see Section P11-4).

As radiation from the primary is absorbed, radial compressive forces are exerted along the entire cylinder at almost the same instant. The problem of time delays in the propagation of thermal shocks is thus overcome, and the way is clear to build a bomb of virtually any size.

The detailed design of a system based on these principles is obviously very complicated. Further, the bombs must be built to fit into the limited physical space of missiles, artillery shells, bomb bays, etc. They must be able to withstand extremes of temperature, humidity, and shock without losing their reliability and without changes in their yield. Clearly, there are enough problems to keep large crews of scientists occupied for long periods of time.

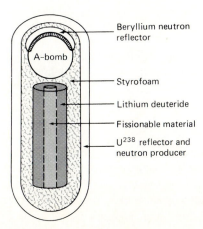

FIGURE 11-4
A schematic diagram of an H-bomb.

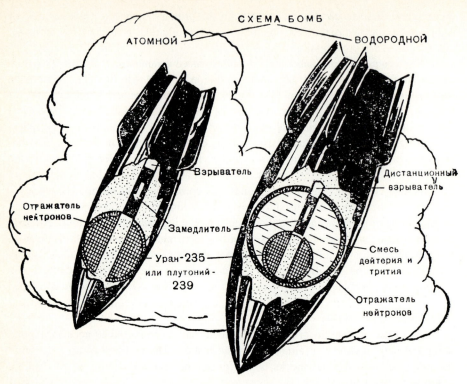

Одна из возможных схем устройства атомной и водородной бомб.

FIGURE 11-5

A schematic representation, from a Soviet textbook, of nuclear bombs mounted in missiles.

The basic principle, though—the "secret of the H-bomb"—remains relatively simple. Any nation with the technical and scientific skills to build a reliable A-bomb will be able to build an H-bomb if they should so desire. So far five nations—the United States, France, the Soviet Union, the United Kingdom, and the Peoples Republic of China—have built H-bombs.

Figure 11-5 is a schematic representation, from a Soviet text on atomic energy, of an A-bomb and an H-bomb mounted in missiles. While vague, the figure does convey a few of the important ideas.

Neutron Bombs

A neutron bomb is a variety of small hydrogen bombs, lacking the uranium jacket, that is designed to produce a large amount of nuclear radiation relative to thermal and shock-wave energy. (See Kaplan, 1981.) (The neutron bomb is also described as an *enhanced radiation* bomb, a more descriptive term from a technical point of view.) The military merit of such a bomb is twofold. First, it may permit use of nuclear weapons in situations in which use of conventional nuclear weapons would not be feasible. Second, because of the low level of blast relative to radiation released, neutron bombs would result in relatively small destruction of physical objects as compared with other nuclear bombs. Furthermore, the neutron energies are higher than for a fission bomb and therefore the neutron attenuation by the atmosphere is less. Table 11-3 contrasts the energy distribution from a typical fission weapon of 1 kiloton with a neutron bomb of the same yield. Figure 7-1 gives the neutron yield for a 1-kt neutron bomb.

The technical idea behind the neutron bomb is to build an H-bomb with the minimum possible amount of fissionable material. This requires three things: (1) building the smallest possible atomic bomb primary; (2) eliminating as much as possible of the fissionable material in the core; and (3) eliminating as much as possible of the neutron absorbing material in the outer jacket. The design problem is that the fissionable material on the axis of the cylinder (Figure 11-4) is important in the ignition process, while the material on the outside, in the casing, is important for momentum balance. It is thus clear that development of the neutron bomb presented technical challenges. How these challenges were resolved has never been made public.

The high radiation levels and relatively limited blast mean that neutron bombs are more effective against people than against physical objects. This is an advantage from the perspective of a military commander who would like to knock out personnel in tanks while minimizing collateral damage. What is perceived as an advantage to the military commander, however, is perceived as a great disadvantage by many protest groups, who have described the weapon as particularly inhumane. Further, the relatively small area of destruction makes the neutron bomb appealing as a battlefield weapon, and thus tends to blur the line of demarcation—already growing murky— between wars fought with nonnuclear bombs and wars fought with nuclear bombs.

A decision to build neutron bombs was announced by President Ronald Reagan on August 9, 1981. While these weapons are now in the U.S. stockpile, they are reportedly not actually deployed in Europe. The stated intent of the United States is to hold them in reserve until situations develop in which they may be needed and then to airlift them rapidly to Europe or elsewhere.

TABLE 11-3
Energy distribution of fission bombs and neutron bombs

	Percentage	
Energy type	Ordinary fission bomb	Neutron bomb
Blast	50	40
Thermal radiation	35	25
Prompt radiation (gamma rays, neutrons)	5	30
Delayed radiation (fallout)	10	5

Third-generation Weapons

Third-generation weapons are one of the most technically interesting of these new directions. These are weapons designed to convert a significant portion of the energy released in a nuclear explosion to a specific form, and to focus it. The most discussed example is **the x-ray laser** (see Chapter 20), which converts bomb energy into soft x-rays and focuses these x-rays into a narrow beam. However, one can imagine designs which would concentrate energy into virtually any part of the electromagnetic spectrum. An example would be an enhanced EMP weapon.

Testing of nuclear weapons is largely for the purpose of developing new technologies, for assuring stockpile reliability, and for maintaining technical skills. Typically only a few percent of actual tests in the United States are for the assuring stockpile reliability. If test-constraining treaties lower the allowable testing limits, this will increasingly constrain the ability of weapons designers to develop new concepts. To some, this is damaging to the national security while to others such constraints are stabilizing.

It is certainly true that with highly constrained testing, experience would deteriorate. It is also possible that the reliability of stockpiled weapons would deteriorate. Whether such deterioriation is a good or a bad thing depends on one's point of view. Some argue that a little deterioration will damage the ability of the United States to deter nuclear war. It is worth noting in this context that this is at best an idea subject to debate. Some of the arguments given for pursuing the Strategic Defense Initiative (SDI, Chapter 20) are that this will introduce uncertainty into the planning process of any prospective aggressor nation. An agreement to severely constrain or to ban nuclear testing will affect both the United States and the Soviet Union. If one's goal is to introduce uncertainty, then a test ban agreement moves in the same directions as does the SDI.

Another argument often raised is that Soviet nuclear bombs may be more robust than U.S. weapons, and that therefore constraints on testing may hurt the United States more than the Soviet Union. It is obviously not known to the United States how robust Soviet weapons are. However, Soviet delivery vehicles have larger throw weights than those of the United States and Soviet technology is generally a number of years behind that of the United States. One response to this concern is to phase in a test ban over several years (e.g., 5 years), thereby allowing time for the United States to develop weapons designed to remain reliable without testing.

Nuclear weapons have been developed to a high art. The next phase will be either a move to new technologies—the third-generation weapons—or else severe constraints on testing, which will slow down or prevent the development of new technologies. It is important to recognize and understand these trade-offs, and to form views on which direction is most likely to lead to a more stable world.

Observations

It appears that with the present state of technology H-bombs of virtually any size can be produced. The largest H-bomb ever tested (by the Soviet Union) released 58 megatons, far more than enough to destroy any city or any military target in the world. Smaller weapons have become much more interesting militarily. With the dramatic improvements in aiming accuracy in recent years (see Chapter 3), there is little use for the larger weapons. Present research focuses on reliability, safeguards, compatibility with delivery systems, and easy field adjustability of yield.

The design of secondaries (the thermonuclear component of thermonuclear weapons) has apparently become so reliable that there is little need to test them at their full yield. Hence testing programs focus on primaries; testing of secondaries is done with the fusion materials partially or entirely replaced by dummy material. This permits both the United States and the Soviet Union to test without violating the 150-kiloton limit of the (still unratified) limited test ban treaty. Testing still goes on (see Figures 11-6 and 11-7) to assure reliability, to validate refinements, to increase safety, to assure the weapons builders retain their skills, and to test warheads for new weapons systems.

The development of nuclear weapons appears today to be moving in several directions. Examples of current challenges to bomb designers are:

Bombs which are relatively invulnerable to shock, such as that which can occur if a weapon is dropped from a plane or pierced by a bullet

Thermonuclear systems that do not require an atomic bomb as a primary

Weapons for use in space; for example, as drivers for x-ray lasers

FIGURE 11-6
Aerial view of a nuclear test at the Nevada Test site.

FIGURE 11-7
Close up of a text assembly being lowered into a bore hole. The instrument package is located above the device being tested. Testing nuclear weapons requires heavy engineering. The crane has a capacity of about one million pounds. After assembly is in place the hold will be carefully sealed to prevent radiation from escaping after the test.

Improved security—against tampering and theft and against unauthorized arming

Improved stockpile reliability

ADDITIONAL PHYSICS SECTION

P11-3 ATOMIC BOMBS

The energy release of 200 MeV per fission may be converted into joules as follows:

$$(200 \times 10^6 \text{ eV/MeV}) \times (1.6 \times 10^{-19} \text{ J/eV}) = 3.2 \times 10^{-11} \text{ J} \quad \text{(P11-1)}$$

How Long Does an Explosion Take?

The speed of a neutron released in the fission process can be estimated as follows. The average neutron energy is about 1 MeV. The neutron mass is 5×10^{-26} kg. Using the expression relating kinetic energy to velocity, we have:

$$KE = \tfrac{1}{2}mv^2 \tag{P11-2}$$

Then

$$KE = (1 \text{ MeV}) \times (1.6 \times 10^{-13} \text{ J/MeV}) \tag{P11-3}$$
$$= 1.6 \times 10^{-13} \text{ J}$$

From this we calculate the neutron speed:

$$v = \left(\frac{2KE}{m}\right)^{1/2}$$
$$= \left[\frac{2 \times (1.6 \times 10^{-13} \text{ J})}{1.67 \times 10^{-27} \text{ kg}}\right]^{-1/2} = 1.4 \times 10^7 \text{ m/s} \tag{P11-4}$$

Initiators

One simple initiator design uses a radioactive source of alpha particles surrounded by beryllium powder. Between the alpha-particle emitter and the beryllium powder is a spherical shell of thin metal such as 0.001-in aluminum. (This is about the thickness of the heavy-duty aluminum foil one can find at the supermarket.) The range of alpha particles of a few MeV energy is less than the thickness of the metallic spherical shell. Together, the alpha emitter, the spherical shell of metal surrounding it, and the beryllium powder surrounding the shell form an initiator. It is placed in the center of the plutonium sphere that is to be compressed by the high explosive. This is shown schematically in Figure 11-8.

When the plutonium is compressed by the high explosive surrounding it, the metallic shell ruptures, allowing the alpha particles to bombard the beryllium powder.

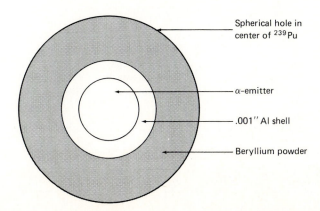

Spherical hole in center of ^{239}Pu

α-emitter

.001″ Al shell

Beryllium powder

FIGURE 11-8
A schematic representation of the initiator mechanism of an implosion bomb.

The following nuclear reaction is an efficient means for producing neutrons in a controlled manner:

$$\text{}^4_2\text{He} + \text{}^9_4\text{Be} \rightarrow \text{}^{12}_6\text{C} + \text{}^1_0 n$$

Helium-4 + beryllium-9 → carbon-12 + neutron

Assembly Speed: ^{235}U vs. Plutonium: Fizzles

This section provides some more technical detail on the characteristics of plutonium and uranium which are important for weapons design. See Table 11-4 for an overview of these characteristics.

The high heat output of ^{238}Pu makes it an excellent isotope for operating thermoelectric generators. The emissions are low-energy alpha particles which are very easily stopped by a thin layer of metal. Thus a packaged ^{238}Pu heat source is quite safe. It can be held comfortably in the hand. One does not, of course, want to hold too large a piece, or bring two small pieces together. This could create a critical mass, with high neutron fluxes which can prove fatal. ^{238}Pu heat sources are routinely used in NASA space missions that go to the far reaches of the solar system, where there is inadequate sunlight to operate photovoltaic power sources (e.g., the missions to Saturn, Neptune, and Uranus).

On the other hand the spontaneous neutron emission rate makes ^{238}Pu a poor choice for a bomb. It is high enough to guarantee a **fizzle** if ^{238}Pu is used in a bomb configuration. ^{239}Pu, which is much better in this regard, is the isotope of choice for a plutonium bomb.

Let us compare ^{235}U and plutonium, with the goal of estimating whether a fizzle will occur or not. We consider a gun-type bomb. A fizzle has a good chance of happening if during, say, the last 10 centimeters of assembly a neutron should initiate the chain reaction prematurely. Let us assume that the piece of fissionable material which will mate with its counterpart at rest to form a critical mass is traveling at 1 km/sec, a rather high speed for an artillery shell. (The actual plutonium gun bomb design called for a 3000 ft/s muzzle velocity, or 914 meter/s). It then requires 10^{-4} seconds, or 100 microseconds, to travel the final 10 centimeters of its path.

TABLE 11-4
Properties of plutonium and uranium

Isotope	Half-life, yr	Primary emission, MeV	Heat, W/kg	Spontaneous fission neutron emission rate, neutrons/g · s	Half-life for spontaneous fission (years)
^{238}Pu	86.4	5.5 alpha	560	2400	4.77×10^{10}
^{239}Pu	24,100	5.2 alpha	1.9	0.025	5.50×10^{15}
^{240}Pu	6600	5.2 alpha	7.0	1030	1.34×10^{11}
^{241}Pu	13.2	0.02 beta	4.5	— —	— —
^{242}Pu	326,000	4.9 alpha	0.1	1800	6.75×10^{10}
^{235}U	0.70 billion	4.4 alpha	0.00005	0.0004	3.50×10^{17}

To avoid a fizzle, a bomb must be assembled in a time short enough that there is only a small chance for emission of a neutron. Once any neutron at all is loose inside a critical mass, the exponential growth process can proceed very rapidly, typically in 10^{-8} s or faster per generation. This growth process is thus fast in comparison with assembly times.

So our criterion for a fizzle is to ask whether there is a good chance or not that a neutron will arise from spontaneous fission in the fissionable material within the critical 100 microseconds of final assembly.

For ^{235}U the spontaneous fission neutron emission rate is given in Table 11-4 as 0.0004 neutron per gram per second. Let us assume that the critical mass is 5 kilograms, which is approximately the value when the fissionable material is surrounded by a natural uranium reflector. The number of neutrons per second produced in the 5 kilograms of ^{235}U is then

$$^{235}U: (0.0004 \text{ neutron/g} \cdot \text{s}) \times (5000 \text{ g}) = 2 \text{ neutrons/s}$$

Therefore, the average time between neutron emissions is 1/2 s = 500,000 microseconds. So the chance that a neutron from spontaneous fission would cause a fizzle is very small. For this reason the Hiroshima gun-type bomb made of uranium 235 was never tested.

If we calculate the case for pure plutonium 239 similarly we have:

$$^{239}Pu: (0.025 \text{ neutron/g} \cdot \text{s}) \times (5000 \text{ g}) = 130 \text{ neutrons/s}$$

The average time between neutron emissions is 1/130 s, or 8000 microseconds. Again, the chance of a neutron from spontaneous fission of pure plutonium 239 causing a fizzle is small. That is, the neutron has only one chance in 80 of arriving within the final 100 microseconds of assembly.

However, when plutonium is made in a reactor from capture of a neutron in uranium 238, the resulting plutonium 239 can in turn capture a neutron forming plutonium 240. In order to produce usable quantities of plutonium 239, the plutonium 240 contaminant is unavoidable. Since its spontaneous fission rate is about 40,000 times greater than plutonium 239, a small amount can cause a significant number of neutrons to be produced. For example, if there is 1 percent contaminant of plutonium 240 in the reactor-produced plutonium, we have:

$$1\% \ ^{240}Pu: (1030 \text{ neutrons/g} \cdot \text{s}) \times (50 \text{ g}) = 52,000 \text{ neutrons/s}$$

The average time between neutron emissions is 1/52,000 s, or 20 microseconds. In this case it is *very likely* that a neutron from the spontaneous fission of the plutonium 240 contaminant would initiate a premature chain reaction in the final 100 microseconds of assembly. In fact, on the average *about five* neutrons would be emitted at this time. The discovery of the high spontaneous fission rate of plutonium 240 was made by Segrè's group at Los Alamos in 1944 (see Chapter 2). This nuclear physics measurement made it clear that the gun-type bomb would not be satisfactory for plutonium, and a crash program was begun to explore the implosion idea discussed earlier in this chapter. This idea had enough uncertainties that a full-scale nuclear test was necessary. The successful test and first nuclear explosion, code-named Trinity, took place July 16, 1945, in the Alamogordo desert in New Mexico.

P11-4 TEMPERATURE OF THE FUSION REACTION

In order for the fusion reaction to take place, the nuclei must be heated to a very high temperature. The deuterium and tritium nuclei are both positively charged and hence tend to repel each other by Coulomb's law (Chapter 7). However, if they approach each other fast enough, the coulomb repulsion is overcome and the attractive nuclear forces take over, pulling the nuclei together and permitting fusion to occur. The effect of heating the atoms is to increase their kinetic energy and hence their velocity. The energy needed to overcome the coulomb barrier is about 10 keV = 10,000 eV. Since roughly 1 eV is approximately 10^4 °K, the temperature must be 1×10^8 °K (or degrees Celsius—the temperature is so large that the difference between the two is negligible).

P11-5 MOMENTUM BALANCE

Momentum is one of the quantities which is conserved in all physical processes. The law of conservation of momentum complements the conservation of mass-energy (Chapter 8). Momentum (in nonrelativistic systems) is defined as the product of mass times velocity. One way to gain a physical feel for momentum is through a simple example. Consider a girl standing on a stationary skate board holding a heavy rock. When she throws the rock in one direction, the skateboard begins to move in the other. Conservation of momentum assures that the mass of the rock times its velocity is equal to the mass of the girl plus the skateboard times their velocity. (In practice there will be friction, so some of the momentum may be transmitted to the earth.)

Another example is in rocketry. The momentum of the rocket fuel leaving the rear of the rocket must be exactly balanced by momentum transmitted to the rocket body. The fuel moves backward, and the rocket is accelerated forward.

The Teller-Ulam idea makes use of the momentum of the x-radiation emitted by the primary. This radiation is absorbed by the styrofoam, which then reemits additional soft x-rays isotropically. Isotropic means that the radiation is emitted uniformly in all directions. There is momentum balance between the radiation transmitted outward and momentum moving inward. The inward-moving momentum serves to compress the lithium-deuteride in the bomb's secondary, which then heats. Radiation balance within a hydrogen bomb is very complex, and understanding it is one of the important issues in bomb design.

Since x-rays move at the speed of light, this technique allows compression of the secondary to begin very quickly after detonation of the primary. Timing is another crucial issue in bomb design. There are a number of different time scales, some associated with the primary, some with the secondary, and some with coupling between the two. All these time scales are short by human standards, since all major energy-release processes are complete within a fraction of a microsecond.

QUESTIONS

1. Explain the role of the reflector in a fission bomb.
2. What is a critical mass?
3. What function does the plastic foam perform in a hydrogen bomb?
4. Why is a fission bomb needed as part of a hydrogen bomb?
5. Why can't a 10-megaton fisson bomb be made?
6. Why is it a good idea to surround an H-bomb with a jacket of ^{238}U?
7. Why can't plutonium be used in a gun-type nuclear bomb?
8. How does implosion technique work?
9. What is a neutron bomb and why is it militarily attractive to some?
10. What is an initiator and why is it necessary?

PROBLEMS

1. How do the elements used in producing a plutonium bomb differ from those used in producing a uranium bomb?
2. How is plutonium produced?
3. Glasstone asserts (Glasstone and Dolan, 1977, Figure 1.25). "For a fission weapon exploded at an altitude of less than 40,000 feet. . . 35% of the explosion energy is in the form of thermal radiation and 50% produces air shock." He observes that for a burst at low altitudes the air shock energy from a fission weapon will be about half of that from a conventional high explosive with the same total energy release. Calculate the size of a conventional bomb that would deliver roughly the same amount of air shock as the Hiroshima bomb. Could a Boeing 747 carry it? (A Boeing 747 weighs about 700,000 pounds.)
4. Show that half the energy in a chain reaction is released in the last doubling.
5. Show that 99 percent of the energy in a chain reaction is released in the last 7 generations.
6. In Section 11-2 a story is told involving grains of wheat on a checker board. Calculate the quantity of wheat on the last four squares. Express your answer in tons.
7. The world population is now nearly 5 billion souls. The growth rate is about 1 percent per year. How long will it take for the population to double?
8. The growth rate of the population in some developing countries (Mexico is one) is about 3 percent per year. In how many years will the population of Mexico double?
9. At a population growth rate of 1 percent per year, how many years will it take before there is standing room only (one square meter per person) on the earth's surface? (The diameter of the earth is about 8000 miles, and about 20 percent of the surface is land.)
10. The energy release from one fission is about 200 MeV. How many fissions are required to release an energy of 10 kt?
11. A car weighing 1 ton is moving at 60 mi/h. What is the quantity of TNT that contains the energy equivalent to the kinetic energy of the car?
12. Calculate the velocity (in meters per second) of a neutron moving with an energy of 2 MeV. This is the energy of a "fast neutron," which is typical of neutrons in bombs and in fast reactors [such as the liquid metal fast breeder reactor (LMFBR)]. Neutrons in light water-power reactors of the sort which now provide about 15 percent of the electrical energy used in the United States use slow neutrons (thermal neutrons), with energies of a fraction of an electron volt. Calculate the speed in (meters per second) of a thermal neutron

with an energy of 0.05 eV. How long does such a thermal neutron require to travel the diameter of a reactor (about 12 ft)?

13. *Inertial containment* is the primary mechanism used to hold a bomb together during the time of energy release. This problem is designed to yield a very rough estimate of the pressures that exist inside an exploding bomb—which we can compare with pressures we are familiar with, such as atmospheric pressure (15 psi). We consider the force F on a uranium 235 atom: $F = ma$. For constant acceleration the speed is given as a function of time by $s = at$, and the distance is given by $x = \frac{1}{2}at^2$. Finally, the force is the pressure times area: $F = PA$. Let m be the mass of the ^{235}U. Take the diameter of the atom as about 10 Å $= 1 \times 10^{-9}$ m. Assume that the bomb disassembles after about 10 shakes $= 10 \times 10^{-8}$ s, and by this time the atom has moved about 1 cm $= 0.01$ m. You can now calculate the acceleration of the nucleus, and hence the force. Knowing the diameter of the atom, you can calculate the pressure that is acting. Compare this with atmospheric pressure. You will find that the pressure is very large indeed—so large that any known material will be instantly torn apart. Thus the only confinement available is due to the acceleration of the atoms—hence the name *inertial containment*.

14. Normally only a small fraction of the mass of a nuclear bomb is transformed into energy. If a fission bomb of ^{235}U has a mass of 4 kg that is completely transformed into explosive energy, what is the yield of the bomb in megatons? (1 Mt $= 4.2 \times 10^{15}$ J.)

15. If hydrogen bombs were constructed using tritium instead of lithium deuteride, then instead of the tritium being formed during the explosion process, it would always be present, decaying with a half-life of 12 yr. (*a*) If a hydrogen bomb so constructed had 10 kg of tritium when new, how much would be present after 12 yr? (*b*) After 24 yr?

16. What is the characteristic generation time (doubling time) in the chain reaction of a fission bomb?

17. The reaction deuterium + tritium $\rightarrow$ helium-4 + neutron + energy is the principal fusion reaction of the hydrogen bomb. Calculate the energy released (in MeV) from the above reaction.

$$\text{Mass of deuterium} = 3.344548 \times 10^{-27} \text{ kg}$$
$$\text{Mass of tritium} = 5.008347 \times 10^{-27} \text{ kg}$$
$$\text{Mass of helium-4} = 6.64658 \times 10^{-27} \text{ kg}$$
$$\text{Mass of neutron} = 1.674954 \times 10^{-27} \text{ kg}$$
$$c = 3.0 \times 10^8 \text{ m/s} \qquad 1 \text{ MeV} = 1.6 \times 10^{-3} \text{ J}$$

18. If 1 kg of tritium is "burned" in the above reaction, how much energy is released? (1 mole of tritium consists of 3 g and contains Avogadro's number of tritium nuclei.)

KEY WORDS

atomic bomb   a generic term which can refer to either a fission or a fusion weapon.

boosted primary   a primary which includes tritium. The result is to allow a much higher energy yield from a given amount of fissile material.

compressional shock wave   a wave moving through a material faster than the speed of sound in that material, thereby creating high pressure.

critical mass   a mass just large enough to sustain fission.

cross section   the effective stopping area of a nucleus or other particle. Cross section depends both on what is interacting and on the energy of interaction.

disassembly   nuclear jargon for something exploding.

explosive lens   high explosives arranged so as to produce a converging shock wave, thereby leading to implosion.

exponential growth   a process in which the number of events or objects doubles in equal time intervals. Often used imprecisely in reference to any rapid growth process.

fission bomb   a nuclear bomb based on the concept of releasing energy through the fissioning (splitting) of heavy elements such as ^{235}U or ^{239}Pu

fizzle   a nuclear explosion which fails to go off, or if it does go off produces a yield far less than anticipated.

fusion bomb   a nuclear bomb based on fusing of light elements. Fusion bombs use fission bombs for ignition.

generation time   the time required for the number of neutrons to double.

half-life   the time required for half of a group of radioactive nuclei to decay.

ignition   the introduction of neutrons into a critical mass.

implosion   increasing the density of a fissile material by crushing it, thereby decreasing the loss of neutrons and creating a critical mass.

intertial containment   confinement of a material by balancing of the momentum of material pushing outward against material pushing inward.

initiation   the start of a nuclear explosion.

initiator   the device which starts ignition.

neutron leakage   neutrons which escape from a bomb or reactor, and which therefore don't contribute to further fissions.

neutron bomb   a nuclear weapon designed to increase the fraction of total energy released as neutrons, so as to injure humans and biota more than objects.

one-point-safe   a weapon designed so that it will not produce a nuclear explosion if the high explosive in it is detonated at any one place.

primary   the fission part of a fusion bomb. The ''match'' which ignites the fusion reaction.

reflector   a mass of material designed to reflect escaping neutrons back into the fissionable material, thereby reducing leakage.

secondary   the thermonuclear part of a fusion bomb.

spontaneous fission   natural decay of a nucleus by splitting apart (fissioning)

tamper   a device surrounding a bomb designed to hold it together longer than otherwise by providing the explosion something to push against. Tampers can also serve as neutron reflectors.

third-generation weapon   an advanced nuclear weapon in which some of the released energy is intensified in one direction or in a particular part of the electromagnetic spectrum, or both (e.g., x-ray weapons, EMP weapons).

trigger   a means of starting a fission bomb.

x-ray laser   a proposed third-generation weapon which would produce intense low-energy x-rays, focused into very small solid angles.

CHAPTER
12

ELECTROMAGNETISM

To strive with difficulties, and to conquer them is the highest human felicity . . .

Samuel Johnson

12-1   THEMES

Electromagnetism is concerned with the electric and magnetic fields produced by stationary and moving electrons and nuclei. Electromagnetism plays a central role in much of the technology of modern society. Understanding electromagnetism permits insight into the operation of electric circuits in cars and houses and the functioning of radios, televisions, microwaves, and radar systems. In more direct application to the nuclear arms race the study of electromagnetism gives us a deeper understanding of nuclear structure (Chapter 10), the radiations from nuclear weapons (Chapters 14 and 15), the electromagnetic pulse (Chapter 17), radiation damage to biological systems (Chapter 18), and possibilities for ballistic missile defense that include lasers and particle-beam weapons (Chapter 20).

Electricity and magnetism are two aspects of the same phenomenon. The protons and electrons, which are elementary constituents of matter, are charged positively and negatively, respectively. The forces which exist between charged particles are called *electromagnetic* forces. Like charges repel each other (protons repel protons; electrons repel electrons), and opposite charges attract each other, through interactions operating according to the principle known as Coulomb's law.

When electric charges are stationary, only **electric forces** occur. Charges in motion produce currents, which in turn produce magnetic fields. Individual atoms and nuclei can have magnetic moments and exert magnetic forces even when not in motion. This internal magnetism makes possible permanent magnets and compasses.

When electric currents change rapidly, they radiate energy (*electromagnetic radiation*), which propagates through space at the speed of light and can carry information.

12-2 MACROSCOPIC ELECTRICITY: VOLTAGE, CURRENT, AND POWER

Electric circuits provide us with **power** which is used (for example) to run our houses and the electrical systems of cars. Light bulbs are labeled with their operating voltage and wattage. A typical household bulb might operate at 115 *volts,* with a power of 100 *watts.* An automatic battery typically operates at 12 volts. An automobile spotlight typically operates with a power of 10 watts.

Voltage is a measure of the energy added per electron by a battery or other source which pushes electrons through a wire. It is analogous to the pressure of water in a water hose or the pressure of air in an air line. The voltages detected by a radio or television set are typically millionths of a volt (microvolts), while high-voltage electric power transmission lines operate above 100,000 volts (100 kilovolts). The flow of **electric current** in a wire is analogous to the flow of fluid through a pipe. In the case of fluid flowing through a pipe, the flow is measured in volume per unit time (e.g., gallons per minute). In wires, electrons are flowing. Each electron carries a single unit of charge. Charge is measured in *coulombs.* (The charge on a single electron is -1.602×10^{-19} coulomb and that on a proton is $+1.602 \times 10^{-19}$ coulomb.) Flow of current is measured in **amperes**; the ampere is a measure of the amount of charge passing a particular point in one second (one coulomb per second passing a point is exactly one ampere). Since the charge on an electron is very small, 1 ampere corresponds to a large number of electrons passing per second: an electron flow of $1/(1.602 \times 10^{-19}) = 6.3 \times 10^{+18}$ electrons per second. Typical currents in devices you are familiar with range from the currents in transistor circuits, which are measured in millionths of an ampere (microamperes), to the currents in house light bulbs, which are typically a few amperes, to the currents in starting motors of cars, which are 100 amperes or more.

Currents flow easily in **conductors**, such as copper, or metals of any kind. They cannot flow readily in **insulators**, such as glass or ceramics.

The *rate* of energy produced or consumed, or *power,* is measured in *watts.* Power is the energy delivered per unit of time, and is measured in joules per second. If volts correspond to the hydrodynamic head in a water system (the height of the dam, or the water tower), and amperes correspond to the flow, in gallons per minute, then watts are the energy flow, which is the product of the pressure and the flow rate. Thus power, in watts, times time of flow, in seconds, yields energy involved, in joules. Electric energy can be converted to mechanical energy (e.g., in a motor), and mechanical energy can be converted to electric energy (e.g., in a generator).

Battery terminals are labeled *plus* and *minus.* (It is important not to get these signs confused. If you are using jumper cables to start a car, and you get the cables reversed, you are likely to destroy the transistors in the alternator and the voltage regulator.)

The plus and minus sign convention was originated by Benjamin Franklin. He chose it arbitrarily. We now know that the charge carriers in wires are electrons, and that the electrons flow from the battery terminal we call "negative" to the one we call "positive." We usually think of current flowing from plus to minus, but in fact the electrons go the other way.

Atoms are composed of nuclei (see Chapters 9 and 10), which are surrounded by an appropriate number of electrons. The nuclei are positively charged electrically, with a charge equal to the atomic number. The charge on the nucleus is due to protons, which are, by definition, positive in sign. Atoms are normally electrically neutral. This means that the positive charge on the nucleus must be counterbalanced by offsetting negative charges. The negative charges are located on *electrons*. Each neutral atom has precisely as many negative electronic charges as there are positive charges on the nucleus.

12-3 ELECTRICITY ON THE ATOMIC SCALE

Charges are *quantized*. The charge on the electron (1.602×10^{-19} coulomb) is the smallest free charge ever found in nature. The first experiment which demonstrated that charges are quantized was the oil-drop experiment of Robert A. Millikan. He placed a small charge on oil droplets and then measured the electric force needed to offset precisely the downward force of gravity on them. He found that all charges were precise multiples of a minimum charge.

> **Aside** A qualification on the indivisibility of the electron charge is in order. Experiments on nuclei performed at extremely high energies have provided evidence that there are, within the nucleus, particles known as *quarks*, with charges $\pm\frac{1}{3}$ and $\pm\frac{2}{3}$ of that of an electron. Free quarks have not been observed, although their existence has been convincingly inferred.

Electrons can be removed from atoms through a process known as **ionization**. An atom which has lost one electron is *singly ionized*; if it has lost two, it is *doubly ionized*; and so on. An *ion,* therefore, is an atom that has lost one or more electrons. A gas consisting of ionized atoms is called a *plasma*. In conductors, some of the electrons are mobile. In insulators no electrons are mobile. Ionization is important in understanding biological effects of radiation (Chapter 18).

12-4 ELECTRIC FIELDS

It is possible to discuss electromagnetism entirely in terms of the forces exerted on charges. However, physicists have found that it is convenient to introduce a more abstract concept—the **electric field**—which simplifies many types of discussion. An electric field may be defined as the force on a unit positive test charge placed at a point in space. The unit of the electric field is *volts per meter*. If one connects a 12-volt battery between two plates spaced 2 meters apart, the electric field between the plates will be 12 volts divided by 2 meters, or 6 volts per meter.

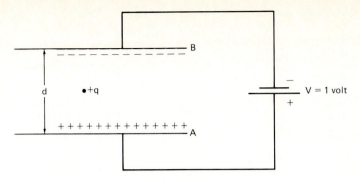

FIGURE 12-1
A pair of parallel plates connected to a battery.

A *battery* (see Figure 12-1) produces 1 volt of potential between a pair of parallel plates. The electric field between the two plates is proportional to the applied voltage and inversely proportional to the spacing. The electric field is directed upward in Figure 12-1. That is, it is directed from the positive charges on the plates to the negative ones. A positive charge placed between the plates experiences a force proportional to the electric field and in the direction of the electric field. The electrical force on the positive charge, $+q$, is therefore upward in this case.

Each proton within a nucleus creates an electric field that is directed radially outward from itself since each proton contains a unit positive charge. Therefore, the electric field of every proton produces an electric force on every other proton and directed away from it. The net result of all these mutual repulsions of protons in the nucleus is to lower the nuclear binding energy, particularly for heavy nuclei which contain the most protons. It is thus energetically more favorable (i.e., greater nuclear binding energy is obtained) if there are more neutrons than protons in heavy nuclei, such as uranium (see Chapter 10).

12-5   THE MAGNETIC FIELD

Electric charges in motion create **magnetic fields**. One of the simplest magnetic fields is created by the current in a long, straight wire (see Figure 12-2). In this case the magnetic field B surrounds the wire concentrically. It is constant at any given distance from the wire and is directed along circles surrounding the wire. If one's right-hand thumb points in the direction of the current, then the fingers will point in the direction of the magnetic field.

A compass needle responds to magnetic fields. A compass needle is a permanent magnet, composed of atoms which are naturally (intrinsically) magnetic. A compass needle will align itself with the local magnetic field. The heavy arrows in Figure 12-2 are schematics of compass needles, and they illustrate how a compass needle can be used to show the direction of the field lines of a magnet.

Just as the electric field is directed from positive to negative charges, the magnetic field is defined to be directed from north poles to south poles. As in the case of

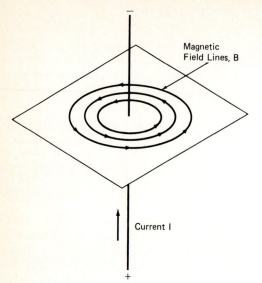

Magnetic Field Lines, B

Current I

FIGURE 12-2
The magnetic field from a long, straight wire. The magnetic field surrounds the wire in concentric circles.

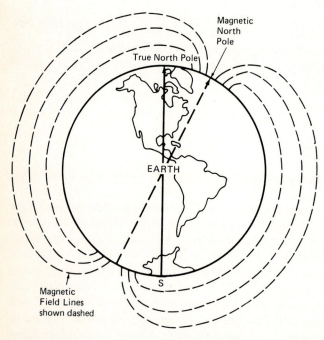

Magnetic North Pole

True North Pole

EARTH

S

Magnetic Field Lines shown dashed

FIGURE 12-3
A schematic picture of the magnetic field of the earth. The field is similar to that which would be obtained by a bar magnet whose south pole was located at the earth's magnetic north. The actual mechanism which produces the earth's magnetic field is not known with certainty.

238

charges, like poles repel each other and unlike poles attract each other. Unlike the situation with electrical charges, there is no experimental evidence that free magnetic charges exist. The south magnetic pole of the earth is located in far northern Canada and attracts the north-seeking (north pole) of a compass. This is shown in Figure 12-3. The figure exaggerates the difference between the magnetic north pole and the true north pole. The earth's magnetic field is essential for the production of the high-altitude **electromagnetic pulse** (EMP) to be discussed in Chapter 17.

The unit of the magnetic field is the *tesla,* or *weber per square meter*. The unit *gauss,* which is 1×10^{-4} tesla, is also sometimes used. The earth's magnetic field is about 0.0001 tesla, or about 1 gauss. A simple electromagnet can produce about 1 to 2 tesla, and modern superconducting magnets produce fields of 10 tesla and more.

12-6   CURRENTS DUE TO FIELDS: SHIELDING

Just as a current can produce a magnetic field, so can a magnetic field produce a current. However, a changing magnetic field is required. The observation that a changing magnetic field creates an electric field is known as *Faraday's law*.

If a conductor is present, the electric field produced by a changing magnetic field will produce a current. These induced currents are called *eddy currents*. The changing magnetic field can arise from an electromagnetic wave from the EMP (see Section P12-4 and Chapter 17). The large currents resulting from the EMP can destroy sensitive electronic equipment. Electronic equipment designed for military use is shielded from the induced currents of the EMP by metal enclosures and filters. Electronic circuits for civilian use are generally not so protected (see Chapter 17).

12-7   MOTION OF A CHARGE IN A MAGNETIC FIELD

A charge moving in a magnetic field experiences a force at right angles to the direction of motion and to the magnetic field. In a uniform magnetic field the charge will move in a circle or spiral. The situation is similar to that of an object that is whirled about on the end of a string: the object is constrained to follow a circular path. As Figure 12-4 illustrates, charged particles are subjected to a similar constraint by the magnetic field.

As discussed in Chapter 2 hundreds of electromagnetic isotope separators were built during World War II during the Manhattan Project. These separators, or "calutrons," had large magnetic fields into which uranium ions were introduced (see Figure 12-5). (An ion is an atom which has one or more of its electrons removed so that it has a net positive charge.) The ions were introduced at high velocities by accelerating them with negatively charged electrodes, S1 and S2 in the figure. Upon entering the magnetic field the uranium 235 ions and the uranium 238 ions described circles of the order of a meter in radius. The uranium 235, which has a slightly smaller

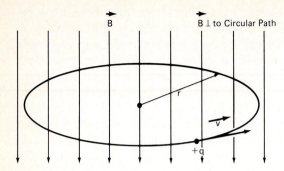

B   **B ⊥ to Circular Path**

FIGURE 12-4
A charged particle is shown making a circular path of radius r as it travels perpendicular to a magnetic field, denoted by the symbol B. The magnetic field is depicted by the vertical lines.

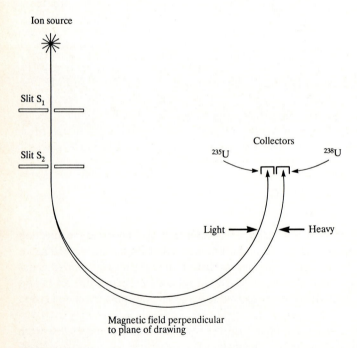

Ion source

Slit S_1

Slit S_2

Collectors

^{235}U ^{238}U

Light ⟶   ⟵ Heavy

Magnetic field perpendicular
to plane of drawing

FIGURE 12-5
Schematic diagram of the operation of a "calutron" for separation of uranium 235 from uranium 238. The uranium ions formed by an electric arc in the ion source are accelerated by negatively charged slits S1 and S2 and then enter a strong magnetic field perpendicular to the plane of the figure. The magnetic field causes the ions to traverse a circular path with the heavier uranium 238 having a slightly larger radius than the uranium 235 ion beam. The ions are then collected as shown. In practice the separation was only partial so that it was necessary to repeat the process to obtain 90 percent pure uranium 235 that is suitable for a nuclear bomb. The Hiroshima bomb was made in part by this process.

mass than uranium 238, described a slightly smaller radius in the magnetic field so that it could be separated from the uranium 238 in an appropriate collector.*

Another instance in which magnetic fields play a role in nuclear arms is the case of the high-altitude electromagnetic pulse, or EMP. For a nuclear explosion taking place above the earth's atmosphere the gamma rays produced proceed radially outward from the explosion point without absorption until they strike the atmosphere. Then they interact with atmospheric atoms to form high-velocity electrons. The electrons in turn describe circular paths in the magnetic field of the earth, since they are charged particles traversing a magnetic field. This motion produces electromagnetic radiation (see Section 12-8 below), which is called the EMP. It will be discussed in more detail in Chapter 17.

12-8 ELECTROMAGNETIC WAVES, RADIO WAVES, AND THE SPEED OF LIGHT

Electric charges in motion create electric current. When a charge (either a free charge or one constrained to move inside a conducting wire such as an antenna) *accelerates,* it produces changing electric and magnetic fields. These changing fields can propagate through space. When electric and magnetic fields propagate, they are called *electromagnetic waves*. Radio waves, television waves, and radar signals are all examples of electromagnetic waves. In air electromagnetic waves travel nearly with the speed of light in a vacuum. (They travel more slowly in media with high dielectric constants.) Since the speed of light is very great, **electromagnetic radiation** moves from one place to another very quickly. The speed of light in a vacuum is often denoted by the symbol c:

$$c = 2.99793 \times 10^8 \text{ meters per second}$$

Thus

$$c \simeq 3 \times 10^8 \text{ meters per second}$$

or 186,000 miles per second, or 1 foot per nanosecond. The time required for the light of the sun to reach the earth is about 8 minutes (from which you can calculate the distance from the earth to the sun). Stationary satellites used for long-distance telecommunications are located about 23,300 miles above the earth (only at this altitude do the satellites remain fixed over a point on the earth's surface). At this distance the round trip signal time delay is about 0.25 second. This delay is noticeable if you are talking to someone you know well, but not if you are talking to a stranger or someone you know only casually.

Modern mainframe computers perform addition or subtraction calculations in times that are typically tens of nanoseconds. Even time delays this small are significant

---

*^{235}U experiences the same magnetic force as the ^{238}U. However, since its mass is less, because of Newton's law ($F = ma$), it is accelerated more.

and must be taken into account when considering a computer's applications. The most modern computers, such as the Cray supercomputers, go to considerable lengths to keep internal distances small because the electromagnetic fields in the computer's signals must travel at velocities less than the velocity of light. In the Cray all the electronics are located around a common core; the machine is so compact that only one person can fit inside for final assembly. The lengths of connecting wires are carefully measured so that the signal transit times are balanced. In the future, as computers get faster and faster, the length of signal delays will be even more important. [The cycle time in the IBM AT computer, which was used to type this book, is about one-tenth of a microsecond (one ten-millionth of a second). The IBM AT operates so slowly that the speed of light is not important in its design.]

Electromagnetic radiation is characterized by a frequency and a wavelength. *Frequency* refers to the number of oscillations the radiation makes per second. Frequency is expressed in *hertz* (Hz), or *cycles per second*. The *wavelength* is the length of the wave in space. In terms of water waves, the frequency is the number of waves passing a given point per second and the wavelength is the distance between two wave crests, or troughs. The product of the frequency and the wavelength is the speed of propagation, which is the speed of light for electromagnetic waves in a vacuum. Thus

$$c = f\lambda$$

where
$$c = \text{speed of light, meters per second}$$
$$f = \text{frequency, seconds}^{-1}$$
$$\lambda = \text{wavelength, meters}$$

The *electromagnetic spectrum* is the set of frequencies (and associated wavelengths) where electromagnetic waves are found. The range is vast. Broadcast radio waves have a frequency of about 1 megahertz (1×10^6 hertz) and a wavelength of 300 meters. Television and FM radio operate at about 100 megahertz, and the signals have a wavelength of about 3 meters. (TV antennas are about a half wavelength long, or about 1.5 meters.) Visible light and gamma rays are also electromagnetic radiation. The electromagnetic spectrum is shown in Figure 12-6.

Visible light has a wavelength of about 0.5 micrometer (sometimes called microns and denoted by the Greek letter μ) or 0.5×10^{-6} meter. The frequency of this light in hertz is,

$$f = \frac{c}{\lambda}$$

$$= \frac{3 \times 10^8}{0.5 \times 10^{-6}} \frac{\text{m/sec}}{\text{m}}$$

$$= 6 \times 10^{14} \text{ sec}^{-1}$$

Radiant heat, which is one of the principal causes of casualties from air-burst nuclear weapons, is transferred by waves whose lengths range from a fraction of a centimeter (0.01 m) to 8×10^{-5} centimeter (8×10^{-7} m) (infrared). The wavelengths of microwaves are in the centimeter region.

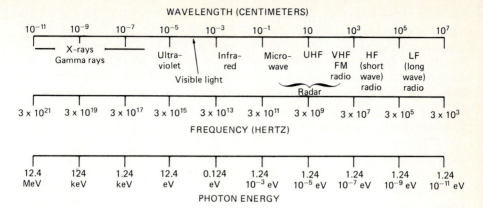

FIGURE 12-6

The spectrum of electromagnetic waves. The spectrum extends from very long wavelength radio waves to very short wavelength gamma rays. The visible spectrum occupies only a small portion of the electromagnetic spectrum.

The visible portion of the electromagnetic spectrum is only a very small part of the total spectrum: 7.5×10^{-7} to 4.0×10^{-7} meter. This is the region of the most intense radiation from the sun at the earth's surface. Human eyes adapted over evolutionary time to be most sensitive to the brightest sunlight. In the short-wavelength end of the spectrum, the ultraviolet extends from the violet, in the visible, down to about 5×10^{-9} meter, at which point the x-ray region begins. X-rays and gamma rays are electromagnetic radiation; they are identical in all ways except wavelength — and hence frequency — with light waves and radio waves. X-rays arise from atomic processes, whereas gamma rays arise from processes taking place in nuclei (see Chapter 10).

The U.S. Navy has built an extremely low frequency transmitter in Michigan to communicate with submerged nuclear submarines. The frequencies used are only a few hertz. The wavelengths therefore are exceedingly long, about 100,000 kilometers. The long wavelengths are needed to avoid attenuation of the radio signals by seawater, which is a good electrical conductor and a very poor medium for the propagation of electromagnetic signals. Because the wavelength is so long, enormous antennas — many miles in length — carrying sizable currents are needed. At very low frequencies it is not possible to communicate large amounts of information quickly. Submarines normally communicate by towing wires near the surface, which can pick up higher frequencies.

12-9 GAMMA RAYS, X-RAYS, AND PHOTONS: WAVES AS PARTICLES

So far we have described electromagnetism in terms of waves. In Chapter 10 we discussed gamma radiation as a particle, i.e., a photon. We now need to unify these two perspectives. All electromagnetic radiation can be described using either the language of particles or the language of waves. Some experiments are best described using one type of description, while others are clearer with the alternative presentation. This duality may violate our intuition, yet there is no reason why we should expect our intuition to work well in areas where we have no experience. In the decades since the particle nature of light was first discovered, many experiments have been performed which, taken together, make a convincing case that this "wave-particle duality" is a fundamental aspect of nature—one that we must simply accept if we are to make sense of our experimental observations of the world.

In situations in which we experience electromagnetic radiation directly there are so many of the fundamental particles, or **photons**, that they act in many ways as waves. Yet if the intensity of illumination is lowered, the particle nature of the radiation becomes important. Consider light falling on a photocell—a device which converts the incoming light to an electric current. At high levels of illumination a continuous current is found. As the light is made weaker and weaker, the current is found to be made up of individual signals, which occur whenever a photon strikes the detector. Signals due to very weak light sources are often examined by counting individual photons.

The history of physics has led to the use of different names for different parts of the electromagnetic spectrum. Yet the entire spectrum illustrated in Figure 12-6 consists of photons. The photons that make up radio waves, microwaves, visible light, gamma rays from an atomic nucleus, and x-rays from atomic electrons or from interstellar space differ only in their frequencies and wavelengths.

Each photon possesses an energy. A photon may collide with an electron much as one ball collides with another, or its energy may be absorbed in ejecting an electron from an atom (see Section P18-2). The energy of a photon is uniquely determined by its wavelength and is proportional to its frequency. The constant of proportionality is usually designated by Planck's constant h (see Section P12-3). Figure 12-6 shows the relationships between energy, wavelength, and frequency.

12-10   RADAR

When radio waves hit an object, part of the energy in the wave is absorbed and part is reflected. Some portion of the reflected energy returns to the transmitting antenna and can be used to gain information about the object. In a **radar** system (*radar* is an acronym for *Radio Detection and Ranging*) a transmitter emits a short burst of electromagnetic radiation which bounces off a target. The time delay between the emitted burst and the returned signal tells how far away the object is. The time t it takes for a signal to reach an object at a distance of 100 miles (about 160,000 meters) is

$$t = \frac{d}{c} = \frac{1.6 \times 10^5 \text{ meters}}{3 \times 10^8 \text{ meters/second}}$$

$$= 0.00053 \text{ second (530 microseconds)}$$

The round-trip time is twice this, or 1060 microseconds. In order for the object to be identified, the wavelength of the emitted radiation should be small compared to the size of the object. Typical radar used for tracking airplanes uses microwave radiation having frequencies of a few gigahertz and wavelengths of a few centimeters. At these wavelengths it should be possible to gain considerable detailed information about a target, although the antennas used are generally designed for detection, rather than detailed shape analysis.

Old-style radar antennas are mechanically rotated and are unsuited for tracking large numbers of fast-moving objects. Modern military radar uses *phased array* antennas which can track electronically. One of the most advanced of these is the *PAVE PAWS* phased array warning system located on Cape Cod, which is designed to identify and track enemy missiles passing over the North Atlantic Ocean.

Sonar is analogous to radar, but relies on sound propagating through water instead of on electromagnetic radiation. *Sonar* systems are used by the U.S. military to identify submarines entering regions close to the continental United States. Advanced sonar might someday be used to track submarines over large portions of the ocean, which would destroy the ability of today's submarines to hide. Obviously sonar research is a high-priority area for both the United States and the Soviet Union (see Tsipis, 1983).

12-11 NAVIGATION AND TARGETING

Electromagnetic waves are used for many types of navigation and targeting. The previous section discussed radar as a ranging device. Radar can also be used to help home in on targets. A variety of techniques are used for navigation. Low- and medium-frequency radio waves have long been used in ship and aircraft navigation. Most of these systems rely on *triangulation*. In triangulation systems a highly directional antenna is aimed to point toward a transmitter. A bearing is then taken. The receiver must be somewhere on the line passing through the transmitter, the location of which is, of course, precisely known. A second bearing on another transmitter yields another line. The receiver must be located at the point of intersection. The approach is similar to that used in stellar navigation for obtaining the coordinates of a star with a transit compass and a watch.

Satellite navigation systems such as NAVSTAR are based on accurate timing of signals emitted from low-orbit satellites. Comparing the arrival times of signals from several satellites allows one to determine precisely the position and velocity of the receiver.

12-12 LASERS

Lasers are an acronym for *Light Amplification by Stimulated Emission of Radiation*. Specifically they are designed to amplify electromagnetic radiation and to produce a very nearly parallel beam. Laser operation is made possible by the fact that if an atom is in an appropriate excited state, it can be stimulated to emit a photon if there is a photon incident on the atom of precisely the same frequency. If this occurs there will now be two photons—the original stimulating photon and the one it produced. This process can be repeated millions of times in a region of excited atoms, produced, for example, by an electrical discharge in a gas. Large amplifications are possible. In this way intense laser beams of visible light, and ultraviolet light and infrared electro-magnetic radiation can be formed. By using a nuclear explosion it is also possible to produce an x-ray laser. Lasers of all types may have application in ballistic missile defense. See Chapter 20 for a more detailed discussion of lasers and such applications.

ADDITIONAL PHYSICS SECTION

P12-4   ELECTRIC FIELDS AND ELECTRIC POTENTIAL

The electric field E is defined as the force F per unit positive charge q:

$$E = \frac{F}{q} \tag{P12-1}$$

The electric field is measured in volts/meter, the force in newtons, and the charge in coulombs. The electric field arising from a single charge Q obeys an inverse square law. That is, the electric field decreases as the inverse of the distance from the charge, squared:

$$E = \frac{kQ}{r^2} \tag{P12-2}$$

If Q is positive the electric field is directed outward radially from the position of Q. Here the experimentally determined constant $k = 8.988 \times 10^9 \, \text{N} \cdot \text{m}^2/\text{C}^2$. The electric field is expressed in newtons per coulomb, joules per coloumb-meter, or volts per meter. All of these are correct in the SI system of units.

The electric field is a measure of how the potential varies with distance. For the parallel plate example shown in Figure 12-1, the field is uniform and the electric field is

$$E \, (\text{V/m}) = \frac{V(\text{V})}{d(\text{m})} \tag{P12-3}$$

If, for example, $d = 0.5$ meter and $V = 1$ volt, then the electric field is 2 V/m.

How are we to reconcile the inverse square law given in Eq. (P12-2) with the assertion that the field is uniform (the example of Figure 12-1)? The inverse square law applies when there is a point charge. But in the figure there are many charges spread out uniformly over the two metal plates. Added together, the inverse square fields due to these many charges give a uniform field. The proof of this striking result may be found in many texts on electromagnetism (see, e.g., Lorrain and Corson, 1970).

The fact that the exponent in Eq. (P12-2) is precisely 2 is important when designing equipment to shield electronic gear. It makes possible a crucially important device known as the *Faraday cage*. This is a conducting box used to surround a piece of gear which is sensitive to electric fields. No electric fields can enter the box; thus the electronic gear is shielded from the electromagnetic pulse and other disturbances. The Faraday cage works because the area of a sphere increases as the radius squared, while the field due to a charge decreases as the radius squared.

Electric fields are the primary cause of damage by nuclear radiation to biological systems. This is explained in detail in Chapter 18. The mechanism for biological damage by both neutrons and gamma rays is the production of charged particles of considerable energy. These particles, recoiling ions in the case of neutrons or electrons in the case of gamma rays, have intense electric fields associated with them. The electrical forces these fields generate produce breaks in DNA and chromosomes, for example, that are deleterious to cell division or to genetic material.

Calculation of Fission Fragment Kinetic Energies

In Section P10-5 we calculated the kinetic energy released from fission of a uranium 236 nucleus into two unequal fragments. This result (about 170 MeV) was obtained from nuclear mass differences.

Since Eqs. (P12-1) and (P12-2) permit us to calculate the forces between electrical charges, it is possible to obtain an alternative estimate of the kinetic energy released in the fission process by calculating the repulsive force between the two fragments. This force acting through a distance does work on the fragments (see Chapter 9) which results in their acquiring kinetic energy. The calculation is somewhat complicated due to the fact that the force between the fragments decreases rapidly with distance so that we are obliged to add up small increments of distance multiplied by the appropriate force.

For ease in calculation we assume that the fission creates (somewhat improbably) equal spherical fragments. We further assume that the nuclear charge in the fragments is distributed uniformly. In this case the force acting between two spherical fragments is the same as if all the charge of each fragment were concentrated at the center of each fragment. This situation is illustrated in Figure 12-7. We begin the calculation when the two fragment spheres are just in contact, and then allow them to fly apart due to their mutual repulsion. If R is the radius of each fragment sphere, we break down the distance increment into steps of $R/2$. These steps are depicted in the figure successively as (1), (2), and (3), corresponding to center-to-center distances, r, of $2R$, $2.5R$, $3.0R$, and finally in (4) schematically separated a distance of $3.5R$.

The repulsive force between the two fragments is obtained by combining Eqs. (P12-1) and (P12-2):

$$\text{Force} = F = Eq = kQq/r^2 \qquad \text{(P12-4)}$$

This equation is also known as Coulomb's law.

In our case $Q = q = 46 \times 1.6 \times 10^{-19}$ coulomb's, since the uranium nucleus of 92 charges is assumed to divide into equal fragments. In position (1) $r = 2R$ and in (2) $r = 2.5R$. The force in position (1) is

$$F = 8.988 \times 10^9 \times (46 \times 1.6 \times 10^{-19}) / (2 \times 6.38 \times 10^{-15})$$

$$= 2990 \text{ newtons (N)}$$

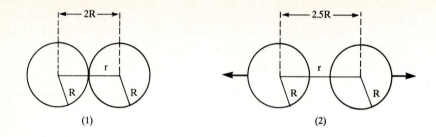

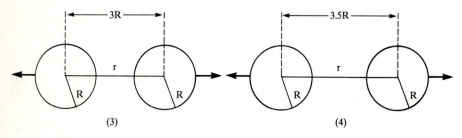

FIGURE 12-7

The kinetic energy given fission fragments is calculated by adding up the contributions of the repulsive force between the positively charged fragments acting through successive distances taken as one-half the fragment radius, R. It is assumed for simplicity that the fragments are spherical and that they are of equal size. Shown are the initial configuration in which the fragments are just in contact, (1), and successive separations of $R/2$. The numbered stages in the figure correspond to the calculation of contributions to the kinetic energy shown in Table 12-1.

Here R is calculated from the empirical relation that reflects the uniform density of nuclear matter:

$$R = 1.3 \times 10^{-15} A^{1/3} \text{ meters} \qquad \text{where } A \text{ is mass number} \qquad \text{(P12-5)}$$

Here we assume $A = 118$ giving the result above. Similarly if we calculate the force at position (2) we find

$$F = 8.988 \times 10^9 \times (46 \times 1.6 \times 10^{-19}) / (2.5 \times 6.38 \times 10^{-15})$$
$$= 1914 \text{ N}$$

The average force between the fragments as they fly apart from (1) $\rightarrow$ (2) can be estimated roughly as $(2990 + 1914)/2 = 2452$ N. This average force acting through the distance $(2.5R - 2.0R) = 0.5R$ will do an amount of work equal to 2452 N $\times$ 0.5R.

$$2452 \text{ N} \times 6.38 \times 10^{-15} /2 \text{ N-meters} = 7.82 \times 10^{-12} \text{ J}$$

Since there are 1.602×10^{-13} J/MeV, this is

$$\frac{7.82 \times 10^{-12} \text{ J}}{1.602 \times 10^{-13} \text{ J/MeV}} = 48.8 \text{ MeV}$$

TABLE 12-1
Calculation of fission fragment kinetic energies

Interval	Average force	K.E. increment (MeV)	Total K.E. (MeV)
(1) → (2)	2452	48.8	48.8
(2) → (3)	1621	32.3	81.1
(3) → (4)	1153	23.0	104.1
(4) → (5)	862	17.2	121.3
(5) → (6)	669	13.3	134.6
(6) → (7)	535	10.6	145.2
(7) → (8)	437	8.7	153.9
(8) → (9)	364	7.2	161.1

This energy appears as kinetic energy of the fragments and is divided equally between them.

We next calculate the force similarly at $r = 3R$. It is found to be 1329 N. It is then averaged with that at $2.5R$ (1914 N) to give an average force in the (2) → (3) distance interval of 1621 N. This average force acting again through $(3.0R - 2.5R) = 0.5R$ gives an increment to the fragment kinetic energy of 32.3 MeV and a total kinetic energy of $48.8 + 32.3 = 81.1$ MeV.

To find the total kinetic energy released it is necessary to continue this process until the fragments are infinitely separated. Table 12-1 gives the average force, the increment in kinetic energy, and the total kinetic energy for the first eight distance intervals.

If the sum is performed on a computer for the first 2000 terms, the total kinetic energy is found to be 240.1 MeV and the average force has decreased to 0.012 N. The total fragment kinetic energy calculated is higher than the correct value. The error is due to the crudeness of the model and the approximations made by assuming a finite distance interval.

The latter error can be avoided through the use of the integral calculus, which permits us to employ infinitesimal distance intervals, dr. In this case we may write the total kinetic energy as

$$\text{Total K.E.} = 8.988 \times 10^9 \, (Ze)^2 \int_{2R}^{\infty} \frac{dr}{r^2}$$

$$= 8.988 \times 10^9 \, (Ze)^2 / 2R \qquad \text{(P12-6)}$$

$$= 3.815 \times 10^{-11} \, \text{J} = 238 \, \text{MeV}$$

which compares favorably with the result above using finite distance intervals.

P12-7 MOTION OF A CHARGED PARTICLE IN A UNIFORM MAGNETIC FIELD

The radius of the circle described by a charged particle traveling perpendicular to a uniform magnetic field can be obtained by equating the **magnetic force** direct toward the center of the circle to the **centripetal force** directed outward from the center. Please refer to Figure 12-4. The situation is analogous to twirling a ball in a circle when held by a string. The force supplied by the string keeps the ball in a circular path and is analogous to the magnetic force.

The magnetic force is given by

$$F_m = qvB \tag{P12-7}$$

where q and v are the particle's charge and velocity, respectively, and B is the strength of the magnetic field (in teslas).

The centripetal force is found from the equation:

$$F_c = \frac{mv^2}{r} \tag{P12-8}$$

Here m and v are the particle's mass and velocity, respectively, and r is the radius of the circle.

If we equate F_c and F_m, and solve the resulting equation for r, we have

$$r = \frac{mv}{qB} \tag{P12-9}$$

The angular frequency of rotation of the particle is given by v/r, or

$$\text{Angular frequency} = \frac{qB}{m}$$

The frequency of rotation is the angular frequency$/2\pi$ so that

$$\text{Frequency of rotation, } f = \frac{qB}{2\pi\, m} \tag{P12-10}$$

The reader is referred to the discussion of synchrotron radiation that forms the electromagnetic pulse as an application of this equation (see Section P17-3).

P12-8   ELECTROMAGNETIC WAVES

The radiated electric and magnetic fields of an electromagnetic wave are perpendicular to each other and also to the direction of propagation (the direction away from the source). This is shown in Figure 12-8. The radiated electric field produced by a charge in motion is proportional to the acceleration of the charge and is in the plane that is formed by the direction of the acceleration and the direction of propagation. The field is perpendicular to the direction of propagation.

The radiated electric field E gets smaller with distance R from the accelerated charge, diminishing inversely with the distance:

$$E = \text{const} \times \frac{a}{R} \tag{P12-11}$$

where a is the acceleration of the charge.

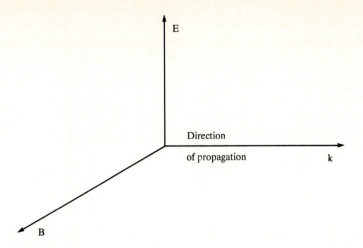

FIGURE 12-8
In an electromagnetic wave the electric field and the magnetic field are perpendicular to each other and to the direction of propagation.

Many charges accelerating together in some direction produce a *time-varying current*. The electric field of the radiated wave is proportional to the current in the source, I, and inversely proportional to the distance from the source, R:

$$E = \text{const} \times \frac{I}{R} \qquad \text{(P12-12)}$$

In the formation of the EMP (see Chapter 17) Eq. (P12-12) gives the result that the pulse would be diminished by only a factor of 2 from the center of the United States to either coast if a nuclear bomb were exploded at 500 kilometers over Nebraska. The electric field from EMP will induce currents in any conductor (see Section 12-6). These currents can seriously damage unshielded electronic equipment or induce large currents in power lines (tens of thousands of amperes) for a short period of time. In turn, these large current surges could lead to excessive voltages in electrical apparatus. The EMP radiation could also induce high voltages by direct induction (Faraday's law), even if the equipment was not connected to the power grid.

P12-9 PHOTONS: WAVES AS PARTICLES

The energy, W, in joules, of a photon of frequency f, in s^{-1}, is

$$W = hf \qquad \text{(P12-13)}$$

where h is Planck's constant, 6.62×10^{-34}; $J \cdot s$ (or $4.1 \times E^{-15}$ eV $\cdot$ s). Or, using the ideas in Section 12-8,

$$W = \frac{hc}{\lambda} \qquad \text{(P12-14)}$$

(Note that the conversion of Planck's constant from joule-seconds to electron-volt-seconds was done on the basis of the fact that 1 eV equals 1.6×10^{-19} J.) Electromagnetic radiation thus has a wave-particle duality. It has a wave aspect, giving rise to concepts like wavelength; but it also has a particle aspect in that each photon of electromagnetic radiation acts as if it were a particle possessing a specific amount of energy.

Planck's constant is very small, so the energy of an individual photon is small in comparison with energy we can readily detect. One of our most sensitive detectors is the eye, which is able to detect only a few photons.

The energy of a blue optical photon (one you can see) of wavelength 0.5 μm $(0.5 \times 10^{-6}$ m) is

$$W = \frac{hc}{\lambda} = \frac{(4.1 \times 10^{-15} \text{ eV} \cdot \text{s}) \times (3 \times 10^8 \text{ m/s})}{0.5 \times 10^{-6} \text{ m}}$$

$$= 2.5 \text{ eV}$$

It turns out that the binding energy of electrons in many materials is a few electron volts, so that optical photons are able to knock these electrons loose under the proper conditions. This is a crucial physical accident that makes possible television tubes and cameras, photovoltaic cells, and many other devices.

QUESTIONS

1. How many electrons per second are in a current of 1 A?
2. What is an electron-volt?
3. What creates a magnetic field?
4. What creates an electric field?
5. What happens when a charge is accelerated?
6. Do like charges repel or attract one another? Unlike charges?
7. What is a watt?
8. What is an electric field?
9. What happens to charged particles that cross a magnetic field?
10. About what wavelength is visible light?
11. What is meant by a photon?

PROBLEMS

1. One watt is a unit of power equal to one joule expended per second. What is the number of kilowatt-hours given by a 1-kt nuclear explosion? (Home consumption is about 500 kWh per month.)
2. Show that 1 kWh is equal to 3.6×10^6 J using the definition of a watt from Problem 1.
3. What is the wavelength of 1-GHz microwaves? (1 GHz $= 1 \times 10^9$ Hz)
4. What is the wavelength of 1000-Hz acoustic waves traveling at the speed of sound in air (about 750 mi/h)?

5. If the electric field from a radiating system is known to give a field strength of 1000 V/m at a distance of 500 mi, what would be the field strength 1000 mi from the source? Assume the radiating system is small enough to be considered a point source (when viewed from 1000 mi).

6. If a photon has a frequency of 100 MHz (TV broadcast frequency), how much energy does each photon carry?

7. Some x-rays are emitted during the first microsecond of a nuclear burst, with a wavelength of 1.0×10^{-9} m. What is the energy of each x-ray photon?

8. What is the frequency of a green light whose wavelength is 0.5 μm? (0.5×10^{-6} m)

9. Two large plates are separated by 20.0 cm. One plate is maintained with a battery at potential of 12 V and the other is grounded (i.e., maintained at zero V). What is the electric field between the plates, in volts per meter?

10. If the earth's magnetic field is 0.5 gauss high in the atmosphere and an electron of 10 keV enters it perpendicularly, what is the radius of the circle the electron will describe (origin of the high-altitude EMP)? [*Hint*: First calculate the electron speed from $\frac{1}{2}mv^2 = 10$ keV $= 10 \times (1.6 \times 10^{-16}$ J).] The mass of the electron is 9.11×10^{-31} kg.

11. How would you expect the electric field from the EMP to vary with the yield of an explosion, assuming that the currents that produce the electric field are proportional to the yield?

12. What is the frequency of rotation of the electron in Problem 10?

KEY WORDS

conductor   a material through which electric current passes easily, usually a metal.

electric current   a stream of charged particles usually carried by a conductor. The stream is of electrons which travel in the opposite direction to the positive current. The current is measured in coulombs per second or amperes.

electric field   the force that a unit positive charge would experience in a region of other electric charges.

electric forces   forces of repulsion between like charges or of attraction between unlike charges. Sometimes called coulomb forces.

electromagnetic pulse   an electromagnetic pulse, or EMP, is produced by a nuclear explosion. It is formed by accelerated electrons in the atmosphere that are created by the gamma radiation from the explosion.

electromagnetic radiation   electric charges that are accelerated produce electromagnetic radiation. Light is such radiation of a particular frequency. Gamma radiation and x-rays are of higher frequencies.

insulator   a material through which electric current passes with difficulty, such as glass, many plastics, or ceramics.

ionization   a process in which one or more electrons are removed from an atom or molecule leaving it with a positive electric charge.

magnetic field   the force that a unit magnetic charge (such as a north pole of a compass) would experience in a region where electric currents are flowing. Actually single magnetic charges do not exist in nature, but the magnetic field concept is useful nevertheless.

magnetic force   the force experienced by a moving charge in a magnetic field. It is equal to the product of the magnetic field and the velocity and charge of the particle.

photon   a photon is a quantum of electromagnetic radiation. According to quantum theory electromagnetic radiation is quantized in packets or quanta of energy such that the energy of a quantum, or photon, is equal to Planck's constant, h, multiplied by the frequency of the radiation.

power   the rate of doing work. Power has the dimensions of energy per unit time. The unit in MKS is the watt, which is equal to one joule per second.

radar   an acronym for radio detection and ranging. Radar functions by directing an electromagnetic wave of short duration at an object and observing the reflected wave. Radar frequencies are much less than those of visible light, but greater than television or radio waves.

sonar   similar to radar, but uses sound waves in water to "range" or detect objects by observing the reflected sound waves.

CHAPTER
13

NUCLEAR WEAPONS EFFECTS I: BLAST EFFECTS

13-1 THEMES

Nuclear explosions in the air produce blast effects qualitatively similar to, though generally larger than, the blast effects of conventional explosives. Other major effects of nuclear weapons (thermal radiation, initial nuclear radiation, electromagnetic pulse, and fallout) are unique.

Blast effects depend primarily on the overpressure, which is usually measured in pounds per square inch (psi). The overpressure decreases in proportion to distance as the bomb yield to the one-third power: a 1-megaton (1000-kiloton) bomb produces the same overpressure as a 1-kiloton bomb at $(1000)^{1/3} = 10$ times the distance away. An overpressure of 6 psi occurs about 4 miles from a 1-megaton bomb exploded in air at 10,000 ft altitude. This pressure will destroy most buildings and kill about half their occupants. Specially hardened structures (e.g., missile silos) can withstand 1000 psi or more, a pressure which is produced only if nuclear weapons hit relatively close (typically a few hundred feet for a 1-megaton weapon).

13-2 SHOCK WAVE

The blast effect of a nuclear explosion is produced by the almost instantaneous heating of air by a nuclear fireball. In nuclear explosions below 40,000 feet, about 50 percent of the energy released goes into blast energy. Temperatures at the beginning of the nuclear explosion are comparable to the interior of the sun, about 1×10^7 °C. The enormous amount of energy released in a small volume of air produces intensely hot gases at extremely high pressures. The result is a shock that proceeds outward from the explosion. Near the explosion the speed of the shock wave is several times the speed of sound in air (1100 feet per second, or about 0.2 mile per second). As the wave moves outward, it gradually slows to the speed of sound.

If one detects the flash of a nuclear explosion (which arrives almost instantaneously) and survives the heat radiation, it may be possible to seek shelter before the blast wave arrives. The distance to the detonation point may be estimated in the same way one estimates the distance of thunder—by counting seconds and allowing 5 seconds per mile.

Overpressure

The shock wave produces an overpressure that can be large enough to destroy virtually any structure.

The overpressure is the amount by which the pressure in the shock wave front exceeds atmospheric pressure. An overpressure of 5 psi is sufficient to destroy normal residential structures and kill half of the occupants of those structures. An overpressure of several thousand psi would destroy most hardened silos. Figure 13-1 shows how overpressure decreases with time and distance from the explosion. The figure shows the shock front at six successive times. The curve labeled ''t6'' illustrates how a negative overpressure develops as the shock front passes. Structures are first buffeted

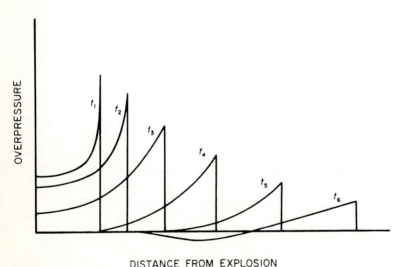

FIGURE 13-1
The overpressure shock front proceeds to the right in the figure at velocities exceeding that of sound. Successive times are denoted by the subscripts. A negative overpressure can develop after the passage of the initial positive shock wave. (*From Glasstone and Dolan, 1977.*)

TABLE 13-1
Overpressure and wind velocity

Peak overpressure, psi	Maximum wind velocity, mi/h
200	2078
100	1777
72	1415
50	934
20	502
10	294
5	163
2	70

by forces away from the explosion. A short time later there is a force toward the explosion. The positive and negative overpressures resulting from a 1-megaton explosion each last several seconds.

The shock front is followed by a wind which can be of hurricane force. In regions where the overpressure exceeds 5 psi, the wind speed is over 150 miles per hour. The wind, sometimes called the dynamic pressure, arises because the shock front disturbs the normal equilibrium of the atmosphere (see Table 13-1).

The Mach Stem

When the shock wave hits the earth's surface, it reflects. The reflected wave combines with the original shock wave, increasing the peak overpressure. This increase in pressure is called the *Mach stem*. Figure 13-2 illustrates how the original wave and the reflected wave merge to produce the Mach stem for an air burst.

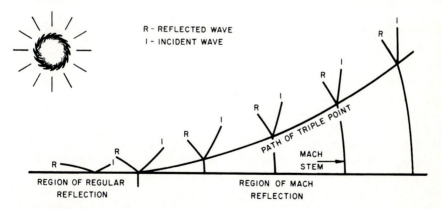

FIGURE 13-2
The original or incident wave and the reflected wave from the ground combine to form a Mach-stem shock wave that has approximately double the overpressure of the original shock wave. The Mach-stem wave propagates horizontally in the figure (actually radially in all directions from the burst point). (*From Glasstone and Dolan, 1977, figure 3.25.*)

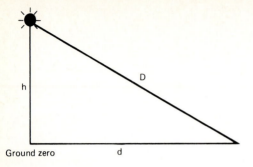

FIGURE 13-3
Geometry of the slant height D. h is the burst height and d is the distance on the ground from ground zero.

Ground zero   d

Slant Range

The distance from an explosion to an observer is called the *slant range*. The geometry is shown in Figure 13-3. For a burst at height h and distance d from ground zero to a given point, the slant range D is, from the Pythagorean theorem,

$$D = \sqrt{d^2 + h^2} \tag{13-1}$$

13-3   SCALING LAWS AND BLAST EFFECTS

Scaling laws allow one to extrapolate from the effects of a weapon of one size to the effects of a weapon of a different size. Scaling laws for nuclear weapons are analogous to those used in extrapolating from wind-tunnel tests of model airplanes to the behavior of full-size aircraft.

The energy released by a bomb may be considered roughly as spread out within the volume of a sphere of radius D, where D is the slant range (or a segment of a sphere, if part is cut off by the ground). Doubling the size of a weapon doubles the volume of the region in which similar blast effects occur. Since the volume of the region is proportional to the cube of the slant range, the scaling law for yield varies as the yield to the one-third power. (This is discussed in more detail in Section P13-3.)

Thus overpressure from a weapon of a given size depends on the height of the burst. If the goal is to maximize the distance at which a particular overpressure occurs, then the burst height can be adjusted accordingly. This is shown in Figure 13-4 for a 1-kt bomb. Figure 13-4 can be used for any weapon yield if height of burst and distance from the burst point are scaled. If one bomb releases 1000 times the energy of another, a given pressure will occur at a distance which is increased by a factor equal to the cube root of the ratio of the yields, or $(1000)^{1/3} = 10$. A 1-megaton bomb exploded at an altitude of 10,000 feet will give an overpressure of 6 psi at 20,000 feet from ground zero, whereas for a 1-kiloton bomb, a 6-psi overpressure occurs at 2000 feet from ground zero if the bomb is exploded at 1000 feet. Figure 13-4 shows how to select the burst height that will create the largest possible circle of blast damage with a particular weapon and a particular overpressure.

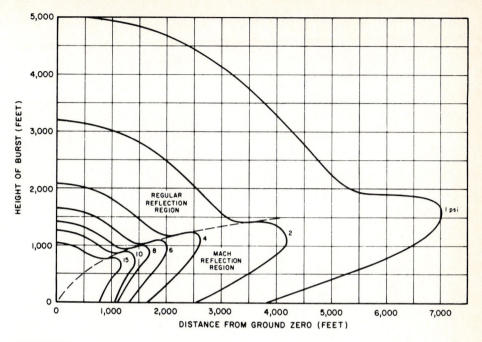

FIGURE 13-4
Peak overpressures on the ground for a 1-kiloton burst (low-pressure range). The distance is measured from ground zero. (*From Glasstone and Dolan, 1977, figure 3.73c.*)

Figure 13-5 is similar to Figure 13-4 except that it gives overpressures in the high-pressure range, which are needed to discuss hardened targets. The overpressures and scale are again those for a 1-kiloton bomb.

13-4   DAMAGE FROM AIR BLAST

The shock wave from an explosion can reflect from walls. This effect can give rise to forces up to eight times larger than those discussed in the previous section. In addition, the wind effects (termed *drag loading*) can cause extensive damage because they last longer than the shock wave. For example, at 1 mile from a 1-megaton explosion the overpressure lasts only a fraction of a second, whereas the duration of drag loading from wind effects caused by the same explosion is 3 seconds. These effects depend on the detailed shape of the structure and the incident angle of the blast wave.

Ordinary unreinforced residences of the type common in the United States are completely destroyed by an overpressure of 5 psi. Figure 13-6 shows a brick house exposed to a bomb exploded at the Nevada test site in 1955 at a point where the overpressure was 5 psi. Figure 13-7 shows the damage to a two-story steel frame building with a 7-inch reinforced concrete wall panel that was 0.4 mile from ground

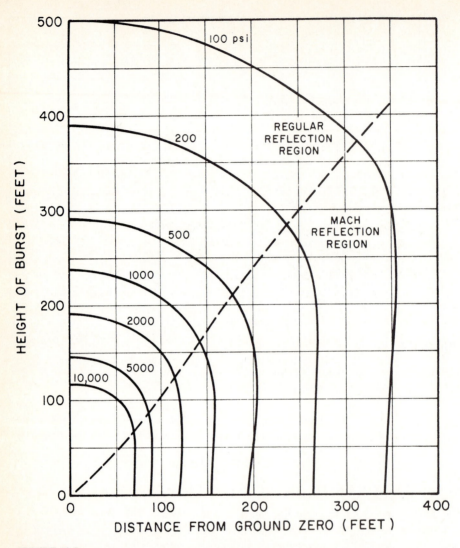

FIGURE 13-5

Peak overpressure on the ground for a 1-kiloton burst (high-pressure range). The figure is similar to Figure 13-4, except that it depicts the overpressure nearer ground zero. The distance is again that from ground zero (or *d* of Figure 13-4). Note that in order to achieve very high overpressures, such as those necessary to destroy a missile silo, the burst must be near the surface. (*From Glasstone and Dolan, 1977, figure 3.73a.*)

zero at Hiroshima. In this building the first-story columns buckled away from ground zero and dropped the second story to the ground. Figure 13-4 can be used to estimate the overpressure experienced by this building as follows: The building was 0.4 mile, or 2110 feet, from ground zero. The Hiroshima bomb was 15 kilotons. The distance

FIGURE 13-6
An unreinforced brick house subjected to a 5-psi overpressure at the Nevada test site in 1953. (*From Glasstone and Dolan, 1977, figure 5.67.*)

from ground zero for the same overpressure for a 1-kiloton bomb is calculated by dividing 2110 by the cube root of 15 which gives 856 feet (2110 ÷ 2.46 = 856). We know that the Hiroshima bomb was exploded at 1900 feet, which scales to 772 feet for a 1-kiloton bomb. The point on Figure 13-4 that is 856 feet from ground zero and has a burst height of 772 feet is between the 10 psi and 15 psi overpressure contours. We therefore conclude that about 10 psi overpressure (with some vertical component in this case) is sufficient to cause severe damage to commercial reinforced concrete structures.

Massive reinforced concrete structures can protect a missile silo against overpressures of 2000 psi or more. Figure 13-5 can be used to estimate the missile accuracy needed to attack hardened targets. For a 1-megaton surface blast, an overpressure of 2000 psi occurs at a distance of 0.23 mile (1200 feet) from ground zero. To obtain an overpressure of 2000 psi, a 1-megaton bomb must be exploded at a height of less than 1900 feet. This means that the harder the silo, the lower the height of burst required, the more the fireball touches the ground, and the greater the radioactive fallout produced.

FIGURE 13-7
Damage to a two-story steel-frame building at Hiroshima with 7-inch reinforced-concrete wall panels. The overpressure was about 10 psi, with some vertical component. (*From Glasstone and Dolan, 1977, figure 5.26.*)

Effect of Blast on Human Beings

The direct effect of overpressure on human beings begins with lung damage; this occurs at a threshold of 12 psi, and severe damage occurs at 25 psi. Eardrum rupture can occur at 15 psi in some individuals, but others can withstand up to 40 to 50 psi before rupture occurs. About 50 percent of eardrums rupture in the region of 15 to 20 psi. Damage to the viscera and tympanic membrane is also caused by blast pressure. The 50- to 75-psi region is one of 50 percent lethality, whereas at 100 psi there is almost 100 percent lethality. The reflected shock wave experienced by a person next to a wall can have a magnitude from 2 to 8 times greater than that of the incident wave. Therefore, in some cases casualties will occur that are associated with higher overpressures than the average in the vicinity.

Most blast injuries and fatalities occur because of indirect effects. Objects become missiles. The body may itself become a missile and strike objects. An overpressure of 4 psi can shatter a glass window into hundreds of fragments, traveling about 120 miles per hour, which can cause serious wounds.

Figure 13-8 shows blast injuries experienced at Hiroshima. The dashed line, at less than 1.2 kilometers, is only an estimate, and was drawn on the assumption that there were no other causes of death than blast. It was based on an estimate of 130,000 fatalities and a similar number of injuries. (Because of the chaotic conditions following

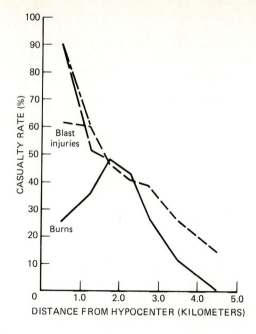

FIGURE 13-8
Blast injuries at Hiroshima. The dotted curve
is an estimate of blast casualties. (*From the
Committee for Compilation of Materials,
1981.*)

the bombing, the figures are necessarily approximate.) There was about a 50 percent
casualty rate at 1.5 kilometers in the civilian population housed principally in residential structures. Using Figure 13-4 and the known yield of the Hiroshima bomb (15
kilotons), we can estimate the blast pressure at 1.5 kilometers as follows: 1.5 kilometers is 4920 feet. We obtain the scaled distance by dividing 4920 by the cube root
of 15, which gives 2000 feet (4920 ÷ 2.46 = 2000). The scaled burst height is 772
feet (see Section 13-4). The point on the figure where 772 feet (ordinate) and 2000
feet (abscissa) intersect is about 5.8 psi.

Summary of Air-Blast Effects

Table 13-2 is a modification of one given by Sartori (1983). It gives the blast effects
of a 1-megaton nuclear explosion at 4000 feet altitude.

13-5   UNDERWATER EXPLOSIONS

A nuclear explosion underwater forms a very hot gas bubble which generates a shock
wave that is analogous to the air burst generated by a nuclear bomb exploded in the
atmosphere. However, since water is much less compressible and more dense than
air, there are important differences from an air burst. The velocity of sound in water
is about 1 mile per second—5 times greater than the velocity of sound in air. The
initial shock wave travels several times faster than that, but eventually, at large distances from the burst, the velocity approaches 1 mile per second.

TABLE 13-2
Blast effects of a 1-megaton nuclear explosion at 4000 feet

Peak overpressure, psi	Wind velocity, mi/h	Distance from ground zero, mi	Effects
100	1415	0.53	A
20	502	1.53	B
10	294	2.35	C
5	163	3.6	D
2	70	6.3	E
1	37	9.5	F

A: Almost 100 percent fatalities from direct pressure effects on the human body. Complete destruction of all structures except those especially hardened, such as missile silos.
B: Serious lung damage, ear rupture in 50 percent of persons exposed. Multistory reinforced concrete buildings demolished.
C: Threshold of lung damage, some eardrum rupture. Most factories and commercial buildings collapsed.
D: Threshold of eardrum rupture. Unreinforced brick and wood houses destroyed and 50 percent fatality to occupants due to flying debris and persons being thrown about. Heavier construction severely damaged.
E: Moderate damage to houses, cracked frames, interior walls knocked down, severe damage to roofs. Some injuries flying glass and debris. Fatality level about 15 percent due to indirect effects.
F: Light damage to commercial structures, moderate damage to residences.

The peak overpressures are much larger than in air, but the duration is shorter. At 3000 feet from a 100-kiloton burst in deep water, the peak overpressure is 2700 psi. The duration, however, is only about 0.05 second. A 100-kiloton air burst at the same distance would have an overpressure of only about 18 psi, but it would last about 1 second.

If the detonation is in shallow water, a reflection of the overpressure wave occurs when the wave reaches the water surface. The reflected wave has a negative overpressure, which tends to cancel the overpressure of the original wave underwater when it arrives. This is called the *cutoff time*. In addition positive reflections from the bottom increase the overpressure; this effect is analogous to the Mach stem effect for air bursts.

Damage to ships or submarines from an underwater burst is of two types: damage to the vessel's hull and damage to components and equipment within the ship due to indirect effects. Main steam lines, boiler brickwork, and electronic equipment are particularly sensitive to overpressure shock. Inadequately secured articles and personnel are thrown about with great violence.

The surface wave a nuclear explosion produces can also cause damage to vessels and harbor installations. In the Baker tests of 1946, a 20-kiloton bomb that exploded in shallow water produced a wave 94 feet high 900 feet from the explosion.

ADDITIONAL PHYSICS SECTION

P13-2   SHOCK WAVES IN AIR

Speed

Glasstone gives an approximate expression for the speed S of the shock wave for a ground burst as

$$S = c_0\left(1 + \frac{6p}{7p_0}\right)^{1/2} \tag{P13-1}$$

Here c_0 is the speed of sound in air (1100 ft/s or 335 m/s at sea level), p_0 is normal atmospheric pressure (15 psi), and p is the overpressure.

Mach Stem

The behavior of the Mach stem is influenced by the fact that the incident wave has previously passed through the air and has heated and compressed it. This causes the reflected shock wave to move faster than the original wave. The reflected wave catches up with the original wave to form a single combined wave, the Mach stem, which propagates along the earth's surface. The pressure in the Mach-stem region can be twice that of the original shock wave.

FIGURE 13-9
Crater formed at the Nevada test site code-named Sedan. This 110-kt nuclear explosion took place several hundred feet below ground level in order to maximize crater size. The test was part of Project Plowshare of the 1960s. One of the objectives of the project was to possibly construct canals or other excavations by means of nuclear explosion. Environmental concerns about the released radioactivity were a major factor in discontinuance of the program. The crater formed was 1,200 feet across and 600 feet deep with a crater lip of the order of 100 feet. *Source*: Lawrence Livermore National Laboratory.

For a surface burst the reflected and original waves combine immediately at the burst point to form a Mach stem. In a tall building or in an aircraft two distinct shock waves will be experienced—the incident and the reflected waves (above the triple point in Figure 13-2).

P13-3 SCALING LAWS

If we know the overpressure at a certain slant distance D_0 which corresponds to a yield Y_0, then the distance at which the same overpressure is experienced for a different yield is

$$D = D_0\left(\frac{Y}{Y_0}\right)^{1/3} \tag{P13-2}$$

The burst height and distance from ground zero to yield the same overpressure also vary as the cube root of the weapon yield. Thus

$$h = h_0\left(\frac{Y}{Y_0}\right)^{1/3} \tag{P13-3}$$

where h is the height appropriate for a weapon of yield Y.
Similarly

$$d = d_0\left(\frac{Y}{Y_0}\right)^{1/3} \tag{P13-4}$$

where d is the ground zero distance appropriate for a weapon of yield Y.
These equations may be used to scale Figures 13-4 or 13-5 to other yields.

Example: The 15-kiloton bomb that devastated Hiroshima was exploded at an altitude of 1900 ft. If we divide 1900 ft by 2.46 ($15^{1/3} = 2.46$) then we may use Figure 13-4 to find the bulge that gives the overpressure as a function of distance from the burst point. The burst height scales to 1900 ft ÷ 2.46 = 772 ft burst height for a 1-kt bomb. Following the ordinate at 772 feet, we find that the optimum overpressure is about 9 psi and occurs at a distance of 1500 ft for a 1-kt bomb. Then 9 psi occurs 2.46 times farther away, or 3690 ft, for the 15-kt bomb. The distance from ground zero (the point directly beneath the bomb) at which 4 psi overpressure (adequate to destroy residential buildings) occurs is 2.46 × 2500 = 6150 ft.

P13-5 UNDERWATER BURSTS

In shallow water the wave height varies as the fourth root of the weapon yield, so for a 320-kt explosion the wave height would be 188 feet.

In deep water, if the burst is not too deep but deep enough so that the gas bubble does not vent, the peak-to-valley wave height H is given by

$$H = \frac{40{,}500 \, Y^{0.54}}{R} \tag{P13-5}$$

where Y is the yield in kilotons and R and H are given in feet. At 1000 ft from a 100-kt underwater burst H is 490 ft! The gas-bubble diameter is given by

$$d = 256 \, Y^{0.25} \qquad \text{(P13-6)}$$

where d is in feet and Y in kilotons. For the above example the fourth root of 100 is 3.16, and so the gas-bubble diameter is 810 ft.

QUESTIONS

1. What is the difference between peak overpressure and peak dynamic pressure?
2. If the overpressure is 20 psi, what is the associated wind velocity?
3. What is the Mach stem? In what direction does it propagate?
4. What is the slant distance?
5. What is the effect on reinforced concrete buildings of a 20-psi overpressure? On the internal organs of human beings?
6. Why is an overpressure of "only" 5 psi likely to result in a 50 percent mortality rate for the occupants of residential structures?

PROBLEMS

1. The overpressure for a 1-kt bomb ground burst is 10 psi at 1100 feet. What is the distance from ground zero that the same overpressure will occur for a 64-kt bomb?
2. With a 5-psi overpressure what force is extended on a human being if his or her "area" is 12 in by 60 in? What will this force do?
3. In a 1-Mt underwater explosion that does not vent, what is the peak-to-valley wave height 2000 ft from sea zero?
4. What is the diameter of the gas bubble that would be produced in the explosion in Problem 3?
5. Given a specific bomb size and the desired overpressure, how is the optimum height of burst calculated?

CHAPTER
14

NUCLEAR WEAPONS EFFECTS II: THERMAL EFFECTS

14-1 THEMES

This chapter begins with a description of a nuclear fireball. It goes on to explore the physical concepts of temperature and thermal radiation, and this background is used in discussions of the characteristics of thermal radiation and the effects of thermal radiation on things and on people. The destructiveness of thermal radiation is then compared with that of blast effects.

14-2 THE FIREBALL

Roughly 35 percent of the energy released in a nuclear explosion in the atmosphere goes into thermal energy. Thus a 1-megaton bomb releases about 350 kilotons of thermal energy. Initially, most of this energy goes into heating of the bomb materials and of the air in the vicinity of the bomb. The temperature within the bomb itself reaches tens of millions of degrees, producing an extremely bright fireball. The initial brightness decreases quickly, but the fireball continues to glow for many seconds. The brilliance of a 1-megaton bomb explosion at a distance of 50 miles is far greater than the brilliance of the sun at noon, even after many seconds.

Some distance away the color spectrum is similar to that of a blackbody at a temperature of 6000 to 7000 centigrade (temperature scales and blackbody radiation are discussed later in this chapter), although it is somewhat deficient in the ultraviolet region. This is hotter than the sun. The surface temperatures of the fireball do not vary much with bomb size.

The fireball from a 1-megaton weapon is about 440 feet in diameter within a millisecond. It increases to the maximum diameter of 7000 feet in about 10 seconds, then begins to decrease as the air cools. The heat causes the air in the vicinity of the fireball to expand, which in turn causes the fireball to rise at rates of 250 to 350 feet per second. The rising column of air creates the famous mushroom cloud, which consists of a rising cloud of hot gases in the stem and a toroidal circulation of hot gas as the cloud reaches the upper atmosphere and begins to cool. After 20 seconds the cloud is 2 miles high and is rising at 330 miles per hour. After 1 minute the cloud is 6 miles high and is rising at 220 miles per hour. After about 4 minutes the cloud has reached its maximum height of about 12 miles, or 65,000 feet. The diameter of the cloud is about 10 miles. Clouds from smaller bombs do not rise so far. For example, a 10-kiloton bomb rises to about 20,000 feet, or 4 miles.

The initial red or reddish color of the mushroom cloud is due to oxides of nitrogen. As the fireball cools, water condensation leads to the white color character-istic of clouds.

Bursts near or just below the surface of the earth carry material high into the atmosphere. In underwater tests, water columns are produced. The location of the blast affects thermal radiation, but, except for deeply buried or very high altitude explosions, the mushroom cloud forms regardless of location.

The fireball radiates thermal energy, which can damage unprotected eyes, even at distances of many miles (see Figure 14-5). The intense energy causes combustible material to break into flame. The resulting fires contribute to the total destruction through many effects, including firestorms.

14-3   TEMPERATURE

The concept of temperature is as familiar and intuitive as three of the other fundamental concepts we have discussed: length, time, and mass. From ordinary experience we are aware that one property of matter is its temperature—its hotness or coldness. The ranges of temperature that we are likely to be directly familiar with are typical of weather and of cooking. These temperatures lie in a range of, say, $-20°F$ to $+600°F$. Elsewhere in the universe we find a very much wider range of temperatures, from near absolute zero to many millions or even billions of degrees—in the interior of some of the more exotic stellar objects and in nuclei.

What do we mean by temperature? Temperature is a concept used to describe the random motion of atoms and molecules within a substance (a solid, liquid, or gas). Temperature is related to (though not the same as) the amount of kinetic energy associated with the random motion of the constituents of a substance. Very high levels of energy of motion are associated with high temperatures, and low levels of motion are associated with low temperatures. If all the internal energy of a substance could somehow be removed (it cannot be), the substance would have a temperature of absolute zero.

Temperature Scales

Temperature scales are usually defined with respect to some fixed reference temperatures. Until recently, the melting of ice and the boiling of water, at a pressure of one atmosphere, which are readily reproducible, served to define the Fahrenheit and the Celsius (or Centigrade) systems. By definition, these temperatures are:

	Celsius (°C)	Fahrenheit (°F)
Boiling temperature of water	100	212
Melting temperature of ice	0	32

As the importance of absolute zero was recognized, it became clear that for many purposes it would be useful to define another scale, one based on the lowest conceivable temperature. Two systems were developed. In the kelvin scale the size of a degree is exactly equal to one degree Celsius. In this system absolute zero is defined as 0 K (read "zero kelvin"), and the melting point of ice is 273.16 K. In the Rankine system, used primarily by engineers, the size of a degree is the same as in the Fahrenheit system. Absolute zero is defined as 0°R (read "zero degrees Rankine"), and the melting point of ice is 459.67°R. These definitions imply that absolute zero is -273.16°C, or -459.67°F, and that water boils at 373.16 K, or 671.67°R.

As temperatures drop, gases turn into liquids and the liquids freeze. At absolute zero all thermal energy is absent. All materials except helium are solid.

14-4 THERMAL RADIATION

A primary means by which the energy is delivered from a nuclear explosion to an object is by *thermal radiation*. (This is one of the three ways in which heat energy is transported. The other two are conduction and convection). An object which is heated emits energy in the form of photons. High-energy photons are identical to gamma radiation (Chapter 10). The photons which account for visible light are much lower in energy than gamma radiation, and the photons which are emitted by a red-hot object (such as a fire, or a toaster) are still lower in energy. (See Section P12-9 for a discussion of the conversion of photon frequency to energy.)

Thermal damage is determined by (1) the amount of energy delivered to an object; (2) the time over which the energy is delivered (if it is delivered slowly, the body can cool); and (3) the susceptibility of the object to damage. The emission of thermal radiation from a nuclear fireball is approximated by the radiation behavior of a blackbody obeying Planck's radiation law. This law describes the amount of energy emitted per second by a body for each unit of emitting surface, within a specified energy range. In the first few microseconds of the fireball's existence its temperature is in the millions of degrees Celsius. The radiation law then shows that the most probable photon energies are emitted in the x-ray or extreme ultraviolet region. When the fireball reaches its maximum diameter, its temperature is about 7000°C (or 7000 K—the difference is negligible for such high temperatures) and the radiation is similar to that from the sun, which has a surface temperature of about 5000°C. A graph of the Planck distribution is shown in Figure 14-8.

Thermal radiation can be absorbed or reflected by an object. The more reflective the object is, the less energy will be absorbed. Black objects tend to have high coefficients of absorption, while white or aluminized objects tend to absorb far less. Thus a dark-skinned person is burned by thermal radiation more readily than a light-skinned person. Thermal radiation passes through some objects (e.g., windows) with little of it being absorbed. The best way to protect against thermal effects is with shielding made of appropriate material, e.g., a wall or light-covered clothing.

When thermal radiation is absorbed by an object, it causes heating. If the energy arrives very quickly, the surface heats up so fast that conduction and convection are unable to move the heat away. If the thermal energy arrives slowly, conduction and convection operate to keep the overall rise in temperature lower.

Effects of Thermal Radiation on Materials

In a nuclear explosion the heat arrives in a few seconds. This is called the *thermal pulse*. The thermal energy per unit area (thermal density) is high, and temperatures rise rapidly. Burning often occurs. Since the duration of the fireball increases with the size of the blast, there may be time for some cooling. This means that a given amount of energy delivered per unit area by a large bomb (at a given distance) produces somewhat less effect than the same amount of energy per unit area delivered by a smaller one.

The energy flux, or energy per unit per unit time, of bright sunlight is 2 calories per square centimeter per minute. If one uses a lens to concentrate the sunlight by a factor of 10 (to 20 calories per square centimeter per minute), in 20 seconds about 7 calories per square centimeter are delivered. This is enough to ignite newspaper or tinder.

Table 14-1 gives data on the burning and ignition of various types of fabric. The variation of effect with bomb size and with color is apparent. A white cotton fabric ignites when exposed to 32 calories per square centimeter from a 35-kiloton bomb, but similar fabric colored olive ignites with only 14 calories per square centimeter. This difference in ignition temperature can be translated into distance from the explosion using the data from Figure 14-9. Ignition of the light fabric occurs at a distance of about 1 mile, whereas the darker fabric may still be ignited at distances up to about 2 miles.

Similar data for a variety of other materials are given in Table 14-2. Paper is very easily ignited. It has low heat capacity, and hence the temperature rises to the ignition point of about 450°F (remember Ray Bradbury's book, *Fahrenheit 451?*) at an exposure of only about 5 calories per square centimeter.

A painted wooden building exposed to thermal radiation from a nuclear fireball responds in two stages. The first stage is the burning of the paint, which is shown in Figure 14-1. If a building is far enough from the explosion, the energy density will be low enough so that the underlying wood will not ignite immediately (see Figure 14-2). However, if the thermal energy density is high enough, the building will

TABLE 14-1

Approximate radiant exposures for ignition of fabrics for low air bursts

Material	Weight, oz/yd^2	Color	Effect on material	Radiant exposure,* cal/cm^2		
				35 kilotons	1.4 megatons	20 megatons
Clothing fabrics						
Cotton	8	White	Ignites	32	48	85
		Khaki	Tears on flexing	17	27	34
		Khaki	Ignites	20	30	39
		Olive	Tears on flexing	9	14	21
		Olive	Ignites	14	19	21
		Dark blue	Tears on flexing	11	14	17
		Dark blue	Ignites	14	19	21
Cotton corduroy	8	Brown	Ignites	11	16	22
Cotton denim, new	10	Blue	Ignites	12	27	44
Cotton shirting	3	Khaki	Ignites	14	21	28
Cotton-nylon mixture	5	Olive	Tears on flexing	8	15	17
		Olive	Ignites	12	28	53
Wool	8	White	Tears on flexing	14	25	38
		Khaki	Tears on flexing	14	24	34
		Olive	Tears on flexing	9	13	19
		Dark blue	Tears on flexing	8	12	18
	20	Dark blue	Tears on flexing	14	20	26
Rainwear (double neoprene-coated nylon twill)	9	Olive	Begins to melt	5	9	13
		Olive	Tears on flexing	8	14	22
Drapery fabrics						
Rayon gabardine	6	Black	Ignites	9	20	26
Rayon-acetate drapery	5	Wine	Ignites	9	22	28
Rayon gabardine	7	Gold	Ignites	†	24	28
Rayon twill lining	3	Black	Ignites	7	17	25
Rayon twill lining	3	Beige	Ignites	13	20	28
Acetate-shantung	3	Black	Ignites	10	22	35
Heavy cotton	13	Dark colors	Ignites	15	18	34
Tent fabrics						
Canvas (cotton)	12	White	Ignites	13	28	51
Canvas	12	Olive drab	Ignites	12	18	28
Other fabrics						
Cotton chenille bedspread		Light blue	Ignites	†	11	15
Cotton venetian blind tape, dirty		White	Ignites	10	18	22
Cotton venetian blind tape		White	Ignites	13	27	31
Cotton muslin window shade	8	Green	Ignites	7	13	19

*Radiant exposures for the indicated responses (except where underlined) are estimated to be valid to ±25 percent under standard laboratory conditions. Under typical field conditions the values are estimated to be valid within ±50 percent with a greater likelihood of higher rather than lower values. The underlined ignition levels are estimated to be valid within ±50 percent under laboratory conditions and within ±100 percent under field conditions.

†Data not available or appropriate scaling not known.

Source: Glasstone and Dolan, 1977, table 7.35.

TABLE 14-2
Approximate radiant exposures for ignition of various materials for low air bursts

Material	Weight, oz/yd^2	Color	Effect on material	Radiant exposure,* cal/cm^2		
				35 kilotons	1.4 megatons	20 megatons
Household tinder materials						
Newspaper, shredded	2		Ignites	4	6	11
Newspaper, dark picture area	2		Ignites	5	7	12
Newspaper, printed text area	2		Ignites	6	6	15
Crepe paper	1	Green	Ignites	6	9	16
Kraft paper	3	Tan	Ignites	10	13	20
Bristol board, 3-ply	10	Dark	Ignites	16	20	40
Kraft paper carton, used (flat side)	16	Brown	Ignites	16	20	40
New bond typing paper	2	White	Ignites	24	30	50
Cotton rags		Black	Ignites	10	15	20
Rayon rags		Black	Ignites	9	14	21
Cotton string scrubbing mop (used)		Gray	Ignites	10	15	21
Cotton string scrubbing mop (weathered)		Cream	Ignites	10	19	26
Paper book matches, blue head exposed			Ignites	11	14	20
Excelsior, ponderosa pine	2 lb/ft^3	Light yellow	Ignites	†	23	23
Outdoor tinder materials‡						
Dry rotted wook punk (fir)			Ignites	4	6	8
Deciduous leaves (beech)			Ignites	4	6	8
Fine grass (cheat)			Ignites	5	8	10
Coarse grass (sedge)			Ignites	6	9	11
Pine needles, brown (ponderosa)			Ignites	10	16	21
Construction materials						
Roll roofing, mineral surface			Ignites	†	>34	>116
Roll roofing, smooth surface			Ignites	†	30	77
Plywood, douglas fir			Flaming during exposure	9	16	20
Rubber, pale latex			Ignites	50	80	110
Rubber, black			Ignites	10	20	25
Other materials						
Aluminum aircraft skin (0.020 in thick) coated with 0.002 in of standard white aircraft paint			Blisters	15	30	40
Cotton canvas sandbags, dry filled			Failure	10	18	32
Coral sand			Explodes (popcorning)	15	27	47
Siliceous sand			Explodes (popcorning)	11	19	35

*Radiant exposures for the indicated responses (except where underlined) are estimated to be valid to ±25 percent under standard laboratory conditions. Under typical field conditions, the values are estimated to be valid within ±50 percent with a greater likelihood of higher rather than lower values. Underlined ignition levels are estimated to be valid within ±50 percent under laboratory conditions and within ±100 percent under field conditions. †Data not available or appropriate scaling not known. ‡Radiant exposures for ignition of these substances are highly dependent on moisture content. *Source*: Glasstone and Dolan, 1977, table 7.40.

FIGURE 14-1
Thermal effects on a wood-frame house 1 second after explosion (about 25 calories per square centimeter of energy have been received). This initial radiation causes the paint to burn off the house. (*From Glasstone and Dolan, 1977, figure 7.20a.*)

eventually burst into flame. Even if a building survives the thermal radiation, it may well be destroyed by blast (see Chapter 13).

Barriers against thermal radiation cause "shadows" that can be used to determine the exact location of a detonation. Figures 14-3 and 14-4 show two kinds of shadows that were used to calculate the detonation site at Hiroshima. Tables 14-1 and 14-2 show that a thermal flux of 20 calories per square centimeter is enough to ignite most combustible materials. In metric units 20 cal/cm^2 is (4.2 joule/calories)* (20 cal/cm^2) = 84 joule/cm^2. This is far below the level required to destroy military equipment, such as ICBMs.

In Chapter 20 we discuss missile defense and the Strategic Defense Initiative. We note that the amount of energy required to destroy an ICBM during launch phase is about 20,000 joule/cm^2. This is a factor roughly 200 larger than the energy density needed to kill people or to ignite combustible materials. This is an enormous difference. It means that any system capable of destroying ICBMs using radiation which can penetrate to ground level would prove a highly potent weapon against things and people.* We discuss this potential offensive use of such weapons in Chapter 20.

---

*Some systems being explored by the Strategic Defense Initiative make use of particle beams or of radiation which would not penetrate the earth's atmosphere. Such systems clearly would not threaten objects or people on the earth's surface.

FIGURE 14-2
The house shown in Figure 14-1 but 0.75 second later. The building is charred, but not burning.
Depending on the thermal energy density, the building may or may not catch fire. If it does not catch
fire, it may still be destroyed by the blast wave which will arrive shortly thereafter. (*From Glasstone
and Dolan, 1977, figure 7.28b.*)

The part of human anatomy most sensitive to thermal radiation is the eye. At
low intensities flash blindness occurs, but the eye recovers. At higher intensities the
retina is burned and permanent eye damage or blindness results. Figure 14-5 shows
the critical distances as a function of yield for burst heights (HOB) of 10,000 and
50,000 feet. The data are for daytime bursts on a clear day. At night the pupil is
dilated and damage occurs farther away. In some of the Johnston Island tests in the
1950s retinal burns were found in animals several hundred miles away. Reflex action
causes the eye to blink in about 0.25 second, so only the very early stages of a fireball
cause eye damage.

Skin burns in humans are divided into three major categories. First-degree burns,
such as sunburn, are characterized by pain and redness. There is no scar formation.
Second-degree burns are painful, and lead to loss of skin. They heal in about 2 weeks
without scarring, but require hospital treatment if over 25 percent of the body is
burned. Third-degree burns destroy the nerve endings in the skin. Initially they are
not as painful as first- and second-degree burns. Scarring occurs because the skin cells
lose their ability to regenerate. Third-degree burns are among the most difficult wounds
to treat. Even with specialized medical attention in burn centers, extensive third-degree
burns over 50 percent of the body are often fatal.

The response of human skin to thermal radiation depends on skin color; darker
skins are more easily burned because they absorb thermal radiation more easily.

FIGURE 14-3
Flash marks produced by thermal radiation on asphalt of a bridge in Hiroshima.

FIGURE 14-4
A gas holder 1.33 miles from ground zero at Hiroshima. The paint was scorched by the thermal radiation, except where protected by the valves.

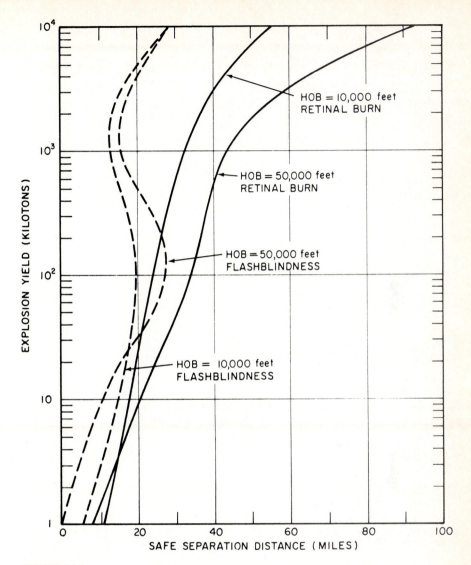

FIGURE 14-5

Safe separation distances for flash blindness and retinal burn for an individual on the ground. Distances are calculated as a function of explosion yield. Because of the focusing action of the eye's lens, the distance at which one is safe from flash blindness is almost independent of weapon yield. (*From Glasstone and Dolan, 1977, figure 12.88a.*)

Second-degree burns occur at about the energy density required to ignite newspaper (4 to 6 calories per square centimeter). Figure 14-6 shows these effects. It is likely that virtually everyone exposed to more than about 6 calories per square centimeter from a 1-megaton blast would be incapacitated. This exposure level occurs at a range of about 8 miles (an area of about 200 square miles).

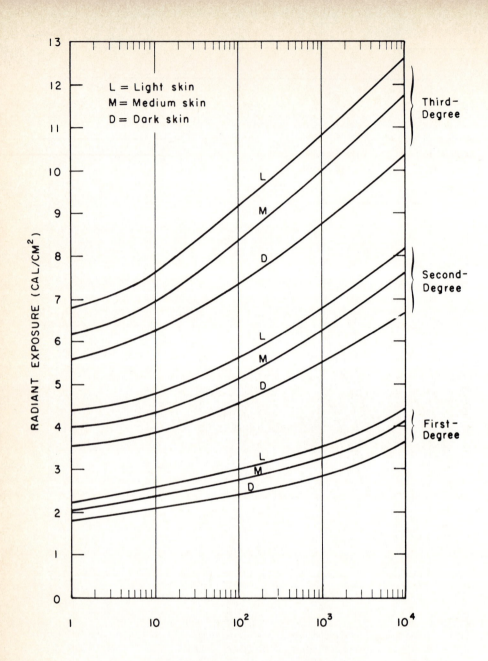

FIGURE 14-6

Curves used to estimate the damage to human skin that has been exposed to a nuclear explosion. In conjunction with Figure 14-5, this information can be used to calculate the distance from nuclear blasts at which an individual would be safe from burns. Note that darker skin pigmentation, which absorbs thermal radiation more readily, permits burn damage at lower radiant exposures. (*From Glasstone and Dolan, 1977, figure 12.64.*)

A small amount of protection against thermal radiation makes a great difference. A building offers virtually complete protection from direct radiation—although there may well be damage from reflected thermal energy. The type of clothing one is wearing also makes a difference. Figure 14-7 shows a patient who was burned in a pattern corresponding to the dark portions of a kimono worn at the time of the explosion.

The thermal radiation from an explosion may be greatly attenuated by fog, smog, and other atmospheric conditions. Thus thermal effects are weather-dependent.

14-4   FIRESTORMS

In an area where many combustible materials exist firestorms can occur. Firestorms are the result of the joining together of many smaller fires, which heat the air and cause winds of hurricane strength directed toward the fire, which in turn fan the flames. World War II experience showed that firestorms developed if (1) there are at least 8 pounds of combustibles per square foot, (2) at least one-half of the structures in the area are on fire simultaneously, (3) there is initially a wind of less than 8 miles per hour, and (4) the burning area is at least 0.5 square mile.

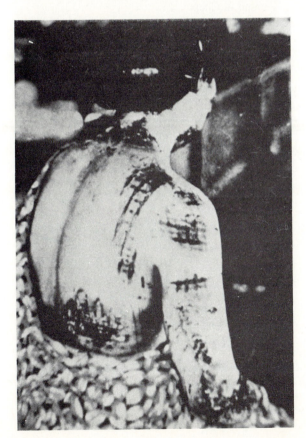

FIGURE 14-7
Burn patterns on a woman exposed to the Hiroshima explosion. The burned areas correspond to the dark pattern on the kimona she was wearing at the time. (*From Glasstone and Dolan, 1977, figure 12.72.*)

The saturation bombing of Dresden, Germany, with conventional weapons in 1956 led to a firestorm. The temperatures were so high that many persons in bomb shelters were killed—either by the high temperatures acting directly or by the attendant loss of air. Kurt Vonnegut was an American prisoner of war in Dresden during this bombing. He and some other prisoners survived because they were being kept in a well-protected slaughterhouse. He described some of these events in his book *Slaughterhouse Five*.

14-6 COMPARISON OF BLAST AND THERMAL EFFECTS

Both blast and thermal radiation are important in understanding weapons effects. In this section we show how to determine which effects are likely to dominate. See also Figures 7-1 and 7-2.

We are concerned here with effects during the first few minutes after detonation. Immediate nuclear radiation is intense only very close to the burst point. The rapid (exponential) attenuation of nuclear radiation due to absorption by the atmosphere makes it initially relatively unimportant as compared to blast and thermal effects. Nuclear radiation effects will be discussed in Chapter 15.

The effects of overpressure and of thermal radiation overlap. Table 14-3 shows how. The 6000-foot altitude maximizes the area receiving overpressures above 15 to

TABLE 14-3
Comparison of blast and thermal effects from a 1-megaton explosion at 6000 feet

Distance, mi	Area, mi^2	Peak overpressure, psi	Thermal energy density, cal/cm^2	Effect
1.8	10	20	150	A
2.7	23	10	80	B
4	50	5	35	C
7	154	2	9	D
10	310	1	3	E

A: Multistory reinforced-concrete buildings demolished. All unprotected combustible material ignited. Winds of 500 mi/h.

B: Most factories and commercial buildings collapsed. Wood and brick houses destroyed. All unprotected combustible material ignited. Winds of 300 mi/h.

C: Unreinforced brick and wood houses destroyed; heavier construction severely damaged. Clothing ignites unless protected. Wood chars but does not ignite. Winds of 160 mi/h.

D: Moderate house damage: wall frames cracked, interior walls knocked down. People injured by flying glass and debris. Newspapers and dry leaves ignite. Some plastics melt. Winds of about 70 mi/h.

E: Light damage to commercial structures; moderate damage to residences. Little thermal damage (except to eyes of people looking toward the blast).

20 psi. The thermal effects are calculated from Figure 14-9. The effects shown in the table are immediate. Later effects may include firestorms and fallout. The major effects cover a circle with a diameter of 20 miles and an area of over 300 square miles. A single 1-megaton bomb would completely demolish the entire core of any city in the nation.

ADDITIONAL PHYSICS SECTION

P14-2   THE FIREBALL

A nuclear explosion in air produces two bursts of thermal radiation. An explosion in space produces only one. The first radiation burst in an air explosion is fast (of the order of milliseconds), is dominated by ultraviolet energy, and contains only a small fraction (1 percent or so) of the total energy. The radiation associated with the first emission produces heating of the air around the bomb, making the initial fireball.

The second burst of thermal radiation lasts for a time which depends on the bomb yield. It is produced by the incandescent shock wave as it penetrates the initial fireball, which is opaque to optical radiation. For explosions below an altitude of 15,000 ft about half the total thermal energy is released in the time

$$t_{1/2} = 1.9Y^{0.44} \text{ s} \tag{P14-1}$$

where Y is the yield in megatons.

Thus for a 1-Mt bomb half of the thermal radiation is released in 1.9 s, while for a 1-kt bomb half the energy is released in 0.09 s.

The remainder of the energy is released over a much longer time period: 80 percent of the energy is released in a period 4.5 times longer than the time calculated from Eq. (P14-1). Thus 50 percent of the energy from a 0.5-Mt explosion is released within the first 1.4s, and 80 percent of the energy is released within $4.5 \times 1.4 = 6.3$ s. At higher altitudes (above 15,000 ft) the air density decreases, which reduces the duration of the fireball somewhat.

The double thermal radiation burst is a characteristic of nuclear explosions that is useful for verification of nuclear explosions in the atmosphere. Satellite detection of such a double burst in the South Atlantic in the vicinity of South Africa led to questions as to whether some nation had conducted a nuclear test. The U.S. government has indicated that it is probable that this was a false alarm.

Empirically it is found that the time for the second thermal pulse to begin is

$$t_2 = 60 \ Y^{0.4} \text{ milliseconds} \tag{P14-2}$$

(measured from the time of detonation). Here Y is the weapon yield in megatons. Therefore a measurement of the time difference between the first thermal pulse and the second gives information as to weapon yield.

The maximum radius of the fireball for an airburst is given approximately by

$$R = 1.1Y^{0.39} \tag{P14-3}$$

where R is in kilometers and the yield in megatons. This expression gives a radius of 1.1 km or 0.66 mi for a 1-Mt bomb and 3.53 km or 2.2 mi for a 20-Mt bomb. In the case of a ground burst the fireball is larger due to reflection of the shock wave from the ground. The maximum radii are then 0.88 mi and 2.9 mi for 1 Mt and 20 Mt respectively.

P14-3 TEMPERATURE CONVERSIONS

Since the distance (in degrees) between the freezing point of ice and the boiling point of water is known for both the Celsius and the Fahrenheit scales, a conversion factor between them can be worked out as follows: When $T = 0°C$, $T = 32°F$. Also, an increase of 100°C is the same temperature difference as an increase of 212°F − 32°F = 180°F. Thus:

$$T \; (°F) = 32 + \frac{212 - 32}{100} \, T \; (°C) \tag{P14-4}$$

$$= 32 + \tfrac{9}{5} \, T \; (°C)$$

Similar, by inverting Eq. (P14-4), we find

$$T \; (°C) = [T \; (°F) - 32] \times \tfrac{5}{9} \tag{P14-5}$$

To convert to absolute degrees, use

$$T \; (K) = T \; (°C) + 273.16$$
$$T \; (°R) = T \; (°F) + 459.67$$

P14-4 THERMAL RADIATION

Figure 14-8 shows the distribution of blackbody radiation as given by the Planck equation. The units are ergs/(cm²·s·Å). (1 Å = 1.0×10^{-10}m; 1 erg = 1.0×10^{-7}J.) The figure shows how a blackbody emits radiation which peaks at a certain wavelength and drops off on either side. The sun, with a surface temperature of about 5000 K, emits maximum energy in just the region to which the human eye is most sensitive.

Bodies at temperatures in the range of 100 million K emit most of their energy at very much shorter wavelengths. Photon energies are in the vicinity of 1 to 1000 keV, which are typical x-ray or gamma-ray energies. These are the temperatures within the interior of an H-bomb, which are required to create the fusion reactions which release thermonuclear energy.

Total Energy Radiated per Unit Time

The total power radiated per unit area, J, from a blackbody depends on the fourth power of the absolute temperature. This means that the emitted radiation increases

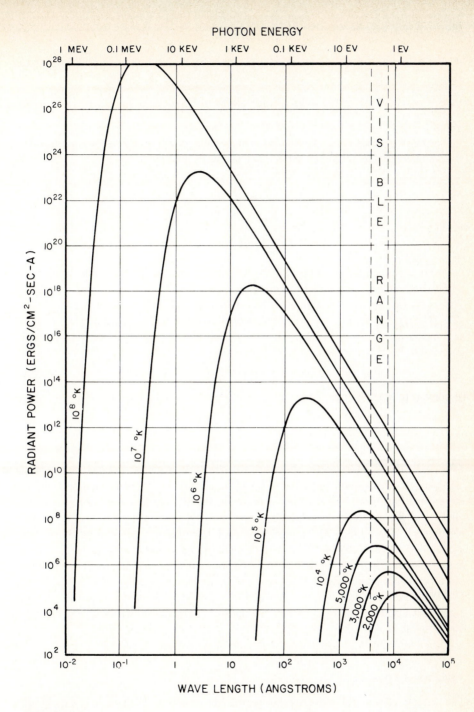

FIGURE 14-8

Radiant heat of a blackbody as a function of temperature. The energy emitted per unit wavelength for a blackbody is shown. The frequency of maximum energy output increases as the temperature increases. The maximum energy output of the sun corresponds closely to the region of greatest sensitivity of the human eye.

extremely rapidly as the temperature goes up. The Stefan-Boltzmann law expresses this:

$$J = 5.7 \times 10^{-12}T^4 \qquad \text{J/cm}^2 \cdot \text{s} \qquad \text{(P14-6)}$$

where 5.7×10^{-12} is the Stefan-Boltzmann constant.

The wavelength λ_{max} at which the maximum power is emitted varies linearly with temperature according to Wien's displacement law:

$$\lambda_{max} = \frac{C}{T} \qquad \text{(P14-7)}$$

where

$$C = 2.9 \times 10^7 \text{ Å} \cdot \text{K}$$

For a surface temperature of 7000 K, which corresponds to the nuclear fireball at the beginning of the second thermal pulse, the wavelength λ_{max} is about 4100 Å. This is on the short-wavelength side (blue-violet) of the visible region.

The total power of the thermal radiation is obtained by multiplying by the surface area of the fireball, $(4\pi R^2)$. With the fireball radius expressed in meters (R) and the temperature in kelvins, the resulting expression is

$$P = 1.7 \times 10^{-7}T^4R^2 \qquad \text{cal/s} \qquad \text{(P14-8)}$$

The units in Eq. (P14-8), calories per second, are standard in discussing thermal effects; 4.2 J = 1 cal.

Thermal Partition

The fraction of the total energy that appears in the form of thermal radiation is called the *thermal partition*. The fraction increases as the altitude increases and also as the total yield increases. A 10-kt explosion at an altitude of 10,000 ft has a thermal partition of 35 percent. A 1-Mt explosion also has a thermal partition of 35 percent at altitudes below 15,000 ft. The fraction increases to 42 percent by 100,000 ft. The many other uncertainties about nuclear explosions are so great that a guideline number of 35 percent is appropriate.

In a ground burst, water vapor and dust impede the thermal radiation so that an effective thermal partition of only 19 percent is obtained for a 10 kt explosion at 40 feet altitude.

Thermal Exposure

The energy of thermal radiation propagates through the air. The intensity of the radiation is decreased by two factors: (1) the inverse square effect and (2) atmospheric attenuation.

The inverse square law results from the fact that all the thermal energy emitted by a bomb must, at any distance r, pass through a shell of area $4\pi r^2$. The initial thermal energy is fY, where f is the thermal partition factory and Y is the yield. The energy delivered at some distance r is then

$$Q = \frac{fY}{4\pi r^2} \quad \text{cal/cm}^2 \tag{P14-9}$$

In addition the energy is reduced by atmospheric attenuation caused by such things as dust and clouds. The actual condition of the atmosphere at the time of a nuclear explosion is one of the largest uncertainties in calculating thermal effects at large distances. At distances at which the delivered thermal energies are large enough to cause fires, atmospheric attenuation is relatively unimportant if the weather is clear. Under very severe weather conditions the thermal effects of explosions can be almost totally absorbed in the atmosphere within a few miles from ground zero.

Figure 14-9, which expresses exposure to targets at specified line-of-sight distances (in calories per square centimeter) for a range of yields, assumes clear weather

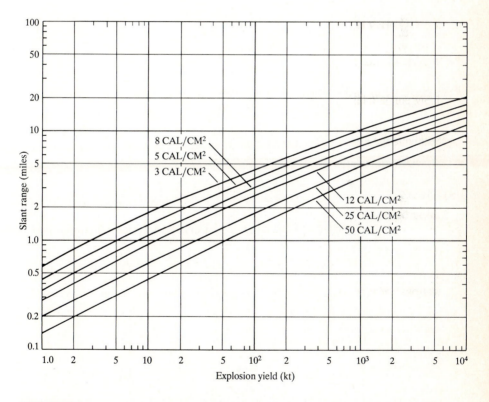

FIGURE 14-9
Energy delivered by thermal radiation to an object on the ground as a function of weapon yield and distance. These curves are used to estimate damage to exposed objects or to estimate burn casualties. To convert the curves to metric (SI) units, multiply by 4.2 joule per calorie. Thus the curve labeled 12 cal/cm² corresponds to about 50 joule/cm².

conditions. A burst height of $200Y^{0.4}$ ft (Y in kilotons) and visibility of 12 mi are assumed. The curves are adequate for air bursts at any height up to 15,000 feet. The data in the figure include various approximations. The uncertainty in any real situation is greatly compounded by the fact that the atmospheric visibility and the size of the actual weapon are likely to be unknown.

QUESTIONS

1. What fraction of the total energy released by a thermonuclear bomb goes into thermal radiation?
2. What is the temperature of the surface of the fireball when it is at its maximum extent?
3. What is temperature?
4. How long does it take for the fireball of a thermonuclear weapon to reach its maximum diameter for a 1-Mt weapon?
5. How far must one be from a 1-Mt nuclear explosion to avoid the possibility of receiving a retinal burn if the height of burst is 10,000 feet?
6. What are the conditions that must be present if a firestorm is to be produced?
7. How many calories per square centimeter are required to produce a third-degree burn from a 1-Mt bomb in a person with light skin?
8. At what distance from a 1-Mt bomb does the thermal energy deposited reach about 5 cal/cm^2?
9. How many calories per square centimeter are required to produce a second-degree burn in a person with dark skin from a 1-Mt bomb?
10. For a 1-Mt bomb at a distance of about 7 mi from the burst point, which effect is most dangerous to human beings in a residential environment, blast or thermal radiation? Discuss.

PROBLEMS

1. What is absolute zero?
2. Assume that the temperature (in kelvins) of a blackbody radiator is doubled. By what factor does the emitted thermal energy increase?
3. How long does it take for 80 percent of the thermal energy of a 10-kt nuclear explosion to be radiated?
4. Will unprotected newspaper ignite if located 1 mi from a 10-Mt explosion on a clear day?
5. Describe how one would go about finding the location of the Hiroshima blast from the kind of data contained in Figures 14-3 and 14-4.
6. At a distance of 4 mi for a 0.5-Mt blast, how do the effects of blast and of thermal radiation compare?
7. What aiming accuracy is required for a 100-kt bomb targeted against a silo hardened to 200 psi?
8. How far from a 10-kt explosion must one be in order that the pressure be less than 1 psi?
9. The Hiroshima bomb was 13 kt and was exploded at 1900 feet, or 580 m. Find the distance from ground zero where second-degree burns began. (Use the graph of Figure 14-6, the figures for medium skin, which are probably appropriate for Japanese casualties. Remember that in Figure 14-9 the slant range is plotted.)

10. For the Hiroshima bomb, find the distance from ground zero where third-degree burns began. (Then look at Figure 13-8, which gives burn normalities experienced at Hiroshima.)

11. Assume that initally the fireball of a nuclear explosion expands radially to 1 m in 1×10^{-6} s and at this time the temperature is 1×10^8 K. What is the rate at which energy is radiated? (The area of a sphere is $4\pi r^2$.)

12. How much thermal energy is radiated by a 20-kt bomb in the first second if it has an average temperature of 5000 K and the average radius is taken to be 200 m? (The area of a sphere is $4\pi r^2$.)

13. How does the answer in Problem 12 compare to the total energy released in a 20-kt bomb? (The total thermal energy released is about 35 percent of the total energy.)

14. The temperature of a room is 68°F. What is the temperature in degrees Celsius?

15. Assume that after the first ten microseconds (1×10^{-5} s) of a nuclear explosion the temperature is 1×10^7 K, but that initially it was 1×10^8 K. What is the ratio of the energy radiated per square centimeter per second initially and after 1×10^{-5} s?

16. Particles that have a temperature of 10,000 K have approximately 1 eV of kinetic energy. If 20 keV is the energy required for a fusion reaction to take place between deuterium and tritium (to overcome the coulomb repulsion of the nuclei), how hot must the "trigger," which is a fission bomb, be in order to initiate the thermonuclear reaction?

17. If a bomb's temperature is 1×10^8 K initially, what is the most probable wavelength emitted at that time? (Use Figure 12-5 to find the region of the electromagnetic spectrum to which this wavelength corresponds.)

18. If the temperature of the fireball of a nuclear explosion is 1×10^{6}°C, what is the most probable wavelength of the emitted thermal radiation?

19. Calculate the number of joules per second (watts) radiated by the fireball from a 1-Mt weapon at its maximum extent. (Assume the fireball is 0.9 km in radius and the temperature is 7000 K.)

CHAPTER
15

NUCLEAR WEAPONS EFFECTS III: INITIAL NUCLEAR RADIATION

15-1 THEMES

The explosive burst of a nuclear weapon is accomplished by nuclear radiation, mostly gamma rays and neutrons. The *initial nuclear radiation* is arbitrarily defined as the radiation arriving during the first minute after an explosion. Almost all neutrons arrive within this time, but gamma rays may be delayed much longer because of the radio-activity of the fission products and other bomb debris or, in the base of a new-surface burst, because of the radioactivity induced in the vicinity of ground zero. This later radiation also has important effects, and it is considered separately in Chapter 16.

The initial nuclear radiation, gamma rays and neutrons combined, represents about 3 percent of the total energy of a nuclear explosion. It is only about 10 percent of the thermal radiant energy considered in Chapter 14, but is much more penetrating and hence generally more harmful to biological systems.

We discuss the mechanisms of absorption of gamma rays and neutrons and give values for the shielding required for protection. Chapter 7 compares all the immediate effects of nuclear explosions that would affect human beings directly [blast (Chapter 13), thermal radiation (Chapter 14), gamma rays and neutrons (this chapter)] for a 1-kiloton fission weapon and a 1-megaton thermonuclear bomb.

15-2   GAMMA RADIATION

Gamma radiation is given off when a nucleus in an excited state returns to its ground state. A useful measure of the effect of gamma radiation on biological systems is the amount of energy absorbed from the radiation per gram of tissue, the *radiation absorbed dose*, or *rad*. One rad represents the deposition of 1×10^{-5} joule of energy per gram of absorbing material. When a human being in good health is exposed to 400 rad, there is a 50 percent chance of death within a month's time. A dose of 200 rad produces severe radiation sickness.

Figure 15-1 gives gamma-ray doses to tissue, in rad, as a function of yield and slant (line-of-sight) distance from a fission-bomb explosion. The delivered dose increases as the yield increases (the slope of the curves becomes steeper). This is partly the result of the lower-than-normal air density created by the passage of the shock wave: the lower pressure reduces the gamma attenuation. This *hydrodynamic enhancement* therefore produces more gamma radiation per kiloton for a large, generally thermonuclear, weapon than it does for a smaller weapon.

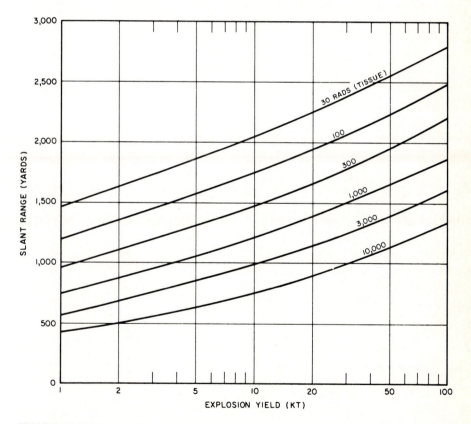

FIGURE 15-1
Slant ranges for specified gamma-ray doses for targets near the ground versus energy yield for fission bombs (0.9 sea-level air density). (*From Glasstone and Dolan, 1977, figure 8.33a.*)

Figure 15-2 gives slant ranges for specified gamma-ray doses for a thermonuclear weapon. Half of the energy is assumed to be derived from fission. The ranges given in Figures 15-1 and 15-2 depend on the design of the weapon and on atmospheric conditions; they are valid to within a factor varying from 0.5 to 2.0 for fission weapons and from 0.25 to 1.25 for thermonuclear bombs.

Gamma-Ray Absorption

If there were no atmospheric attenuation of the gamma rays, their intensity would decrease from the burst point as the inverse square of the distance. However, gamma rays may collide with electrons in air molecules. After a collision with an electron, a gamma ray has a reduced energy. This process is called the *Compton effect*, and is schematically represented in Figure 15-3.

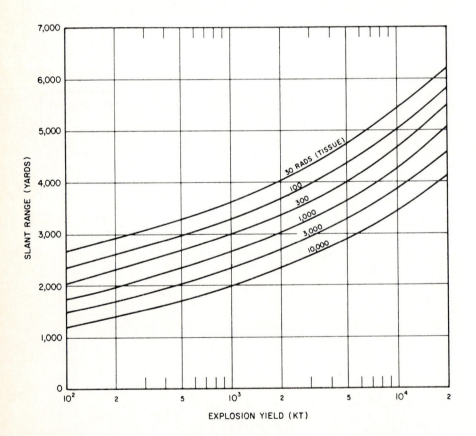

FIGURE 15-2

Slant ranges for specified gamma-ray doses for targets near the ground versus energy yield for a thermonuclear weapon with a 50 percent fission yield (0.9 sea-level air density). (*From Glasstone and Dolan, 1977, figure 8.33b.*)

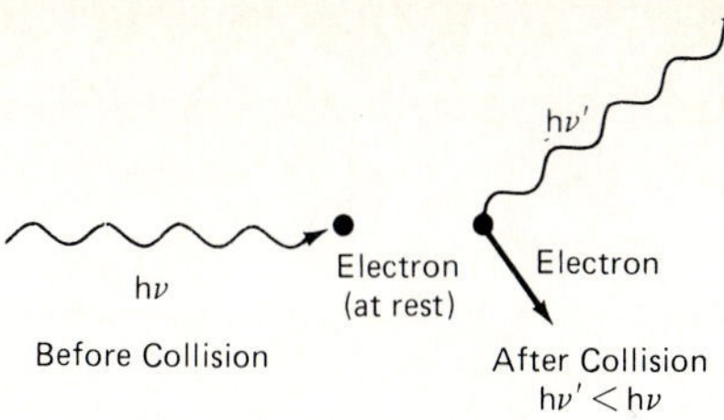

FIGURE 15-3
Schematic representation of the Compton effect. An incoming photon strikes an electron in an atom. The electron recoils with a certain amount of kinetic energy and the photon has its energy reduced by this amount.

In air the Compton effect is the principal cause of the attenuation of gamma rays. Each time a Compton process occurs, a photon which has a certain initial energy is removed from the gamma-ray beam and replaced by a lower-energy photon, which is more readily absorbed. This gives rise to the concept of the *half-value thickness* of an absorber, which is the amount of absorber necessary to reduce the gamma-ray intensity to one-half of its original value (see Chapter 10). Since the probability that the Compton process will occur decreases with increasing gamma-ray energy, half-value thicknesses are greater at higher gamma-ray energies. It is for this reason that the gamma rays from neutron capture in nitrogen, which have energies of up to about 7 MeV, are more difficult to attenuate than lower energy gamma radiation. Table 15-1 gives the half-value thickness in air at normal density and in concrete for a range of monoenergetic gamma radiations. The term *monoenergetic* means that all the gamma rays are assumed to have the same energy.

Since the gamma radiation from fission products and neutron-capture radiation in nitrogen is in both cases a mixture of many gamma rays, and is hence not mono-energetic, the half-value thicknesses given in Table 15-2 are more useful for calculating protection factors than those given in Table 15-1.

An attenuation factor of 1024 (2^{10}) is obtained from a shield equal to 10 half-value thicknesses, or about 1730 yards of air for fission-product gamma rays and 2520 yards for neutron-capture gamma rays from nitrogen. The rapid attenuation means

TABLE 15-1
Half-value thicknesses for monoenergetic gamma rays

Gamma-ray energy, MeV	Half-value thickness	
	Air, yd	Concrete, in
0.5	68.3	1.24
1.0	93.6	1.82
2.0	133.0	2.48
3.0	165.0	3.10
4.0	185.0	3.50
5.0	217.0	3.84
10.0	292.0	4.54

TABLE 15-2
Effective half-value thicknesses

	Half-value thickness	
Gamma-ray type	Air, yd	Concrete, in
Fission-product gamma rays	173	3.31
Neutron-capture gamma rays in nitrogen	252	4.82

that the initial gamma radiation is not as likely to cause fatalities as thermal or blast effects, especially for large weapons. A comparison is made in more detail in Section P15-4.*

Time of Arrival of Gamma Rays

Gamma-ray emission takes place over a considerable time. The reason for this is that considerable gamma radiation is emitted by the fission fragments which exist in abundance after the explosion. These fission fragments decay with a range of lifetimes, but gamma emission is especially important for the shortest-lived isotopes. Those gamma rays emitted while the shock wave is expanding encounter less attenuation than those emitted during the explosion. This is especially true for large-yield weapons, since the hydrodynamic enhancement of the fission-product gamma rays is larger. This is shown in Figure 15-4.

For a 20-kiloton weapon it would not be practical to move out of the way of the gamma rays given off by the initial nuclear radiation, since only about 1 second is available. However, for a 5-megaton weapon, falling prone behind a substantial object might make a difference, since only about half of the gamma-ray exposure arrives in the first 5 seconds. Since blast overpressure would also be severe in the region where gamma-ray exposure would be a hazard, shielding from radiation alone might not guarantee survival. Even a very thin shield suffices to reduce exposure to thermal radiation (see Chapter 14), which is also emitted for several seconds after a thermonuclear burst, so evasive action should be taken.

15-3   NEUTRON RADIATION

General

Neutron radiation accounts for only about 1 percent of the energy of an explosion. In contrast to gamma rays, neutrons are emitted only *during* the explosion. They scatter

---

*In calculations for thick shields it is necessary to take into account the buildup of a secondary gamma-ray flux arising from the Compton recoil photons. The buildup can be quite serious, increasing the gamma-ray intensity by an order of magnitude or more over what would be calculated from simple half-thickness considerations. Actual shielding calculations are carried out with elaborate computer codes.

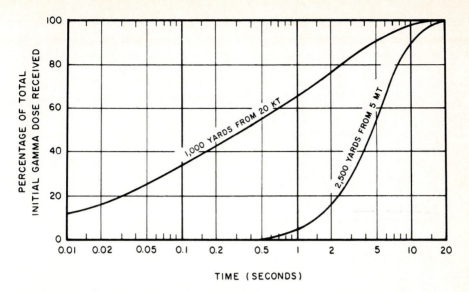

FIGURE 15-4

Time arrival of gamma rays. Gamma rays from thermonuclear weapons are particularly delayed as a result of hydrodynamic enhancement. (*From Glasstone and Dolan, 1977, figure 8.47.*)

inelastically in the weapon material and the intervening atmosphere so that their initial energy is degraded to some degree. Neutrons range in energy from a few electron volts to up to about 10 MeV for fission weapons to up to 14 MeV for thermonuclear weapons. A neutron of 0.1 MeV has a velocity of 4400 kilometers per second (see Section P15-3). This is so fast (1.5% of the speed of light) that it is impossible for a human being to take evasive action to avoid exposure to neutron radiation.

Neutron Sources in Nuclear Weapons

In fission bombs the neutrons are produced in the fission process. They are emitted from the highly excited fission fragments on a time scale of the order of 1×10^{-20} second after the fission fragment is formed. Neutrons emerging after interactions with the weapon material have energies from a few kilovolts up to 10 MeV, but the average energy is about 1 to 2 MeV.

The following reactions contribute to the neutron flux in a thermonuclear weapon:

$$^2_1D + {}^3_1T \rightarrow {}^4_2He + {}^1_0n + 17.6 \text{ MeV}$$
$$\text{(3.5 MeV)} \quad \text{(14.1 MeV)}$$

$$^3_1T + {}^3_1T \rightarrow {}^4_2He + 2{}^1_0n + 11.3 \text{ MeV}$$
$$\text{(up to 11.3 MeV)}$$

$$^2_1D + {}^2_1D \rightarrow {}^3_2He + {}^1_0n + 3.2 \text{ MeV}$$
$$\text{(0.8 MeV)} \quad \text{(2.4 MeV)}$$

The numbers in parentheses show how the kinetic energy is divided among the decay products. The first two nuclear reactions produce neutrons of high energy, so that the spectrum of neutrons emerging from a thermonuclear explosion has relatively more neutrons above 5 MeV than the spectrum of neutrons emerging from a fission bomb. In addition there are neutrons produced from fission fragments in the weapon's primary and in the ^{238}U jacket surrounding the secondary (the thermonuclear) portion of the bomb.

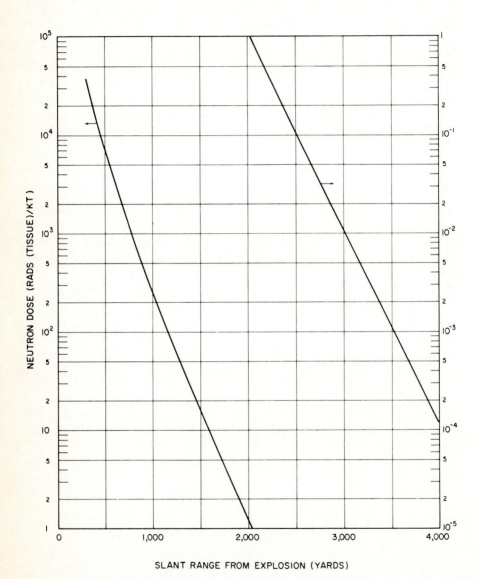

FIGURE 15-5
Neutron dose per kiloton yield for thermonuclear air bursts (air density is assumed 0.9 sea-level density). (*From Glasstone and Dolan, 1977, figure 8.123b.*)

Neutron Interactions with Matter

The way that neutrons interact with matter is quite different from the way that gamma rays interact. Neutron have negligible interactions with atomic electrons. Their only direct interaction is with nuclei (Section P15-3). The interactions cause the neutrons to deviate from a straight-line path (elastic scattering), to lose energy (inelastic scattering), or to become absorbed (neutron capture).

Neutron Dose from Nuclear Weapons

Neutron interactions in the human body can produce ionizing radiations and subsequent doses of radiation (see Chapter 18). Figure 15-5 shows the neutron dose, in rad, for a thermonuclear weapon as a function of slant distance. The atmospheric density is assumed to be nine-tenths that at sea level, or that at about 3000 feet average elevation. The neutron radiation dose from a fission bomb is similar.

There is no hydrodynamic enhancement for neutrons since they arrive before the blast wave.

Shielding against Neutrons

Shielding against neutrons is more complex than shielding against gamma radiation. For gamma shielding one need only interpose a sufficient mass of material. Iron and lead therefore are especially effective gamma-ray shields. For neutrons it is useful to begin the shield with iron or steel, since iron has a high inelastic scattering probability, which reduces the neutron energy. After the neutrons have been slowed to about 1 MeV, it is most effective to use a material containing hydrogen. Water, damp soil, or concrete (which contains a good deal of water) are effective. Capture of the slow neutrons produces gamma radiation, which must be absorbed. In practice, concrete or damp soil makes a good and relatively inexpensive shield. The shield must, of course, be sufficiently thick. Table 15-3 gives the dose-reduction factors for gamma

TABLE 15-3
Dose-reduction factors* for various structures

Structure	Gamma rays		Neutrons	
Frame house	0.8	–1.0	0.3	–0.8
Basement	0.1	–0.6	0.1	–0.8
Multistory apartment				
Upper stories	0.8	–0.9	0.9	–1.0
Lower stories	0.3	–0.6	0.3	–0.8
Concrete blockhouse shelter				
9-in walls	0.1	–0.2	0.3	–0.5
12-in walls	0.05	–0.1	0.2	–0.4
24-in walls	0.007	–0.02	0.1	–0.2
Three ft underground	0.002	–0.004	0.002	–0.01

*The ratio of the dose received behind the shield to the dose at the same location in the absence of shielding.

Source: Glasstone and Dolan (1977).

rays and neutrons for several types of structures. The radiation dose received is the product of the shielding factors given in the table times the dose that would be received by an unprotected individual.

ADDITIONAL PHYSICS SECTION

P15-2 SOURCES OF INITIAL GAMMA RADIATION

Prompt Gamma Rays

In the tenth of a microsecond following a nuclear explosion there is a burst of *prompt* gamma rays. These arise from the fission process itself as well as from inelastic scattering of neutrons from the weapon material. Fast neutrons emitted during the explosion can interact inelastically with nuclei of weapon material and raise them to excited states. As the excited nuclei deexcite, they emit gamma rays (see Chapter 10). The prompt gamma rays give rise to the electromagnetic pulse (EMP) (Chapter 17).

Gamma Rays from Inelastic Neutron Scattering in Air

In a time interval of from 10^{-7} s to 10^{-5} s, the fast neutrons from the explosion scatter inelastically from the atoms of oxygen and nitrogen in the air. These nuclei are raised to an excited state; they then return to the ground state, emitting gamma rays. Figure 15-6 shows the calculated time dependence of gamma rays for the initial nuclear radiation.

Isomeric Decays

Isomers are relatively long-lived (metastable) excited states of nuclei. Normally a nucleus deexcites, as in elastic neutron scattering, in 10^{-12} s or less, but in the case of isomers the excited state may have a half-life of up to hours or even days. The half-lives of the isomers arising from fission lie for the most part in the region from 1 μs to 1 ms, which is very much shorter than the half-lives of fission products (see below). For bursts in the lower atmosphere, where interactions in the air produce secondary gamma rays, the relative contribution of isomeric gamma rays to tissue dosages is very small.

Neutron-Capture Gamma Rays

Within the first minute after a nuclear explosion a large contribution to the gamma-ray flux is the result of capture of neutrons released during the fission process, both

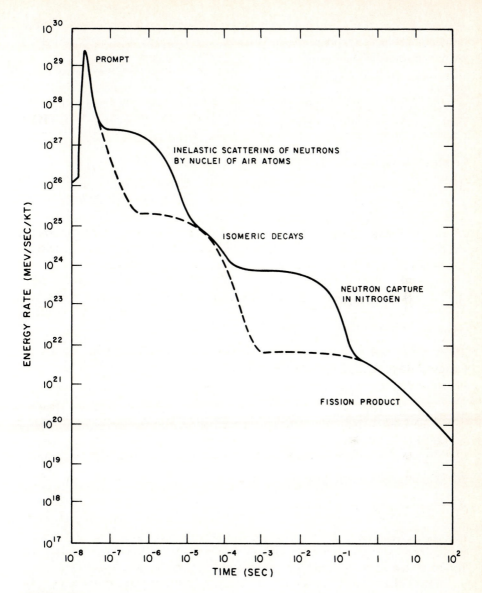

FIGURE 15-6
Calculated time dependence of gamma-ray energy output per kiloton of energy yield. The dashed line refers to an explosion outside the atmosphere. (*From Glasstone and Dolan, 1977, figure 8.14.*)

by weapon materials and, if the weapon is exploded in air, by nitrogen in the surrounding atmosphere. When a nucleus captures a neutron, its neutron number is increased by 1 and a new isotope is formed. The capture process leaves the nucleus in a highly excited state. The nucleus deexcites by emitting neutron-capture gamma radiation. The gamma rays arising from the capture of the neutrons by nitrogen in the air have high energies, some of them in excess of 7 MeV, and therefore are difficult to attenuate. This fact has a bearing on the shielding needed for protection against the initial nuclear radiation.

If the nuclear weapon is exploded above the atmosphere, the formation of gamma radiation from inelastic neutron scattering or neutron capture in air is suppressed. The resulting changes in gamma-ray distribution as a function of time are shown by the dotted line in Figure 15-6.

Gamma Rays from Fission Fragments

An appreciable number of gamma rays also arise from the radioactivity of the fission products, which is very intense just after the explosion. Some of the fission products have half-lives for beta emission of a few seconds or less. After beta emission, the resulting daughter nuclei are often left in excited states. As they deexcite, they emit gamma rays. Fission products contribute to the gamma-ray flux on a time scale from a millisecond to many years (see the discussion of fallout in Chapter 16).

P15-3   NEUTRON RADIATION

Velocity of a 0.1-MeV Neutron

The velocity of a 0.1 MeV neutron may be calculated by using the definition of kinetic energy (see Eq. P9-3, Chapter 9):

$$\tfrac{1}{2}Mv^2 = (0.1 \text{ MeV}) \times (1.6 \times 10^{-13} \text{ J/MeV}) = 1.6 \times 10^{-14} \text{ J} \quad \text{(P15-1)}$$

The neutron mass M is 1.675×10^{-27} kg. Solving, one finds the neutron speed

$$v = 4.37 \times 10^6 \text{ m/s} \ (4370 \text{ km/s})$$

Interactions of Neutrons with Matter

Neutrons have negligible interactions with atomic electrons (e.g., there is no Compton effect). Their only direct interaction is with the nuclei of the atoms through which they are passing. Since the human body is about 80 percent water and there are two protons per water molecule, the interaction of neutrons with hydrogen is critically important in neutron-induced radiation damage to living things (Chapter 18).

The chief neutron interactions are elastic scattering, inelastic scattering, and capture.

ELASTIC SCATTERING. In elastic scattering a neutron collides with a nucleus much like one billiard ball collides with another billiard ball. The neutron loses energy, which is taken up by the nucleus as it recoils. After a head-on collision with a proton (hydrogen nucleus), a highly ionizing particle which has almost the same mass as that of the neutron, all the kinetic energy of the neutron is taken up by the proton. Collision with the nitrogen or oxygen nuclei of the air reduces the energy of the neutron only slightly, because the nuclear masses of nitrogen and oxygen are about 14 and 16

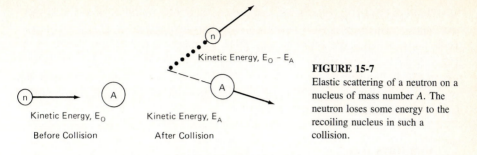

FIGURE 15-7
Elastic scattering of a neutron on a nucleus of mass number A. The neutron loses some energy to the recoiling nucleus in such a collision.

times, respectively, the mass of the neutron. However, an elastic collision with air nuclei will scatter the neutron almost isotropically. Figure 15-7 illustrates the elastic scattering of a neutron with a nucleus of mass number A.

INELASTIC SCATTERING. If a neutron has a kinetic energy greater than the difference in energy between the ground state of a nucleus and one of its excited states, the neutron may lose kinetic energy in an amount that is equal to this difference. This leaves the nucleus in an excited state, and it then decays by gamma emission. Figure 15-8 shows this process schematically. Inelastic scattering can be important in shielding from high-energy neutrons. Iron, for example, is useful at the beginning of a shield because inelastic scattering substantially reduces the neutron energy.

Inelastic scattering of neutrons of a few MeV is quite probable in ^{238}U. Since about 1 MeV of the kinetic energy of the neutron is required to induce fission in ^{238}U, the inelastic scattering is often sufficient to lower the neutron energy below the fission threshold for ^{238}U. This and a high neutron-capture probability make it impossible to use ^{238}U for a chain-reacting fission bomb.

Inelastic scattering in nitrogen and oxygen occurs only when the neutron energy is greater than 1.6 and 6 MeV, respectively. Nitrogen (80 percent abundant in air) accounts for the major part of the inelastic scattering of the neutrons from nuclear weapons. The effect is to degrade the initial neutron spectrum toward lower neutron energies.

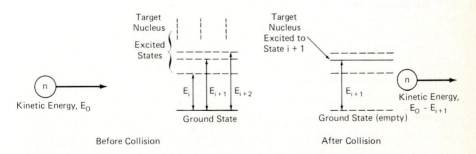

FIGURE 15-8
Inelastic scattering of a neutron. The neutron loses kinetic energy by raising a nucleus to an excited state. When the nucleus in the excited state subsequently decays, a gamma ray is emitted.

NEUTRON CAPTURE. In neutron capture the neutron combines with the nucleus encountered and disappears. The nucleus becomes another isotope of the same element, but with one more neutron than before the interaction. Neutron capture is the least important process as far as attenuation of the neutrons from a nuclear weapon is concerned. If nuclear weapons are exploded on the ground, or near the ground, neutron capture in the nuclei of the soil will produce isotopes that are often radioactive. The residual radioactivity can be appreciable.

The Hiroshima bomb exploded at an altitude of 1900 ft. At ground zero the radiation dose was about 3900 rads of neutrons and 5800 rads of gamma rays (U.S.–Japan Study, 1987). The neutron flux was also estimated later from activation of the soil and human bones by neutron capture (Hiroshima, 1981). The aluminum 28 (2.3-min half-life) and manganese 56 (2.6-h half-life) radiation levels were initially 500 rad/h and 5 rad/h, respectively. The neutron exposure required to immediately incapacitate tank personnel is about the same as the neutron exposure at ground zero at Hiroshima.

From Figure 15-5 we see that a 1-megaton weapon exploded at 1900 ft would yield a neutron exposure of about 3×10^6 rads at ground zero. In this case neutron activation would be higher by about a factor of 770 than was the case at Hiroshima, and so the initial radiation levels of aluminum 28 and manganese 56 would be 390,000 and 3,900 rad/h respectively. A ground burst would produce these radiation levels at approximately 1900 ft radially from the explosion point, since the air attenuation would be similar.

Neutron Fluence and Radiation Dose as a Function of Slant Range

The combined effect of the radial dispersion of the neutrons (which leads to a decrease of neutron intensity as the inverse square of the distance) and the interactions of the neutrons with the intervening air produces a rapid decrease in neutron intensity with distance from burst point. The neutron *fluence* (the number of neutrons passing through 1 cm^2 at a specified distance) is shown in Figure 15-9 for a thermonuclear bomb. Curve 10 in the figure is the fluence for all neutrons with energies greater than 0.0033 MeV; curve 1 illustrates the decrease in fluence with distance of the highest-energy neutron component, between 12.2 and 15 MeV. The higher-energy neutrons are degraded to lower energy with distance by interactions with the atmosphere so that successive curves, starting from curve 10, have steeper slopes at a given distance from the burst point. The figure gives the fluence per kiloton; thus the neutron fluence from a 1-Mt weapon, for example, is obtained by multiplying the ordinate by 1000.

P15-4 COMPARISON OF GAMMA RAYS AND NEUTRON EFFECTS WITH BLAST AND THERMAL EFFECTS

The reader is referred to Figures 7-1 and 7-2 to compare the effects of gamma rays and neutrons (dosage) with blast and thermal effects. For a small nuclear weapon

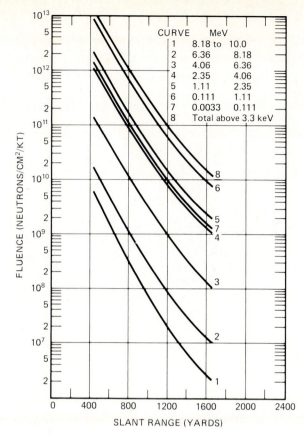

FIGURE 15-9

Neutron fluence per kiloton energy yield for a thermonuclear bomb. (*From Glasstone and Dolan, 1977, figure 8.17b.*)

(Figure 7-1), the gamma ray and neutron radiation can be the primary cause of casualties. For a thermonuclear weapon the situation is reversed. This is due to the air attenuation of gamma rays and neutrons which becomes relatively more important at the larger distances associated with weapons in the megaton range.

QUESTIONS

1. Why is the neutron bomb more effective at low weapon yields?
2. Discuss the various mechanisms for the formation of gamma rays and their associated times of emission with respect to time of burst.
3. What is the Compton effect? How do materials absorb gamma rays via the Compton effect?
4. Why is its possible to avoid some of the gamma radiation from a 1-Mt bomb by quick evasive action but it is not possible to thus avoid the neutron component?
5. How do neutrons interact with matter?

PROBLEMS

1. What are the blast, thermal, neutron, and gamma-ray effects at 4000 ft from ground zero for a 1-Mt bomb having a burst height of 6000 ft?

2. Compare the neutron effect and the blast effect at a distance of 1500 ft from a 1-kt neutron bomb exploded at 600 ft. See Chapter 7.

3. How much air at sea-level density is required to reduce the number of 2-MeV gamma rays by one-half?

4. For the gamma rays associated with neutron capture, what thickness of concrete is necessary to reduce the gamma-ray intensity to 1/32 of its original value?

5 What is the shielding offered by a blockhouse with 9-in concrete walls to the neutron flux of a nuclear weapon?

CHAPTER 16

NUCLEAR WEAPONS EFFECTS IV: FALLOUT

The awareness that we are all human beings together has become lost in war and through politics.

Albert Schweitzer

16-1   THEMES

Fallout consists of the radioactive particles that fall to earth as a result of a nuclear explosion. In the previous chapter we considered initial nuclear radiation. Radioactive fallout occurs later.

Fallout is one of two major types: **early fallout**, defined as that which occurs up to 24 hours after an explosion, and **delayed fallout**, which occurs days or years later. Delayed fallout is further subdivided into that which comes from the **troposphere** (lower atmosphere) and falls to earth via rain or snow within 1 or 2 months after the explosion, and that which comes from the **stratosphere** (upper atmosphere) and falls to earth from 1 to 3 years later. Much depends on the size of the weapon and the altitude at which it was exploded. For example, for low-altitude air bursts of less than 100-kilotons, all of the fallout is tropospheric, whereas for a ground burst of 1 megaton about 40 percent of the fallout is stratospheric. For a given megatonnage the stratospheric proportion is higher for air-burst explosions than for ground bursts.

Fallout consists of neutron-activated weapon debris, fission products, and, in the case of a ground burst, activated particles of soil. For explosions in the sea there

303

will be activation of seawater minerals, and, with shallow-water bursts, possible activation of materials from the ocean floor.

Fallout particles from a ground burst vary in diameter from thousandths of a millimeter to several millimeters. Stratospheric fallout is composed of the finer particles.

Predictions of fallout radioactivity levels are difficult because of variations in burst conditions and types of weapon. Particles of different sizes fall at different rates, and the vagaries of the winds at different levels in the atmosphere, as well as local terrain conditions, must be taken into account.

Heavy particles of fallout descend quickly, while less massive ones can be carried hundreds of miles downwind. If the fireball does not touch the ground there is very little early fallout because the radioactive residue consists only of fine particles (0.00001 to 0.02 millimeters) which descend slowly.

16-2 EARLY FALLOUT

Early fallout consists of over 300 radioactive species. One kiloton of fission yield produces about 3.0×10^{23} fission-product atoms. One minute after an explosion the radioactivity level is 1.0×10^{21} disintegrations per second. If the fallout were distributed over 1 square mile, the radioactivity level 3 feet above the ground plane would be about 2900 rad per hour 1 hour after the explosion.

The Spatial Distribution of Fallout for Surface Bursts

Predictions of fallout distribution can only be made under idealized assumptions as to wind speed and rate of descent of the fallout particles. The latter depends on the nature of the material engulfed by the fireball, and so fallout patterns observed in nuclear tests serve only as a rough guide to what might actually be the case for a surface burst in a city, for example.

Predictions of fallout are made by computer calculation. The fallout dose contours in Figure 16-1 were calculated assuming a constant 15 miles per hour wind carrying the radioactive cloud at all altitudes and negligible wind shear (the wind is in the same direction at all altitudes). If there were no wind, the fallout would be centered on the explosion point and would decrease radially with distance. The winds produced by the explosion carry some fallout upwind against the prevailing wind direction, but the major part of the fallout occurs downwind. The figure gives the spatial distribution of fallout as a function of time after the explosion of a thermonuclear weapon with 1-megaton fission yield (total yield being 2 megatons).

Decay of Fallout Radioactivity with Time

Some fallout continues to arrive after the 18-hour period shown in Figure 16-1, but radioactive decay is taking place continuously. Because fallout is composed of about 300 different radionuclides, each with a different half-life, the decay process is com-

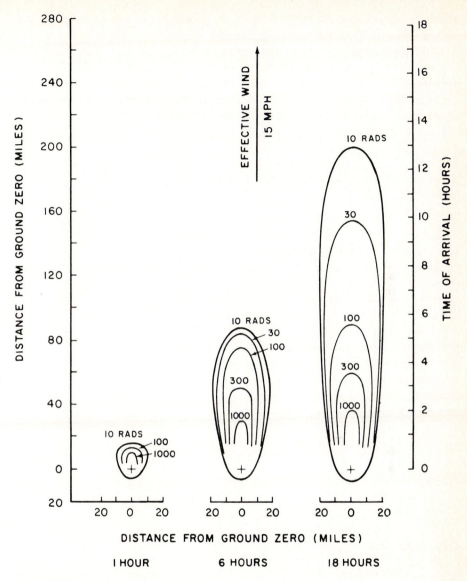

FIGURE 16-1
Total dose contours from early fallout at the times indicated for surface burst of a bomb with a
1-megaton fission yield. (*From Glasstone and Dolan, 1977, figure 9.86b.*)

plex (see Section P16-2). The intensity of the radioactivity decreases roughly in proportion to the time that has elapsed since the explosion. For example, if the radiation
level from fallout is 100 **rad** per hour 1 week after the explosion, it will be about
50 rad per hour 2 weeks later, 25 rad per hour 4 weeks later, and so on.

The difficulty of predicting fallout was tragically demonstrated after the Bravo
test carried out by the United States in 1954 in Marshall Islands. Many hundreds of

Marshallese were exposed to about 180 rad and narrowly missed a lethal dose of radiation. Had they been on the north side of Rongelap Atoll, where some normally resided, instead of attending a religious ceremony on the south side, they would have received several thousand rad. See Figure 16-2.

Note that the dose contours in Figure 16-2 are different from the idealized contours given in Figure 16-1. In practice there will be local hot spots of radioactivity due to terrain, wind conditions, and precipitation.

16-3   DELAYED FALLOUT

Structure of the Atmosphere

Delayed fallout is defined as that occurring more than 24 hours after a nuclear explosion. It consists of particles which are less than a few micrometers (1 micrometer = 0.001 millimeter) in diameter and which descend extremely slowly. About 40 percent of a 1-megaton surface burst and a much higher percentage of air bursts of all yields contribute to delayed fallout. The fallout is carried by winds hundreds and sometimes thousands of miles from the explosion. With weapons of 100 kilotons or more some of the fallout finds residence in the stratosphere, or upper atmosphere, which begins at an altitude of about 25,000 to 40,000 feet in polar and temperature zones and at about 55,000 feet in the tropics. The stratosphere is above the weather and is thus a very stable region. The residence time of fallout in the stratosphere is from 1 to 3 years. Below the stratosphere is the troposphere, or lower atmosphere. Tropospheric fallout is precipitated in rainfall or snowfall, usually within 1 or 2 months after the explosion.

Figure 16-3 shows the structure of the atmosphere during July and August. Note that the *tropopause*, the boundary between the stratosphere and the troposphere, lowers during the winter period in the southern hemisphere.

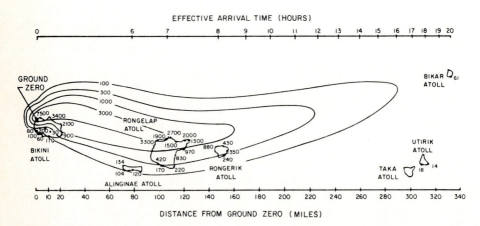

FIGURE 16-2
Accumulated doses at times up to 96 hours for the Bravo test explosion in the Marshall Islands. (*From Glasstone and Dolan, 1977, figure 9.105.*)

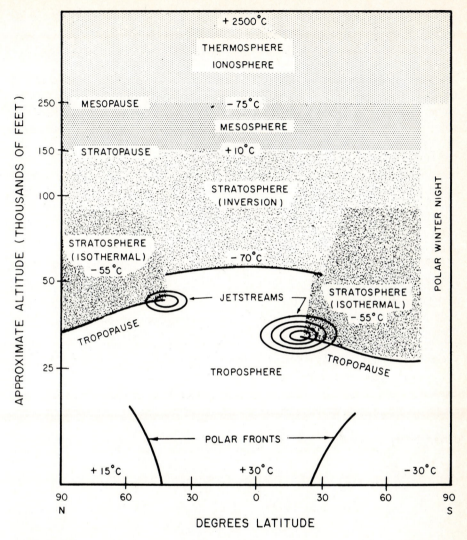

FIGURE 16-3
Structure of the atmosphere during summer months in the northern hemisphere. (*From Glasstone and Dolan, 1977, figure 9.126.*)

In each temperature zone there is a marked gap or discontinuity in the height of the troposphere at the latitude where jet streams are found. Here, mixing of stratospheric and tropospheric air masses can occur.

Tropospheric Fallout

Delayed fallout from lower elevations comes to earth chiefly through precipitation and so tends to be in higher concentration where precipitation is greatest. The smaller particles of delayed fallout in the troposphere may be carried by winds for thousands of miles. Winds at these upper tropospheric altitudes are generally from west to east. Table 2-1 (page 32) shows the radioactivity observed in Chile a few days after French atmospheric tests in the South Pacific.

Clouds of radioactive dust particles from atmospheric tests have been observed to circumnavigate the earth in a period of about 2 weeks. Figure 16-4 shows observations of the trajectory of such a cloud after a Chinese test at Lop Nor on May 9, 1966. The numbers on the figure indicate that day of the month. The cloud passed over the United States about 6 to 8 days after the test. Its speed was 20 to 30 meters per second (1400 miles per day).

Studies by Turco et al. (see Chapter 19) of global nuclear war show that the effect of precipitation of radioactive fallout from the troposphere in the first few months after the nuclear exchange would indeed be serious, especially for inhabitants of the northern hemisphere.

Stratospheric Fallout

In the lower stratosphere (below 70,000 feet) it takes about 10 months for particles to transfer to the troposphere, from which they precipitate in another 1 to 2 months. Such transfer takes place at the discontinuity in the tropopause, and the material is injected into the temperature zone. Even though there is considerable precipitation in

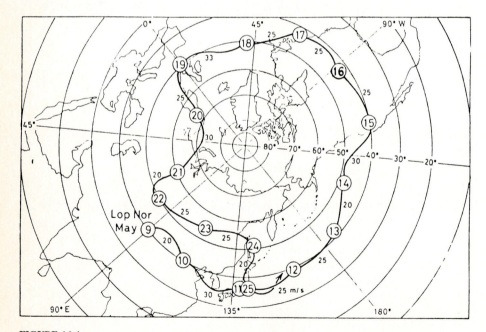

FIGURE 16-4

Passage around the earth of the radioactive cloud from a Chinese atmospheric test. (*From Hibakusha, 1977.*)

the tropics, tropical latitudes receive little fallout from the stratosphere. The mixing time between hemispheres is about 5 years in the lower stratosphere, so that fallout from explosions in the northern hemisphere mostly occurs there. However, this mixing time might be shortened to a few months if a larger scale nuclear exchange produced an overall cooling of the continents. This possibility is known as ''nuclear winter'' and is discussed in Chapter 19.

Large nuclear explosions or explosions at high altitudes deposit fallout in the upper stratosphere (above 70,000 feet). Here the transfer of material between hemispheres is much more rapid and the half-residence-time for transfer to the troposphere is longer. Both of these factors operate to produce a more even distribution of fallout between the hemispheres. Again, in the southern hemisphere most of the fallout precipitates in the temperature zone. The residence time in the stratosphere is of the order of a year. This additional time allows for radioactive decay and reduces the radioactivity level as compared with fallout originating in the troposphere, which is deposited on the earth's surface within a month or so.

The fallout that takes up residence in the stratosphere eventually finds its way to earth by interaction with the troposphere at the discontinuity in the tropopause. It is then precipitated by the weather in the temperate zone over long periods of time.

Figure 16-5 shows how the strontium 90 component of stratospheric fallout changed during the period 1951 to 1974. (One megaton of fission yield produces about 0.11 megacurie of strontium 90.) The burden of strontium 90 in the 1962-1963 period was due principally to an extensive series of atmospheric nuclear tests conducted before the Limited Test Ban Treat (LTBT) came into force in 1963 (38 by the United

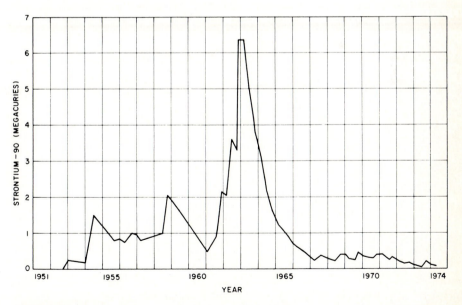

FIGURE 16-5
Stratospheric burden of strontium 90. (*From Glasstone and Dolan, 1977, figure 9.143a.*)

States and 71 by the Soviet Union). After the LTBT, no new strontium 90 was injected into the stratosphere, and by 1966 the strontium 90 found there had declined to relatively low levels. The remaining burden could be due to French and Chinese atmospheric tests.

Figure 16-6 shows the accumulation of strontium 90 on the earth's surface and in the biosphere as a result of the atmospheric tests.

Japanese scientists (Hibakusha, 1977) have assembled worldwide data on surface accumulations of strontium 90. Figure 16-7 shows the distribution of strontium 90 with latitude relative to the amount measured in Tokyo in 1975. The Tokyo value was 48.6 millicuries per square kilometer. The latitude effect due to deposition in the temperate zones can be seen in the figure.

16-4 LONG-LIVED RADIOACTIVE CONSTITUENTS OF FALLOUT

Ingestion of long-lived radioactive material can be a serious biological hazard. Table 16-1 (in the Additional Physics Section) lists the major constituents of fallout due to fission products (typically one-half of the yield of thermonuclear weapons is due to fission). Considerable radioactivity also results from activation of weapons components, soil components, and other nonfission sources. The principal radioisotopes in

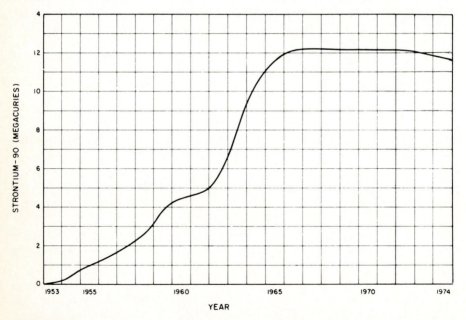

FIGURE 16-6

Surface inventory of strontium 90. The maximum amounts of strontium 90 on the earth's surface are reached when the rate of decay due to the 27.7-year half-life just begins to exceed the rate at which the isotope comes to the ground. (*From Glasstone and Dolan, 1977, figure 9.143b.*)

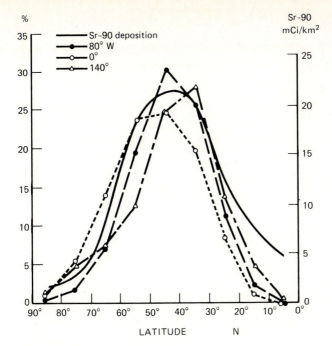

FIGURE 16-7
Distribution of strontium 90 with latitude. (*From Hibakuska, 1977.*)

fallout from these sources are listed in Table 16-2. Chapter 18 discusses the biological effects of some of these radioisotopes.

16-5 WATER-SURFACE AND UNDERWATER BURSTS

In explosions near water, fission products and radioactive weapons debris are partially contained in water droplets. When the water evaporates, the remaining solids consist chiefly of sea salt mixed with these materials. The particles are less massive than those from land bursts and hence there is reduced fallout near ground zero. If the explosion is in shallow water, part of the sea bottom, activated by neutron-induced reactions, mixes with the airborne radioactivity.

Considerable radioactivity is generated in the seawater near ground zero. In the Castle test series conducted by the United States in March 1954, which included the Bravo test mentioned above, the surface seawater was initially heavily polluted with fission products. Later, the contamination was moved by ocean currents to depths of several hundred feet. By the end of November 1954, 682 Japanese fishing boats holding radioactive fish had been found. Many of these fish were too contaminated for human consumption. One of the main radioactive contaminants was zinc 65, which is not a fission product but is formed by neutron activation of sea water. This experience revealed that ocean currents and fish migration can spread radioactive contam-

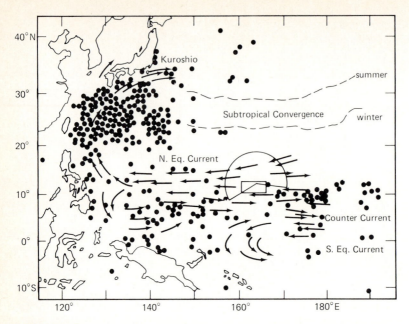

FIGURE 16-8
Distribution of fishing sites where contaminated fish were caught in 1954. (*From Japan Fisheries Agency.*)

ination thousands of miles from ground zero. Figure 16-8 shows the distribution of contaminated fish over the North Pacific in 1954 (Hibakusha, 1977).

ADDITIONAL PHYSICS SECTION

In this section we examine the time dependence of fallout radioactivity and provide tables of the principal radioactive species present in fallout both from fission products and from nuclear reactions and weapons residues.

P16-2 TIME DEPENDENCE OF FALLOUT RADIOACTIVITY

Since there is a complex mixture of fission products and weapons residue, the radioactivity from fallout does not follow an exponential decay law. While each radioactive constituent does so, the aggregate follows a $1/t^{1.2}$ law for about the first 6 months after the explosion. After 6 months, the decay is more rapid. Figure 16-9 shows radioactivity levels, or dose rates, from a few minutes up to about 1 month after an explosion. The **dose rate** at 1 h after the explosion is the *reference* dose rate, which is unity in the figure. The other dose rates are defined relative to the reference dose

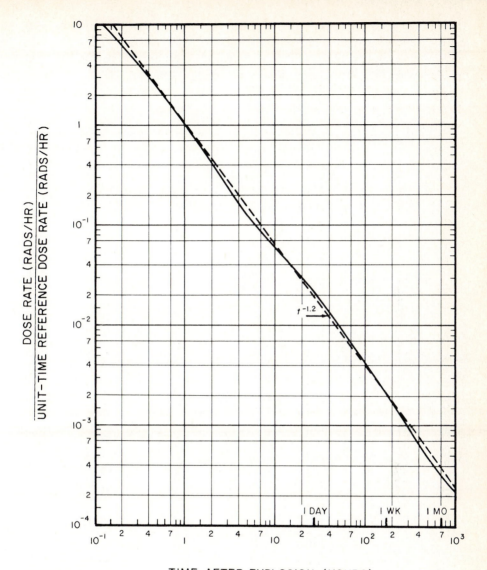

FIGURE 16-9
Dependence of the dose rate from early fallout during the first month upon time after explosion.
(*From Glasstone and Dolan, 1977, figure 9.16a.*)

rate. Note the close approximation to the $1/t^{1.2}$ law. We may often approximate the decay behavior as

$$I \approx \frac{I_R t_R}{t} \qquad \text{(P16-1)}$$

The equation gives the intensity 10 h after a nuclear explosion as 0.10 of the intensity at 1 h. The value read from Figure 16-9 is 0.06.

For times from 1 month to 25 years Figure 16-10 can be used to calculate decay rate. Departure from the $1/t^{1.2}$ law begins after about 6 months.

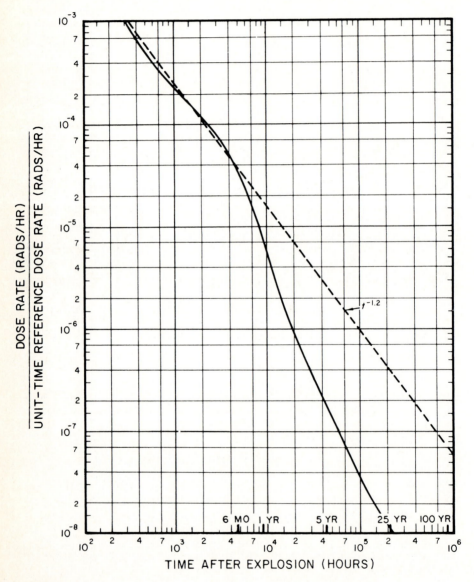

FIGURE 16-10

Dependence of dose rate from early fallout on time after explosion (1 week to 25 years). (*From Glasstone and Dolan, 1977, figure 9.16b.*)

Sometimes we are interested in *total* **accumulated dose** rather than dose rate. The accumulated dose can be calculated from Figure 16-11 if the dose rate at a reference time is known (see example below).

An Estimate of the Radioactivity Doses in the United States That Would Result from a Full-Scale Nuclear Attack by the Soviet Union

The graphs in Figures 16-9 to 16-11 can be used to make a very rough estimate of the levels of radioactivity that would occur after a full-scale Soviet attack. First, we make the following simplifying assumptions:

1. The fallout activity is distributed uniformly over the area of the United States (excluding Alaska).
2. The exposure begins (on the average) 3 h after the attack and continues indefinitely. That is, the people of the United States do not have shelter from the fallout and do not leave the country.
3. The dose rate for the radioactivity of a 1-kiloton fission-yield bomb, if the radioactivity is spread uniformly over 1 mi^2, is 2900 rad/h 1 h after the explosion.
4. The Soviets drop 5000 Mt of their 8000-Mt arsenal on the United States.

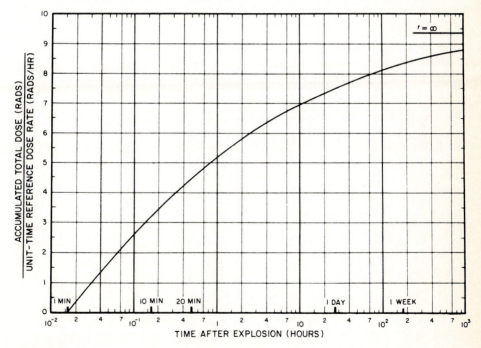

FIGURE 16-11
Curve for calculating accumulated dose from early fallout if the unit-time reference dose rate is known. (*From Glasstone and Dolan, 1977, figure 9.20.*)

First, we find from Figure 16-9 the radioactivity level 3 h after the attack. Remember that in the figure the dose rate at 1 h is arbitrarily taken as unity. Thus the dose rate at 3 h is about 20 percent of that at 1 h. Using assumption 3 above, we calculate the dose rate 3 h after the attack as 20 percent of 2900 rad/h, or 580 rad/h.

We now distribute this radioactivity over the area of the United States excluding Alaska, which is roughly 3×10^6 mi^2, and multiply by 5 million (the number of kt in 5000 Mt). Thus we estimate the dose rate at 3 h to be (580 rad/h) $\times$ (5×10^6)/ (3×10^6), or 970 rad/h.

The next step is to find the *accumulated* dose from 3 h to an infinite time ahead for the dose rate of 970 rad/h. This is done with Figure 16-11. Remember, the unit time is still one hour. The ordinate of the figure is 6.1 at 3 h and at infinite time it is 9.4. Therefore, the accumulated dose is

$$(9.4 - 6.1) \times 2900 \times \frac{5 \times 10^6}{3 \times 10^6} = 16,000 \text{ rads}$$

Although the above is a crude estimate, the calculation shows clearly that radioactive fallout would be a major cause of casualties. An exposure level of 16,000 rads is 40 times the level (400 rads) that will kill 50 percent of normal adults in 30 days. Even if somehow a person was able to find shelter from the radioactivity for the first two weeks following the exchange, the accumulated exposure would still be lethal. In this case the ordinate of Figure 16-11 is 8.6 and the corresponding accumulated exposure

TABLE 16-1
Long-lived fission products

Nuclide	Half-life	Major radiation
Krypton 85	10.8 years	Beta, gamma
Rubidium 87	4.8×10^{10} years	Beta
Strontium 89	52.7 days	Beta
Strontium 90	27.7 years	Beta
Yttrium 91	58.8 days	Beta
Zirconium 95	65.5 days	Beta, gamma
Niobium 95	35.0 days	Beta, gamma
Ruthenium 103	39.5 days	Beta, *gamma**
Ruthenium 106	368 days	Beta, *gamma**
Antimony 125	2.71 years	Beta, gamma
Tellurium 127 (isomer)	109 days	Beta, gamma
Tellurium 129 (isomer)	34.1 days	Beta, gamma
Iodine 131	8.05 days	Beta, gamma
Xenon 133 (isomer)	2.3 days	Gamma
Cesium 137	30.0 years	Beta, *gamma**
Barium 140	12.8 days	Beta, *gamma**
Cerium 141	32.5 days	Beta, gamma
Cerium 144	284 days	Beta, gamma
Neodynium 147	11.1 days	Beta, gamma
Praesodynium 147	2.62 years	Beta
Samarium 151	87 years	Beta, gamma

Gamma refers to gamma radiation from a radioactive daughter.

TABLE 16-2
Radionuclides from nuclear reactions and weapons residue (plutonium fission bomb and thermonuclear bomb)

Nuclide	Half-life	Major radiation
Tritium	12.3 years	Beta
Beryllium 7	53.6 days	Gamma
Carbon 14	5730 years	Beta
Sulfur 35	87.9 days	Beta
Argon 39	269 years	Beta
Chromium 51	27.8 days	Gamma
Manganese 54	303 days	Gamma
Iron 55	2.6 years	Gamma
Iron 59	45.6 days	Beta, gamma
Nickel 59	8×10^4 years	Gamma
Cobalt 60	5.3 years	Beta, gamma
Zinc 65	245 days	Beta +, gamma
Molybdenum 93	>100 years	x-ray
Tantalum 182	115 days	Beta, gamma
Uranium 237	6.75 days	Beta, gamma
Neptunium 239	2.35 days	Beta, gamma
Plutonium 238	86.4 years	Alpha
Plutonium 239	24,100 years	Alpha
Plutonium 240	6580 years	Alpha
Plutonium 241	13.2 years	Beta, gamma

is 3,900 rads. Further, internal exposure due to ingestion of radioactive materials will add significantly to the lethality of the radiation.

In an actual attack it is certain that the fallout would not be distributed uniformly: some areas would receive more and some less than the average. Nevertheless, the "order of magnitude" of the dose estimate is so high that we can conclude that it would have a catastrophic impact on human and other populations of the American ecosphere.

A similar intensity of fallout from U.S. nuclear explosions on the Soviet Union would probably also occur, thereby producing lethal radiation exposures in target regions. In a matter of two weeks time the fallout from the Soviet and U.S. explosions would form a belt encircling the earth in the latitudes of the initial explosions (see Figure 16-4). This would result in high levels of radiation exposure for all inhabitants of the northern hemisphere in those latitudes (30 to 60 degrees north latitude). See Chapter 19 for more information on fallout estimates from a global exchange.

P16-4 LONG-LIVED RADIOACTIVE SPECIES IN FALLOUT

Table 16-1 is a list of long-lived fission products, their half-lives, and the kind of radiation they give off.

Radioactive nuclei can also be produced or released in a nuclear explosion by neutron-induced reactions with the atmosphere or with weapons components and by reactions such as deuterium + deuterium and lithium 6 + deuterium to give tritium during a thermonuclear explosion. The intrinsic radioactivity of bomb components that are not completely utilized in the explosion, such as plutonium 239, can also be a factor. Major radioactive species of this type found in the ecosphere after a nuclear explosion are given in Table 16-2.

QUESTIONS

1. Define the stratosphere. The troposphere.
2. How far away were the Marshallese islanders from ground zero when they were exposed to 180 rad?
3. What was the radioactive species that was not a fission product observed by the Japanese in contaminated fish as a result of the Bikini tests? How is it formed? *Hint*: Neutrons are produced in abundance by H-bombs.
4. Describe delayed fallout. What is the delay time?
5. How is delayed fallout distributed according to latitude?
6. Why is strontium 90 a particularly dangerous component of delayed fallout?
7. What was the increase in radioactivity levels in air observed in Chile from French atmospheric tests in the South Pacific in 1972? (Use the data in Table 2-1.)
8. How long did it take for the nuclear cloud from the Chinese atmospheric test of 1966 to circle the earth?

PROBLEMS

1. If the fallout activity level is 300 rad/h 1 day after a nuclear explosion, what will the activity level be 2 days after the explosion? 3 days later? Use the $1/t^{1.2}$/law.
2. Use Figures 16-9 and 16-10 to find the fallout level for the explosion in Problem 1 1 year later.
3. Find the accumulated dose, in rad, for a person who emerges from a fallout shelter 1 week after the explosion in Problem 1.

KEY WORDS

accumulated dose   the dose rate multiplied by the time interval for that dose rate and summed over all time intervals (integrated dose rate), often given in rads.

delayed fallout   radioactive debris that falls to the earth at times later than 24 hours, perhaps days or even years later.

dose rate   the radiation received by a person per unit time, often measured in rads per hour.

early fallout   radioactive debris that falls to earth up to 24 hours after the explosion.

rad   the energy absorbed by the body per unit of body weight. One rad is defined as 0.01 joule absorbed per kilogram (see Chapter 18).

stratosphere   the atmosphere above the weather patterns. The stratosphere begins in altitude where the troposphere ends, at about 13 kilometers.

troposphere   that part of the atmosphere that contains the weather patterns. It extends up to about 40,000 ft, or about 13 kilometers.

CHAPTER

17

THE ELECTROMAGNETIC PULSE

We need a moral about-face.

Pope John Paul II

17-1 THEMES

When the gamma radiation emitted by a nuclear explosion hits atoms of the air or of an object, some of the electrons are stripped from the atoms (ionization) and are given a large part of the gamma energy. With air (which consists of elements with low atomic numbers), this occurs chiefly as a result of the Compton effect, and, with many solid objects (composed of elements with relatively high atomic numbers), as a result of the photoelectric effect (see Chapter 18). As these free electrons move, they create strong electromagnetic fields, which can cover very large areas and produce severe damage to electrical and electronic systems. For a nuclear explosion above the atmosphere, electric fields on the order of 10,000 volts per meter could be produced over the entire United States. These effects are known as the **electromagnetic pulse (EMP)**. A single 1-megaton nuclear explosion high over the central United States or the Soviet Union could destroy much of the nation's telecommunications, wipe out its electric power distribution grid, destroy transistorized ignition systems in vehicles, and damage military equipment, such as radar, aircraft, and missiles. A nuclear explosion in space could produce **system-generated EMP** (SGEMP) in satellites and missiles thousands of miles away, which could destroy their ability to function.

319

17-2 EMP DAMAGE

EMP damage results from the extremely powerful electric fields caused by the acceleration of free electrons produced by gamma radiation and x-rays from a nuclear blast. The electric fields in turn produce large pulses of voltage and electric current. They are rapidly created mainly during the last few generations of energy release—in about 10 nanoseconds, or one-hundredth of a millionth of a second. They decay relatively slowly as the electrons recombine. As a result the frequency spectrum is extremely broad, ranging from above 100 megahertz to below 1 megahertz.

EMP can demolish electronic equipment at distances very far from the blast. It has the potential to destroy or incapacitate a large part of the nation's communications and electric power distribution system. The EMP from a single nuclear blast in space above the United States or the Soviet Union could incapacitate virtually everything which relies on transistors and is not protected by an electromagnetic shield. This includes automobile ignition systems and the ignition and control systems of airplanes in flight. It also includes the electronic systems of missiles and other elements of United States or Soviet defense systems.

The entire civilian telephone network might be paralyzed. There is a considerable risk that every unprotected piece of electronic equipment—computers, television sets, radios, electronic controls in planes and cars, instruments in laboratories and hospitals, controls on nuclear reactors, and electronic networks in industry—either would be destroyed or would begin to malfunction. Successive high-altitude bursts could then damage backup systems.

Power lines serve as enormous antennae for picking up EMP, as Figure 17-1 shows. The EMP resulting from a nuclear explosion could cause the fault current sensors on power transmission and distribution grids to trip. This would open protective relays. Since electrical systems are interconnected, it is possible that just one EMP pulse would be sufficiently destabilizing to shut down an entire grid, leading to blackout over large areas. (In 1965 electricity to most of the northeastern United States was shut down for many hours as the result of the failure of one tiny relay.) If several EMP pulses were produced in succession, the relays that automatically close after one EMP pulse would open again and probably stay open, triggering automatic generator shutdown. In the millisecond before protective devices interrupted, power pulses of massive voltage would be conducted to all electric apparatus connected to the power grid. These pulses would be sufficient to cause malfunctioning or destruction of such apparatus as television, radios, broadcasting stations, and computers.

Figures 17-2 and 17-3 demonstrate the damage that is produced by voltages of up to 1 kilovolt (in this case energies in the range 0 to 0.5 microjoule) in metal-oxide-semiconductor field-effects transistors (MOSFETs). Figure 17-2 shows the craters produced in a MOSFET device, and Figure 17-3 shows one of the craters, highly magnified. Such craters cause the MOSFET to fail permanently.

Protection against the EMP requires that entire facilities be encased in metal cages (Faraday shields) and that special attention be paid to avoiding ground loops. Every electric apparatus must be connected directly to a common ground. To bury or shield the nation's power grid or telephone grid would require hundreds of billions of

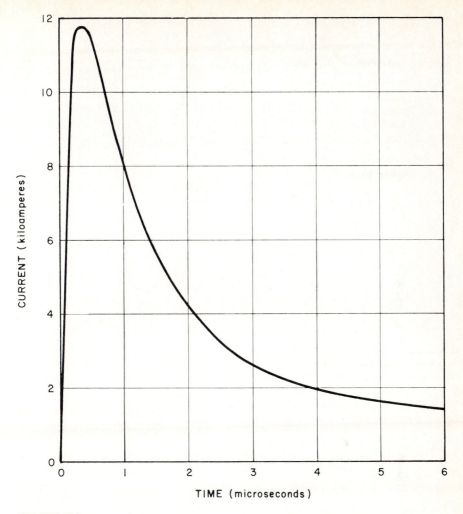

FIGURE 17-1
Currents in a power line that might be anticipated from a high-altitude nuclear explosion.
(*From Glasstone and Dolan, 1977, figure 11.50.*)

dollars and many years to complete. Although power lines are protected to some degree from voltage surges by lightning arrestors, present designs offer little protection against the EMP, which has a faster rise time than lightning and bypasses the arrestors.

The EMP might also severely cripple the military command and control system, impairing its ability to respond to an attack. Indeed, military communications systems could be viewed as so vulnerable that an attacked country might feel it had no choice but to launch an all-out retaliation to *any* attack or risk losing the ability to respond. Therefore EMP is a potentially valuable tool in any proposed "decapitation" strategy.

FIGURE 17-2
Damage to a metal-oxide-semiconductor device by an electric pulse. (*Courtesy Hewlett-Packard Corporation.*)

Protection against the EMP is also essential to any strategy calling for protracted nuclear war fighting capability.

The shift from vacuum tubes to transistors has exacerbated the problem of protection from the EMP. Some years ago a Soviet pilot defected to Japan. The electronic equipment in his plane contained many more vacuum tubes than electronic equipment in U.S. military aircraft. The question was: Were the Soviets just using antiquated technology, or were they attempting to make their aircraft secure against the EMP?

17-3 THE ORIGIN OF THE EMP

About 0.3 percent of the energy released in a nuclear explosion appears as prompt gamma radiation. The gamma rays that produce the EMP are those emitted in nuclear reactions of the primary explosion plus those produced by neutron reactions with surrounding weapon residues. The gamma rays interact with air molecules and atoms through *Compton scattering* and produce an ionized region called the **deposition region**, where the electron currents are formed. The location of the deposition region depends on where the blast occurs.

The Compton electrons produce EMP radiation in two primary ways: (1) The accelerating electrons produce electromagnetic radiation directly. (2) If the electrons

FIGURE 17-3
Magnification of the damage in Figure 17-2. (*Courtesy Hewlett-Packard Corporation.*)

are released high in the atmosphere, they spiral in the earth's magnetic field and emit synchrotron radiation.

The Compton electron recoil mechanism was discussed in Chapter 15 as one of the principal effects of the absorption of gamma radiation. Figure 15-3 gives a schematic representation of the Compton effect. In Chapter 12 it was explained that when a charged particle is accelerated, it produces electromagnetic radiation. The acceleration of electrons produced by the Compton effect is the basic origin of the EMP.

The earth's magnetic field distribution was discussed briefly in Chapter 12. This magnetic field extends through the atmosphere into outer space surrounding the earth. In that chapter it was explained that in a magnetic field a charged particle (here an electron) will describe a circular motion. To remain in a circular path the electron must be continually accelerated inward toward the circle's center. In this case the acceleration is due to the continual change in the direction of the electron's velocity as the electron describes a circle. This inward acceleration produces electromagnetic radiation, known as synchrotron radiation.

High-Altitude Explosions

There is one recorded case of EMP effects due to a high-altitude explosion. In the early 1960s, just before the Limited Test Ban Treaty went into effect, a high-altitude nuclear test of 1.4 megatons took place over Johnson Island, about 800 miles from

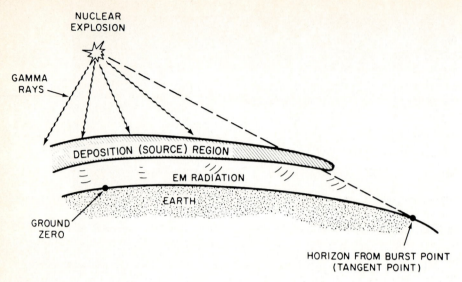

FIGURE 17-4

EMP produced by a high-altitude nuclear explosion. The electrons are deposited over a large volume, called the deposition region. The size of this region depends on the weapon yield and the altitude of the explosion. (*From Glasstone and Dolan, 1977, figure 11.13.*)

Oahu in the Hawaiian chain. In Oahu hundreds of burglar alarms were set off and strings of street lights went out as a result of failure of fuses and circuit breakers.

EMP from a high-altitude explosion is produced in two steps. (1) The electron deposition region is formed, and (2) synchrotron radiation within the deposition region is emitted. For nuclear explosions above about 20 miles, the gamma rays proceeding

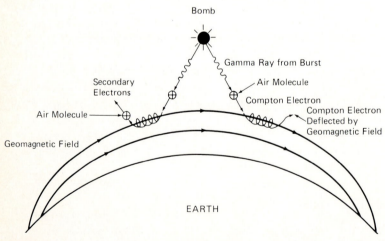

FIGURE 17-5

Helical paths of Compton electrons in the earth's magnetic field.

radially outward travel long distances in the thin atmosphere. The formation of the deposition region for a high-altitude nuclear explosion is shown schematically in Figure 17-4. Most of the radiation produced from a high-altitude explosion is the result of **synchrotron radiation** emitted by the **Compton electrons** spiraling in the earth's magnetic field (Figure 17-5).

The EMP from an explosion 500 kilometers high would blanket the entire United States. The effect of burst height on range for high-altitude EMP is shown graphically in Figure 17-6.

Medium-Altitude EMP

Air bursts 3 to 20 miles above the earth are medium-altitude air bursts. At these altitudes, the deposition region does not reach the ground but is still well within the earth's atmosphere. If the explosion were spherically symmetrical, gamma rays would be emitted isotropically (uniformly) in all directions. Because the earth's atmosphere becomes less dense with height, there is a loss of symmetry, causing a net electron current upward. Medium-altitude EMP is relatively weak relative both to high-altitude EMP and to EMP produced by surface bursts. The frequencies of the emitted radiation are low—from a few kilohertz to a few megahertz.

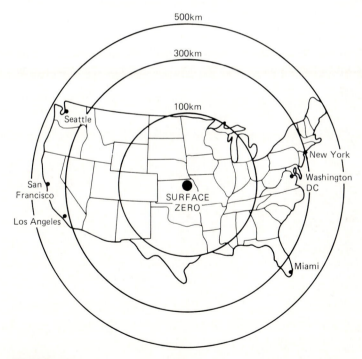

FIGURE 17-6
Effect of a burst height on range of high-altitude EMP.

EMP from Surface Bursts

The ground absorbs neutrons and gamma rays more strongly than air. Therefore in a surface or near-surface nuclear explosion the deposition region approximates a hemisphere in the air. There is a strong net acceleration of electrons upward. The electron current that is produced returns through the relatively highly conducting round. This give a circulating current through the burst point and produces a strong azimuthal magnetic field (see Figure 17-7). The result is a much stronger EMP effect than that from a medium-altitude air burst. The region of substantial **EMP** damage **from** a 1-megaton **surface burst** is about 8 miles, but very sensitive devices, such as very large scale integrated (VLSI) circuits and field-effect transistors, could be affected at much greater distances.

System-Generated EMP (SGEMP)

In a nuclear explosion in space the gamma radiation and x-rays from thermal radiation can propagate long distances, colliding with satellites, missiles, and other objects. When gamma or x-radiation is absorbed by an object in space, it produces large electron currents in the object which can burn out transistors and other components. Military satellites are reported to be protected to some degree against SGEMP (Griffith and Cooper, 1982). Civilian satellites are not, so any nuclear explosion in space is likely to destroy a large number of civilian communications networks (e.g., TV and telephone relays), as well as remote sensing and navigational capabilities. Since the United States and Europe are far more dependent on satellites than in the Soviet Union, the relative greater vulnerability of the West is substantial.

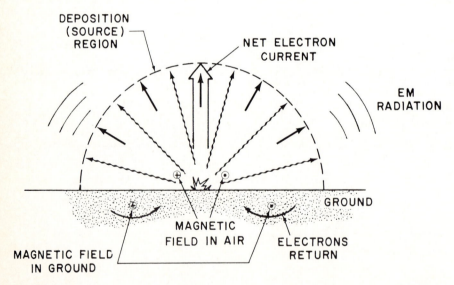

FIGURE 17-7
Schematic of the EMP effect from a surface burst. (*From Glasstone and Dolan, 1977, figure 11.10.*)

17-4 OTHER ELECTRICAL EFFECTS OF NUCLEAR EXPLOSIONS

The gamma radiation of a nuclear explosion in the upper atmosphere will disturb the ionized layers which are important for long-distance radio transmission. The atmospheric turbulence from the explosion also produces breakup of high-frequency radio communication. The results of these various effects is that no radio frequency band can be counted upon for reliable radio communication for many hours after an atmospheric explosion. Thus the management of the postattack environment would be extremely complicated.

ADDITIONAL PHYSICS SECTION

P17-2   CIRCUIT DAMAGE

Table 17-1 shows data on the energy needed to destroy some typical circuit elements. According to the table, burnout of integrated circuits, for example, can occur with as little as 8×10^{-6} J. Burnout could occur as a result of power line pulses or through direct induction. In the latter case, integration over a typical EMP pulse time distribution for EMP of 10,000 V/m give the energy flux as 0.047 J/m^2. The area of an integrated circuit that could be burned out is therefore $(8 \times 10^{-6})/0.047$, or 1.7×10^{-4} m^2 (1.7 cm^2). An area this large can contain an enormous number of logic elements.

TABLE 17-1
Minimum energies needed for damage to various circuit elements

Element	Minimum energy, J	Malfunction
Logic circuit	2×10^{-9}	Circuit upset
Integrated circuit	4×10^{-10}	Circuit upset
	8×10^{-6}	Burnout
Memory core	3×10^{-8}	Core erasure by wiring
Amplifier	4×10^{-21}	Interference (noise)
Relay	1×10^{-1} to 1×10^{-3}	Welded contacts
Microammeter	3×10^{-3}	Slammed meter
Transistors		
PNP audio	3×10^{-2}	Burnout
NPN switching	1×10^{-3} to 1×10^{-5}	Burnout
PNP switching	1×10^{-3} to 1×10^{-4}	Burnout
Diodes	1×10^{-3} to 1×10^{-5}	Burnout
SCR	3×10^{-3}	Burnout
Vacuum tubes	1 to 2	Burnout

Source: Waters, 1983.

P17-3 THE ORIGIN OF THE EMP

Direct Induction

The electric field from the EMP can enter equipment through voltage surges in power lines or by direct induction of voltages. In the latter case even if the equipment is disconnected from the power line, damage can result. Waters (1983) calculates the energy absorbed by a Yagi TV antenna as an example. Such an antenna has an effective area of about 280 m^2 so that it will capture a huge amount of EMP energy in its most sensitive direction. He calculates the energy flux that would be induced for a 10,000 V/m EMP electric field as 0.047 J/m^2. This figure is obtained by summing the energy flux over the time of the EMP pulse, which is about 20 μs (see Figure 17-1). Therefore the antenna would absorb 13.3 J. This energy value is many orders of magnitude above the failure level for typical receiver input circuits (see Table 17-1).

The General Mechanism for Production of EMP in the Atmosphere

If a photon has an energy of several million electron volts (a typical energy for gamma rays accompanying a nuclear explosion), then a large part of this energy can be transferred to electrons on atoms in the atmosphere via the Compton effect (see Chapter 15). Since the electron is *accelerated* by the collision with the photon, electromagnetic radiation is produced. For gamma rays with energies appreciably above the rest energy of the electron (0.511 MeV), the recoiling electrons are formed mostly in the direction of the incoming gamma ray, thereby producing an outward current of accelerating electrons.

For a 1-Mt nuclear explosion about 1×10^{24} gamma rays are emitted in all directions from the burst point. The resulting EMP is found by combining the contribution of the individual electron currents.

High-Altitude EMP

In the case of high-altitude EMP an extensive deposition region is formed as the gamma rays that are emitted downward encounter the upper atmosphere. Since the density of the atmosphere is very low, the Compton recoil electrons can make circular or, in general, helical paths in the earth's magnetic field. This is not possible for medium-altitude or surface bursts because the electrons are scattered by the air molecules.

In general, the centripetal acceleration of an electron which is traversing a circular or helical path produces radiation; in this case, it produces what is known as synchrotron radiation.

Synchrotron Radiation

The frequency of rotation of a nonrelativistic free electron in a magnetic field is given by

$$\text{Freq} = \frac{eB}{2\pi m} \qquad \text{(P17-1)}$$

where e is the charge on the electron, B is the magnetic field, and m is the electron mass (refer to Section P12-7). The earth's magnetic field is about 0.5 gauss $= 5 \times 10^{-5}$ Wb/m^2. The mass and charge of the electron are, respectively,

$$m = 9.11 \times 10^{-31} \text{ kg}$$

$$e = 1.60 \times 10^{-19} \text{ C}$$

Thus the frequency of the electron's circular orbit is

$$\text{Freq} = \frac{(1.60 \times 10^{-19}) \times (5 \times 10^{-5})}{2\pi(9.11 \times 10^{-31})}$$

$$= 1.4 \times 10^6 \text{ Hz}$$

or 1.4 MHz, or Mcps.

When the energy given the electron by Compton scattering of a gamma ray is comparable to or greater than rest mass, relativistic effects are important. The rest energy of an electron is 0.511 MeV, so the energy transferred by a 2-MeV electron can be about four times the rest energy. In this case the emitted radiation has a frequency spectrum that extends above that calculated from Eq. (P17-1) by a factor approximately equal to the cube of the ratio of the electron's energy to its rest energy, or about $4^3 = 64$ (Jackson, 1962). This gives a peak frequency (peak spectral component) of 89 MHz. There will actually be some higher frequencies because there are a few gamma rays with energies above 2 MeV in the burst. The reciprocal of the frequency gives the rise time of the EMP, which is of the order of 1/89 MHz, or about 1×10^{-8} s (10 ns).

The Geometry of a High-Altitude Burst

Let D be the distance to the horizon from the burst point of an explosion and h the height of the burst above the earth. R is the radius of the earth (6400 km) (see Figure 17-8).

Then

$$R^2 + D^2 = (h + R)^2 \approx R^2 + 2hR \qquad \text{(approximately)}$$

Solving for h, we obtain

$$h = \frac{D^2}{2R}$$

$$= \frac{(2500 \text{ km})^2}{2(6400 \text{ km})} \qquad \text{(P17-2)}$$

$$\approx 500 \text{ km}$$

(D, 2500 km, is one-half of the distance across the United States.)

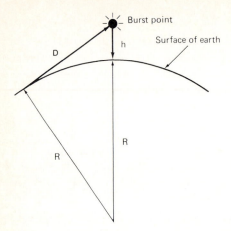

FIGURE 17-8
Geometry of high-altitude EMP.

The electric field on the earth's surface from high-altitude EMP varies slowly with distance. As a first approximation it varies inversely as the slant range D in Figure 17-8. This is in accord with Eq. (P12-5). That is, the radiated electric field E from the EMP is $E = $ constant/D. (Note that a radiated electric field from an accelerating charge falls off inversely with the distance, not the inverse square of the distance as from a static charge.) In the section below the electric field strength is estimated at 15,000 V/m at 1000 km from a 1-Mt explosion. The electric field is then given as

$$E = 15,000 \times (1000/D) \text{ V/m} \qquad \text{(P17-3)}$$

for the case of a 1-Mt explosion and where D is measured in kilometers and D is greater than 1000 km.

Since the source is really extended and not a point source because of the formation of the deposition region (see Figure 17-4), the electric field from high-altitude EMP will diminish with distance even more slowly than Eq. (P17-3) predicts. For example, for $D = 2500$ km, which is the distance from Nebraska to either coast of the United States, it is probably more reasonable to predict a higher value than 6000 V/m, which is given by Eq. (P17-3) for this case. Roughly one may say, taking into account the expended source, which would be hundreds of kilometers across, that the electric field of the EMP would be one-half of its value at 1000 km, or 7500 V/m.

Estimate of the Electric Field for a High-Altitude Burst

An estimate of the electric field of the EMP pulse from a high-altitude 1-Mt burst can be made as follows:

1. Energy released is 4.2×10^{15} J.
2. Assume 0.3 percent of the energy is emitted in prompt gamma rays.
3. Assume 0.6 percent of the gamma rays escape and form Compton electrons.

4. The gamma rays have an average energy of about 1 MeV.

5. The gamma rays are emitted over about 1.0×10^{-8} s.

The amount of energy available for the EMP pulse is

$$\text{Energy} = (4.2 \times 10^{15} \text{ J})(0.006)(0.003)$$

$$= 7.6 \times 10^{10} \text{ J}$$

This energy is distributed in a spherical shell whose radius is the distance from the nuclear explosion to the observer, r. The thickness of the shell is the distance the gamma rays go during a time $t = 1.0 \times 10^{-8}$ s at a speed of 3×10^8 m/s:

$$\text{Distance } d = \text{velocity of light} \times (1.0 \times 10^{-8} \text{ s}) = 3 \text{ m}$$

One-half of the stored energy of the EMP, or 3.8×10^{10} J, is in the electric field; the other half is in the magnetic field. The stored energy is given by

$$U = \tfrac{1}{2}\epsilon_0 E^2 V$$

where E is the electric field amplitude in volts per meter, U is the energy density in joules per cubic meter, and V is the shell volume, $4\pi r^2 d$.
   Then

$$3.8 \times 10^{10} \text{ J} = \tfrac{1}{2}\epsilon_0 E^2 4\pi r^2 d$$

Here the constant $\epsilon_0 = 8.85 \times 10^{-12}$ farads/m.
   Solving this equation for the electric field, we find that if r is 1000 km (1.0×10^6 m), the electric field is 15,000 V/m. For a 10-Mt burst the electric field would be a factor of $\times 10^{1/2}$ times larger, or 47,000 V/m.
   The EMP increases as the square root of the weapon yield because the energy in the electromagnetic field varies with the square of the value of the electric field and the energy available for the EMP is proportional to the yield of the nuclear weapon.

The Electric Field from Surface-Burst EMP

An equation from Mindel (1977) gives the electric field from a surface burst as

$$E = \frac{1 \times 10^7}{r} \qquad \text{V/m} \quad \text{where } r \text{ is in meters} \tag{P17-4}$$

This equation gives a pulse strength of 780 V/m at 8 mi, or about 13,000 m. This is of sufficient magnitude to damage electronic equipment, as indicated in Section P17-2. In fact, the distance in which EMP damage from a surface burst can occur is very dependent on the sensitivity of the affected devices. Very large scale integrated circuits or field-effect transistors, for example, can be damaged at distances greater than 8 miles. Due to saturation effects Mindel states that the electric field is not very dependent on weapon yield.

System-Generated EMP (SGEMP)

The SGEMP electric field is formed by emission of electrons from the solid materials of the equipment. Both the Compton effect and the photoelectric effect are important. The latter effect is proportional to the fifth power of the atomic number, and therefore is not very important in atmospheric EMP, which is formed from low-atomic-number air molecules. The photoeffect is increasingly important for lower photon energies so that x-rays from the thermal radiation need to be considered as well.

The photoeffect is caused by the ejection of the electron from an atom when hit by a photon. The kinetic energy of the electron is equal to the photon energy $h\nu$ less the binding energy of the electron to the atom, W:

$$KE = h\nu - W \tag{P17-5}$$

These electrons can in turn react (see Additional Physics Section, Chapter 18, for a further discussion of the photoelectric effect) with the solid material to release more electrons, called **secondary electrons**. The electrons are primarily produced on the surfaces of the solid material. Since they have a component of velocity perpendicular to the surface, some of them will be emitted from the surface. This results in an electric field near the surface and in the generation of large surface currents. This holds for a vacuum environment, such as a satellite in space. If the equipment one is concerned with is located in the atmosphere, then x-ray-generated photocurrents in the surrounding air are also important to consider.

The protection of satellites from SGEMP is difficult. The large currents generated by the SGEMP cause burnout of sensitive electronic components. Protection is provided by shielding the equipment with a metal shell. This is much more practical for small systems, such as a satellite, for example, than for large ones. It is, however, expensive and requires testing by exposing the equipment to x-ray fluxes to see whether it will continue to perform. Waters (1983) states that the satellites of the United States are protected from SGEMP at an x-ray flux density substantially greater than 1×10^{-5} cal/cm^2 (4.2×10^{-5} J/cm^2).

We can calculate the number of x-rays per square centimeter, which are assumed to have some average energy, as follows. Assume the x-rays are produced by a bomb's thermal radiation at 10^8 °C in the first microsecond of the explosion. The average x-ray energy will be about 10 keV = 0.01 MeV. The number of joules per x-ray is then

$$(0.01 \text{ MeV}) \times (1.6 \times 10^{-13} \text{ J/MeV}) = 1.6 \times 10^{-15} \text{ J/x-ray}$$

The required flux of x-rays in joules per square centimeter to produce damage is

$$(1 \times 10^{-5} \text{ cal/cm}^2) \times (4.2 \text{ J/cal}) = 4.2 \times 10^{-5} \text{ J/cm}^2$$

$$\frac{4.2 \times 10^{-5} \text{ J/cm}^2}{1.6 \times 10^{-15} \text{ J/x-ray}} = 2.6 \times 10^{10} \text{ x-rays/cm}^2$$

How far from a 1-Mt explosion must a satellite be in order not to sustain damage? According to Glasstone and Dolan, for a high-altitude burst about 80 percent of the energy of the nuclear explosion appears as radiant energy. Now 1 Mt liberates $4.2 \times$

10^{15} J, and 80 percent of this, or 3.3×10^{15} J, will appear as electromagnetic radiation. If we define the x-ray region to be above 1 keV in photon energy, then almost all the radiant energy is in the form of x-rays. This can be calculated by integration of the Planck blackbody law or estimated using Figure 14-8. Gamma radiation consists of photons produced by processes within nuclei. X-radiation (which also consists of photons) results from electronic transitions outside of the nucleus. Typically only 0.3 percent or so of the energy from a thermonuclear bomb is released as gamma radiation, while a much higher proportion of the energy (80 percent, typically) appears as thermal radiation from the fireball. For explosions in space the fireball temperature is high, and most of the thermal radiation is at high frequencies and is x-radiation.

If we imagine a sphere of radius R with its center at the explosion, then the energy associated with the x-ray flux at distance r from the explosion is

$$4\pi r^2 \times \text{flux density} = 3.3 \times 10^{15} \text{ J}$$

The critical flux density of 4.2×10^{-5} J/cm^2 occurs at a distance of 25,000 km! We can infer from this very rough estimate that nuclear explosions in space are a major threat to satellites or space warfare stations, even at considerable distances.

If a missile is to be protected while in flight, the ionizing action of the x-ray photoeffect on surrounding air must also be taken into account. X-ray-generated skin currents on a missile in space produce 10 A/m in a vacuum, but up to 10,000 amp/m is in air (Woods, 1981). These skin currents in turn generate electromagnetic fields internal to the missile, possibly damaging its control system. The size of the nuclear weapon or its range that would produce the above currents is not given in the reference and is presumed to be classified information.

QUESTIONS

1. Why is medium-altitude EMP relatively weak?
2. Describe the process by which high-altitude EMP is produced.
3. Why isn't low-altitude EMP produced by the same process that produces high-altitude EMP?
4. Discuss the impact of EMP on the civilian and military sectors in the event of a nuclear war.
5. What is SGEMP?
6. Why does ground-burst EMP only extend a limited distance?
7. Describe the Compton effect.
8. How much energy need be absorbed in an integrated circuit to produce a malfunction?

PROBLEMS

1. For high-altitude EMP how does the electric field change if the yield of the weapon is quadrupled? The energy absorbed by a circuit?
2. If a nuclear bomb is exploded at 400 km, what is the effective diameter of the circle on the earth's surface in which the EMP will be experienced?

3. Calculate the magnitude of the EMP electric field from a surface burst at a distance of 10 km.
4. Calculate the EMP voltage pulse amplitude (of electric field) at a point 2000 km away from a 2-Mt bomb exploded at 500 km.
5. Distinguish between direct induction of EMP and EMP pulses that come from the power grid, acting as an antenna.
6. Find the frequency with which an electron describes a circular orbit if it is nonrelativistic (kinetic energy less than 100 keV) and the magnetic field of the earth is 1.0 gauss.
7. What is the approximate highest frequency observed in the harmonics of the frequency obtained in Problem 6?

KEY WORDS

Compton electrons   electrons produced by the collision of a gamma ray with electrons in atoms. In the case of EMP the electrons are in atoms of air in the atmosphere (nitrogen and oxygen).

deposition region   a region in the atmosphere in which the gamma rays from a nuclear explosion produce Compton electrons.

EMP from surface burst   an electromagnetic pulse formed by radiation from upward-accelerating Compton electrons produced by the gamma rays accompanying a nuclear explosion.

high-altitude EMP   an electromagnetic pulse formed by the synchrotron radiation that is produced by a nuclear explosion above the atmosphere.

secondary electrons   electrons produced by the primary electrons that are formed by x-rays in the SGEMP.

synchrotron radiation   electromagnetic radiation produced by Compton electrons traversing circular or helical paths in the earth's magnetic field.

system-generated EMP   system-generated EMP, or SGEMP, is formed principally in outer space on satellites and other equipment by the action of x-rays from a nuclear explosion. Photoelectrons and Compton electrons liberated by the x-rays may produce large and damaging currents which in turn may damage sensitive electronic components.

CHAPTER
18

THE BIOLOGICAL AND MEDICAL EFFECTS OF RADIOACTIVITY, GAMMA RAYS, AND NEUTRONS FROM NUCLEAR WEAPONS

. . . and whoever walks a furlong
without sympathy walks to his own
funeral drest in his shroud.

Walt Whitman

18-1   THEMES

Nuclear weapons cause casualties and affect the ecosystem through several effects: blast, thermal radiation, nuclear radiation, and fallout. Chapters 15 and 16 discussed the initial nuclear radiation and the radiation from fallout. In this chapter we examine the effects of this and other radiations on biological systems, particularly on human beings. The primary units used in discussing radiation damage, the rad and the rem, are introduced. Background radiation (naturally occurring radiation) is about 100 millirem (0.1 rem) per year, while the dosage required to kill 50 percent of the humans exposed to it (denoted *LD 50*) is about 400 rem.

335

18-2 THE PHYSICAL MECHANISMS THAT CAUSE BIOLOGICAL DAMAGE

The fundamental physical mechanism of nuclear radiation that harms living organisms is **ionization**—the separation of one or more electrons from an atom or molecule. The electric field created by a positively charged ion or electron can damage sensitive constituents of cells, such as the DNA, causing the cell to die, to be incapable of reproduction, or to reproduce in a changed manner (mutation). Ionization causes energy to become available within the cell that can form free radicals such as OH^- or produce oxidants, such as hydrogen peroxide, which act as poisons. If a sufficient number of cells in an organism are so affected, the organisms begins to show adverse physiological effects. If the exposure is sufficient, these effects can cause the organism's death.

Figure 18-1 shows a schematic diagram of the production of high-speed electrons and free radicals by gamma radiation that in turn can produce damage to the double-helix DNA molecule. The initial particle need not be electromagnetic radiation. High-speed atomic particles, protons, neutrons, alpha particles, and electrons can also produce significant biological damage via the ionization process, as explained below.

Gamma Rays and X-Rays

If one is close to a nuclear explosion, both gamma rays from excited nuclei and also x-rays from excited atoms may cause radiation damage. Later, there is risk from radioactive fallout, which emits a great number of gamma rays.

The gamma rays or x-rays produce recoiling charged particles or electrons in tissue (see the Additional Physics Section at the end of the chapter), which form deleterious products within the cells.

Alpha Particles and Beta Particles

Alpha particles (helium nuclei) and beta particles (free electrons or positrons) are two of the products emitted during the decay of radioactive nuclei. Their range is small and they are stopped by the surface layers of the body. Beta burns on human skin due to fallout particles that were not washed off have been observed. Loss of hair can also occur in humans and animals if beta radioactivity on the scalp or on clothes is sufficiently intense. The principal danger from beta and alpha radioactivity is the damage of internal organs that results if the radiation is ingested. Alpha particles produce ionization at a much higher rate than do beta particles, and so alpha particles are particularly carcinogenic in lung and bone tissues.

Neutrons

Neutrons do not have an electric charge and hence do not produce ionization directly. However, neutrons have a fairly high probability of interacting with the hydrogen nuclei, or protons, in the body—after which ionization can occur. A great deal of

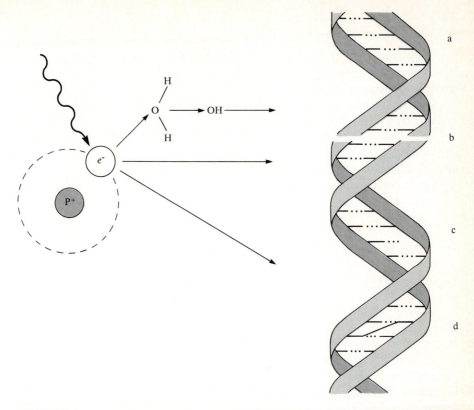

FIGURE 18-1
Damage to DNA is the most critical effect of low-level radiation. The effect can be direct or indirect. At the left a hydrogen atom is ionized by absorbing electromagnetic radiation. The electron is ejected from the atom with high velocity. In the indirect effect (top arrow) a secondary electron interacts with a molecule of water to give rise to a free radical (OH), which does the damage to the DNA. In the direct effect (lower arrows) the electron itself interacts with the DNA. The schematic representation of DNA at the right shows a normal segment of the molecule (a) and three of the many types of damage that can be caused by either direct or indirect effects of ionization: a double-strand break in the DNA double helix (b), the deletion of a base (c), and the chemical cross-linking of the two DNA strands (d). (*Source: "The Biological Effects of Low Level Ionizing Radiation," Arthur C. Upton, Scientific American, February 1982.*)

hydrogen is present in the body, not only in proteins, fat, and other complex molecules but also in water, which comprises about 80 percent of body weight. If the interaction with hydrogen is a glancing collision, the neutron may lose very little energy; in a head-on collision, the neutron may lose all its energy. The energy that is lost by the neutron is gained by the recoiling proton. The recoiling proton is a heavily ionizing particle, like the alpha particle, and can produce extensive cell damage. For example, 1 rad (defined in Section 18-3 below) of fast neutrons (with energy greater than about 1 MeV) is about 5 times more likely to produce cataracts in the eye than is 1 rad of gamma radiation.

18-3   UNITS OF RADIATION

The **roentgen** (R) is a measure of how much ionization is produced by radiation. By definition, 1 roentgen is equal to 2.58×10^{-4} coulomb of free charge produced in one kilogram of air (or 1 e.s.u. of charge of each sign per cubic centimeter of air). This is equivalent to about 2×10^9 ion pairs per cubic centimeter. Approximately 1 roentgen per hour is produced at a 1-meter distance from 1 gram of radium (in equilibrium with its daughter products).

The *radiation absorbed dose* (**rad**) is a measure of radiation energy *absorbed* by the body. In principle, different parts of the body absorb a given amount of radiation slightly differently. A practical definition is that one rad corresponds to absorption of 0.01 joule per kilogram of body weight.

Thus:

$$1 \text{ rad} = 1.00 \times 10^{-2} \text{ joule/kilogram}$$

Relative biological effectiveness (**RBE**) is a measure of the biological damage to a given tissue caused by a given type of radiation. The RBE depends on both the type of radiation and the particular tissue through which it passes. The *roentgen equivalent mammal* (**rem**) is defined such that 1 rem = 1 rad × RBE.

The quality factor, or QF, is a measure of the density of ionization produced by a given kind of radiation at a specified energy. It is a factor in the RBE that depends on the type of radiation. For beta rays and gamma rays the QF is 1, for neutrons from 1 to 10 MeV it is about 5, and for plutonium alpha particles, it is 10. For the low-energy beta rays of tritium (18 keV maximum energy) the QF is 1.7. The other factor in the RBE is biological, i.e., it depends on the particular part of the body involved. Often the biological factor is approximately unity so that the quality factor and RBE become the same. Hence, 1 rad of plutonium alpha particles or neutrons is more dangerous than 1 rad of beta particles or gamma rays, especially if the former is ingested.

Generally the RBE for gamma rays and x-rays is about unity so that measurement of radiation dose in rads or rems is about equivalent. The more precise measure is in rems, however, which takes into account biological sensitivity to the particular radiation as well as the quality factor.

18-4   EXPOSURE TO IONIZING RADIATION

Low-Level Radiation

BACKGROUND RADIATION. We live in a sea of radiation, as human beings have for millions of years. Humans and other organisms have adapted to this exposure, at least to some degree. It is known, for example, that cells have repair mechanisms. Such mechanisms were developed to repair cell damage produced by spontaneous mutations in cell structures. Only a small fraction of such mutations are caused by the natural background radiation, however. Hence it is not clear how effective the cell repair mechanisms would be in reversing damage due to radiation. Typical background radiation levels are about 100 millirem per year (1 millirem is one one-thousandth of a rem). It is an open question whether there is a threshold below which radiation levels are "safe."

Background radiation comes to us by several routes.

1. Cosmic rays, which are energetic particles from outer space, arrive at the rate of about one per square centimeter per minute. The highly energetic primary particle interacts with atoms in the atmosphere to produce showers of electrons, mesons, and other particles. These particles are highly penetrating, and to avoid them it is necessary to go deep underground. Cosmic rays contribute about 44 millirem per year to total background radiation. Cosmic rays are more abundant at high altitudes, and if we take a jet flight across the United States, we receive about 4 millirem. At high-altitude locations such as Denver, Colorado (5000 feet above sea level), there is an increased exposure of a few tens of millirem per year.

2. External radioactivity produces gamma radiation in our environment which gives us about 40 millirem per year. For example, in a brick house there is increased external radioactivity due to minute quantities of uranium and other radioactive nuclei in the bricks. Soil contains radioactivity, and some areas of the earth are more radioactive than others because of the variation in soil radioactivity.

3. Internal radioactivity accounts for about 18 millirem per year. One of the principal causes is the natural radioactivity of potassium 40, which is a constituent of the potassium in our diet. Trace amounts of uranium and thorium alpha emitters are incorporated in the bone marrow of the body, as is carbon 14 produced by cosmic rays in the atmosphere.

Atmospheric nuclear tests contribute strontium 90 and cesium 137 to the ecosphere. In 1970 an individual in the northern hemisphere would have been exposed to about 4 millirem per year from this source. During the extensive atmospheric testing of the 1950s and early 1960s, in latitudes above 40 degrees, the yearly exposure from fallout was greater. Since the half-lives of strontium 90 and cesium 137 are 27.7 and 30.0 years, respectively, their presence in the environment is slowly decreasing (Chinese and French atmospheric tests have slightly slowed the decrease).

Cosmic radiation, external radiation, and internal radiation together provide a normal background of about 102 millirem per year (44, 40, and 18 millirem per year, respectively). This figure can vary by as much as 30 percent depending on individual circumstances. In addition there is an average dose of about 50 millirem per year from medical x-rays, medical therapy, and industrial exposure to radiation.

A recently discovered and potentially important effect can occur inside houses built on earth or of materials containing traces of uranium. The radioactive uranium decays to radon, which is a gas. Radon is an alpha particle emitter with a high RBE (of the order of ten) in lung tissue. In some houses the increase in the probability of developing cancer has been found to be as much as that due to smoking several cigarettes a day.

EFFECTS OF LOW DOSES OF RADIATION. There is an ongoing controversy about the effects of low doses of ionizing radiation. It is argued by some that body repair

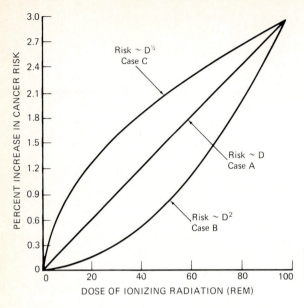

FIGURE 18-2
Cancer induction as a function of dose of ionizing radiation.

mechanisms may be effective at low doses and so radiation levels even a few times greater than the levels of natural background radiation may be safe. It is also argued that for certain cases of animal exposure a given dose is less harmful if the dose rate is lower. This would be expected if repair occurs. It is possible that near the threshold for damage in humans the same thing occurs (Goldman, 1982). Morgan (1978) suggests that there may be several curves approaching zero dose depending on the person's age and type of cancer being produced—but that linearity is the most reasonable assumption if we are ignorant. Figure 18-2 shows the various possibilities. The figure is a plot of $E = kD^n$, where E is the cancer risk (percent of persons who will get cancer) as a result of exposure to a dose of D rem of ionizing radiation. Case A, in which $n = 1$, illustrates the *linear hypothesis*, in which one would expect 3×10^{-4} cancers per person per rem. Case B, in which $n = 2$, illustrates that *threshold hypothesis*, in which the cancer risk becomes negligible, or statistically insignificant, at a low average dose per person. (Strictly speaking, the threshold hypothesis means that *no* damage occurs at sufficiently low dose rates.) It may typify the low risk of leukemia for middle-age persons exposed to beta or gamma radiation. Case C, or some other curve with n less than 1, may apply to leukemia among the old and young or possibly to other forms of cancer regardless of age. A dose of 1 rem, for example, would produce cancer in 300 members of a population of 1 million in case A, in 3 people (which is statistically insignificant) in case B, and in 3000 people in case C.

Upton (Upton, 1982) compares breast cancer induced by the atomic bombing of Hiroshima (which was a large instantaneous exposure) to breast cancer induced by fluoroscopy studies of patients with collapsed lungs who were suffering from tuberculosis. The latter women received radiation doses of from 10 to 50 rem in exposures over many months. The excess in cancer cases over the normal rate per unit radiation

TABLE 18-1
Cancer risk and known range of linearity

Linearity of dose, down to	Risk, per million persons	Comments
10 rad	30–100 (L) 50–170 (C)	Hiroshima and Nagasaki atom bomb survivors
0.2–0.8 rad	300 (L) 600 (C)	X-ray exposures to the pelvic region
About 1.0 rad	300–3000 (L)	X-ray exposures to the pelvic region
20 rad	50–110 (T)	X-ray therapy
6.5 rad	120 (T)	X-ray for ringworm

L = leukemia risk; C = total cancer risk; T = thyroid cancer risk.
Source: Morgan, 1978.

dose is not different in the two cases, which suggests a linear response to breast cancer induction down to about 10 rem exposure level.

Table 18-1 gives some known cancer risks in humans at low dose levels. An average conservative figure from these data, assuming linearity, is about 200 cancers induced per million population per rem of exposure. This figure is for the lifetime of the individual. For comparison the normal cancer induction *rate* in a population of one million persons from natural causes is about 1500 cancer deaths *per year*.

Figure 18-3 gives the lifetime risk of various types of cancer from low-level radiation. The number of cancers given are in terms of exposure of a population of one million persons to a whole-body dose of 1 rem. Cancer deaths are given in black and total cancers of a given type are given in gray in the figure. The total number of cancers of all types produced in a lifetime from this figure is 872 per million persons exposed to one rem. The total number of cancer deaths is 520 per million persons exposed per rem.

Najarian (1978) discusses cases of low-level occupational exposure in the nuclear industry for accumulated radiation dose. Since the latency period for cancer induction can be up to 40 years, the data should be regarded as the lower limit of the effect. Figure 18-4 gives the aggregate of several studies of cancer deaths for workers in the nuclear industry and in nuclear tests versus the exposure above natural background. The heavy line represents a linear extrapolation of data from higher exposures (similar to case A in Figure 18-2, except that this figure gives cancer **rate** rather than lifetime risk as given in Figure 18-2). The cancer rate at zero occupational exposure is the normal rate, or about 1500 cancers per million persons per year. The principal feature of the figure is that the points (B), each of which represents the cancer death of an individual, are *all* above the line (A).

The study represents about 0.5 million cases. The results indicate that the risk is *greater* than the linear assumption (an example of case C of Morgan' study above). An accumulated exposure of 20 rem results in about 1000 additional cancer deaths per million persons exposed *per year*, or about 50 deaths per million per rem per year. If one assumes an average lifetime of 30 years beyond exposure, then the lifetime

SITE

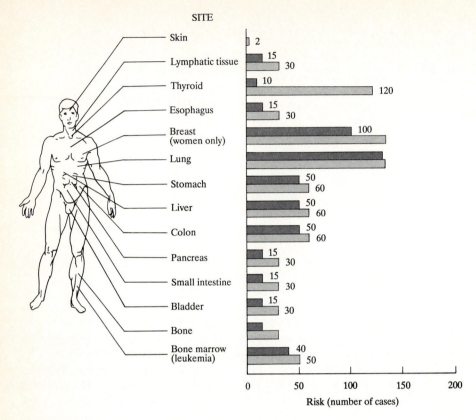

Risk (number of cases)

FIGURE 18-3
Lifetime risk of various types of cancer from low-level radiation is shown on the basis of a number of investigators. The risk is per million persons per rem of exposure over a lifetime. The figures given are the maximum estimates for fatal cancers (black) and number of cancer cases (gray). In each instance, the estimates actually cover a range in which the minimum figure is much lower (for example, for bone marrow cancer the minimum figure is 15 cases and 15 deaths). (*Source: "The Biological Effects of Low-Level Ionizing Radiation," Arthur C. Upton, Scientific American, February 1982.*)

risk is 1500 cancer deaths per millon per rem for this occupational exposure study. Otherwise stated, if the response is linear, and *if* persons in this study received 600 rem accumulated dose, then the cancer induction rate from radiation would equal the normal cancer rate, 1500 cancer deaths *per year*; i.e., the cancer death rate would double. The lifetime cancer deaths from the Najarian study is about three times that given by Upton (Upton, 1982) in Figure 18-3, and both of these studies are somewhat higher than the cancer risk given by Morgan above.

A conservative overall estimate of the cancer death risk might be about 300 cancer deaths per million persons exposed to one rem over a lifetime. Such an estimate assumes a **linear** response to low radiation exposures, such as in case A of Figure 18-2. This estimate is conservative in the sense that it is somewhat low in magnitude

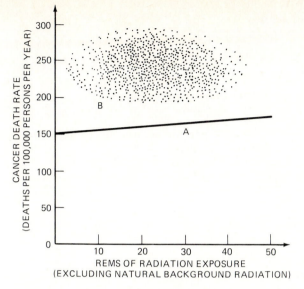

FIGURE 18-4
Cancer death rate for occupational exposures. (*From Najarian, 1978.*)

and also that it does not make the optimistic assumption that there is a threshold below which radiation is not harmful. In the absence of evidence that there is a threshold the prudent response would seem to be that there is none unless demonstrated to the contrary. Demonstration of cancer induction by radiation at low exposures is especially difficult in human populations because radiation-induced cancers would be a small addition to the normal cancer rate, which itself is subject to variability, making statistical analysis difficult.

However, just because demonstration of cancer induction by low-level radiation is difficult does not mean it does not exist as is sometimes claimed or implied; i.e., "there was no measurable effect of the radiation exposure." In the discussion in Chapter 19 of the effects of a global nuclear war or the effects of radiation releases from reactor accidents, the assumption will be made that there would be a linear response to radiation exposure.

High-Level Radiation

WHOLE-BODY EXPOSURE. The acute effects, in human beings, of whole-body exposure to radiation are summarized in Table 18-2. At high doses, radiation-induced lesions and their consequence are essentially nonreversible. Large total-body doses have a particularly serious effect on the regenerative cells of the intestinal epithelium, on the regenerative cells of the bone marrow, on the microvascular system's endothelial cells, and on embryos. After irradiation a number of effects evolve in which phagocytic function is impaired and electrolyte containment alters. Massive gastrointestinal hemorrhages occur, permitting entry into the body of the gastrointestinal contents.

TABLE 18-2
Acute effects of whole-body irradiation

Dose, rem	Effect
5–20	Possible late effect; possible chromosomal aberrations
20–100	Temporary reduction in leukocytes; after 50 rem temporary sterility in men
100–200	Mild radiation sickness within a few hours: vomiting, diarrhea, fatigue; reduction in resistance to infection; possible bone growth retardation in children
200–300	Serious radiation sickness; effects as in 100–200 above and also bone marrow syndrome (loss of blood-producing tissue), hemorrhage; LD 10-35/30*
300–400	Serious radiation sickness as above; also marrow and intestine destruction; permanent sterility in women; LD 50-70/30
400–1000	Acute illness, early death; LD 60-95/30
1000–5000	Acute illness, early death in days; intestinal syndrome; LD 100/10
Over 5000	Acute illness; death in hours to days; central nervous system syndrome; LD 100/2

*Lethal dose to percentage of population in number of days (for example, LD 10-35/30 means a lethal dose in 10 to 35 percent of the population in 30 days).
Source: Goldman, 1982

ACUTE DOSES FOR ANIMALS. The effects of high-level radiation on mammals are similar to the effects on humans. Horses, cattle, and sheep also receive internal radiation as a result on ingesting food contaminated by radiation from fallout (see Section 18-5). LD 50 (the dosage which, if received in a short time, will kill half the exposed population) for mammals is in the range from 350 to 800 rem. Chickens have an LD 50 of about 900 rem and rodents have an LD 50 of 600 to 800 rem. Bacteria have an LD 50 in the 5000-rem range. With insects there is considerable variability between species with some species having an LD 50 considerably greater than 5000 rem. For example, moths can withstand 25 to 40 kilorems with slight somatic effects, and to kill insects that destroy grain in storage requires 100 to 500 kilorems. This high somatic resistivity to radiation is due to the fact that adult insect cells are not continuously dividing as is the case in mammals. However, radiation doses of 10 kilorems will cause sterility in most insects because cell division must take place in this case.

ACUTE DOSES FOR PLANTS. Plants vary considerably in their response to radiation. For most plants LD 50 is in the range of kilorads. Conifers are more sensitive to radiation than deciduous trees, and seeds and buds are more sensitive than other plant tissue because of their high cell division rate.

Long-Term Radiation Effects

BLOOD DISORDERS. According to Japanese data (Hibakusha, 1977) there was an increase in anemia among persons exposed to the bomb. In some cases the decrease in white and red blood cells persisted for up to 10 years after the bombing.

CATARACTS. Table 18-3 shows the cataract incidence in Nagasaki in survivors who were lightly shielded and suffered partial loss of hair. In order to investigate the factor

TABLE 18-3
Cataract incidence at Nagasaki

Distance from ground zero (km)	Cataract incidence, %
1.0–1.2	96
1.2–1.4	60
1.4–1.6	41
1.6–1.8	15

of age a study was also made of junior and senior high school students exposed to the Hiroshima bomb (ages 12 to 18). The results are presented in Table 18-4.

According to Auxier (1977), the Hiroshima bomb had relatively many more neutrons than that of Nagasaki. However, recent reevaluation of the atomic bombing data using more elaborate computer codes disputes the earlier work (Loewe, 1981 and U.S.–Japan Joint Study, 1987). Even though the neutron flux is now reduced, it could be of some importance in cataract formation since the RBE for neutrons in this instance may be from 4 to 6, as this is observed in animals. According to the U.S.–Japan Study, at 1.05 km from ground zero the calculated neutron and gamma-ray exposures were respectively (including all neutron and gamma-ray energies) 14.9 rad and 112 rad at Hiroshima, and 9.6 rad and 235 rad at Nagasaki.

As was discussed in Chapter 15 and also given graphically in Chapter 7, both gamma-ray and neutron dose levels increase rapidly as ground zero is approached.

MALIGNANT TUMORS. All ionizing radiation is carcinogenic, but some tumor types are generated more readily than others. A prevalent type is leukemia, a disease in which there is an unlimited proliferation of leukocytes, or white blood cells. Figure 18-5 shows the death rates from leukemia in the period 1946-1975 among survivors of Hiroshima. The figure shows that the latent period for leukemia mortality was at

TABLE 18-4
Cataract incidence 12 years after the Hiroshima bombing for survivors exposed during childhood

Distance from ground zero (km)	Eyes examined	Cataract incidence	
		No.	%
0.0–1.0	18	10	56
1.0–1.2	20	10	50
1.2–1.4	18	4	22
1.4–1.6	50	6	12
1.6–1.8	30	0	0
1.8–2.0	38	1	6
2.0–3.0	56	0	0
Total	230	31	13

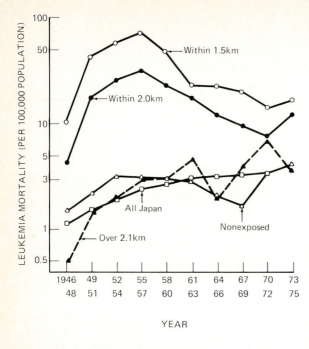

FIGURE 18-5
Changes in leukemia mortality from
Hiroshima survivors by 3-year
intervals from 1946 to 1975. (*From
Hibakuska, 1977.*)

least 2 or 3 years, with a maximum mortality occurring about 10 years after the bombing. The correlation with distance from ground zero is also evident; persons beyond 2.1 kilometers had the same mortality as the general Japanese population.

The cancer incidence among survivors of Hiroshima and Nagasaki is significantly larger than that of the general population, and there is a significant correlation

FIGURE 18-6
The parents of Sadako. Kasuga City, Fukoka, Japan, October 14, 1984. Fujiko Sasaki, beside her husband Shingeo holds a portrait of Sadako, their 12-year-old daughter. Sadako and her mother were in Hiroshima when the atomic bomb exploded. Sadako was 2 years old at the time. The words under the photograph read: Sadako Sasaki. First year, 3. Nobori-machi Junior High School. Subacute lymphatic leukemia. Died: October 25, 1955. A children's story about Sadako is very popular in Japan and has been published in the United States under the title ''Sadako and the Thousand Paper Cranes'' (Coerr, 1977). The title comes from the belief that if Sadako had been able to cut out one thousand paper cranes she would recover from her fatal leukemia. (*Source: ''At Work in the Fields of the Bomb,'' Robert del Tredici, Harper & Row, New York, 1987.*)

between exposure level and degree of increase of malignancies. Inceased incidence has been reported for thyroid cancer, breast cancer, lung cancer, and cancer of the salivary gland. Often a decade or more passes before radiation-caused malignancies appear. Figure 18-6 is a photograph of the parents of Sadako, a girl of junior high school age, who died of leukemia from the atomic bombing of Hiroshima.

In an article in *Science* Leslie Roberts reported (Roberts, 1987) that as a result of the U.S.–Japan Study the excess cancer deaths resulting from a single dose of 1 rem to one million persons had risen from 230 (BEIR, 1980) to between 500 and 1000. The latter numbers were based on a linear-quadratic relationship (something between curves A and B in Figure 18-2). If the response curve is in fact linear then the number of cancer deaths produced by a *single exposure* of 1 rem to a million persons would rise to 1600, according to this article. This figure should be compared with the conservative number recommended earlier in this section of 300 cancer deaths per million persons exposed to an *accumulated* exposure of 1 rem due to low-level radiation exposure. The large range in values reported (300 to 1600) may also be partly due to the large statistical uncertainties in the data.

OTHER SOMATIC EFFECTS. Ionizing radiation from nuclear weapons can also cause hypothyroidism due to destruction of the thyroid gland. Exposure in utero can cause congenital malformation of the fetus, delayed or suppressed growth and development, and mental retardation, as well as an overall increase in infant mortality. Neurosis-like complaints (dizziness and mental instability) were also reported, but were not correlated with radiation level.

GENETIC EFFECTS. The chromosome is the carrier of genes in the nucleus of a cell. Its basic constituent is deoxyribonucleic acid, or DNA. Radiation biology has firmly established that chromosomes are highly vulnerable to ionizing radiation. Radiation provides sufficient energy to break chromosomes apart. When the fragments rejoin, they often reconsitute themselves as they were before the damage, but aberrations can result. Highly ionizing radiation, such as protons recoiling from neutrons, produces a large number of such genetic abberations.

Schull et al. (1981) studied a group of Hiroshima and Nagasaki survivors who had children. Although their study was extensive, they could not find a statistically significant result because of the smallness of the sample. This does not mean that genetic damage from the bombings does not exist or is insignificant. In fact Schull et al. suggested that their findings might be taken in a preliminary way at face value in order to obtain some idea of the possible effect. If this is done, they concluded that exposure to about 156 rem, distributed between the parents, doubled the spontaneous mutation rate. According to James Neel, a new U.S.–Japan study (Marx, 1988) corroborates Schull's result. It gives the doubling dose as in the range from 145 to 255 rems. The genetic indicators used by Schull et al. were fourfold: frequency of abnormal pregnancy outcomes, death of live-born children prior to age 17, frequency of children with sex chromosome aneuploidy (abnormality), and frequency of children with mutation resulting in an electrophoretic variant (alterations of specific proteins).

The doubling dose of 156 is about a factor of 4 higher than the doubling dose obtained in experimental studies on mice. The Hiroshima and Nagasaki study is based on an acute radiation exposure. If accumulated (chronic) lower-level exposures are experienced in mice, the mutation rate is lowered by a factor of 3. If mice and humans are the same in this respect, the doubling dose of humans exposed to chronic lower-level doses should be 468 rem.

The effects of a "genetically significant" 5-rem dose to the gonads of a parental generation on the first generation and descendants is summarized in Table 18-5 in terms of "current incidence." Current incidence describes what is acutally observed in terms of genetic disease in a population and is somewhat higher than the mutation rate since some individuals with mutations continue to reproduce. The data of Parker et al. from the table would require at least 60 times 5 rem, or 300 rem, to double the current incidence of genetic disease in the first generation. According to these data a radiation exposure of 300 rem to a population of one millon persons would produce from 6000 to 60,000 genetic diseases in the first generation and from 18,000 to 420,000 in the second and all later generations.

It is to be noted in conclusion that exposure of a population to several hundred rads of radiation would very likely produce genetic disease, leading to death in some cases, for a significant percentage of that population in either the first or succeeding generations. Over many generations these diseases will be gradually eradicated from the population, since such afflicted individuals are less likely to reproduce. The human misery for those with the diseases and their loved ones would be very real, however.

TABLE 18-5
Estimated effects of 5 rem to the gonads of the parental generation on ensuing generations

Disease classification	Current incidence per million live births	First generation	Second and all later generations
Dominant diseases	10,000	50–500	200–2000
Recessive diseases	1,500	Very few	Very few per generation
Chromosomal diseases	5,000	65	15
Congenital anomalies	15,000		
Anomalies expressed later	10,000	5–500	45–4500
Constitutional and degenerative diseases	15,000		
Totals	60,000	100–1000	300–7000

Source: Parker et al., 1975.

18-5 BIOLOGICAL HAZARDS FROM FALLOUT

Many constituents of fallout are especially hazardous biologically. We review here some of the most important.

Strontium 90

There is an appreciable yield of strontium 90 in the fission process. This isotope, which has a half-life of 27.7 years, is a bone seeker. That is, it behaves chemically, and thus physiologically in a manner similar to calcium. Strontium 90 decays to a daughter nucleus, yttrium 90, which emits beta particles ranging in energy up to 2.27 MeV. This beta radiation can cause serious local damage to bone tissue, producing bone necrosis, tumors, leukemia, and other blood abnormalities.

When animals eat vegetation contaminated with strontium 90, it is not concentrated in their soft tissue. Thus meat has a smaller strontium 90 to calcium ratio than does animal feed. This is also true for cow's milk. This barrier does not operate if an animal inhales or ingests the strontium 90 directly. Contamination of dairy products can be serious. In 1972 60 kilograms of French atmospheric tests conducted some 4000 miles westward of Chile caused a doubling of the radiation dose that lactating infants were exposed to—from the normal 18 millirem per year to 33 millirem. (See Chapter 2, Table 2-2, p. 35.)

The amount of strontium 90 in the body should not exceed 0.027 microcurie per kilogram of calcium. (An adult has about 2 kilograms of calcium.) Amounts greater than that can cause bone cancer. The limit is placed at this low level in part because the residence time of strontium 90 in the skeleton is long-term. Children have a higher metabolic rate in their bones, permitting faster ^{90}Sr uptake. Since a 1-megaton fission explosion releases 0.11 megacurie into the ecosphere, or about 2×10^{12} maximum permissible doses, exposure to strontium 90 fallout represents a serious health problem.

Fallout distribution and ^{90}Sr inventories on the earth from atmospheric testing are given in Figures 16-6 and 16-7.

Cesium 137

Physiologically, cesium behaves in a manner similar to potassium, and is distributed fairly uniformly throughout the body. Its biological half-life is from 50 to 200 days. Cesium 137 is a prominent component of fission products. It has a 30-year half-life and its decay is accompanied by an energetic gamma ray. The result of ingestion of cesium 137 is a fairly uniform irradiation of the body, with a slightly higher concentration in muscles. Cesium 137 can be ingested in material deposited on the leaves of plants. It contributes to gonadal irradiation and genetic damage.

Carbon 14 and Tritium

Carbon 14 is produced by a nuclear reaction of fast neutrons (n, p reaction) with the nitrogen 14 of the atmosphere. It has a half-life of 5730 years and emits beta particles of about 50 keV with no gamma rays. ^{14}C does not concentrate in any particular body organ, but is distributed throughout the body. It is present in nature as a result of interaction of cosmic rays with the atmosphere (making possible radiocarbon archeological dating). In 1952 the background dose of ^{14}C was about 1 millirem per year. Because of nuclear testing this dose had been doubled by 1964. It will take about 100 years for the ^{14}C from these nuclear tests to be removed from our immediate environment by dissolution into the oceans as carbon dioxide. ^{14}C in the gonads can contribute to genetic damage.

Tritium is produced in copious amounts during a thermonuclear explosion. It has a half-life of 12.3 years and is incorporated in the body by ingestion of food and water or inhalation of tritiated water vapor (in which one or both of the hydrogen atoms in the water molecule is replaced with tritium). The average energies of the beta particles from tritium are only 6 keV. Nevertheless, they are dangerous; for example, they can cause lung cancer. The annual radiation level of tritium in the 1960s was less than 0.1 millirem, even at the height of the atmospheric testing.

Plutonium

When a plutonium fission weapon is exploded, not all of the plutonium is fissioned. In Section P9-6 a calculation was made for a uranium bomb which showed that if 10 percent of 5 kilograms of uranium were fissioned, 10 kilotons of explosive energy would result. A calculation for plutonium would give a similar result. The Nagasaki bomb, made from plutonium, had a yield of 21 kilotons. About 1.1 kilograms of plutonium was fissioned. The actual amount of plutonium in this bomb is not declassified, but it is likely to have been less than 5 kilograms. Thus about 90 percent of the plutonium was released to the biosphere. Presumably the fission yield has been improved in recent years, yet it is likely that some vaporized plutonium will be released in the environment after the explosion of any bomb containing plutonium.

Plutonium is handled in reprocessing plants for material used in weapons and in military nuclear power reactors. (Used fuel rods from civilian reactors are not at present reprocessed in the United States.) Plutonium is extremely toxic, so great care must be taken to prevent its release into the environment. Unfortunately, such releases did occur at the plutonium processing facility at Rocky Flats, Colorado, requiring permanent evacuation of some of the immediate surrounding area.

Plutonium 239 has a half-life of 24,400 years. It has a biological half-life of 100 years in the skeleton and 40 years in the liver. If it is in the form of insoluble dioxide, it also has a long residence time in the alveolar spaces of the lungs. Its short-range but highly ionizing (high-RBE) alpha particles can cause serious injury, such as the formation of bone and lung tumors. Ingestion of as little as 1 microgram of plutonium—a barely visible speck—is a serious health hazard.

Iodine 131

Although ^{131}I has a relatively short half-life, 8.05 days, ingestion of ^{131}I is followed by a large uptake of the radioactivity by the thyroid gland. The biological residence time is about 80 days. In sufficient amounts ^{131}I radioactivity can destroy all or part of the gland, leading to hypothyroidism. The effect can be partially averted by blocking the thyroid with large intakes of iodine. During the Three Mile Island nuclear power accident in 1979 plans were under way to distribute potassium iodide to the population of eastern Pennsylvania. However, delays made it impossible to provide the potassium iodide blocking agent during the critical period. Fortunately, only relatively small releases of ^{131}I actually took place. Had large ^{131}I releases taken place, the area's inhabitants would have been at risk for hypothyroidism and other thyroid diseases.

In the Bravo test, the Marshallese on Rongelap Atoll were exposed to fallout (see Section 16-3). Of 19 children under 10, 17 developed thyroid abnormalities, including one malignancy and two cases of hypothyroidism.

ADDITONAL PHYSICS SECTION

In this section we give more detail about the mechanisms by which gamma rays, x-rays, and neutrons interact with matter in biological systems. The ionization produced in such interactions damages cells by assisting in the formation of poisonous chemical compounds or by direct molecular breakage.

P18-2   THE PHYSICAL MECHANISMS FOR BIOLOGICAL DAMAGE

Gamma Rays and X-Rays

Gamma rays produce ionization via the Compton effect and the photoelectric effect. For gamma energies above several MeV, pair production occurs, but this can generally be neglected because most gamma rays from substances of biological interest are of lower energy. *Pair production* refers to the process by which an electron-positron pair is created from a gamma ray.

The photoelectric effect refers to a process in which a photon is completely absorbed by an atom and the photon's energy is given to an atomic electron, which is then ejected from the atom with an energy which is the proton energy $h\nu$ less the binding energy of the electron to the atom, W.

$$\text{Ejected electron energy} = h\nu - W \qquad \text{(P18-1)}$$

In contrast to the Compton effect, there is no scattered photon at all. With both the Compton effect and the photoelectric effect some of the inital photon energy is trans-

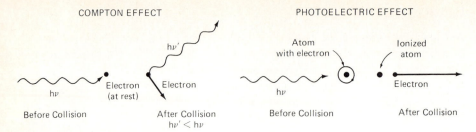

FIGURE 18-7
The Compton effect and the photoelectric effect.

formed into the kinetic energy of a recoiling electron. The electron produces ionization, leading to cell damage, as discussed above. Figure 18-7 shows these two effects schematically.

Neutrons

Neutrons do not have an electric charge. An interaction with nuclei of atoms in biological tissue needs to take place before they can produce ionization. Neutrons have a fairly high probability of interacting with the hydrogen nuclei (protons) in the body. A great deal of hydrogen is present—in proteins, fat, other complex molecules, and water, which comprises about 80 percent of body weight. In the interaction with hydrogen the energy lost by the neutron is gained by the recoiling proton, a heavily ionizing particle which can produce extensive cell damage. One rad of fast neutrons (neutrons with a neutron kinetic energy greater than 1 MeV) is about 5 times more likely to produce cataracts in the eye than is 1 rad of gamma radiation. That is, fast neutrons have an RBE of 5 in the eye.

Figure 18-8 shows the scattering of a neutron by a hydrogen nucleus. After the collision, the neutron has reduced kinetic energy and the energy lost by the neutron appears as kinetic energy of the recoiling proton. Since the proton is a charged particle, it produces ionization in the biological tissue by means of its electric field.

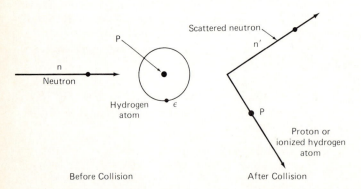

FIGURE 18-8
Elastic scattering of a neutron by a hydrogen nucleus.

QUESTIONS

1. What are the two principal mechanisms by which gamma radiation (and x-radiation) produce ionizing particles in biological tissue?
2. How do neutrons produce ionization in tissue?
3. How is the quality factor related to RBE?
4. Define a rad?
5. Discuss carcinogenesis at low doses of radiation.
6. What radioisotope can cause hypothyroidism and how does this occur?
7. Why is plutonium dispersed finely in the air a health problem?

PROBLEMS

1. If a person is exposed to 100 rad of neutrons which have an RBE of 5 for production of eye cataracts, how many rem of neutrons radiation is the eye exposed to?
2. How many rad does it take to produce death in 50 percent of normal individuals within a month's time?
3. If a person survives a nuclear attack, but is exposed to 200 rad of radiation, what is the chance of cancer in some form in subsequent years?
4. If a population of 100 million is exposed to 200 rad of radiation, how many genetic abnormalities will occur in the first generation of children of the survivors? How many abnormalities will occur in the second and future generations?

KEY WORDS

background radiation   background radiation is that found naturally in our environment. It is formed from cosmic rays and natural radioactivity.

carcinogenic   producing cancer (in terms of this text via exposure to ionizing radiation).

ionization   process in which one or more electrons are removed from an atom or molecule leaving it with a positive charge.

LD50   a lethal dose for 50 percent of a normal population for radiation administered over a small interval of time.

linear hypothesis   the assumption that any dose of radiation will have a biological effect even though the effects of low-level doses are difficult or impossible to measure. The assumption is that effects clearly seen at higher radiation levels will still persist at lower levels in a manner proportional to the radiation dose or exposure.

mutation rate   the rate at which genetic material (DNA in cells) is altered to produce genetic changes. The mutation rate can be **spontaneous** as it occurs naturally or be increased due to ionizing radiation.

rad   the energy of ionizing radiation absorbed by a body per unit of body weight. One rad is defined as 0.01 joule absorbed per kilogram.

RBE   relative biological effectiveness. A measure of the response of given biological material to a particular kind of ionizing radiation. For example, neutrons of over 1 MeV have an RBE of about 5 in forming cataracts in the human eye.

rem   roentgen equivalent mammal (or man); rem is the product of rads with RBE and hence is a more precise measure of the biological effect of radiation.

roentgen   the intensity of ionizing radiation that can produce 2.58×10^{-4} coulombs of free charge per kilogram of air (or 1 e.s.u. of charge per cubic centimeter of air).

PART
III

CONSEQUENCES

Power is like a drug: the need for either is unknown to anyone who has not tried them, but after the initiation, which can be fortuitous, the dependency and need for even larger doses is born, as are the denial of reality . . .

[T]he syndrome produced by protracted and undisputed power is clearly visible: a distorted view of the world, dogmatic arrogance, the need for adulation, convulsive clinging to the levers of command, and contempt for the law.

Primo Levi, *The Drowned and the Saved*, p. 67

CHAPTER
19

STRATEGIC NUCLEAR EXCHANGE BY THE SUPERPOWERS

The storm . . . this storm you talk of. . . . It will be such a one, my son, as the world has not seen before. There will be no safety by arms, no help by authority, no answer in science. It will range till every flower of culture is trampled and all human things are leveled in a vast chaos. . . . The Dark Ages that are to come will cover the whole world in a single pall; there will be neither escape nor sanctuary.

James Hilton, *Lost Horizon*, 1922

Convictions are more dangerous foes of truth than lies

Friedrich Wilhelm Nietzche

19-1 THEMES

In previous chapters we studied the effects of individual nuclear weapons. We are now in a position to consider the consequences of general nuclear war in which all the weapons effects would occur simultaneously and there would be over ten thousand nuclear explosions within a short period of time. (In the following discussion we neglect the effects of the possible use of tactical nuclear weapons.)

If deterrence should fail and the superpowers deliver against each other most of the megatonnage in their strategic nuclear arsenals—using ICBMs, SLBMs, cruise missiles, and long-range bombers, what would be the effects? The total number of strategic warheads in the United States and the Soviet arsenals in 1982 was 19,000, and about 23,000 in 1985 (see Chapter 3). The megatonnage in 1988 was about 4000 and 8000 megatons in the strategic arsenals of the United States and the Soviet Union,

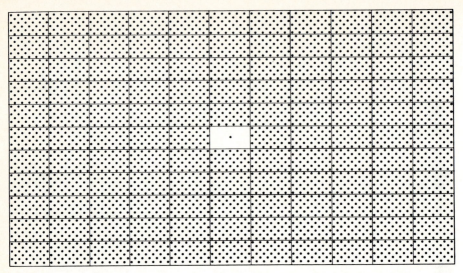

- The one middle dot represents all the bombs used in WWII including the atomic bombs exploded on Hiroshima and Nagasaki (3 MT).
- The weapons of one square are enough to destroy all the large and medium-sized cities of the world (100 MT).
- Eight dots represent the destructive power of a Trident submarine (24 MT).
- The total number of dots, about 4,000, represents the 12,000 MT in the arsenals, of the superpowers, or about one million Hiroshima bombs.

FIGURE 19-1
Comparison of different kinds of explosive power.

respectively. This chapter explores the short-term effects of a nuclear exchange by the superpowers defined as the aggregate effects of blast, thermal radiation, initial nuclear radiation, and early fallout, and the long-term effects, which include extended fallout, smoke and dust obscuration, and ozone depletion.

The conclusion that emerges is that the target nations would almost certainly cease to exist as functioning societies. Also, a major exchange would probably cause massive fires, which would deposit fine smoke particles in the upper atmosphere. This would reduce the temperature and sunlight intensity at the earth's surface, and could cause serious problems for agriculture and the ecosphere. There would also be ozone depletion of the upper atmosphere, a large residual radiation level, and dissemination of toxic gases from the fires. The result might be the destruction of large portions of the ecosphere, including the capability to raise food. The effects would be particularly pronounced in the northern hemisphere, but could possibly extend to tropical areas and the southern hemisphere as well. Thus, although nonparticipants in an all-out nuclear exchange might not be affected immediately, eventually they could suffer seriously. Figure 19-1 compares the megatonnage dropped in World War II with the megatonnage that is now estimated to be available to the superpowers in their strategic arsenals. The one middle dot in the figure represents all the bombs used in World War II, including the atomic bombs exploded on Hiroshima and Nagaski (3 megatons).

FIGURE 19-2
All the warheads in the U.S. nuclear arsenal. This field of ceramic nose cones represents in miniature all the warheads in the U.S. nuclear arsenal. Estimates set the total at about 25,000. Amber Waves of Grain installation, Boston Science Museum, Boston, MA. (*Source: At Work in The Fields of the Bomb, Robert del Tredici, Harper & Row, New York, 1987.*)

The weapons of one square (100 megatons) would be enough to destroy all the large and medium-sized cities of the world.

Eight dots represent the destructive power of a Trident submarine (24 megatons). The total number of dots, 4000, represents the 12,000 megatons in the arsenals of the superpowers, or about 1 million Hiroshima bombs. Figure 19-2 shows an artist's model of the total number of nuclear warheads of the United States (about 25,000) in the form of ceramic nose cones.

19-2   LOCAL, OR DIRECT, EFFECTS

The **direct effects** of blast, thermal radiation, and initial nuclear radiation can be estimated using calculations given in Chapters 13 to 18. For the large bombs in strategic arsenals, the effect of the initial nuclear radiation is masked by blast and thermal effects.

The OTA Study

The Office of Technology Assessment (1979) made an estimate of the effects of a large-scale attack by the Soviets on U.S. military and economic targets. This scenario assumes a direct attack on 250 U.S. cities, with a total yield of 7800 megatons. The study concludes:

> A large Soviet attack against the United States would be devastating . . . (with) physical destruction of a high percentage of the U.S. economic and industrial capacity. . . . The full range of effects resulting from thousands of warheads—most having yields of a megaton or greater—impacting near U.S. cities can only be discussed in terms of uncertainty and speculation. . . . The DOD 1977 study estimated that 155 million to 165 million Americans would be killed by this attack if no civil defense measures were taken and all the weapons were ground burst. . . . [The] Arms Control and Disarmament Agency analysis of a similar attack where only one half the weapons were ground burst gave 105 million to 135 million.

OTA also estimated that U.S. fatalities would be reduced to about 22 to 50 million if relocation and sheltering were possible. No attempt was made by OTA to estimate serious injuries, but they would be in the tens of millions. Further, there would be little prospect of medical treatment, since most medical facilities are in the cities and would thus be destroyed. There would be additional millions of deaths from radiation sickness and from weakening of the body's immune system.

OTA estimates that a similar attack by U.S. forces on the Soviet Union would kill 50 to 100 million Soviet citizens; at least 80 percent of these deaths would be due to direct effects of blast and thermal radiation. Estimates of the total number of U.S.

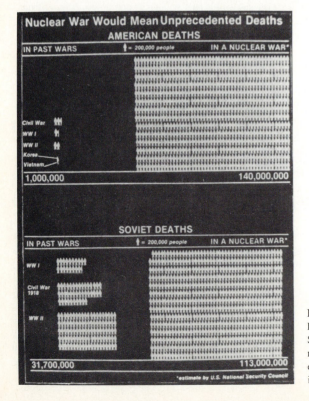

FIGURE 19-3

Expected fatalities in the United States and the Soviet Union as a result of a full-scale nuclear exchange compared with fatalities in previous wars.

and Soviet citizens that would be killed in such an exchange range from 155 million to 265 million if no civil defense measures were taken.

Figure 19-3 compares the estimated fatalities in the United States and the Soviet Union after an all-out nuclear exchange with previous losses in wars. Such losses are unimaginable. We have no experience with which to compare them. The Soviet Union suffered 20 million fatalities in World War II, an experience which has permanently affected the attitudes of its citizens. But a loss of 20 million is small compared with the losses that would be sustained after a full-scale nuclear exchange.

Figure 19-4 shows possible fallout patterns from a nuclear attack on the 400 sites designated by the Federal Emergency Management Administration as high-risk areas.

Fallout areas at 1 hour after detonation

Fallout areas at 24 hours after detonation

FIGURE 19-4
Local fallout patterns from a nuclear strike on 400 high-risk areas in the United States.

Ambio Studies

The Royal Swedish Academy of Sciences has examined the possible human and ecological consequences of nuclear war. Its studies, published in the journal *Ambio* in 1982, were later collected and published in book form (*Aftermath*). In the *Ambio* scenario, nuclear war is assumed to have spread to truly global dimensions (*Ambio*, 1983):

> In this reference scenario North America, Europe and the Soviet Union are regarded as the main strategic areas in a nuclear war, although a number of other countries are considered important for strategic and political purposes. The great powers might decide to target some countries to prevent them from dominating international politics following a nuclear war. . . . The Soviet warheads are targeted mainly on North America, Europe, and China, which is a more widespread and complicated pattern of targets than that of the U.S., whose targets are mainly concentrated in the Soviet Union.
>
> There are three categories of targets in this scenario: population targets, military targets and economic/industrial targets. It should be noted that military/industrial targets are often located in or near cities. . . .
>
> This scenario assumes that bombs detonated at ground level will maximize the number of casualties from local fallout, but will greatly reduce the number of immediate deaths from the effects of blast. The division between ground and air bursts chosen in this scenario differs from that assumed in most other descriptions of nuclear war. The effect is to emphasize the immediate environmental impact of the explosions.

The *Ambio* study assumes that cities in the United States, Canada, Western Europe, Eastern Europe, the U.S.S.R., Japan, North and South Korea, Vietnam, Australia, South Africa, and Cuba are targeted with the megatonnages given in Table 19-1. For example, according to the table there are (630 cities) × (163,000 deaths per city) = 103,000,000 people killed in cities of 100,000 to 300,000 population.

TABLE 19-1
Ambio estimates of injuries and death following a global exchange

Population* range injured, millions	No. of cities	Weapons used†	People killed, millions per city	People injured, millions per city	Total killed, millions	Total injured, millions
0.1–0.3	630	300 kt × 3 100 kt × 1	0.163	0.008	103	5
0.3–1.0	600	300 kt × 3 100 kt × 1	0.414	0.103	248	62
1.0–3.0	219	1Mt × 3	1.14	0.430	250	94
3.0–10.0	52	500 kt × 10 1 Mt × 5	4.10	1.000	213	52
Over 10	13	500 kt × 10	4.00	5.150	52	67
Total	1514				866	260

*The population density is assumed to be uniform and to be 8000 persons per square kilometer.
†The energy release and number of warheads used on each city in the specified populations class; for example three 300-kiloton weapons is 300 kt × 3.

The *Ambio* study thus gives the total number killed initially in all cities as about 866 million. Many of the injured would die within a few weeks from latent effects of radiation and infectious diseases, making the overall death figure about 1 billion people. In this study cities receive a total of 4970 warheads and 1941 megatons; 4845 warheads are targeted in the northern hemisphere. The study assumes that most industry will be destroyed with the cities, and that air bursts are used to destroy remaining industries, power plants, oil refineries, and oil fields. This accounts for 3136 more warheads and 701 more megatons.

Military targets, such as air bases, army bases, naval ports, straits, ICBMs, and nuclear submarines, are targeted with 6641 warheads and 3100 megatons. Many of the military installations are located close to cities, subjecting the cities to additional damage and casualties.

The total is 14,747 warheads, delivering a total of 5741 megatons, or about two-thirds of the warheads and one-half of the megatonnage in the superpowers' arsenals.

The WHO Study

The World Health Organization (WHO) estimated that a large-scale nuclear exchange might kill 1.1 billion people outright and seriously injure an equal number. This study estimates that nearly one-half of the human population would be immediate casualties of a nuclear war (Borgstrom et al., 1983). These figures do not take into account environmental effects.

19-3 GLOBAL, OR INDIRECT, EFFECTS

Delayed Fallout

R. P. Turco and his coworkers calculate that in a 10,000-megaton exchange, 2 × their baseline (5000-Mt) case, the northern hemisphere *average* dose of **delayed fallout** (that which falls out after 2 days) would be about 40 rad (Turco et al., 1983).

This calculation assumes no sheltering or weathering of the dust. In northern midlatitudes the radiation level would be 2 to 3 times greater, or about 100 rad. These authors also estimate that there would be an additional 100 rad of exposure to specific body organs from internal beta and gamma emitters that had been ingested, giving a total of 200 rad to some body organs. Those doses, according to the authors, are "roughly an order of magnitude larger than previous estimates, which neglected intermediate-timescale washout and fallout of tropospheric nuclear debris from low-yield (less than 1 megaton) detonations." Because of the inhomogeneity of the actual fallout deposition, there would be midlatitude areas where individuals would receive appreciably more, perhaps lethal doses, of this delayed fallout, and there would be other areas where less exposure would be encountered. It should be emphasized that the above fallout exposures are in *addition* to the dose received from the early fallout in the direct plume of a nuclear explosion (see Chapter 16).

"Oooooooooooooooo!"

Fallout can be a serious health hazard, both because of external radiation, principally from gamma rays, and because of internal radiation due to ingestion of radioactive materials (see Chapters 16 and 18). In Chapter 18 the number of deaths from cancer induced by accumulated external radiation was estimated conservatively to be about 30,000 per million persons exposed to 100 rem. Recent analysis of data from Hiroshima indicate that the figure might be larger for a single exposure to direct atomic bomb radiation rather than low-level exposure. This analysis gives from 50,000 to 100,000 deaths per million persons per 100 rem of exposure (Roberts, 1987). *Ambio* (1983, p. 66) gives a figure of 12,500 deaths per million persons per 100 rad. For exposure in utero in the first trimester, the same source states that "100 rad might engender a fatal childhood cancer risk of 10 percent," which would be 100,000 per million so exposed. This is because embryonic tissue is rapidly dividing and is very sensitive to radiation.

Ambio made estimates of radiation levels, cancer deaths, and genetic deaths for various regions of the northern hemisphere for the direct-effect scenario described

TABLE 19-2
A summary of the effects of external radiation from fallout in the northern hemisphere in the *Ambio* scenario

	North America	Western Europe	Soviet Union
Percent receiving more than 100 rad	60.4	52.8	48.3
Acute radiation deaths	52,000,000	68,000,000	44,000,000
Cancer deaths	2,100,000	2,800,000	1,900,000
Genetic deaths	1,000,000	1,200,000	800,000
Permanent sterility	5,000,000	7,000,000	4,000,000

above, i.e., for 5740 Mt. (See Table 19-2.) The term *acute radiation death* refers to death occurring within a few weeks, whereas death from cancer can occur any time over a period of years. Genetic deaths are given for the first generation only. If all succeeding generations were included, the number of deaths would be about 2 to 3 times larger (see Chapter 18).

The total consequence of external radiation is estimated by Coggle and Lindpop (*Ambio*, 1983): "By the most conservative estimates the survivors of a nuclear war will suffer from 5.4 to 12.8 million fatal cancers; 17 to 31 million people will be rendered sterile; and 6.4 to 16.3 million children will be born with genetic defects during the subsequent 100 years." If the figure 30,000 cancer deaths per million given previously (see Chapter 18) is used, the TTAPS study indicates cancer fatalities of at least 30 million people, assuming one billion people are exposed in northern mid-latitudes.

The above estimates are for external radiation and do not include the effects of internal radiation due to ingestion of iodine 131, cesium 137, strontium 90, and other radioactive materials present in the fallout. Bonidetti (*Ambio*, 1983) estimates that during the first week after fallout deposition 1 quart of milk would give an infant thyroid a dose of 200 rem, enough to cause serious damage to the thyroid gland. This exposure was calculated for a deposition of 0.5 curie per square kilometer of strontium 90, which, it is estimated, would occur about 200 miles downwind from a 1-megaton explosion.

Ambio also estimates that agricultural workers at the same location would receive about 200 rem of exposure in the first year after the explosion due to ingestion of radioactive materials. This is about 10,000 times the normal internal radiation exposure, which is 18 millirem per year (Chapter 18). Eventually about 0.4 curie per square kilometer of strontium 90 would be deposited over the northern hemisphere. This estimate is obtained by multiplying the observed ^{90}Sr from atmospheric tests in the early 1960s by the ratio (23) of the megatonnage assumed in the *Ambio* scenario to that of the tests.

If the calculations of Turco et al. for global fallout levels are used, as well as the conservative estimate from Chapter 18 of cancer deaths induced by low-level external radiation, a much larger prediction of cancer deaths results. To make the prediction the following is assumed:

1. The global fallout is concentrated in the 30 to 60 degree region of north latitude, the fallout region. This results in a concentration of fallout about a factor of 2.5 greater than the value obtained by Turco et al. in which the fallout was averaged over the entire northern hemisphere.
2. The Turco et al. base case of 5000 Mt is used in order to compare more directly with the *Ambio* study. Their result is then an exposure of 50 rem per person in the fallout region.
3. Assume there are one billion persons living in the fallout region.

The number of cancer deaths from a 5000-Mt exchange is then 30,000 cancer deaths/100 rem/million × 1 billion people × 50 rem, or 15 million deaths. Turco et al. estimate a similar exposure to internal radiation, which would add another 15 million cancer deaths. If the global exchange was at the 10,000-megaton level (some 80 percent of the superpower arsenals), then the total number of cancer deaths from global fallout could reach 60 million persons in the northern hemisphere according to the calculations of Turco et al. Many of these deaths would occur in countries other than the superpowers.

Reactors as Targets

If nuclear reactors were destroyed in an attack, the fallout would contain much longer-lived radioactivity. One year after an attack the fallout from a demolished 1000-megawatt reactor which had been in operation for some time would be about 30 times greater than that from a 1-megaton bomb. The area of contamination where one would receive 100 rad or more during the 12 months after detonation—starting 1 month after detonation—is 2000 square kilometers for a 1-megaton bomb—but 34,000 square kilometers, extending 500 kilometers downwind, for a 1-megaton bomb on a 1000-megawatt nuclear reactor (Fetter, 1981). The additional exposure could upset civil defense plans. Reactor targeting has not been included in the scenarios discussed above. Since at present there are about one hundred power reactors in the northern hemisphere, an attack targeting reactors could make an already serious situation very much worse (Ramberg, 1980).

The Chernobyl Experience

On April 26, 1986, the Chernobyl graphite reactor in the Soviet Union suffered a catastrophic internal explosion and fire due to operator error. As a result this 1000-megawatt (billion watt) reactor released about one-half of its volatile radioelements such as cesium 137 (half-life 30 years), and iodine 131 (half-life 8.05 days), and many others. Fortunately the refractory elements such as strontium 90 (half-life 27.7 years) and plutonium 239 (half-life 24,400 years) were released in much less quantity.

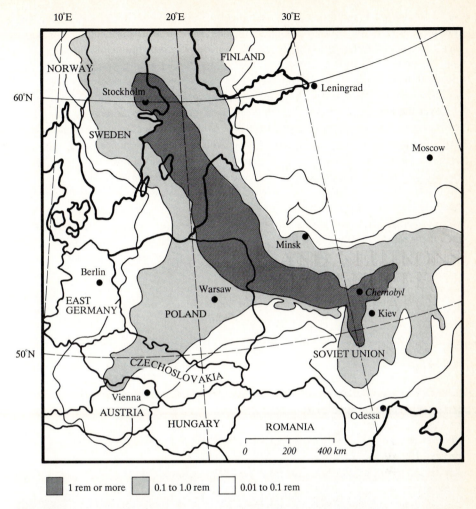

FIGURE 19-5
Inhalation doses to the thyroid gland from iodine 131 released by the Chernobyl reactor three days after the accident according to data assembled by the Lawrence Livermore National Laboratory. (*Source: "Estimating Long-Term Health Effects," Frank von Hippel and Thomas B. Cochran, Bulletin of the Atomic Scientists, August/September 1986.*)

This would not be the case if the reactor were subject to nuclear attack, whereupon its contents might be vaporized.

This incident is an interesting case study of the fact that radioactive fallout is no respecter of national boundaries and of the fragility of modern civilizations to its impact. Figure 19-5 shows the extent to which radioactive fallout had dispersed in three days, by April 29, and gives the radiation exposures to citizens of the respective countries involved. The radioactivity on the ground was particularly pronounced when rainfall occurred in subsequent days in Great Britain (May 2) and Italy.

Von Hippel and Cochran (von Hippel, 1986) estimated the exposure to the European population by correlating radiation levels with population. They concluded that there would be 2000 to 40,000 thyroid tumor cases (from iodine 131 inhalation) and that a few percent of these would be fatal. There would be 10,000 to 250,000 potential thyroid tumor cases from iodine 131 absorbed via the grass-cow-milk route in the absence by public health authorities to block this exposure route. Cesium 137 was predicted to produce 3500 to 70,000 cancer cases of which approximately one-half would be fatal. These cancers will not develop for the next few decades. The West German government did indeed block the distribution of powdered milk that came from milk contaminated with cesium 137. Figure 19-6 shows the "whey train" parked on a siding and filled with 250 tons of contaminated milk.

The Chernobyl fallout was detected in about two weeks in the United States but had dispersed and decayed to such an extent that it was barely detectable.

Using Figure 19-5 we can make a very crude estimate of cancer deaths to be expected from Chernobyl. Assume that about 50 million persons in the heavily affected area received eventually one rem of radiation. Actually more persons were exposed

FIGURE 19-6
The whey train. The whey train sits in an out-of-the-way trainyard in the small town of Kolbermoor, outside Munich. Its cargo is 250 tons of radioactive whey powder from the Meggle milk factory in Bavaria. The powder is contaminated with cesium 137 from the Chernobyl cloud. The Bavarian government tried unsuccessively to bury the powder, incinerate it, and sell it as food to Egypt. Kolbermoor, West Germany, December 28, 1986. (*Source: At Work in the Fields of the Bomb, Robert del Tredici, Harper & Row, New York, 1987.*)

to varying degrees of radiation and in more countries than Figure 19-5 shows. According to Chapter 18 a conservative estimate is 300 cancer deaths in a lifetime per rem of exposure per million persons exposed. We would then predict 300×50, or 15,000, radiation-induced cancer deaths to occur over the lifetimes of the exposed populations.

To compare with the radiation exposure from a nuclear exchange, according to Fetter (Fetter, 1981), the radiation level from a 300-kt thermonuclear weapon is about the same as from a 1-gigawatt reactor (such as Chernobyl) if it is measured one day after the explosion in each case. At 10 hours it is the same as a 70-kt thermonuclear weapon. After a year it is the same as 30 1-megaton weapons. The ratio is time-dependent because nuclear weapons have a much larger proportion of short-lived radioactivity than a reactor that has been in operation for a year or more, such as the one at Chernobyl. Since only about one-half of the radioactivity was released, the sizes of the equivalent nuclear weapons referred to above should be reduced by a factor of two. Or we may say that at 10 hours after a nuclear war began using 10,000 megatons of the arsenals, the resulting radioactivity level would be the equivalent of

$$\frac{10{,}000 \times 1000 \text{ kt}}{35 \text{ kt/Chernobyl}} = 290{,}000 \text{ Chernobyls!}$$

Ozone Depletion

When a 1-megaton bomb explodes in the air, chemical reactions produce copious quantities of nitrogen oxides, NO and NO_2. After the fireball cools, these oxides [about 1×10^{32} molecules for a 1-megaton explosion (Glasstone and Dolan, 1977)] are carried into the upper atmosphere, where they reduce the concentration of ozone.*

The normal amount of ozone in the atmosphere is about 10 parts per million. This small amount is effective in absorbing ultraviolet radiation from the sun.

In the tropics, a 50 percent decrease in ozone increases the amount of sunburn in a given time by a factor of 6, and a 70 percent decrease in ozone increases the sunburn by a factor of 16. The ozone layer at a latitude of 40 degrees is about 20 percent thicker than in the tropics, so that a 60 percent decrease at 40 degrees latitude has about the same effect as a 50 percent decrease in the tropics. After such a 60

---

*Ozone is formed principally in the stratosphere through the Chapman cycle:

$$O_2 + h\nu \rightarrow O + O$$
$$O + O_2 + M \rightarrow O_3 \text{ (ozone)} + M$$

where M is a nonreacting molecule that absorbs energy and $h\nu$ represents an optical photon. Oxides of nitrogen form a catalytic cycle to reduce ozone:

$$NO + O_3 \rightarrow NO_2 + O_2$$
$$\underline{NO_2 + O \rightarrow NO + O_2}$$
$$\text{net } O + O_3 \rightarrow 2O_2$$

The reactions $NO_2 + h\nu \rightarrow NO + O$ and $NO_2 + O \rightarrow NO + O_2$ also occur, so either NO_2 or NO can be important in reducing ozone.

percent reduction in ozone, detectable sunburn (erythema) occurs in about 2 minutes and an incapacitating sunburn (blistering or hemorrhage) in 30 minutes. When unshielded eyes encounter an environment with 60 percent **ozone depletion,** snow blindness occurs within minutes. Human beings wearing sunglasses might avoid this. Some animals, however, would be blinded.

According to Duewer et al. (1978), after a nuclear explosion nitrogen oxide pulse injections occur at stabilization altitudes (the altitude at which the mushroom cloud flattens out) as follows:

Weapon size, Mt	Altitude, km
0.025	9.5–16.5
1.00	12.5–21.5
4.00	17.5–28.5

The stratosphere extends roughly from 40,000 to 100,000 feet, or 12 to 30 kilometers, in the summer and begins at approximately 30,000 feet, or 9 kilometers, in the winter. Therefore weapons of 1 megaton or greater yield will inject a major part of the nitrogen oxides into the stratosphere, while weapons of lower yield will deliver them predominantly to the troposphere.

In the troposphere a complex series of photochemical reactions produces ozone from methane. If the weapon yield is such that only the lower limit of the stratosphere is reached by the mushroom cloud, then it is possible to actually have an ozone *increase*. However, if a large pulse of nitrogen oxides reaches the middle stratosphere, it will cause a substantial ozone reduction which can overwhelm the relatively modest ozone increase in the lower stratosphere and troposphere.

The model of ozone depletion in Figure 19-7 assumes uniform changes in ozone over the entire northern hemisphere and calculates ozone depletion for 1.0- and 4-megaton bombs used in 1000-, 5000-, and 10,000-Mt exchanges. In midlatitudes, where the nuclear explosions would probably take place, there would be considerably greater changes (by factors of 2 or 3 at least).

A substantial reduction in ozone would produce significant changes in the ecosystem. Plankton in the sea are quite sensitive to ultraviolet radiation and would be killed in great numbers. These small marine animals are the basic food supply for many other marine species. Ultraviolet exposure also inhibits plant growth, reduces photosynthesis, and influences the pollination behavior of insects. It is possible that continuous exposure to greatly increased ultraviolet radiation could cause permanent corneal damage in mammals (permanent snow blindness), with catastrophic consequences for the ecosystem.

A 50 percent decrease in ozone produces a 10 percentage increase in skin cancer. This type of cancer is 99 percent curable, but only if adequate medical facilities exist and there is early detection. A small number of skin cancers are malignant melanomas.

Calculations done by the *Ambio* group have shown that the ozone-depletion effect depends to a large extent on the nuclear scenario chosen. For a scenario using relatively small weapons, ozone is deposited in the troposphere and there is little ozone depletion. Another model, which distributes 10,000 megatons equally between 1- and 5-megaton bombs, suggests ozone reductions of 70 percent (Whitten et al.,

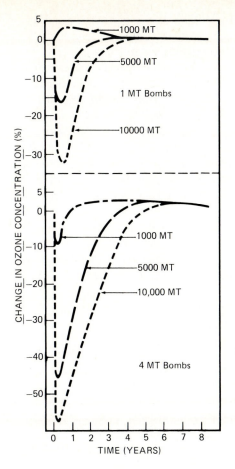

FIGURE 19-7

Calculated ozone depletion vs. time for bombs of (a) 1 megaton and (b) 4 megatons. Long dashes and dots: 1000-megaton exchange; long dashes: 5000-megaton exchange; short dashes: 10,000-megaton exchange. (*From Duewer et al., 1978.*)

1975). Ozone recovery is exponential, with a time constant of about 3 years. That is, ozone concentrations would be back to 63 percent of normal in 3 years and 86 percent of normal in 6 years.

The fact that ozone levels take some years to return to normal is important in that the ozone-depletion effect may still be present after any major smoke and dust effect has dissipated.

Ozone Depletion from Nuclear Weapon Tests in the Atmosphere

Nuclear tests in the atmosphere provide us with some empirical evidence as to ozone reduction through scavenging by the oxides of nitrogen in the stratosphere.

Analysis of nuclear weapons tests in 1961–1962 (300 megatons total) by Chang et al. (1979) predicted a maximum ozone depletion of 4 percent in 1963. During the period 1960–1962 there was a decrease of about 2 percent from normal, and this was followed by an increase of 4.4 percent in the 1963–1970 period. These data are consistent with the expected magnitude of ozone depletion, but a cause-and-effect relationship was by no means established. The timing of the observed changes suggests that effects other than nuclear weapons tests were also present.

More recent analysis with a two-dimensional atmospheric model rather than the one-dimensional model of Chang has shown as much as a 5 percent diminution of the protective ozone layer over the central United States as a result of atmospheric nuclear tests in the late 1950s and early 1960s (Wuebbles, 1988). The effect was maximum in 1963 at 45° latitude and slowly decreased to normal at the end of the 1960s. The damage was even greater in the Arctic where as much as 12 percent of the ozone layer reportedly vanished. These results were obtained by comparing the improved model with known global ozone data of the period. A high correlation resulted, giving confidence in some of the model's predictions. Ozone monitoring stations during the period of nuclear testing were not nearly as good as they are at present, so the correlation is not as precise as could be obtained currently; nevertheless there is a definite effect from nuclear testing in this new study. A total of 477 nuclear bombs were exploded in the atmosphere from 1946 until the Limited Test Ban Treaty went into effect in 1963, with a considerable number in the megaton range.

Estimates of Ozone Depletion in a Global Nuclear Exchange

As Figure 19-7 illustrates, if the warhead yield is smaller, then less ozone change is predicted. Since warheads are now typically about 300 kilotons rather than in the megaton range of the late 1950s and early 1960s, the ozone change produced by the *nuclear fireball alone* would be predicted to be less, since less of the nitrogen oxides would reach the stratosphere.

However, recent studies indicate that in a nuclear war the smoke from burning cities and forests, as well as oil and gas-well fires may seriously affect the ozone layer (Glatzmaier, 1989). This new mechanism results from the fact that the soot absorbs sunlight which heats the troposphere causing the smoke and air in the troposphere to rise and eventually reach the stratosphere. The rising tropospheric air brings with it nitrogen oxides from the nuclear explosions which then deplete the stratospheric ozone.

Another result of this heating effect is to cause a temperature inversion in the atmosphere that lowers the top of the troposphere from nine to about five kilometers, isolating the smoke from the troposphere and decreasing its rainout and that of the nitrogen oxides. The soot that reaches the stratosphere also causes additional heating there, which increases the rate of the chemical reactions that absorb ozone.

Air rising into the stratosphere of the northern hemisphere drives ozone there to the southern hemisphere, thereby depleting the ozone layer of the northern hemisphere. Preliminary results by Glatzmaier and the Los Alamos group indicate that displacement of ozone to the southern hemisphere would decrease the ozone protective layer in the northern hemisphere by an average of 15 percent during the first 20 days (limit of calculation). Coupled with the diminution of stratospheric ozone by the nitrogen oxides, the total diminution in the northern hemisphere *could rise to as much as 30 percent.* The effect probably increases when the calculation extends beyond 20 days. The ozone depletion effect would indeed be very serious; it has been dubbed by some as **ultraviolet spring.** Ultraviolet spring might be an additional shock to the ecosphere after **nuclear winter.**

Present calculations show that the ozone concentration would initially rise in the southern hemisphere due to the tropospheric displacement, but that eventually some decrease in ozone protection would be expected there also when the solar-heated smoke and nitrogen oxides blow into the southern hemisphere.

The model used is three-dimensional and will eventually be able to account more precisely for rainout of the smoke from the troposphere. If this is a large effect, the ozone depletion prediction will be much reduced. It should also be stated that the chemical reactions in the stratosphere that reduce ozone are complex and temperature-dependent so that additional study is required to be more certain of the quantitative value of the ozone depletion.

Smoke and Dust Effects—Nuclear Winter

In the 1980s a previously unappreciated effect of a global nuclear exchange was explored. In 1982, Crutzen and Birks were investigating the effects on the atmosphere of the dust produced by nuclear explosions. At the end of the investigation as an afterthought they examined the effect of the fires that a nuclear war would create and in particular the effect of the production of large quantities of soot from the fires. Since soot is highly absorbent of sunlight, they found that the climatic effect of relatively small amounts of soot in the atmosphere might be large changes in climate. They examined the atmospheric effects of the burning of 1 million square kilometers of forest adjacent to urban areas; the firestorms resulting from burning cities; the burning of most of the 1.5 billion tons of U.S. fossil fuel reserves; and the burning of natural gas and oil wells. (A 300-kiloton bomb would uncap all gas wells within a radius of 1 kilometer and set them on fire.) They concluded that the fires would produce a thick smoke layer that would ''drastically reduce the amount of sunlight reaching the earth's surface The darkness would persist for many weeks, rendering any agricultural activity in the northern hemisphere virtually impossible if the war takes place during the growing season'' (Creutzen, 1983).

The TTAPS Study

In 1983, R.P. Turco, O.B. Toon, T.P. Ackerman, J.B. Pollack, and Carl Sagan (often referred to as TTAPS) published a paper entitled ''Global Atmospheric Consequences of Nuclear War'' (Turco et al., 1983). The TTAPS paper attempted to quantify the complex atmospheric problem that was posed by the work of Crutzen and Birks. Their work focused particularly on the global atmospheric effects of small particles of soot produced by fires from nuclear explosions, but also included an estimated contribution from dust.

The TTAPS research used various nuclear war scenarios, but their baseline case was a 5000-Mt nuclear exchange with 0.33 megaton of dust mass lofted into the atmosphere per megaton exploded for a surface burst, and 0.10 megaton of dust for a near surface burst. They also made detailed assumptions as to smoke yields (grams of smoke per gram burned) for urban and suburban emissions as well as wildfires. In the baseline case total smoke emission was 225 megatons of which 5 percent reached the stratosphere, and 960 megatons of dust were injected into the atmosphere, with 80 percent reaching the stratosphere.

The results of these calculations showed large climatic effects indeed. For the baseline case the vertical **optical depth** immediately after the war was calculated to be about 4.5. The optical depth is defined as the distance in which the intensity of light is diminished by $1/e$ ($e = 2.71828 . . .$), or to 37 percent of the original intensity. So for the baseline case it was predicted that sunlight would be reduced to about 2 percent of its normal value at noon. Such darkness was furthermore predicted to last for several months. Physically the TTAPS model forecast that 98 percent of the incident sunlight would be absorbed by the soot and dust in the upper atmosphere, producing a large heating effect there, and a severe cooling effect on the earth below. The baseline case predicted freezing conditions in continental interiors of the northern hemisphere for over 3 months after the nuclear war began.

By way of comparison, the El Chichon volcano erupted in Mexico in March 1982. This eruption gave a maximum vertical optical depth of 0.3. During May and June of that year a cloud formed completely around the earth between 5 degrees south latitude and 25 degrees north latitude. The intensity of direct sunlight in Hawaii was reduced by 21 percent. By September and early October the cloud had spread as far north as Boulder, Colorado, and by November it had caused reductions in intensity at solar noon in Boulder of 15 to 20 percent.

The severe climatic changes predicted by TTAPS would produce catastrophic changes in the ecosystem on which humankind is so dependent. In April 1983 an emergency conference of 40 prominent biologists was assembled and published a paper of their conclusions (Ehrlich et al., 1983). Using a more pessimistic 10,000-megaton exchange from the TTAPS paper, Ehrlich et al. concluded that:

> The possibility exists that the darkened skies and low temperatures would spread over the whole planet (TTAPS). Should this occur a severe extinction event could ensue, leaving a highly modified and biologically depauperate Earth. Species extinction could be expected for most tropical plants and animals and for most terrestrial vertebrates of the north temperate region, a large number of plants, and numerous freshwater and some marine organisms.

The TTAPS study confirmed quantitatively Crutzen and Birks' ideas about the possible severe climatic consequences of nuclear war. Research at the Computing Center of the Soviet Academy of Sciences in turn confirmed the TTAPS results (Aleksandrov and Stenchikov, 1983). From these researches and their popularization, the term ''nuclear winter'' was coined.

The TTAPS paper stressed the tentativeness of their results and the need for continued research. The model used by them and others that confirmed their results suffered from several unrealistic assumptions:

1. The model is one-dimensional; that is, it does not take into account north-south and east-west directions, but instead treats the earth as a homogeneous all-land sphere having a temperature that depends only on the up-down direction, atmospheric altitude.

2. Because the model is one-dimensional it has no winds, no feedback of atmospheric circulation changes or the rate of smoke and dust precipitation by rainfall or snowfall. (The three-dimensional model discussed below shows that three-fourths of the smoke is removed in the first month by precipitation.)

3. The amount of smoke lofted into the atmosphere may have been too large (225 megatons instead of 20 to 180 megatons in later studies).

4. The ameliorating effect of the large heat capacity of the oceans could not be taken into account adequately.

5. The infrared "greenhouse" effect of the smoke, which produces a warming effect, was not included.

Three-Dimensional Models

It was recognized that the deficiencies noted above could be taken into account by three-dimensional models of the atmosphere. The first such calculation was reported by the Los Alamos group, Robert Malone et al. (Malone, 1986).

A later paper by Thompson and Schneider (Thompson, 1986) also uses a three-dimensional model of the atmosphere in which the deficiencies enumerated above of the TTAPS calculation are removed. The calculations of Thompson and Schneider and Malone et al. are in substantial agreement. Thompson and Schneider carried out their research at the National Center for Atmospheric Research (NCAR) in Boulder, Colorado. Their model divides the atmosphere into small "cells" of five degrees in latitude by seven degrees in longitude, and with vertical divisions extending to a height of 30 kilometers (about the middle of the stratosphere). It takes into account the removal of smoke and dust particles in each "cell" by rainfall, transport by winds, the energy brought to the cell by sunlight, and the result of the infrared greenhouse effect on the cell because of the reflection of radiant energy back from other cells at higher altitude.

The results of the three-dimensional calculations of Thompson and Schneider show a marked diminution of the surface cooling compared with the TTAPS study (about 3 or 4 times less), and the effect is of shorter duration. So the term "nuclear fall" is perhaps more apt than "nuclear winter." Some results of their calculations are shown in Figure 19-8. The several curves denoted by "Tg" refer to teragrams of smoke lofted into the atmosphere (one teragram is 10^{12} grams or one million metric tons or one megaton). The TTAPS baseline case is also given in the figure. Thompson and Schneider also investigated the land surface temperatures resulting from a pessimistic assumption of 180 megatons of lofted smoke as a function of latitude in the northern hemisphere. The results are shown in Figure 19-9. The minimum temperature reached is seen to drop markedly as the latitude decreases so that this calculation

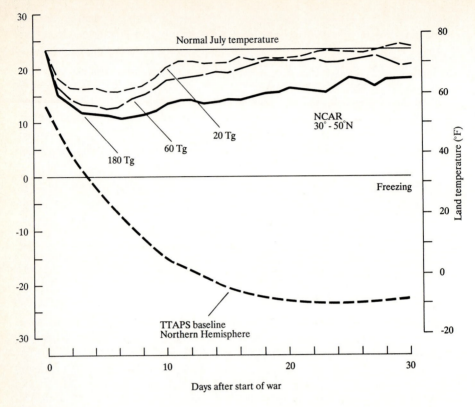

FIGURE 19-8
The three curves denoted as "NCAR" (National Center for Atmospheric Research) give the average July surface temperature of land areas within the 30 to 50 degree latitude zone for the 30 days following a hypothetical nuclear war. Three different amounts of moderately black smoke are used. "Tg" refers to the amount of smoke in teragrams or 10^{12} grams. The TTAPS model was one-dimensional and predicted an average northern hemisphere temperature for an all-land planet and for annually averaged conditions. One difference between an annual average and July cases can be seen in the colder Day 0 for the TTAPS curve. (*Source: Starley L. Thompson and Stephen H. Schneider, Foreign Affairs, Summer 1986.*)

indicates that tropical areas and the southern hemisphere might not suffer major effects.

Thompson and Schneider caution that the *blackness* of the smoke that would be produced in a nuclear war is not well determined, and that the blackness is as important as the amount of smoke lofted. It is for this reason that they have used several amounts of smoke in Figure 19-8 in order to "bracket" this uncertainty in their best judgment. They also caution that:

The curves in the figures represent averages over all the land areas in wide latitude zones. At any specific location in the model, however, the temperatures are considerably more variable. For example, some large areas in the interiors of the North American and Eurasian continents, particularly in Canada and Siberia, fall below freezing intermittently

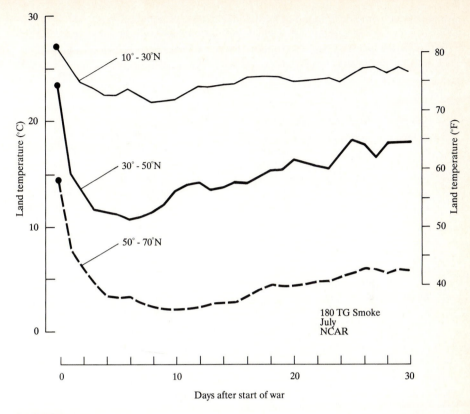

FIGURE 19-9

This figure is similar to Figure 19-8 except that the curves give land surface temperatures for different latitude zones in the northern hemisphere for the case in which 180 million metric tons (teragrams) of smoke are lofted. The black dots at the start of each curve indicate the normal temperature of each latitude zone. It is to be noted that the minimum temperature reached in the 10 to 30 degree zone is considerably less than in the 30 to 50 degree zone. (*Source: Starley L. Thompson and Stephen H. Schneider, Foreign Affairs, Summer 1986.*)

in the two cases of large amounts of smoke. On the other hand, some areas near coasts experience little effect. Thus, it can be misleading to interpret the curves in the figures without taking into account geographic and weather variability as well. Indeed, for certain biological impacts it would be sufficient to have only a few hours below some critical level—e.g., subfreezing for wheat, or 10–15 degrees centigrade for rice.

It should be noted that underdeveloped countries are often dependent on the agriculture of developed nations for their food supply. A disruption of agricultural production in these nations could lead to serious famines not only for their own populations, but for those in third-world countries as well.

Thompson and Schneider further state: "The effects of climatic change also should be considered synergistically with other effects of nuclear war. For example, persons weakened by radiation from fallout will be more subject to epidemic disease brought about by the destruction of normal health care of populations. In turn if famine results from a lack of agricultural production, these persons will be subjected to further risk in their already weakened condition.''

Thompson and Schneider also address the long-term effects of nuclear war as follows:

> The difficult issue of chronic climatic effects (months to years) has not received nearly as much attention as the acute nuclear winter effects (one to 30 days), but will undoubtedly receive greater research importance in the future. A substantial fraction (perhaps ten to 30 percent) of smoke injection from any massive nuclear war would likely reside in the stratosphere for months before finally being removed from the atmosphere. Although the obscuration of sunlight caused by such a shroud would not be sufficient to cause severe surface cooling, it could create other serious climatic effects, e.g. anomalous late spring and early autumn frosts, or a disruption of normal monsoons and summer rainfall over continental areas. Such effects could greatly hamper agricultural recovery in those areas still having sufficient social stability and economic resources to carry out viable agricultural practices.
>
> The previously discovered chronic environmental problems of global radioactive fallout and ozone layer depletion continue to be studied. It now appears that the trend to smaller warheads has made the intermediate-term (days to weeks) and global fallout problems somewhat more serious.

In terms of lofting nitrogen oxides directly into the stratosphere the smaller warheads make the ozone problem less serious. On the other hand, as noted above, *smoke and nitrogen oxides together* may produce serious ozone depletions.

> Each problem—ozone depletion, climatic change, and delayed radioactive fallout—*considered separately* may not pose a global threat that is substantial compared to the direct effects of a nuclear war. But considering all the chronic, indirect effects of a large nuclear war separately may be a misleading exercise; all the chronic effects would, to some degree, act synergistically with each other, and with the direct weapons effects, to produce unprecedented worldwide human misery.
>
> The interaction between a failure of the Asian summer monsoon and the disruption of international trade in food, for example, would be a potent prescription for mass starvation on the Indian subcontinent. Many other interactions can be speculated upon, such as those of radiation-induced depression of the human immune system, disruption of medical services and epidemics of contagious diseases; such synergisms deserve the serious study that might allow us to draw less speculative conclusions. *Therefore it is still quite plausible that climatic disturbances, radioactive fallout, ozone depletions, and the interruption of basic societal services, when taken together, could threaten more people globally than would the direct effects of explosions in a large nuclear war.*

For further detail on the effect of a global nuclear war on food and nutrition in the United States, Soviet Union, and the developing nations the reader is referred to a special report to the *New England Journal of Medicine* by Nevin Scrimshaw (Scrimshaw, 1984).

INTERHEMISPHERIC TRANSPORT. Under normal ambient conditions interhemispheric transport (principally via the stratosphere) requires a year or more. Heating of the airborne nuclear debris by the sun would create new circulation patterns. For the TTAPS 5000-megaton baseline case, the heating amounts to about 40°C over normal conditions at an altitude of 10 kilometers and 80°C at 15 kilometers. An abnormal temperature difference in the upper atmosphere is thus set up between this region and those where there is less nuclear debris. As a result, high-velocity winds can be created. For example, the winter monsoon in India is driven by about a 10°C temperature difference between the cool land mass and the relatively stable ocean.

The three-dimensional calculations referred to earlier in connection with ozone depletion in the northern hemisphere (p. 372) also show tropospheric transport from the northern to southern hemispheres.

Dust storms on Mars are apparently driven by solar heating of dust aloft. They are observed to develop on one hemisphere and to spread over the entire planet in a matter of about 10 days. The Martian data may be applicable to earth, since the atmosphere there is about the same density as the earth's stratosphere and the period of rotation is very similar to the earth's.

Following the El Chichon eruption, at 14 degrees north latitude, about 15 percent of the stratospheric aerosol was transported to the southern hemisphere in 7 weeks.

Covey et al. (1984) of the National Center for Atmospheric Research also have made a three-dimensional calculation that shows the potential for enhanced interhemispheric transport of nuclear debris. Their result is in agreement with similar Soviet research carried out at the Computing Center of the Academy of Sciences, Moscow (Aleksandrov and Stenchikov, 1983).

Conclusion

The conclusions of the various studies of a global nuclear exchange underscore the statement made in Chapter 1 that the nuclear fire is orders of magnitude more energetic than the chemical reactions involved in previous weapons systems, and hence has a potential for destruction which is larger by the same factor. In previous wars casualties were numbered in the millions. After a general thermonuclear war, casualties would be numbered in the billions. Indirect effects—radiation from delayed fallout, ozone depletion, climatic changes, famine, and disease—would probably cause as many deaths as the direct effects of nuclear explosions. Nations far removed from the "line of fire" would suffer seriously. In an all-out nuclear war there are no bystanders.

QUESTIONS

1. According to the *Ambio* study how many people would be killed outright in a nuclear war? How many wold be seriously injured?
2. According to the *Ambio* study how many acute radiation deaths would there be in North America? Cancer deaths?
3. According to Turco et al., what would be the average dose external radiation to an individual living in midlatitudes of the northern hemisphere from a 10,000-Mt exchange (2 times their baseline exchange)?

4. Discuss why it might be possible for nuclear debris from a global nuclear exchange to reach the southern hemisphere in greater quantities and more rapidly than was previously thought.

5. In a 5000-Mt nuclear war using 1-Mt warheads, what is the maximum ozone depletion predicted by Duewer, et al. and when is it predicted to occur? What is your estimate of the ozone depletion if the effect is confined to the 30° to 60°N latitude zone?

6. According to Thompson and Schneider what is the average minimum temperature that would be reached on land in the 50 to 70 degree latitude region if 180 teragrams of smoke were lofted into the atmosphere in a general nuclear war?

7. Discuss the difference between the TTAPS model and that of Thompson and Schneider.

8. According to the OTA study, how many Americans would be killed in a massive Soviet attack on the United States?

9. Discuss the additional fallout hazard if a nuclear reactor is a target of a nuclear bomb.

KEY WORDS

delayed fallout radioactive debris from the global exchange that remains in the troposphere for up to several months and in the stratosphere for a year or more. It is distinguished from early fallout, which was defined in Chapter 16 as being fallout that occurs less than 24 hours after the nuclear explosion. Turco et al. define the time boundary of delayed fallout as being greater than 2 days.

direct effects these are the direct effects of the nuclear explosions including blast, thermal, initial nuclear radiation, and early fallout (less than one day).

indirect effects general term for the effects that would follow after the direct effects in a global nuclear war. Indirect effects include ozone depletion, nuclear winter, epidemics, and radiation exposure due to delayed fallout, and the disruption of normal social services and international trade leading to famine.

interhemispheric transport refers to the disruption of the normal separation of weather patterns between the northern and southern hemispheres because of the heating of the upper atmosphere by the sun. The heating is caused by the deposition of smoke and dust particles there by nuclear explosions.

nuclear winter the prediction of dramatic climatic change due to the smoke and dust obscuration of sunlight from a global nuclear exchange. Nuclear winter was originally used and popularized as a result of some one-dimensional calculations of expected climatic effects (Turco et al. and others). Newer three-dimensional calculations confirm the effect, but predict quantitative results that are much smaller. The new results have been termed ''nuclear fall'' by some authors.

optical depth the depth at which smoke and dust obscuration of sunlight reduces the original intensity of the sunlight to $1/e$ or about 37 percent of its original value. An optical depth of 2, for example, would reduce sunlight to 37 percent of 37 percent, or about 14 percent of the original value.

ozone depletion large thermonuclear bombs deplete the ozone layer in the upper atmosphere due to formation of massive amounts of nitrogen oxides. The ozone layer protects the ecosphere from ultraviolet radiation from the sun. A decrease in ozone of 50 percent would have serious consequences for the ecosphere.

ultraviolet spring the period following a global nuclear exchange when the smoke and dust have cleared and the depleted ozone layer in the atmosphere permits extraordinary amounts of ultraviolet radiation from the sun to reach the earth's surface.

CHAPTER
20

STRATEGIC NUCLEAR MISSILE DEFENSE

Mr. President, if . . . we were to immediately launch an all out and coordinated attack on all their airfields and missile bases, we'd stand a damn good chance of catching them with their pants down. . . . An unofficial study which we undertook of this eventuality indicates that we would destroy 90 percent of their nuclear capabilities. We would therefore prevail and suffer only modest and acceptable civilian casualties. . . . Mr. President, we are rapidly approaching a moment of truth. . . . Now truth is not always a pleasant thing, but it is necessary now to make a choice, to choose between two admittedly regrettable but nevertheless distinguishable postwar environments. One where you got twenty million people killed and the other where you got 150 million people killed. . . . I am not saying we wouldn't get our hair mussed. But I do say, no more than ten to twenty million killed tops.

General Buck Turgidson
in *Dr. Strangelove, or How I Learned to Stop Worrying and Love the Bomb.*
A Stanley Kubrick Film, 1963

20-1 THEMES

Can't we defend ourselves? The threat of use of nuclear weapons inevitably raises the question of defense against them. Is defense possible? If we prepare to defend, will that stabilize or destabilize the arms race? How will the Soviets respond?

The nuclear strategy of the United States is based on a modified version of the concept of mutual assured destruction, or **MAD.** Flexible response, built into the present single integrated operational plan, or **SIOP,** goes well beyond pure MAD; it includes plans for limited nuclear war and protracted nuclear war.

The result of nuclear utilization strategies (**NUTS**) has been to increase the "need" for strategic nuclear weapons from a few hundred (the McNamara number—see Chapters 2 and 4) to about ten thousand. The Soviets have countered with a concomitant increase in their arsenal. Any nuclear ballistic missile defense system must therefore be effective against many thousands of warheads. In this chapter we examine the prospects for missile defense.

In thinking about missile defenses, it is advisable to use empathy, and to try to imagine how the U.S. would respond if the Soviet Union began to install systems such as those the U.S. is proposing.

In 1983, President Reagan proposed that the United States develop a technical way to defend itself against intercontinental ballistic missiles. A major program was started. Unfortunately it turned out that the problem is extremely difficult, even if the Soviet Union doesn't seek to overcome U.S. defenses. In fact an OTA study indicated (OTA, 1985) that Soviet cooperation was necessary in order to have an effective ballistic missile defense. If the Soviets are uncooperative, then the problem seems hopeless at present levels of ballistic missile warheads (over 10,000 for each super-power). Nuclear weapons are so destructive and large numbers of ballistic missiles are so difficult to destroy in the time available that it turns out to be much easier and cheaper to overcome defenses than to install them. If the superpowers wish to be safe from ballistic missiles, the best (and perhaps the only) way to accomplish this will be by mutual actions to get rid of them.

20-2   ABM HISTORY

The ABM Treaty

In the 1960s both the United States and the Soviet Union explored the possibility of building missile defense systems (antiballistic missile systems, or **ABMs**). The Soviet Union actually deployed an ABM system around Moscow, and the United States deployed one around a midwestern ICBM base. As it became apparent to both sides that it was relatively cheap for the other side to install enough more missiles to overpower any given ABM installation (favorable exchange ratio), there developed a commonality of interests strong enough that a treaty could be negotiated. The SALT I treaty (the name results from the Strategic Arms Limitation Talks during which it was negotiated) came into force on October 3, 1972. It prohibits the deployment of ABM systems, except in two areas of each country—the capital and one ICBM base. This exception was included so neither country would be required to dismantle its existing ABMs—though they were eventually taken out voluntarily in the United States. (The treaty was later modified to allow only one ABM site per nation.) The SALT I treaty had other provisions, which are discussed in Chapter 2.

The agreement by the two superpowers not to deploy ABMs was an admission that ABM technologies for defense against ballistic missiles were inadequate. This recognition of a technical limitation went against the grain of many. After all, self-defense has a long tradition, and a specific agreement *not* to engage in self-defense is very unusual. It is not surprising, therefore, that a great deal of attention has been given to concepts that might make possible an effective missile defense system.

President Reagan's "Star Wars" Speech, The Strategic Defense Initiative

On March 23, 1983, the idea of defense against nuclear attack again became important in United States planning when President Reagan gave what became known as the "**Star Wars**" speech. In it he stated:

> Since the advent of nuclear weapons United States strategy has been directed toward deterrence of aggression through the promise of retaliation—the notion that no rational nation would launch an attack that would inevitably result in unacceptable losses to themselves. The approach to stability through offensive threat has worked. . . .
>
> I have become more and more deeply convinced that the human spirit must be capable of rising above dealings with other nations and human beings by threatening their existence. . . .
>
> Would it not be better to save lives than to avenge them? . . . Let me share with you a vision of the future which offers hope. It is that we embark on a program to counter the awesome Soviet missile threat with measures that are defensive. Let us turn to the very strengths in technology that spawned our great industrial base and that have given us the quality of life we enjoy today. . . .
>
> What if free people could live secure in the knowledge that their security did not rest upon the threat of instant United States retaliation to deter a Soviet attack; that we could intercept and destroy strategic ballistic missiles before they reach our own soil or that of our allies? . . .
>
> I call upon the scientific community who gave us nuclear weapons to turn their great talents to the cause of peace: to give us the means of rendering these nuclear weapons impotent and obsolete.

This is an exciting concept, since it seems to hold out the means of ridding humanity of the terrifying threat of strategic nuclear weapons. But is it technically feasible? What does it imply strategically, technically, and politically?

The challenge raised by President Reagan has led to much discussion about the technical feasibility of accomplishing the goal; it has also led to substantial increases in the military budget in many areas relating to missile defense. Administration responses to the "Star Wars" speech are often referred to as the **Strategic Defense Initiative,** or **SDI.**

20-3   GENERAL COMMENTS

Considerations valid for either space-based or land-based ABMs include the following:

A missile defense system should not be designed to deal only with today's Soviet missiles, but to cope with prospective measures for defeating them. Many measures are possible.

An anti-ICBM system is not by itself adequate to protect the nation from nuclear attack. A total defense system would have to deal simultaneously with warheads delivered by airplanes or cruise missiles, which might enter our airspace at high altitudes, at low altitudes, or both at once. It would also have to consider low-trajectory offshore-launched missiles, nuclear torpedoes launched at coastal cities from close-in submarines, and nuclear warheads planted clandestinely in United States cities.

At present strategic missile levels, a program to build a missile defense system could be severely destabilizing. If one side anticipated that the other was on the verge of having an effective defense first, there would be incentive for a first strike. Ballistic missile defense therefore has the potential to accelerate the arms race, despite the appeal of self-defense. Since no one knows where such acceleration might lead, we could end up with higher expenses but reduced security—as occurred when MIRVed warheads were introduced a few years ago.

While a missile defense system might or might not be effective against a nation with the resources of the Soviet Union, it would certainly provide useful defense against third party nations or terrorist groups. If a large number of nations should gain access to nuclear weapons and delivery systems (the "N-country problem"), there might be value to a limited defense even if it were incapable of defending against a full-scale attack.

It is much easier to defend hardened missile silos against attack than to protect our cities. Viable defense of cities with present missile levels is so remote a possibility that is is deceptive to think of it as a reasonable expectation.

Terminal defense (not space-based, or "star wars," defense) is possible for hardened missile silos and may be possible for cities if missile levels are reduced to a few hundred rather than ten thousand.

Paul Nitze has served under many presidents. In the Reagan administration he was an influential arms control negotiator. He proposed that any missile defense should be evaluated as to whether it is "cost effective at the margin" and also whether it is "survivable," that is, not easily destroyed by countermeasures. If it costs the offense less to counter a defense than it costs the defense to deploy one, then it is usually disadvantageous to proceed with the defense. Such a system would fail the "cost effectiveness at the margin" test (Nitze, 1985).

Five years after President Reagan's "Star Wars" speech it has become clear that the problem of defeating ICBMs is vastly more complex than many had believed. Major research programs have been undertaken. However, as new information is developed it has become increasingly clear that many of the technologies proposed will require may years of development, and may simply not prove feasible. A study undertaken by the American Physical Society (1987) of the potential for directed energy weapons showed that with many technologies it will require at least a decade of intense research to determine whether the approach is feasible. Further, during the time of development the Soviet Union will certainly be hard at work finding ways to counter the new technologies.

It has also become clear that the problem of destroying satellites is far simpler than that of destroying ICBMs. Hence any move to place anti-ICBM weapons in space will have a devastating impact on satellite systems. This is a serious problem for the United States, for it is far more reliant on space assets for c-cube-I functions than is the Soviet Union. Some proponents of early deployment of an SDI system oppose treaties that would forbid testing and deployment of ASAT systems, since such systems in their early phases of development are difficult to distinguish from an ABM system.

For a review of key SDI issues the reader is referred to studies of the Office of Technology Assessment of the U.S. Congress (OTA, 1985, 1988). For an introduction to SDI systems and their political ramifications see Schroeer (1987) and Jungerman (1988).

20-4   TECHNICAL CONSIDERATIONS

A comprehensive missile defense system must be able to defend against attacks on two types of target—hardened military targets and "soft" targets, such as cities and industrial installations. The requirements are very different.

An attack on an ICBM installation must have a very high probability of success, since any failure means that the surviving missile could do enormous retaliatory damage; for example, a single MIRVed ICBM, such as the MX, might destroy 10 cities. To have high confidence, an attacker would have to target two or more warheads on each hardened silo. Defense of hardened targets, therefore, must plan on dealing with many incoming missiles simultaneously. On the other hand, the defending system need not be 100 percent successful, since survival of even a few missiles assures devastation of the enemy.

Defense of soft targets (cities, oil refineries, power plants, factories, etc.) is much harder. A loss of even a single city would be a major disaster, and the loss of several dozen major cities could lead to collapse of the nation. Therefore any system used to defend cities must have virtually 100 percent reliability. Without major arms limitations this goal cannot be reliably achieved with any prospective technologies of which we are aware.

Collateral Effects of Defense

An effective defense system must operate so that the after-effects of the defense do not severely damage the nation. Destroying incoming weapons by exploding nuclear warheads in their path, for example, is a defense that may not be feasible, because of fallout.

Incoming warheads must be prevented from detonating at low altitudes. A 1-megaton bomb must be intercepted at an altitude of at least 20 miles to avoid most retinal burns and thermal radiation effects.

General Technical Requirements for a Defense System

A defense system may be divided into four parts: search and track, battle management, kill (destruction of the incoming warheads), and kill verification. The "kill" category has received much popular emphasis, but the other functions present formidable challenges. Radar has impressive search-and-track capabilities. Objects of a few square centimeters can be detected at distances up to 1000 kilometers by a ground-based array. However, radar is vulnerable to attack and to electronic countermeasures— e.g., jamming. One way to reduce such vulnerability would be to build many small units.

Radar would be used to detect and track reentry vehicles as they enter the space and atmosphere near the United States.

When a missile is launched, fuel burns for 3 to 5 minutes, emitting great quantities of thermal radiation. This is termed the *boost phase*. The radiation can be detected with short-wave infrared sensors mounted in satellites. The missile bus, or its warheads, can also be detected high above the atmosphere, in midcourse of the missile's trajectory.

The information from the sensors is relayed to a central data processing facility, where it is interpreted. An attack involving 10,000 warheads and possibly 10 to 100 times as many decoys—which are deployed concurrently to confuse the defense— presents formidable battle-management problems. The computers and their codes must function satisfactorily the first time they are used. Instructions to interceptors must be given within minutes, particularly for boost-phase interception. As the battle progresses, the system must keep track of kills or misses and interceptor status.

After detection and analysis, attack is authorized. In the ABM system the United States deployed in the late 1960s, which has since been dismantled, the kill was to be accomplished with 5-megaton nuclear warheads. The present Soviet system deployed around Moscow also uses nucler warheads on its interceptors. At present in the United States, nonnuclear interceptors appear more promising. Their deployment does not violate the Limited Test Ban Treaty, but would violate the ABM treaty. The ability of a defensive nonnuclear missile to successfully destroy an incoming warhead has been demonstrated by the United States military under carefully controlled conditions.

Layered Defense

Much analysis focuses on a *layered defense* concept. There are three places where an attack may be made on an enemy missile (Fig. 20-1):

Boost-phase intercept. Satellite-mounted infrared sensors are used to detect the exhaust from a missile as it is launched. Weapons mounted on space platforms attack the missile either while it is still in the atmosphere or shortly after it leaves the atmosphere. Unless directed-energy weapons are used, the satellites would have to be in low orbit to respond quickly. This means they cannot be geostationary, and many would be needed so that a few would be over the launch sites at any time—one current

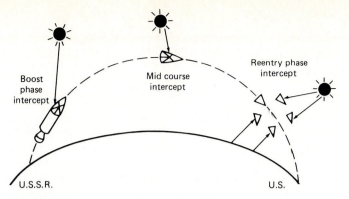

FIGURE 20-1

A schematic representation of the three areas of opportunity for destroying an attacking missile. During the boost phase the missile is moving slowly. During early midcourse it has not yet released its MIRVs; later in midcourse it may release decoys as well as MIRVed warheads.

estimate is that about 400 satellites would be necessary for this purpose. [Geostationary orbits are at 40,000 kilometers (if in an equatorial orbit) and permit a satellite to be always over one point on the earth's surface.]

Boost-phase intercept is attractive because a missile in boost phase is moving slowly and has not dispersed its MIRVed warheads. However, such interception is difficult because boost phase lasts for only a few minutes, the attack must be made over enemy territory, and there is minimal warning. Weapons to attack the boost phase must originate from space or must "pop up" quickly from ground or sea stations. All such systems present formidable technical obstacles. For example, a pop-up rocket would have to be larger than the Saturn V rocket that carried U.S. astronauts to the moon in order to be able to reach a sufficient altitude within the current booster burn time.*

Midcourse intercept. Following launch a missile coasts through space. During this phase it can be tracked from satellites and attacked. During midcourse the bus of a MIRVed vehicle disperses up to 10 warheads, which then must be separately tracked and killed. The offense could also include decoys that simulate warheads, warheads made to look like decoys (antisimulation), or conducting chaff or the like to confuse the defense.

Reentry-phase intercept (Terminal Defense). Missiles not destroyed in boost phase or warheads not destroyed in midcourse must be killed as they approach their targets. Reentry-phase intercept must deal with each one of the warheads of a MIRVed system. Decoys burn up in the atmosphere, so that only true warheads need be attacked. Destruction must occur at an altitude of some 20 miles to avoid major damage, although there will always be fallout if the warhead explodes.

---

*Currently about 3 minutes, but it might be shortened to about half of that.

Suppose that each phase of a defense system is 90 percent effective. A single kill in boost phase (when MIRVs and MIRV decoys have not been deployed) destroys more warheads than a kill during midcourse or reentry phase. Thus boost kills are high-priority. If 90 percent of the warheads are destroyed in boost phase, 10 percent survive. If 10 percent of these survive midcourse phase, there remain $(0.1) \times (0.1) = 0.01$ (1 percent) which reach reentry phase, and 10 percent of these, or $(0.1) \times (0.01) = 0.001$ (0.1 percent) reach their targets.

This isn't good enough. If the enemy launched 10,000 warheads, 10 of them would get through—and could destroy 10 cities. Further, the enemy might well decide to deploy 100,000 warheads, in which case 100 would get through. Any defense system that is to protect soft targets must be spectacularly effective. One must be careful about a mode of analysis which makes use of layer arguments. Obviously the apparent effectiveness of layers can be improved indefinitely by simply adding more layers. A major problem with this approach is the implicit assumption that the layers operate independently. In fact, they can't. There are likely to be "common mode" failures. Suppose that one layer works relatively poorly. This means that the next layer will see far more incoming warheads or decoys than it is designed to cope with. Its performance may deteriorate, or the layer could fail entirely. Analysis in terms of layers is useful, but can also be misleading.

ABM Research

The SDI research program was structured to explore a very wide range of possible systems. These ranged from some based on known technologies to the very exotic. In addition to individual weapons systems heavy attention was given to the development of control systems, which would require some of the most complex computer control ever proposed. Because of the very short time between booster lift-off and the separation of the "buses" and the individual warheads and decoys, the entire system would have to operate virtually without human intervention.

Some of the technical systems which are receiving attention include:

1. Directed-energy weapons, including nuclear-pumped x-ray lasers, beams of neutral particles, free electron lasers, and visible and infrared high-energy lasers. (For a technical discussion of these devices see Section 20-5 and the Additional Physics Section at the end of this chapter.)
2. Precision sensors with optics for search and tracking, laser imaging radar, and millimeter wave radar.
3. Computer systems capable of 1 billion operations per second, and integration of precision sensors with computers to permit using precise small interceptors.
4. Devices capable of accelerating mass to high speeds. Material moving at speeds of many kilometers per second has kinetic energies per gram which are a few percent of the energies of high explosive. These kinetic kill devices (sometimes called **"smart rocks"** or **"brilliant pebbles"** because of their ability to guide themselves toward an incoming warhead) rely largely on existing technology or

relatively simple improvements on existing technologies. Some devices use rocket propulsion; others rely on new developments such as a hypervelocity gun based on electromagnetic rail-gun technology (which uses a magnetic field to accelerate mass). **Kinetic kill devices** move at a very small fraction of the speed of light, and hence the platforms from which they are launched must be much closer to the targets than those for particle beam or light weapons, where the beam moves at or near the speed of light.

5. Massive computer simulation systems for exploring battle management. These computers must respond to complex threats rapidly, and must be able to retain reliability even if a part of the system is destroyed.

20-5 POSSIBLE ABM SYSTEMS

Space-Based Systems

Most of the space-based defense techniques are nonnuclear. All rely on extremely high-level technology. Here we explore a few of the concepts that are particularly important to the understanding of such techniques.

Our discussion is confined to the boost phase, which is the most crucial from the point of view of battle management. In midcourse MIRVs have separated from the booster and an attacker can deploy a large number of decoys, so analysis is more complex.

Space-based missile defense systems would be extremely expensive. Figures in the hundreds of billions of dollars, and occasionally in the trillion-dollar range, are mentioned.

Kinetic-Energy Weapons

Kinetic-energy weapons kill by direct collision. The kinetic energy of mass moving at satellite speeds is comparable to that of a high explosive. A rocket (located in space and directed from a satellite base) would home in on the thermal plume of the booster (Graham, 1983).

In the slow-burning SS-18 (the largest Soviet ICBM), the boost phase lasts 5 minutes, during which the missile reaches an altitude of 400 kilometers. If an interceptor rocket has a velocity of 5 kilometers/second, then in the 300 seconds of burn, the interceptor can travel 1500 kilometers.

Since the attacking satellites can be only 1500 kilometers from the booster, they must be in low orbit around the earth. They cannot be in geosynchronous orbit at 36,000 kilometers. About 50 are needed to ensure that at least one is over all parts of the Soviet Union at all times (Drell et al., 1984). Since the Soviet missile sites are scattered over much of that country, about 240 satellites would be needed to handle the 1400 boosters that the U.S.S.R. now possesses. Each satellite would have to have at least 140 interceptors.

A rocket capable of accelerating a 15-kilogram guided projectile to a velocity of 5 kilometers per second (required for kill) has a mass of about 200 kilograms. The mass of a suitable launch rocket is about 28,000 kilograms. The space shuttle can bring to orbit about 15,000 kilograms, so to establish the 240 satellites would require (28,000 × 240)/15,000, or about 450 shuttle trips. If the Soviets used an MX-type booster (with higher acceleration than the SS-18) that had only 200 seconds of burn, then each attacking weapon could travel only 1000 kilometers. This would mean that 400 satellites would be necessary. Carter (1984) concludes that "a rocket-propelled kinetic energy system operating against today's Soviet ICBM . . . would be a dubious investment." According to Carter, a defense system with only 400 satellites would represent "meager coverage of Soviet ICBM fields" and "the concept would have no capability whatsoever against an MX-like booster . . . even if the interceptor were fired straight down."

Carter also points out that if the Soviets elected to use ICBMs with fast-burn boosters (boosters that burn out in 50 seconds, while still in the atmosphere at 100 kilometers), an interceptor launched from a satellite at 400 kilometers could not be used to defend against it because the interceptor could not descend straight down to 100 kilometers in the required 50 seconds.

Directed-Energy Weapons

Directed-energy weapons evolved from a beam of light or x-rays (produced by lasers) or one of particles produced by an accelerator (particle beam) that travels to a target at or near the speed of light (300,000 kilometers per second). Lasers have the potential for depositing enough energy in a target to destroy it, and particle beams can destroy sensitive electronic components by causing radiation damage.

SPACE-BASED LASERS. A laser functions as follows: A molecule or atom can store energy in an excited, or metastable, state. Such a state can be produced by various energy sources, for example, by chemical action. The process that forms the excited state is called *pumping*.

When a molecule or atom in a metastable state is stimulated by the passage of a wave of the correct frequency, it sheds its energy in the form of a light quantum. The transition from the metastable level to a lower energy level provides energy to reinforce the energy of the stimulating wave. The wave of increased amplitude in turn stimulates additional atoms or molecules. The result is a powerful beam of almost monochromatic (single-frequency) light that is highly parallel. Its energy can traverse large distances and still be confined to a relatively small area. Lasers are described more fully in Section P20-5.

The lethality of a laser weapon is measured by the amount of energy that the laser can deposit per unit time per unit area. This *power density* is determined in part by the diameter of a mirror or lens that is part of the laser and the wavelength of the light it provides.

Nearly 500 laser satellites of 100 megawatts each would be needed to handle a launch of 1400 Soviet missiles. A hydrogen fluoride laser of a few megawatts is now under construction on the ground, and there is no fundamental technical reason why a 100-megawatt laser of this type could not be built. The fuel requirements would be about 15 million kilograms or 600 shuttle loads. At an estimated cost of placing material in low orbit of $3000 per kilogram, the cost for the fuel alone would be $45 billion.

If the Soviets chose to spin their boosters, then the power would be distributed over an area triple that affected by stationary boosters and three times as much laser energy and fuel would be needed. If the Soviets used fast-burn boosters, the U.S. lasers might have only 40 rather than 200 seconds in which to attack. This would require increasing the laser power by a factor of 5.

GROUND-BASED LASERS WITH SPACE-BASED MIRRORS. It may be possible to place lasers on the ground and then send their beams through the atmosphere to mirrors about 100 feet in diameter located in space. A system of several mirrors (perhaps 10) would carry such a laser beam around the curve of the earth.

About 100 mirrors, each 15 feet in diameter, would be used to focus the laser beam on the target. The atmosphere and mirrors would attenuate the laser beam so that about 10 percent of the initial emitted laser light would reach the target. Thus a laser of 400 megawatts power would be needed. This is about 100 times larger than any laser now available.

Atmospheric turbulence could deflect ground-based laser beams. However, a pilot beam (steering beam) might be used to correct for this.

X-RAY LASERS PUMPED BY NUCLEAR BOMBS. An exploding nuclear bomb produces a fireball that emits mostly in the x-ray part of the optical spectrum. These x-rays might be used to produce a lasing action in a bundle of fibers, forming a directed beam of x-rays.

An x-ray laser would self-destruct, and could thus be used only once. X-rays are difficult to focus, and x-ray beams have much greater angular divergences than optical lasers do. The Union of Concerned Scientists (1984) estimates that an x-ray beam would form a spot 450 yards in diameter 2500 miles away. Carter (1984) states that under optimal conditions, a 1-megaton x-ray laser could deposit 300 kilojoules of energy per square centimeter over a spot 200 meters wide at a range of 10,000 kilometers. Since about 10 kilojoules per square centimeter are needed for a kill at the booster stage, it might be possible to target Soviet boosters from a geosynchronous orbit at 40,000 kilometers. The power per unit area would then be $\frac{1}{16}$ of the above, or about 20 kilojoules per square centimeter.

X-rays are readily absorbed by the atmosphere. Hence x-ray lasers would have to attack the boosters after they have left the atmosphere but before burnout. The large divergence angle of an x-ray laser means that less precision is required to direct its beam to a target.

X-ray lasers in low orbit might use multiple lasing rods, pumped by one nuclear explosion, each directed toward a separate booster. Because any given x-ray laser would not be over the U.S.S.R. most of the time, aiming problems are severe.

Since a nuclear-bomb-pumped x-ray laser is relatively small, it could be "popped up" at the moment of attack. As with kinetic-energy weapons, this would require a massive rocket. Any testing of such weapons would violate the ABM Treaty, the Outer Space Treaty, and the Limited Test Ban Treaty.

PARTICLE BEAMS. Charged particles (electrons or protons) could be produced in beams from accelerators orbiting in space. These particles would stop in a few centimeters of material, producing copious quantities of nuclear radiation and heat. In order to transport a particle beam to a target, it would be necessary to electrically neutralize the beam. Otherwise, the charged particles would be bent from a straight-line path by the earth's magnetic field. Particle beams produce more damage than laser beams for the same energy deposited. They can be readily switched from one target to another by electric or magnetic deflection of the primary, i.e., charged-particle beam. They share with lasers the advantage of near speed-of-light action on a target.

Measuring the energy and intensity of the x-rays or gamma rays produced when a particle beam hits a target might be a way to distinguish warheads from decoys.

Particle beams do not penetrate the atmosphere readily, and the accelerators would probably have to be located in space. The fuel requirements for such a system would be substantial.

A prestigious panel of the American Physical Society concluded a two-year study of the development of directed-energy weapons (DEW weapons) for strategic missile defense in 1987 (APS, 1987). Their conclusion was that it would be at least ten years before it could be decided on technical grounds whether or not a DEW system was feasible, since the science and technology to make an assessment were not available at that time.

Countermeasures

A space defense system should not be designed only to cope with the present Soviet arsenal. The situation is not like sending a person to the moon (with which missile defense is often compared), because it must be assumed that the Soviets will do whatever is possible to defeat the system. There are many ways to defeat the systems described above.

As mentioned above, the Soviets could use fast-burn boosters that completed their burns in the atmosphere. This would

1. Increase the number of attacking weapons required and decrease the warning time
2. Make systems based on kinetic energy impractical (because of atmospheric attenuation)
3. Make optical and x-ray lasers unreliable (again, because attenuation would protect the booster)

It is also possible to produce "atmospheric heave" by exploding a nuclear weapon in the atmosphere at the moment of attack, thus lifting the atmosphere and providing an additional shield of air around the boosters (Drell and Ruderman, 1962). For x-ray lasers and particle beams, atmospheric heave accomplishes the same objective as the short-burn booster.

The infrared radiation accompanying a nuclear explosion at an altitude of 100 kilometers causes the atmosphere to glow brightly over areas 200 kilometers in diameter for 1 minute. This would disrupt infrared booster detectors located on satellites.

A decoy used to simulate a booster plume would require a rocket, but such a rocket would be considerably cheaper than an ICBM. Another good way to protect a booster is to provide it with an ablative heat-shielding coating (that is, a coating that burns off instead of conducting the heat inward). The hardness of a missile can be tripled by adding about 1 gram per square centimeter of such material. If spinning boosters are used, the required dwell time of directed-energy beams is increased by an additional factor of 3.

Lightweight, cheap decoys which would follow the actual "bus" or its dispersed warheads and which would be difficult to distinguish from those targets could be deployed in space.

All space-based defensive systems are themselves extremely vulnerable to attack with antisatellite weapons. Space mines could be launched and situated within kill distance of a satellite and exploded on command by radio signal. (An x-ray laser would make a powerful space mine.) Homing vehicles could be directed against satellites from base satellites.

Land-Based Systems—Terminal-Phase Defense

Terminal-phase defense has several advantages:

1. The systems are based on the ground, in friendly territory. They are much less expensive than space-based systems.
2. Decoys are burned up by the atmosphere so that the system need deal only with actual warheads.
3. The systems are much less vulnerable to attack than space-based systems.
4. They are much less threatening to the other side.

The disadvantages of land-based systems include the following:

1. An intercepted warhead may explode, resulting in fallout, EMP, and blast and thermal radiation effects. Thermonuclear weapons of very large yield can produce substantial damage to cities even if exploded high above the earth. A 50-megaton weapon exploded at an altitude of 20 miles in clear weather would create fires in an area of over 1000 square miles.
2. Incoming warheads are traveling about 8 kilometers per second upon entering the atmosphere and 3 kilometers per second upon impact. These high speeds and marked deceleration due to air drag make tracking difficult.
3. Because of MIRVing there are likely to be a very large number of warheads to destroy, virtually simultaneously.

Warheads can be protected during reentry by ablation shields, but they are still vulnerable to being struck by any object. One proposed device is the *hypersonic interceptor* (*Aviation Week,* 1983). The warhead, consisting of pellets spread out so as to cover a substantial area, would be launched from the ground on detection of incoming warheads. It would rise rapidly (5 to 6 kilometers per second, or 3.5 miles per second, or 12,600 miles per hour), would have a 15- to 50-kilometers-latitude capability, and would have an intercept range of 200 kilometers.

Nuclear explosions in the vicinity of incoming warheads damage them by radiation. Radiation from a nuclear explosion is not attenuated in outer space. The intensity per unit area decreases as the inverse square of the distance. The thermal radiation can melt the warhead, and the nuclear radiation (especially x-rays) can produce SGEMP which can damage electronic components. Megaton-sized weapons can produce substantial damage at a range of a mile or more.

The ABM system deployed by the United States in the early 1970s used a 5-megaton warhead (Spartan), to be exploded above the atmosphere (at 100 kilometers), and a 1-kiloton neutron-bomb warhead (Sprint), to be used in the atmosphere. The Soviet system deployed currently to protect Moscow uses about 50 nuclear warheads.

One disadvantage of nuclear warheads is that they cannot be tested for their efficacy in an ABM system without violating the Limited Test Ban Treaty. Also the EMP and other electronic noise from early explosions would make tracking of incoming missiles difficult.

Land-based nonnuclear interception of a single Minuteman missile was achieved in 1984 at an altitude of over 100 miles as it approached reentry at Kwajalein island in the Pacific. The interceptor was another Minuteman missile with an on-board computer and a long-wave infrared sensor for detecting the missile in space.

Control Systems

Control of a full-scale SDI system is immensely complex. The launch phase of ICBMs (the time the booster plume is visible, before the system deploys its individual warheads and decoys) is only a few minutes. Thus an SDI system must react so rapidly that there is virtually no time for human intervention. Tens or hundreds of thousands of enemy decoys must be detected and discriminated in midcourse. These requirements, and many more, dictate a computer control system of vast complexity. In the case of the x-ray laser (see above) that is proposed to be ''popped up'' in time to attack the boost phase (five minutes or less) complete automation will be required. Thus, the launch of the x-ray laser defenses and the accompanying nuclear explosions would not have any human intervention in the decision loop.

20-6   CONCLUSIONS

In a report dated April 11, 1983, the Scowcroft Commission (a panel appointed by President Reagan to consider the role of the MX missile in the national defense) stated:

Substantial progress has been made in the last decade in the development of endo-atmospheric and exo-atmospheric ABM defenses. However, applications of current technology offer no real promise of being able to defend the United States against massive nuclear attack in this century. An easier task is to provide ABM defense for fixed hardened targets, such as ICBM silos. . . . At this time, however, the Commission believes that no ABM technologies appear to combine practicality, survivability, low cost, and technical effectiveness sufficiently to justify proceeding beyond the stage of technology development.

Sidney Drell (1984), who has long experience and has recently worked intensely on the ABM problem, stated in testimony before the Senate Foreign Relations Committee:

We do not know how to build an effective nation-wide defense, nor is there any prospect of achieving one in the foreseeable future, unless the offensive threat is first tightly constrained technically and greatly reduced numerically as a result of major progress in arms control.

At best, a practical ABM system for the defense of cities and other soft targets—if it could be developed at all at present ICBM levels—would not be operational until the end of this century or later.

To the authors a more reasonable course would be to reduce—either by negotiations or by sequential unilateral actions—ICBM levels down to a point (perhaps a few hundred on each side) at which an ABM system could play a useful role. This is the perspective explored by Freeman Dyson (1984):

Until the negotiated reduction of offensive [nuclear] weapons has made substantial progress it would be foolish to raise the question of ABM at all. Nevertheless, if we are ever fortunate enough to see offensive weapons reduced to low levels, ABM defenses would be helpful in giving us confidence to make the next big jump from low levels to zero, and it would be foolish then not to take advantage of whatever benefits ABM defenses have to offer.

Both the process of developing an ABM system, and its eventual deployment if the R&D project is successful, could prove destabilizing to the arms race if conducted at the present threatening levels of offensive nuclear weapons. The expenditures would be massive, and would certainly trigger similar expenditures on the other side. William Burrows (1984) states that:

An ABM system would in fact fuel the arms race, not curtail it, by forcing the Russians to vastly increase the number and variety of their missiles and warheads, improve their quality, develop new ways of delivering them, perfect advanced penetration aids and deploy specific counterweapons, such as anti-satellite systems to counter American defenses. . . . And not least, an American ballistic missile defense effort would seriously damage American political credibility by violating the Limited Test Ban Treaty, the Outer Space Treaty, and the extremely important ABM treaty, while distracting interest and attention from far more important initiatives such as a comprehensive verifiable freeze on weapons testing, which is what is really needed.

In 1983 the Soviet Union introduced into the United Nations a draft of a treaty to ban the deployment of weapons in space. This idea found no takers within the United States government. However, there are signs of progress in extragovernmental circles. One of the most interesting of these is an informal agreement that relates to the banning of reactors in space. This was proposed by academicians of the Soviet Academy of Science and representatives of the Federation of American Scientists. The agreement states that the Soviet Union will remove its reactors in space if the United States agrees not to place reactors there. The Soviet Union presently uses reactors to power its radar satellites used for tracking United States naval vessels. The United States is interested in reactors in space for powering certain SDI systems such as space-based lasers. While the agreement has no official weight, the coordination of the Soviet Academy of Sciences and the Gorbachev government is so close that there is good reason to believe that the Soviet government wants to negotiate in this area.

This is one of many constructive directions in which negotiations among the superpowers might move. Space is rapidly being militarized in areas of information collection. These directions are generally stabilizing. However, to place weapons in space would likely lead to rapid escalation of competition between the United States and the Soviet Union, which would almost certainly lead to reductions in the security of both nations.

The United States government has not responded positively to the idea. Under the Reagan administration United States policy was generally that such agreements are not in the national interest. Several considerations may lead to change, however. The United States is placing increasingly more reliance on space-based assets for intelligence and communications. Research carried out in conjunction with the Strategic Defense Initiative has made the problems of such systems increasingly clear. In particular, it has become apparent that virtually all weapons with the capability of attacking ICBMs are even more capable of attacking satellites. The advantages of placing limits on weapons in space are becoming increasingly clear, and it appears to us likely that treaties will be explored seriously under the Bush administration.

ADDITIONAL PHYSICS SECTION

P20-5 TECHNICAL CONSIDERATIONS OF POSSIBLE ABM SYSTEMS

Kinetic-Energy Weapons

A mass of 1 kg moving at 20,000 mi/h (about 10 km/s) toward an incoming warhead moving at equal speed toward it has relative kinetic energy of $\frac{1}{2}(2 \times 10^4)^2 = 2 \times 10^8$ J/kg. This is 5 percent of the energy of TNT (4.2×10^9 J/kg). Proposed techniques for ejecting antimissile projectiles (such as use of the rail gun) might achieve speeds

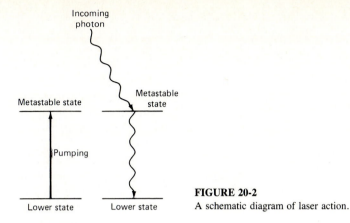

FIGURE 20-2
A schematic diagram of laser action.

at which the kinetic energy would exceed that of TNT. A small fraction of a kilogram of such a projectile would destroy any warhead.

Lasers

Lasing occurs when atoms or molecules are energized to an excited, or metastable, state that lasts for a considerable period of time. The state is depopulated by stimulated emission to a lower state if a photon corresponding to the transition energy to the lower state interacts with the atom or molecule. This process is illustrated in Figure 20-2.

Since the photon released by the stimulated emission has the same frequency as the incident photon, the beam amplitude is increased by the addition of the stimulated photon. Thus the laser acts as a light amplifier. The acronym *laser* stands for *l*ight *a*mplification by *s*timulated *e*mission of *r*adiation.

Laser light is said to be *coherent*. This means the atoms that produce it act in unison, or in phase. The result is a beam of highly collimated (parallel) light. Laser light diverges mainly because of the aperture limitations of optics. The divergent angle of a light beam is limited by the diffraction of the beam by a finite aperture (a lens or a reflecting mirror, for example) that limits the diameter of the beam. The expression that gives the diffraction limit for the divergence of a light beam is

$$\text{Angle of divergence} = 1.2 \times \frac{\text{wavelength}}{\text{diameter of aperture}} \quad \text{(radians)} \quad \text{(P20-1)}$$

If the wavelength is 1 μm and the mirror diameter of the laser is 1 m, the divergence angle is 1.2×10^{-6} radian. The relation between the laser beam diameter at the target, the distance to the target, and the angle of divergence is

$$\text{Beam diameter} = \text{distance} \times \text{angle of divergence} \quad \text{(P20-2)}$$

For the above case, if the target is at 1000 km, the beam diameter is 10^6 m $\times$ 1.2×10^{-6} radian $= 1.2$ m.

In order to destroy a booster or warhead it is necessary to deliver energy of about 20 kJ/cm^2.* A perfect 1-m mirror forming a perfect hydrogen fluoride laser beam with a power of 100×10^6 W (optimistic but probably feasible) would produce a spot 120 cm in diameter (area = 11,300 cm^2) at 1000 km. The power density is 8.8 kW/cm^2, or 8.8 kJ/cm$^2 \cdot$ s. Thus a kill would occur in about 2.3 s.

Suppose we allow the satellite 2.3 s to accomplish a kill. To this we must add time to track, aim, and assess damage. If the total time for all this is 3 s, and if the boost phase lasts 3 min, then each satellite can kill at most 60 ICBMs. If the Soviets launch 1400 ICBMs, then 24 satellites must be on station at all times.

Since the earth has a circumference of 40,000 km and a satellite can attack only if it is within 1000 km of a target, each satellite can at most be on station only about 5 percent of the time. Thus a total of 24/0.05 = 480 satellites would be required (Drell, 1984, p. 47).

To destroy a single ICBM requires a laser power of 100 MW operating for 2.3 s, or 230 MJ. If the laser efficiency is 30 percent, the fuel requirement is 767 MJ. Each laser carries fuel to destroy 60 ICBMs, and there are 480 satellites, so $767 \times 60 \times 480$ or about 2.2×10^7 MJ must be placed in orbit. Fuel (e.g., hydrogen fluoride) might be provided at an energy density of about 1.5 MJ/kg, so 15×10^6 kg of material would have to be placed in orbit. If an advanced shuttle carrying 25 t (25,000 kg) were used, 600 shuttle loads would be needed just to carry the fuel. This would not allow for any redundancy or for any expansion of the Soviet ICBM installation.

Offensive Use of Lasers Deployed in Space

The Soviets label SDI components as "space-strike weapons" and view them as threatening. If one were to imagine a U.S. first strike under crisis circumstances, than an operating SDI could serve to protect the United States from a ragged retaliatory strike by the U.S.S.R. SDI can therefore be viewed as part of a first-strike capability of the United States. As was pointed out in Chapter 22, it is the perception of the opponent that is the reality that fuels the nuclear arms race.

A laser beam in space at a frequency capable of penetrating the earth's atmosphere would be an exceedingly powerful weapon for use against a variety of earth-based targets. Energy depositions of about 10 calories/cm^2 (42 joule/cm^2) are sufficient to produce third-degree burns on individuals (see Chapter 14). Such energies are a fraction of those required to melt through the metal of an ICBM booster (about 10,000 joule/cm^2). A beam can therefore be spread out considerably, and still prove lethal to human beings.

One can envisage a situation of the sort which occurred frequently in Vietnam or in Central America where soldiers are under attack from an enemy machine gun or mortar emplacement (Craig, 1987). A soldier wearing a back-pack-mounted nav-

---

*Modern boosters are able to withstand energy pulses of about 1 kJ/cm^2 delivered over times of a few seconds. Increasing the skin thickness to a fraction of a centimeter and using specialized materials (e.g., carbon) might make it possible to raise the resistance to destruction by heating to 20 kJ per cm^2 (Drell et al., 1984).

igation/communication systems would request assistance from SDI headquarters. Within a few moments a blast of laser energy could be directed from space against the enemy installation, destroying it virtually instantly. Since the satellite orbits required to provide continuous coverage of the Soviet Union necessarily cover almost all the inhabited regions of the world, virtually all present or prospective enemies of the United States or of the Soviet Union or their allies would be vulnerable.

Similarly, a leader of an enemy nation could be killed while reviewing the troops. There is also the possibility that an American president could be incinerated while standing in the Rose Garden outside the White House, or the Soviet leadership could be killed while reviewing Soviet troops from atop Lenin's tomb during the traditional May Day celebration.

Many other military and quasimilitary applications of SDI laser technology can be imagined. Very low intensity radiation of fields during critical parts of a growing season could severely damage crop germination. High-intensity beams could destroy aircraft in flight. The tracking requirements are modest compared with those which a system capable of destroying ICBMs during launch phase would necessarily have. While the cost of such systems would be high, once they are installed, the cost of using them would be relatively low.

Space-deployed lasers of SDI specifications would also have a direct technical capability for offensive use. Let us consider in particular lasers of about one micron wavelength, a wavelength for which the atmosphere is transparent. Such a laser would be tempting to develop in order to attack ICBM boosters before they leave the atmosphere, i.e., early in the boost phase. To meet SDI specifications the laser would have a range of at least 1000 kilometers and should deliver the required kill flux of 20 kilojoules per square centimeter in a short time in order to attack hundreds of ICBMs during the five minutes or less of boost phase. Let us suppose the beam on target time is one second and that the laser is orbiting at 300 kilometers above the earth. So we assume that it would deliver 20 kilowatts of beam power at 1000 kilometers. Directly below the laser the beam power would be increased by a factor of $(1000/300)^2$ because of the beam divergence. This factor arises because at a given distance the beam is spread out over an area that is proportional to the square of the distance from the laser.

That is, if the beam power is P_1 at d_1 and P_2 at d_2, then

$$P_2 = P_1 \times (d_1/d_2)^2 \qquad \text{(P20-3)}$$

Therefore, the beam power directly below the laser on the ground would be about 11 times greater than at 1000 km which would be 220 kilowatts/cm^2 or 53,000 calories/cm^2. Since 20 calories/cm^2 will start a fire in combustible material (see Chapter 14), the laser has the inherent capability to start over 2500 fires per second by slewing the beam about from space. As the laser passes over a city it could in principle start thousands of fires.

If desired, the power available could melt through tank armor or other military assets, or it could be used as an antipersonnel weapon. According to the information in Chapter 14, third-degree burns are caused by just 10 calories/cm^2 so a person could be given such a burn in a fraction of a millisecond.

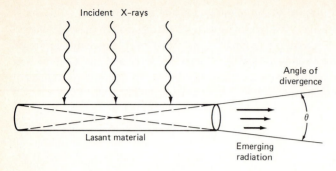

FIGURE 20-3
A schematic diagram of an x-ray laser.

X-Ray Lasers

In an optical laser the parallel beam of light is formed by multiple reflections from two accurately parallel mirrors. An x-ray laser is "pumped" by the thermal x-rays of a nuclear explosion. Near the explosion is a rod of thin fibers which can be made to "lase" by the thermal x-rays. Figure 20-3 shows schematically the geometry of an x-ray laser.

The divergence angle of an x-ray laser is determined by the ratio of the width of the rod to its length—until the diffraction limit intervenes. Thus the divergence angle is limited by the smallness of the rod and is, at best, about 20 μ radians. This gives 20 kJ/cm^2 from an 800-kt bomb producing x-rays at 3 percent efficiency (Carter, 1984), in geosynchronous orbit at 40,000 km altitude, over a spot 800 m in diameter.

Experiments to develop x-ray lasers have been going on in the United States for several years. Work at Lawrence Livermore National Laboratory has apparently demonstrated the possibility of producing laser action. Despite highly publicized claims (especially by Edward Teller) that the x-ray laser is ready to move into the engineering phase, this technology is still in a very early research stage, and far from being ready for any practical military application.

Long before x-ray lasers capable of destroying ICBMs during launch phase can be built, there will exist the capability of building lasers able to destroy virtually any space asset. The x-ray laser would be a truly formidable antisatellite weapon. Rather than being a device for destroying ICBMs, if usable at all as a weapon it is much more likely to play a role in destroying major space-based elements of any strategic defense system.

Particle Beams

The angular divergence of a beam of neutral particles is, at best, about 10 μ radians. At 1000 km the diameter of the beam spot is therefore 10 m and the area is 7.9×10^5 cm^2. The power in the beam is beam energy, in MeV, times current, in microamperes. For a 100-MeV beam of 10 A, the power is 1000 MW and the power density is 1.3 kW/cm^2. The beam would therefore deposit 20 kJ in about 15 s. Since the particle accelerator will not be 100 percent efficient in converting the energy from the power source into beam energy, but rather perhaps 10 percent efficient, an orbiting power source of 10,000 MW is required. The power output of a large nuclear power reactor is about 1000 MW. The problems of developing, installing, maintaining, and defending such systems are all immense. The beam power is several orders of magnitude larger than any accelerator on earth.

QUESTIONS

1. Describe how a laser works.
2. What are the difficulties in killing a booster with an x-ray laser?
3. Give arguments to support the idea that deployment of an effective ABM system would be destabilizing at the present time.
4. Give arguments to support the idea that deployment of an ABM system would be stabilizing.
5. What are some of the technical problems involved in developing an effective space-based ABM system?
6. Give an estimate of the budget requirement for developing an optical laser booster intercept system (assume that no countermeasures are taken).
7. Give arguments for and against terminal-phase ICBM defense.

PROBLEMS

1. What is the divergence angle from a laser mirror 10 m in diameter with wavelength one micron?
2. What would be the power density of the laser in Problem 1 at 1000 km if 2 MW are in the laser beam?
3. What would be the diameter of the beam spot from a perfect laser with a mirror diameter of 1 m if the light is 0.5 μm in wavelength (green) and the target is at 5000 km?
4. If the fibers (rods) in an x-ray laser are 30 μm in diameter and the rods are 2 m in length, what is the diameter of the beam spot at 1000 km?
5. What would the power density be if the laser in Problem 2 were located in geosynchronous orbit at 40,000 km?
6. How long would it take the laser in Problem 2 to deposit 20 kJ/cm^2?

KEY WORDS

ABM   antiballistic missiles.
brilliant pebbles   see kinetic kill device. These are an advanced version of smart rocks. They are to be smaller and cheaper, and with much enhanced computing power.
directed-energy weapon   a beam of light, particles, or x-rays which can be focused onto a target. The beam propagates with almost the speed of light.
kinetic-kill weapon   a space-based device for detroying ICBM components. It destroys by direct collision, rather than through the use of explosives.
MAD   Mutual Assured Destruction.
NUTS   Nuclear Utilization Strategies. Similar to flexible response; a parody on MAD.
SDI   Strategic Defense Initiative. Same as Star Wars.
SIOP   Single Integrated Operations Plan. The key targeting plan of the United States.

smart rocks   see kinetic kill weapon.

Star Wars   popular name for the Reagan administration's plan for deploying antiballistic missile technology. Same as Strategic Defense Initiative.

terminal defense   a missile defense system which defends during the last moments, when a missile has almost reached its target. Can be either an independent system or a part of a larger system (e.g., a component of SDI).

x-ray laser   a laser producing soft (low-energy) x-rays, driven by a nuclear explosion. Whether such a weapon can ever be made is highly conjectural.

CHAPTER
21

CIVIL
DEFENSE

A close look at the facts shows with fair certainty that with reasonable protective measures, the United States could survive nuclear attack and go on to recovery within a relatively few years.

Federal Emergency Management Agency, Dec. 1980

Optimism: A cheerful frame of mind that enables a teapot to sing though up to its nose in hot water.

Anonymous

21-1 THEMES

Civil defense refers to those aspects of the defense of the nation that are not specifically concerned with military installations. We define civil defense broadly, in order to provide some understanding of the diverse measures that might be taken before, during, or after a nuclear war. All aspects of civil defense, especially when a broad interpretation is being used, as here, are fraught with uncertainty. Further, even a highly effective plan to protect people in fallout shelters during the days or weeks immediately after a war might not be adequate to assure their survival over months or years. Civil defense might be of little benefit in the event of a full-scale nuclear war. However, civil defense could be of substantial benefit as protection against terrorist attacks, or at a time when nuclear arsenals are greatly reduced.

21-2 INTRODUCTION

From a technical point of view, it is possible to take civil defense measures that will reduce the death and injuries resulting from any given attack. Blast shelters and radiation shelters are technically feasible. Yet the issues involved are complex. For example, civil defense measures may lead to overconfidence. Or the very existence of civil defense planning may be perceived by an enemy as an aggressive posture. National resources spent on civil defense are not available for other purposes.

Any discussion of civil defense must take into account the fact that there are so many nuclear weapons in the stockpiles of the United States, the Soviet Union, Britain, and France that a war which involved only a small fraction of them would probably destroy the nations involved for many decades, possibly forever. This is not to say that there would be no survivors of such an exchange. But these survivors would lack most of the infrastructure that is essential to the functioning of a modern industrial society.

The fact that a large-scale nuclear war could destroy civilization as we know it is not, per se, an argument against civil defense. If war is going to come anyway, shouldn't we make our plans so as to save as many as possible? Shouldn't we stockpile the technological essentials that survivors would need in order to reestablish a civilization? Suppose there is a limited nuclear war, which does not endanger the entire society. Is it not proper to put into place equipment (e.g., medical supplies) which could save lives and ease the suffering of survivors? These are very difficult questions, on which people can and do disagree.

A federal agency, the Federal Emergency Management Agency (FEMA), has proposed developing evacuation plans for virtually every city in the United States and development of a massive array of shelters throughout the nation. In contrast, a group known as Physicians for Social Responsibility (PSR) asserts that it is improper for physicians to collaborate in any program of civil defense against nuclear attack. The primary grounds given by the PSR for its position is the impossibility of coping with nuclear devastation and the social damage that would be caused by devoting resources to meaningless preparation. A PSR analysis of a 1-megaton attack on San Francisco concluded that even if surviving physicians could get to all the injured within the first week, they would be able to devote only 10 minutes to each person.

The United States has vacillated on civil defense programs. There was a large burst of civil defense activity in the early 1960s at the time of the Cuban missile crisis. Then interest waned, and existing programs became moribund. Government policy on civil defense a decade ago is represented by Presidential Decision Document 41 (September 1978). This included the following guidelines:

1. The United States civil defense program should enhance the survivability of the American people and its leadership in the event of a nuclear war.
2. The civil defense program should enhance deterrence and crisis stability, contribute to perceptions of overall United States/Soviet strategic balance, and also reduce the possibility that the Soviets could coerce us in times of increased tension.
3. The civil defense program will include planning for population relocation during times of international crisis, and be adaptable to help deal with natural disasters and other peacetime emergencies.

These quotations are reproduced from a FEMA planning document released in September 1980. While not representing today's policy of doing virtually nothing in the way of civil defense, they do represent a view which has periodically found expression in governmental policy, and which may again attain prominence. The document continues by discussing the importance of integrating civil defense with national defense programs so as to make clear to the Soviets that they cannot intimidate us. According to the document, "In Soviet military thinking, the threat to commit suicide does not constitute meaningful deterrence. Effective deterrence has to involve not only the ability to inflict damage on the enemy, but also the ability to limit damage to oneself." Civil defense is thus viewed not purely as a matter of protection—it is explicitly intended to communicate to the Soviets that we intend to win any exchange.

Present nuclear strategy in the United States is based, fundamentally, on a balance of terror. We and the Soviet Union are each other's hostages. With present levels of nuclear weaponry, civil defense measures can play but a small role. Eventually, however, the world's nuclear arsenals may be reduced to a far more modest level. At that stage we can envision a situation in which nations have a limited number of weapons for security, and civil defense programs to protect themselves. This form of strategy is described by Freeman Dyson (1984) as "live and let live." Such a world may be a dream. But it is a dream worth pondering.

21-3 ISSUES

Bomb shelters are probably the classic example of civil defense. They were widely used in World War II. Upon warning of attack, sirens sounded and people rushed to designated shelters. There can be no doubt that shelters saved large numbers of lives, particularly in cases of massive attacks against cities, such as those in 1940 during the Battle of Britain.

When the Battle of Britain began, there was no alternative but to defend the cities and to counterattack. The use of bomb shelters in this instance was as pure an instance of passive defense as one is likely to find. Passive defense strategies are those which make use of technologies which are intrinsically difficult to use for offensive purposes. Some examples from ordinary experience are bulletproof vests, bulletproof glass in banks and gas stations, stocks of emergency food, and a strategic petroleum reserve.

Stockpiling emergency food, medical supplies, strategic materials, and petroleum is one way to prepare for shortages which might occur in case of war or other disaster. Stockpiling of a year's food supply, a routine part of Mormon practice, is an individual measure which, when adopted by many families, can add resilience to an entire society. The planned stockpiling of 1 billion barrels of oil (one-half billion barrels are now stored) by the United States in salt domes along the Texas gulf— enough oil to permit the United States to avoid importing oil for several months—is an example of a national strategy designed to impart resilience to our economy. It decreases United States vulnerability to disruption of oil imports, particularly those originating in the highly vulnerable Persian Gulf.

Would a potential adversary regard such measures as purely defensive, or as aggressive? Civil defense in a nuclear age will probably never be viewed as a purely defensive activity.

Some questions one might want to consider in developing a civil defense program are the following:

What are the physical characteristics of an attack which the program might defend against? A single small terrorist weapon? An attack on a single city? A concerted attack on many cities?

What is the time scale of the potential attack? A single strike in a short period? A continuing bombardment lasting months?

How will the number of lives saved vary with the amount of warning?

What kind of an environment will exist after the attack? Will people be able to resume normal lives? When?

How much loss of life is "acceptable" in a war?

If the civil defense measures require action well before the outbreak of war, to what extent will these actions themselves tend to increase the probability of the outbreak? (An example would be evacuation of cities in a time of global tension.)

What can an enemy do to overcome any specific civil defense action? (For example, an enemy might increase the megatonnage of attacking weapons so as to destroy shelters, or retarget so as to attack people in whatever locations they have been moved to.)

What is the cost of civil defense? To what extent will civil defense expenditures remove human and material resources from the productive part of the economy and damage the ability of the nation to compete economically with the rest of the world?

What are the psychological effects of a civil defense program? Will a civil defense program produce a false sense of confidence in civilians and political leaders, thereby making war more likely? Will children brought up in an atmosphere of continuing preparation for war be more likely to accept it as inevitable?

What are the key points of vulnerability of the society? How does one protect the industrial and agricultural infrastructure so that the nation can recover should a war be fought?

What would the regional and global effects of nuclear war be? If, after a nuclear war, the nation has no real opportunity to recover from the destruction of physical facilities and ecosystems, then what would a civil defense system based on fallout shelters have accomplished, other than a delay of death for a few months or years?

Are there reasons why a civil defense program might make sense for nations without nuclear weapons (such as Switzerland)?

Does the special position of the United States as a nuclear superpower give special meaning to any civil defense activities we might engage in?

To what extent does a nuclear civil defense program provide protection against other emergencies (flood, earthquake, etc.)?

These questions cover virtually every aspect of our society. We turn now to a much narrower question—the potential of civil defense for saving lives following a nuclear attack on a single city.

21-4   CIVIL DEFENSE OF CITIES

An Attack on Detroit

The Office of Technology Assessment (1979) examined several attack scenarios, from which we select one—a weapon dropped over Detroit, which has a metropolitan population of about 4.3 million. The scenario assumes the following:

1. A 1-megaton air burst dropped over downtown Detroit
2. No warning
3. Night detonation
4. Clear weather
5. Altitude chosen to maximize the area of 30-psi overpressure
6. No other cities attacked

Inside the 12-psi contour (Figure 21-1) there would probably be no survivors; beyond the 2-psi contour there would be little direct damage, *provided* that a fire storm did not occur. OTA estimates immediate deaths at 470,000 and injuries at 630,000. There would thus be some 3.7 million survivors. (OTA notes that if a 25-megaton bomb were used, there would be virtually no survivors.) However, the infrastructure for dealing with the survivors is woefully inadequate. The 63 hospitals included in the area shown on the map have 18,000 beds. However, 55 percent of these are inside the 5-psi circle and would be totally destroyed; another 15 percent are inside the 2- to 5-psi band and would be severely damaged, leaving just 5000 beds. (In 1977 there were only about 1 million hospital beds in the United States. Further, many of the injured would be burn victims requiring intensive care, and there are only about 2000 beds equipped for burn care in the entire United States.)

Fallout from the blast would be carried downwind, requiring evacuation or protection over many square miles. Electricity, gas, and water lines would be destroyed inside the core area, but service outside this area could probably be restored fairly quickly—provided there were no EMP effects (Chapter 17). If EMP damage did occur, virtually all functions relying on electricity might be inoperable for a considerable period of time.

A single 1-megaton bomb hitting Detroit would create a disaster far beyond anything ever experienced in the United States, or indeed anywhere in the world. Nevertheless, while the devastation would be enormous, the survivors would far outnumber the injured, and support services could be brought in from outside the city. Furthermore, the casualty estimates assume no shelter, and deaths could be substantially reduced by installation of fallout shelters. Stockpiling of food and medical supplies could also reduce casualties. Such preparations could save many tens of thousands of lives during and after an attack on a single city, and at a modest cost per life saved. It is this conclusion that motivates much civil defense planning in the United States.

After a nuclear explosion over a single city, help—including food, water, and medical supplies—unquestionably would be available from the outside. An attack on

FIGURE 21-1
A 1-megaton bomb exploded over Detroit. The air burst occurs at the civic center. Overpressures at various ranges are indicated. (*From Office of Technology Assessment, 1979.*)

many cities would change the picture drastically. In a multicity scenario there would be no outside.

Shelters

At a 5-mile distance from a 1-megaton air burst there is overpressure of 5 psi and a thermal deposition of over 25 calories per square centimeter. Most persons within an area of about 80 square miles who are not shielded will be killed. Given a typical urban population density of 10,000 persons per square mile, this amounts to 800,000 immediate fatalities. However, civil defense could help substantially to decrease death and injury. With adequate shielding, substantial protection, even from ground bursts, is conceivable.

There are many possible civil defense measures. Blast shelters capable of withstanding 20 to 30 psi are relatively simple to construct. The building of shelters that can withstand the heat and oxygen shortage of fire storms is more complex. Outside the immediate area of destruction, simple shelters could provide shielding from fallout. Thirty-six inches of dirt would reduce radiation levels by a factor of 100, which would reduce the cumulative dose rate from fallout in the region immediately downwind from the blast from an estimated 4000 rem in the first week to 40 rem—a low enough level so that there would be few immediate effects on persons able to remain sheltered for weeks.

A fallout-shelter program capable of shielding from overpressures up to 100 psi would also save everyone outside a circle of radius 3500 feet, or two-thirds of a mile from a ground burst (the range at which a 100-psi overpressure occurs for a ground burst). Within this 1.4-square-mile circle in Detroit there are only 14,000 persons. Thus 100-psi fallout shelters could, in principle, save the great majority of the population. It is assumed that the walls of the shelters would be thick enough to attenuate the initial nuclear radiation to "acceptable" levels.

It is this technical capability of fallout shelters to save lives that underlies all arguments for massive civil defense programs. There have been many proposals. One interesting concept examined at the Oak Ridge National Laboratory (Haaland, 1970)— involves a system of deeply buried corridors, arranged so as to form a grid under a city. As in the OTA study, Detroit was used as the example city. Tunnels buried to a depth of about 120 inches of earth, or 80 inches of concrete, could provide protection up to 1000 psi, which is the pressure attained only a short distance out from the crater lip. At these close ranges, protection from neutrons and gamma rays is needed. Shielding requirements for earth and concrete at the 1000-psi level are given in Table 21-1. The study assumed citizens would have warning of the attack and would proceed to the shelters—95 percent of them arriving within 10 minutes.

At a walking speed of 3 miles per hour a person could go 2640 feet in 10 minutes, which determines the required spacing of the tube entrances. (No time was allowed for leaving buildings or for crowding. This time could be substantial.) Once the population was inside the tubes, blast doors would be closed. Except for those very close to ground zero, everyone would be sheltered, and could then walk gradually through the tunnels to points where supplies were stockpiled, and eventually to regions

TABLE 21-1
Shielding* requirements at the 1000-psi level

	Radius, feet		Million rem, no shielding		Earth cover, inches		Concrete, inches	
Yield, Mt	1000 psi contour	Crater edge	Neutrons	Gammas	Neutrons	Gammas	Neutrons	Gammas
0.1	700	630	5.5	1	71	103	47	72
1.0	1500	1300	5	3.3	70	117	47	81
10.0	3200	2700	0.9	5	59	122	39	85

*The shielding is that required to reduce the initial dosage of 100 rem. Assumes ground burst.

Source: Based on Haaland, 1970.

outside the city. It was estimated that such a system could save up to 95 percent of the city's population.

The Oak Ridge design examined the requirements for food, air, water, and sanitation over a 2-week period. Air would have to be filtered to prevent entry of fine particles of fallout, and cooled in case of fire storm. Communications services would be desirable, as would emergency lighting. It was estimated that after 2 weeks in these shelters, the external radiation level would be 100 rad per hour, which would permit people to leave the shelters briefly. The fallout would then decay slowly (according to the $t^{-1.2}$ law, see Chapter 16), so that longer excursions outside the shelter would become possible.

A grid system of passage does, in theory, permit evacuation of a city after an attack, but it has several problems. For example, it assumes adequate warning and almost instant response; it does not take account of the possibility of a staged attack, with missiles coming at intervals over a long time; it does not attempt to deal with the postattack environment after 2 weeks, when nuclear-winter effects might be felt; and it does not attempt to address the problem of restoring basic services, industry, or agriculture.

The Oak Ridge approach to fallout shelters emphasizes a system that can be used with very little warning if the citizenry are well trained. An alternative approach, the one currently favored by the federal government, is based on dispersal. This approach places little emphasis on shelters. It assumes that there will be a long warning time (a week or more) that would permit residents of cities to move into new locations—with an overall reduction in population density. Among the disadvantages of a system based on dispersal is the long warning time needed and the possibility that an enemy would retarget as people were relocated, as well as the act being viewed as provocative by the adversary.

21-5 AN ATTACK ON OIL REFINERIES

The United States could absorb the loss of any single city and continue to function. However, as the number of attacking nuclear weapons increases, different types of effects become important and the necessary civil defense measures change qualitatively. The OTA explored a large attack directed against oil refineries. The energy sector is a particularly vulnerable part of any industrialized nation. Oil, in particular, runs most of the transportation system, including tractors on farms, the trucks which move food and factory output, oil-fired electric generating plants, and the diesel trains which run on most of the nation's tracks and which carry a great deal of the coal used to generate electricity. Nuclear-fired power plants and hydropower plants could continue to operate, but together these produce only about 15 percent of the nation's electricity. Oil stockpiles are adequate for only a few months, even if the strategic petroleum reserve, which is itself vulnerable to attack, is included. The replacement of oil refineries would take years—and require a great deal of oil in the process.

OTA considered a hypothetical attack directed at U.S. oil refineries by 10 Soviet SS-18 ICBMs, each MIRVed with eight 1-megaton warheads. Because of the clustering of MIRVs, each SS-18 could hit only eight targets, within an area of about 125,000 square miles. Since oil refineries are geographically concentrated in both the United States and the Soviet Union, this is not a serious limitation. One possible approach to targeting is shown in Figure 21-2.

The eight warheads were assumed to be targeted on the 77 largest U.S. oil refineries. Since these plants have many tanks and pipes in open, above ground structures, they are vulnerable to low overpressures—perhaps 5 psi. Thus the probability

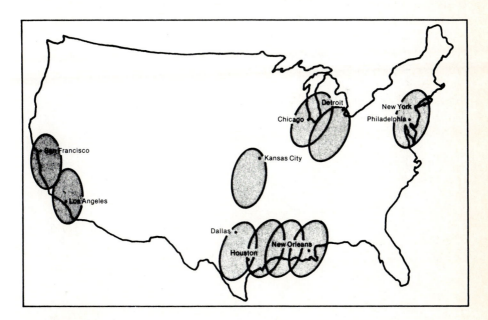

FIGURE 21-2
"Footprints" of ten MIRVed SS-18s targeted on United States oil refineries. (*From Office of Technology Assessment, 1979.*)

TABLE 21-2
Long-term effects from nuclear attacks (casualties in thousands)

	Somatic effects			Genetic effects	
	Cancer deaths	Thyroid cancers	Thyroid nodules	Abortions due to chromosomal damage	Other genetic effects
Air bursts					
Worldwide* effects from a 1-Mt airburst over Detroit (OTA case 1)	0.2– 2	≈0.7	≈1	0.1– 1	0.3– 3.5
Worldwide* effects from an attack using 78 air bursts of 1 Mt each (OTA case 2 attack on the U.S.)	16– 160	≈55	≈78	8– 80	27– 270
Total† effects from an attack using 72 air bursts of 40 kt each (OTA case 2 attack on U.S.S.R)	6– 60	≈50	≈80	2.5– 25	5– 50
Limited surface bursts					
Estimated total‡ effects of an attack on U.S. oil refineries using surface bursts, with fallout sheltering treated parametrically PF = 5:	2,000–5,500	≈2,000	≈2,500	250–2,500	900–9,000
PF = 10:	1,000–3,000	≈1,000	≈1,500	150–1,500	50–5,000
PF = 15:	300–1,000	≈300	≈500	50– 500	150–1,500
Estimated effects outside the U.S. from this attack	8– 80	≈30	≈50	0.4– 40	13– 130
Counterforce attacks (mixed air and surface bursts—OTA case 3)					
Estimated total† effects of an attack on U.S. ICBM silos, using one air burst and one surface burst (each 1 Mt) against 1054 solos. A case in which bomber and submarine bases are also attacked with air bursts gives similar results. Fallout sheltering is treated parametrically. PF = 5:	1,000–6,000	≈2,000	≈3,000	300–3,000	900–9,000
PF = 10:	700–5,000	≈2,000	≈3,000	250–2,500	750–7,500
PF = 40:	500–4,500	≈1,500	≈2,500	200–2,000	650–6,500

Estimated effects outside the U.S. from this attack	400–3,800	≈1,400	≈2,000	170–1,700	600–6,000
Estimated total‡ effects of an attack on Soviet ICBM silos, using one air burst and one surface burst (each 100 kt) against 1477 silos. The overwhelming bulk of deaths are from "worldwide" (between 30° and 60° north latitude) fallout, and hence fallout sheltering in the Soviet Union makes little difference.	300–3,300	≈2,500	≈3,600	120–2,500	400–4,000

Comprehensive attacks (OTA case 4)

Estimated effects inside the U.S. of an attack on military and economic targets in the U.S. consisting of 3325 weapons with a total yield of 6500 Mt. A mixture of air bursts and surface bursts was assumed, and the ranges include variations in fallout protection available.	1,000–5,500	1,000–2,000	1,500–2,500	150–6,000	400–9,000
Estimated effects outside the U.S.	900–9,000	≈3,200	≈4,500	500–5,000	1,500–15,000
Estimated total‡ effects of an attack on military and economic targets in the Soviet Union consisting of 5660 weapons with a total yield of 1300 Mt. A mixture of air bursts and surface bursts was assumed, and the ranges include variations in fallout protection.	1,200–9,300	≈5,500	7,700–8,400	320–8,000	1,000–12,500

*Most worldwide fallout would be in the northern hemisphere, and it would be concentrated between 30 and 60 degrees north latitude.

†Includes worldwide totals, but effects are greater in the target country.

‡PF = protection factor.

Source: Office of Technology Assessment, 1979. (See this document for a detailed specification of the various cases.)

413

that they would be destroyed is very high. The attack would be devastating. Two-thirds of the oil-refining capacity of the United States would be destroyed, and about 5 million persons would be killed directly.

Civil defense against an attack of this sort would be extraordinarily difficult. The major elements would include stockpiling vast quantities of oil in protected sites, hardening and dispersing oil refineries, and protecting citizens against fallout. Each of these undertakings would be both complex and expensive. The first, however, is partially under way. The U.S. strategic petroleum reserve is located in salt domes along the Texas gulf. This reserve is designed to ultimately hold about 1 billion barrels of oil, or about a 2-month supply if all other sources of oil cease. (The value of the oil in storage will be about $30 billion, and billions of dollars were spent in constructing the domes.) The second and third steps would be far more difficult and expensive, since refineries are among the more vulnerable parts of the U.S. industrial infrastructure and fallout would be intense and widespread.

Table 21-2 summarizes the long-term effects of several nuclear scenarios examined by the OTA, including the attacks on Detroit and on oil refineries discussed above.

21-6   OTHER POINTS OF VULNERABILITY

The United States and the Soviet Union are both centralized, the Soviet Union being slightly more so in its industrial infrastructure. The example of oil refineries described above indicates a systemic vulnerability to nuclear attack in both nations.

Much heavy industry is highly concentrated, and in the United States there are fewer than 100 nuclear power reactors. The reactors are an especially sensitive point of vulnerability since they contain large amounts of radioactivity. Though they are heavily shielded, even a small nuclear weapon could break them open.

In a study carried out for FEMA, Lovins and Lovins (1982) identified many components of the United States energy system that are particularly susceptible to disruption. They explore various types of attack, including sabotage and limited warfare. Their enumeration of vulnerable points includes:

Communications systems. Telephones, electronic data transfer, banking services.

Liquefied natural gas facilities. These include tankers, terminals and deliquefaction plants, storage tanks, pipelines, and other transportation systems.

Oil and gas. In addition to refineries discussed above there are oil and gas fields, shipping facilities, offshore drilling platforms, natural gas processing plants, oil and gas pipelines and pumping stations (e.g., The Trans Alaska Pipeline System, TAPS), and juncture points among pipelines. The United States relies heavily on oil from the Middle East, especially Saudi Arabia. An industrial civil defense program for the United States must take into account disruption of foreign supplies. The international system includes wells, pipelines, ship terminals, and supertankers, all of which are extremely vulnerable.

Electric power system. This includes generators, the transmission grid, substations, and control systems. The power grid is an enormous antenna. EMP would probably trigger a full shutdown by tripping relays and destroying control circuits. Nuclear plants are particularly appealing targets for nuclear attack because of the radiation release. Hydropower dams, if destroyed, would release floods on populations downstream.

An effective civil defense program would have to provide for protection of all of these systems, or for backup systems. To accomplish this would certainly require relocating virtually every one of the above facilities into heavily protected environments. Even if such a massive restructuring (burying) of the society were undertaken, the Soviets could still design weapons to demolish the society.

21-7 LONG-TERM EFFECTS

Repairing an industrial nation's destroyed infrastructure following nuclear attack would be extraordinarily difficult. We have come a long way from the time of self-contained cottage industries. Specialization has yielded great benefits in terms of industrial output, but at the price of a system in which many components must be transported long distances. Manufactured items are assembled from components brought from all over the nation or the world. A civil defense program that would permit the nation to recover from a major nuclear attack would have to include plans for stockpiling virtually everything. Since the industrial composition of the nation's economy is always changing, the stockpiling would have to be a continuing process, and, no matter how it was carried out, many of the items stored would become obsolete before they could ever be of use.

Not only would a comprehensive civil defense program have to deal with the problems of stockpiling manufactured items, it would have to take into account the climatic changes which might occur during the year or more following a large-scale nuclear exchange. (See the discussion of nuclear winter in Chapter 19.) Preliminary calculations suggest that the detonation of as little as 100 megatons over 1000 or so cities could lead to temperature reductions lasting for months. A civil defense program designed to cope with this kind of change would have to stockpile food and other essentials to sustain the population—including heating fuel—perhaps for several years. And this would have to be done for every part of the nation, since even the regions that escaped the initial blast and fallout might experience severe effects. Thus a truly comprehensive civil defense program would probably absorb a large portion of the nation's GNP for many years. Even a "limited" nuclear attack on strategic weapons systems could lead to destruction of many major cities and the deaths of tens of millions of people. Some of the problems of limited nuclear war and flexible responses are explored in Chapter 4.

21-8 WHAT ABOUT SOVIET CIVIL DEFENSE?

Soviet literature suggests that civil defense plays a more important role in their planning than it does in the United States. To some extent this is to be expected, because the two nations have had very different experiences with war. The Soviet Union lost 20 million citizens when it was invaded by Nazi Germany. Virtually every person there had relatives killed in the war. The United States, of course, has never been invaded, and its losses in recent wars, while very great, are dwarfed by those sustained by the Soviet Union. One result of this has been that Soviet doctrine places an extremely high priority on defense of the homeland. For a typical book on the subject, see Yegorov (1970).

Soviet civil defense literature leads to the impression that massive civil defense facilities have been installed and that most citizens are prepared to act in a coordinated way in the event of an imminent nuclear war. The results of some U.S. studies tend to confirm Soviet estimates that the protective measures provided by their plan would be highly effective. In testimony before the Civil Defense Panel of the Subcommittee on Investigations of the Committee on Armed Services, T. K. Jones claimed that ''if a U.S. retaliatory attack were directed against Soviet urban-industrial areas and weapons were detonated above ground, Soviet fatalities would be slightly over 2 percent of their population [about 6 to 7 million fatalities]'' (*Civil Defense Review,* 1976). It is pointed out that more people than this were killed by the Soviets themselves in the great purges of the 1930s. The size of the hypothetical U.S. attack is not specified. There is a clear implication, however, that a similar attack on the United States would lead to very much greater damage. The conclusions reached by Jones, who went on to become a high-ranking official in the Department of Defense under the Reagan administration, are highly controversial.

Just what does Soviet civil defense planning consist of, and how effective is it? Soviet training manuals emphasize moving citizens out of urban areas and building many simple fallout shelters out of dirt and branches, using simple equipment such as picks and shovels. The reduction of fatalities to a low level assumes that all citizens will have warning of attack so that they can walk for one day, thus moving about 30 miles from the cities. According to visiting westerners, there is no extensive civil defense preparation visible within the cities.

If this type of evacuation could be carried out, how effective would it be in preserving Soviet society? The Soviet industrial infrastructure is even more concentrated than that of the United States. Virtually any civil defense measure that the Soviets might introduce to save their society could be frustrated through the use of existing U.S. weaponry if the United States (1) targeted critical industrial installations, (2) allocated a few warheads for destruction of protected facilities, and (3) attacked before defensive preparations were completed (Kincade, 1977).

The Soviet civil defense system may prove useful against low-level or terrorist attacks, but does not provide much protection against a large-scale war. Furthermore, the Soviets are even more vulnerable to food shortages than is the United States because of the poor productivity of Soviet agriculture, the severe climate, and the long distances over which food must be transported. Thus any climatic changes resulting from nuclear war would affect them even more than they would affect the United States.

21-9 THINKING ABOUT CIVIL DEFENSE

There is a strong tendency in thinking about civil defense to concentrate on a limited subset of the issues that arise. This is a consequence, in part, of a natural tendency to try to reduce problems to manageable size. It is appealing, for example, to examine a question such as: what is the number of lives that might be saved in city X if it is attacked by a single warhead of Y megatons, through the installation of shelters, the stockpiling of medical supplies, the stockpiling of food, etc.? Formulating a problem this way permits quantification, so that the methods of systems analysis can be applied and numerical results obtained. A characteristic of nuclear weapons, however, is that there are so many possiblities and uncertainties that such a restricted, detailed analysis may completely overlook critical effects.

The most important need in civil defense planning is to include a sufficiently broad array of possible issues. This by itself will not assure that planning focuses on the most important issues, but it will improve the odds. This section suggests some ways of encouraging such breadth of approach.

Figure 21-3a and b gives schematic representations of a system that could help identify different types of nuclear threats and the civil defense options which might be used to mitigate them. The approach is modeled after that often used in studying the possible environmental impact of hypothetical events. Using the figures, one should be able to qualitatively order threats and possible responses, taking into account both severity and potential for destruction.

Figure 21-3a takes as its starting point threats which occur at some given (though generally unknown in advance) time. The magnitude of the threat is the variable: A

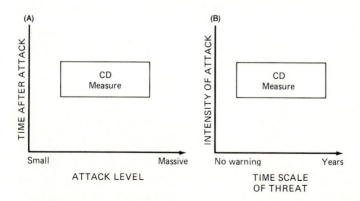

FIGURE 21-3
A schematic means for thinking about nuclear threats. Such diagrams can help identify areas in which civil defense might be feasible.

small threat might be a terrorist blackmail threat to use a nuclear device against a city; a large one would be the prospect of an all-out strategic attack by one nuclear power against another. Civil defense planning for dealing with any threat should explore all the implications of the situation. These include the immediate crisis that would result from the explosion of a nuclear bomb or bombs; the intermediate-time-scale effects; and the long-term effects, which might range from the need for industrial reconstruction to the psychological trauma suffered by the survivors of such an attack and their children.

Figure 21-3*b* introduces the "threat matrix," which focuses on the idea that nuclear threats can go on for very long periods. We live under the shadow of the possibility of massive nuclear attack. We have lived under this shadow for decades, and we may do so indefinitely. Against this all-pervasive backdrop occur instances of high tension, such as the Cuban missile crisis of 1962 and the deployment of cruise and Pershing II missile systems in Europe. A civil defense system designed to cope with continuing stress must maintain itself over long periods, without degradation of performance. Evacuation of cities, for example, is a possible civil defense measure over a time scale of a few days or weeks. It is not practical over a period of months or years. At the opposite extreme, entire cities might be hardened or rebuilt underground. This would be a civil defense measure designed to operate over years or decades. Such an approach to civil defense would totally change the character of our society and, if they responded in kind, that of the Soviet Union as well.

Civil defense in the United States and the Soviet Union is necessarily coupled with nuclear strategies. The reason may be understood by thinking about swords and shields. A shield is a purely defensive weapon only in the absence of a sword. In the presence of a sword, a shield is an adjunct to an offensive weapon, and is therefore itself properly perceived as to some extent offensive. If a nation is contemplating a first strike, a civil defense system will make it less vulnerable to whatever retaliation may occur with whatever weapons are left.

This reasoning allows us to understand better the civil defense measures employed in Switzerland. That nation has for hundreds of years (including all of World War II) maintained a policy of neutrality. Virtually all of Switzerland's male population serves in the military, and retains reserve status until age 50. Switzerland has well-trained troops, and a large supply of materiel. Swiss building codes require that all new buildings be equipped with fallout shelters.

Shelters in Switzerland are properly perceived differently than the same type of shelters would be perceived in the United States or the Soviet Union. The reason is that Switzerland clearly has shelters as a means of protection against fallout from nuclear war in other parts of Europe, or as protection against nuclear weapons that might inadvertently hit their nation. A nation which lacks offensive capability—as Switzerland does—need not worry that its defensive efforts are perceived by other nations as being a part of an offensive strategy. Civil defense in Switzerland is nonthreatening to other nations—in contrast to the same technology in the United States or the Soviet Union.

Each element in the complex web of nuclear strategies has civil defense implications, and it is often unclear whether a particular civil defense activity will prove stabilizing or destabilizing. For example, the doctrine of mutual assured destruction (MAD) is based on the ability of each nuclear power to destroy its enemies. Each nation possessing nuclear weapons is thus at the mercy of the others, and a civil defense program capable of protecting one of the nations will inevitably be seen as a threat to the others. If a successful defense could be carried out, the final stages of installation would be particularly critical. If one superpower perceived that the other was about to complete successful installation of a defense system, there would be incentive for it to strike before the shield was in place. This issue has also been raised in conjunction with the Strategic Defense Initiative (Star Wars defense, see Chapter 20).

Civil defense clearly has a role to play in national planning. Civil defense measures designed to cope with natural disasters such as floods, earthquakes, and tornadoes save lives, and many of these measures would be of aid in dealing with a limited nuclear disaster, such as the explosion of a terrorist nuclear weapon in a city. However, it seems unlikely that civil defense measures capable of coping with full-scale nuclear war are either institutionally or technically feasible, and, in addition, they serve to increase the likelihood of the very event which they are designed to protect against. A critical policy issue for the United States relates to decisions on what to defend against—taking into account the potential benefits of lives saved and the risks and costs of installing the civil defense measures involved. In civil defense, as in nuclear weaponry, the critical question remains: How much is enough?

Are there circumstances in which a substantial shelter program might be reasonable? If the nuclear powers ever reduce their nuclear arsenals from thousands down to a few hundred, a civil defense program perhaps in conjunction with defensive weapons might provide real protection. It would also be useful in the event of a threat by a terrorist or a smaller nuclear nation. A national civil defense program might have most appeal in a world making significant progress toward a workable defensive strategy—a world in which the concept of mutual assured destruction had been abandoned. Whether such a world is a dream or a realistic long-term goal we cannot say. What is clear is that it would be vastly different from the world we live in now.

QUESTIONS

1. Make your own list of the advantages and disadvantages of a civil defense program designed to cope with initial fallout (i.e., one focused on the first several weeks following a nuclear attack).

2. How would the list you made in Question 1 change if the nation were in a state of continuing high international tension? Take "continuing" to mean that there is a high level of confrontation over a period of many months.

3. Reflect on what you have learned in your own life about U.S. civil defense preparations (through, say, observing training programs in schools, noticing buildings marked as fallout shelters, reading articles in the press). If you were a strategic analyst in the Soviet Union and had access to this same information, what is the strongest case you could make that the United States had a significant civil defense program? (The purpose of this exercise is to get you to think in terms of "worst-case" analysis from the perspective of a Soviet planner.)

4. What are some of the design considerations you would use in planning a shelter to protect yourself at a distance of 3 miles from ground zero of a 1-megaton nuclear blast (burst height 6000 ft; see Chapter 7)? Estimate the blast effects at this distance and take into account the fact that you will be on your own for quite a while.

5. What would be the elements of a civil defense program designed to cope with a 1-month period of darkness following a nuclear exchange? Assume the exchange takes place at the worst possible time—spring, at the start of the crop-growing season.

6. What would be the elements of a civil defense program designed to cope with a Soviet attack on U.S. oil refineries?

7. Under what circumstances do you believe that evacuation of cities should be ordered by the government? How much planning for such evacuation should be a part of our national civil defense program? Should civil defense be a part of required curricula in junior high school? High school? College?

8. Switzerland has an elaborate civil defense program. All new buildings in Switzerland must, by law, be equipped with fallout shelters, emergency food and water, and manually operated air pumps equipped with particle filters. Should the United States have such a program? Should the Swiss? If you see differences between the situations in the two nations, explain what they are.

9. Assume you are downwind of a nuclear explosion. An hour after you hear the blast, your radiation meter begins to show rapidly rising readings. In a few moments it is reading 1000 rem/h. Design a system that will keep you reasonably safe from radiation injury. (You might want to assume that the sensor on the meter is located outside your shelter.) You will need to use information from Chapter 16.

CHAPTER
22

THE PSYCHOLOGICAL EFFECTS OF NUCLEAR WEAPONS

The unconscious is not a demoniacal monster. . . . It only becomes dangerous when our conscious attitude to it is hopelessly wrong. To the degree that we repress it, its danger increases.

C. G. Jung

22-1 THEMES

The psychological effects of nuclear weapons may be divided into two distinct categories: (1) the present and past psychological effects of the nuclear arms race, with its ever-present threat to individual and societal survival and (2) the probable psychological effects on the survivors of a nuclear war. The present effects we can understand by looking around us. The actual psychological experiences of the **hibakusha,** or survivors of the atomic bombings of Hiroshima and Nagasaki, offer our only guidance to the impact of actual nuclear war.

In a very real sense psychology is a paramount feature of the nuclear arms race. The amassing of increasing levels of nuclear weapons by the superpowers and other nations is in large measure a result of the desire to influence the perception of the opponent. Each nation wants its opponent to believe that whatever steps are necessary to achieve its national security will in fact be taken. Stand firm and be strong. Those steps to be taken are themselves based on perceptions of what will influence the opponent. In turn the opponent reacts in a similar fashion and the spiral of perceptions takes another step of escalation.

22-2 THE PSYCHOLOGICAL EFFECTS OF THE NUCLEAR ARMS RACE

Denial

The threat of nuclear war casts a shadow over all our lives. In an effort to cope with the threat, many people choose not to face it or to dilute it. Robert Jay Lifton (1983) speaks of this process as "psychic numbing." The problem is that such numbing, while probably necessary for living a reasonably stress-free life, makes it more difficult to generate the atmosphere needed to produce awareness of the nuclear threat. Our feelings are further blunted by the absurdity of our predicament—that is, two human societies, the United States and the Soviet Union, in their massive effort to be capable of destroying each other, may well destroy civilization, if not humanity itself.

Psychic numbing can take several forms. We have heard highly placed government officials state that because Hiroshima and Nagasaki were rebuilt, a nuclear war, although undoubtedly horrible, is something that we can survive with our civilization intact, and perhaps even "win." This is a massive denial of the evidence of many studies that show that the United States would cease to exist as a functioning society (see Chapter 19) and that there would be no outside help to rebuild, as there was for the isolated cases of Hiroshima and Nagasaki.

Joanna Rogers Macy (1983) speaks eloquently of the emotions that the prospect of nuclear war engenders:

> The responses that arise, as we behold what we are doing to our world, are compounded of many feelings. There is fear—dread of what is overtaking our common life and terror at the thought of the suffering in store for our loved ones and others. There is anger—yes and bitter rage that we live our lives under the threat of so avoidable and meaningless an end to the human enterprise. There is guilt; for as members of society we feel implicated in this catastrophe and haunted by the thought that we should be able to avert it. And above all, there is sorrow. Confronting so vast and final a loss as this brings sadness beyond telling.
>
> Even these terms, however—anger, fear, sorrow—are inadequate to convey the feelings we experience in this context; for they note emotions long familiar to our species as it faced the inevitability of personal death. The feelings that assail us now cannot be equated with dread of our own individual demise. Their source lies less in concerns for the personal self than in apprehensions of collective suffering—of what happens to others, to human generations to come, and our green planet herself, wheeling there in space.
>
> What we are really dealing with here is akin to the original meaning of compassion: "suffering with." It is the distress we feel on behalf of—or more precisely in connection with—the larger whole of which we are a part. It is our pain for the world.
>
> Yet we tend to repress that pain. We block it out because it hurts, because it is frightening, and most of all because we do not understand it and consider it to be a dysfunction, an aberration, a sign of personal weakness.

Human beings are programmed to pay attention to immediate, pressing needs. Anything else seems unreal, leading to an ostrichlike attitude toward the nuclear world in which we live. We seem to have the attitude that nuclear issues are "too complicated" and are better left to the experts. We may have faith that somehow a benevolent and parental government will protect us and do what is best. We assure ourselves that MAD is working and that the contradictions between a growing capability to destroy life and the desire to live our lives and fulfill our potentials can somehow be resolved. Richard Garwin, for example, is one of the more thoughtful critics of many aspects of U.S. defense posture. Yet he writes (Garwin, 1980):

> There is no technical solution in existence or in sight that would enable a modern society to survive a determined attack by strategic nuclear forces such as those of the United States or the Soviet Union. But fear of the destruction of American society by nuclear attack from the Soviet Union is not high among concerns of thoughtful people in the United States (and vice versa). This is not because we have an effective defense or because the Soviets wish American society well; rather, it is because the Soviet Union is deterred from initiating such an attack by the knowledge that it would likely destroy them in turn.

We, the authors, are not so sanguine, nor are we at all convinced that this statement accurately reflects the consensus "of thoughtful people in the United States," though it may well reflect a consensus among those individuals who are required by their jobs or dispositions to study war for large parts of their days.

Adaptability is a useful human trait, one which has contributed to survival of our species over millennia. We attempt to adapt also to the nuclear threat. Another term for this process, with a different connotation, is *habituation*. If there is no *apparent* change in a situation, we get used to it and it ceases to impinge upon our consciousness. Such habituation can be life-threatening. A frog, for example, will not jump out of a pan of water that is being slowly heated—until it is too late. The changes in the water temperature, which are the forerunners of impending catastrophe, occur so slowly that the frog does not notice them.

Our language is altered to soften the threat. As Robert Lifton points out, we "domesticate" nuclear weapons in our language and attitudes. We call them "nukes" as if they were cute. The bombs dropped on Hiroshima and Nagasaki were nicknamed "Little Boy" and "Fat Man," suggesting a newborn baby or an affectionate tribute to Winston Churchill. Judith E. Lipton (1983a) refers to "nukespeak":

> Language can be a great cover-up. It can hide what we are doing, not only from others, but also from ourselves as well. Nowhere is this more apparent—and more dangerous—than in the case of "nukespeak," that strange and bloodless language by which the planners of nuclear war drain the reality from their actions. Nukespeak is the sanitization of the world's dirtiest words. It is at least partly because of nukespeak that hundreds of otherwise decent Eichmanns can go about their work with sanity and a feeling of personal decorum, removed from what they are actually doing. It is because of nukespeak that the targeting centers and institutes of strategic planning seem more like banking offices or accountancy firms than designers of death. Hitler spoke of "the final solution" to the Jewish problem—not mass murder. And our own strategists speak of "demographic targeting"—not the incineration of people. But genocide by any other name still stinks.
>
> Here are just a few examples: "delivery vehicle" = bomber or missile, "reentry vehicle" = missile warhead that enters the atmosphere, "overkill" = the ability to kill more people than actually exists, "collateral damage" = the murder of innocent civilians

(especially women, children, and the elderly) as well as the destruction of homes, businesses, farms, etc., "device" = bomb, "counterforce" = blowing up an opponent's missiles or bombers, "countervalue" = blowing up the opponent's cities.

Dr. Lipton refers to Glasstone and Dolan, who speak of "translational velocities" of a human body produced by blast effects. She says that such language causes "us to think about something without really thinking about it—or rather, without feeling it. 'Translational velocity' is a problem in physics, not crushed lungs and fractured skulls."

According to psychologist Chellis Glendinning (1983):

We have dealt with the horror of impending atomic holocaust by deadening ourselves. In the process we have blocked our capacity to feel both joy and other emotions that make joy possible by contrast. Once we have deadened ourselves by psychic numbing our threshold of sensation rises. In order to feel anything at all, we must bombard ourselves with ever coarser stimuli. We need more sensationalized depictions of sex, more violence, more brassy-braying media and entertainment. . . .

Once we face the possible loss of a collective future, we lose all sorts of things. There's no longer a rationale for caring: there's no longer a reason to take pride in our work. The concepts of heroism and altruism become pointless. With no human future, why sacrifice anything in the present? . . . People want to get theirs before the big one drops.

Our denial and deadening also leave us with a flimsy basis for making moral judgments. Yet at its root, nuclear war is a moral problem. In his book *The Undiscovered Self,* C. G. Jung wrote:

It is not that present-day man is capable of greater evil than the man of antiquity or the primitive. He merely has incomparably more effective means with which to realize his proclivity to evil. As his consciousness has broadened and differentiated, so his moral nature has lagged behind. That is the great problem before us today.

Some people, it has been suggested, could be well-adjusted in hell itself. But we can ask whether "adjustment" has any meaning in a world devoid of moral values. A young launch control officer at an ICBM base described such a world well when he stated the operational policy of the base: "We have two tasks. The first is not to let people go off their rockers. That's the negative side. The positive side is to ensure that people act without moral compunction."

Although we often do not think of generals as being concerned with morality, Omar Bradley, chairman of the joint chiefs of staff from 1949 to 1953, was very sensitive to the moral problem pointed out by Jung. He stated: "We have grasped the mystery of the atom and rejected the Sermon on the Mount. The world has achieved brilliance without wisdom, power without conscience. Ours is a world of nuclear giants and ethical infants. We know more about killing than we know about living. . . ." Bradley further stated that he was not so much distressed by the magnitude of the problem as by "the average citizen's colossal indifference to it."

According to psychiatrist Roger Walsh (Walsh, 1984):

Repression and denial are the crutches we use to help us avoid it (reality). One of the most persistent sources of despair to those working in these areas is the recognition of just how hard it is to sustain awareness of the true state of the world. "I'd rather not think about it," "It's not really so bad," or, "It will all work out somehow" are just some of the statements that spring from repression and denial. The result is "ostrichism" which narcotizes us and saps our motivation to respond in appropriate ways.

But the mechanisms of repression and denial extend further. We wish to deny not only the state of the world, but also our role in producing it. Hence we use the mechanism of projection to attribute to others the unacknowledged aspects of our self-image and motives (what Jungians call the "shadow"), and thus create "the image of the enemy."

The image is usually stereotypic and mirror-like. That is, no matter who "the enemy" is—Germans or British, Russians or Americans—they tend to be ascribed similar stereotypic traits and motives. These perceptions are mirror-like because enemies tend to perceive each other similarly, each ascribing hostility and untrustworthiness to the other and seeing themselves as well-intentioned and benign. The process is further exacerbated by the "mote-beam phenomenon" that allows us to recognize the faults of others with crystal clarity while somehow missing our own. Moreover, what we deny in ourselves we tend to attack in others, a process that clearly operates as destructively at the international level as it does at the interpersonal.

The net result of all these defense mechanisms is "psychic numbing." This is a narcotizing of our awareness that denies the world's reality (and our own), replacing it with distorted self-serving illusions that justify our misperceptions and deceptions, fuel our addictions and aversions, separate and alienate us from others, and further exacerbate the problems they were created to deny.

Helplessness

The prospect of a nuclear confrontation between the superpowers is so awesome that we can become filled with feelings of helplessness and despair. One individual seems to count for so little in the vast sweep of history—in a world of proliferation of nuclear weapons and delivery systems, refinement of weapons technology, and the institutionalization of the nuclear arms race by various government bureaucracies and their constituencies in both the United States and the Soviet Union.

A Japanese psychiatrist was particularly struck by westerners' lack of appreciation for and inability to alleviate feelings of helplessness in themselves or others. Rather than understanding and trying to assuage such feelings, our stance is to ask ourselves and others to "shape up" or "get on with it." In his book, *The Anatomy of Dependence,* Takeo Doi (1983) explains that the Japanese have a special verb, **amaeru,** which means to presume upon a person, particularly when one is feeling helpless. It permits a person to be the passive recipient of the love and support of another, the infant suckling at the mother's breast. In contrast to western society, in Japanese culture, "to amaeru" is a pervasive and completely acceptable form of behavior.

Our cultural intolerance of feelings of helplessness makes it difficult for us to express them and leads to suppression and psychic numbing. Herman Kahn, in his book *On Thermonuclear War* (1961), gives an example of this western attitude. In an imagined postnuclear world one person tells another: ''You have only received 10 roentgens, why are you vomiting? Pull yourself together and get to work.''

Dr. Macy says that ''opening to our despair opens us to the love that is within us, for it is in deep caring that our anguish is rooted. . . .'' Facing the tiger of despair permits us to be more fully human. When our feelings are not deadened, we can be open to others who have had the same experience. Deep reserves of strength emerge and possibilities for collective action arise. In action, feelings of helplessness are transformed to excitement, and power is generated for societal change.

Children and the Nuclear Threat

Although parents would perhaps have it otherwise, most children are aware of the nuclear threat. It is natural to try to shield children from this folly perpetrated by the adult world, but the information is too pervasive for such an effort to be successful. In children the terror of a possible nuclear war is not as suppressed as in adults, and they can be easily encouraged to describe their feelings. In the words of a third-grader: ''In Boston there's going to be a war and there's going to be fire coming to earth and from the sky a bomb is coming to earth and the earth is going to split open and fire is going to come down to earth.'' The film *In the Nuclear Shadow: What Can the Children Tell Us?** is a particularly poignant chronicle of the feelings and concerns about nuclear war that even very young children have.

In a Society of Friends meeting a father told of an experience during a late-night thunderstorm in the Sacramento Valley—a rare occurrence there. His small son, who had never experienced a thunderstorm, came running into his bedroom in panic shouting, ''It's nuclear war—they're hitting Sacramento.''

It is vital that we share our concerns with the children and not leave them to struggle with their fears alone. Children believe that their parents are all-powerful. Parents are their world and their support system. Thus it is reassuring to children when parents are involved in political action that concerns the nuclear threat. Then when they see frightening things on television or hear them elsewhere, they will be able to think that their parents are doing something about it, that it will be taken care of.

In Japan in the third and fourth grades children study the effects of the atomic bombing of Hiroshima and Nagasaki and discuss what students might do to promote peace. Older grades read material written by the victims of the atomic bombings.

A study by John E. Mack (1981) shows that children feel that their future is in danger, and many believe that ''planning ahead'' is pointless. Although most of them said that they still plan on careers, marriage, and families, all expressed doubts and fears as to the validity of long-term planning. This sense of ''radical futurelessness'' leaves some of these children bitter and cynical. They feel helpless, in an uncertain world, and are likely to lead their lives impulsively and selfishly.

---

*Educational Film and Video Project, 1725 Seabright Ave., Santa Cruz, CA 95062.

A task force report on psychosocial aspects of nuclear developments conducted by the American Psychiatric Association (R.R. Rogers, 1981) corroborates Mack's findings. They report that "profound uncertainty about whether or not mankind has a forseeable future exerts a corrosive and malignant influence upon important development processes in normal and well-functioning children."

A joint Soviet-American study of adolescent attitudes toward nuclear weapons and nuclear war is reported in the *New England Journal of Medicine* by Chivian et al. (Chivian, 1988). The study involved large samples of adolescents from both cultures. The American sample used 3370 students from the Maryland area and the Soviet sample employed 2148 students from the Rostov-Tambov region. Both samples were from heartland areas away from more cosmopolitan centers such as Leningrad or Moscow in the Soviet case. For both the Maryland and the Tambov-Rostov teenagers the two greatest worries were "your mother or father dying" and "nuclear war." The U.S. students worried more about their parents' death and the Soviet students worried more about nuclear war. The Soviet students were slightly younger than their American counterparts, 11 to 17 years, whereas the American students were from 12 to 18 years in age. Analysis of variance in responses by age or sex revealed no major differences for either country in the responses. Table 22-1 is taken from the joint study.

TABLE 22-1
Mean scores and ordering of worries

Subject of worry	U.S. teenagers (N = 2305)	Soviet teenagers (N = 2148)
1. Your mother or father dying	3.20	3.75 (2)
2. Nuclear war	3.11	3.89 (1)
3. Poor grades	2.83	3.24 (7)
4. Your own death	2.71	3.07 (9)
5. Illness, disability, accident	2.71	3.28 (6)
6. Not finding a satisfying job	2.71	2.50 (17)
7. World hunger	2.70	3.64 (3)
8. Being a victim of violent crime	2.65	3.11 (8)
9. Nuclear-power plant accident	2.54	3.62 (4)
10. Getting cancer	2.46	2.54 (16)
11. Getting or making someone pregnant	2.30	2.54 (15)
12. Environmental pollution	2.24	3.44 (5)
13. Insufficient family resources	2.17	2.38 (19)
14. Being considered physically unattractive	2.16	2.54 (14)
15. People not liking me	2.02	2.69 (12)
16. Overpopulation of the planet	1.93	2.94 (11)
17. Getting hooked on drugs	1.85	2.66 (13)
18. Divorce of parents	1.84	2.98 (10)
19. Earthquakes	1.69	2.50 (18)

Taken from a joint Soviet-American study of teenagers' concerns about nuclear war by Chivian et al. Mean scores given above were derived from a scale in which "not at all worried" was equal to 1 and "very worried" was equal to 4. The Soviet ranking is indicated in parentheses.

Source: *New England Journal of Medicine.*

Illusions

In Chapter 4, we spoke of "nuclear diplomacy." Unfortunately, some U.S. strategists even today seek security through "nuclearism" — the reliance on nuclear weapons to further our foreign policy.

Beilenson and Cohen (1982) illustrate this approach:

> The United States is on the wrong road [because it is not] . . . fully exploiting the military consequences of the nuclear revolution. . . . Current security arrangements are catastrophe-prone [because of] . . . our well-intentioned but misconceived readiness to fight wars with conventional weapons all over the world.

Their recommendation for increasing the nation's security is through shifting our defense spending priorities toward even more emphasis on nuclear weaponry. Considering the dilemmas of the arms race, the concept seems illusory.

A prevalent illusion among nuclear strategists is that a nuclear conflict could be conducted rationally. This is exemplified in an article by Colin Gray and Keith Payne (1980) entitled "Victory Is Possible" in which they state: "If American nuclear power is to support U.S. foreign policy objectives, the United States must possess the ability to wage nuclear war rationally. . . . The United States should plan to defeat the Soviet Union and to do so at a cost that would not prohibit U.S. recovery [and] . . . identify war aims that in the last resort would contemplate the destruction of Soviet political authority and the emergence of a post-war world order compatible with Western values." Such considerations ignore the grave risk that nuclear conflict involving superpowers, however limited initially, would escalate into a full-scale exchange.

Implicit in the arguments for a policy of limited nuclear war is the assumption that there will be recovery. This is a particularly dangerous illusion. Lipton writes (1983b):

> The illusion of limit and control [is related] . . . to virtually all false assumptions about the bomb. . . . The psychological key is the assumption that a preplanned combination of bold, limited nuclear action and equally bold, more or less unlimited nuclear threat can enable us to control the situation and keep it limited. This assumption defies virtually all psychological experience. Having nuclear weapons dropped on one or even on a close ally can readily be perceived as threatening to a nation's overall existence. A response to that kind of threat is likely to include full expression of one's potential for violence, which means full use of one's available nuclear arsenal.

President Carter embraced the concept of limited nuclear war toward the end of his administration (in Presidential Directive 59). The same policy was endorsed by the Reagan administration. On October 16, 1981, President Reagan discussed nuclear policy in a meeting with a group of visiting editors. He asserted on that occasion that a nuclear exchange could occur "without it bringing either one of the major powers to pushing the button." When asked 25 days later at a press conference whether he still held to that belief, he appeared uncomfortable, made a long rambling response, and concluded by saying that "limited nuclear exchange was a 'possibility' that could take place." He then added, "You could have a pessimistic outlook on it or an optimistic one. I tend to be optimistic."*

22-3 THE PSYCHOLOGICAL EFFECTS OF THE USE OF NUCLEAR WEAPONS

Since there has not been a nuclear war, the assessment of the psychological consequences of such a war must rest on professional opinion, impossible to verify, which represents extrapolation from known psychological responses to predicted responses to an unprecedented situation. The only time that human beings have been exposed to nuclear weapons was at the end of World War II—at Hiroshima and Nagasaki. A study of the Japanese reactions to these events is a basis for trying to understand what the psychological implications of a full-scale nuclear war might be.

The Japanese Experience

Robert Lifton (1982) interviewed survivors of Hiroshima. He was able to formulate the responses of the victims into four general stages:

1. Death immersion
2. Invisible contamination
3. Atomic bomb disease
4. Lifelong identification with the dead

The **death-immersion** experience involved the image of a grotesque and absurd death not related to the life cycle. Survivors recalled not only feeling that they themselves would soon die but experiencing a sense that the whole world was dying. In the words of one survivor:

> I just could not understand why our surroundings changed so greatly in one instant. . . . I thought it must have been something which had nothing to do with the war, the collapse of the earth, which was said to take place at the end of the world, which I had read about as a child. . . . There was a fearful silence, which made me feel that all people . . . were dead.

In the second stage, invisible contamination, victims began to experience the symptoms of acute radiation sickness: diarrhea and weakness, ulceration of the mouth, bleeding from bodily orifices.

> The symptoms gave rise to a special image in the minds of the people of Hiroshima— an image of a force that not only kills and destroys on a colossal scale, but also leaves behind in the bodies of those exposed to it deadly influences that may emerge at any time and strike down their victims. (Lifton, 1968.)

---

*Boston Globe, Nov. 11, 1981, p. 1.

In describing the third stage—the long-term effects and anxieties called *atomic bomb disease* by the Japanese—a Japanese physician referred to fatal malignancies in blood-forming organs, such as leukemia, as well as thyroid, breast, stomach, lung, and other cancers. The cancers occurred with a latency period of years or even decades after the bombing. The anxiety is everpresent:

> Yes, of course, people are anxious. Take my own case. If I am shaving in the morning and if I should happen to cut myself slightly, I dab the blood with a piece of paper—and then when I notice that it has stopped flowing, I think to myself, "Well, I guess I'm all right." (Lifton, 1968.)

The Hiroshima experience culminates in the fourth stage—a lifelong identification with the dead. The survivors are in their own eyes and the eyes of others a tainted group—the hibakusha. They are poor marriage risks because of the possibility of somatic or genetic damage. They are also poor risks for employment because of physical and psychological impairment. They are also reminders, with their keloid burn scars, of a fearful event that people do not want to be reminded of. The Japanese government belatedly recognized them in the late 1950s as a group eligible for special consideration. (Earlier, the U.S. occupation authorities had forbidden any discussion of the atomic bombings and their effects.)

The Committee for the Compilation of Materials on Damage Caused by the Atomic Bombs in Hiroshima and Nagasaki (Committee, 1981) discussed the psychological effects of the atomic bombings:

> Certainly the most sweeping and searing destruction ever visited upon mankind left an enormous, abhorrent, and lifelong impression in the minds and memories of all its victims. Even today, over thirty years after the bombings, there is no end to the hundreds of diaries, testimonies, and drawings that annually come from the hands of victims, some of which gain the attention of the mass media. Despite the passage of time, the memories of these survivors are strikingly vivid and concrete. . . . The startling lucidity of the A-bomb victims' memories is surely one proof of the enormity of the psychological shock they suffered.
>
> The severity of this shock, along with other disabling conditions, has robbed the victims of their psychological equilibrium; indeed, the psychological damage was so great that it may be said that they were deprived of their "humanity." At the same time, the victims have struggled to overcome psychological disintegration and to recover their humanity. Such psychological breakdown, continuing and growing in severity, and the efforts to surmount it have been shared by all A-bomb victims. . . .
>
> The overpowering situation of "total collapse" left the A-bomb victims incapable of affirming life—their world was completely ruled by "death and desolation." The bombing and its continued effects constantly pulled them back into that world. But these victims were surrounded daily by other people whose silent testimony was that mankind still lives; that babies are being born; and that the victims too are in fact part of that living community. Passage from death to life became a matter of pressing necessity, and most victims chose life. It was not an easy choice.

The following is a letter written by an operations officer who was sent to Nagasaki to remove U.S. prisoners of war before the occupation troops arrived. His widow gave permission for its publication in the *Bulletin of Atomic Scientists* (Bryson, 1982):

Nagasaki
September 14, 1945

The atomic bomb damage is a story in itself. Rubble and ruins I know and can look upon without any particular emotions. This is indescribably different. As you enter the harbor and look at the buildings from a distance they appear to be intact. As you come closer you see that the houses are windowless. The shingles on the roofs have the appearance of a moulting hen. The ridge rafters are broken, allowing the roofs to sag in the middle. Many of the older houses have just collapsed like a tired beast of burden which has fallen from exhaustion. A smell of death and corruption pervades the place, ranging from the ordinary carrion smell to somewhat subtler stenches with strong overtones of ammonia (decomposing nitrogenous matter, I suppose).

The general impression, which transcends our physical sense, is one of deadness, the absolute essence of death in the sense of finality without hope of resurrection. And all this is not localized. It's everywhere, and nothing has escaped its touch. In most ruined cities you can bury the dead, clean up the rubble, rebuild the houses and have a living city again. One feels that it is not so here. Like the ancient Sodom and Gomorrah, its site has been sown with salt and ichabod is written over its gates.

Tons of newsprint will be devoted to the things written about this place, and all is far better written than I can write, but the real thing can't be put into words. Therefore I shall stop trying.

Captain William C. Bryson (U.S.N.)

The Psychological Effects of General Nuclear War

Extrapolation of the experiences of the hibakusha to the situation that would prevail after a general nuclear war can only dimly serve as a starting point. It is most unlikely that there would be anyone from the "outside" to reinstill a sense of humanity in the survivors and break their psychological bonds with death. The loss of one's entire culture and the fact that there would be no succor from healthy fellow citizens would add to the almost unbearable personal losses.

We have found no medical professionals who do not believe that general nuclear war would be a psychological catastrophe. Exactly what the response would be to such an unprecedented calamity no one can say with certainty. However, to provide some awareness of what might occur, we conclude this chapter by quoting Kai Erickson and Robert Jay Lifton (1983), who attempted to address the question of the psychological effects of a nuclear war.

Hiroshima and Nagasaki, however, can provide us with no more than a hint of what would happen in the event of nuclear war. A single weapon today can have the power of one thousand Hiroshima bombs and we have to imagine one thousand of those exploding in the space of a few minutes. Moreover, in the case of Hiroshima and Nagasaki—and this is absolutely crucial—there was still a functioning outside world to provide help.

In nuclear war the process of psychic numbing may well be so extreme as to become irreversible.

Imagine the familiar landscape turning suddenly into a sea of destruction. Everywhere smoldering banks of debris, everywhere the sights and sounds and smells of death. Imagine that the other survivors are wandering about with festering wounds, broken limbs, and bodies so badly burned that their features appear to be melting and their flesh is peeling away in great raw folds. Imagine on the generous assumption that your children are alive at all—that you have no way of knowing whether the radiation they have been exposed to has already doomed them.

The suddenness and the sheer ferocity of such a scene would not give survivors any chance to mobilize the usual forms of psychological defense. The normal human response to mass death and profound horror is not rage or depression or panic or mourning or even fear; it is a kind of mental anesthetization that interferes with both judgment and compassion for other people.

In even minor disasters, the mind becomes immobilized, if only for a moment. But in the event of a nuclear attack, the immobilization may reach the point where the psyche is no longer connected to its own past and is, for all practical purposes, severed from the social forms from which it drew strength and a sense of humanity. The mind would, then, be shut down altogether.

The resulting scene might well resemble what we usually can only imagine as science fiction. The landscape is almost moonlike, spare and quiet, and the survivors who root among the ruins seem to have lost contact with one another, not to mention the ability to form cooperating groups and to offer warmth and solace to people around them.

In every catastrophe for which we have adequate records, survivors emerge from the debris with the feeling that they are (to use anthropologist Anthony Wallace's words) "naked and alone . . . in a terrifying wilderness of ruins."

In most cases—and this, too, is well recorded in the literature of disaster—that sense of isolation quickly disappears with the realization that the rest of the world is still intact. The disaster, it turns out, is local, confined, bounded. Out there beyond the peripheries of the affected zone are other people—relatives, neighbors, countrymen—who bring blankets and warm coffee, medicines, and ambulances. The larger human community is gathering its resources to attend to a wound on its flank, and survivors respond to the attention and the caring with the reassuring feeling that there is life beyond the ruins, after all. That sense of communion, that perception that the textures of social existence remain more or less whole, is a very important part of the healing that follows.

None of that will happen in nuclear war.

There will be no surrounding human community, no undamaged world out there to count on.

No one will come in to nurse the wounded or carry them off to hospitals. There will be no hospitals, no morphine, no antibiotics.

There will be no succor from the outside—no infusion of vitality, the confidence in the continuity of life that disaster victims have always needed so desperately.

Rather, survivors will remain in a deadened state, either alone or among others like themselves, largely without hope and vaguely aware that everyone and everything that once mattered to them has been destroyed.

Thus survivors would be experiencing not only the most extreme forms of individual trauma imaginable, but an equally severe form of collective trauma stemming from a rupture of the patterns of social existence.

Virtually no survivors will be able to enact that most fundamental of all human rituals, burying their own dead.

The bonds that link people in connecting groups will be badly torn, in most cases irreparably, and their behavior is likely to become muted and accompanied by suspiciousness and extremely primitive forms of thought and action.

Under these conditions, such simple tasks as acquiring food and maintaining shelter would remain formidable for weeks and months, even years. And the bands of survivors would be further reduced not only by starvation but also by continuing exposure to radiation and by virulent epidemics.

For those who manage to stay alive, the effects of radiation may interfere with their capacity to reproduce at all or their capacity to give birth to anything other than grossly deformed infants. But few indeed would have to face that prospect.

The question often asked, "Would the survivors envy the dead?" may turn out to have a simple answer. No, they would be incapable of such feelings. They would not so much envy as, inwardly and outwardly, resemble the dead.

QUESTIONS

1. How do we "domesticate" nuclear weapons?
2. Give some examples of psychic numbing.
3. What is atomic bomb disease?
4. How were the hibakusha treated by Japanese society?
5. Describe some of the probable differences in the psychological effects experienced in a postattack Hiroshima or Nagasaki and those that could be expected after a global nuclear war.
6. What are some positive steps one can take to transform feelings of helplessness in connection with the nuclear threat?
7. Describe some of the feelings engendered by the nuclear threat.
8. Can children be protected from the knowledge of the nuclear threat? If not, why not?
9. What is the Japanese concept of "amaeru"? Is this an acceptable concept in western culture?
10. Do you think that any of the "illusions" concerning nuclear war or nuclear weapons mentioned in this chapter are not illusions, but are valid?
11. Explain why perceptions are so important to stability in our nuclear world.
12. Do you agree with Carl Jung's judgment of the moral character of the modern world?
13. According to Chellis Glendinning what is the effect of the perceived loss of a collective future?
14. What is nukespeak?
15. What is the experience of "death immersion" that was pervasive in the survivors of Hiroshima and Nagasaki?
16. Describe your own reactions to the atomic bomb. As a child. Today. As you imagine yourself reacting in 10 years. Try to use any particularly clear incidents to clarify your reactions and feelings about nuclear war.

17. Find some quotations concerning nuclear war in current newspapers or news magazines that you believe provide illustrations of dehumanization.
18. Compare Soviet and American teenagers' chief worries.

KEY WORDS

amaeru   the Japanese verb which means to presume upon a person and that it is O.K. to feel helpless.

death immersion   the experience of atomic bombing victims that the whole world is dying.

hibakusha   the Japanese survivors of the atomic bombings.

psychic numbing   a psychological mechanism of denial of a reality that is too painful to face: "I'd rather not think about it" or "It will work out somehow" are expressions that betray psychic numbing.

CHAPTER 23

PROLIFERATION

The atomic bomb is a paper tiger which the U.S. reactionaries use to scare people. It looks terrible, but in fact it isn't.

Mao, 1960

Two men look out through the same bars. One sees the mud, and one sees the stars.

Frederick Langbridge

23-1 THEMES

The United States and the Soviet Union both wish to control and limit nuclear weapons not under their own jurisdiction. This has been an area of substantial agreement between the superpowers. Two broad issues are involved. First, nuclear weapons may be sought by the developed nations, particularly those nations which are, or may be, perceived as enemies. Second, other nations may seek to acquire the ability to build nuclear weapons. These two issues constitute the proliferation problem.

The massive buildup of large numbers of nuclear weapons in the arsenals of the United States, the Soviet Union, the United Kingdom, and France is often referred to as **vertical proliferation.** The spread of nuclear weapons to other nations is called **horizontal proliferation** or, occasionally, the "**N country** problem." Most of this book deals with vertical proliferation. In this chapter we examine horizontal proliferation, including the connection between research and power reactors and the production of nuclear weapons. Chapter 24 explores the problems of determining what other nations are doing and of verifying treaties and other agreements designed to limit both vertical and horizontal proliferation.

23-2 POLITICAL FACTORS

The term *horizontal nuclear proliferation* refers to the acquisition of nuclear weapons by nations or terrorist organizations. Members of the nuclear "club" now include the United States, the Soviet Union, the United Kingdom, France, and China. In addition, in 1974 India tested one "peaceful" nuclear device. Many other nations have the technical potential for producing nuclear weapons—either by using enriched uranium or plutonium produced in research or power reactors or by using material purchased surreptitiously or stolen.

The major nuclear powers have great interest in selling their civilian reactor technologies to developing nations. This leads to a fundamental difficulty. On the one hand, the exporting of nuclear technologies increases international trade; on the other, it increases the likelihood that nuclear weapons will be produced elsewhere.

The Nonproliferation Treaty

The most significant international agreement that attempted to address this problem was the **Nonproliferation Treaty (NPT)** of 1968. This was an attempt to limit the spread of nuclear weapons by providing incentives to other nations not to build them. Under the terms of the NPT, the nations that have developed nuclear weapons are committed not to give or sell them, or the technology to manufacture them, to other nations. Similarly, the nonnuclear states agree not to acquire nuclear weapons or the technology to manufacture them. Nonnuclear states also agree to inspection of their facilities by the **International Atomic Energy Agency (IAEA).** Members of the nuclear club permit inspection of their nonmilitary nuclear installations on a voluntary basis. The inspections are done to assure compliance with the treaty and to prevent diversion of fissionable material from peaceful uses for weapons programs. Under the NPT, the nuclear nations agree to assist the nonnuclear nations in developing peaceful uses of nuclear energy. To date over 130 countries have signed the NPT, and the number of nations having tested nuclear weapons has not expanded, except for India (a nonsigner). One of the brighter spots in the picture of the nuclear arms race is the fact that so few nations have chosen to develop nuclear weapons.

The authority of the IAEA is limited. Several countries (Argentina, Israel, India, Pakistan, and South Africa) have extensive nuclear power programs, yet will not permit IAEA inspections in all facilities. Israel cited lack of confidence in the IAEA safeguards as justification for their 1981 bombing of the Iraqi Osiraq reactor near Baghdad, which the Israelis believed would be used to produce weapons-grade nuclear material.

One NPT provision requires members of the nuclear club to reduce their nuclear arsenals and seek arms control agreements. At review conferences in 1975 and 1980, nonnuclear states complained strongly that the nuclear states, particularly the superpowers, have shown a lack of good faith in not carrying out such reductions and making such agreements. Instead, the nuclear arms race has continued. Arms control agreements and genuine steps to deescalate the arms race by the superpowers would be a positive factor in support of nonproliferation. (See also Chapter 2.)

Why Nations Build Nuclear Weapons

A nation's decision to begin or not to begin a nuclear weapons program is a complex matter. For example, after World War II, the United Kingdom decided secretly to launch a nuclear program partly because the British wished to be independent of the

United States in nuclear matters and partly because they had actively participated in the Manhattan Project and for them the development of nuclear weapons had a "technological momentum."

The Soviet Union did not pursue the development of nuclear weapons in the early part of World War II because of more pressing military priorities and also because older members of the Soviet Academy of Sciences did not wish to jeopardize their positions in the new field of nuclear energy. In 1940, they won out in a power struggle with younger scientists (Holloway, 1979). When, in 1942, it became known to the Soviets that the United States and (as they believed) Germany were working on a nuclear bomb, Stalin decided to begin a low-priority program—perhaps as a hedge for the postwar world. After Hiroshima and Nagasaki, the Soviet nuclear program was given high priority.

Israel offers another example. Israel has pursued an active nuclear program since becoming a nation in 1948 and is thought by many to have nuclear weapons in nearly complete form. The knowledge that Israel might have nuclear weapons held in reserve as a last resort could serve to deter hostile neighbors from initiating a conflict.

India developed an atomic bomb in 1974, both for domestic reasons and to enhance international prestige. India had had a series of border skirmishes with the Chinese, who by then had a modest nuclear arsenal.

Pakistan is reputed to be working on a nuclear weapons program, possibly in response to India's development—but perhaps also to gain the attention of the superpowers. In the case of Pakistan there are substantial economic reasons for not giving nuclear development a high priority since the necessary resources are scarce and could be better used for other purposes.

Potter (1982) has analyzed the political factors affecting proliferation. Table 23-1 reflects the complexity of the issue.

Many foreign policy experts are concerned that the acquisition of nuclear weapons by developing and other countries could lead to involvement of the superpowers in a nuclear catastrophe if a weapon were used in one of the many wars that take place regularly throughout the world. Both the United States and the Soviet Union support regimes in many countries with potential nuclear capability. Israel is one example.

23-3 TECHNICAL FACTORS

One of the principal technical aspects of the proliferation problem is the "weapons connection." By this is meant the fact that power reactors and research reactors produce plutonium, a weapons material, as a by-product of their operation. Some reactors also use enriched uranium or plutonium, a fuel which can be diverted to use for weapons.

Light-Water Reactors

While power reactors have much in common with fission bombs, there are important differences. Both rely on the facts, discussed in Chapter 11, that neutron-induced

TABLE 23-1
Summary of proliferation determinants

Country	Most likely precipitating factor	Underlying pressures		Underlying constraints	
		Primary	Secondary	Primary	Secondary
Argentina	18	4, 5	7	9, 11, 13	12, 14
Brazil	18	4, 5		9, 11, 13	12, 14
Canada*		2		11, 12	5, 15, 16
France		4, 5, 8			15
India	18, 19, 22	4, 5	1, 7, 8	18	9, 10, 12, 13, 15
Israel	18, 19, 22	1, 3	2, 5	9, 13	16
People's Republic of China		1, 4, 5			9, 15, 17
Pakistan	18, 20, 21	1, 2, 5	7	9, 13	10
Taiwan*	20, 22	1, 2, 3, 5	4	9, 13	10
South Korea*	20	1, 2	5	9, 13	10
United Kingdom*					
World War II	19	2	6		
Postwar	19	4, 5	8		
United States*	19	2	8		
Soviet Union*	18	1		17 (WW II)	

1 Deterrence	12 International norms
2 Warfighting advantage	13 Economic and political sanctions
3 Weapon of last resort	14 Unauthorized seizure
4 Status and prestige	15 Economic costs
5 Autonomy and influence	16 Public opinion
6 Economic spillover	17 Bureaucratic politics
7 Domestic politics	18 Nuclearization of other states
8 Technological momentum	19 International crisis
9 Military reaction by other states	20 Weakening of security guarantees
10 Strategic credibility gap	21 Increased accessibility of knowhow and material
11 Absence of perceived threat	22 Domestic crisis/leadership

*NPT signer.

Source: Potter, 1982.

fission of uranium or plutonium releases about 200 MeV of energy, plus the emission of several neutrons. The major difference between a reactor and a fission bomb is that a fission bomb releases a very large amount of energy very quickly in a self-destructive explosion, while a reactor accomplishes the controlled release of energy over an extended period of time.

The operation of a power reactor may be understood using the ideas developed in the technical discussion in Chapter 10 on radioactivity and that of Section 11-3 on how fission bombs work. You should refer to that material to help you understand the discussion here. In that discussion we discussed why bombs must be assembled quickly, and how a few neutrons injected by the trigger at just the right time lead to exponential growth of the number of fissions. After a small number of **shakes** (hundredths of a microsecond) so much energy has been released that the bomb blows itself apart and the fission process stops.

Like a bomb, a power reactor contains enough fissionable material to sustain a chain reaction. However, the rate at which the chain reaction proceeds is carefully controlled. This is accomplished by inserting into the reactor control rods made of a material which efficiently absorbs some of the neutrons. The arrangement is shown schematically in Figure 23-1. The reaction is started slowly and carefully by gradually withdrawing the control rods. As this is done the number of fissions occurring per second gradually increases until it reaches a desired rate of energy release.

Most of the energy released in a fission appears as kinetic energy of the fission fragments. These fragments are slowed down by multiple collisions with the atoms of the reactor, which become hot. The heat is transferred to a coolant, usually water, which heats up and produces steam. The steam then drives a turbine connected to a generator of electricity.

Most power reactors designed in the United States and in Europe use fuel composed of uranium enriched in ^{235}U as a fuel, and ordinary water as a coolant. Such reactors are called **light-water reactors,** or **LWRs.** Some power reactors use heavy water (deuterium oxide) or graphite for thermalization, slowing down the neutrons. Reactors in which the water is turned to steam within the reactor are called **boiling-water reactors (BWRs).** Reactors where the water is pressurized so that it cannot boil within the reactor vessel are called **pressurized-water reactors (PWRs).** In a PWR the hot pressurized water leaving the reactor is run through a heat exchanger where steam is produced.

The neutrons in a fission bomb have energies of about 1 MeV (see Section P11-3). They move at a speed of a few percent of the speed of light. In power reactors the neutrons are slowed down, or thermalized by scattering (from water in United States power reactors). The term thermalization means that the neutrons are cooled so that their temperature is about the same as that of the hot water in the reactor, typically about 600°F.

In most United States commercial reactors slowing down of the fast neutrons is by collisions with the cooling water. Some research reactors and a few power reactors (Chernobyl, for example) use scattering from other materials, such as graphite (carbon) atoms.

A few percent of the neutrons released in fission are delayed by a fraction of a second. These neutrons come from decay of fission products. Even though there aren't very many of them, the delayed neutrons are extremely important, for they allow time to control the power of the reactor.

In a bomb it is essential that no neutrons are present while the critical mass is being assembled (see Chapter 11). The fissionable material used for bombs must be chosen so that it emits very few neutrons spontaneously. ^{235}U and ^{239}Pu have this property (see Table 11-4). In reactors spontaneous neutrons do little harm. Weapons-grade uranium or plutonium must be highly enriched in these low-neutron-emitting isotopes. However, a reactor can be built with material which emits many neutrons, and which would be unsuitable for bomb construction.

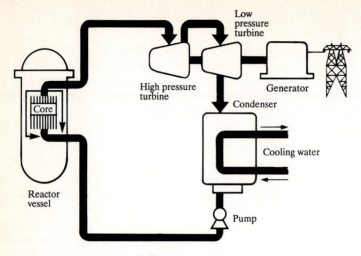

Boiling-water reactor

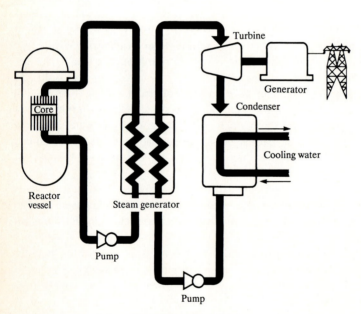

Pressurized-water reactor

FIGURE 23-1
Light-water reactors. The top illustration shows a boiling water reactor (BWR). Water is heated by a nuclear reaction, producing steam, which drives a turbine. The lower illustration is a pressurized water reactor (PWR). Boiling of the water is prevented by maintaining a system pressure of about 2250 pounds per square inch. The hot water passes through a steam generator, where steam is produced, which drives a turbine. (*Source: Department of Energy ERDA-76-107.*)

Weapons-grade material contains 90 percent or more ^{235}U or ^{239}Pu. Reactor-grade uranium typically only need contain about 2 to 3 percent ^{235}U, which is produced by enrichment of naturally occurring uranium which contains about 0.7 percent ^{235}U, with most of the rest being ^{238}U. A uranium-fueled reactor produces plutonium from ^{238}U through the process described in Chapter 2, p. 15. The process involves capture of a neutron by ^{238}U which subsequently decays by emitting a beta particle and an antineutrino to form neptunium 239. The neptunium 239 in turn beta-decays to plutonium 239. In nuclear physics language (see Chapter 10):

$$^{238}_{92}\text{U} + ^{1}_{0}n \rightarrow ^{239}_{92}\text{U} \rightarrow ^{239}_{93}\text{Np} + ^{0}_{-1}e + ^{0}_{0}\bar{\nu} \rightarrow ^{239}_{94}\text{Pu} + ^{0}_{-1}e + ^{0}_{0}\bar{\nu} \quad (23\text{-}1)$$
$$\underset{\text{23 min}}{} \underset{\text{2.4 days}}{}$$

$^{239}_{94}$Pu has a half-life of 24,100 years and therefore can be isolated and purified (although it is dangerously radioactive).

The most critical point is that plutonium differs chemically from uranium, and therefore can be separated in relatively simple chemical processes rather than the much more complex isotopic separation processes required for separating isotopes of uranium.

The power reactors used in most of the world are light-water-cooled (boiling-water reactors and pressurized-water reactors) which use uranium enriched to 2 to 3 percent in ^{235}U. Uranium at this low enrichment level cannot be used to produce bombs directly. However, these reactors produce plutonium as a by-product. There are at present a total of about 412 commercial reactors in the world, of which 110 are in the United States, 52 in the Soviet Union, 50 in Great Britain, and 38 in France. About 560 nuclear reactors are installed in naval vessels: United States (165), Soviet Union (362), Great Britain, France (9), and China (5) (Nuclear Notebook, 1988). A 1-gigawatt (1000-megawatt) commercial light-water reactor produces about 220 kilograms of plutonium a year. One such reactor could produce enough plutonium for at least 40 to 50 fission bombs per year (the critical mass of plutonium metal is less than 4 or 5 kilograms). 412 reactors × 40 bombs per year gives us the possibility of making over 16,000 bombs per year from reprocessing of fuel rods of commercial reactors. Fortunately reprocessing facilities are not easy to conceal since they require special handling equipment for the extremely high-level radioactivity contained in the fuel rods. Since plutonium is a fissionable material, it can be recycled in the reactor, making the fuel cycle more economical and also burning up some of this long-lived, dangerous isotope. Alternatively, a nation could use the plutonium to surreptitiously develop a nuclear weapons program. Spent fuel rods can be reprocessed to produce weapons-grade fuel. Thus a key nonproliferation objective has been to introduce controls on spent fuel rods, so that all reprocessing is done under strict international control. The IAEA monitors the nuclear fuel cycle to make sure that uranium and plutonium are not diverted.

Figures 23-2 and 23-3 show schematically the process by which nuclear power is produced and the similar process by which nuclear weapons are produced (for more detail see Nero, 1979).

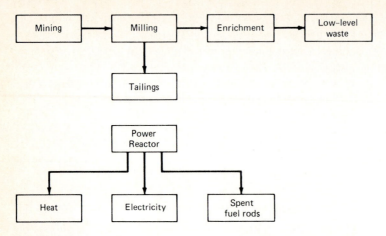

FIGURE 23-2
The open fuel cycle for the production of nuclear power. This cycle, like that of the production of nuclear weapons (Figure 23-3), begins with the mining, milling, and enriching of uranium. The enrichment process can be refined to produce weapons-grade uranium, or the plutonium produced in the power reactor can be "harvested" for a nuclear weapons program.

Uranium Enrichment

It is possible to separate ^{235}U from ^{238}U by physical means. This was the method used to produce the fissile material for the Hiroshima bomb (see Chapter 2). There are several different enrichment methods. One common method in use at this time employs a gas centrifuge; the more massive ^{238}U moves preferentially to the periphery of the centrifuge. This is the method that Pakistan is reputed to be using for its nuclear program.

Another method for uranium enrichment involves gaseous diffusion. The United States has several gigantic facilities, many built during World War II, that use gaseous diffusion. A gaseous compound of uranium is forced through porous barriers; the

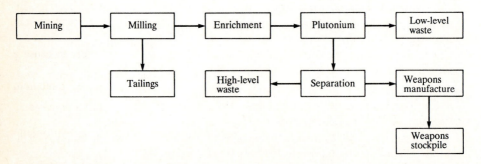

FIGURE 23-3
The fuel cycle for the production of nuclear weapons.

compound containing ^{235}U diffuses slightly faster than that containing the heavier ^{238}U. These facilities require very large investments in physical plant and power.

During the period of Chinese-Soviet cooperation in the 1950s a uranium enrichment plant was constructed in Manchuria. It is likely that the fissionable material for the first Chinese bomb came from this facility.

Research is under way at present to find a way of using lasers to perform isotopic separation. This method relies on the fact that the atomic energy levels of ^{235}U and ^{238}U are slightly different because of their different nuclear masses. It is possible to ionize preferentially an atom or molecule containing a particular uranium isotope by using a laser of the proper frequency. The ionized atom or molecule can then be separated by means of an electric or magnetic field (Palmer, 1984).

If isotopic separation by laser is successful, it will permit production of high-purity ^{235}U with much less electric power than present methods. It might also permit separation of ^{240}Pu and ^{241}Pu from ^{239}Pu. This could lead to serious nuclear proliferation. It is not yet clear whether laser separation technology will be simpler and cheaper than other enrichment methods.

Breeder Reactors

Breeder reactors, which have been extensively developed in France, form more fuel than is "burned" because extra neutrons are produced which are used to convert ^{238}U to ^{239}Pu. The plutonium is separated chemically, after which it can be used as reactor fuel—or it can be used to produce nuclear weapons. A breeder of 1000 megawatts of power might have about 5000 kilograms of plutonium in its core, with about 2500 kilograms being processed, transported, or stored at any given time. The potential for using this plutonium to produce nuclear weapons is enormous.

Denaturing Nuclear Fuel

A number of ideas have been proposed by which the plutonium from nuclear reactors would be "denatured" to make it unsuitable for nuclear weapons. One proposed approach would require that the plutonium remain in the reactor for long enough that large percentages of plutonium isotopes with high spontaneous fission rates would be formed. The best isotope for bomb building, ^{239}Pu, is dominant when fuel rods are relatively new, but as they are used, the relative proportion of the heavier plutonium isotopes (^{240}Pu, ^{241}Pu, and ^{242}Pu) increases. These heavier isotopes produce more spontaneous fissions, and hence more stray neutrons, and are thus likely to cause a bomb to explode prematurely, producing a "fizzle" (see Chapter 11).

Unfortunately, with sophisticated weapons design even denatured plutonium could be used to produce viable bombs, and denaturing of plutonium does not appear to offer a promising route to nuclear safety (Lovins, 1980).

Another idea involves "spiking" weapons-grade fuel with radioactive (usually gamma-ray-emitting) isotopes. This would make the fuel easy to trace and to identify. It could also make the material so radioactive (hot) that it could only be handled in special facilities not likely to be accessible to most organizations.

The CANDU Design

It is possible to build power reactors that do not use enriched uranium. The Canadian CANDU (CANadian DeUterium) reactor is moderated by deuterium oxide (heavy water) instead of light water. It uses natural instead of enriched uranium and thus bypasses all export controls on enriched uranium. The fissionable material used in the A-bomb exploded by India in 1974 may have been produced in a deuterium oxide moderated research reactor of this type (the Canadians had assisted the Indian nuclear program).

23-4   NUCLEAR TERRORISM

Nonnational Groups

A team of skilled terrorists could probably produce a low-yield weapon. Nuclear weapons are small, and a terrorist organization could probably place one in any major city, with little danger of being caught. The industrialized nations have learned to deal with aircraft hijacking and other acts of terrorism. It is possible that they may at some stage have to learn how to deal with nuclear blackmail and terrorism. It is not, however, easy to obtain fissionable material, and a high level of technical knowledge is needed to make even a crude bomb. In addition, because nuclear weapons can cause such enormous damage, a terrorist group that threatened to use one could alienate supporters. Further, there are many easier ways a terrorist group could cause disruption (e.g., with biological or chemical weapons).

Small Nations

The potential for terrorism exists in nations as well as in aberrant groups. In areas in the world with centuries-old bitter rivalries the lure of nuclear weapons may be particularly strong. For example, there are persistent rumors that Pakistan is attempting to build nuclear weapons, with Libya supplying the enriched uranium. The Middle East is a region where nuclear weapons might very well be used if they became available to the antagonists.

It is conceivable that a number of smaller nations may also develop the ability to deliver nuclear weapons far from their borders. Some third nation might even destroy a Soviet or United States city and attempt to make it appear that the other superpower was responsible. Such possibilities underscore the need for setting up a joint United States–Soviet intelligence center where continuous communication would take place as a means to decrease the chance that an error, or an act of aggression by another nation or a terrorist group, might plunge the world into nuclear war.

23-5   CONCLUSIONS

Preventing proliferation of nuclear weapons is a complex problem. To be successful it must take into account changing technology and a host of political and economic realities.

The Nonproliferation Treaty has been remarkably successful, if success is judged by the fact that only one new nation has exploded a nuclear weapon since it went into effect in 1970. Nevertheless, the superpowers have not pursued arms control with the vigor the treaty demands, nor have they seriously assisted the nonnuclear states in acquiring the technology to use nuclear energy for peaceful purposes. This has created dissatisfaction among the nonnuclear states, and this, in itself, might be an incentive for those states to develop a nuclear weapons program.

The IAEA is inspecting nuclear facilities, but in a limited way. One way to further discourage proliferation is to strengthen its role in the future. However, if proliferation is to be really avoided in the future, the superpowers and other nations— particularly those which produce nuclear facilities—must be truly dedicated to nonproliferation. Such dedication does not now exist.

QUESTIONS

1. Discuss the connection between nuclear power and nuclear weapons.
2. How many nuclear weapons could the Rancho Seco reactor (near Sacramento) make in one year if the fuel rods were recycled and the plutonium recovered? Assume the reactor operates 80 percent of the time and its operating level is 1000 MW. (In the United States the production of fissionable material for weapons is done in specialized facilities and is not linked to nuclear power generation.)
3. Which nations do you think could make nuclear weapons from their nuclear power programs? What kinds of technology and skills would be required?
4. How can nuclear weapons be clandestinely produced?
5. How did India make a nuclear bomb?
6. What is Pakistan's possible program for nuclear weapons development?
7. According to Potter, what is the principal reason that Taiwan refrains from producing nuclear weapons?
8. What is meant by denatured plutonium?
9. What are some of the requirements that would have to be met to use denatured plutonium or denatured uranium in a bomb? List several approaches (refer to Chapter 11).
10. How is weapons-grade plutonium produced?
11. Why is it difficult to make a bomb using reactor-grade plutonium?
12. How might you denature ^{235}U?
13. Describe how ^{235}U might be separated from ^{238}U.

KEY WORDS

boiling-water reactor   a reactor in which water is boiled directly in the reactor vessel. Compare pressurized-water reactor.

BWR   see boiling-water reactor.

horizontal proliferation   acquisition of nuclear weapons by many nations. Same as "N-country problem."

IAEA   see International Atomic Energy Agency.

International Atomic Energy Agency   an international agency headquartered in Vienna with responsibility for inspection of nuclear power plants and other technologies which might be used for weapons production.

light-water reactor   a reactor which uses ordinary water to slow down (moderate) the fission neutrons (LWR).

LWR   light-water reactor.

N-country problem   same as horizontal proliferation.

nonproliferation treaty   a treaty to slow the spread of nuclear weapons (NPT).

NPT   see nonproliferation treaty.

pressurized-water reactor   a reactor in which energy released by fission heats pressurized water, which is then used to produce steam to run a turbine. Combine boiling-water reactor.

PWR   see pressurized-water reactor.

shake $\frac{1}{100}$ millionths of a second.

vertical proliferation   buildup of nuclear weapons by the superpowers. Compare horizontal proliferation.

CHAPTER
24

VERIFICATION

In the beginning God created the heaven and the earth. And the earth was without form, and void; and darkness was upon the face of the deep. And the Spirit of God moved upon the face of the waters. And God said, Let there be light: and there was light.

Genesis

A Cowardly act? You may be sure that I would never fear to commit one if it were to my advantage.

Napoleon

24-1 THEMES

Treaties are agreements between or among nations which constrain them in various ways. Nations enter into treaties because they believe that the advantages outweigh the disadvantages. Treaties never enter into force unless all participants believe they will gain. Treaties do not rely primarily on trust. Nations must be assured through factual information that treaties are bing honored. The gathering and interpretation of such information is a part of the verification process. The United States and the Soviet Union have entered into many treaties in the past, and it appears likely there will be many more in the near future. Development of verification techniques is essential to this process since if a proposed treaty can't be adequately verified, it is extremely unlikely to be approved.

24-2 GENERAL

One objective of any nation is to minimize its need to devote resources to armaments, and to otherwise increase its security, by concluding agreements to limit deployment of weapons or to limit the ways in which weapons are used. Such international agreements often take the form of treaties or conventions, although there are other approaches, such as tacit agreements or understandings which do not rely on written documents.

Examples of various forms of agreements include the international convention prohibiting the use of biological agents in warfare; the comprehensive test ban, lasting from 1958 to 1961, which was initiated unilaterally by the Soviet Union and which was not supported by written agreements but was observed by the United States; and the Limited Test Ban Treaty signed by the Soviet Union, the United States, and a number of other nations. The SALT II agreement, though signed by the governments of the Soviet Union and the United States, was not ratified by the U.S. Senate and hence is not legally in force. It is nevertheless being observed by both nations (1988).

The INF Treaty (see Chapter 2), which entered into effect in 1988, requires dismantling of 1591 nuclear weapons delivery systems.* The treaty contains elaborate provisions for monitoring of the dismantling process and for stationing of observers at plants used for construction of the missiles. Under the INF Treaty Soviet inspectors will continuously monitor the Hercules Plant Number 1 at Magma, Utah, and U.S. inspectors will monitor the Votkinsk Machine Building Plant in the Udmurt Autonomous Soviet Socialist Republic.

The Stockholm Accords of 1986 (SIPRI Yearbook, 1987, Chapter 10) are an important agreement which does not have treaty status. These accords require notification of troop movements and authorize the presence of observers at major troop movements.

An unusual set of arrangements is being explored through informal agreements between the Soviet Union and individuals in the United States. The Natural Resources Defense Council (NRDC) signed an agreement with the Soviet Union to emplace seismometers in the vicinity of nuclear test sites. These exchanges of equipment and people led quickly to great improvements in knowledge of the seismic characteristics of regions where nuclear tests are performed. Soviet and U.S. experts are now officially directly observing nuclear explosions on each other's territory. These matters are discussed more fully in Section 24-3.

Agreements which permit United States inspectors within the Soviet Union and vice versa are a very new feature of negotiations between the superpowers. On-site inspection has been discussed for decades, but until recently has not been achieved. On-site inspection issues were given as a reason for the failure of the 1946 Baruch proposal for international control of all fissionable material (see Chapter 2). The first real sign of change occurred in negotiations over on-site inspection for a comprehensive test ban treaty under the Carter administration. However, that negotiation was unsuccessful (York, 1982).

On-site inspection is critical to many approaches to the control of nuclear weaponry and delivery systems. One must be careful not to become too optimistic about

---

*Especially U.S. Pershing II's **IRBMs** and BGM-109G GLCMs; and Soviet SS-20 [RSD-10] SS-4 [R-12], and SS-5 [R-14] IRBMs. The designations in brackets are those used by the Soviets. Only within the past few years have the Soviet designations even been made available in the west.

what is feasible. One problem has to do with the very small size of nuclear weapons. They are so small that it is almost inconceivably difficult to imagine an inspection scheme that could find all nuclear weapons in nations the size of the Soviet Union or the United States. What is more, there are several compelling reasons why a comprehensive inspection procedure would not be acceptable within this nation. One of these is the Constitution, which prohibits government officials from entering private property without a search warrant. Another is the need to maintain secrecy for many parts of the military system (would a search of the White House, the Pentagon, or the Central Intelligence Agency be acceptable?). A final compelling reason why inspections must be limited relates to industrial security. It is easy to understand that many businesses would be quite unhappy to have Soviet inspectors looking around their factories.

Whatever their form, agreements among nations always stem from a belief by each party that it will benefit. No altruism is involved. Thus all agreements, written or understood, must be verified. No nation can afford to trust another nation in matters affecting its fundamental security. Here we focus attention on the verification of treaties. This is especially important because of the atmosphere of distrust between the superpowers. The detailed wording of treaties is always conditioned to a substantial degree by problems of verification of compliance. It is for this reason that one finds treaties addressing testing of weapons (in the atmosphere, underground, or in space) but does not find treaties limiting early stages of research. A treaty attempting to limit laboratory-stage research would be virtually impossible to verify.

Verification of compliance with treaties covering testing of nuclear weapons and rockets is obtained by a variety of methods, including satellite surveillance, seismic detection of underground tests, atmospheric monitoring, and other intelligence-gathering methods. Remote techniques are collectively designated as **national technical means**.

Detection Errors

The detection of cheating in any treaty is subject to a fundamental tension because two types of error can occur. One can miss a test that was actually carried out, or one can erroneously identify a test when in fact none has been carried out.

The problems are roughly analogous to those of control of nuclear weapons. There is continual conflict between "negative control," which is designed to prevent unintended launch of nuclear weapons delivery systems, and "positive control," which assures that launch actually does occur when a properly authorized order is given. The situation can also be compared with the problems of a "hair trigger" versus a tight trigger on a gun (see Chapter 3).

In order to explain how these issues work out in practice we examine an analysis of the 150-kiloton limit of the 1976 (unratified) Threshold Test Ban Treaty (discussed below). Seismic signals from nuclear explosions provide estimates of how large the explosions are. In a typical situation the monitoring uncertainty might be a factor of two. This means that a test with an actual yield of 150 kt is equally likely to be

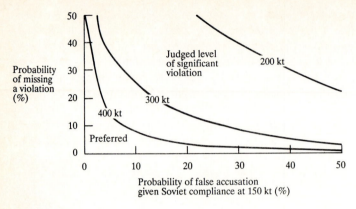

FIGURE 24-1

Sensitivity of the trade-offs between the probability of a false accusation given Soviet compliance with a 150-kt testing limit and the probability of missing an actual violation at various yields. The curves assume a factor-of-two in monitoring of yields, so that it is equally likely that an explosion actually yielding 150 kt will be thought to yield 75 kt and 300 kt. If a 300-kt violation is thought significant and one is willing to accept a situation in which one misses 25 percent of all violations, then one will make false accusations about 10 percent of the time. (*Source: Lawrence Livermore National Laboratory Verification Project. Report UCRL-53830.*)

interpreted as having a yield of 300 kt (twice the actual yield) or as 75 kt (half the actual yield).* This ratio is known as the **monitoring uncertainty factor**.

This uncertainty leads to the following problem. If one insists on a very small chance of missing a violation, then one is quite likely to often make the error of claiming a violation occurred when in fact none did. Similarly, if one wants to minimize the number of times when one will incorrectly claim a violation occurred, then one will often miss an actual violation.

These ideas are captured in Figure 24-1. The curve allows one to examine the probability of making a false accusation against the probability of missing an actual violation of the 150-kt limit, both expressed as the percent of the time that errors will be made, and both assuming a factor of two for the monitoring uncertainty factor. Consider the curve labeled "300 kt." This curve is calculated assuming that a measurement of 300 kt will be considered a violation. Suppose one is content with making false accusations 25 percent of the time. From the curve, this would imply that one would miss actual violations about 12 percent of the time. This is probably not acceptable, since erroneous accusations of cheating which occur 25 percent of the time would lead to an enormous amount of tension, and would certainly prove diplomatically unacceptable.

---

*More precisely, the probability distribution is approximately described by a "log-normal probability distribution" with a standard deviation of a factor of two. A discussion of log-normal distributions can be found in most standard textbooks on statistical techniques. The normal probability distribution is discussed in Chapter 3.

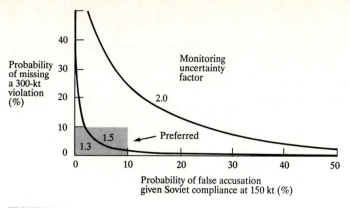

FIGURE 24-2

This figure shows how improvements in monitoring accuracy lead to reductions in uncertainty. The curve labeled "2.0" is identical to the curve labeled "300 kt" in Figure 24-1 for a 300-kt violation. The other curves examine how the probability of making errors decreases as the monitoring uncertainty error is improved to a factor of 1.5 and a factor of 1.3. At a factor of 1.3 the probability of missing a 300-kt violation is 0.25 percent when the probability of making a false accusation given actual compliance at 150 kt is 0.25 percent. These error probabilities are so low that enforcement problems should be negligible. (*Source: Lawrence Livermore National Laboratory Verification Project. Report ULRL-53830.*)

Similarly, the curve labeled 400 kt means that the United States decides to make an accusation of violation only if the seismic signal indicates that a 400-kt test was performed. From the curve labeled "400 kt," a decision to make false accusations 10 percent of the time means that actual tests at 150 kt will be missed only 8 percent of the time. This might be more acceptable politically, but on the other hand it might prove militarily unacceptable to the United States to have a substantial probability of Soviet tests as large as 400 kt.

Clearly the solution to this dilemma is to improve detection accuracy. This can be done with arrays of seismometers, and especially with seismic stations located within the Soviet Union.

As monitoring accuracy improves, the probability of error decreases rapidly. This is shown in Figure 24-2. In this figure the monitoring uncertainty error is decreased from 2 to 1.5 and to 1.3.* A monitoring uncertainty factor of 1.5 means that if one is content with making false accusations of violations only 5 percent of the time, there is only about a 3 percent chance of missing an actual violation at 300 kt. If the monitoring uncertainty factor is improved to 1.3, then when the probability of a false accusation is 0.5 percent, the probability of missing a 300-kt violation is only 0.5 percent. This level of error is probably acceptable both politically and technically. With modern monitoring techniques a monitoring uncertainty factor of 1.3 is probably possible.

---

*A factor of 1.5 monitoring uncertainty error means that there is a 50 percent chance that a test actually releasing 150 kt of energy will be detected as one with 1.5×150 kt = 225 kt, or at 150 kt/1.5 = 100 kt. Similarly for a factor of 1.3.

Seismic verification of yields is by far the most commonly used technique. This results from the fact that it can be done remotely, though only within an accuracy of a factor of about two. Local calibration permits some improvement in the precision. A technique being extensively explored is called CORRTEX. It was developed at the United States weapons laboratories. The CORRTEX technique relies on the fact that very close to a nuclear explosion the rock flows like a fluid. The speed of propagation of a signal very soon after a nuclear explosion can be related to the yield, and is largely independent of the geological environment. In CORRTEX a cable is buried within a few meters of a nuclear explosion. Electronic signals determine the length of the cable. As the cable is crushed by the explosion, the shortening of the cable yields information which can be interpreted in terms of the yield. This method offers the possibility of reducing uncertainties from a factor of two down to perhaps a factor of 1.3.

Any complex military system necessarily requires a great deal of testing. Systems that require only a few tests are usually of limited military importance. Thus no single test is of great importance; it is a series of tests that matters. Consequently, a detection system that misses a few events is unlikely to give a major advantage to the side that is testing.

As detection techniques become more sensitive the chance of the second type of error (an identification of a test that has not taken place) becomes more likely. This is especially true for underground tests, since more sensitive detection techniques must contend with ever larger numbers of natural events—hence a larger chance of false alarms. Hannon (1983) states that if underground explosions are monitored by seismic methods that detect events at a level of magnitude of 2 to 3,* about 1500 "false alarms" will be picked up. This is because small shallow earthquakes are seismically indistinguishable from nuclear explosions of a few kilotons if the explosions take place in a special cavity. At levels in the vicinity of a kiloton or so a significant number of chemical explosions occur. These too can be difficult or impossible to distinguish from nuclear explosions.

Monitoring SALT Compliance

A comprehensive analysis of U.S. verification capabilities was the subject of a conference held at the University of California, Los Angeles, in 1979. The following is an excerpt of a statement made by Joseph Kruzel concerning SALT II verification by the United States (Potter, 1980):

> A number of different intelligence systems are involved in monitoring compliance with SALT II. Basically, satellite photography is used to monitor the numbers and types of deployed weapons. Telemetry and other sources are used to analyze the characteristics of Soviet strategic weapons and provide evidence of their production and operational

---

*The intensity of earthquakes and nuclear explosions is measured using a scale in which the intensity level is proportional to the logarithm of the energy. The Richter scale may be familiar to you through its use in reporting earthquakes in the public press. (See Section 24-3.)

status. This intelligence system is highly sophisticated, overlapping and well coordinated. What is learned from one source—photography for example—can often be checked against information from other sources such as radar or telemetry monitoring. The use of multiple sources complicates any effort to disguise or conceal a violation. . . . The actual deterrent value of verification depends on the extent of a potential violator's uncertainty. This may be the most compelling reason for preserving the security of intelligence capabilities and techniques.

24-3   DETECTION OF NUCLEAR EXPLOSIONS

Atmospheric Testing

The United States detected the first nuclear tests by the Soviet Union and other nations by sampling radioactivity in the air at high altitudes with special aircraft. Because the signature of the fission products of a nuclear explosion is quite specific, there is little doubt when such a detection method is used. Further, by examining carefully the constituents of the radioactive cloud, much can be learned about the details of the bomb's design. Measurements of the presence and relative amounts of isotopes of uranium, plutonium, fission fragments, and other materials permit detailed reconstruction of the test events.

When satellite surveillance became routine, direct observation of the flash provided an independent method for detecting aboveground nuclear explosions. After the Limited Test Ban Treaty went into effect in 1963, the United States, the Soviet Union, and the United Kingdom discontinued aboveground nuclear testing. However, France, China, and India continued to test in the atmosphere, and, until recently, verification using satellite surveillance was important.

Underground Testing

The Limited Test Ban Treaty did not slow testing; testing of nuclear weapons continued underground. (See Chapter 2.) Once testing by the superpowers moved underground in 1963 after the ratification of the Limited Test Ban Treaty the environmental impact noted by the public was sharply reduced. Public protest vanished until the 1980s when the Reagan administration made clear that the official U.S. policy was to be able to fight and "prevail" in limited nuclear war. Political sentiment gradually shifted such that in 1987 and again in 1988 the House of Representatives voted for a halt in funding for nuclear tests above one kiloton. This action was not sustained by the Senate, however.

The largest underground test was carried out by the United States in the Aleutian Islands in 1971. The Cannikin explosion was about 5 megatons—a greater explosive yield than all the munitions used in World War II, though far less than the 58-megaton 1961 Soviet air test. Since 1976 the **Threshold Test Ban Treaty (TTBT),** which limits underground explosions to 150 kilotons, has been observed, even though the treaty has not been ratified by the United States (1988). Evidence for conformity with

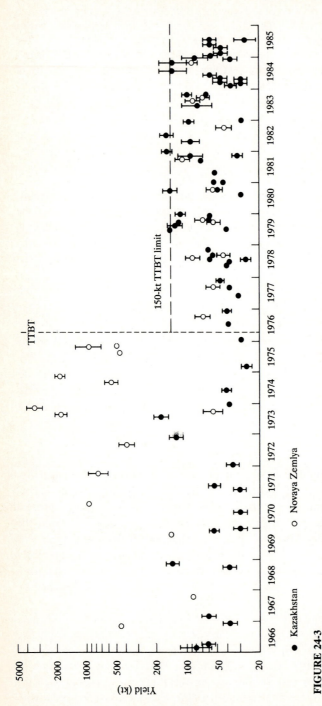

FIGURE 24-3

U.S.S.R. nuclear tests 1966–1986 according to Sykes and Davis. These yields are calculated using P-wave and surface-wave magnitudes, M_s and m_b. The few tests that do appear to have exceeded 150 kt after the TTBT was signed in 1976 are well within the expected scatter. (*Source: L. R. Sykes and D. M. Davis, Scientific American, vol. 256, No. 1, January 1987, pp. 29–37.*)

the TTBT as given by seismic data is shown in Figure 24-3. We discuss such seismic measurements in some detail below.

Seismic monitoring offers virtually the only technique for determining the occurrence and size of underground tests. Seismic techniques have been extensively developed, and all treaties rely heavily on arrays of detection stations with **seismometers.** (A seismometer consists of a mass connected to the earth by a damped spring. A detector senses relative motion between the mass, which serves as an inertial reference point, and the earth.) Most motion of the earth occurs at frequencies far below the audible range, so seismometers are designed to operate at frequencies below a few hertz (cycles per second) and to be insensitive to higher frequencies. (Some recent results suggest that somewhat higher frequencies, in the vicinity of 10 to 30 Hz, may be useful for discriminating between natural events and explosions.)

The challenge to the analyst is to devise ways to reliably separate signals produced by nuclear explosions from those produced by other sources, particularly signals from earthquakes.

Seismic waves due to nuclear explosions differ qualitatively from those due to earthquakes, making it possible to monitor nuclear explosions as small as a few kilotons with suitable arrays of seismic stations (Sykes, 1983). The nuclear explosion creates a symmetrical radial expansion, forming predominantly compressional waves (called **P waves**). Earthquake waves are formed by one plate sliding on another, and hence include a large component of shear waves (**S waves**) along with the *P* waves.

In addition to the *S* and *P* waves, which propagate through the body of the earth, two types of surface waves—Rayleigh waves and Love waves—are generated by the complex reflection of the *S* and *P* waves from the earth's surface. A nuclear explosion generates some Rayleigh waves but very few Love waves. Furthermore, the amplitude of the Rayleigh wave for an isotropic nuclear explosion is much less than that for an earthquake of the same released energy. Figure 24-4 shows the paths of various seismic waves.

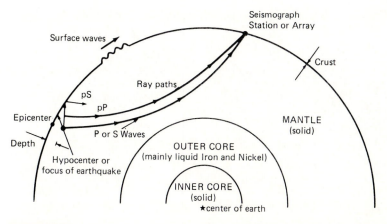

FIGURE 24-4

A cross section of the earth's crust, showing paths of various seismic waves. The hypocenter is the focal point of an earthquake, or of a nuclear explosion, from which the seismic waves radiate. (*From Sykes, 1983.*)

Seismologists describe the size of a seismic event in terms of an event's *magnitude*, that is, the logarithm of the amplitude of a particular type of wave. Two such magnitudes, M_S and m_b, are important for distinguishing earthquakes from nuclear explosions. The former is the magnitude of the vertical amplitude of the Rayleigh surface waves, with periods of typically 20 seconds, whereas the latter is the magnitude of the P waves, with periods near 1 second. As the size of the nuclear explosion is decreased, the relative importance of the earthquake "noise" increases, so that eventually the signal from the nuclear explosion is lost in the noise of a large number of earthquakes. For example, when the P-wave magnitude is 4.0, there are about 15,000 earthquakes per year that must be examined. Nevertheless, even for this magnitude, a clear separation of nuclear explosions and earthquakes is possible. A plot showing the discrimination between earthquakes and nuclear explosions is shown in Figure 24-5.

Discrimination between earthquakes and explosions can probably be enhanced by filtering out the low seismic frequencies. Figure 24-6 shows the effect of such filtering in distinguishing between a large earthquake and a $\frac{1}{2}$-kiloton explosion. The earthquake occurred in the eastern part of the Soviet Union, and the nuclear explosion took place at Kasakhstan in that country. The seismograph was located in Norway about 3800 kilometers from the explosion.

A further enhancement of sensitivity of detection of nuclear explosion is by means of **seismic arrays** which utilize several detectors in given locations perhaps a few kilometers apart. By combining their signals the background noise can be con-

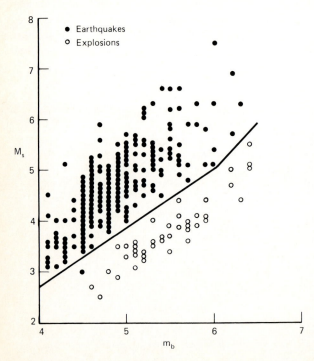

FIGURE 24-5

Surface-wave magnitudes of long-period Rayleigh waves as a function of 1-second-compression body-wave magnitude. The earthquakes represented here all have depths of less than 30 kilometers, and so might be mistaken for nuclear explosions. (The deepest nuclear explosion has been at 2 kilometers.) Only one earthquake from the southwest Pacific (and not the Soviet Union) falls within the explosion population and it occurred in an area where the seismic-array coverage was poor. (*From Sykes, 1983.*)

Conventional recording using low frequencies

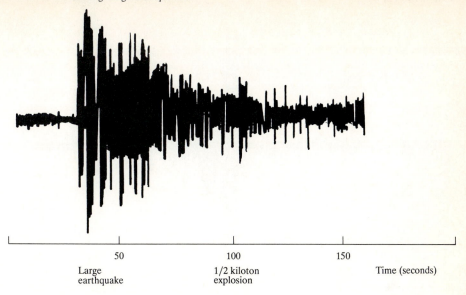

Same recording but with high frequency passband

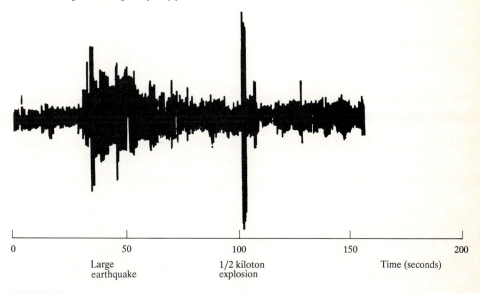

FIGURE 24-6

Seismic detection of nuclear explosion and earthquake. The upper and lower seismograms were recorded near Oslo, Norway, and cover the same period of time. The upper seismogram was obtained conventionally allowing low frequencies to be recorded. The lower seismogram was equipped with a passband filter allowing only seismic waves of a limited band of frequencies (of the order of several tens of cycles per second) to be recorded. In both seismograms a large earthquake that occurred in the eastern part of the Soviet Union is registered at about the 30-second region. About one minute after the earthquake, at about 100 seconds on the time scale, the Soviet Union exploded a very small nuclear bomb (about ½ kt) at the Kasakhstan test site about 4000 kilometers away. The explosion is clearly revealed in the high-frequency passband of the lower figure, even in the presence of the large earthquake. (*From Semiannual Technical Summary for the Norwegian Seismic Array for 1984, Royal Norwegian Council for Scientific and Industrial Research, Scientific Report 1-84/85.*)

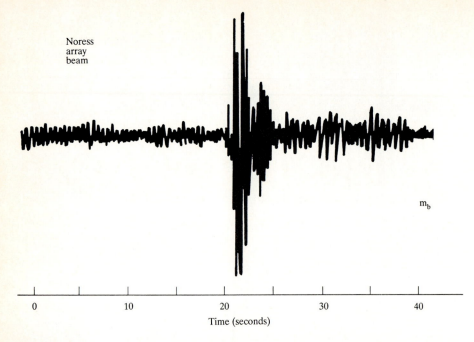

Noress
array
beam

m_b

0   10   20   30   40

Time (seconds)

FIGURE 24-7

Detection of a 0.25-kiloton explosion with a seismic array. The seismic signal came from a 0.25-kt explosion at the Soviet test site near Semipalatinsk. The signal was recorded 3800 km away near Oslo, Norway, by using an array of seismometers. There is a clear signal to noise ratio of 30:1. This result indicates that even smaller explosions could be detected even at this great distance. (*From R. W. Alewire III, "Seismic Sensing of Soviet Tests," Defense 85, December 1985, pp. 11–21.*)

siderably reduced. The Norwegian Regional Seismic Array (NORESS) is located north of Oslo and consists of 25 individual sensors arranged in 4 concentric rings with a maximum diameter of 3 km (OTA, 1988). Figure 24-7 shows the detection of a 0.25-kiloton explosion 3800 kilometers away in the Soviet Union with a signal to noise ratio of 30:1.

Further sensitivity can be obtained by **networks** of arrays located around the perimeter of a country to be monitored. If in-country arrays (tamperproof) can be negotiated, then great improvement in detection efficiency can be obtained. Networks also permit the location of the explosion by triangulation methods, since the propagation velocities of the seismic waves are known.

In 1988 the Soviet and U.S. nuclear tests were monitored within each nation by scientists of the other nation by an arrangement negotiated between the National Resources Defense Council (NRDC) and the Soviet Academy of Sciences.

Various scenarios for avoiding seismic detection have been proposed, such as exploding a nuclear weapon in coincidence with an actual earthquake, exploding multiple nuclear weapons to simulate an earthquake, and exploding a bomb in a cavity to "decouple" the explosion from the surrounding earth. The first is impractical because the number of appropriate earthquakes would only be a few per year and the testing team would have to be in constant readiness. The second could evade one screening method, but if other seismic discriminators were used, it would fail. The third method would be limited to relatively small explosions because of the large size of the cavity needed and the possibility of detection, via satellite, of large-scale preparatory earth removal. For example, holes adequate to decouple a 10-kiloton explosion would require the removal of about 0.5×10^6 cubic meters of dirt, or a cube 75 meters (almost the length of a football field) on a side.

It requires political as well as technical judgment to determine the sensitivity level of detection that would be specified in a threshold test ban treaty that could be agreed to by the nuclear states. In 1973 John Foster, then Director of Defense Research and Engineering for the Department of Defense, told a U.S. Senate committee that monitoring devices would have to have the capability of detecting explosions of 0.25 kiloton or less in order not to endanger national security interests. However, in more recent testimony to the House Armed Services Committee, Harold Agnew, former director of the Los Alamos Scientific Laboratory, was quoted as saying that "I don't believe testing below 5 to 10 kilotons can do much to improve [as compared to maintaining] our strategic posture."

According to Sykes et al. (1983):

> If one can replace Foster's 0.25 kiloton with Agnew's 5 kilotons, a nearly intractable monitoring problem is converted into one of simplicity itself. . . . If in addition to the 15 external stations, 15 simple stations are also operated within the U.S.S.R., greater identification capabilities can be obtained. Fully-coupled explosions of 0.1 kiloton could then be identified at 0.90 probability in much of the U.S.S.R.

The judgment of Livermore scientists (Foster is a former director of Lawrence Livermore National Laboratory) is more conservative. Hannon (1983) states: "It would take a more extensive network, one that includes *more than 30 high-quality in-country* arrays, to detect explosions with yields of *about 1 kiloton* (not 0.1 kiloton) with 90 percent confidence." Hannon also raises the possibility of evasion of detection by conducting explosions in dry alluvium. He says that explosions in dry alluvium with yields of one to several kilotons could remain undetected or unidentified. However, Sykes et al. (1983) state that dry alluvium could be used for cheating only for explosions of a *maximum* of 1 kiloton. Also, alluvium is unstable, and an explosion might well produce enough deformation to form a surface depression which could easily be detected by satellite photography or other national technical means. Some nonseismologists (Hughes, 1982) suggest that detection of 5- to 10-kiloton Soviet tests carried out in alluvium would not be possible. The Military Geology Branch of the U.S. Geological Survey and the Defense Advanced Research Projects Agency consider such tests would in fact be detected.

It is important to evaluate the *source* of information on alleged Soviet treaty violations or on seismic monitoring requirements. For example, it should be remembered that the Comprehensive Test Ban Treaty was always opposed by the Lawrence Livermore National Laboratory, which holds that nuclear testing is necessary to ensure reliability and safety, to make sure that there are no surprises with new technology, and to keep a well-trained cadre of technical staff available in case all-out testing is somehow needed in the future.

Example: Erroneous accounts of Soviet testing

Harold M. Agnew (letter to *Science,* April 8, 1983): "Subsequent tests appeared to us to range as high as 400 kt."

Alewine and Bache (letter submitted to *Science,* June 1983): "In the U.S. experience an m_b greater than 6.2 (as measured for the largest Soviet events) has only been seen for yields of 600–800 kt and larger."

Judith Miller (*The New York Times,* July 26, 1982): "One official said that there had been several Soviet tests, many at one particular site, that had been estimated at 300 kt."

According to Sykes et al., all Soviet tests to date have been 150 to 200 kilotons or less. They say that Jack Anderson's report (of a 350-kt test in 1980 and a 260-kt test in 1982) was simply "silly" and that the others (above) were based on faulty intelligence reports that overestimated yields by a factor of 3 because of an error of 0.4 in the *P*-wave-magnitude parameter.

Present States

According to the study of seismic verification by the Office of Technology Assessment of the U.S. Congress (OTA, 1988):

> Based on cautious assumptions for a network of 30 internal arrays or about 50 three-component internal stations (to measure three directions of seismic motion), it appears likely that a detection threshold of *m* 2.5 (90 percent probability of detection at four or more stations) could be reached. This corresponds to a well-coupled explosion of 0.1–0.01 kt, or a fully decoupled nuclear explosion with a yield of about 1 kt. Based on more optimistic assumptions that the conditions to be encountered and prospective improvements in data processing capability, this same network could have a detection capability as low as *m* 2.0.

This sensitivity would correspond to detection of nuclear yields well below 0.1 kt for many geological environments. Given the present attitude of the Soviet government toward "glasnost," or openness, it is conceivable that negotiations to provide in-country seismic arrays in each superpower's territory may indeed be possible. In this manner a TTBT with much lower threshold or a Comprehensive Test Ban Treaty could be monitored effectively by seismic means.

For further detail on seismic verification the reader is referred to the OTA study (OTA, 1988), and articles by W.J. Hannon (Hannon, 1985) and Sykes (Sykes, 1982, 1983). A paper by David Hafemeister et al. (Hafemeister, 1985) discusses satellite verification techniques as well (see below).

Satellite Surveillance

Early in the arms race, information about what was occurring on the surface of another nation's territory was difficult to obtain, particularly in the case of the Soviet Union and China. Such information was deemed so necessary that secret U-2 missions to overfly those countries were authorized by President Dwight David Eisenhower. In a celebrated incident a U-2 plane was shot down over the Soviet Union. The pilot, Gary Powers, survived. This was embarrassing to Eisenhower, who had denied the existence of such flights. As a result Khrushchev snubbed Eisenhower at a subsequent summit meeting in France to discuss arms control. Krushchev took a tour of French villages instead of meeting with Eisenhower.

With the development of orbiting satellites in 1960, a new ear in information about the surface activities of nations became available. Satellites are now one of the principal national technical means available for detection of troop movements, counting missile installations, monitoring missile tests, etc. A Vela satellite reportedly picked up a double light pulse (typical of nuclear explosions) in the South Pacific near the coast of South Africa. This "evidence" of a clandestine nuclear explosion has been discounted by U.S. experts as inconclusive. South Africa and Israel have denied their participation.

About half of the spy satellites are in geosynchronous orbit at an altitude of 23,300 miles. This altitude is suitable for electronic intelligence collection, but too high for photography. These are called "staring" satellites because they keep a single area under constant surveillance rather than circle the earth. Most of them are used for early warning of the launch of ballistic missiles and for communications.

The U.S. Air Force has deployed a reconnaissance spacecraft (KH-11) at an altitude of about 160 miles which provides high-resolution images by digital-image transmission. Digital-image transmission provides a longer useful life for reconnaissance spacecraft than does film (which is returned to earth) because the craft's lifetime is not limited by film-pod depletion. Film-return satellites are used in concert with digital vehicles, but will shortly be replaced with new high-resolution all-electronic technologies using charge-coupled detectors. It is claimed that satellite film-return techniques yield resolutions of 6 inches, permitting very detailed information to be obtained for particular areas of concern in another nation's territory.

Table 24-1 gives a summary of some of the satellite capabilities of the United States.

Other Verification Issues

Our discussion has focused largely on verification of nuclear testing. However, nuclear weapons are only one aspect of the nuclear arms race As noted, nuclear weapons are themselves very small and hard to detect. Thus there is relatively little emphasis on their detection. On the other hand, delivery systems are much larger, and so a great deal of attention is given to identifying them. This is the approach taken in the INF treaty of 1988.

When systems are totally banned, detection of a single unit is clear evidence of a violation. When treaties limit numbers, life is much more complex. The problem is especially severe with cruise missiles, which can be used with either conventional or nuclear warheads. A great deal of work is ongoing to find ways to write treaties for such systems. One approach is to use unique tags, similar to fingerprints. The United

TABLE 24-1
Some of the satellite capabilities of the United States

Designation	Altitude, mi	Function
Big Bird	100	Television pictures or photographs of land or ocean objects
Rhyolite	23,300	Interception of telemetry from test flights of Soviet missiles
USAF High-resolution satellite	80	Highly detailed photographs of objects on the ground
KH-11	160	Enhanced color and television pictures of objects on the land or ocean
TRW Code 647	23,300	Early warning (3 to 4 min after launch) of a missile launch; monitoring of Soviet missile tests
Ferret	400	Eavesdropping on other satellites and ground communications
Vela	60,000	Nuclear explosion detection; detection of flash and radiation from nuclear explosions and missile launches

Source: Center for Defense Information.

States would provide tags which would be placed on Soviet cruise missiles, and vice versa. Each nation would be permitted to inspect the tags so as to ensure that they could not be used to signal the location of the weapons system. Actual suggestions for how to write treaties for cruise missiles are technically and institutionally extremely complex (Stanford, 1988).

What Is the Significance of Violations?

The Threshold Test Ban Treaty uses a limit of 150 kt. It is far from obvious what the significance of this limit is. Does it really matter if the Soviet Union tests at 200 kt, or even at 300 kt? What can they learn that is likely to significantly change the overall military balance? This kind of question is exceedingly difficult to assess. Such questions may become even more difficult if thresholds are lowered to levels (probably around 10 to 15 kt) where it is possible to test primaries but not secondaries of nuclear weapons. Often levels used in treaties have large arbitrary elements in them. That is, a search for a treaty requires that levels be set, even though these levels may be based only loosely on technical considerations. This situation is not unique to testing treaties. A good example is automobile speed limits. Once one accepts the idea that a limit is desirable, then a specific number must be chosen. There may be no good reason for selecting 60 miles per hour (say) rather than 55 or 65 mph. Once a number is chosen, though, it becomes a part of the law, and becomes a standard for enforcement.

In nuclear testing one can identify several general principles, but not specific numbers. At 150 kt secondaries can be tested, and probably weapons can be designed capable of yields several times the threshold. At 10 to 15 kt, primaries can be tested but not secondaries. At 5 kt primaries probably can't be tested, but seismic detection is still possible. At 1 kt seismic detection becomes very difficult—there are many natural events, and even many chemical explosions that might be detected. A comprehensive test ban means that cheating is relatively easy at low levels (up to one or perhaps a few kilotons), and hence there is concern about the possibility that the Soviet Union may be able to cheat because of the high level of secrecy in that nation, while the United States may be forced to conform to the treaty. However, the fundamental question is whether clandestine testing at the level of one kiloton would be significant compared with the advantage of a comprehensive test ban.

Our discussion thus far has focused on assessing the probability of a violation of a treaty or agreement, and the technical significance of a violation. Such analysis provides input to the political process. Determination of the significance of a violation is not primarily a technical matter—though it may draw heavily on technical analysis. If, for example, political leaders have decided to seek rapprochement with another nation, they will be very reluctant to make a major issue of a possible violation of an agreement. On the other hand, if political leaders are seeking excuses for attacking another nation, technical data which show that the probability of a violation is small but not negligible may well be used as justification for mounting an attack. This was the situation under President Reagan, where his staff was seeking every possible excuse to accuse the Soviet Union of violating the 150-kt limit. Scientists could and did tell the administration that the probability that a violation had occurred was small. Yet this was not enough to prevent use of this small probability for accusations against the Soviet government.

It is often asserted by military analysts that their analysis is value-netural, and is based on facts alone. One way in which this assertion appears is in the assessment of the risk to the United States from the military forces of another power. Normal procedure is to argue that the analyst must ignore military doctrine and base the assessment entirely on military capability. It is what a potential enemy *can do* that matters, not what it claims it *will do*.

While this argument is not without merit, it is at least worth noting that both Britain and France have the technical capability with their ballistic missile equipped nuclear submarines to destroy the United States. Despite this technical reality, analyses of military problems routinely ignore this capability and focus instead on the Soviet Union. The fact that the Soviet Union has far more destructive capability in its arsenal than does either France or Britain is true, but misses the point. The reality is that perceptions of the attitude of a potential aggressor affect both analysts and political figures (see Chapter 22) and thereby assessments of which issues are appropriate for a high ranking on the national political agenda. Political reality is that we worry about the nuclear arsenals of the Soviet Union but not about those of Britain or France.

QUESTIONS

1. Discuss the types of problems in a verification agreement that are likely to arise if there is too much emphasis on detecting every single violation.
2. Discuss the types of problems in a verification agreement that are likely to arise if there is too much emphasis on not rocking the political boat.

3. What are S waves, P waves, and Rayleigh waves and how can they be used to distinguish between underground nuclear explosions and earthquakes?

4. What features would you search for in a photograph of the Soviet Union if you were (a) interested in underground tests and (b) interested in the number of deployed missiles?

5. What indicators other than seismic signals could you look for that might give some indication of Soviet underground tests?

6. What advantages do the Soviets have over the United States in negotiating treaties on (a) testing weapons, (b) testing missiles, and (c) testing missile-detection systems (ABM intelligence)?

7. Do you believe that the structure of our society places us at a significant advantage or disadvantage in negotiating with the Soviet Union? Why?

8. According to Sykes et al., what would be the threshold for seismic detection of nuclear explosions if there were 15 seismic stations inside and 15 outside the Soviet Union?

9. Try to design the optics of a detection system to be located on a satellite. How big must camera optics be at an altitude of 100 miles to read a license plate? At a 24,000-mile geosynchronous orbit? (This problem requires more physics background than is included in the text. One needs to consider diffraction limited otpics and detector resolution. See, for example, David Hafemeister, "Science and Society Test IX: Technical Means of Verification," *American Journal of Physics,* 1985.)

10. Design a treaty that will limit SLBMs. Focus on verification issues.

11. Design a treaty to limit cruise missile deployment. How might you deal with the problem of distinguishing cruise missiles with nuclear warheads from those without nuclear warheads? Is a treaty banning "nuked" cruise missiles plausible? Why? Would on-site inspection help?

12. The ABM treaty excludes new radar systems except on national borders (interior radars are precluded). Why was this provision included? How might the United States determine whether the new Soviet radar installation in central Siberia, near the Soviet Union's six SS-18 heavy ICBM complexes, violates the ABM treaty? Why should the United States worry about this radar?

13. Design a treaty to slow "star wars" technology. Be sure to include in your proposal adequate verification provisions using feasible technology.

KEY WORDS

IRBM   intermediate-range ballistic missile. A missile with a range of a few hundred to a few thousand kilometers.

monitoring uncertainty factor   uncertainty in yield estimation due to intrinsic detection problems. Seismic signals have noise due to general earth motion. Improved techniques can decrease but not eliminate this noise.

national technical means   techniques for verification which do not require entering another nation's territory. Typical techniques use satellite photography, radio, and radar.

P waves   compressional waves set up in the earth by seismic disturbance. Explosions give strong P wave signals.

seismic network   seismometers or arrays of seismometers located at distances of hundred or thousand of kilometers apart, but synchronized so that an explosion or earthquake can be more sensitively detected and its location determined by triangulation.

seismometer   a device that will measure minute displacements of the earth at a given location. Often seismometers measure not only the two horizontal displacements (north-south and east-west) as a function of time, but the vertical displacement as well so that a three-dimensional measurement of the motion of the earth's surface is made at that point.

S waves   shear waves. They are formed by one plate of the earth sliding over another; hence S waves are prominent in earthquakes.

threshold test ban treaty   a treaty (unsigned but followed by both the United States and the U.S.S.R.) which would limit nuclear testing to 150 kilotons.

TTBT   see threshold test ban treaty.

CHAPTER
25

THE ECONOMICS
OF THE
ARMS RACE

Global war has become a Frankenstein to destroy both sides. No longer is it a shortcut to international power. If you lose you are annihilated. If you win you stand only to lose. . . . [War] contains now only the germs of double suicide.

General Douglas MacArthur, 1961

Every gun that is made, every warship launched, every rocket fired signifies in the final sense a theft from those who hunger and are not fed, those who are cold and are not clothed. This world in arms is not spending money alone. It is spending the sweat of its laborers, the genius of its scientists, the house of its children.

President Dwight D. Eisenhower

25-1 THEMES

This chapter raises some broad issues associated with nuclear weaponry: the economic implications of the arms race between the United States and the Soviet Union and the dynamics of the nuclear weapons business. The United States spends about 7 percent of its gross national product (**GNP**) on defense. That amount is larger than the entire government budget of every other nation except the Soviet Union. The DOD budget in 1980 was $144 billion (1980$), and in 1987 $296 billion (1987$). Of the latter amount $66 billion was for nuclear forces. This figure doubled during the Reagan administration from $35 billion in 1981. Because of the increasing national debt, Congress has restricted the military outlay since 1985 to approximately $300 billion. From the fiscal years 1982 to 1988, $2 trillion dollars was spent by the United States on military forces. This amounts to about $8000 per American citizen, whether child or adult. About one-half this amount (about $150 billion dollars per year) is for the defense of Europe (NATO).

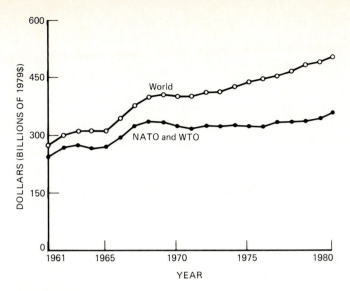

FIGURE 25-1
World expenditures on arms. (*From SIPRI, 1982.*)

The military expenditures of the Soviet Union and its Warsaw Pact allies have been roughly equal to those of NATO. Under the regime of Chairman Gorbachev it has been realized that these expenditures have been placing a heavy burden on the Soviet economy. Part of the campaign of **perestroika,** or restructuring, is to find ways to reduce military expenditure in order to bolster the civilian economy.

25-2 GLOBAL ARMS EXPENDITURES

Global arms expenditures have been increasing by about 3 percent per year for several years. This is substantially faster than population has grown (1.7 percent), and very much faster than world economic growth. A critical issue, to which we return later, is the connection between arms expenditures and economic growth. Figure 25-1 shows global military expenditures since 1961 through 1980.

According to the Stockholm Peace Research Institute (SIPRI, 1987) the United States and the U.S.S.R. together accounted for about 80 to 83 percent of the world military research and development expenditure. The total for the United Kingdom, France, China, and the Federal Republic of Germany was about 14 percent. For value of exports of weapons to Third World countries the U.S.S.R was first with $7.7 billion and the United States second with $5.1 billion in 1986. About one-half of scientists and engineers in the United States are employed by the military or military-related industries. It is clear that the economies of the superpowers are involved in a major way with the military. Budget reductions for the military that might be the result of an improved international climate would have to be made in conjunction with the buildup of other programs in order to avoid serious economic dislocations.

25-3 COMPARISONS OF U.S. AND SOVIET EXPENDITURES

The substantial discrepancy between the above data and those in Figure 25-1 is typical of the uncertainties in this area. There is no such thing as a "correct" number. In order to understand why, we will focus on the problems of comparing expenditure figures in the Soviet Union with those in the United States. (For a detailed discussion, see Holzman, 1980.)

The controversy stems from a number of sources. First, while the United States publishes detailed military budgets, the Soviet Union publishes only a single figure, and there is consensus that this figure substantially understates actual expenditures. Second, even if an accurate ruble figure were available, there would be doubt about how to convert rubles to dollars, since the ruble exchange rate is set by the government and not controlled by market forces. The approach used by the CIA (a primary source of these data) is to estimate the quantity of everything that is included in the defense activities of the Soviet Union (e.g., number of soldiers and number and type of weapons) and then to estimate what it would take for each element to be reproduced in the United States, taking into account quality differentials.

The United States has many ways of estimating the size and capabilities of the Soviet military, and it is believed that the estimate of characteristics is substantially correct. A bigger problem is in assigning dollar figures to specific Soviet military items. In the Soviet Union, labor is relatively cheap. When the cost of Soviet military personnel is estimated using the pay rates of U.S. soldiers, the Soviet military expenditures in this area appear greater than those of the United States.

On the other hand, capital-intensive goods are very expensive in the Soviet Union, and the cost to the Soviets of reproducing the U.S. military arsenal in terms of material would be extremely high. Since military planners on both sides are under pressure to do worst-case contingency planning, it is quite likely that each side believes the other is spending more on defense than is actually the case, and is urging increases in order to catch up. As Holzman put the matter:

> It is important to recognize that there are undoubtedly Soviet counterparts to the CIA. At the aggregate level, for purposes of comparison, they probably calculate U.S. expenses in rubles. . . . It seems reasonable to argue that the vested interest of those making the calculations in the U.S.S.R. is to build up, as much as possible, the Soviet military-industrial complex. In this event, they would probably make a ruble calculation or, at least, would stress the ruble calculation just as our policymakers stress the dollar calculation. . . . The frightening thing about this highly probable scenario is that each nation, viewing the other's defense expenditures through exaggerated . . . lenses . . . is apt to increase its own defense expenditures beyond what is necessary to achieve any preassigned goal. So, for example, if both nations would be satisfied with aggregate expenditure parity, and actually have parity, each would nevertheless chase the other forever in upward escalation under the impression that it was behind. A ruble's-eye view of U.S. defense expenditures . . . might even offer a plausible explanation for the continuous rise over the past decade in Soviet defense expenditures.
>
> If one fleshes out the "ruble's-eye view" one finds the Soviets eyeing a competitor which is spending only 5 percent of GNP in comparison with their own 11 to 13 percent

and yet which can generally (1) produce weapons of superior technology as well as (2) higher quality weapons at the same technological level and (3) has better-trained forces.

The differences associated with these two methods of comparison of military strength are very large. In 1977, the CIA estimate, which was made on the basis of converting rubles to dollars, was that the U.S.S.R. was spending 40 percent more on defense than the United States. A calculation by Holzman in which he converted to rubles suggests that the United States is outspending the Soviet Union by somewhere between 3 and 43 percent. He concludes (in agreement with the conclusions of SIPRI) that there is little basis for claiming that either nation is outspending the other.

25-4   INTERNATIONAL ARMS TRADE

The international arms trade is very big business: $26.1 billion worth of arms were exported in 1980. In that year total foreign economic aid from all governments was $38.8 billion (Sivard, 1983). The United States in 1981 delivered $7.9 billion worth of arms. The largest amounts ($ in billions) went to Saudi Arabia, $1.4; Israel, $1.0; Australia, $0.5; Federal Republic of Germany, $0.4; Taiwan, $0.4; Japan, $0.3; Belgium, $0.3; Netherlands, $0.3; United Kingdom, $0.3; and Korea, $0.3 (SIPRI, 1982).

25-5   COSTS OF PREVIOUS WARS

Figure 25-2 shows that over one-half of U.S. tax dollars are used for financing current U.S. military programs or for paying off the debts incurred in past wars. Many of these costs continue for many years. The last veterans of the Civil War died only a few years ago at ages well above 100, and some veterans of World War I will be

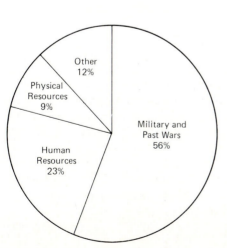

1982 Federal Budget

Other 12%

Physical Resources 9%

Human Resources 23%

Military and Past Wars 56%

FIGURE 25-2
Federal budget priorities in the United States.

TABLE 25-1
Trends in U.S. military spending, 1940–1985

Year	Current $, billions	Constant 1972$, billions	% of federal budget	% of GNP
1940	1.490	6.0	15.8	1.6
1945	81.858	252.0	88.3	37.7
1948	7.845	20.3	26.3	3.2
1950	12.407	29.4	29.1	4.7
1953	49.912	96.3	65.6	13.8
1955	39.834	75.8	58.1	10.5
1960	45.168	73.8	49.0	9.1
1965	47.456	69.3	40.1	7.2
1968	78.755	101.4	44.0	9.5
1970	78.553	90.3	40.0	8.2
1975	85.552	67.1	26.2	5.9
1980	125.830	70.4	23.7	5.0
1985	277.3	122	29	8.0

Source: Page, 1983 (updated).

collecting benefits for years to come. By the early 1990s millions of World War II veterans will reach age 65, at which time they will become eligible for taxpayer-supported medical care at Veterans Administration hospitals even if they did not suffer war-related injuries.

Table 25-1 summarizes trends in military expenditure from 1940 to 1980. As Page (1983) observes, there is a "ratchet effect" in that expenditures do not decline as rapidly after wars as they rise during them. New weapons systems are retained, troops are not completely demobilized, and veteran's benefit and interest programs rise.

25-6 ARMS EXPENDITURES AND ECONOMIC GROWTH

The Direct Cost of Defense Expenditures

A nation must be able to defend itself, and defense costs are therefore a necessary part of its economy. Yet a balance must somehow be struck between defense and other needs. (Figure 25-2 shows federal budget priorities.) Zero defense expenditure is surely unacceptable—but it would be equally unrealistic for the nation to spend the entire GNP on defense. Is the 7 percent of its GNP that the United States presently spends on defense too much or too little? How much is enough? The Soviet Union spends 11 to 13 percent of its GNP on defense. Is it this high primarily because they are seeking to match United States and NATO capabilities, because of bureaucratic inertia, or because the Soviet Union has a desire for world domination?

Under the Reagan budget proposals the United States spent $350 billion in 6 years on nuclear weapons. This raised the fraction of military spending devoted to nuclear weapons from 10 to 15 percent to about 22 percent. The uncertainty in present spending stems from problems of deciding how to allocate costs between nuclear and nonnuclear categories. How do we decide if the balance is reasonable?

How should we balance military expenditures against other uses of our finite national resources? Military expenditures by their very nature do not contribute to, but rather detract from, production of consumer goods and from the nation's ability to compete economically with the rest of the world. This means, for example, that resources devoted to the construction of tanks are not available for the manufacture of television sets. Men and women serving in the military are not available to work in factories, build roads and bridges, or perform nonmilitary services. According to Olvey et al. (1984):

> Defense expenditures impose opportunity costs on the rest of the economy. At the macroeconomic level, the costs are either increased inflation, lower consumption and investment in the private sector, or reductions in competing government programs. The defense budget has enormous implications for the national economy. . . . It is our clearest political statement of the opportunity costs we are willing to impose on the nation in order to reduce perceived threats to our national security. . . . By any criterion, the defense budget claims a huge share of our national resources.

There can be economic benefits from military expenditures. If the economy is running slowly then, at least in the short run, a decision to expand the Army will have the effect of reducing unemployment. In the long run, however, the matter is more complex. For example, the same resources could be used to replace obsolete steel mills with the kind of modern technology which now exists in Japan—and which has made it possible for Japan to underbid United States steel companies.

Distribution of Military Spending

The distribution of military spending in the United States is very uneven. Every state has major military projects, and every representative and senator spends a significant amount of time working with his or her constituents to bring in new contracts and to maintain and expand the old. Some of the toughest political battles that secretaries of defense have to fight occur when they want to close down obsolete military bases. Some typical numbers for state-level military expenditures in 1981 are shown in Table 25-2.

The impact of these expenditures of the economy is uncertain and controversial. The Council on Economic Priorities (1982) quotes Pentagon sources as asserting that 5.7 million jobs were created by military spending in 1982, of which 1 million were civilian DOD employees, 2.1 million were uniformed personnel, and 2.6 million were employed by private companies working on DOD projects. Military projects are highly concentrated in a few areas of the nation: Dallas–Fort Worth (General Dynamics), Los Angeles (Rockwell, Northrop and Hughes), San Francisco (Lockheed), Seattle (Boeing), Boston (General Electric), Connecticut (General Dynamics, Electric Boat Division, and United Technologies), St. Louis (McDonnell Douglas), Long Island

TABLE 25-2
Military involvement at the state level (selected states, 1981)

State	Contract awards ($ in millions)	Payroll ($ in millions)	Civilian employees, thousands	Military employees, thousands
Alabama	790	964	24	24
California	16,600	6,900	128	195
Massachusetts	4,596	442	12	10
New York	6,481	658	18	21
Vermont	167	13	0.5	0.08
Total U.S.	96,653	43,688	891	1368

Source: Statistical Abstract of the United States, 1984.

(Grumman), and Newport News (Tenneco). There is a net shift of income from the northeastern part of the nation to the south and west (Council of Economic Priorities, 1982).

Economic Comparison between Military and Civilian Expenditures

The military certainly employs people, but not in such a way as to produce more jobs in the long run. Employment in much civilian industry not only gives people jobs but contributes to the production of more jobs and more output. Anderson (1982) examined what would have happened in the period 1977–1978 had the investment of federal tax funds among the states in military-related activities been used for typical non-military projects. The analysis showed that even some states that received substantial DOD money had fewer jobs than they would have had if the money had been spent in the civilian sector. Those states which paid more than their share of the military budgets were the largest losers. Such states are taxed, but they don't get funds back which might be reinvested.

Anderson concluded that about 1 million jobs were lost in that period for the entire nation. The largest losers were (in thousands, negative numbers mean a job loss to the state): New York, − 288; Illinois, − 160; Michigan, − 139; Ohio, − 131; Pennsylvania, −112; New Jersey, −72. The largest winners were Virginia, +126; Hawaii, +45; South Carolina, +29; North Carolina, +24. Surprisingly, California—the recipient of the largest amount of military funding—would lose only 13,800 jobs if military expenditures were shifted to civilian investment.

This type of "what if" analysis is interesting, but difficult to defend precisely. For example, it uses an input-output methodology with fixed coefficients. The actual economy is dynamic.

It is often observed that military spending has civilian-sector spin-offs. For example, the military need for advanced large-scale integrated circuits led to heavy investments in new technology—technology which has been used in the civilian sector in developing advanced computers and other products. A spin-off effect undoubtedly exists. The questions are: How big is it? And how much more might have been accomplished had the same resources been fully devoted to civilian-sector development?

The transfer of military-related skills and technologies to the civilian sector is less direct than might appear. Military equipment is very specialized and must be extremely reliable, and cost plays a very minor role in its design. Many contracts are written on the basis of cost plus fixed fee, and so there is no penalty for cost **overruns.** Indeed, there is often an advantage to be gained. As a result, engineers trained to work on military systems generally have a hard time making the transition to civilian-sector work, where cost control is essential. Retraining is of course possible, but the fact remains that military and civilian technologies have very different priorities.

In a time of general underemployment one can argue that since there is a surplus of labor the nation does not lose by expanding the military sector. If this is true, then from an economic point of view, not only is the arms industry ''costless,'' but it benefits the nation by utilizing idle resources. This view has led some Marxist-Leninist economists to argue that capitalism tends to encourage militarism. It does not, however, take account of the limited supply of skilled labor. On the other hand if there is little unemployment, the military sector will compete for labor needed in the civilian economy with adverse effect.

Use of Skilled Labor by the Arms Industry

The military uses a great deal of sophisticated equipment, and thus draws disproportionately upon skilled labor. There are of course unskilled military personnel at low levels, but military expenditures overall tend not to help the unskilled laborers who form the bulk of the unemployed. About 90 percent of workers in all United States industry are production employees, who tend to be relatively unskilled. The corresponding percentages for some specific industries are (Council on Economic Priorities, 1982):

Industry	Percentage of production employees
Aircraft and parts	53.8
Complete guided missiles	27.8
Shipbuilding and repair	79.1
Communications equipment	50.0
Ordnance and accessories	47.3
Motor vehicles	73.5
Electronic and computing	34.2

Since skilled workers are generally paid more than unskilled workers, the total number of jobs produced by investments in military technologies is less than for investments in other sectors. ''Total jobs'' include not only those created directly but also those which result when a company which has received a government contract orders components from another company, and when employees buy personal goods and services such as food and houses. The economic technique known as input-output analysis is used to estimate such indirect effects. The total number of jobs generated by an expenditure of $1 billion in 1980 would have been (Anderson, 1982):

Area	Jobs created
Retail trade	65,000
Education	62,000
Hospitals	48,000
Newspapers	30,000
Apparel manufacturers	28,000
Fabricated metals	16,000
Guided missiles and ordnance	14,000

Overall, according to this analysis, every $1 billion spent on the military creates 9000 fewer jobs than would be created if the same money were spent in the average private sector and 35,000 fewer jobs than would be created if the money were spent in the state and local government sector.

Anderson's (1982) analysis of the B-1 bomber program compared its effects on the economy with (1) a tax cut of the same size and (2) a public housing program. Over a 5-year period the tax cut would have yielded 30,000 more jobs and the housing program 70,000 more jobs.

Further, the nation's stock of truly gifted individuals is limited. Those who are hired to work on weapons development are not available to work on the high-technology innovations that will be essential if the United States is to effectively compete in the increasingly competitive international environment. (Because the number of very highly skilled persons is so small, this effect does not show up in aggregate statistics.)

Research and development has a particular need for skilled persons. The United States invests about 1 percent of GNP in civilian R & D and about 2 percent in military R & D. The percentages spent in the civilian sector are about the same in the United Kingdom, France, the Federal Republic of Germany, and Japan. However, the percentages of GNP spent on military R & D in these countries are, respectively, 0.6, 0.5, 0.2, and less than 0.1 percent.

Inflationary Pressures due to Military Expenditure

When defense expenditures are increased rapidly, inflation rates in the defense sector tend to be large. The Council on Economic Priorities quotes a DOD Defense Science Board report which found that in 1979–1980 the overall defense-sector inflation rate was 10 to 20 percent per year and the rate in certain subsectors, such as jet engines and electronic memories, was as high as 35 percent. For industries involving raw materials critical to the defense industry, rates were even higher.

Some argue that the inflationary pressures associated with the current military buildup are not unreasonable, given the fact that defense outlays as a percent of GNP have been substantially less in the early 1980s (7 percent) than they were at the height of the war in Vietnam, when they ranged from 10 to 14 percent of the GNP.

It can also be argued that since military expenditure is not labor-intensive, conversion of the military machine to civilian activities would have minimal impact on the economy. Many analysts say that military expenditures do not have to be justified in terms of their contribution to economic growth, but are a national security requirement only. Such a distinction is difficult to demonstrate in practice, and the preponderance of the evidence indicates that in the long run excessive military expenditures are erosive to any nation's long-term economic interests.

25-7   COST ESCALATION AND OVERRUNS

Military systems are renowned for cost increases. There are two major reasons: (1) military systems have become increasingly complicated, and hence expensive, and (2) many aspects of the weapons procurement process do not lend themselves to cost control.

The complexity of military systems was bound to increase with the development of advanced electronic technologies. However, the U.S. focus on complexity is in contrast with the Soviet Union's emphasis on simplicity and reliability. In a comparison of areas in which the United States is ahead of and behind the Soviet Union, Donald Kerr, Director of Los Alamos Scientific Laboratory, identified simplicity and ease of field maintenance as an area in which the Soviet Union is ahead.

Recently aircraft carriers have carried price tags approaching $2 billion. The cost escalation of virtually every military system is far beyond the cost escalation that would be expected as a result of normal inflation. There is little doubt that military costs will continue to rise as the level of technology and the complexity of missions increase. But it does need to be asked how much of the increases are unavoidable and how much are the result of factors that should be controlled.

Cost escalation that skyrockets beyond original estimates is probably an example of the latter.

The costs of replacement parts are notorious. The *San Francisco Chronicle* carried a typical article in 1983:

34 Cents Buys a $1280 Navy Part

Two senior Navy chiefs at Lemoore Naval Air Station near Fresno, California, thought $1280 was a bit excessive for a diode and tried to find one cheaper. They did, for 34 cents, a Navy spokesman said Friday. Charles Oliver, who with Len Claycomb was monitoring the performance of a multi-million dollar weapons training flight simulator for the F-18 Hornet, told a base newspaper reporter many of the prices on a list of 10,000 parts from prime contractor Hughes Aircraft seemed exorbitant.

"I think the first item questioned was a diode that the contractor wanted the Navy to pay $1280 for," he said. "We checked the Navy supply system and found the same diode costing 34 cents."

A Hughes spokesman confirmed the price and said it was high because it would be very costly to set up a special system to test and stock only four diodes.

Contracts are often written on a cost plus fixed fee basis, which means the contractor has little incentive to save. They are also frequently written so the contractor is paid a percentage of the cost, which is based on actual expenses rather than on a fixed price bid. This system—in which the higher the price goes, the more money the contractor makes—is not conducive to cost control. Once the development of a system is at a certain point, there is little chance of cancellation, and a contractor can often renegotiate at higher prices. Then, when a system is in operation, there is a continuing market for parts, and generally these are sold on a "sole-source" basis, which means that there is no competition. In such contracts there are few limits on the prices that can be charged—as the above news article indicates.

Many actions could be taken to make the weapons procurement process more efficient, with no decrease in performance. However, institutional structures that have developed around the military have made cost control virtually impossible. An occasional scandal leads to some local improvements, but major reform appears unlikely.

One of the best analyses of these problems is found in *National Defense,* by James Fallows (1981), which includes many case studies.

25-8 ARMS EXPENDITURES AND ECONOMIC GROWTH

Comparing percentages of gross national products spent on the military with growth in manufacturing output (a key indicator of ability to compete internationally) shows that in recent years nations with the highest military expenditures have experienced the lowest rates of productivity growth (Table 25-3). The industrial nations with which the United States must compete spend a smaller proportion of their resources on the military, and they tend to have higher economic growth rates and faster improvement in worker productivity. See Figure 25-3. The negative correlation is strong. Although there may be other factors involved, there is reason for concern that U.S. investment in military buildup may be exacting substantial long-run costs in terms of ability to compete internationally. One possible approach would be for the United States to ask its allies to pay a larger share of the costs of armaments.

TABLE 25-3
Relationship between military spending and growth in productivity

	Percentage of GNP devoted to military spending in 1960–1979	Rate of change of output per hour in manufacturing productivity 1960–1970, %
U.S.	7.4	2.6
U.K.	5.4	2.9
France	4.6	5.5
West Germany	3.9	5.4
Sweden	3.8	5.3
Italy	2.9	6.1
Canada	2.7	3.9
Japan	0.9	8.1

Source: Council on Economic Priorities, 1982.

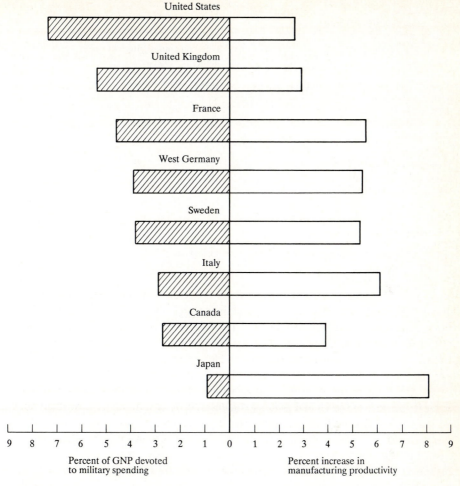

United States

United Kingdom

France

West Germany

Sweden

Italy

Canada

Japan

9 8 7 6 5 4 3 2 1 0 1 2 3 4 5 6 7 8 9

Percent of GNP devoted
to military spending

Percent increase in
manufacturing productivity

FIGURE 25-3

Economic productivity and military spending in 11 industrialized nations for the period 1960–1979. The data are taken from the Council on Economic Priorities, 1982.

In a release to the Associated Press in September 1988 (Chronicle, 1988), the Council on Competitiveness, chaired by John Young, chairman of Hewlett-Packard Corporation, contended that the United States has been far too complacent in the face of foreign competition and recommended a major effort by government, industry, and schools to reverse the trend. Young said he wanted to challenge the illusion that high-technology industries would provide the "economic panacea we all need" to offset job losses in traditional industries. The report said that U.S. companies' market share in technical areas had shrunk so dramatically in the past two decades that in 1986 the country suffered a trade deficit in high-technology goods for the first time ever. Table 25-4 illustrates this trend for a few technical products.

TABLE 25-4
U.S. share of technology

Technology	Pioneered by	U.S. companies' share of domestic American market				Estimated 1987 value of U.S. market (millions)
		1970	1975	1980	1987	
B&W television	U.S.	65	30	15	2	175
Audio tape recorders	U.S.	40	10	10	1	500
Video cassette recorder	U.S.	10	10	1	1	2,895
Ballbearings	Germany	88	83	71	71	41,687
Telephone sets	U.S.	99	95	88	25	2,000
Semiconductors	U.S.	89	71	65	64	19,100
Semiconductor manufacturing equipment	U.S.	100	90	75	75	1,865
Cellular telephones	Scandinavia/U.S.	—	—	—	40	740
Facsimile machines	U.S./Japan	—	—	—	0	750

Source: International Trade Administration, U.S. Department of Commerce.

The same kind of considerations which apply to the relation between economic growth and military expenditures in the United States also apply to the Soviet Union. Since military expenditures in the Soviet Union are a much greater fraction of the GNP than they are in the United States, it is certain that they are paying a large price in terms of their economic development. The economy of the Soviet Union is not strongly coupled to world markets, and they have less of a problem than the United States does with competition from other nations. But because their standard of living is far below that in the United States (as measured, for example, by how many hours an individual must work to earn her or his daily food or a pair of shoes), the cost of the arms race for Soviet citizens is substantially higher than for U.S. citizens.

In the period from fiscal year 1981 to fiscal year 1987, the annual federal budget deficit grew from $79 billion to $178 billion. To pay for the deficits the United States has borrowed from foreign countries and in the process has gone from the world's largest creditor nation to the world's largest debtor. This situation if prolonged could lead to serious consequences; for example, major decisions concerning the U.S. economy will be made by foreign investors. In the case of a contracting world economy, foreign investors would probably withdraw funds from the United States, thereby creating more downward pressure on the U.S. economy. This happened to the United Kingdom in 1929 when U.S. investors withdrew funds.

A serious problem in the military in the next few years will probably occur because of the development of too many new and expensive weapon systems in the 1981–1988 period. These systems are discussed in detail in the next section, particularly in Table 25-5. In an era where budgets may be shrinking in order to combat the increase in national debt, new weapons will just be coming off the production lines. Production expenses will be large and it will be necessary for the Pentagon to rethink priorities imposed by the momentum of earlier program commitments for expensive new weapon systems. According to Stephen Daggett (Daggett, 1986), as a result of the "funding wedge" of the new programs, funding for readiness and sustainability may become fodder for the fiscal retreat. According to Daggett:

> The US faces the real prospect of entering the 1990's with shiny, new, high-technology forces that look impressive but cannot roll or sail or fly to where they might be needed. Nor will they have enough tactical missiles to fire when they get there.

The Bush administration will have to make some hard decisions about defense priorities. This situation is similar to that facing the Soviets. Since it is in the best interest of both nations to reduce defense expenditures in order to bolster their civilian economies, it is possible that real opportunities may be created for substantial reductions in military commitments. For example, there might be incentive on both sides to reduce conventional forces in Europe and to proceed effectively with the START talks for reduction in strategic nuclear weapons. Since the United States is presently spending $150 billion annually for the defense of Europe, it may be timely to re-examine the magnitude of this commitment. It is, after all, well over forty years after World War II, and further the European economies, with early U.S. assistance, are now fully recovered from that war.

According to Gordon Adams (Adams, 1986), a genuine economic dimension needs to be added to the concept of national security. So in framing the federal budget, for example, the questions of who needs jobs and where those jobs are needed should be addressed. Adams states:

> The problem posed by conversion advocates (from military to civilian needs) is, in fact, a small facet of a much larger dilemma: how to develop and handle economic transitions in a way that is fair to all. The U.S. economy goes through many transitions every year, some of them brutal. The steel industry is shrinking; the automobile industry shook out 250,000 workers; what was once called the Midwest is jokingly described as the "rust bowl." Economic adjustment is a major problem generally handled in an inadequate and wasteful way. Economically productive resources are thrown away, with no retraining or relocation benefits, while taxpayers spend billions on low-income programs that maintain living standards, but do not provide employment.

25-9   COSTS OF NEW MILITARY SYSTEMS

As noted, the strategic (nuclear) component of the U.S. defensive system consumes about 22 percent of all military spending (Center for Defense Information, 1987). About $350 billion was spent on the nuclear arsenal in the period 1981–1987. About 17,000 new nuclear weapons were built, replacing some 6000 older weapons. The costs of many of these new systems are huge. A single B-1B bomber will cost $300 to $400 million. A B-52 (now three decades old, but still the cornerstone of the bomber leg of the strategic triad) costs $7500 per hour to operate. The annual operating cost of the B-52 fleet is $1.9 billion.

Many new weapons systems are proposed as part of the buildup; most of these will be enormously expensive. Table 25-5 lists some of these systems and gives estimates of what they will cost. There is certain to be controversy over whether the

TABLE 25-5
Examples of very expensive nuclear weapons systems

Weapons system	Number	First year operational	Money spent through FY83, $ billions	Money requested FY84, $ billions	Number requested FY84	Money proposed FY85, $ billions	Unit cost, $ millions	Estimated total cost, $ billions*	Remarks
MX missile	223	1986	6.7	6.2	27	5.3	123	27.4	50 deployed by 1989, balance test and spares.
Trident submarine	20–25	1982	13.0	1.8	1	2.0	1600	31–39	Cost for first 15 subs, $23.6 billion.
Trident I missile	595	1979	7.4	0.6	52	0.210	19	11.2	For 12 backfitted subs and first 8 Trident subs with 211 test and spares.
Trident II missile	740	1989	0.682	1.5	0 (R & D)	2.3	50	37.6	For 15 subs. For 20–25 subs cost would be $45–53 billion.
B-1B bomber	100	1986	11.5	6.9	10	8.5	400	40.0	90 operational aircraft will be deployed at four bases.
Stealth bomber (B2)	132	Early 1990s	?	0.292	0 (R & D)	1.05	?	40–50?	Classified program.
B-52 bomber modifications	263	On-going	2.5	0.720	—	0.752	20 per plane	5.8	Radar, engines, avionics, and other improvements.

System	Number	Year							Comments
Air-launched cruise missile	1739	1982	3.5	0.493	240	?	2.7	4.7	Production canceled at 1739 of original 4348.
Sea-launched cruise missile	4068	1984	2.1	0.528	124	0.768	2.8	11.5	Total is for all versions; includes 74 for R & D, 758 for nuclear attack.
Advanced cruise missile	2600	1987–88	?	?	0 (R & D)	?	5–7	7.0	Classified program: figures are estimates.
Command, control, communications, and intelligence	Many programs	On-going	?	7.5	—	9	—	40–50	Hundreds of programs.
Air defense	Many programs	On-going	?	0.482	Various	1	—	7.8	Radar, F-15 aircraft, AWACS aircraft.
Midgetman missile	1000	1992	0	0.604	0 (R & D)	0.604	38–70	38–70	20-year costs could be $107 billion.

*Does not include DOE costs for nuclear warheads and bombs which normally are an additional 10 to 20 percent of the weapons system cost.

Source: DOD, DOE, CDI. Chart prepared by Center for Defense Information, 1983.

costs of many of these systems are justified in terms of their contribution to the security of the nation.

Nuclear arms are far cheaper than conventional arms for the same amount of destructive capability. The cost of maintaining the present level of military strength (in Europe, for example) would be greater if reliance on nuclear systems were decreased. What does this mean in terms of a trade-off between military security and economic well-being? What kind of procedures and methodology might be devised for helping to think about such trade-offs?

QUESTIONS

1. What percentage of the GNP has the United States been spending on the military?
2. What fraction of the total military budget is for nuclear weapons and their delivery systems?
3. What was the percentage of gross national product devoted to military spending by the United States and Japan in the 1960 to 1979 period? What was the percent change in manufacturing productivity in output per hour for the United States in the same period?
4. Discuss the correlation (if any) between the productivity of an industrial nation and the expenditure on the military sector.
5. Why does the expenditure of national resources on the military produce less employment than a comparable amount spent on civilian programs?
6. Why is it difficult to compare Soviet and United States military expenditures?
7. Which nations are the leading sellers of armaments to developing countries?
8. What is the approximate expenditure on armaments per year if all the major nations are considered?
9. Compare labor and material costs of the United States and the Soviet Union.
10. What fraction of the GNP is spent on the military by the United States? The Soviet Union?
11. Identify some military projects or technologies which you believe contribute to civilian productivity.
12. How much do you pay each year to support the defense of the nation? How much do you pay to support arms shipments to other nations?
13. Make a list of some of the secondary effects that result when a dollar is spent on a military project in a given area (e.g., the restaurants and clothing stores and schools that are needed to care for workers and their families.

KEY WORDS

GNP   gross national product. The aggregate of all the goods and services produced by the United States annually.

overruns   cost escalation beyond original estimates or contracts.

perestroika   restructuring. Part of the effort of perestroika in the Soviet Union is to restructure the economy to make it more efficient and to reduce arms expenditure to release more monies for the civilian economy.

CHAPTER
26

VISIONS

Where there is no vision, the people perish.

Proverbs 29:18

Turning and turning in the widening gyre
The falcon cannot hear the falconer
Things fall apart, the center cannot hold
Mere anarchy is loosed upon the world
The blood-dimmed tide is loosed, and everywhere
The ceremony of innocence is drowned
The best lack all conviction, while the worst
Are full of passionate intensity

Surely some revelation is at hand. . . .

William Butler Yeats,
"The Second Coming," 1921

The unleashed power of the atom has changed everything except our modes of thinking, and so we drift toward unparalleled catastrophe.

Albert Einstein, 1945

26-1 THEMES

In this, the concluding chapter, we reassess our nuclear predicament in the light of material contained in this book. We discuss briefly several views of aggression and warfare. Finally, we give our own views of short-range and long-range goals that we believe would be helpful in extricating our nation from the danger of nuclear war.

26-2 THE PREDICAMENT

Since the invention of the atomic bomb, the United States and the Soviet Union, assisted by France and the United Kingdom, have at enormous expense developed

483

and installed weapons systems that can destroy the civilizations of all nations. Global nuclear war would devastate the northern hemisphere, and the shock to the ecosphere might well be worldwide. Billions of human lives would be lost in combatant and noncombatant nations. Some say that the existence of human life itself would be threatened. No matter how one looks at it, therefore, our lives have become far less secure as a result of the invention of the A-bomb.

The incentive to build the first nuclear weapons was overwhelming. Once given scientists' knowledge of fission, it is hard, even with hindsight, to imagine any circumstances that might have postponed the construction of such weapons for long. Nuclear technology exists, and we have no choice but to learn to live with it.

Many students of world affairs believe that the buildup of nuclear arsenals in the past four decades has led to a stable balance of power between the nations that are so armed. They argue that mutual assured destruction (MAD) has worked, and is still working.

As we have said repeatedly, we are less sanguine. No one can deny that nuclear weapons have not been used against people since 1945, but it does not appear possible to make any strong statements about the effectiveness of MAD. In fact that strategy is not "mutual," since the Soviets have never subscribed to it. All we know is that war has not occurred. We have no idea what might have happened had the nations of the world pursued different nuclear strategies—such as, for example, the Oppenheimer-Baruch plan.

Four decades is a very short time in human affairs. If the United States, as well as other major cultures of the northern hemisphere and perhaps the world, is to survive for centuries, the arms race will somehow have to be brought under control. Yet ideas on how to accomplish this are very scarce indeed. If there is a typical view within the U.S. establishment, it is that in the short run we *have* to persist in at least matching the Soviets—which means continuing to build up nuclear weapons systems—and that changes from this strategy will have to await the next generation.

We do not agree. We see the risks of our present approach growing ever larger. We strongly suspect that there is not time enough to leave these matters to another generation. One reason is that warfare has been a part of human history for the last 6000 years, and weapons, once invented, tend to be used.

By the end of World War II, human destructive powers had reached a point at which they could be used, with great effort, to destroy entire cities. In August 1945, nuclear weapons were first used in warfare—and one bomb destroyed a city. The meaning of war changed forever because the potential for destruction in war increased by a factor of millions. Since Hiroshima, the nuclear arms race has realized this potential. The superpowers' arsenals now contain the firepower of a million Hiroshimas.

Given present levels of nuclear arsenals, there is no relief from vulnerability to nuclear attack. Nuclear weapons possessing unprecedented power can be readily delivered by the thousands in a few minutes' time. The technical possibility of a defense system effective enough to provide confidence in any nation's ability to withstand a nuclear attack is remote. Those who support research exploring defense systems say that such research will at the least help the United States avoid surprises, but, in reality, much of the research is likely to prove a waste of money. Worse, it can raise false hopes in the citizenry and encourage denial of the stark fact that America is vulnerable and will remain so until political progress is made that will permit dramatic reductions in nuclear arsenals. Furthermore, when vulnerable weapons systems (such as the MX missile) are part of the overall picture, deployment of a defensive system could easily be perceived by the Soviets as part of a first-strike capability, thereby destabilizing the arms race.

A terminal defense for some areas might become feasible at strategic arsenal levels of about 100 megatons (see Chapter 20). In our society it is customary to seek technical solutions to problems of vulnerability. But unless levels are drastically reduced, reliable defense is an unrealizable dream.

Our lives are linked to decisions made in other nations—particularly decisions made in the Soviet Union. Any nuclear weapons policy that is to assure our survival, either as individuals or as a nation, must take this fact into account.

Meanwhile, we need to remember that alliances and enmities change with time. The Kaiser's Germany, Nazi Germany, Japan in the 1940s, and later China in the 1950s and 1960s were our bitter enemies. Many Americans lost their lives in fighting those countries. The war propaganda of the United States during those times portrayed our enemies in the worst possible terms, attempting to totally dehumanize them. Times change, and these nations are now our friends and allies. Germany and France have fought each other many times; their border is now peaceful.

In their book *The Wages of War 1816–1965,* J. David Singer and Melvin Small (1972) conclude that:

> Of the 209 pairs who ever fought in opposition . . . 19 percent had fought against each other at least once before; but . . . 21 percent had been partners on at least one occasion in the past. . . . There seems to be only modest evidence in support of the notion that nations have highly consistent sets of fundamental relationships with each other. . . . If most nations find it possible to cooperate with almost any other ones in wartime, such cooperation in the avoidance of war may not be as impossible to achieve as the pessimists might have us believe.

Singer and Small (1982) have also examined the number of wars taking place in the world, and find that a Poisson distribution fits quite well, meaning that wars tend to occur randomly.

26-3 NEW POLITICAL VALUES

Citizens of the Soviet Union share many of our deepest values: love of family, friends, and homeland—and the desire for survival itself. Their nation's experiences of war have been very different from ours. Twenty million Soviet citizens were killed during the German invasion in World War II. Russia has been invaded over the centuries dating back to the time of the Mongol campaigns. As a result, the Soviet Union has an ingrained horror of invasion that is hard for us to imagine. Yet they have also fostered repressive regimes and have repeatedly moved to expand their power into new areas of the globe. We deplore their repression in the recent past of citizens striving for freedom in Poland, Hungary, Czechoslovakia, and Afghanistan, as we do the defensiveness that resulted in the destruction of Korean Airlines Flight 007. It is encouraging to note that under the Gorbachev policies of perestroika (restructuring) and glasnost (openness) the sense of repression felt by visitors to the Soviet Union has lessened considerably in comparison with past experience.

It is sobering to recall, on the other hand, that the United States has acted in ways far removed from our professed national ideals. In the eyes of many Vietnamese, we engaged for years in a devastating and unsuccessful attempt to repress their centuries-old striving for independence. In so doing we used more munitions on their nation than all combatants used during all of World War II. Over 50,000 Americans were killed in that war, and there were far more casualties among Vietnamese civilians. The United States also remains to this date the only nation to have used nuclear weapons on cities, with their massed human targets.

The central fact of the nuclear age is that we—the people of the nations of the earth—must cooperate or we shall perish. Pierre Teilhard de Chardin expressed this succinctly in 1936 when he said, ''The Age of Nations is past. The task before us, if we would not perish, is to build the earth.''

Meanwhile, it is well to remember that we are in the midst of an age of extremely rapid technological transition. Fission was discovered only in 1939, and already we are threatened with extinction of our nation and much of humankind. The times call for a political vision to match our technological advance—if we are to survive. We see a need for a vision of a future that might be complemented by here-and-now actions that will start us on the way.

Too often we seek a ''technological fix'' for political and human problems. Ever since the industrial revolution we have tried to conquer nature and make it submit to human desires. In the process we have become alienated from our fundamental being and from the earth itself. We pollute the environment and speak with cool logic of megadeaths.

What is needed are new values appropriate to the postindustrial nuclear age. We are entering a more advanced phase of human existence. With new powers over life and death, a new maturity is demanded of us; from this we might create a new vision of individual and planetary behavior. One goal should be supreme: the preservation of the human species.

Konrad Lorenz, in *King Solomon's Ring* (1952), describes the instinctive species-preserving behavior of wolves. The fangs of a wolf are deadly weapons in any contest for power with another wolf. If evolution had not provided some means to control the use of these weapons, the species might have disappeared. But such a control did evolve. If two wolves are in a teeth-bared battle, and one wolf realizes it is losing, it ends the conflict by exposing its jugular vein to the attacker. At this signal the other wolf will cease fighting, even if it has been on the verge of sinking its teeth into the opponent's throat.

Humans, too, need to evolve some sort of self-regulation that grows out of our instinct for survival. Our weapons were not created by nature, but by ourselves. The social inhibitions that can enable us to survive must come from the same source. As Herman Wouk stated in *War and Remembrance* (1978):

Either war is finished or we are. . . . War is an old habit of thought, an old frame of mind, an old political technique, that must now pass as human sacrifice and human slavery have passed. I have faith that the human spirit will prove equal to the long heavy task of ending war.

The political scientist Louis Beres (1981) expands this image. He calls for a new planetary identity.

> Steps must be taken to satisfy two interrelated objectives: a strengthened tapestry of international treaties and agreements directed at non-proliferation, arms control and disarmament; and a generalized renunciation of the long-discredited principles of *realpolitik*.
>
> We must transform the characteristic behavior of the superpowers in world politics. We must create the conditions whereby the United States and the Soviet Union consider cooperation in the world interest to be in their respective national interests. . . . The United States and the Soviet Union must retreat from increasing acceptance of counterforce principles and return to the relative sanity of minimum deterrence.
>
> Without necessarily seeking fundamental changes in the prevailing state-centric structure of global authority, the two superpowers must learn to associate their own security with a more far-reaching search for worldwide stability and equity. To prevent nuclear war between the superpowers, the prescribed nuclear regime must be augmented by a new awareness of the "connectedness" of states.
>
> The centerpiece of this universal regimen must be the cosmopolitan understanding that all states, like all people, form one essential body and one true community. Such an understanding, that a latent oneness lies buried beneath the manifold divisions of our fractionate world, need not be based on the mythical attractions of universal brotherhood and mutual concern. Instead, it must be based on the idea that the individual states, however much they may dislike one another, are tied together in a struggle for survival.

Obviously the world will go on, regardless of what we do. However, good management and massive global cooperation could lead to a far better world. Other approaches, including the approach of doing nothing, may lead to severe deterioration. Management of "spaceship earth" appears to us to be the proper successor to the nuclear arms race as a primary focus of attention for concerned citizens of all parties and all political outlooks.

There is a story that if one tosses a frog into a pot of boiling water he hops out. But if one places him in a pot of cold water and heats it slowly he doesn't notice, and is cooked. The story may be apocryphal, but it illustrates an important point. The biosphere, which includes us, may be in a "frog" situation. Whether we can react and prevent being cooked remains to be seen. For further reading about these issues, good places to start are Mathews (1989) and Goldemburg et al. (1988).

In recent years there has been an enormous growth in awareness of the interconnectedness of the world. The so-called "ozone hole" in the Antarctic is a direct result of mankind's use of a particular type of chemical—chlorofluorocarbons. This compound was long believed harmless, yet it turns out that it plays a major role in destroying ozone in the upper atmosphere.

Carbon dioxide and other "greenhouse" gases are increasing rapidly. Already there are indications that mankind is altering the climate of the world. It appears likely that within only a few more years there will be unambiguous data showing that man's activities are leading to global warming. Associated with warming could be large fluctuations in weather. This could have profound implications for agriculture and for many industries. It could lead to drought in some areas, and flooding in others.

Population growth is already leading to enormous stresses on the biosphere. The writer Isaac Asimov has captured the problem of crowding and of limited resources in what he calls the "bathroom analogy." If two people live in a house or apartment having two bathrooms, there is no stress. Each can use a bathroom whenever he or she wishes, as long as he or she wishes. If the occupancy of the apartment or house is increased to a dozen or more, then the situation changes. Even with the best will in the world there will be stress. No amount of planning can change this. The demand simply exceeds the availability of the limited resource.

It took the world 130 years to grow from one to two billions, and only a decade to climb from 5 billion to 6 billion. Population growth is fastest in developing countries. It is hard to see how these nations will ever be able to industrialize. In fact, they may even go backwards, as has occurred in some parts of Africa in recent years as gross national product has actually declined. Drought in the African Sahel, and destruction of tropical forests are probably irreversible.

We see a situation emerging in which the urgency of dealing with superpower relations and nuclear weaponry is replaced by an awareness that all peoples of the earth must work together if we are not to irreversibly destroy so much of the earth that global standards of living decline.

26-4   RENUNCIATION OF ARMS

Have there been instances in history when nations have voluntarily renounced the use of particular weapons? There are a few. The horrible experiences with mustard gas in World War I gave rise to the Convention on the Use of Chemical and Biological Weapons. Thus far, with the exception of the war between Iran and Iraq, this accord has been obeyed. After World War I the United States, Great Britain, and Japan signed a naval treaty which led to the sinking of a number of ships. This treaty lasted well into the 1930s, after which those nations began to rearm. But it does show that weapons can be destroyed by mutual agreement.

Giving up the gun: Japan, 1543–1879. A unique instance of voluntary constraints on weapons occurred in Japan, which for over three centuries forswore use of the gun for other than ceremonial occasions. During this period Japan had the technical knowledge to manufacture and use guns, but chose not to do so. The story, told by Noel Perrin (1980), is given in some detail here.

In 1543 a Chinese cargo ship anchored at the harbor of Tanegashima. Two Portuguese on board had with them arquebuses and ammunition. They demonstrated their weapons—the first known to have reached Japan—to the increasingly excited Lord Tokitaka, who purchased them for a large sum. The incident is documented in a famous drawing by one of the greatest of all Japanese artists, Hokusai.

Manufacture began, and a few years later guns were widely available and cheap. In 1560 the first large battle with firearms took place. Manuals on the use of guns were prepared, and the process of integration of this powerful new technology was institutionalized. During this period Japan was in the midst of interminable wars. The samurai warrior class was powerful and its members were numerous, making up about 7 to 10 percent of the population. (The U.S. military now constitutes about 1 percent of the population, perhaps double this if one includes armaments makers.)

Despite all these incentives, when Commodore Perry began the process of opening up Japan in 1854, there were virtually no guns to be found. The few that were there were used for ceremonial occasions only. What had happened?

The answer will never be known for certain, but Perrin speculates that at least four different factors were involved. First, the samurai class came to recognize that the use of guns removed the highest level of skill from the hand of the samurai to that of the gunsmith. The samurai were spectacular swordsmen, and they gradually came to agree among themselves that the only way to preserve their status and their livelihoods (as well as their lives) was to preserve the old ways of fighting.

The second reason was geopolitical. Japan, an isolated group of islands, was difficult to invade. The land could be defended with conventional weaponry.

The third reason seems strange to us. To the samurai the sword had an importance far beyond its use in fighting. Swords were the embodiment of honor. They were works of art. Swords acquired a symbolic value quite independent of any practical use. A shift to other weapons, therefore, would have required major changes in the imagery of power.

The anthropologist Ruth Benedict is quoted as having pointed out that the Japanese still speak of self-indulgent behavior as ''the rust of my body''—referring to the crime against one's sword of allowing even a speck of rust to mar the blade. A Japanese warrior would have felt unsexed as well as defenseless without his sword. Much in the same way, Perrin observes, a cowboy in an American western movie feels unsexed without his six-shooter.

The fourth reason for rejection of the gun resulted from a reaction against all outside ideas including the idea of the gun. The country was closed to foreigners in 1636 in order to keep out missionaries.

The firearm entered Japan in 1543. It played a major role for a century or so. It then gradually faded out of use for two centuries, until contact with the west forced its reintroduction.

26-5 RENUNCIATION OF NUCLEAR WEAPONS

Although we seek a world without armed conflict, this may not be attainable in the near future. Warfare among the peoples of the world is likely to persist. The difference today is the unique destructiveness of nuclear weapons. We need not eliminate all weapons, but we must avoid the use of these. Direct high-stakes conflict, even with conventional weapons, must be strictly avoided between nations armed with nuclear weapons.

But how shall we proceed? A useful approach should start with recognition of the dual causes of nuclear arms escalation: external threats and internal dynamics. While not ignoring the external threat, we observe that all too often in the last decades the United States—for internal reasons—has taken the lead in an outdated realpolitik that involves introduction of weapons systems and aggressive unilateral international action. If we are to survive, we must accept our responsibilities as a world leader. We must have the courage to recognize that nuclear weapons have no practical war-fighting utility. This means abandoning the nuclear war-fighting counterforce doctrine. As a nation, we now act as if our defense objective is to have more weapons than the Soviets. That is an immature goal.

If we adopt for the immediate future a deterrence posture, we need only enough nuclear weapons so that we cannot be intimidated; this is the essence of assured destruction. We do not need enough nuclear weapons to fight any conceivable war—or indeed any war at all.

Our immediate objective should be only to deter the Soviets, as well as any other nation that may contemplate aggression against us. To accomplish this, we require (for the immediate future, in any event) a minimal nuclear arsenal, together with a delivery capability and a control system. Such an arsenal could be, and should be, only a small fraction of what we now possess.

For the longer term we believe it is possible to avoid completely our reliance on nuclear weapons—but this will be a long process, as we discuss below.

Short-Term Goals

It appears to us possible—indeed likely—that within only a few years the character of the relations between the United States and the Soviet Union may change enormously. Rather than being implacable enemies, the two superpowers may well come to recognize that they not only can coexist but in many areas can contribute to each other's well-being.

It has now been over two decades since essential nuclear parity developed between the United States and the Soviet Union. Since then, and for the foreseeable future, the superpowers will retain the capability to destroy each other. Recognition of this essential fact of life in the nuclear age has come far more slowly. There are still many individuals who retain the unrealizable dream of America's being able to overpower the Soviet Union.

Political recognition of the implications of nuclear parity may well have occurred sooner in the Soviet Union than in the United States. This is perhaps not surprising, since the Soviet Union has national memories of invasion and the death of many millions of citizens which finds no parallel in the United States.

Under President Reagan, negotiations with the Soviet Union about nuclear matters moved in directions many had believed impossible under any president. The INF treaty is the first agreement calling for the scrapping of nuclear weapons. It is also the first which allows inspectors from each of the superpowers on the territory of the other. Agreements have also been reached for monitoring of nuclear explosions. A start has been made on crisis centers in both nations, which will remain in continuous contact with each other. This is a major extension of the hot line agreement which has been in existence for many years.

On the Soviet side the advent of glasnost and perestroika under Gorbachev's leadership is providing many signs of change and opening up. The Soviet decision to pull out of Afghanistan is among the most prominent indicators of change, but many are appearing in every sector of Soviet life.

All this leads us to be optimistic that even larger positive changes lie ahead. In this section we summarize some of the directions which we believe are both possible and desirable over the next decade.

1. SALT II should be ratified by the United States. This treaty has been signed by both sides, but not ratified by the United States Senate. It has the effect of putting a ceiling on strategic weapons. Under today's conditions it should be possible to go far beyond SALT II. However, the existence of an unratified treaty of this sort presents a poor image to the world.

2. We should negotiate with the Soviet Union over deep cuts in all aspects of the nuclear strategic arsenals. A goal of 50 percent cuts has been discussed (the START talks), but much deeper cuts could be made without sacrificing (indeed with improvement in) United States overall security.

3. We should reconfigure American forces so that nuclear weapons are not so closely integrated with conventional forces and modify the present policy of ''flexible response'' to downplay the role of nuclear weapons. This should include a move toward a renunciation of the policy of ''first use'' of tactical nuclear weapons if there is an attack on NATO. This can be partially accomplished by negotiations with the Soviets toward a massive reduction, particularly of offensive forces, in the Warsaw Treaty Organization, with appropriate reduction of NATO forces. The U.S. contribution to NATO is presently about $150 billion dollars annually, or about one-half of the defense budget (see Chapter 25). Force reductions would not only save money on for both sides but also would permit modification or abandonment of NATO's anachronistic and dangerous policy of ''first use.''

4. The comprehensive test ban treaty, which is in an advanced stage of negotiation, should be completed and signed. This would prevent ever-new developments in nuclear weapons and their deployment in places where they do not now exist (e.g., space). There is great divergence of opinion within the United States about reliability of our nuclear stockpile relative to that of the Soviet Union. If necessary to address this problem, the CTBT might be phased in over several years, thereby permitting both superpowers to replace or modify any weapons which they believe to be inadequately reliable. By changing U.S. nuclear weapon design policy, preparation for a CTBT could begin immediately. Research into new domains of nuclear weapons, such as the x-ray laser, would not be permitted under the guise of preparing for a CTBT. An agreement for a CTBT between the superpowers, and other states if possible, would be most important symbolically as it would be a clear message that development of ever new generations of nuclear weapons is not in the best interest of the United States, the U.S.S.R., or other nations.

5. Creating nuclear-free zones in Europe, as we have in Latin America, should be a high priority. We now have thousands of tactical nuclear weapons there on both sides that could easily bring about general nuclear war should armed conflict break

out on the East-West border. In order to create a nuclear-free zone in Europe, it may be necessary to negotiate an agreement with the German Democratic Republic and the Federal Republic of Germany that would neutralize both countries and demilitarize them along the lines of the post-World War II Austrian peace treaty. This treaty negotiated a withdrawal of both Soviet and NATO forces from Austria and has been very successful. Such a treaty may well be the key to a lasting detente in Europe. The force structure in Europe should be reconfigured so as to be less threatening. Restructuring should reduce mobility, range, and the physical capability of both sides to rapidly concentrate military force and to conduct surprise attacks. The ideas of Non-Offensive-Defense (NOD) should be explored in detail in Europe, and incorporated into treaties. The Stockholm Accords (SIPRI 1987) provide one possible starting point for this restructuring.

6. The United States and the Soviet Union should act with renewed vigor to stop the proliferation of nuclear weapons. We have cooperated well on this issue in the past. With the example of real reductions in nuclear arsenals by the superpowers, other nations would be put under great pressure to forego development of nuclear weapons.

7. We should expand considerably the crisis control centers being set up by the two superpowers. A major focus should be on bringing together military and civilians from the superpowers at a variety of different levels in situations where they can get to know each other better, and understand the problems each faces when international tensions grow. Simulation games provide a particularly good vehicle for these interactions.

8. The United States should develop a policy not to seek supremacy over the Soviet Union in research and development of new military technology. The current Strategic Defense Initiative (SDI) (''star wars'') program is a clear example of an effort to move ahead of the Soviets in military space technology. Experience with other military systems (the MIRV is a classic example, and cruise missiles will soon be another) shows that the Soviet Union has both the technical capability and the will to follow close on our heels. The dream of defensive technologies is appealing, but it must be modified feasibly.

9. None of the above will come about without renewal of the spirit of detente. Polarizing rhetoric for domestic consumption should be discouraged as well as rhetoric linking arms control agreements and other international events. Arms control and arms reduction are in the best interests of both the United States and the Soviet Union. To promote this, exchange of all sorts between the Soviet Union and the United States—economic, cultural, and people-to-people—should be vastly augmented. The more they understand about us and we about them, the less each will be dehumanized by each other. Dehumanization is the traditional path to war. We must cooperate or perish, and cooperation begins with mutual understanding.

These changes could bring about a new era in our nuclear world, making us far safer than we presently are, as well as saving resources which are desperately needed for coping with an ever-growing list of major global problems, such as overpopulation, climate change due to carbon dioxide and fluorocarbon emissions, economic development in the Third World, and the incessant wars which are taking place throughout the developing world.

Long-term Goals

Our basic long-term goal is to recognize that nuclear weapons are useless except as a threat and should be discarded as soon as possible. Their use in warfare between the superpowers would amount to mutual extermination. Although it can be argued that the existence of strategic nuclear weapons has kept the peace between the United States and the Soviet Union for the last 40 years, it is unlikely, in our view, that the balance of terror can persist into the indefinite future without nuclear conflict. Any miscalculation, accident, or escalation of a conventional regional conflict could lead to catastrophe.

We urge that concepts such as "limited nuclear war" and "protracted nuclear war" be abandoned as both unrealistic and incredibly dangerous. Initially, as stated above, perhaps we can return to the concept of the capacity for minimum deterrence. However, we should recognize that if such a policy were actually carried out, millions would be incinerated, and thus even deterrence policy is basically immoral and inhuman. As the Catholic Bishops' Conference carefully pointed out, such a position can only be justified on a temporary basis (see Chapter 4).

What should we do beyond deterrence? The answer is simple, but it will be difficult to accomplish. We must give up the deceptive idea that offensive nuclear weapons can provide us with security. This means abandoning them as soon as possible. Such an abandonment would be a tremendous psychological shift for both superpowers and particularly for the United States. The idea is deeply imbedded that more-powerful weapons—ever greater numbers of them—somehow give us greater security. This attitude is in consonance with our history—"get there first with the most"—and is not easily given up. But the fact is that in the nuclear age this attitude has led us into a situation of unprecedented danger.

The nuclear sword of Damocles must be lifted from the world, but it will not be easy. We have spent hundreds of billions of dollars and 40 years of effort in pursuing the illusory goal of security through nuclear weapons. There are entrenched constituencies and, even more influential, an all-pervasive dogma that nuclear weapons are necessary.

In order to reach the long-term goal of a world free of nuclear weapons it is essential to have some sort of long-range plan to replace the transitory security that nuclear deterrence is providing for us. Without some sort of plan we drift toward the day that through accident or miscalculation the nuclear holocaust is loosed upon us. Any plan would be modified by the course of history, but it is important to begin. It should also be recognized that we must be imaginative, persistent, and patient, for the nuclear age demands nothing less than a complete restructuring of the relation between states—certainly states with nuclear weapons.

As an example of long-range plan we would like to briefly outline a proposal by Randall Forsberg (Forsberg, 1984). The paper cited gives considerable detail. It should be emphasized that the Forsberg proposal is only one of many. Our purpose here is to stimulate the reader's thinking including the possible renunciation of long-cherished ideas or world views, if need be.

The following is a plausible route to a world free of nuclear weapons. It is surely a route that would take decades to implement, but that is precisely the meaning of a long-range plan.

Step 1. Stop the production of U.S. and Soviet nuclear weapons and shut down their nuclear weapon facilities. This goes beyond a CTBT in that it envisions no further production of weapons or the fissionable material for them.

Step 2. End large-scale military intervention—the maintenance of military bases and the use of troops, air forces, or naval forces—by the industrialized countries of the northern hemisphere in the developing countries of the southern hemisphere.

Taken together with step 1, the nonintervention regime of step 2 would stabilize and defuse one of the most provocative aspects of the east-west confrontation. There is always the danger that the superpowers in providing proxy nations with conventional weapons could find a conflict escalating to a nuclear confrontation. Fortunately, so far they have been circumspect in this regard, but there is no guarantee that it would always be so.

Step 3. Cut by 50 percent the nuclear and conventional forces of the NATO and Warsaw Pact nations, plus those of China and Japan. This step would stabilize conventional forces and arrest the wasteful and destabilizing trade in major conventional weapon systems. It would also build confidence that war could be deterred with much smaller forces than exist at present. To proceed with further reductions the regime of perestroika and glasnost would have to extend to the satellite nations of the Soviet bloc so that large Soviet forces would not be needed to maintain Soviet hegemony.

Step 4. Strengthen the economic development of the Third World nations, promote civil liberties in all countries, and improve international institutions for negotiation and peacekeeping.

The funds freed by steps 1 to 3 would make the economic development of step 4 possible. When the Europeans are sufficiently secure that they do not fear a reunified Germany, and the United States is sufficiently sure that neither Europe nor the Soviet Union will rearm, it will be possible to move to the next step.

Step 5. Abolish all military alliances and foreign military bases and restructure conventional military forces to limit them to short-range border defense, air defense, and coastal defense.

When the nations observe that this narrow definition of defense is in fact providing security and there is no perceived external threat (e.g., such as relations of the United States with Canada or Mexico), nuclear weapons aren't really needed, so that the next step can be taken.

Step 6. Abolish nuclear weapons.

After a considerable period of time nations may become sufficiently secure that armed force will not be used against them that they would find national armed forces for defense unnecessary. Only national police would be needed to keep internal order. At this stage the final step can be taken:

Step 7. Eliminate national armed forces altogether and replace them with international peacekeeping forces.

Several other alternative plans are given by Joseph Nye, Jr., Graham Allison, and Albert Carnesale in a thoughtful book addressing ten possible answers to the question: How can we create a safer world in the nuclear age (Nye, 1988).

It is encouraging that influential Soviet officials have expressed views that are in considerable agreement with the suggestions we have made above. It is important that the language they use to describe the nuclear predicament is now similar to that of the west.

In April 1987 a report in English was issued in Moscow (Sagdeev, 1987). The supervisors of this large committee report were academician Roald Sagdeev, director of the Institute of Space Research of the U.S.S.R. Academy of Sciences, and Andrei Kokoshin, deputy director of the Institute of the U.S.A. and Canadian Studies of the U.S.S.R. Academy of Sciences. They propose several levels of reduction of nuclear forces. One option proposes a reduction of nuclear forces by 95 percent, leaving only several hundred strategic warheads on each side. They further propose that "in order to lower the probability of surprise attack and offensive operations, there should be reductions in the armed forces and conventional weapons of the NATO and the Warsaw Treaty Organization." They also propose that "nuclear weapons of the 'third' nuclear powers would be reduced proportionally or completely eliminated; the ABM treaty would be still in force; there would be a ban on space-strike weapons (SDI) and ASAT weapons of all types; an agreement on a general and full test ban would be in force (CTBT); and the production of fissionable material for nuclear munitions would be stopped."

Both Jonathan Schell (1984) and Freeman Dyson (1984) have argued, in one form or another, for abandonment of nuclear weapons. Schell introduces the concept of "weaponless deterrence." He assumes that we shall have negotiated nuclear weapons all the way to zero and then addresses the question of possible nuclear "cheating" by a nation bent on aggression. Schell believes the widespread knowledge of how to produce nuclear weapons would be sufficient deterrence because in a few months — or possibly weeks — an industrial nation could recreate nuclear weapons if necessary.

Dyson argues for a "live and let live" policy which assumes that it is better to have live Americans than dead Russians. That is, we maintain the ability to damage the Soviets as badly as they can damage us — but we prefer our own protection to their destruction. This policy rests on a much more solid ground of morality and common sense than does the strategy of assured destruction. It is also consistent with Soviet ideas concerning their own security and survival.

Both Schell and Dyson recognize the crucial fact — the uselessness of nuclear weapons. The first steps in acting on that fact must be something like those outlined in the section above on short-term goals. We need to negotiate patiently, sincerely, and with determination to achieve levels of nuclear weapons substantially lower those we have today. Eventually, as their uselessness became manifest to all, the goal would be zero nuclear weapons.

When nuclear arsenals are reduced through bilateral negotiations to levels that are 30 to 100 times less than we have today, it may be possible to devise a defense system against the remaining strategic nuclear weapons. Such a defense would protect not only against the Soviet Union but also against other possible aggressor nations. Neither the United States nor the Soviet Union could be subjected to nuclear blackmail.

A defensive system would require modification of the ABM treaty. The authors believe that such a system should be undertaken cautiously and nonprovocatively. If a defensive system were deployed now, it could easily be perceived as part of a first-strike threat and escalate the arms race—and in any event would not be effective against the present level of strategic nuclear warheads. (See Chapter 20.)

In order to reduce nuclear weapons all the way to zero, multilateral negotiations would be necessary. Although the obstacles to such negotiations appear formidable at present, successful bilateral negotiations, carried out by the United States and the Soviet Union, could pave the way for fruitful multilateral discussions.

Lifting the threat of nuclear apocalypse would be a tremendous step forward for humanity. It would rekindle hope for the future. In the words of Dyson:

> We should not worry too much about the technical details of weapons and delivery systems. The basic issue before us is simple. Are we, or are we not, ready to face the uncertainties of a world in which nuclear weapons have been negotiated all the way down to zero? If the answer to this question is yes, then there is hope for us and our grandchildren.

A decision by the United States to reduce our nuclear arsenal and deescalate the arms race would have many positive effects. Among other things, vast amounts of human and material resources would be released; these could be used to address the many other problems the world is facing, such as the fact that two-thirds of the world's peoples are underfed. The nonmilitary jobs created by redirecting our economy would be personally far more satisfying to most individuals than working on weapons.

The signals sent to the Soviet Union by United States unilateral actions to slow the arms race would likely lead to decisions on the Soviet Union's part to alter its strategy and provide more goods and services to its citizens—who are in far more need than most of us are.

The process must start at home, in the United States of America. As citizens of a democratic superpower, we have a great responsibility because our voices and votes make a difference to our government. The freedom of action and expression that has made this nation great also provides us with the flexibility to move in new directions. Because of the authoritarian character of the Soviet Union, there is little chance that the needed leadership can come from the Soviet people. The responsibility must be ours.

We bear the ultimate responsibility for our government's actions. We shall also bear, along with many innocents of other nations, the catastrophic consequences should we fail to find new policies capable of halting what Herbert York has called the "race to oblivion."

We live in unique and trying times. But we do live, and most of us live well. We have the physical and cultural resources to move in almost unlimited directions— to improve our lives and the lives of our children and grandchildren. Or we can stand by and allow those lives to be destroyed. We need dreams to live by, and the drive to convert these dreams into a more secure future. It is far from assured that we can accomplish this. Not to try would be to forswear our heritage and deny our humanity.

CONVERSION
FACTORS
AND OTHER
USEFUL
DATA

A-1 RADIATION

Natural Sources

	Annual dose rate per person, mrem*/yr
Cosmic rays, ground level	44
Rocks, soil, etc.	40
Internal sources (e.g., ^{40}K)	18
Total	102

Artificial Sources

Fallout from weapons	4
Medical and dental	73
Occupational exposure	1
Miscellaneous	2
Total (artificial)	80
Overall total	**182**

---

*The abbreviation rem stands for roentgen equivalent mammal. It is that amount of ionizing radiation that produces the same damage to humans as 1 roentgen of high-voltage x-rays. The SI equivalent is the sievert, which has the unit joule per kilogram. One rem is equal to one rad (radiation absorbed dose) × RBE (relative biological effectiveness).

Variation of Radiation with Altitude

Altitude, ft	Dose rate, mrem/yr
0	50
2,500	52
5,000	68
10,000	190
15,000	460
20,000	1,100
100,000	13,000

A-2 EXPONENTIAL GROWTH

Growth rate, %/yr	Doubling time, yr
0	Infinite
2	35.0
5	14.0
10	7.3
20	3.8
50	1.7
100	1.0

A-3 ENERGY CONTENT

Substance	Common unit	Btu/ton (Btu/1000 kg)	J/kg
Coal (varies widely)		25×10^6	29×10^6
Crude oil	5.6×10^6 Btu/bbl	3.5×10^5	4×10^6
Gasoline	5.2×10^6 Btu/bbl	38×10^6	44×10^6
Hydrogen gas	333 Btu/ft^3	107×10^6	124×10^6
Natural gas	1030 Btu/ft^3	47×10^6	55×10^6
Wood (varies widely)	20×10^6 Btu/cord	12×10^6	14×10^6
Bread	1100 kcal/lb	9×10^6	10×10^6
Butter	3600 kcal/lb	29×10^6	33×10^6
High explosive (varies)	1000 cal/g	4×10^6	4.2×10^6
Fission	200 MeV/fission	7×10^{14}	8×10^{14}
D-D fusion	4 MeV/reaction		
D-T fusion	17.6 MeV/reaction		
"$E = mc^2$"* conversion	931 MeV/amu	7.7×10^{16}	9×10^{16}

*E is in joules, m in kilograms, and c in meters per second. The complete conversion of 1 kg yields 8.9 $\times 10^{16}$ ($\approx 9 \times 10^{16}$ J).

Source: Adapted from R. Romer: *Energy, An Introduction to Physics.*

TNT Equivalents for a 1-kt Weapon

Fission of 57 g mass
10^{12} cal
10^9 kcal
2.6×10^{25} MeV
4.18×10^{19} ergs
4.18×10^{12} J
1.16×10^6 kWh
3.97×10^9 Btu

Solar Energy

Solar constant (power per unit area outside the earth's atmosphere): 1.353 kW/m^2 (2 cal/cm^2 · min).

Solar energy delivered to horizontal surface in a sunny part of the United States, averaged over the year: 200 W/m^2 (approx. 1 bbl oil equivalent/m^2 · yr).

A-4 PHYSICAL CONSTANTS

Acceleration due to gravity g	9.8 m/s^2; 32 ft/s^2
Avogadro's number	6.022×10^{23}
Gas constant R	8.314 J/(mol · K)
Boltzmann's constant k	1.381×10^{-23} J/K
Stefan-Boltzmann's constant	5.67×10^{-8} W/m^2 · K
Wien's displacement law constant for λ_{max}	$0.0029/T$ (K)
Planck's constant ν	6.626×10^{-34} J · s
Electron charge e	1.602×10^{-19} C
Coulomb's law constant	9×10^9 N · m^2/C^2
Speed of light in vacuum c	$\approx 3 \times 10^8$ m/s; 3×10^{10} cm/s; 186,000 mi/s; 1 ft/ns
Speed of sound in air, sea level	331 m/s; 1087 ft/s; 741 mi/h
Density of air at sea level	1.29 kg/m^3
Atomic mass unit, amu	1.661×10^{-27} kg; 1.661×10^{-24} g
Average radius of the earth	6371 km; 3959 mi

Masses of Fundamental Particles

Electron	5.49×10^{-4} amu; 9.11×10^{-31} kg
Proton	1.0072766 amu; 1.6726×10^{-27} kg
Neutron	1.0086652 amu; 1.6749×10^{-27} kg
Hydrogen atom	1.0078252 amu; 1.6735×10^{-27} kg

Atomic Size

Atomic sizes are typically a few times 10^{-10} m, or a few angstroms.

Nuclear Size

Nuclear size varies as the atomic mass to the one-third power:

$$r = 1.4 \times 10^{-15} A^{1/3} \text{ m}$$

Hydrogen: $\qquad r = 1.4 \times 10^{-15} \text{ m}$

Uranium: $\qquad r = 8.7 \times 10^{-15} \text{ m}$

A-5 WAVELENGTHS AND FREQUENCIES (RANGES ARE APPROXIMATE)

[frequency (Hz) $\times$ wavelength (m) $= 3 \times 10^8$ m/s]

	Frequency, Hz	Wavelength, m
X-rays and gamma rays	$>10^{17}$	$<3 \times 10^{-9}$
Ultraviolet	3×10^{15}	10^{-7}
Visible	10^{15}	4×10^{-7}–7×10^{-7} (4000–7000 Å)
Infrared	3×10^{12}–3×10^{13}	10^{-4}–10^{-5}
Microwaves and radar	3×10^9–3^-10^{11}	10^{-1}–10^{-3}
TV, FM	10^8	3
AM radio	10^6	300
ELF (extra low frequency) signals	10–1000	3×10^5–3×10^7

A-6 PREFIXES

pico	10^{-12}
nano	10^{-9}
micro	10^{-6}
milli	10^{-3}
centi	10^{-2}
kilo	10^3
mega	10^6
giga	10^9
tera	10^{12}

One billion is 10^9 in the United States, but it is 10^{12} in Europe. It is better to use units analogous to 1000 million kW or 1 GW to avoid confusion.

A-7 CONVERSION FACTORS

1 angstrom Å $= 10^{-10}$ m

1 in $= 2.54$ cm

1 cm = 0.01 m
1 ft = 12 in
1 yd = 3 ft
1 mi = 5280 ft
1 nautical mile = 6076 ft
1 km = 0.621 mi
1 mi = 1.609 km

$T\ (°F) = \frac{9}{5} T\ (°C) + 32$
$T\ (°C) = \frac{5}{9}[T(°F) - 32]$

Absolute zero: 0 K (kelvin)
                     0°R (Rankine)
                     $-273.15°C$
                     $-459.67°F$

Water freezes at: 0°C
                     32°F
                     273.15 K

Water boils at: 212°F
                     100°C
                     373.15 K

Energy Conversion Factors

1 kcal = 1 cal = 1000 cal = 1 cal = 4.184 J
1 eV = 1×10^{-6} MeV = 1.602×10^{-19} J
1 Btu (British thermal unit) = 1054 J = 252 cal
1 kWh = 3413 Btu = 3.6×10^{6} J
1 horsepower = 746 W = 0.746 kW
1 kt (explosive) = 1×10^{12} cal = 4.2×10^{12} J
1 a.m.u. = 931.5 MeV

Energy and Power

Power is energy per unit time. Energy is power times time.
1 W = 1 J/s
1 J = 1 W · s

APPENDIX
B

ABBREVIATIONS
AND ACRONYMS

Note: The abbreviations marked with an asterisk are defined in the Glossary.

ABM   antiballistic missile.

AEC   Atomic Energy Commission. *See* Nuclear Regulatory Commission and Department of Energy in the Glossary.

ALCM   air-launched cruise missile.

ASAT   antisatellite system. An antisatellite system is one capable of damaging or destroying a satellite.

ASBM   air to surface ballistic missile.

ASW   antisubmarine warfare.

AWACS   Airborne Warning and Communications System.

BEIR   Committee on Biological Effects of Ionizing Radiations.

BMEWS   ballistic missile early warning system.

BWR   see boiling-water reactor in the Glossary.

C-cubed-I (C³I)   command, control, communications, and intelligence.

*CEP   circular error probable.

CIA   Central Intelligence Agency.

COMINT   communications intelligence.

CONUS   continental United States.

CORRTEX   Continuous Reflectometry for Radius versus Time Experiments.

*CTBT   comprehensive test ban treaty.

DCA   Defense Communications Agency.

*DEFCON   defense condition.

DMZ   demilitarized zone.

DOD   Department of Defense.

*DOE   Department of Energy.

*EHF   extremely high frequency.

*ELF   extremely low frequency.

ELINT   electronics intelligence.

EMP   electromagnetic pulse.

*ERCS   Emergency Rocket Communications System.

ERDA   Energy Research and Development Agency. *See* Department of Energy in the Glossary.

EMT   equivalent megaton, defined as the yield expressed in megatons, raised to the two-thirds power.

EUCOM   European command.

ERW   enhanced radiation warhead.

*FEMA   Federal Emergency Management Agency.

GLCM   ground-launched cruise missile.

*HF   high frequency.

IAEA   see International Atomic Energy Agency.

ICBM   intercontinental ballistic missile.

INF   intermediate nuclear forces.

IRBM   intermediate-range ballistic missile.

JCS   Joint Chiefs of Staff.

*kt   kiloton.

*LF   low frequency.

*LOW   launch on warning.

LTBT   Limited Test Ban Treaty.

*LUA   launch under attack.

LWR   light-water reactor.

MAD   mutual assured destruction.

*MARV   multiple adjustable target reentry vehicle.

MIRV   multiple independently targetable reentry vehicle.

*MRV   multiple reentry vehicle.

*Mt   megaton.

MX   missile experimental.

NASA   National Aeronautics and Space Administration.

NATO   North Atlantic Treaty Organization.

NAVSTAR-GPS   Navigational Satellite Timing and Ranging–Global Positioning System.

*NCA   National Command Authority.

NCAR   National Center for Atmospheric Research.

NOD   nonoffensive defense, also called nonprovocative defense.

*NORAD   North American Air Defense.

NORESS   Norwegian Regional Seismic Array.

NPT   see nonproliferation treaty in the Glossary.

*NRC   Nuclear Regulatory Commission.

NSA   National Security Agency.

*NSC   National Security Council.

*NTM   national technical means.

NUTS   nuclear utilization strategies. Similar to flexible response; a parody on MAD.

PNE   Peaceful Nuclear Explosion Treaty (signed in 1976).

PWR   see pressurized-water reactor in the Glossary.

rad   radiation absorbed dose. A measure of radiation absorbed by the body. One rad is equivalent to the absorption of 0.01 joule per kilogram of body weight. One rad equals 0.01 gray.

RAF   Royal Air Force (Britain).

RBE   relative biological effectiveness. The RBE is a measure of the biological damage caused by a particular type of radiation in a particular body organ.

R&D   research and development.

RD&D   research, development, and demonstration.

rem   roentgen equivalent mammal. Equal to the number of rads multiplied by the relative biological effectiveness, RBE.

RF   radio frequency.

*SAC   Strategic Air Command.

*SAGE   semiautomatic ground environment.

*SALT   strategic arms limitation treaty.

SDI   Strategic Defense Initiative.

*SIGINT   signals intelligence.

*SIOP   single integrated operational plan.

SLBM   submarine-launched ballistic missile.

SLCM   submarine-launched cruise missile (''sliccom'').

*SRAM   short-range attack missile.

SSBN   strategic submarine, ballistic nuclear.

*START   strategic arms reduction talks.

*TNF   theater nuclear forces.

TNT   trinitrotoluene.

TTBT   Threshold Test Ban Treaty (signed in 1976).

UHF   ultra high frequency.

UV   ultraviolet.

*VHF   very high frequency.

*VLF   very low frequency.

WWMCCS   World Wide Military Command and Control System (Wimex).

WTO   Warsaw Treaty Organization. The nations of Eastern Europe, plus the Soviet Union.

ABM   antiballistic missiles.

acceleration   the change in velocity in a certain time, or the change in velocity divided by the elapsed time.

accumulated dose   the dose rate multiplied by the time interval for that dose rate and summed over all time intervals (integrated dose rate), often given in rads.

air to surface missile   a missile launched from aircraft to surface targets.

ALCM   air-launched cruise missile ("alcom").

alpha particle   a helium 4 nucleus that emerges spontaneously from some heavy nuclei, e.g., plutonium.

amaeru   the Japanese verb which means to presume upon a person and that it is O.K. to feel helpless.

antineutrino   a particle with very little or no mass and no electric charge which is emitted along with an electron in beta decay.

ASAT   antisatellite system. An antisatellite system is one capable of damaging or destroying a satellite.

atomic bomb   a generic term which can refer to either a fission or a fusion weapon.

atomic number   the number of protons in a nucleus.

Avogadro's number   the number of atoms or nuclei contained in one mole. It is numerically equal to 6.023×10^{23}.

background radiation   background radiation is that found naturally in our environment. It is formed from cosmic rays and natural radioactivity.

ballistic missile   a missile that consists of one or more rocket stages with a warhead, usually nuclear, that detaches to proceed to target.

beta decay   the process taking place within a nucleus in which a neutron changes into a proton. Beta decay therefore increase the atomic number by one.

beta particle   a high-energy electron that is released spontaneously by some radioactive nuclei.

binding energy per nucleon   the energy required to remove a nucleon from a nucleus. In the region of iron in the periodic table the binding energy per nucleon is greatest, over 8 MeV.

boiling-water reactor a reactor in which water is boiled directly in the reactor vessel. Compare pressurized-water reactor.

boosted primary a primary which includes tritium. The result is to allow a much higher energy yield from a given amount of fissile material.

booster that portion of a missile that contains the rocket engines.

brilliant pebbles see kinetic kill weapon. These are an advanced version of smart rocks. They are to be smaller and cheaper, and with much enhanced computing power.

broken arrow military jargon for an accident involving nuclear weapons.

bus the part of a booster assembly carrying the MIRV warheads. After the bus is launched into space by the booster the warheads are individually launched.

BWR see boiling-water reactor.

C-cube-I command, control, communication, and intelligence. Sometimes written C^3I.

carcinogenic producing cancer (in terms of this text via exposure to ionizing radiation).

CEP circular error probable. A measure of the aiming accuracy of a missile or other weapon.

chain reaction a process taking place in an atomic bomb or nuclear reactor in which a given fission releases neutrons and energy. The neutrons in turn produce more fissions releasing more energy and form a chain of nuclear fissions.

circular error probable the radius of a circle around a target within which 50 percent of the missiles will fall. If the CEP is 100 yards, then half the missiles will hit within a radius of 100 yards.

chain reaction a self-sustaining nuclear reaction using fissionable material.

comprehensive test ban treaty a treaty that would prohibit nuclear tests in all environments.

compressional shock wave a wave moving through a material faster than the speed of sound in that material, thereby creating high pressure.

Compton electrons electrons produced by the collision of a gamma ray with electrons in atoms. In the case of EMP the electrons are in atoms of air in the atmosphere (nitrogen and oxygen).

conductor a material through which electric current passes easily, usually a metal.

counterforce attack attack primarily on military targets.

countervalue attack attack primarily on economic targets, e.g., cities.

critical mass a mass just large enough to sustain fission.

cross section the effective stopping area of a nucleus or other particle. Cross section depends both on what is interacting and on the energy of interaction.

cruise missile a low-flying pilotless aircraft capable of delivering nuclear or conventional weapons at subsonic speeds. The wings are small, so the cruise must be given a moderate speed by its launching device.

death immersion the experience of atomic bombing victims that the whole world is dying.

decay constant the number of radioactive atoms decaying per unit time is proportional to the number of such atoms present. The constant of proportionality is the decay constant. It is also the reciprocal of the mean life.

deep penetrator a warhead now under development designed to penetrate several meters into the earth before exploding. The device couples its energy into the ground more efficiently than existing nuclear weapons. It would be useful in attacking command structures or hardened targets. Some argue that the deep penetrator is an example of a highly destabilizing weapon.

defense condition DEFCON, the "alert" status of the military, ranges from DEFCON 5, during peacetime, to DEFCON 1, when war is extremely likely. DEFCON 1 is sometimes referred to as "cocked pistol."

delayed fallout radioactive debris that falls to the earth at times later than 24 hours, perhaps days or even years later.

Department of Energy   established in 1977 the DOE absorbed most of the research functions of the Atomic Energy Commission, the Federal Power Commission, and some branches of the Department of the Interior.

deposition region   a region in the upper atmosphere in which the gamma rays from a nuclear explosion produce Compton electrons.

deuterium   hydrogen with an extra neutron in its nucleus: heavy hydrogen.

directed-energy weapon   a beam of light, particles, or x-rays which can be focused onto a target. The beam propagates with about the speed of light.

disassembly   nuclear jargon for something exploding.

dose rate   the radiation received by a person per unit time, often measured in rads per hour.

early fallout   radioactive debris that falls to earth up to 24 hours after the explosion.

electric current   a stream of positively charged particles usually carried by a conductor. Actually the stream is of electrons which travel in the opposite direction to the positive current. The current is measured in coulombs per second or amperes.

electric field   the force that a unit positive charge would experience in a region of other electric charges.

electric forces   forces of repulsion between like charges or of attraction between unlike charges. Sometimes called coulomb forces.

electromagnetic pulse   an electromagnetic pulse, or EMP, is produced by a nuclear explosion. It is formed by accelerated electrons in the atmosphere that are created by the gamma radiation from the explosion.

electromagnetic radiation   electric charges that are accelerated produce electromagnetic radiation. Light is such radiation of a particular frequency. Gamma radiation and x-rays are of higher frequencies.

electromagnetic separation   separation of uranium isotopes by electromagnetic means (to produce uranium 235 for an atomic bomb).

electron   a subatomic particle, carrying one unit of negative charge, that orbits around the nucleus of an atom. It has only 1/1837 the mass of the proton or the hydrogen nucleus.

element   a fundamental chemical unit made up of atoms. The nature of an element is determined by the number of protons in the nucleus of the atom. For example, the nucleus of hydrogen contains one proton; the nucleus of uranium has 92 protons.

ELF   extra low frequency communications channels. ELF signals propagate better through sea (salt) water than do high frequencies, and so are useful for communicating with submarines.

Emergency Rocket Communications System   a system which would use Minuteman missiles to communicate critical commands (fire, cease fire) if other communications channels were destroyed.

energy   the ability to do work. Force times distance.

EMP from surface burst   an electromagnetic pulse formed by radiation from upward-accelerating Compton electrons produced by the gamma rays accompanying a nuclear explosion.

EMT   equivalent megaton, defined as the yield expressed in megatons, raised to the two-thirds power.

energy   energy is the capability of doing work. It is the product of the force multiplied by the distance through which the force acts.

enhanced-radiation warhead   a warhead that is designed to have maximum neutron yield in the few kiloton range. Also called the neutron bomb.

explosive lens   high explosives arranged so as to produce a converging shock wave, thereby leading to implosion.

exponential growth   a process in which the number of events or objects doubles in equal time intervals. Often used imprecisely in reference to any rapid growth process.

extremely high frequency   EHF communications are in the gigahertz range. They are relatively invulnerable to EMP, but are suitable only for line-of-sight communications.

extremely low frequency   ELF communications are in the range of a few 100 hertz or less. Radio waves at these frequencies penetrate the ocean and are hence useful for communicating with submarines. The antennas are extremely large.

fallout   radioactive debris from a nuclear explosion that drifts to the earth.

Federal Emergency Management Agency   this agency is responsible for all federal disaster-related activities, in both wartime and peacetime.

fiber optics   transmission of communications signals through small glass fibers. Fiber optics provides the ability to move very large amounts of information (high bandwidth) and high security against electromagnetic pulse. Like all physical linkages, the fibers are vulnerable to blast.

fission bomb   a nuclear bomb based on the concept of releasing energy through the fissioning (splitting) of heavy elements such as ^{235}U or ^{239}Pu.

fizzle   a nuclear explosion which fails to go off, or if it does go off produces a yield far less than anticipated.

flexible response   a policy doctrine emphasizing the ability to respond to threats selectively, using a carefully chosen level of force, ranging from conventional weaponry through tactical nuclear weapons to strategic systems.

footprint   the region within which a set of warheads from a MIRVed missile can be targeted.

force   the physical means by which an acceleration is produced. According to Newton's second law force is the product of an object's mass and the acceleration produced by the force. If there is no force, the acceleration is zero and the velocity does not change.

fratricide   the damaging influence of one attacking warhead on a later-arriving warhead. The dust or wind raised by a first bomb may damage a second one.

fusion bomb   a nuclear bomb based on fusing or burning of light elements. Fusion bombs use fission bombs for ignition.

gamma radiation   electromagnetic radiation of high frequency emitted from nuclei when they decay from excited states.

gamma ray   a high-energy photon released by a nucleus.

gaseous diffusion   separation of isotopes by the process of diffusion through a barrier.

generation time   the time required for the number of neutrons to double.

GLCM   ground-launched cruise missile ("gliccom").

GNP   gross national product. The aggregate of all the goods and services produced by the United States annually.

gray   a gray is equal to 100 rads or 1 joule of absorbed radiation energy per kilogram of body weight.

ground zero   the point on the earth's surface where a nuclear weapon detonates. If an explosion is an air burst, ground zero is directly beneath the burst.

half-life   the time in which a given amount of radioactivity will decay to one-half its initial value. It is also the time for the number of radioactive atoms to be one-half their initial value.

half-value thickness   the thickness of shielding that will reduce radiation to one-half of its incident value.

hardened   reinforced (usually with steel and concrete) so as to be able to withstand the blast of a nearby nuclear or conventional explosion. Hardening is expressed in terms of the blast overpressure (in pounds per square inch) which an object can withstand.

hibakusha   the Japanese survivors of the atomic bombings.

high-altitude EMP   an electromagnetic pulse formed by the synchrotron radiation that is produced by a nuclear explosion above the atmosphere.

high frequency   the band of frequencies from 3 to 30 MHz in the radio spectrum.

horizonal proliferation   acquisition of nuclear weapons by many nations. Same as ''N-country problem.''

IAEA   see International Atomic Energy Agency.

ICBM   intercontinental ballistic missile. A missile with a range of about 6000 miles or 10,000 kilometers that can attack the heartland of either superpower from launching sites in the other.

ignition   the introduction of neutrons into a critical mass.

implosion   increasing the density of a fissile material by crushing it, thereby decreasing the loss of neutrons and creating a critical mass. Also a technique for compressing plutonium with chemical high explosives in order to make its mass ''critical'' and produce a nuclear explosion.

inertial containment   confinement of a material by balancing of the momentum of material pushing outward against material pushing inward.

initiation   the start of a nuclear explosion.

initiator   the device which starts ignition.

insulator   a material through which electric current passes with difficulty, such as glass, many plastics, or ceramics.

intermediate nuclear forces   ballistic missiles with a range from 500 to 5000 km that are banned by the INF treaty for deployment by either the United States or the U.S.S.R. Sometimes termed theater nuclear forces.

International Atomic Energy Agency   an international agency headquartered in Vienna with responsibility for inspection of nuclear power plants and other technologies which might be used for weapons production.

ion   an atom which has one or more electrons removed and hence has a positive charge.

ionization   process in which one or more electrons are removed from an atom or molecule leaving it with a positive charge.

IRBM   intermediate-range ballistic missile. A missile with a range of a few hundred to a few thousand kilometers.

isotope   forms of the same element having identical properties, but differing in their atomic masses due to different numbers of neutrons in their respective nuclei.

kill ratio   a measure of the ability of a particular weapon system to attack a target. Kill ratio depends on weapon yield and accuracy of the delivery system.

kiloton   typically a kiloton of TNT equivalent. An energy release of 4.2×10^{12} joules.

kinetic energy   energy possessed by an object in motion. It is numerically equal to one-half of the product of the mass and the square of the object's velocity.

kinetic kill weapon   a space-based device for destroying ICBM components. It destroys by direct collision, rather than through the use of explosives.

laser   light amplification by stimulated emission of radiation.

launch on warning   a nuclear-weapons-release strategy in which nuclear delivery systems are fired automatically when detection systems show an attack may be underway. See launch under attack.

launch under attack   similar to launch on warning, except that the response is delayed until an attack has actually occurred.

LD50   a lethal dose for 50 percent of a normal population for radiation administered over a small interval of time.

light-water reactor a reactor which uses ordinary water to slow down (moderate) the fission neutrons (LWR).

Limited Test Ban Treaty a treaty signed by the United States, the U.S.S.R., and the United Kingdom that forbids nuclear testing in the atmosphere, in the oceans, or in outer space.

linear hypothesis the assumption that any dose of radiation will have a biological effect even though the effects of low-level doses are difficult or impossible to measure. The assumption is that effects clearly seen at higher radiation levels will still persist at lower levels in a manner proportional to the radiation dose or exposure.

LOW launch on warning. The policy of launching weapons upon warning that an attack may be imminent.

low frequency the band of frequencies from 30 to 300 kHz in the radio spectrum.

LWR light-water reactor.

MAD mutually assured destruction. The capability of two superpowers to destroy each other.

magnetic field the force that a unit magnetic charge (such as a unit north pole of a compass) would experience in a region where electric currents are flowing. Actually single magnetic charges do not exist in nature, but the magnetic field concept is useful nevertheless.

magnetic force the force experienced by a moving charge in a magnetic field. It is equal to the product of the magnetic field and the velocity and charge of the particle.

MaRV maneuverable reentry vehicles. MaRV warheads can be aimed during reentry or final approach phase, thereby allowing improved accuracy.

mass-energy conversion a result of Einstein's famous equation that $E = mc^2$ or that a given mass m is equivalent to energy if multiplied by the square of the velocity of light.

mass number the number of protons and neutrons in a nucleus or the total number of nucleons in a nucleus.

mean life the average time required for a radioactive atom to decay. The mean life is approximately 1.44 times as long as the half-life.

megaton 1000 kilotons. A unit of explosive energy. One megaton is the energy that would be released in the explosion of one million tons of TNT explosive.

MIRV multiple independently targetable reentry vehicles. MIRVing permits individual warheads contained on a single rocket to be targeted independently.

mole the mass in grams corresponding to the mass number of the element. For example, one mole of uranium 238 is 238 grams.

monitoring uncertainty factor uncertainty in yield estimation due to intrinsic detection problems. Seismic signals have noise due to general earth motion. Improved techniques can decrease but not eliminate this noise.

multiple independently targetable reentry vehicle the several warheads of a MIRV may be aimed independently of each other so as to permit precise selection of multiple targets.

multiple reentry vehicles these carry several warheads but the individual warheads cannot be separately aimed, as in a MIRV system.

mutation rate the rate at which genetic material (DNA in cells) is altered to produce genetic changes. The mutation rate can be spontaneous as it occurs naturally or be increased due to ionizing radiation.

N-country problem same as horizontal proliferation.

National Command Authority the chain of command governing release of nuclear weapons. It ranges from the President down to the military elements controlling individual nuclear weapons.

National Security Council an arm of the executive branch having responsibility for high-level planning and review.

national technical means a remote technique for gathering information about another country.

Such means include seismic information obtained outside the country's borders, satellite information, and atmospheric monitoring (say for radioactivity from a possible nuclear explosion).

NATO North Atlantic Treaty Organization. Most of the nations of Western Europe, plus the United States and Canada.

negative control a system to assure that weapons will not be launched unless an order to launch is given. Compare positive control. Provides safety against "trigger itch."

network a number of seismometers or arrays covering a large region, or many regions, possibly including several arrays. A network reduces seismic noise and increases locational accuracy.

neutron An uncharged subatomic particle, contained in the nucleus of an atom, having almost the same mass as the proton.

neutron bomb a nuclear weapon designed to increase the fraction of total energy released as neutrons, so as to injure humans and biota more than objects.

neutron capture the process in which a neutron is absorbed by a nucleus thereby creating a new nucleus with a mass number one greater than the original nucleus.

neutron fluence the number of neutrons per unit area. In the MKS system, the number of neutrons per square meter.

neutron leakage neutrons which escape from a bomb or reactor, and which therefore don't contribute to further fissions.

nonoffensive defense a proposed military posture that excludes offensive armaments, such as tanks and bombers. Also called nonprovocative defense. The focus is on low-mobility systems which cannot be easily moved fast or far.

nonproliferation treaty a treaty to slow the spread of nuclear weapons (NPT).

normal distribution a bell-shaped curve describing the distribution of events, such as the spread of shots aimed at a particular point.

North American Air Defense the NORAD command is located in a mountain near Colorado.

NPT see nonproliferation treaty.

nucflash military jargon for nuclear detonation.

nuclear fall the global climatic effect of a general nuclear war caused by smoke and dust obscuration of sunlight. Nuclear fall is less intense and less dark than nuclear winter.

nuclear fission the process whereby the nucleus of a heavy element splits into two nuclei of lighter elements. Fission can occur spontaneously or by the absorption of neutrons.

nuclear forces the forces which hold nuclei together. Nuclear forces are strong and short-range and can overcome the repulsive forces of the protons for distances of nuclear dimensions (about 10^{-15} to 10^{-14} meters).

nuclear fusion release of nuclear energy by combining light nuclei to form heavier ones.

nuclear reactor a device for producing a controlled chain reaction in order to produce plutonium or electric power.

Nuclear Regulatory Commission absorbed the regulatory functions of the AEC in 1974. Consists of Office of Nuclear Reactor Regulation, Office of Nuclear Materials Safety and Safeguards, and Office of Nuclear Regulatory Research.

nucleon refers to either a proton or a neutron, a nuclear constituent.

nucleus the central part of an atom where almost all the mass is found.

nudet military jargon for nuclear detonation report.

NUTS nuclear utilization strategies. Similar to flexible response; a parody on MAD.

one-point-safe a weapon designed so that it will not produce a nuclear explosion if the high explosive in it is detonated at any one place.

overruns cost escalation beyond original estimates or contracts.

P waves compressional waves set up in the earth by a seismic disturbance. Explosions give strong *P* wave signals.

Pauli exclusion principle the principle states that some particles such as neutrons (or protons) must be in a unique quantum state. Thus when two or more neutrons are in a nucleus, they must all be in different quantum states.

perestroika restructuring. Part of the effort of perestroika in the Soviet Union is to restructure the economy expenditure to release more monies for the civilian economy.

phased array radar an antenna controlled electronically, usually by computer, to permit extremely accurate aiming.

photon A photon is a quantum of electromagnetic radiation. According to quantum theory electromagnetic radiation is quantized in packets of quanta of energy such that the energy of a quantum, or photon, is equal to Planck's constant *h* multiplied by the frequency of the radiation.

plutonium an artificial element produced in a nuclear reactor and suitable as fissionable material for an atomic bomb.

positive control a system to assure that weapons can be launched when the order to launch is given. Compare negative control.

potential energy energy possessed by an object because of its position, usually in the gravitational field of the earth. The higher an object is the greater is its potential energy, which is equal to the product of its weight and height.

power the rate of doing work. Power has the dimensions of energy per unit time. The unit in MKS is the watt, which is equal to one joule per second.

pressure force divided by the area over which the force acts. Usually expressed as pounds per square inch.

pressurized-water reactor a reactor in which neutrons heat pressurized water, which is then used to produce steam to run a turbine. Compare boiling-water reactor.

primary the fission part of a fusion bomb. The "match" which ignites the fusion reaction.

proliferation the process by which nations acquire nuclear weapons.

proton a subatomic particle, carrying one unit of positive charge, that is contained in the nucleus of an atom.

psychic numbing a psychological mechanism of denial of a reality that is too painful to face: "I'd rather not think about it" or "It will work out somehow" are expressions that betray psychic numbing.

quality factor measures the density of ionization produced by a given kind of radiation at a specified energy. It is about 1 for beta and gamma rays, 5 for neutrons of 1 to 10 MeV, and about 10 for plutonium alpha particles. It is a component of the RBE.

rad radiation absorbed dose. A measure of radiation absorbed by the body. One rad is equivalent to the absorption of 0.01 joule per kilogram of body weight. One rad equals 0.01 gray.

radar an acronym for radio detection and ranging. Radar functions by directing an electromagnetic wave of short duration at an object and observing the reflected wave. Radar frequencies are much less than those of visible light, but shorter than television or radio waves.

RBE relative biological effectiveness. A measure of the response of given biological material to a particular kind of ionizing radiation. For example, neutrons of over 1 Mev have an RBE of about 5 in forming cataracts in the human eye.

reflector a mass of material designed to reflect escaping neutrons back into the fissionable material, thereby reducing leakage.

rem   roentgen equivalent mammal (or man). rem is the product of rads with RBE and hence is a more precise measure of the biological effect of radiation.

roentgen   a measure of how much ionization is produced by radiation. Equal to 0.000258 coulomb of free charge produced in one kilogram of air (or 1 e.s.u. of charge per cubic centimeter or air)

S waves   shear waves. They are formed by one plate of the earth sliding over another; hence *S* waves are prominent in earthquakes.

SDI   Strategic Defense Initiative, also called ''star wars'' by some critics. Originally proposed as a missile defense to shield the U.S. population from nuclear attack.

secondary   the thermonuclear part of a fusion bomb.

secondary electrons   electrons produced by the primary electrons that are formed by x-rays in SGEMP.

seismic array   a number of seismometers located in one particular region, operating in tandem to reduce noise.

seismic network   seismometers or arrays of seismometers located at distances of hundreds or thousands of kilometers apart, but synchronized so that an explosion or earthquake can be more sensitively detected and its location determined by triangulation.

seismometer   a device that will measure minute displacements of the earth at a given location. Often seismometers measure not only the two horizontal displacements (north-south and east-west) as a function of time, but the vertical displacement as well so that a three-dimensional measurement of the motion of the earth's surface is made at that point.

semiautomatic ground environment   a large computer system active in the 1960s for detecting and tracking enemy missiles and aircraft.

shake   100 millionths of a second.

short-range attack missile   U.S. nuclear aircraft carry SRAMs for attacking at short distances.

signals intelligence   military intelligence gained from examining electromagnetic and acoustic signals emitted by an enemy nation.

single integrated operational plan   the U.S. nuclear war plans which integrate the activities of all elements of the military.

SIOP   single integrated operations plan. The key targeting plan of the United States.

SLBM   submarine-launched ballistic missile. A missile (possibly MIRVed) launched from a submarine.

SLCM   submarine-launched cruise missile (''sliccom'').

smart rocks   see kinetic kill weapon.

sonar   similar to radar, but uses sound waves in water to ''range'' or detect objects by observing the reflected sound waves.

spontaneous fission   natural decay of a nucleus by splitting apart (fissioning).

Sputnik   the first Soviet satellite, launched in 1957. A generic Soviet term for a satellite.

Star Wars   popular name for the Reagan administration's plan for deploying antiballistic missile technology. Same as Strategic Defense Initiative (SDI).

stealth technology   aircraft, cruise missiles, etc., designed so as to be very difficult to detect from their radar, thermal, or other signatures. Stealth systems can sneak into enemy territory with low risk of detection. Even if detected, they are hard to track.

Strategic Air Command   SAC headquarters are near Omaha, Nebraska.

Strategic Arms Limitation Treaty   SALT I is active; SALT II was not ratified by the U.S. Senate.

strategic arms reduction talks   the Reagan administration term for negotiations on strategic arms. Successor to the SALT II negotiations.

strategic nuclear weapon by U.S. definition a nuclear weapon that can be launched from the U.S or a U.S. submarine and reach the Soviet Union. The U.S.S.R views some U.S. nuclear weapons in Europe as strategic since they can strike the Soviet homeland.

stratosphere the atmosphere above the weather patterns. The stratosphere begins in altitudes where the troposphere ends, at about 8 miles.

synchrotron radiation this is radiation produced by electrons spiraling in the earth's magnetic field. The electrons are produced by the Compton effect in the upper atmosphere as a result of the gamma radiation emitted from a nuclear explosion in space. Synchrotron radiation is responsible for high-altitude EMP, electromagnetic pulse.

system-generated EMP system-generated EMP, or SGEMP, is formed principally in outer space on satellites and other equipment by the action of x-rays from a nuclear explosion. Photoelectrons and Compton electrons liberated by the x-rays may produce large and damaging currents which in turn may damage sensitive electronic components.

tactical nuclear weapons nuclear weapons of relatively ''small'' yield in the kiloton range to be used on the battlefield or at sea.

tamper a device surrounding a bomb designed to hold it together longer than otherwise by providing the explosion something to push against. Tampers can also serve as neutron reflectors.

terminal defense a missile defense system which defends during the last moments, when a missile has almost reached its target. Can be either an independent system or a part of a larger system (e.g., a component of SDI).

theater nuclear forces nuclear forces deployed in a particular theater, defined by some to have a range from 1000 to 4000 kilometers. The INF treaty provides an elimination of these forces in the arsenals of the U.S. and U.S.S.R.

third-generation weapon an advanced nuclear weapon in which some of the released energy is intensified in either direction or in a particular part of the electromagnetic spectrum, or both.

threshold test ban treaty a treaty (unsigned) which would limit nuclear testing to 150 kilotons.

throw weight the useful weight that a ballistic missile can place on its trajectory. This weight does not include the rocket itself.

TNF (See Theater Nuclear forces).

triad the combination of ICBMs, SLBMs, and bombers that independently can bring nuclear warheads to a target.

trigger a means of starting a fission bomb.

tritium an isotope of hydrogen containing one proton and two neutrons.

troposphere that part of the atmosphere that contains the weather patterns. It extends up to about 40,000 ft or about 13 kilometers.

TTBT see threshold test ban treaty.

Vela satellites a system for detecting nuclear explosions that was first deployed in the late 1950s.

velocity the change in distance in a certain time, or the distance traversed divided by the elapsed time.

vertical proliferation buildup of nuclear weapons by the superpowers. Compare horizontal proliferation.

very high frequency the band of frequencies in the 30- to 300-MHz range in the radio spectrum.

very low frequency the band of frequencies in the 3- to 30-kHz range in the radio spectrum.

weight   the attraction of gravity (usually that of the earth) for a mass. It is equal to the object's mass multiplied by the acceleration of gravity g.

WTO   Warsaw Treaty Organization. The nations of Eastern Europe, plus the Soviet Union.

x-ray laser   a laser producing soft (low-energy) x-rays, driven by a nuclear explosion. Whether such a weapon can ever be made is highly conjectural.

x-rays   electromagnetic radiation from an atomic transition.

REFERENCES

KEY TO REFERENCE CATEGORIES

1 Historical

2 Political

3 Physical Effects of Nuclear Weapons, Nuclear Weapons Design

4 Medical and Biological Effects of Nuclear Weapons

5 Psychological and Social

6 Delivery Systems, Missile Defense, Satellites

7 Proliferation and Verification

8 Economics and Civil Defense

9 General and Fiction

10 Alternative defense, nonoffensive defense, NATO

8 Adams, Gordon: "Economic Conversion Misses the Point," *Bulletin of Atomic Scientists,* February 1986, pp. 24–28.

10 *ADIEU Report* (1988), vol. 10, No. 1, January–February 1988. Armament and Disarmament Information Unit, Science Policy Research Unit, Mantell Building, University of Sussex, Falmer, Brighton, East Sussex BN1 9RF, UK.

2,7,10 Ahfeldt, Horst: *Defensive Verteidigung,* Reinbek, Rowohlt Taschenbuch Verlag, Hamburg, 1983.

2,6 Aldridge, Robert C: *First Strike, The Pentagon's Strategy for Nuclear War,* South End, Boston, 1983.

3 Aleksandrov, V. V., and G. L. Stenchikov: *On the Modeling of Climatic Consequences of the Nuclear War,* U.S.S.R. Academy of Sciences, Proceedings on Applied Mathematics, Computing Center, Moscow, 1983.

3 *Ambio: Aftermath, The Human and Ecological Consequences of Nuclear War,* Jeannie Peterson (ed.), Pantheon, New York, 1983.

6 American Physical Society: "Report to the American Physical Society of the Study Group on Science and Technology of Directed Energy Weapons," N. Bloembergen and C. K. Patel co-chairs, American Physical Society, 335 E. 45th Street, New York, NY, 1987.

3,6 American Physical Society: Science and Technology of Directed Energy Weapons Study. American Physical Society, 335 E. 45th St., New York, NY. *Reviews of Modern Physics,* summer 1987.

8 Anderson, Marion: *The Empty Pork Barrel,* Employment Research Associates, 400 South Washington Ave., Lansing, MI, 1982.

2 Arkin, William M.: "Why SIOP-6?" *Bulletin of the Atomic Scientists,* April 1983, p. 9.

4 Auxier, J. A.: "Ichiban: Radiation Dosimetry for the Survivors of the Bombings of Hiroshima and Nagasaki," *ERDA Critical Review,* Oak Ridge National Laboratory Report No. 71D-27080, 1977.

2,7 Bajusz, William: "Deterrence, Technology and Strategic Arms Control," Adelphi Paper 215. International Institute for Strategic Studies, London, 1986/1987.

2 Beilenson, Lawrence W., and Samuel T. Cohen: "A New Nuclear Strategy," *The New York Times Magazine,* Jan. 24, 1982, pp. 34, 38, 39.

4 BEIR, Committee on the Biological Effects of Ionizing Radiations, 1980, National Research Council, Washington, DC, National Academy of Sciences.

2 Beres, Louis Rene: "Steps Toward a New Planetary Identity," *Bulletin of the Atomic Scientists.* February 1981, pp. 43–47.

1 Bernstein, B. J.: Address to the Summer Seminar on Global Security and Arms Control, sponsored by the University of California Institute on Global Cooperation and Conflict, Santa Barbara, June 1983.

2,7 Biddle, Stephen: "The European Conventional Balance: A Reinterpretation of the Debate," *Survival,* published by the International Institute of Strategic Studies, March/April 1988, pp. 99–121.

1,2 Bishops: "The Challenge of Peace: God's Promise and Our Response," Office of Publishing Services, United States Catholic Conference, Washington, DC, May 1983.

3,4,5 Bonidetti: in *Ambio, Aftermath, The Human and Ecological Consequences of Nuclear War,* Jeannie Peterson (ed.), Pantheon, New York, 1983.

4 Borgstrom, S., et al.: *Effects of a Nuclear War on Health and Health Services.* World Health Organization Publication A36.12, Geneva, 1983.

2,7,8 Boserup, Anders: Non-offensive Defenses in Europe. In *Defending Europe: Options for Security,* Derek Paul (ed.), Taylor and Francis, London and Philadelphia, 1986.

6 Bracken, Paul: *The Command and Control of Nuclear Weapons,* Yale University Press, New Haven, CT, 1984.

9 Bradbury, Ray: *Fahrenheit 451,* Simon and Schuster, New York, 1967.

4 British Medical Association Board of Science and Education: *The Medical Effects of Nuclear War,* Wiley, New York, 1983.

3 Broad, J.: "Nuclear Pulse, I: Awakening to the Chaos Factor," *Science,* vol. 212, May 29, 1981, p. 1009.

2 Brodie, B.: *The Absolute Weapon,* Harcourt Brace, New York, 1946, p. 76.

2,7,8 Brody, Richard I.: "Strategic Defenses in NATO Strategy," Adelphi Paper 225. International Institute for Strategic Studies, London, 1987.

Brown, Harold: *Arms Control Today,* April 1987, p. 28.

1 Bryson, William C.: Letter, *Bulletin of the Atomic Scientists,* December 1982, p. 35.

1,2 Bucheim, Robert: Address to the Summer Seminar on Global Security and Arms Control, sponsored by the University of California Institute on Global Cooperation and Conflict, Santa Barbara, June 1983.

10 *Bulletin of the Atomic Scientists* (1988), September 1988, entire issue.

2 Bundy, McGeorge: "The Bishops and the Bomb," *New York Review of Books,* June 16, 1983, p. 3.

2 Bundy, McGeorge: " 'No First Use' Needs Careful Study," *Bulletin of the Atomic Scientists,* June 1982, p. 6.

2,6 Bunn, Mathew, and Kosta Tsipis: "The Uncertainties of a Preemptive Nuclear Attack," *Scientific American,* November 1983, pp. 38–47.

2,6 Burrows, William E.: "Ballistic Missile Defense: The Illusion of Security," *Foreign Affairs,* Spring 1984, p. 854.

2 Burt, Richard (ed.): *Arms Control and Defense Postures in the 1980s,* Westview, 1982.

1,2 Carnendale, Albert, et al.: *Living with Nuclear Weapons: The Harvard University Study Group,* Bantam, New York, 1983.

6 Carter, Ashton B.: *Directed Energy Missile Defense in Space,* Office of Technology Assessment, Government Printing Office, Washington, DC, 1984.

6 Center for Defense Information: US Military Force—1980: An Evaluation, CDI, Washington, DC, 1980, updated annually.

3 Chang, J. S., W. H. Duewer, and D. J. Wuebbles: "The Atmospheric Nuclear Tests of the 50's and 60's: A Possible Test of Ozone Depletion Theories," *Journal of Geophysical Research,* vol. 84, 1979, p. 1755.

5 Chivian, Eric, John P. Robinson, Jonathan R. H. Tudge, Nikolai P. Popov, and Vladimir G. Andreyenkov: "American and Soviet Teenagers' Concern about Nuclear War and the Future," *New England Journal of Medicine,* vol. 319, No. 7, 1988, pp. 407–413.

8 Chronicle, Associated Press; "Why U.S. May Lose Tech War," *San Francisco Chronicle,* Thursday, September 8, 1988, p. C1.

8 *Civil Defense Review,* Hearings before the Civil Defense Panel of the Subcommittee on Investigations of the Committee on Armed Services, U.S. House of Representatives, 94th Congress, February–March 1976.

6 Cochran, T. B., W. M. Arkin, and M. M. Hoenig: *U.S. Nuclear Forces and Capabilities,* vol. I, *Nuclear Weapons Databook,* Ballinger, 1984.

3,6 Cochran, Thomas B., William M. Arkin, and Milton M. Hoenig: *Nuclear Weapons Data Book,* vol. I, U.S. Nuclear Forces and Capabilities. Ballinger, 1984.

3,6 Cochran, Thomas B., William M. Arkin, Robert S. Norris, and Milton M. Hoenig: *Nuclear Weapons Data Book,* vol. II, *U.S. Nuclear Warhead Production,* Ballinger, 1987.

1,4 Coerr, Eleanor: "Sadako and the Thousand Paper Cranes," Dell Publishing Co., P.O. Box 3000, Pine Brook, NJ, 07058, 1977.

1,3,4,5 Committee for the Compilation of Materials on Damage Caused by the Atomic Bombs in Hiroshima and Nagasaki: *Hiroshima and Nagasaki, The Physical, Medical, and Social Effects of the Atomic Bombings,* Basic Books, New York, 1981.

1,8 U.S. Congress: "Civil Defense Review Hearings," House of Representatives, 94th Congress, February and March, 1972 (H.A.S.C. 94–92).

1,2 U.S. Congress: "Effects of a Comprehensive Test Ban Treaty on U.S. National Security Interests," August 14–15, 1978 (H.A.S.C. 95–99).

8 Council on Economic Priorities: *The Costs and Consequences of Reagan's Military Buildup. A Report to the International Association of Machinists and Aerospace Workers, AFL-CIO,* New York, 1982.

3 Covey, C., S. J. Schneider, and S. L. Thompson: "Global Atmospheric Effects of Massive Smoke Injection from a Nuclear War: Results from General Circulation Model Simulations," in press. Preliminary results were printed in "Search and Discovery," *Physics Today,* February 1984.

6 Craig, Paul: "The Sword of Jehovah. Physics and Society," *Journal of the Forum on Physics and Society of the American Physical Society,* vol. 16, No. 3, July 1987, p. 12.

2,8 Craig, Paul P., and Mark D. Levine: in D. W. Hafemeister and D. Schroeer (eds.), *Physics, Technology, and the Nuclear Arms Race,* chapter 10, American Institute of Physics Conference Proceedings, No. 104, New York, 1983.

1 Craig, William: *The Fall of Japan,* Dial, New York, 1967.

3 Crutzen, P. J., and J. W. Birks: "The Atmosphere after a Nuclear War: Twilight at Noon," in *Ambio, Aftermath, The Human and Ecological Consequences of Nuclear War,* Jeannie Peterson (ed.), vols. 11, 15, Pantheon, New York, 1983.

8 Daggett, Stephen: "Up the Mountain and Along the Plateau: New Adventures of the Military Budget," *Arms Control Today,* April 1986, pp. 12–16.

3,4,8 Daugherty, William H., Barbara G. Levi, and Frank M. von Hippel: "The Consequences of 'Limited' Nuclear Attacks on the United States," *International Security,* vol. 10, No. 4, spring 1986, pp. 3–45.

2 Dean, Jonathan: "Military Security in Europe," *Foreign Affairs,* fall 1987, pp. 22–40.

2,8 *Defending Europe: Options for Security,* Derek Paul (ed.), Taylor and Francis, London and Philadelphia, 1986.

10   "Defense and Disarmament Alternatives (1988)," *Bulletin of the Institute for Defense and Disarmament Studies,* 2001 Beacon Street, Brookline MA 02146. Various issues.

2,3 DeWitt, Hugh, and Gerald E. March: "Stockpile Reliability and Nuclear Testing," *Bulletin of the Atomic Scientists,* April 1984, p. 40.

2,7 Disarmament and Security, *1987 Yearbook of the USSR Academy of Sciences,* Institute of World Economy and International Relations, Novosti Press Agency Publishing House, Moscow, 1988.

5 Doi, Takeo: *Anatomy of Dependence,* Kodansha International, Tokyo and New York, 1981.

2 Douglass, Joseph D., Jr., *What Happens if Deterrence Fails? Air University Review,* November–December 1982, pp. 8, 9.

2 Draper, Theodore: *New York Review of Books,* Aug. 18, 1983, p. 27.

3 Drell, S. D., and M. A. Ruderman: *Infrared Physics,* vol. 1, 1962, p. 189.

6 Drell, Sydney: Testimony on Space-Based and Space Directed Weapons, Senate Foreign Relations Committee, Apr. 25, 1984.

6 Drell, Sydney D., Phillip J. Farley, and David Holloway: *The Reagan Defense Initiative: A Technical, Political, and Arms Control Assessment,* Stanford University Press, Stanford, Calif., 1984.

  Duewer, W. H., D. J. Wuebbles, and J. S. Chang: "The Effects of a Massive Pulse Injection of NO_x Into the Stratosphere," UCRL-80397, 1978.

2 Dulles, John Foster: Address to the Council of Foreign Relations, Jan. 12, 1954.

9 Durenmatt, F.: *The Physicists,* Grove, New York, 1965.

2,6,9 Dyson, Freeman: *Weapons and Hope,* Harper & Row, New York, 1984.

2 *Effects of a Comprehensive Test Ban Treaty on United States National Security Interests,* Hearings before the United States House of Representatives Armed Services Committee Hearings, No. 95–99, Aug, 14, 15, 1978.

3,4 Ehrlich, Anne: "Nuclear Winter," Special Supplement, *Bulletin of the Atomic Scientists,* April 1984, pp. 1S–15S.

4 Ehrlich, Paul R., et al.: "Long-Term Biological Consequences of Nuclear War," *Science,* vol. 222, Dec. 23, 1983, p. 1293.

2 Ellsberg, Daniel: *Nuclear Armaments: An Interview with Dr. Daniel Ellsberg.* The Conservation Press, Berkeley, Calif., 1980.

2 Enthoven, Alain, and Wayne Smith: *How Much Is Enough?* Harper & Row, New York, 1973.

5 Erickson, Kai, and Robert Jay Lifton: "Nuclear War's Effect on the Mind," *The New York Times,* 1982.

10 ESECS: "Strengthening Conventional Deterrence in Europe: Proposals for the 1980s," *Report of the European Security Study* (ESECS), Westview Press, Boulder, 1983.

10 European Security Beyond the Year 2000, Robert Rudney and Luc Reychler (eds.), Praeger, 1988.

2 Fallows, James: *National Defense,* Vintage, New York, 1981.

10 Federation of American Scientists (1988): Public Interest Report, 307 Massachusetts Avenue NE, Washington, DC 20002, February 1988.

3 Fetter, S. A., and K. Tsipis: "Catastrophic Releases of Radioactivity," *Scientific American,* vol. 244, 1981, p. 33.

3,7 Fetter, Steve: Stockpile Confidence under a Nuclear Test Ban, *International Security,* vol. 12, No. 3, winter 1987, pp. 132–167.

1 Feynmann, R. P.: *Surely You're Joking, Mr. Feynmann.* Norton, New York, 1985.

2 Forsberg, Randall: "A Bilateral Nuclear-Weapon Freeze," *Scientific American,* November 1982, pp. 52–61.

10,2 Forsberg, Randall: "The Freeze and Beyond: Confining the Military to Defense as a Route to Disarmament," *World Policy Journal,* vol. I, No. 2, winter 1984, pp. 286–318.

3 Garwin, R. L.: "Physics and Technology of the Arms Race," in Hafemeister and Schroeer, op. cit., chapter 2 (1983).

2 Garwin, R. L.: "Reducing Dependence on Nuclear Weapons: A Second Nuclear Regime," in Franklin C. Miller (ed.), *Nuclear Weapons and World Politics: Alternatives for the Future,* McGraw-Hill, New York, 1980.

6 Garwin, R. L., K. Gottfried, and D. L. Hafner: "Antisatellite Weapons," *Scientific American,* June 1984, pp. 45–55.

10   Gates, Davis: "Area Defense Concepts: The West German Debate," in *Survival,* July/August 1987, International Institute for Strategic Studies, London.

2,3,7   Gervasi, Tom: *The Myth of Soviet Military Supremacy,* Harper & Row, 1986.

3   Glasstone, S., and P. J. Dolan: *The Effects of Nuclear Weapons,* Government Printing Office, Washington, DC, 1977.

3   Glatzmaier, G. A., private communication, 1989.

5   Glendinning, Chellis: "Interview with Bill Mandel," *San Francisco Chronicle.* Oct. 23, 1983.

8,9   Goldemberg, Jose, Thomas Johansson, Amulya Reddy and Robert Williams, *Energy for a Sustainable World.* Wiley Eastern International, New Delhi, 1988.

10   Golden, James R., Asa A. Clark, and Bruce E. Arlinhaus: *Conventional Deterrence,* Lexington Books, D.C. Heath and Company, Toronto, 1984.

4   Goldman, M.: "Ionizing Radiation and Its Risks," *The Western Journal of Medicine,* December 1982, p. 137.

1   Goldschmidt, Bertrand: *The Atomic Complex,* American Nuclear Society, 1982, p. 52.

1   Goudsmit, S.: *Alsos, The Failure of German Science,* Sigma, London, 1947.

8   Gouré, Leon: *Civil Defense in the Soviet Union,* University of California Press, Berkeley, Calif., 1962.

6   Graham, Daniel O.: *The Non-Nuclear Defense of Cities: The High Frontier Space-Based Defense against ICBM Attack,* Abt Books, Cambridge, 1983.

2   Gray, Colin S., and Keith Payne: "Victory Is Possible," *Foreign Policy,* summer 1980, p. 14.

9   Greider, Kenneth: *Invitation to Physics,* Harcourt, New York, 1970.

3   Griffith, H. A., and R. S. Cooper: *Science,* vol. 216, 1982, p. 1364.

8   Haaland, Carsten, M.: *Systems Analysis of U.S. Civil Defense via National Blast Shelter Systems,* Oak Ridge National Laboratory Report ORNL-TM-2457, March 1970.

6,7   Hafemeister, David, Joseph J. Romm, and Kosta Tsipis: "The Verification of Compliance with Arms-Control Agreements," *Scientific American,* vol. 252, March 1985, pp. 39–45.

3   Hafemeister, David W., and Dietrich Schroeer (eds.): *Physics, Technology, and the Nuclear Arms Race,* American Institute of Physics Conference Proceedings No. 4, New York, 1983.

1   Haldeman, H. R.: *The Ends of Power,* Time-Life, New York, 1978.

3   Halliday, D.: *Introductory Nuclear Physics,* Wiley, New York, 1955.

7   Hannon, W. J.: "Seismic Verification of a Comprehensive Test Ban," *Science,* vol. 227, Jan. 18, 1985, pp. 251–257.

3   Hannon, W. J., Jr.: "Seismic Verification of a Comprehensive Test Ban," *Energy and Technology Review,* Lawrence Livermore National Laboratory, May 1983.

8   Hartung, William D.: *The Economic Consequences of a Nuclear Freeze,* Council on Economic Priorities, New York, 1984.

3,4   Hibakusha: *A Call from the Hibakusha of Hiroshima and Nagasaki,* working document V, *Nuclear Weapons and Radioactive Pollution of the Earth's Environment,* Proceedings of the International Symposium on the Damage and After-Effects of the Atomic Bombing of Hiroshima and Nagasaki, 1977.

Hiroshima, 1981 (see *Committee,* 1981).

2   Holloway, David: "Nuclear Weapons in Europe," *Bulletin of the Atomic Scientists,* April 1983, p. 17.

1   Holloway, David: *Entering the Nuclear Arms Race: The Soviet Decision to Build the Atomic Bomb 1939–1945,* working paper No. 9, The Wilson Center for International Security Studies, Washington, DC, 1979, p. 18.

2,8   Holzman, Franklyn D.:"Are the Soviets Really Outspending the U.S. on Defense?" *International Security,* vol. 4, 1980, pp. 86–104.

2   Hughes, P. C., and W. Schneider, Jr.: in *Arms Control and Defense Postures in the 1980's,* Westview, 1982, pp. 21–37.

2   Hyland, William G.: "Reagan-Gorbachev III," *Foreign Affairs,* fall 1987, pp. 7–21.

10   IMEMO: "Disarmament and Security," *1987 Yearbook of the USSR Academy of Sciences,* Institute of World Economy and International Relations (IMEMO), Novosti Publishing House, Moscow, 1988.

Institute for Defense and Disarmament Studies. See Wright, Barton.

6   The International Institute of Strategic Studies, *The Military Balance,* 1981–82, IISS. London, 1982.

2 "In the Matter of J. Robert Oppenheimer," Transcript of Hearing before Personnel Security Board, U.S. Atomic Energy Commission, Washington, DC, Apr. 12, 1954–May 6, 1954, p. 710.

1 Irving, David: *The German Atomic Bomb,* Simon and Schuster, New York, 1967.

9 Jackson, J. D.: *Classical Electrodynamics,* Wiley, New York, 1962.

5 Jung, C. G.: *The Undiscovered Self,* translated from the German by R. F. C. Hull, New American Library, New York, 1958.

6 Jungerman, John A.: "Understanding SDI: A Primer and Critique," Institute on Global Conflict and Cooperation, University of California San Diego, La Jolla, CA, 1988.

2 Kahn, Herman: *On Thermonuclear War,* Princeton University Press, 1961, p. 42.

6 Kaldor, Mary: *The Baroque Arsenal,* Andre Deutsch, London, 1982.

6,8 Kaldor, Mary: *European Defense Industries—National and International Implications,* Institute for the Study of International Organizations, Monograph, First Series, No. 8, University of Sussex, Brighton, England, 1972.

3 Kaplan F. W.: "Enhanced Radiation Weapons," *Scientific American,* vol. 238, May 1978, pp. 44–51.

2 Kaplan, Fred: *Strategic Thinkers, Bulletin of the Atomic Scientists,* December 1982, p. 52.

3 Kaplan, Fred: "The Neutron Bomb, What It Is, The Way It Works," *Bulletin of the Atomic Scientists,* October 1981, pp. 6–7.

6 Karas, Thomas: *The New High Ground, Strategies and Weapons of Space Age War,* Simon and Schuster, New York, 1983.

2 Keegan, John: *The Specter of Conventional War, Harper's,* July 1983, pp. 10–15.

10 Kelleher, Catherine McArdle, and Gale A. Mattox: *Evolving European Defense Policies,* Lexington Books, D.C. Heath, 1987.

1,2 Kennan, George F.: "Two Views of the Soviet Problem," *The New Yorker,* November 1981, p. 54.

2 Kerr, Donald M., Steven A. Maaranen, and Robert E. Pendley: *Strategic Trends and Critical Choices,* Los Alamos Scientific Laboratory Report No. LA-8692-MS, January 1981.

6 Kidron, Michael, and Dan Smity: *The War Atlas,* Simon and Schuster, New York, 1983.

1,8 Kincade, William H.: "Repeating History: The Civil Defense Debate Renewed," *International Security,* vol. 2, 1977, pp. 99–110.

1 Kuwahara, Y., and Gordon T. Allred: *Kamikaze,* Ballantine, New York, 1957.

3 Lederer, C. M., and V. S. Shirley: *Table of Isotopes,* Wiley, New York, 1978.

3 Lerner, E. J.: "Electromagnetic Pulses: Potential Crippler," *I.E.E.E. Spectrum,* May 1981, 41.

6 Levi, Barbara G.: "The Nuclear Arsenals of the U.S. and the U.S.S.R." *Physics Today,* vol. 36, no. 3, March 1983, pp. 43–49.

3,4,8 Levi, Barbara G., Frank N. von Hippel, and William H. Daugherty: "Civilian Casualties from 'Limited' Nuclear Attacks on the Soviet Union," *International Security,* vol. 12, No. 3, winter 1987–1988, pp. 168–189.

5 Lifton, Robert Jay: *Death in Life, Survivors of Hiroshima,* Basic Books, New York, 1982.

2,5 Lifton, Robert Jay, and Richard Falk: *Indefensible Weapons,* Basic Books, New York, 1983.

2,3 Lipschultz, R. D.: *Radioactive Waste: Politics, Technology, and Risk,* Ballinger, Cambridge, Mass., 1984.

5 Lipton, Judith Eve: *Thinking and Not Thinking about the Unthinkable,* Proceedings of the Symposium on the Medical Consequences of Nuclear War, Physicians for Social Responsibility and University of California Office of Continuing Education, Davis, CA, Jan. 21, 1983.

5 Lipton, Judith Eve: "The Last Traffic Jam: Psychological Consequences of Nuclear War," *The Western Journal of Medicine,* February 1983, p. 222.

9 Livingstone, Neil C., and Joseph D. Douglas, Jr.: "CBW: The Poor Man's Atomic Bomb," *World Affairs,* vol. 2, 1984.

2 Lockwood, Jonathan Samuel: *The Soviet View of U.S. Strategic Doctrine: Implications for Decision Making,* Transaction Book, New Brunswick, NJ, 1983.

4 Loewe, W. E., and E. Mendelsohn: "Revised Dose Estimates at Hiroshima and Nagasaki," *Health Physics,* vol. 41, no. 663, 1981.

9 Lorenz, Konrad: *King Solomon's Ring: New Light on Animal Ways,* Crowell, New York, 1952.

9 Lorrain, and D. Corson: *Principles of Electromagnetic Fields and Waves,* Freeman, San Francisco, 1970.

7 Lovins, Amory B.: "Nuclear Weapons and Power-Reactor Plutonium," *Nature,* vol. 283, February 1980, pp. 817–822.

2,7 Lovins, Amory B., and L. Hunter Lovins: *Brittle Power: Energy Strategy for National Security.* Brick House, Andover, Mass., 1982.

2,7 Lucas, Michael: "The United States and Post-INF Europe," *World Policy Journal,* spring 1988, pp. 183–232.

2 Luttwak, Edward N.: Strategy: *The Logic of Peace and War,* Belknap Press of Harvard University Press, Cambridge, MA, 1987.

5 Mack, John E.: "Psychosocial Effects of the Nuclear Arms Race," *Bulletin of the Atomic Scientists,* April 1981, p. 19.

5 Macy, Joanna Rogers: *Despair and Personal Power in the Nuclear Age,* New Society Publishers, Philadelphia, 1983.

2 Mahedy, W: Address to the Summer Seminar of Global Security and Arms Control, sponsored by the University of California Institute on Global Cooperation and Conflict, Santa Barbara, June 1983.

3 Malone, Robert C., Lawrence H. Auer, Gary A. Glatzmaier, and Michael C. Wood: "Nuclear Winter: Three-Dimensional Simulations Including Interactive Transport, Scavenging, and Solar Heating of Smoke," *Journal of Geophysical Research,* vol. 91, No. D1, 1986, pp. 1039–1053.

　　　　An earlier publication appeared in *Science:* Robert C. Malone, Lawrence H. Auer, Gary A. Glatzmaier, Michael C. Wood, and Owen B. Toon: "Influence of Solar Heating and Precipitation Scavenging on the Simulated Lifetime of Post-Nuclear War Smoke," *Science,* vol. 230, Oct. 18, 1985, pp. 317–320.

5 Mansfield, Sue: "War as Ultimate Therapy," *Psychology Today,* June 1982, pp. 56–66.

7 Mark, J. Carson, Thomas D. Davies, Milton M. Hoenig, and Paul L. Leventhal: "The Tritium Factor as a Forcing Function in Nuclear Arms Reduction Talks," *Science,* vol. 241, Sept. 2, 1988, p. 1166.

4 Marx, Jean L.: "Lower Radiation Effect Found," *Science,* vol. 241, 1988, p. 1986.

2,5,8 Matthews, Jessica Tuchman: Redefining Security. Foreign Affairs, spring 1989, pp. 162–177.

2,6 Millar, T. B.: *The East-West Strategic Balance,* Allen & Unwin, Boston, 1981.

9 Miller, Walter M.: *A Canticle for Leibowitz,* Lippincott, Philadelphia, 1959.

3 Mindel, I. N.: "DNA-EMP Awareness Course Notes," Defense Nuclear Agency Document No. 2772T, 1977.

9 Molander, E. A., and R. C. Molander (eds.): *Ground Zero, What about the Russians and Nuclear War?* Pocket Books, New York, 1983.

4 Morgan, K. Z.: "Cancer and Low Level Ionizing Radiation," *Bulletin of the Atomic Scientists,* September 1978, p. 30.

1,3 Morland, Howard: "The H-Bomb Secret," *Progressive,* November 1979, pp. 14–23; Errata, December 1979, p. 16.

4 Najarian, T.: "The Controversy over the Health Effects of Radiation," *Technology Review,* November 1978, p. 74.

3,4 National Academy of Sciences, Committee to Study the Long Term Effects of Multiple Nuclear Weapons Detonations: *World-Wide Effects of Multiple Nuclear Weapons Detonations,* National Research Council, Washington, DC, 1975.

2 National Conference of Catholic Bishops: *The Challenge of Peace: God's Promise and Our Response,* Office of Publishing and Promotion Services, United States Catholic Conference, 1312 Massachusetts Ave. N.W., Washington, DC, May 1983.

6 *Naval Warfare Analysis Group: Unclassified Summary of NAVWAG Study No. 5,* Jan. 12, 1958, Office of Staff Secretary, White House Office Files, Subject Series, Alpha Subseries, Box 21, Nuclear Exchange (1) folder, Dwight Eisenhower Library, Washington, 1958.

4 Neel, James V.: private communication, 1988.

7 Nero, Anthony V. Jr.: *A Guidebook to Nuclear Reactors,* University of California Press, Berkeley, 1979.

6 Nitze, Paul: "On the Road to a More Stable Peace," Current Policy No. 657, U.S. Department of State, Washington, DC, Bureau of Public Affairs, Feb. 20, 1985.

6 Norris, Robert S., William M. Arkin, and Thomas B. Cochran: US–USSR Strategic Offensive Nuclear Forces 1946–1986. Nuclear Weapons Databook Working Paper NWD 87-1, NRDC, 1350 New York Avenue NW, Suite 300, Washington DC, 2005.

3,6 Nuclear Notebook, section of the *Bulletin of the Atomic Scientists,* September 1988, p. 64.

6 *Nuclear Weapons Databook,* a project of the National Resources Defense Council. Various references. See Cochran, Thomas B.; also Norris, Robert S.

10 Nye, Joseph S., Graham T. Allison, and Albert Carnesale: *Fateful Visions: Avoiding Nuclear Catastrophe.* Ballinger Press, Cambridge MA, 1988.

6 Office of Technology Assessment: "Ballistic Missile Defense Technologies," Government Printing Office, Washington, DC, September 1985.

3,4,9 Office of Technology Assessment: *The Effects of Nuclear War,* Allanheld, Osmun, 1980.

7 Office of Technology Assessment: *Nuclear Proliferation and Safeguards,* OTA, Washington, DC, 1977.

6,7 Office of Technology Assessment: "Seismic Verification of Nuclear Testing Treaties," Government Printing Office, Washington, DC, 1988.

6 Office of Technology Assessment: *Strategic Defenses: Ballistic Missile Defense Technologies, Anti-Satellite Weapons, Countermeasures and Arms Control,* OTA, Washington, DC, 1985.

8 Olvey, Lee D., James R. Golden, and Robert C. Kelly: *The Economics of National Security,* Avery, Wayne, NJ, 1984.

8 Page, Benjamin: *Who Gets What from Government,* University of California Press, Berkeley, 1983.

7 Palmer, George, and Dan I. Bolef: "Laser Isotope Separation: The Plutonium Connection," *Bulletin of the Atomic Scientists,* March 1984, pp. 26–29.

4 Parker, D. R., et al.: "Genetic Effects on Humans," *Long Term World-Wide Effects of Multiple-Nuclear Weapons Detonations,* National Academy of Sciences, National Research Council, Committee to Study the Long Term Effects of Multiple Nuclear Weapons Detonations, Washington, DC, 1975.

2 Payne, Keith B., and Colin S. Gray: "Nuclear Policy and the Defensive Transition," *Foreign Affairs,* spring 1984, p. 820.

1 Perrin, Noel: *Giving Up the Gun: Japan's Revision to the Sword, 1542–1879,* Shambhala Press, Boulder, CO, 1980.

2 "Perspectives—Ban Space Weapons," *Bulletin of the Atomic Scientists,* November 1983, p. 2.

3,4,8 Postol, Theodore A.: "Possible Fatalities from Superfires Following Nuclear Attacks on or near Urban Areas," in *The Medical Implications of Nuclear War,* National Academy of Sciences, National Academy Press, 1986.

7 Potter, William C.: *Nuclear Power and Proliferation,* Oelgeschlager, Gunn, Hain, Cambridge, MA, 1982.

7 Potter, William C.: *Verification and SALT: The Challenge of Strategic Deception,* Westview, 1980, p. 97.

2 Pringle, Peter, and William Arkin: *S.I.O.P.: The Secret U.S. Plan for Nuclear War,* W. W. Norton, New York, 1983.

1,2 Quester, George: *Nuclear Diplomacy: The First Twenty Five Years,* Dunellen, New York, 1970, p. 125.

3 Ramberg, B.: *The Destruction of Nuclear Facilities in War,* Lexington Books, Lexington, Mass., 1980.

1 Rhodes, R.: *The Making of the Atomic Bomb,* Simon and Schuster, New York, 1987.

2 Richardson, Lewis F.: *Statistics of Deadly Quarrels,* Boxwood, Pittsburgh, 1960.

4 Roberts, Leslie: "Atomic Bomb Doses Reassessed," *Science,* vol. 238, Dec. 18, 1987, pp. 1649–1651.

6 Robinson, G. A. Jr.: "Study Urges Exploiting of Technologies," *Aviation Week and Space Technology,* Oct. 24, 1983.

7 Rochlin, Eugene: *Plutonium Power, and Politics: International Arrangements for the Disposition of Spent Nuclear Fuel,* University of California Press, Berkeley, Calif., 1979.

5 Rogers, R. R. (Chair): "Report of Task Force 20 of the American Psychiatric Association: Psychosocial Aspects of Nuclear Developments," American Psychiatric Association, 1700 18th Street, N.W., Washington, DC 20009.

9 Romer, Robert H.: *Energy, An Introduction to Physics,* W. H. Freeman and Co., San Francisco, 1976.

2,3,4 Sagan, Carl: "Nuclear War and Climatic Catastrophe: Some Policy Implications," *Foreign Affairs,* winter 1983–84, pp. 257–292.

1,2 Sagan, Scott D.: "SIOP-62: The Nuclear War Plan Briefing to President Kennedy," *International Security,* vol. 12, No. 1, summer 1987, pp. 22–51.

2,10 Sagdeev, Roald, and Andrei Kokoshin: "Strategic Stability under the Conditions of Radical Nuclear Arms Reductions," group leaders of a working group of the Committee of Soviet Scientists for Peace, Against the Nuclear Threat. Edited by Sanford Lakoff with commentary by several U.S. political scientists. Available as Policy Paper No. 7 of the Institute on Global Conflict and Cooperation, University of California, Q-068, La Jolla, CA 92093-0068.

3 Sartori, Leo: "Effects of Nuclear Weapons," *Physics Today,* vol. 36, March 1983, pp. 32–42.

8 Scheer, Robert: *With Enough Shovels: Reagan, Bush, and Nuclear War,* Random House, New York, 1982.

2,9 Schell, Jonathan: "Reflections (Nuclear Arms)," *The New Yorker,* Jan. 2, 9, 1984.

2,9 Schell, Jonathan: *The Abolition,* Knopf, New York, 1984.

2 Schelling, Thomas: *The Strategy of Conflict,* Oxford University Press, Cambridge, 1960, p. 252.

9 Schroeer, Dietrich: *Science, Technology and the Nuclear Arms Race,* Wiley, New York, 1984.

6 Schroeer, Dietrich: *Data Tables on the Present Nuclear Balance,* in Hafemeister and Schroeer, op. cit., appendix E.

6 Schroeer, Dietrich: "Directed Energy Weapons and Strategic Deterrence: A Primer." Adelphi Paper 221, International Institute for Strategic Studies, London, 1987.

4 Schull, W. J., M. Otake, and J. V. Neel: "Genetic Effects of the Atomic Bombs: A Reappraisal," *Science,* vol. 213, 1981, p. 1220.

2,6 Scowcroft: Report of the President's Commission on Strategic Forces, Brent Scowcroft, Chairman, The White House, 1983.

4 Scrimshaw, Nevin S.: "Food, Nutrition, and Nuclear War," *New England Journal of Medicine,* vol. 311, No. 4, July 26, 1984, pp. 272–276.

6 SDI: "Technology, Survivability and Software," Office of Technology Assessment, Washington DC, 1988, Report OTA-ISC-353.

1 Seaborg, G. T.: *Kennedy, Khrushchev, Test Ban,* University of California Press, Berkeley and Los Angeles, CA, 1981.

1,8 Singer, J. David, and Melvin Small: *The Wages of War 1816–1965: A Statistical Handbook,* Wiley, New York, 1972.

10 SIPRI: *The Uncertain Course: New Weapons, Strategies and Mindsets,* Stockholm International Peace Research Institute, Oxford University Press, 1987, Carl G. Jacobson (ed.).

1,2,6 *SIPRI Yearbook, 1987. World Armaments and Disarmament.* Stockholm International Peace Research Institute, Oxford University Press, 1987.

2,8 Sivard, Ruth Leger, "World Military and Social Expenditures. World Priorities," 1983. Issued annually: Box 15140, Washington, DC 20007.

1,2 Small, Melvin, and J. David Singer: *Resort to Arms: International and Civil Wars, 1816–1980,* Sage, Beverly Hills, 1982.

1 Smyth, H. D.: *Smyth Report,* Princeton University Press, Princeton, NJ, 1945.

2,6 *Soviet Military Power,* United States, Washington, DC, Stock Number 008-000-00464-1 (1987 edition). Published annually.

6,7 Stanford: "Potential Verification Provisions for Long-Range, Nuclear-Armed Sea-Launched Cruise Missiles," John Harvey and Sally Ride, Co-Chairs, Workshop Report, Center for International Security and Arms Control, Stanford University, 1988.

6 Stockholm International Peace Research Institute: *World Armaments and Disarmament, SIPRI Yearbook,* Taylor and Francis, London, 1981 (issued annually).

6 Stockholm International Peace Research Institute: *Armaments or Disarmaments?* 1982.

7 Sutcliffe, W. G.: "Limits on Nuclear Materials for Arms Reduction: Complexity and Uncertainties," *Science,* vol. 241, Sept. 2, 1988, p. 1166.

7 Sykes, Lynn R., and Jack F. Evernden: "The Verification of a Comprehensive Nuclear Test Ban," *Scientific American,* vol. 247, October 1982, pp. 47–55.

7   Sykes, Lynn R., Jack F. Evernden, and Ines Cifuentes: *Seismic Methods for Verifying Nuclear Test Bans,* In Hafemeister and Schroeer (eds.), *Physics, Technology, and the Nuclear Arms Race,* American Institute of Physics Conference Proceedings No. 4, New York, 1983.

7   Taylor, Ted: "Magnets for Terrorists, Weapons Grade Uranium in University Research Reactors," *Critical Mass Bulletin,* April 1984. Transcript of testimony before the Nuclear Regulatory Commission, Jan. 27, 1984.

2   Thompson, E. P.: *Zero Option,* Merlin Press, London, 1982.

3   Thompson, Stanley, L., and Stephen H. Schneider, "Nuclear Winter Reappraised," Foreign Affairs, summer 1986, pp. 981–1005.

3   Tipler, P. A.: *Modern Physics,* Worth, New York, 1978.

2,8   Tirman, John (ed.): *The Militarization of High Technology.* Ballinger, 1984.

2,6,3   Tsipis, Kosta: *Arsenal: Understanding Weapons in the Nuclear Age,* Simon and Schuster, New York, 1983.

6   Tsipis, Kosta: "How to Calculate the Kill Probability of a Silo," appendix E in Hafemeister and Schroeer, *Physics, Technology, and the Nuclear Arms Race,* American Institute of Physics Conference Proceedings No. 4, New York, 1983.

6   Tsipis, Kosta: "Laser Weapons," *Scientific American,* December 1981, p. 51.

3   Turco, R. P., et al. "Global Atmospheric Consequences of Nuclear War," *Science,* vol. 222, Dec. 23, 1983, p. 1283.

2,7   Ury, W. L., and R. Smoke: *Beyond the Hotline: Controlling a Nuclear Crisis,* Report to the U.S. Arms Control and Disarmament Agency, Nuclear Negotiation Project, Harvard University Law School, Cambridge, MA, 1984.

2   U.S. Department of Defense: *Soviet Military Power,* 1982, rev. 1983.

4   U.S.–Japan Joint Study: "US–Japan Joint Reassessment of Atomic Bomb Radiation Dosimetry in Hiroshima and Nagasaki—Final Report," National Research Council 2101 Constitution Ave., Washington, DC, 1987.

2,6   "United States Military Posture," prepared by the Joint Chiefs of Staff, The Pentagon, Washington, DC. Annual statement.

4   Upton, Arthur C.: "The Biological Effects of Low-Level Ionizing Radiation," *Scientific American,* vol. 246, No. 2, February 1982, pp. 41–49.

2   U.S.S.R.: *Whence the Threat?* (published in 1982 as a rebuttal to the U.S. DOD document *Soviet Military Power*).

3,4   von Hippel, Frank, and Thomas B. Cochran: "Estimating Long-term Health Effects," *Bulletin of the Atomic Scientists,* vol. 43, No. 1, August/September 1986, pp. 18–24.

3,4   von Hippel, Frank N., Barbara G. Levi, Theodore A. Postol, and William H. Daugherty: "Civilian Casualties from Counterforce Attack," *Scientific American,* vol. 259, September 1988, p. 36.

9   Vonnegut, Kurt: *Slaughterhouse Five, or the Children's Crusade,* Dell, New York, 1971.

9   Walker, Paul F.: "Precision-Guided Weapons," *Scientific American,* August 1981, p. 37.

5   Walsh, Roger: *Staying Alive: The Psychology of Human Survival,* Shambala Publications, Boulder, CO, 1984, p. 37.

2   Wang, C.: "China's Nuclear Programs and Policies," *Bulletin of the Atomic Scientists,* March 1983, p. 18.

9,3   Waters, W. E.: *Electrical Induction from Distant Current Sources,* Prentice-Hall, Englewood Cliffs, NJ, 1983.

1,4   Wells, W.: W. Wells' Interview of Dr. Kaovu Shima—His Recollections of Hiroshima after the A-Bomb, *American Surgeon,* vol. 24, September 1958, pp. 668.

3   Whitten, R. C., W. J. Borucki, and R. P. Turco: "Possible Ozone Depletion Following a Nuclear Explosion," *Nature,* vol. 257, 1975, p. 38.

2   Wieseltier, Leon: "When Deterrence Fails," *Foreign Affairs,* spring 1985, p. 827.

2   Wiesner, J. B., and H. F. York: "National Security and the Nuclear Test Ban," *Scientific American,* vol. 211, 1964, p. 4.

1,8   Winkler, Allan M.: "A 40-Year History of Civil Defense," *Bulletin of the Atomic Scientists,* June–July 1984, p. 16.

6   Wit, Joel S.: "Advances in Submarine Warfare," *Scientific American,* February 1981, p. 31.

2 Wohlstetter, Albert: "Bishops, Statesmen, and Other Strategists on the Bombing of Innocents," *Commentary,* June 1983, pp. 15–35.

3 Woods, A. J., et al.: "Air Effects on the External SGEMP Response of a Cylinder," *I.E.E.E. Transactions on Nuclear Science,* vol. NS-28, no. 6, December 1981, p. 4467.

2 Woolsey, R. James: "The Politics of Vulnerability: 1980–1983," *Foreign Affairs,* vol. 62, spring 1984, pp. 805–819.

World Weapons Database: See Wright, Barton.

1,9 Wouk, Herman: *War and Remembrance,* Pocket Books, New York, 1980.

6 Wright, Barton: *World Weapons Database,* vol. I: *Soviet Missiles,* Institute for Defense and Disarmament Studies, Lexington Books, Lexington, MA, 1986.

3 Wuebbles, Donald: private communication, 1988. Some results will be found in "The Present State of Knowledge of the Upper Atmosphere—1988," R. D. Watson and the ozone trends group, M.T. Prather and the ad hoc theory panel, M. J. Kuryllo and the NASA panel for data evaluation, *NASA Reference Publication* 1208, August 1988.

8 Yegorov, P. T., I. A. Shlyakhov, and N. I. Alabin: *Civil Defense,* Publishing House for Higher Education, Moscow, 1970. Translated and published by Oak Ridge National Laboratory, U.S. Government Stock No. 008-070-00382-1.

1,2 York, H.: *The Advisors, Oppenheimer, Teller, and the Superbomb,* W. H. Freeman, San Francisco, 1975.

1,2 York, H.: *Race to Oblivion: A Participant's View of the Arms Race,* Simon and Schuster, New York, 1970, p. 109.

1,2 York, H.: private communication, 1982.

1,2 York, Herbert F., and Neil Joeck: "Countdown on the Comprehensive Test Ban," Institute on Global Cooperation and Conflict, University of California San Diego, La Jolla, CA, 1985.

3 Zimmerman, Peter D.: "The Physics and Employment of Neutron Weapons," chapter 4 in Hafemeister and Schroeer (eds.), *Physics, Technology, and the Nuclear Arms Race,* American Institute of Physics Conference Proceedings No. 4, New York, 1983.

1,2 Zuckerman, Solly: *Nuclear Illusion and Reality,* William Collins Sons, London, 1982.

ANSWERS TO ODD-NUMBERED PROBLEMS

CHAPTER 3

1. (*a*) 22 *Mt*   (*b*) 4.6 *Mt*   (*c*) 1 *Mt*   (*d*) 0.22 *Mt*
(*e*) 0.046 *Mt*   (*f*) 0.01 *Mt*

3. (*a*) 59 ft   (*b*) 127 ft   (*c*) 273 ft   (*d*) 587 ft   (*e*) 1270 ft

CHAPTER 8

1. 19,000 mi/h

3. 6 mi/h/s

5. 588 N

7. 0.15 m ≈ 6 in

9. 11,000 ft

11. 6000 m/s = 19,700 ft/s

13. 39 m/s

15. 125 s

17 (*a*) 3.45×10^{-3} (*b*) 1.23456×10^2 (*c*) 1×10^3 (*d*) 9.3×10^{-7}

19. (*a*) 1.2×10^4 (*b*) 7.7×10^{-3} (*c*) 1.2×10^8(*d*) 1.5×10^{-8} (*e*) 1.0×10^{11}

21. (*a*) 6.9×10^1 (*b*) 1.5×10^6 (*c*) 1.5×10^2 (*d*) -1.7×10^2

23. (*a*) 256   (*b*) 0.00391   (*c*) 64   (*d*) 0.0156   (*e*) 2.83   (*f*) 0.354   (*g*) 1.09
(*h*) 0.917   (*i*) 1.09   (*j*) 0.917

25. 5.6 mi

27. 576 tons
29. 9800 N
31. 2.44 km/s

CHAPTER 9

1. $0.075 \text{ m} \approx 3 \text{ in}$
3. $1.6 \times 10^{-5} \text{ g}$
5. 242 m/s
7. 52 MeV
9. 20 m
11. $8.36 \times 10^{13} \text{ J}$
13. $1.03 \times 10^5 \text{ N/m}^2$
15. 5 m/s^2
17. 19,600 J
19. 0.51 MeV
21. $1.1 \times 10^{10} \text{ g}$
23. $3.6 \times 10^6 \text{ J}$

CHAPTER 10

1. $^{131}_{54}\text{Xe}$
3. (a) 20,000 kg   (b) 5000 kg   (c) 1250 kg
5. 250
7. 2.61 MeV
9. $1.84 \times 10^{17} \text{ kg/m}^3$
11. 0.549 MeV
13. 1.76×10^{20}

CHAPTER 11

1. ^{235}U is an isotope of a naturally occurring element. It has 92 protons and 143 neutrons in its nucleus. ^{239}Pu is a manufactured isotope with 94 protons and 145 neutrons in its nucleus.
3. $7.5 \times 10^6 \text{ lb}$
5. $(\frac{1}{2} + \frac{1}{4} + \frac{1}{8} + \frac{1}{16} + \frac{1}{32} + \frac{1}{64} + \frac{1}{128}) = 0.99$ so last 7 generations gives 99 percent (last 10 generations gives 99.9 percent).
7. 69 years
9. 990 years
11. 7.8×10^{-5} tons, or 0.156 lb
13. 145 lb/in^2 on one atom (using 10^7 atoms in 1 cm of the fissionable material gives 1.5×10^9 lb/in^2 on a 1 cm^3 "chunk" of uranium)
15. (a) 5 kg   (b) 2.5 kg
17. 17.6 MeV

CHAPTER 12

1. 1.16×10^6 kW · hr
3. 0.3 m
5. 500 V/m
7. 2.0×10^{-16} J
9. 60 V/m
11. $Y^{1/2}$

CHAPTER 13

1. 4400 ft
3. 840 ft
5. Use the scaling laws; $h = h_0 \left(\dfrac{Y}{Y_0} \right)^{1/3}$.

CHAPTER 14

1. Absolute zero is the temperature at which there is no kinetic energy associated with the molecules in the solid cooled to this point (except for quantum effects). It is equal to $-273.15°C$.
3. 1.13 s
7. They are about the same.
9. About 9000 ft (for a ground burst).
11. $Q = 6.7$ cal/cm^2 has a slant range of 1.4 mi. This is equivalent to about a 40 percent casualty rate.
13. 1.8×10^9 J
15. 20°C
17. 2×10^8 K
19. 3×10^{-9} m

CHAPTER 15

1. The neutron radiation has a $LD_{50/30}$ (400 rads) (50 percent mortality in 30 d). The blast effects give 40 lb/in^2 overpressure (recall that 20 lb/in^2 can cause rupture of sensitive internal organs). The thermal effects give 280 cal/cm^2, which will cause cloth garments to ignite as well as the wooden frames on houses. The gamma radiation is 2800 rad, which is fatal to all exposed human beings. (See Chapter 7.)
3. 400 ft
5. 30 to 50 percent attenuation

CHAPTER 16

1. (a) 130 rads/h   (b) 80 rads/h
3. 16,500 rads. See Figures 16-10 and 16-11 (assumes perfect shielding for first week).

CHAPTER 17

1. The electric field is doubled and the energy absorbed is quadrupled.
3. 1000 V/m
5. Direct induction EMP occurs when an antenna connected directly to the electronic device receives the pulse and transmits the harmful energy level to the equipment. EMP pulses that come from the power grid are produced by large currents in the power lines, bringing current to the electronic devices which in turn burn out these components that are "plugged into the wall."
7. 180 MHz

CHAPTER 18

1. 500 rem
3. About 1 chance in 25 (4 percent)

CHAPTER 20

1. For a wavelength of 1×10^{-6} m: 1.2×10^{-7} rads.
3. 3 m
5. 0.11 MW/m²

INDEX